MICRO FOCUS WORKBENCH

DEVELOPING MAINFRAME COBOL APPLICATIONS ON THE PC

Alida Jatich and Phil Nowak

Foreword by Jerome Garfunkel, Micro Focus, Inc.

John Wiley & Sons, Inc.

New York • Chichester • Brisbane • Toronto • Singapore

To all COBOL programmers:

May we continue to prosper and to enjoy what we do;

and may COBOL continue to be the most successful

computer language ever invented.

Library of Congress Cataloging-in-Publication Data

Jatich, Alida.
    Micro Focus Workbench : developing mainframe COBOL applications on the PC / Alida Jatich, Phil Nowak.
        p.   cm.
    Includes index.
    ISBN 0–471–55611–4 (pbk.)
    1. COBOL (Computer program language)   2. Micro Focus Workbench.
    3. Computer software—Development.   I. Nowak, Phil.
    QA76.73.C25J38   1992
005.2'22—dc20   92–14038
                                                             CIP

Acknowledgments

Thanks to the following people: John Beggs, Mike McCandless, Dan Gilliland, Mark Warren, Erin Kelley, Larry Simmons, Mark Foster, Andrew Wood, Mike Gilbert, and Jerome Garfunkel of Micro Focus, Inc.; Bruce Zupek and Janet Carissimi of Stingray Software Co.; Jim Graves of Reusable Technologies, Inc.; Cheryl K. Middleton and Glenn Dent of Proximity Software, Inc.; and Dan Dunkel, Sabrina Schultz, and John Cunningham of Command Technology Corporation. Without their help, this book could not have been written.

About the Authors

Alida Jatich graduated Phi Beta Kappa with a B.A. in economics from the University of Chicago. She has worked with computers since 1976 and has been an independent consultant since 1983. She is the author of *CICS Command Level Programming* and has written articles for *CICS Update, Inside DPMA, 73 Amateur Radio,* and *Plane & Pilot* magazines. Her experience includes business and manufacturing applications on IBM mainframes, HP 3000 minicomputers, and IBM personal computers.

Phil Nowak has worked with computers since 1966 and has been an independent consultant since 1972. His experience includes teaching, programming, systems design, technical writing, and publishing. He writes product reviews and other articles for *Ventura Professional, 73 Amateur Radio, Shutterbug, Cat Fancy, Private Pilot,* and *Plane & Pilot* magazines. He holds a commercial pilot's license along with airplane and instrument instructor ratings. Mr. Nowak is a contributing editor for *Plane & Pilot* magazine.

Ms. Jatich and Mr. Nowak created the design for this book, using Ventura Publisher page layout software and Adobe PostScript fonts. They also publish *DPMA NEWS,* the newsletter for the Chicago Chapter of the Data Processing Management Association.

Trademarks

Foreword

These are exciting times in COBOL's 33-year history. Its popularity has never been greater. Created in 1959 as a batch-processing, business-oriented language for mainframe computers, COBOL today is no longer solely for batch processing, no longer strictly business-oriented, and certainly no longer just for mainframes.

COBOL came to the microcomputer in the late 1970s. It took a lot of vision in those days to believe in COBOL's future in this brand new environment. Few saw then what the founders of Micro Focus, Brian Reynolds and Paul O'Grady, had envisioned as the destiny of the COBOL language. What they guessed was that COBOL has two *raisons d'etre* on the microcomputer. First, the microcomputer was a natural workstation for MIS programmers to develop mainframe applications. This entailed making the entire application development process on the microcomputer, including the COBOL language, testing, and file processing, behave as similarly as possible to the COBOL language on the mainframe. Second, microcomputer applications, they believed, were likely to become as sophisticated as their mainframe counterparts; and just as the mainframe world turned to COBOL three decades ago, to solve its problems of unmaintainable systems in low-level languages, so would the microcomputer world.

As it turns out, they were right on both fronts. Each of these COBOL environments—mainframe application development and microcomputer application development—requires its own set of priorities from the COBOL language and its accompanying tools. Each needs its own specific utilities and each addresses a different "universe" of programmers. *Micro Focus Workbench: Developing Mainframe COBOL Applications on the PC,* by Alida Jatich and Phil Nowak, explores in depth the former of these two environments. It will serve today's mainframe developer who uses Micro Focus Workbench as a modern-day "bible." If there is still any doubt about COBOL's popularity in the world of microcomputers, this book should put it to rest.

COBOL has been on the defensive for much of its 33-year history. Cries of COBOL's obsolescence have been heard for three decades, particularly in the academic community. "The teaching of COBOL should be made a criminal offense," said Professor Edsger Dijkstra of Holland, in May 1982; other academicians shared the sentiment. In the mid-1980's, many thought that COBOL's life expectancy was nearing its end. To this day, the legacy of COBOL-bashing is still heard. In 1984, while the COBOL language was bogged down in a siege of protest over the revision of the 1974 American and international standards, in what was to become the ANS COBOL 85 language, the international COBOL committee took some bold action. They changed the process by which COBOL is developed to assure its relevance to contemporary programming and design methodologies. The inclusion of intrinsic functions (42 high-level macros) as an amendment to the ANS COBOL 85 language, as well as the current work being done on Object Oriented COBOL, is a direct benefit that provides evidence of this new approach.

As a result, the COBOL language has never been stronger than it is today. It is truly a state-of-the-art application development tool. Moreover, because of COBOL's presence on PCs, both for mainframe and PC application development, an entire new generation of programmers is discovering COBOL. This new generation of COBOL programmers is being merged with some of the "old timers," who typically are more experienced mainframe COBOL programmers. At first, when the PCs were introduced into the MIS workplace, there was resistance. Changing from 3270-mode "dumb" terminals to stand-alone intelligent PCs with their own COBOL compilers and tools was not a comfortable move for many. There was a new set of "JCL" to learn (i.e., MS-DOS and all its accompanying utility functions), new compiler directives, and an entirely new environment to get used to. How could they be sure that the COBOL application on the PC would behave *exactly* like the application on the mainframe, they wondered? It has taken a few years, and the process is still ongoing, but the sophistication of COBOL compilers like Micro Focus', overwhelmed the skeptics.

Many MIS programmers discovered the power of Micro Focus Workbench accidentally. Multiple dialects offered within the Micro Focus Workbench make it great for "conversion" projects when going from one version of COBOL to another, say from OS/VS COBOL to VS COBOL II. Many installations experimented with Workbench for this one feature alone and discovered all the wonderful "extras" they had inherited. Nearly every area of mainframe compatibility has been addressed by the Micro Focus Workbench. Phil and Alida discuss in depth all of these compatibility issues in their book. Not only do they address Workbench's intrinsic components such as the Animator, the COBOL Source Information (CSI) Analyzer, the Editor, and the Session Recorder, but they cover as well those important add-on facilities such as CICS, IMS, and RCM. In addition, attesting to the currency of their book, they have introduced some of the basic concepts of object oriented programming—which is likely to be the next great milestone in COBOL's evolution.

On the personal side, I first learned of Micro Focus in 1980, while attending a CODASYL COBOL Committee meeting. One Englishman had been sent over to the United States to establish an American presence for Micro Focus and to serve as Micro Focus' first representative to the CODASYL COBOL Committee. A dozen years later, nearly half of the members of the CODASYL COBOL Committee would be microcomputer COBOL vendors, and Micro Focus would grow into a 100-million-dollar corporation, recognized by many as the *de facto* leader in the COBOL world.

My own interest in Micro Focus began when I used their CIS COBOL product to develop and teach COBOL classes. What a treat to be able to personalize the COBOL teaching environment! If I was impressed then, I was "blown away" later when I upgraded to the Micro Focus COBOL/2 Compiler with Animator. I could not think of a better teaching environment. The ability to offer "what-if" scenarios with such ease was wonderful. I often likened it to surrounding a "jet pilot" (programmer) with all of the tools and gadgets he or she needs to "fly" through the application development process. Today's Workbench was unimaginable to me then—the "cockpit" is more high-tech and the accompanying tools make programming even more productive. As for tomorrow's Workbench, it is staggering to think what the next generation of Workbench tools might do for teachers and for application developers.

In 1982, at the National Computing Centre in Manchester, England, I befriended John Triance, a professor at the prestigious University of Manchester Institute of Science and Technology (UMIST). John was a part-time representative on the CODASYL COBOL Committee on behalf of Micro Focus. Years later, John and I and Micro Focus would form *The COBOL Training Company,* affectionately known as TC2. TC2 went on eventually to become the Micro Focus training division. John later became Micro Focus' Vice President in charge of Development. Although John would be the first one to remind you that it was the collective efforts of many individuals, it is a fact that the Micro Focus Workbench evolved into the direction and shape it has today, under the guidance of this man. To this day, John and I remain close friends.

While these times are exciting for the COBOL community, one must note with sadness two important milestones in the history of the COBOL language. On January 1, 1992, Grace Murray Hopper died at the age of 86. Grace's work with Flow-Matic, an early prototype of a third-generation compiling language, contributed much to the early design of the COBOL language. She served on the original CODASYL COBOL executive committee and has been closely identified with the COBOL language ever since. From an historical perspective, she actually contributed more to the concept of high level computer languages in general than to the COBOL language specifically. She has often been referred to as the mother of COBOL.

The other important milestone that has occurred this past year is the demise of the CODASYL COBOL Committee. For the last 30 years of COBOL's 33-year history, the COBOL language has been jointly developed by the CODASYL COBOL Committee and the ANSI COBOL Committee. In 1962, the United States of America Standards Institute (USASI), later renamed the American National Standards Institute (ANSI), became partners with CODASYL in the development and standardization of the COBOL language. CODASYL remained responsible for all new COBOL language features and syntax, while ANSI was responsible for COBOL's standardization and its administration as an official American Standard language. In addition, ANSI served as the designated American liaison to the international (ISO) COBOL community. After years of debate, it was felt that this division of responsibilities between ANSI and CODASYL was artificial and no longer necessary. Some, in fact, saw this division as an impediment to sound language development. Earlier this year, the CODASYL COBOL Committee voted itself out of existence. Its members will become part of an ad hoc group of the ANSI COBOL Committee, technically called ANSI X3J4. The CODASYL COBOL Committee will officially cease to exist upon the completion of the object oriented COBOL report being developed by the CODASYL COBOL Committee Object Oriented COBOL Task Group (OOCTG).

Today, the Object Oriented COBOL Task Group is hard at work to define new COBOL syntax that incorporates the latest object oriented concepts. The COBOL language is proving itself to be more versatile for systems programming, and for other non-business applications, than the original "business-oriented" COBOL language was intended to be. Compilers and runtime libraries are more sophisticated than ever before and they are getting better every year. The robust repertoire of utilities, tools, and add-on extensions to its COBOL language puts the Micro Focus Workbench at the leading edge of application development, in any language and in any environment. *Micro Focus Workbench: Developing Mainframe COBOL Applications on the PC,* by Alida Jatich and Phil Nowak, will take the mainframe COBOL programmer step-by-step through this collection of tools. It will serve both as a teaching text for the newcomer and as a reference book for the experienced Workbench user.

Jerome Garfunkel
Litchfield, Connecticut

Contents

Introduction   **1**

    Purpose of This Book   1

    Brief History of Micro Focus, Inc. and the Workbench Product   1

1   **Overview: What Is the Micro Focus Workbench?** **5**

    1.1 Developing Mainframe Applications on the PC   **5**
        1.1.1 Why Develop Mainframe Applications on the PC?   5
        1.1.2 What You Need to Consider   6

    1.2 Overview of the Three Parts of the Micro Focus Product   **7**
        1.2.1 The COBOL/2 Compiler   7
        1.2.2 The Toolset   11
        1.2.3 The Workbench   11

    1.3 Operating Environments   **13**
        1.3.1 MS-DOS   13
        1.3.2 Windows   14
        1.3.3 OS/2 and OS/2 Extended Services   14
        1.3.4 Unix, Xenix, AIX (separate Micro Focus product)   14

    1.4 Exercises   **14**

2   **Getting Started**   **15**

    2.1 Installation Requirements for MS-DOS, Windows, OS/2   **15**
        2.1.1 Hardware: Processor, RAM, Disk Space   15
        2.1.2 Software: Operating Systems Supported   16

    2.2 Installing the Workbench   **16**
        2.2.1 Overview of the Installation Procedure   16
        2.2.2 Importance of Release Notes and "Read This First"   16
        2.2.3 Setting Up Your Directories   17
        2.2.4 Required Environment Variables: MS-DOS, Windows,
            OS/2   17

2.2.5 Extended Memory Manager (XM)   20
2.2.6 Running the SETUP Program   20

2.3 Sample and Demo Programs Provided with the System   **32**

2.4 Exercises   **32**

3   **Becoming Familiar with the Workbench Menu System**   **35**

3.1 Concept of Integrated Menu System   **35**

3.2 Menu Structure   **36**
3.2.1 Parts of the Screen   37
3.2.2 Selecting Options   38
3.2.3 How the Submenus Are Accessed   38
3.2.4 Navigating with CTRL, ALT, and Function Keys   39
3.2.5 Moving Back to Higher Menus with Escape Key   40
3.2.6 The Help System and On-line Reference   40
3.2.7 The Operating System Prompt   40

3.3 Mainframe Development Environment (MDE) Main Menu   **41**
3.3.1 Help Screen Showing MDE Menu Structure   41
3.3.2 Files: Data Conversion Utilities   41
3.3.3 Develop: Editing, Checking, Animating (the Functions Most Often Used)   41
3.3.4 Execute: Compiling and Running Programs, Access to MS/DOS or OS/2 Prompt   42
3.3.5 Add-On Products, if any (IMS, CICS)   42
3.3.6 Configure: Customizing the Workbench Menus   42
3.3.7 Workbench: Developer's Environment (Alternative Main Menu)   42
3.3.8 Toggling between the MDE and WDE Main Menus   43
3.3.9 Exiting from the System   43

3.4 Exercises   **43**

4   **The Micro Focus COBOL Editor**   **45**

4.1 Concept of ASCII Editor   **45**

4.2 Getting into the Editor   **47**
4.2.1 Items Appearing on the Editor Information Line   47

4.3 Loading Files to Be Edited   **48**
4.3.1 Choosing Files from the Directory   48
4.3.2 Default File Extensions   51
4.3.3 Inserting Another File with Load Operation   51

4.3.4 Clearing the Editor Work Area before Loading the Next
File   52

4.4 Creating a New File   **52**

4.5 Saving a File to Disk   **52**

4.6 Changing Editor Settings   **52**
4.6.1 Insert   52
4.6.2 Caps Lock   52
4.6.3 Num Lock   53
4.6.4 Scroll Lock   53
4.6.5 Word Wrap   53
4.6.6 Margins   53

4.7 Navigating through the File   **55**
4.7.1 Using the Cursor Keys   55
4.7.2 Setting Cursor Position with the Mouse   56

4.8 Copying, Deleting, and Restoring Lines   **56**
4.8.1 The Internal Stack and How it Affects "Cut-and-Paste" 56
4.8.2 Function Keys for Editing Lines   57

4.9 Deleting and Restoring Characters   **58**

4.10 Deleting Words   **59**

4.11 Block Operations   **59**
4.11.1 Defining a Block to be Manipulated   60
4.11.2 Copying or Moving a Block   60
4.11.3 Deleting a Block   60
4.11.4 Using the Block Stack   60
4.11.5 Editing a Block   61
4.11.6 Saving a Block as a New File   61

4.12 Find and Replace   **61**
4.12.1 Entering Find and Replace Arguments   63
4.12.2 Changing Default Settings for Find and Replace   63

4.13 Multiple Editor Windows   **64**
4.13.1 Editor Window Commands   64
4.13.2 Mouse Support   66

4.14 Printing ASCII Files   **66**
4.14.1 The Print Function   66
4.14.2 Printer Setup Considerations   67

4.15 Editor Tips and Tricks   **67**
4.15.1 Using Tags ("Bookmarks")   67
4.15.2 Changing the Default Directory   68
4.15.3 Line Drawing   68

4.15.4 Using the Calculator 69

4.15.5 Editing Files Named in COPY Statements 70

4.15.6 Using On-line Information (Hypertext-Based Help) 70

4.16 Starting Editor from the Command Prompt 76

4.17 Exercises 76

5   **The Micro Focus Syntax Checker**   **79**

5.1 Basic Syntax Checker Concepts 79

5.1.1 What Is the Syntax Checker? 79

5.1.2 Files Used and Produced by the Checker 80

5.1.3 Bringing Up the Checker from Workbench 81

5.2 Checker Directives 82

5.2.1 Types of Directives 82

5.2.2 Passing Directives to the Checker 85

5.2.3 Directives for the Checker's User Interface 88

5.2.4 Directives for Debugging: Animation, CSI 88

5.2.5 Directives for Compatibility with Mainframe COBOL 89

5.2.6 Directives to Tailor Programs for Different Countries 91

5.2.7 More about the Checker Menu 92

5.3 Correcting Syntax Errors from the Checker 92

5.4 Running the Checker from the Command Line Prompt 94

5.5 Exercises 94

6   **The Micro Focus Animator**   **97**

6.1 What Is the Animator? 97

6.1.1 Interactive Testing 97

6.1.2 Basic Animator versus Advanced Animator 99

6.2 Files Used by Animator 99

6.3 Getting Ready to Animate 100

6.3.1 Bringing Up the Animator Menu 100

6.3.2 Navigating through the Source Program Display 102

6.4 Executing under the Animator 104

6.4.1 Step (Manual Single Step through Program) 104

6.4.2 Go (Automatic Step through Program with Adjustable Speed) 105

6.4.3 Zoom (Execute Until End of Program, or Next Breakpoint, Without Animation) 105

6.4.4 Watch (Single Step Showing Data Fields) 105

6.4.5 Animate (Automatic Step Showing Data Fields) 107

6.5 Querying Data Values   **107**
    6.5.1 Displaying and Updating Data Fields   107
    6.5.2 Creating and Deleting Monitor Windows   107

6.6 What Is a Breakpoint?   **109**

6.7 Using Breakpoints on a Source Line   **110**
    6.7.1 Setting Unconditional Breakpoints   110
    6.7.2 Setting Periodic Breakpoints   110
    6.7.3 Setting Conditional Breakpoints   110
    6.7.4 Viewing Breakpoint Settings   111
    6.7.5 Clearing Breakpoints   111
    6.7.6 Animating with Breakpoints   111

6.8 Using Global Breakpoints Associated with Data Items   **112**
    6.8.1 Usefulness of Global Breakpoints   112
    6.8.2 Setting, Clearing, and Using Global Breakpoints 112
    6.8.3 Animator Environment Settings   113

6.9 Backtracking from a Breakpoint   **114**
    6.9.1 Purpose of Backtracking   114
    6.9.2 How to Use Backtracking   114

6.10 Adding New Source Lines While Animating   **115**
    6.10.1 Concepts of Do and Break-Do Functions   115
    6.10.2 Using the Do Function   115
    6.10.3 Using the Break-Do Function   116

6.11 Next-If and Perform Functions   **116**
    6.11.1 Zooming through Portions of Code   116
    6.11.2 Using the Next-If Function   116
    6.11.3 Using Perform Functions   117

6.12 Reset Function to Skip Execution of Portions of Code   **117**

6.13 Split-Screen Function   **118**

6.14 Query Dump Files   **118**

6.15 Adjusting Viewing Windows   **119**

6.16 Analyzer (Statement Execution Counts)   **119**
    6.16.1 Analyzer Concepts   119
    6.16.2 Setup and Execution   120
    6.16.3 Clearing Analyzer Counts   121
    6.16.4 Printing Analyzer Totals   122

6.17 Structure Animation   **122**
    6.17.1 Concepts   122
    6.17.2 Using Structure Animation   123
    6.17.3 Adjusting Diagram Format   125

6.17.4 What Structure Diagrams Reveal 128

6.18 Animating from the Command Prompt 129

6.19 Exercises 129

7 **COBOL Source Information (CSI)** **135**

7.1 Purpose of CSI 135

7.2 Preparation 136
7.2.1 Checking with the CSI Directive 136
7.2.2 Running CSI 136

7.3 Using the CSI Menus 137
7.3.1 Basic Query Functions 137
7.3.2 Querying Additional Names 141
7.3.3 Special CSI Query Keywords 142
7.3.4 Setting CSI Options: Types of Detail to Display 146
7.3.5 Setting CSI Options: Display Format 147
7.3.6 Printing Results of a CSI Query 148
7.3.7 Tags (Bookmarks) 149

7.4 Mouse Support in Text Mode 150

7.5 What About the Command Prompt? 151

7.6 Exercises 151

8 **Compiling and Running Programs** **153**

8.1 Compiling/Linking/Running versus Checking/Animating 153

8.2 The Micro Focus Compiler 154
8.2.1 Files Used and Produced by the Code Generator 154
8.2.2 Compiler Directives 155

8.3 The Execute Menu 157
8.3.1 Compiling from the Execute Menu 157
8.3.2 The Run Menu 159
8.3.3 Operating System Command Prompt 161

8.4 Compiling from the Command Line 161

8.5 Link-Editing and the Shared Runtime System 162
8.5.1 Using the Linker 162
8.5.2 Linking with LCOBOL: Static Linked Runtime
System 163
8.5.3 Linking with COBLIB: Shared Runtime System 163
8.5.4 Using RTE: Toolset Run-Time Environment 163

8.5.5 Link-Editing from the WDE Menu 164

8.6 Running Programs from the Command Line 166

8.7 Performance Considerations on the PC Workstation 167

8.8 Exercises 168

9   Mainframe Testing on the PC 169

9.1 EBCDIC versus ASCII Considerations 169
9.1.1 Bridging the Mainframe and PC Environments 169
9.1.2 Which Files Need Translating? 169
9.1.3 Source Programs with Embedded Hex Codes 171

9.2 Mainframe versus PC File Types 172
9.2.1 Mainframe and PC Sequential Files 172
9.2.2 Mainframe and PC Indexed Sequential Files (VSAM) 173
9.2.3 Relative Files 174
9.2.4 DL/I Databases 174
9.2.5 SQL-Based Databases 174

9.3 MS-DOS and OS/2 versus Mainframe JCL 175
9.3.1 What Mainframe JCL Actually Does 175
9.3.2 Methods for Allocating Disk Files to Programs 176
9.3.3 Using the PC Printer and Other Devices 178
9.3.4 Mainframe SYSIN and SYSOUT 179
9.3.5 Using the PARM Passer Facility 180

9.4 Utilities on the Mainframe Side 182
9.4.1 IDCAMS REPRO 182
9.4.2 VRECGEN (Micro Focus File Format Utility) 182
9.4.3 3270 Send-Receive or IRMA 183

9.5 Utilities on the PC Side 183
9.5.1 File Transfer Aid (Micro Focus Download Utility) 183
9.5.2 MDECONV (EBCDIC/ASCII translation) 189
9.5.3 WFL (Workbench File Loader) 191
9.5.4 HEXEDIT (Hex Editor) 199
9.5.5 Data File Editor (DFED) 201

**9.6 Processing Sequence for Downloading and Converting
Each File Type** 210

9.7 Exercises 211

10   Other Useful Utilities 213

10.1 Introduction 213

10.2 File Finder   214
  10.2.1 What File Finder does   214
  10.2.2 Using File Finder   215

10.3 Source Comparison (DIFF) Utility   216
  10.3.1 What DIFF Does   216
  10.3.2 Using DIFF   216

10.4 Concurrency   219
  10.4.1 Concurrency Concepts   219
  10.4.2 Starting Concurrency   220
  10.4.3 Starting and Switching between Concurrent
         Processes   221
  10.4.4 Background Syntax Checking While Editing   223

10.5 Keystroke Macros (MFKEYMAC)   224
  10.5.1 Keystroke Macro Concepts   224
  10.5.2 Starting Up Workbench with Keystroke Macros   224
  10.5.3 Defining Keystroke Macros   225

10.6 Session Recorder for Regression Testing   226
  10.6.1 What Is Regression Testing?   226
  10.6.2 Session Recorder Concepts   227
  10.6.3 Recording a Testing Session   229
  10.6.4 Comparing Screen Snapshot Files   233
  10.6.5 Viewing Keystroke Files   236

10.7 Exercises   238

**11   Tools for the Workbench System
        Administrator**   239

11.1 What the System Administrator Does   239
  11.1.1 Installing and Upgrading Workbench and
         Add-On Products   239
  11.1.2 Training and Standards   240
  11.1.3 Contact Person for Micro Focus Product Support   240
  11.1.4 Customizing the Menu System   240

11.2 Micro Focus Configuration Files   240
  11.2.1 Overview of Configuration Files   240

11.3 Customizing Menu Color Settings   241
  11.3.1 Configuring Colors   242

11.4 Customizing Editor Default Settings   244
  11.4.1 Editor Configuration Information   244
  11.4.2 Word Wrap, Directives, and Other Toggles   245
  11.4.3 Filename Extensions for Search   246
  11.4.4 Default Margin Settings   246

11.5 Creating New Banners and Text Screens   **246**
11.5.1 Using Forms Facility to Paint Text Screens   246
11.5.2 Installing New Banner Screens   249

11.6 Customizing Function Key Settings   **251**
11.6.1 Function Key Menu Statements   251
11.6.2 Customizing Default Checker/Compiler Directives   252

11.7 Customizing On-line Information (HYHELP) Files   **254**
11.7.1 Where the System Finds HYHELP Files   254
11.7.2 Creating New HYHELP Files   254
11.7.3 Compiling HYHELP Files   257
11.7.4 Testing HYHELP Files   258

11.8 How to Find Answers in the Micro Focus Manuals   **260**
11.8.1 Error Messages: Using the Error Manual   261
11.8.2 The Master Index Volume   261

11.9 Exercises   **261**

12   **Overview of Add-On Options**   **263**

12.1 Mainframe Assembler Support   **263**
12.1.1 Micro Focus 370 Assembler with ANIMATOR/370   263

12.2 MVS JCL Support   **269**
12.2.1 Proximity Software ProxMvs   269

12.3 CICS Support   **276**
12.3.1 MCO2: Micro Focus CICS Option for OS/2
(CICS OS/2)   276
12.3.2 MCO: Micro Focus CICS Option (formerly ISI
CICSVS86)   279

12.4 SQL-based Database Management Systems   **280**
12.4.1 XDB   280
12.4.2 IBM OS/2 Extended Services Database Manager   284
12.4.3 Microsoft SQL Server   285
12.4.4 Oracle   286
12.4.5 Gupta SQLBase   287

12.5 IMS Database and Data Communications Support   **287**
12.5.1 IMS Option (Micro Focus/Stingray Software)   287

12.6 Computer Associates DBMS Support   **292**
12.6.1 The CA-IDMS/PC and CA-DATACOM/PC
Environments   292
12.6.2 CA-IDMS/PC   292
12.6.3 CA-DATACOM/PC   293
12.6.4 For more information.   293

12.7 VM/CMS Emulation   **293**
    12.7.1 KEDIT: Emulator for VM/CMS XEDIT on the PC   293

12.8 Mainframe ISPF Emulation   **296**
    12.8.1 CTC ISPF Editor (SPF/PC and SPF/2)   296
    12.8.2 Micro Focus/Stingray AD/MVS Menu System   297

12.9 Source Code Management and Code Reusability   **301**
    12.9.1 Reusable Code Manager   301

13   The SPF Editor   311

13.1 Why Use the SPF Editor?   **311**

13.2 The SPF/PC and SPF/2 Menu Systems   **312**
    13.2.1 Hierarchy of Functions   312
    13.2.2 Using SPF/PC and SPF/2 with the PC File System 312

13.3 SPF/2 Setup   **312**
    13.3.1 Installing SPF/2   312
    13.3.2 Interfacing SPF/2 with the Workbench   312

13.4 New Features of SPF/2 Version 2.0   **315**
    13.4.1 Overview of New Features   315
    13.4.2 Keyboard Mapping   315
    13.4.3 Text Highlighting   316
    13.4.4 Super Lists   317

13.5 Tailoring SPF/2   **319**
    13.5.1 SPF/2 Options Menu   319
    13.5.2 Profiles   319

**14   The Graphical User Interface Workbench
Organizer   321**

14.1 Reducing the Intimidation Factor   **321**

14.2 Workbench Organizer Concepts   **322**
    14.2.1 What Object Orientation Means   322
    14.2.2 Advantages of Graphical User Interface   324
    14.2.3 SAA CUA Concepts   324
    14.2.4 Organizer Projects and Tools   327

14.3 Workbench Organizer Setup   **327**
    14.3.1 Organizer System Requirements   327
    14.3.2 Installing the Organizer   328
    14.3.3 Starting the Organizer   328

14.4 Using Objects   **329**
    14.4.1 Built-In Tools Supplied with Workbench   329

14.4.2 Using the Template to Define New Tools 330
14.4.3 Using the Template to Create New Projects 332
14.4.4 Using Existing Tools and Projects 333
14.4.5 More about Starting Tools 334

14.5 Customizing the Environment **335**

14.6 Exercises **335**

15 The GUI Animator V2 **337**

15.1 Animator V2 Concepts **337**
15.1.1 Introduction 337
15.1.2 Overview of Animator V2 337

15.2 Animator V2 Setup **338**
15.2.1 Installation 338
15.2.2 Starting Animator V2 338

15.3 The Animator V2 Menu Structure **340**
15.3.1 Appearance of Animator V2 340

15.4 File and Directory Facilities **342**
15.4.1 Loading and Saving Files 342

15.5 Editing Facilities **343**
15.5.1 Basic Editing Operations 343
15.5.2 Configuring Screen Appearance 345
15.5.3 Configuring Editing Behavior 346

15.6 Checking and Compilation Facilities **348**
15.6.1 Checking a Program 348
15.6.2 Compiling a Program 348

15.7 Animation Facilities **349**
15.7.1 Animating a Program 349
15.7.2 Monitoring Data Items 350
15.7.3 Using Breakpoints 353

15.8 COBOL Source Information Facilities **354**
15.8.1 Performing Searches 354
15.8.2 Setting Find Options 357

15.9 Exercises **360**

16 Workbench GUI Utilities **361**

16.1 Introduction **361**

16.2 Directory Facility (MFDIR V2) **361**

16.2.1 Description   361
16.2.2 Invoking MFDIR V2   362
16.2.3 Simple File Commands   363
16.2.4 Searching for Files   364
16.2.5 Directory Commands   364
16.2.6 Configuration Options   367

16.3 On-line Information System (GUI Hypertext Help)   368
16.3.1 Description   368
16.3.2 Command line interface   368
16.3.3 On-line Information menu options   369

16.4 Session Recorder   373
16.4.1 Description   373
16.4.2 Changes from the Text Mode Version   373
16.4.3 Processing Flow   373
16.4.4 Invoking Session Recorder   374

16.5 GUI File Transfer Aid (MFXFER V2)   376
16.5.1 Description   376
16.5.2 Invoking MFXFER V2   377
16.5.3 Operation of MFXFER V2   377

16.6 GUI Source Comparison Utility (DIFF V2)   382
16.6.1 Description   382
16.6.2 Invoking DIFF V2   382
16.6.3 Operation of DIFF V2   382

16.7 Overview of Other New Workbench Functions   384
16.7.1 Probe   384
16.7.2 Build V2   388

16.8 Other Enhancements with Workbench v3.0   388
16.8.1 Improved CICS Support   388
16.8.2 Btrieve Support   389
16.8.3 The RUNPM Shell   389

**A   Appendix A: PC Fundamentals for the
             Mainframe Programmer   391**

A.1 Distinguish MS-DOS, Windows, and OS/2 Environments   391

A.2 Basic Concepts   393
A.2.1 MS-DOS and OS/2 Command Line Prompt   393
A.2.2 Directory Structure   394
A.2.3 Batch Files (MS-DOS)   399
A.2.4 Command Files (OS/2)   399
A.2.5 Environment Variables   399
A.2.6 AUTOEXEC.BAT   400
A.2.7 CONFIG.SYS   400

A.2.8 Text versus Graphic (Windowed) Environment   400

A.3 Commands Most Often Used   **401**
A.3.1 Viewing Directory Contents   402
A.3.2 Making, Removing, and Changing Subdirectories   402
A.3.3 Copying, Renaming, and Deleting Files   403
A.3.4 Running Programs and Batch Files   404
A.3.5 PATH Command   404
A.3.6 SET Command   404

A.4 Installing Both MS-DOS and OS/2   **405**
A.4.1 Dual Boot Using MS-DOS or OS/2   405
A.4.2 Booting from a Diskette   406
A.4.3 Boot Manager   406

A.5 More About the OS/2 2.0 Desktop   **409**
A.5.1 Objects on the OS/2 2.0 Desktop   409
A.5.2 The Settings Menu   409
A.5.3 Shutting Down OS/2 2.0   410

A.6 Where to Find More Information   **410**
A.6.1 The COBOL Language   410
A.6.2 The PC Operating Environment   410

B   **Appendix B: Micro Focus Support Information 413**

B.1 User Groups   **413**

B.2 The Micro Focus Bulletin Board System (BBS)   **415**

B.3 Micro Focus Offices   **415**

Index   **417**

Introduction

Purpose of This Book

If you're a potential purchaser wondering whether or not the Micro Focus Workbench will meet your needs, this book will provide more than enough information on which to base your decision. The variety of examples used in this book will give you a definite feel for the process of using a personal computer to do mainframe development. You'll discover that the Micro Focus Workbench is a useful tool for developing new mainframe applications and maintaining existing mainframe applications. Does your shop have old convoluted, unstructured, and undocumented COBOL programs that no one remembers? This book will explain the Workbench features to help you figure out, modify, or rewrite these programs.

For a new user, the overwhelming amount of reference documentation provided with the Micro Focus Workbench can look like an insurmountable obstacle. This book will provide new users with a clear, step-by-step approach to getting started using this powerful and extensive product. For example, we'll lead you through the setup directives (options) you'll need to install the Micro Focus Workbench for the first time.

Micro Focus offers hands-on classes for new Workbench users. The Workbench class is thorough and moves along at a rapid pace. While we found the Workbench class to be very useful, we couldn't help wondering how well we would retain the material after the class was over. This book will help you remember the hundreds of details that went by so quickly in the class. If you can't take the class, this book will introduce you to those same hundreds of details, as well as other information not covered in a three-day class.

Experienced Workbench users will find this book useful as a single reference source for solving most common problems. During the research for this book, we asked many experienced users of the Micro Focus Workbench just what they'd like to see in a book. We listened to their suggestions and incorporated the best of them into this book.

Brief History of Micro Focus, Inc. and the Workbench Product

According to the 1991 Micro Focus annual report, "Micro Focus was founded in 1976 on the idea that increasing hardware power arising out of the advances in microprocessor technology would eventually lead to computer workstations which would give the power of a mainframe on a desk. . . . COBOL was already by then the industry standard computer language for writing business applications. . . . Micro Focus believed that this plus the massive investment in trained programmers and working applications, often consisting of many hundreds of thousands of lines of COBOL code, would ensure COBOL's pre-eminence for a long time to come."

Brian Reynolds and Paul O'Grady founded Micro Focus in London, England in 1976. According to company background information, Micro Focus developed its first COBOL compiler for a microcomputer in 1977. A year later, Micro Focus introduced CIS COBOL at the National Computer Conference (NCC). The NCC, now defunct, was a major computer industry trade show—the mainframe equivalent of today's Comdex. CIS COBOL ran on the eight-bit, 64K RAM microcomputers then available. It became the first micro COBOL compiler to attain U.S. General Services Administration certification for conformance to ANSI standards.

During the early 1980s, IBM introduced its first personal computer or "PC." The large volume of PC sales, and the ease of connecting it to IBM mainframes, established the PC as a de facto standard for microcomputer architecture. Micro Focus introduced its Level II COBOL compiler in 1981 to run on computers based on the new 16-bit, Intel 808x processors. It attained ANSI '74 high-level certification; this meant that it supported the full extent of the COBOL language features available in many mainframe and minicomputer compilers. In 1982, the Level II compiler was introduced for the Motorola 68000 processor. In 1984, Level II COBOL/ET provided support for the new 32-bit microprocessors. Level II COBOL has been ported to more than 100 different environments, including CP/M-86-, MS-DOS-, and UNIX-based systems. In 1985, it was chosen as the basis for the X/OPEN COBOL specification.

Micro Focus released the VS COBOL Workbench in January 1985. The Workbench added mainframe programming features to the PC-based development environment. Add-on products for CICS and IMS DB/DC emulation followed soon. Micro Focus was a participant of the ANSI COBOL committee and had helped formulate the ANSI '85 standard. This enabled Micro Focus to earn the world's first ANSI '85 certification for its VS COBOL compiler in 1986.

In April 1987, Micro Focus introduced COBOL/2 for the IBM Personal System/2 (PS/2), supporting the new OS/2 operating system as well as MS-DOS. The Micro Focus COBOL/2 Workbench also became available in 1987. As Micro Focus gained more experience with the Micro Focus Workbench, they were able to emulate the mainframe environment more closely. This meant that mainframe COBOL programs could be downloaded to PCs, changed, tested, and uploaded back to the mainframe. Micro Focus COBOL/2 supports many COBOL dialects, including mainframe OS/VS COBOL, VS COBOL II, and COBOL/370.

Micro Focus began holding user conferences in 1989 for their customers. Major new releases of the product are announced at these conferences. The 1991 user conference, held in May in Orlando, Florida, attracted more than 700 attendees. In addition, Micro Focus Workbench user groups have formed in some parts of the country (see the Appendix for more information.) A computerized bulletin board system (BBS) maintained by Micro Focus allows further exchange of information among Micro Focus users.

Micro Focus consists of two divisions. The Packaged Products Division (PPD) develops and sells Micro Focus products under the Micro Focus name to users worldwide. The Computer Industry Division (CID) licenses Micro Focus software and methods to computer manufacturers worldwide, with the exception of IBM® and Microsoft®, which are serviced by PPD. Micro Focus has licensed its COBOL/2 compiler to IBM and to Microsoft, who have resold the compiler under their own names. On May 7, 1991, Micro Focus signed an agreement with IBM to market the Micro Focus Workbench family of COBOL products jointly as part of the AD/Cycle Business Partner relationship. IBM has designated Micro Focus COBOL as IBM's Systems Application Architecture (SAA) COBOL for workstations. The Micro Focus COBOL/2 compiler will therefore replace the IBM COBOL/2 compiler licensed in 1987 by Micro Focus to IBM. This means that you can buy the Workbench products from your IBM branch office, and still get product support directly from Micro Focus. In addition, Micro Focus sells and supports IBM's CICS OS/2 as an add-on option for the Workbench.

Overview: What Is the Micro Focus Workbench?

1.1 Developing Mainframe Applications on the PC

1.1.1 Why Develop Mainframe Applications on the PC?

Developing mainframe applications on the PC can offer advantages in cost savings, quality, security, and flexibility. Let's look at cost first. The most obvious problem faced in large mainframe sites is this: *"Our mainframes are bursting at the seams!"* We all know the symptoms: poor on-line response, slow batch turnaround, and unplanned outages. The simplistic answer, *"We need bigger mainframes,"* is not always the best answer. While there will always be a need for large computer systems for large, high-volume tasks and for centralized coordination, the fact remains that large systems are more expensive to purchase and operate. **In general, it costs much more to provide mainframe CPU cycles, memory, and storage for a mainframe terminal user than it costs to provide the same amount of resources on a PC workstation.** This means that it pays to offload any work that doesn't require a large system.

This is already being done to some extent. Many mainframe shops already have some PCs onsite, typically used for word processing, spreadsheets, small databases, desktop publishing, and project scheduling. Sometimes PCs used by application programmers contain 3270 emulation boards so that they can double as mainframe terminals. While this arrangement avoids the need for two CRTs on each desk, using the PC as a mainframe "dumb terminal" wastes the PC's processing power. The mainframe still has to do nearly all the work. Using the Micro Focus Workbench to provide mainframelike programming resources on the PC allows the PC to do nearly all the work.

Making it more convenient for programmers to do their work translates into cost savings, improved quality, and better morale. In a PC-based testing environment, programmers don't have to wait for COBOL compiles and listings, for on-line test regions to come up, for VTAM communication links to be restored, or for the system programmer to maintain system resources such as CICS tables. On the PC, each application programmer can manage his or her own program libraries, test files, databases, and system definition tables on the PC, without depending on or interfering with anyone else. Programmers don't have to compete with production jobs for batch turnaround,

Calling Operations when the mainframe is down

on-line response, disk space, the printer, or other resources. No more "mainframe politics": jockeying for higher priority when resources are scarce. No more staring at a dead terminal while listening to the busy signal at the help desk. **Whenever programmers are spending their time waiting for something, money is being wasted. Properly equipped PC workstations allow programmers to spend more time working and less time waiting.**

Mainframe programmers are tempted to skimp on testing whenever mainframe test turnaround or response time is slow, or when mainframe testing tools are unavailable or hard to use. The PC environment provides a much richer set of testing tools than anything available on the mainframe. Making application testing easier and more convenient encourages programmers to do a more thorough job, resulting in more reliable applications.

Isolating the program testing environment on the PC can improve security. Errors made by one person during program testing will not bring down the test region, the VTAM network, or the entire mainframe. At most, one programmer will have to reboot one workstation. Production work and other application testing will continue uninterrupted. Even for the affected programmer, it takes much less time to reboot the PC workstation than it does to revive a multi-CPU mainframe with many on-line regions and a big VTAM network. And if programmers corrupt their own files or databases, they can restore them from backup diskettes at any time. Production databases, and other programmers' test databases, remain unaffected.

In a production environment, PC workstations provide more flexibility in applications design. Some production applications can be split between the mainframe and the PC workstations. This is known as **distributed processing.** Keeping some of your data on the PC allows local data entry and lookups even when the link to the mainframe is down. Confidential data not intended for sharing with mainframe users can be isolated on the PC's hard drive, under password protection. Other systems cannot get at the data unless you set up links for them to do so. Complex user interface processing can be done without using any mainframe memory or CPU cycles. Designing applications in this way takes careful planning. When you get to that stage, you will find that some of the add-on products that go with the Micro Focus Workbench can make it easier to write distributed applications in COBOL.

1.1.2 What You Need to Consider

Several major issues will come up when you develop mainframe applications on the PC:

- **Cost of PC hardware and software.** Although you are very likely to save money in the long run, there is a startup cost in providing PC workstations for each programmer. This doesn't always mean that your organization will have to purchase a new machine for each programmer. Some programmers may already have adequate workstations on their desks; others may have

AT-class or better workstations that can be upgraded by adding communications adapters or more memory.

- **Differences between the PC and mainframe environments.** The PC is physically different from the mainframe in several ways. It comes with a graphics display, unlike the 3270-type text display on a mainframe. The PC stores text data in ASCII rather than EBCDIC. The internal architecture is different from the mainframe; it runs a different instruction set. PC operating systems are designed to take all of that into account. When you plan to duplicate the mainframe environment on the PC, you need to be aware that it is impossible to make the environments perfectly identical. There will always be certain minor inconsistencies. However, from a practical standpoint, it will be close enough to let you develop and test mainframe applications on the PC.
- **The learning curve.** Some mainframe programmers may not have much PC experience. Even for those who do have that experience, it takes some time to learn a new programming environment such as the Micro Focus Workbench. To get the benefits, the programmer must be willing to invest the time needed to learn the purpose and function of each of the Workbench features.

1.2 Overview of the Three Parts of the Micro Focus Product

The Micro Focus Workbench is a COBOL application program development environment that runs on an 80286 (IBM AT-class) machine or better. The Workbench contains facilities for editing, compiling, testing, debugging, and running COBOL applications. Three separate parts make up the Workbench environment: the compiler itself, the Toolset, and the Workbench.

1.2.1 The COBOL/2 Compiler

The heart of the Micro Focus Workbench is the COBOL/2 compiler. This compiler gives you the option of using the latest ANSI Standard COBOL or other COBOL standards or dialects to match your mainframe compiler. COBOL standard examples include ANSI '74 or '85 COBOL, IBM OS/VS COBOL, IBM VS COBOL II (1, 2, or 3), X/OPEN, and IBM SAA COBOL. Other COBOL dialects supported by Micro Focus COBOL/2 include Data General Interactive COBOL V1.30, Ryan-McFarland COBOL V2.0, Microsoft COBOL 1.0 AND 2.0, and IBM COBOL 1.0.

The COBOL/2 compiler, which can be purchased by itself, consists of a Checker/Compiler and a basic source-level debugger called the Animator. The package also includes a linker (licensed from Microsoft), a screen painter for the PC environment, and an indexed file rebuild utility. The compiler supports indexed files using the same syntax as mainframe VSAM. It provides support for EXEC SQL commands so that your COBOL program can access OS/2 Extended Services Database Manager, XDB, Gupta, and other SQL-based database management systems. It supports the usual mainframe ANSI ACCEPT/DISPLAY syntax together with various extensions, including full-screen ACCEPT/DISPLAY with SCREEN SECTION. Callable routines provide more extensive support for the PC keyboard, screen, and mouse.

Micro Focus updates the COBOL/2 compiler and the Workbench frequently to keep up with changes in the industry, particularly with new ANSI standards. One example of the evolution of COBOL was the improved support for structured programming that came with ANSI '85. In the past, COBOL programmers sometimes used GO TO statements to get around language limitations. With ANSI '85 COBOL and the 1989 Addendum, there is no longer any reason to use GO TO statements in a COBOL program.

COBOL intrinsic functions are part of the 1989 Addendum to the ANSI 85 COBOL Standard. In May 1991, Workbench version 2.5 began supporting this feature. Intrinsic functions provide calendar arithmetic and conversion, character and string handling, calculations, mathematical and statistical functions, and trigonometric functions. Of these, the date functions are likely to be used the most often. Functions work somewhat differently from other COBOL syntax. You can use functions in place of other COBOL variables, expressions, or parts of expressions. A function gives back a temporary data item whose value is calculated at runtime. It disappears unless you save it somewhere. You are responsible for moving this value to a permanent field or using it in some other calculation. You can even *nest* functions by using one function as an argument of another function.

Figure 1.1 shows an example of COBOL program syntax using an intrinsic function. In Figure 1.1, the REVERSE function has a single *argument,* **ws-my-name.** The MOVE statement saves the *temporary value* returned by the REVERSE function by placing it in **ws-backward.**

```
01  ws-my-name      pic x(12) value "Phil Nowak  ".
01  ws-backward     pic x(12) value spaces.
*
    MOVE FUNCTION REVERSE (ws-my-name) TO ws-backward.
*
*Result: ws-backward now contains "  kawoN lihP".
*
```

Figure 1.1 Example of a COBOL intrinsic function

Micro Focus made intrinsic functions available on the PC before any mainframe COBOL compiler had them. If you want to port a program from the Workbench back to the mainframe, you will be able to use the intrinsic functions only if your mainframe compiler supports them, as does IBM's COBOL/370. It's a good idea to become familiar with new COBOL language elements so that you can begin planning how to make best use of them. Detailed information about COBOL intrinsic functions is in the *Micro Focus COBOL/2 Language Reference.* Figure 1.2 lists available COBOL intrinsic functions.

The COBOL language is in no danger of becoming obsolete. In a presentation to the Midwest Area Micro Focus Users Group, COBOL expert Jerome Garfunkel offered some statistics gathered by Hewlett-Packard Corporation:

- One trillion lines of COBOL code are running worldwide.
- Ten billion lines of new COBOL code are written each year.
- Three million programmers use COBOL.

	Calendar Functions
Name	**Description**
CURRENT-DATE	Current date and time; local variation from Greenwich time
DATE-OF-INTEGER	Translates of integer date to calendar (YYYYMMDD) format
DAY-OF-INTEGER	Translates of integer date to Julian (YYYYDDD) format
INTEGER-OF-DATE	Translates of calendar date (YYYYMMDD) to integer date format
INTEGER-OF-DAY	Translates of Julian date (YYYYDDD) to integer date format
WHEN-COMPILED	Date and time of most recent program compilation
	Character and String Functions
Name	**Description**
CHAR	Character in nth position of collating sequence (EBCDIC or ASCII)
ORD	Ordinal position of this character in collating sequence
LENGTH	Length of argument in bytes
LOWER-CASE	Converts alpha characters to lower case
UPPER-CASE	Converts alpha characters to upper case
NUMVAL	Converts character string to numeric with correct decimal point and sign
NUMVAL-C	Converts character string containing currency signs and commas, with proper de-editing
REVERSE	Reverses order of characters in a string
	Financial Functions
Name	**Description**
ANNUITY	Calculates annuity ratio
PRESENT-VALUE	Calculates net present value

Figure 1.2 COBOL intrinsic functions

Not only is there an enormous installed base of COBOL programs and a large community of experienced programmers, but the COBOL language evolves over time to meet the needs of its users. The American National Standards Institute (ANSI) standardization process ensures that the new language features will be portable across all COBOL programming environments. For example, object-oriented languages, such as Borland C++, have been much in the news lately. **Object-oriented COBOL will be coming soon.** The Object-Oriented COBOL Task Group (OOCTG) is working on standards, and Micro Focus is participating in the standards-making effort. Micro Focus will offer add-on products for object-oriented programming in COBOL, in

Numerical Analysis Functions

Name	Description
INTEGER	Returns the greatest integer that is not greater than the argument.
INTEGER-PART	Returns the integer part of a numeric argument (truncation)
MAX	Value of the largest argument presented
MIN	Value of the smallest argument presented
MIDRANGE	One-half the sum of the maximum and minimum arguments
ORD-MAX	Ordinal position of the largest argument presented
ORD-MIN	Ordinal position of the smallest argument presented
RANDOM	Random number generator
RANGE	Difference of maximum and minimum arguments
REM	Remainder of argument 1 divided by argument 2

Statistical Functions

Name	Description
FACTORIAL	Factorial
LOG	Natural logarithm (base e)
LOG 10	Common logarithm (base 10)
MEAN	Arithmetic mean of arguments
MEDIAN	Median of arguments
MOD	Argument 1 modulo argument 2
SQRT	Square root
STANDARD-DEVIATION	Standard deviation of arguments
SUM	Sum of arguments
VARIANCE	Statistical variance of arguments

Trigonometric Functions

Name	Description
ACOS	Arc cosine
ASIN	Arc sine
ATAN	Arc tangent
COS	Cosine
SIN	Sine

Figure 1.2 COBOL intrinsic functions (cont'd)

conformance with proposed standards. **Reusable Code Manager (RCM)**, for example, provides a library for COBOL source modules. It makes it easy for a group of programmers to reuse the same pieces of tested COBOL program logic in many programs, with whatever minor variations are needed.

A revealing anecdote. At the Micro Focus user conference in 1991, a nonprogrammer asked a group of conference attendees, "What do you use COBOL for?" Several people in the crowd replied, *"Everything!"* This is largely true. The COBOL language is becoming broader in scope. While the name "COBOL" stands for "Common *Business* Oriented Language," the COBOL language is evolving toward greater support for scientific and engineering applications and for systems programming as well as for business applications. At present, only a few specialized applications, such as high-resolution graphic arts and animation, are not being done in COBOL. Even these exceptions are likely to disappear soon. New binary data types that support graphics, audio, and video applications are "in the works." Graphics primitives will become available either with subprogram library calls (as in the C language) or with embedded statements that go through a preprocessor (as is now done with SQL).

1.2.2 The Toolset

Another part of the Micro Focus Workbench is the Toolset. This product includes a COBOL source code editor with windowing capability, a runtime system, and an extended memory manager (XM) for MS-DOS. It also contains PC-specific software such as the Callable File Handler (allows direct interception of all file access), Fileshare (file integrity for networks), Co-Writer (report generator), Setup (program installation utility that you can use for your own applications), and Panels (user-interface design). With version 2.5, besides other enhancements, the COBOL source code editor now has mouse support.

1.2.3 The Workbench

Micro Focus uses the term "Workbench" in two ways. The Workbench is the third part of the environment, containing the utilities that integrate the entire Micro Focus Workbench environment into a coherent whole. In that sense, Workbench is the third product sold by Micro Focus, as distinguished from the COBOL/2 compiler and the Toolset. However, the term "Workbench" also describes the complete Workbench environment, which includes the COBOL/2 compiler, Toolset, and Workbench products integrated under the Workbench menu system.All features in the environment can be run either from the integrated menu system or from the MS-DOS or OS/2 command prompt. Figures 1.3 and 1.4 show the relationship between these Micro Focus products and the Microsoft Windows and IBM OS/2 operating environments. (Note that you can also run the Workbench products in text mode directly under MS-DOS.)

The Workbench includes an Advanced Animator, COBOL Source Information, a Session Recorder, various file handling and conversion utilities, a Data File Editor, on-line help, and a generator for screens and forms. These utilities make it easy to use the Workbench not only for developing new applications, but also for maintaining existing applications now running on

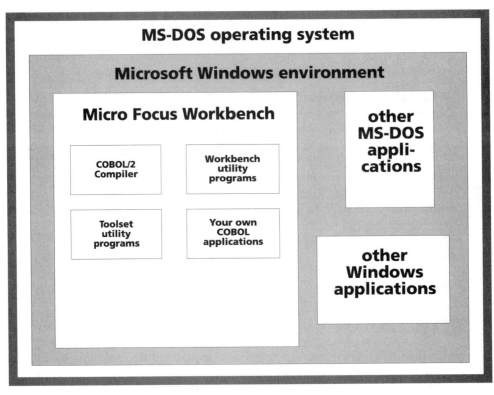

Figure 1.3 Micro Focus Workbench in the Windows environment

other systems. Micro Focus enhanced many of these utilities for versions 2.5 and 3.0.

The Micro Focus Workbench provides features for developing applications that will be run either on mainframes or PCs. Once the Workbench environment is on your workstation, you can tailor it further by installing add-on options to match your mainframe or PC environment. These include mainframe CICS, IMS, IDMS, and even 370 Assembler emulation, as well as SQL-based databases and support for graphical user interfaces on the PC such as Windows and OS/2 PM. One of the latest techniques in application design involves cooperative processing: allowing different parts of the application to run on different systems within the same network. For example, the user interface runs on PCs that communicate with the mainframe handling the database. The Micro Focus Workbench makes it easier to write this type of application.

Workbench v2.5 introduced support for Windows 3.0 applications programming interface (API), floating point numeric processing (using an Intel math coprocessor if available), better network communications support, and a hypertext help system. These new features let you write programs in COBOL that formerly required C or assembler language. Workbench v3.0 introduced the graphical user interface (GUI) Workbench described in Chapters 14-16, as well as COBOL/370 and DOS/VS COBOL support, Btrieve indexed file support, and enhancements to the Workbench File Loader (WFL).

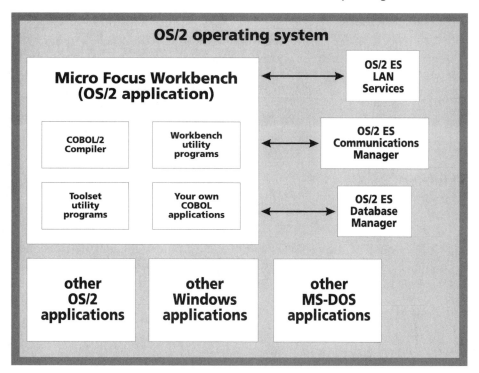

Figure 1.4 Micro Focus Workbench in the OS/2 environment

1.3 Operating Environments

We mentioned that Micro Focus supports a variety of operating environments. The Micro Focus products will run in those environments and will produce code that takes advantage of the features of those environments. If you have the Workbench installed on a workstation running under MS-DOS, it's easy to change it over to Microsoft Windows or OS/2. The same Workbench product takes care of all three environments. The first step is to load the new operating environment; then, if you did not originally install the Workbench to run in both the old and the new operating environments, you will need to reinstall the Workbench. Use the same installation diskettes and the same SETUP utility that you used before. As always, it will ask you what operating environments you plan to install. In this section, we will discuss what types of programming Micro Focus will let you do in each environment. (We will discuss hardware and software requirements in Chapter 2.)

1.3.1 MS-DOS

In the MS-DOS environment, the Workbench runs with the Toolset extended memory manager (XM). In this environment, you can use the Workbench to produce text-mode MS-DOS applications as well as applications for uploading to the mainframe. MS-DOS applications can be run as standalone modules or run with the Toolset runtime system (RTS). You also can distribute XM to the end users with your MS-DOS COBOL applications if they need the space (a royalty fee applies if you distribute XM or the RTS).

As of version 2.5, Micro Focus did not offer a shared PC network server version of Workbench. (By that we mean a version that can be run on a Novell server, for example, to be accessed by many workstations at once.) However, you can run the Workbench on network workstations (each under its own separate license), using the server to hold your libraries of programs, copy members, and data. You also can use the Workbench to write COBOL applications that follow proper methods of file locking for use on a PC network. Micro Focus plans to offer network products for releases that follow 2.5.

1.3.2 Windows

Beginning with version 2.5, the Workbench will run under Microsoft Windows 3.0 and will produce applications that take advantage of that environment. These applications may be text mode, graphics mode, windowed, or full screen. The Micro Focus Workbench provides language extensions and called routines to use the Windows graphics mode application programming interface (API). You can use the Microsoft Windows Software Development Toolkit (SDK) with Micro Focus COBOL/2 programs to write full graphics-mode Windows applications.

1.3.3 OS/2 and OS/2 Extended Services

The Micro Focus Workbench also runs under the OS/2 operating system. You can use it to write OS/2 applications, including those using the Presentation Manager graphical user interface (GUI). You can write the PM portion in COBOL if you also have the PM Developer's Toolkit. Alternatively, you can use the Dialog System add-on product to do the graphical front end. You can also access the OS/2 Extended Services Communications Manager and Database Manager features. SQL precompiler support is part of the COBOL/2 compiler product.

1.3.4 Unix, Xenix, AIX (separate Micro Focus product)

Micro Focus also offers a COBOL/2 compiler and Toolbox utilities for the Unix environment. The Unix products are sold separately; they are tailored for the Unix enviroment and therefore are not the same as the Micro Focus Workbench family of products for the single-user PC discussed above. **The COBOL language support is compatible across both environments.**

1.4 Exercises

1. Define the term "COBOL dialect." Explain the meaning of "COBOL language compatibility across different operating environments" in practical terms.

2. Describe some possible advantages to using the new COBOL intrinsic functions once they are available in your mainframe environment. (Hint: What might you use in place of CURRENT-DATE as the year 2000 approaches?)

2

Getting Started

The Micro Focus Workbench is a powerful product that will support a multitude of needs and situations. It comes with a setup utility that lets you configure it to suit your requirements. However, because of the large number of options available, there are many questions to answer during the setup process. Installation can be intimidating for the new user. The purpose of this chapter is to show you what you need to do to get Workbench running on your system so that you can run the sample exercises. You will be able to add other refinements later.

Be aware that Micro Focus may change the SETUP utility program and script files from release to release. The example here is from the SETUP script for version 2.5 and is intended to give you a general idea of what to do. Older or newer releases will have slightly different menu formats and sets of options.

Simple MS-DOS or OS/2 commands are needed to install and bring up the Micro Focus Workbench. If you are unfamiliar with PC operating systems, we suggest you read the Appendix before continuing with this chapter.

2.1 Installation Requirements for MS-DOS, Windows, OS/2

The installation requirements here apply to version 2.5. Since requirements may change, always read the release documentation before attempting to install the Micro Focus Workbench.

2.1.1 Hardware: Processor, RAM, Disk Space

- You'll need a PC workstation with an 80286 or better processor. Suitable workstations include the IBM PC/AT, PC/XT 286, or PS/2 with 80286, 80386, or 80486 processors, or compatible machines from other manufacturers.
- If you will be running the Workbench under MS-DOS, you'll need a minimum of two megabytes of RAM. In the *Mainframe Programmer's Guide,* Micro Focus recommends two to four megabytes of extended memory together with the usual one megabyte of conventional memory. If you run any TSR utilities that take up your memory, make sure you have at least 1.5 megabytes of free memory remaining. If you will be running the Workbench under OS/2, RAM requirements are much greater. Micro Focus recommends at least eight megabytes of RAM, particularly if you use the OS/2 Extended Edition Database Manager or other add-on products.

- With either MS-DOS or OS/2, you'll need at least 10 megabytes of free space on your hard disk for the Workbench modules, another three megabytes for sample programs that come with the Workbench, and several more megabytes as work space for developing for your own applications.

2.1.2 Software: Operating Systems Supported

The Workbench runs under MS-DOS or PC-DOS version 3.3 or higher, or OS/2 version 1.2 or higher (Standard Edition or Extended Edition). The Workbench also supports Microsoft Windows 3.0.

2.2 Installing the Workbench

2.2.1 Overview of the Installation Procedure

This section will introduce you to the mechanics of starting the installation procedure. However, please read the rest of this chapter and the release notes supplied with your installation package before you actually begin loading any diskettes!

The Micro Focus installation procedure is based on a program called SETUP.EXE, supplied on diskette. SETUP is a generic program that can be used to automate the installation of just about any PC application. (You can even license SETUP from Micro Focus and distribute it to the end user along with PC applications that you write.) In this case, a script file called WB.INI, also supplied on diskette, tells SETUP how to install the Workbench software. SETUP shows you various selection menus to let you configure the software to be installed on your system. You tell it such things as what hard disk drive and directory to use, which language features and system utilities you plan to install, and whether you will be running under MS-DOS, OS/2, or both. Once you've finished making those selections, SETUP will prompt you to insert the diskettes in the proper order. Micro Focus Workbench software is delivered in compressed form. SETUP automatically uses the PKUNZIP utility to expand the files onto your hard disk.

Important: SETUP will not eliminate files and directories left over from previous versions of Workbench. Remove those manually before installing the new version. Back up your own applications, configuration files, and so forth, before removing any old Workbench directories.

2.2.2 Importance of Release Notes and "Read This First"

When you open your installation package, you will see a folder or pamphlet entitled *Read This First*. Human nature being what it is, not everybody reads it before randomly shoving diskettes into the machine! In any case, this document tells you where to find the most current information about how to begin your installation. The first thing it tells you to do is to "Read Chapters 1 and 2 of your *Getting Started* manual." Chapter 1 of *Getting Started* describes the purpose of each Workbench module. This material is easier to understand for those who have used earlier versions of Workbench, but even if you have not, take a look at it anyway. You will also find instructions for contacting tech support and using the Micro Focus bulletin board system (BBS). Chapter 2 tells you how to run SETUP, how to verify that the installation was successful by starting up the Workbench, and how to make sure you have the right variables in your MS-DOS or OS/2 environment table. Additional information is provided for those who intend to run the Workbench on a networked workstation. Be sure to read the parts of Chapter 2 that apply to your own operating environment.

Micro Focus software is updated regularly. The programs are updated more frequently than the manuals. This means that the *Getting Started* manual, and other manuals, might not be completely up to date. The SETUP menu lets you choose to **View essential information** and **View on-disk documentation** before you proceed with your installation. If you select these options, SETUP will let you page through display screens containing the most current information about this release. Always look at these release notes before installing the software.

2.2.3 Setting Up Your Directories

As of version 2.5, the Micro Focus Workbench is set up to be installed in several subdirectories under a parent directory called \COBOL. The creation of subdirectories is automatic, once you have told the SETUP program where to build the \COBOL directory. Usually, you will build the \COBOL directory under the root directory of a hard disk drive. Make sure you have enough free space left on that drive. If you have more than one partition (logical drive) on your physical hard disk drive, choose a partition with plenty of free space. The Micro Focus SETUP program will tell you how much disk space is needed to install the modules you have selected. However, you'll need some space for your own COBOL applications, too.

OS/2 users can install the Workbench either on an OS/2 HPFS logical drive or on an MS-DOS FAT-format logical drive. (See the Appendix for further discussion of HPFS and FAT directory formats.) However, if you want to share the Workbench between MS-DOS and OS/2 on the same machine, don't use an HPFS logical drive because MS-DOS won't recognize HPFS. Workbench version 2.5 will handle HPFS complex filenames as long as the total number of characters in the file or directory name (including periods) is no greater than 65.

2.2.4 Required Environment Variables: MS-DOS, Windows, OS/2

The environment table under MS-DOS or OS/2 contains variables that tell the system where to find files and programs that it needs. Paths specified with the PATH command tell the operating system where to find executable files. Parameters specified with the SET command tell applications such as the Workbench where to find other resources. In addition, the LIBPATH command is used under OS/2 to tell the system where to find executable subroutine libraries (.DLLs). You need to specify these to get the Workbench to run.

Under MS-DOS, the environment variables are set in the AU-TOEXEC.BAT file. Under OS/2, they are set in CONFIG.SYS. You will need to add new directory paths to the beginning of the path lists for some of these variables. The SETUP program will ask you whether or not you want it to update AUTOEXEC.BAT or CONFIG.SYS automatically. If you don't feel comfortable with allowing a program to update your system files, you'll have to perform the updates manually with an ASCII text editor, either before or after you run SETUP. In either case, you should verify that AUTOEXEC.BAT and/or CONFIG.SYS has been updated correctly before you reboot your system. These changes take effect at system boot time.

The *Getting Started* manual describes the updates that need to be made, either by the SETUP program or by the user. However, a few things were omitted. Under both MS-DOS and OS/2, the d:\COBOL\LBR directory path needs to be included in the PATH command following d:\COBOL\EXEDLL. Under OS/2, the d:\COBOL\LBR directory path needs to be included in the LIBPATH command following d:\COBOL\EXEDLL. The correct method is shown in the examples below.

Sample MS-DOS AUTOEXEC.BAT file. The MS-DOS AUTOEXEC.BAT file shown in Figure 2.1 sets up the environment variables needed for the Workbench. The Workbench, in this case, was installed on the K: drive. The last line of this AUTOEXEC.BAT file starts up Microsoft Windows, so that the Windows environment will appear when you turn on the computer.

Under MS-DOS, you may also need to expand the buffers, files, and environment table space by supplying parameters in CONFIG.SYS. Figure 2.2 shows CONFIG.SYS settings needed to run Workbench.

```
L:\WINDOWS\MOUSE.COM/Y
ECHO OFF
SET COMSPEC=C:\DOS\COMMAND.COM
REM ***** Commands updated for Micro Focus Workbench *****
SET COBDIR=K:\COBOL\LBR;K:\COBOL\EXEDLL
SET LIB=K:\COBOL\LIB;
SET COBHNF=K:\COBOL\ON-LINE;
SET INCLUDE=K:\COBOL\INC
SET CWWORK=K:\COBOL\DEMO\COWRITER
SET CWFILES=K:\COBOL\DEMO\COWRITER
SET CWRSYSTEM=K:\COBOL\LBR
PATH K:\COBOL\LBR;K:\COBOL\EXEDLL;C:\DOS;L:\WINDOWS;
REM ********** End of WB commands **********
VERIFY OFF
REM Colorful MS-DOS command line prompt using ANSI.SYS driver
Prompt $e[1m$e[31m[DOS] $e[33m$p $e[36m$t$h$h$h;$e[32m$_
REN ***** Start up Microsoft Windows *****
C:
WIN
```

Figure 2.1 Sample MS-DOS AUTOEXEC.BAT

```
BUFFERS=40
FILES=128
DEVICE=C:\DOS\SETVER.EXE
DEVICE=C:\DOS\HIMEM.SYS
SWITCHES=/W
DOS=HIGH
BREAK=ON
FCBS=20,8
LASTDRIVE=L
REM ***DOS ENVIRONMENT SHOULD BE AT LEAST 512***
REM ***PREVERABLY 1024***
SHELL=C:\DOS\COMMAND.COM /P /E:1024
DEVICE=C:\DOS\ANSI.SYS     /x
INSTALL=C:\DOS\FASTOPEN.EXE C:=(150,150)
```

Figure 2.2 Sample MS-DOS CONFIG.SYS

Warning: If you use the OS/2 dual boot option, be sure you modify the correct AUTOEXEC.BAT and CONFIG.SYS files used for your MS-DOS boot. OS/2 boot options are discussed in more detail in the Appendix. Also, don't confuse the MS-DOS AUTOEXEC.BAT with the OS/2 AUTOEXEC.BAT used with the "DOS compatibility box" (DOS session) running under OS/2. The Workbench is not set up to run in a DOS compatibility box under OS/2.

Sample OS/2 CONFIG.SYS file. Figure 2.3 shows an OS/2 CONFIG.SYS containing environment variables needed to run the Workbench:

```
PROTSHELL=C:\OS2\PMSHELL.EXE C:\OS2\OS2.INI C:\OS2\OS2SYS.INI
C:\OS2\CMD.EXE
SET COMSPEC=C:\OS2\CMD.EXE
REM ***** Commands updated for Micro Focus Workbench *****
SET PATH=K:\COBOL\LBR;K:\COBOL\EXEDLL;C:\OS2;C:\MUGLIB;C:\SQLLIB;
C:\OS2\SYSTEM;C:\OS2\INSTALL;C:\;
LIBPATH=K:\COBOL\EXEDLL;K:\COBOL\LBR;.;C:\OS2\DLL;C:\MUGLIB\DLL;
C:\SQLLIB\DLL;C:\;C:\OS2;C:\OS2\INSTALL;
SET COBDIR=K:\COBOL\LBR;K:\COBOL\EXEDLL;
SET LIB=K:\COBOL\LIB;
SET COBHNF=K:\COBOL\ON-LINE;
SET INCLUDE=K:\COBOL\INC
SET CWWORK=K:\COBOL\DEMO\COWRITER
SET CWFILES=K:\COBOL\DEMO\COWRITER
SET CWRSYSTEM=K:\COBOL\LBR
BUFFERS=60
IOPL=YES
REM ********** End of WB commands **********
SET DPATH=C:\OS2;C:\MUGLIB\DLL;C:\OS2\SYSTEM;
C:\OS2\INSTALL;C:\;C:\SQLLIB;
SET HELP=C:\OS2\HELP;
SET BOOKSHELF=C:\OS2\BOOK;
DISKCACHE=64
MAXWAIT=3
MEMMAN=SWAP,MOVE
PROTECTONLY=NO
SWAPPATH=J:\
THREADS=255
SHELL=C:\OS2\COMMAND.COM /P
BREAK=OFF
FCBS=16,8
RMSIZE=640
DEVICE=C:\OS2\DOS.SYS
COUNTRY=001,C:\OS2\SYSTEM\COUNTRY.SYS
DEVINFO=KBD,US,C:\OS2\KEYBOARD.DCP
CODEPAGE=437,850
DEVINFO=SCR,VGA,C:\OS2\VIOTBL.DCP
SET VIDEO_DEVICES=VIO_IBMVGA
SET VIO_IBMVGA=DEVICE(BVHVGA)
DEVICE=C:\OS2\POINTDD.SYS
DEVICE=C:\OS2\IBMMOU02.SYS
DEVICE=C:\OS2\MOUSE.SYS TYPE=IBMMOU$
DEVICE=C:\OS2\PMDD.SYS
DEVICE=C:\OS2\EGA.SYS
SET KEYS=ON
DEVICE=C:\OS2\COM02.SYS
LOG=ON
SET QRWDR=C:
SET QRWINST=C:\SQLLIB
REM Colorful OS/2 command line prompt!
SET PROMPT=$e[1m$e[31m[OS2]$e[33m$p$e[36m$t$h$h$h;$e[32m$_
```

Figure 2.3 Sample OS/2 CONFIG.SYS file

Alternative method. Some users do not want to add another set of operating system environment variables to the AUTOEXEC.BAT or CONFIG.SYS files whenever they install a new application. AUTOEXEC.BAT and CONFIG.SYS have a systemwide effect, but other applications will not need those same PATH and SET variables. In that case, you may want to run the Workbench from a batch or command file that establishes the PATH and SET variables needed for Workbench before starting it up. The same batch or command file should restore the original environment variables after the Workbench session terminates.

Windows .PIF files. Two kinds of applications can be run under Microsoft Windows: MS-DOS applications, and applications written specifically for Windows. Windows uses .PIF files to find out how to run MS-DOS applications, and .INI files to configure Windows-specific applications. As of version 2.5, the Micro Focus Workbench itself is a text-mode application designed to run under MS-DOS or OS/2. It is not specifically a Windows application in that it was not written to run under the Windows graphical application programming interface. With Workbench v2.5, Micro Focus supplies the WB.PIF file to define the Workbench application to the Windows Program Manager.

2.2.5 Extended Memory Manager (XM)

XM is an extended memory manager supplied as part of the Toolset. It gets around the 640K addressing limitation of MS-DOS so that you can use other memory that you have installed on your system. XM can be used for running the Workbench itself under MS-DOS, or for running your own COBOL applications that take large amounts of memory. **Don't try to run some other third-party memory management utility at the same time you run XM; they will probably conflict.** SETUP will ask you whether you want to install XM. If you will be running under plain vanilla MS-DOS or Windows at least part of the time, you should install XM. XM may be needed to run some COBOL or Workbench features such as COBOL SORT. The WB.PIF file supplied for running the Workbench under Windows 3.0 does invoke XM, using it as an interface to the Windows DPMI memory management. You are not forced to use XM all the time just because you have it on your system. **XM is not needed under OS/2 (and will not work under it) because OS/2 does not have the 640K limitation.** So, if you use MS-DOS, Windows, and OS/2 at different times, you will use XM when you are running Workbench under MS-DOS or Windows, but not under OS/2.

2.2.6 Running the SETUP Program

Considerations for the Mainframe Developer. In this section, we will discuss the menu choices presented by the SETUP program, so that you can get Workbench up and running. We will identify those modules most likely to be needed by the mainframe applications developer. If disk space is in short supply, you can choose to install only those modules. You can always rerun the SETUP program later to add any modules you omitted. On the other hand, if you have plenty of disk space, you can choose to install everything at one time, including modules for which you have no immediate need, so that you can familiarize yourself with those modules at your own convenience.

Mainframe COBOL dialects. What mainframe compiler versions are being used in your shop? Look at some program listings and look at the compile JCL streams and control statements in current use. You may find that older programs have been compiled with OS/VS COBOL LANGLVL(2), which is the IBM mainframe implementation of the ANSI '74 COBOL standard, or OS/VS COBOL LANGLVL(1), which is the even more obsolete ANSI '68 standard. (You aren't still writing programs in that, are you?) The VS COBOL II compiler is a more recent IBM product that has been issued in three releases so far. VS COBOL II release 3 supports the complete ANSI '85 standard, while COBOL/370 supports the 1989 Addendum. In general, it's advisable to compile all new COBOL programs under VS COBOL II or COBOL/370 if available, and to convert older OS/VS COBOL programs as circumstances permit. Here are three major advantages in converting to ANSI '85 COBOL:

- ANSI '85 COBOL provides enhanced COBOL language features: improved support for structured programming, better interface to CICS, and other conveniences. The 1989 Addendum provides intrinsic functions.
- VS COBOL II and COBOL/370 allow use of mainframe virtual memory above the 16-megabyte address line to provide virtual storage constraint relief.
- VS COBOL II and COBOL/370 will continue to be supported when OS/VS COBOL is phased out.

The Micro Focus COBOL/2 compiler can simulate OS/VS COBOL or any of the three levels of VS COBOL II, depending on the **compiler directives** you give it. These directives are parameters that tell the compiler how to behave, similar to CBL statements on a mainframe. As we mentioned in the previous chapter, the COBOL/2 compiler also supports intrinsic functions.

The SETUP script will ask you what compiler version you want to support. When you answer, in effect you are specifying the set of default directives that the Workbench will use when it invokes the COBOL/2 compiler. This is why you need to know which mainframe compiler and language level you use most. For instance, if you choose VS COBOL II release 3, the Workbench COBOL compilation function will simulate mainframe VS COBOL II release 3 unless you override it with another selection at compile time.

Why does the Micro Focus COBOL/2 compiler need so many directives? One problem that Micro Focus faced when emulating other COBOL dialects was the fact that the other compilers didn't always work the way one would expect. Not only did mainframe COBOL compilers have a few limitations or awkwardly implemented features, but they also behaved differently in certain unusual situations from one release to the next. Writers of brand-new PC applications wanted Micro Focus to implement the most advanced form of ANSI-standard COBOL, without any limitations or awkward behavior. Programmers who wanted to test mainframe programs on a PC workstation wanted COBOL on the PC to act as much like their installed mainframe COBOL dialect as possible, even to the extent of simulating the less desirable features. Micro Focus got around this problem by letting the user select a set of directives to configure the compiler's behavior in various situations. The price to be paid for this flexibility is the effort of choosing which directives to select for each site's configuration.

Mainframe Development Environment menu. We mentioned that the Workbench SETUP script is designed to support both mainframe and PC program developers. Since the Workbench menu system is user-configurable, the SETUP utility will configure different main menus for you depending on whether you are primarily interested in mainframe or in PC development. The **Mainframe Development Environment (MDE)** is a main menu tailored for mainframe applications developers, while the **Workbench Development Environment (WDE)** is tailored for PC applications developers. If you are a mainframe developer, you will spend most of your time working from the MDE, so you should select the MDE as the default main menu, and the WDE as the alternative menu. The MDE will come up as the primary selection menu when you start up Workbench. However, you can bring up the WDE from that menu by pressing the F9 key. (The MDE menu is shown in Figure 3.1 and the WDE menu is shown in Figure 10.1.)

What diskette to start with. The SETUP program and script that you want to use to begin the installation process will always be on the Workbench Setup and System 1 diskette. *Important: Do NOT start with the Early Release, Update, Toolset, or COBOL/2 diskettes.* Other diskettes may contain their own SETUP scripts for use in installing separate parts of the system. However, if you start with the Workbench Setup and System 1 diskette, SETUP will automatically tell you to install the Toolset and COBOL/2 diskettes at the proper time, provided that you elected to install the complete system. To begin running SETUP, place the Workbench Setup and System 1 diskette in the diskette drive, make that drive the current default drive, and enter the word **SETUP** at the MS-DOS or OS/2 command prompt. (For a system with a monochrome screen, type **SETUP /M.**)

Recommended selections on each screen. Let's look at some of the installation choices that SETUP will ask you to make. When the SETUP program begins, a line will flash on the screen briefly to tell you what script is being processed. Then, a series of text screens will appear, showing descriptive information. Press the enter key each time to go to the next display. Finally, you will be presented with the following menu choices (Figure 2.4):

```
                    SETUP MAIN MENU
            View essential information
            Customize system
            Start the installation
            View on-disk documentation
            Exit SETUP without installing
```

Figure 2.4 SETUP Main Menu

These choices are provided as a "light bar" menu. Use the arrow keys to scroll up or down through the choices, and use the enter key to activate the selection.

View essential information and **View on-disk documentation** will let you see the release notes and other information. Once you've looked at these, select **Customize system.** This brings up the menu choices for configuring the Workbench installation.

On the following menu, you'll be asked whether to install the COBOL/2 Workbench in its entirety or as an add-on only. What does this mean? If you already have current versions of the COBOL/2 Compiler and the Toolset on your system and you wish to add the Workbench, you would install the Workbench as an add-on product only. In all other situations, choose the option to **Install COBOL/2 Workbench.** Here again, make your selection by scrolling with the arrow keys and pressing the enter key (Figure 2.5):

```
        Install COBOL/2 Workbench
        Install Workbench as an add-on only
```

Figure 2.5 Setup screen: complete vs. add-on

The next light-bar menu will appear with **Select Components** already highlighted. Press the enter key to continue (Figure 2.6):

```
            Customize System
        Select Components
        Configure Compiler
        Return to Main Menu
```

Figure 2.6 Setup screen: Customize System

Let's look at the series of choices provided on the Component Selection submenus. These options are provided as **check box** selections; you can select as many or as few as you need. Note that you don't actually select them by typing the letter "X" between the square brackets. Instead, you toggle the choices on and off by pressing the space bar repeatedly. The cursor arrow keys scroll up and down among the choices. When you have finished making your selections on each screen, press the enter key to go to the next screen.

The screen images shown in this example are from version 2.5, although the same basic steps apply to other versions as well. Versions 3.0 and later will contain additional check boxes for new modules that you may want to install, such as the GUI Workbench functions described in Chapters 14, 15, and 16. In addition, Micro Focus has simplified the compiler configuration process.

On the first component selection screen (Figure 2.7), a mainframe programmer would need to select **Compiler and Animator, File REBUILD Utility,** and **COBOL/2 On-line Reference Files.** You'll probably need REBUILD to maintain your test data files. You can also select **Linking Support** if you plan to link-edit certain routines once they have been tested. The other components are tools for PC applications development.

```
                        Component Selection
     [X]   Compiler and Animator
     [X]   Linking Support
     [ ]   COBOL Communications Module Support (MCS)
     [ ]   Screen/Keyboard Configuration Tools
     [X]   File REBUILD Utility
     [ ]   Screen Painter Utility, SCREENS
     [X]   COBOL/2 On-line Reference Files
```

Figure 2.7 Setup screen: Component Selection #1

On the next screen, **Mixed Language Support** is for programs that call modules written in other languages on the PC. Mainframe programmers generally wouldn't need this, unless they have a library of compiled routines on the PC that simulates some other software on the mainframe. The compatibility options are for PC programmers who want to compile programs written in other microcomputer COBOL dialects. Choose the last three selections so that you will get sample programs and documentation files (Figure 2.8):

```
                        Component Selection
  Further components for you to select if you wish.
     [ ]   Mixed Language Support
     [ ]   Micro Focus COBOL Compatibility Tools
     [ ]   Microsoft(R) COBOL 2.2 Compatibility Tools
     [ ]   RM Compatibility Tools (Conversion Series 3)
     [ ]   DG Compatibility Tools (Conversion Series 5)
     [X]   Installation Verification Programs
     [X]   All COBOL/2 Sample Programs
     [X]   All COBOL/2 Document Files
```

Figure 2.8 Setup screen: Component Selection #2

You will definitely need the **COBOL Editor** and the **Run Time Environment. Panels** is a tool for PC screen painting, not needed for mainframe program development. **XILERATOR** might be needed for debugging complex applications that call outside modules. Choose **XM** if you plan to run under MS-DOS or Windows at least part of the time; ignore it if you run OS/2 only. The **Install-function** is for distributing SETUP with PC applications. Choose, and read, the documentation files; you can always erase them later if you need the hard disk space (Figure 2.9):

```
     [X]   Micro Focus COBOL Editor
     [ ]   Panels
     [X]   Micro Focus Run Time Environment
     [X]   Xilerator
     [X]   XM
     [ ]   Components to build Install-function sub-programs
     [X]   All Toolset documentation files
```

Figure 2.9 Setup screen: Component Selection #3

On the next screen, select the on-line reference files and the demo programs. The remaining items are for PC applications development and are unlikely to be of interest to the mainframe programmer. **Callable Rebuild** lets an application invoke a routine to rebuild an indexed file. **Co-Writer** is a 4GL for reporting. **Fileshare V2** handles file integrity in multi-user programs running on a PC network (Figure 2.10):

```
[ ]   Callable Rebuild
[ ]   Co-Writer
[X]   Toolset On-line Reference files
[ ]   Fileshare V2
[X]   Toolset Demonstration Programs
```

Figure 2.10 Setup screen: Component Selection #4

You might want to select **concurrency support**, which lets you do several things at once within the Workbench, such as editing and checking at the same time. **HLLAPI support** allows COBOL programs on the PC to communicate with the mainframe on the 3270 emulation level, but without using CICS. If you are writing applications to run only on the mainframe, you won't need this. The remaining items on this menu are useful to mainframe programmers (Figure 2.11):

```
[X]   Install Concurrent Workbench startup files
[X]   Concurrent COBOL environment support files
[ ]   HLLAPI support files
[X]   Workbench demonstration programs
[X]   Mainframe variable file conversion (VRECGEN)
[X]   Workbench documentation files
[X]   Mainframe support files
```

Figure 2.11 Setup screen: Component Selection #5

The next screen has **radio buttons** instead of check boxes. Radio buttons are shown using the presence or absence of a dot within curved brackets, as opposed to an X within square brackets. To use radio buttons, scroll among the choices with the cursor arrow keys, select a choice by using the space bar, and press the enter key to activate your selection. Note that radio buttons allow you to select only one choice. If you choose one button, the others are deselected. In other words, the options are mutually exclusive. This is like the buttons on your car radio that let you listen to only one station at a time. On this menu, as we mentioned previously, a mainframe developer should select the **Mainframe Development Environment** to be the default main menu (Figure 2.12):

```
        Workbench Environment Selection
  ( )   Workbench Development Environment
  (*)   Mainframe Development Environment
```

Figure 2.12 Setup screen: Workbench Environment Selection

The next menu (Figure 2.13) will let you install the other menu as an alternative that can be reached using the **F9** key on the main menu. Select **Y**.

```
Do you wish to install the alternative menu system? (Y/N)       Yes
```

Figure 2.13 Setup screen: Alternative menu system

If the menu shown in Figure 2.14 appears, choose **Advanced Animation only.** The Advanced Animator includes all of the animation features. You would need to run the plain vanilla animator only if you are trying to run Workbench on a system with minimal RAM.

```
            Animator Type Selection
    (*)   Advanced Animation only
    ( )   Choose Animator within menu
```

Figure 2.14 Setup screen: Animator Type Selection

On the screen in Figure 2.15, choose the mainframe COBOL dialect you use most often. This choice will determine which compiler directives will go into the **WB.DIR** file. WB.DIR becomes the default directives file when you run the syntax checker or compiler from the command line prompt. You can override these defaults at compile time.

```
            Mainframe Development Environment
Choose the directive set which is most applicable for your application.
        ( )   OS/VS COBOL
        ( )   VS COBOL II release 1
        ( )   VS COBOL II release 2
        (*)   VS COBOL II release 3
```

Figure 2.15 Setup screen: Choose directive set (MDE)

The **Customize System** menu will reappear with **Configure Compiler** already highlighted (Figure 2.16). Press the enter key to continue.

```
            Customize System
        Select Components
        Configure Compiler
        Return to Main Menu
```

Figure 2.16 Setup screen: Customize System menu

On the **COBOL Dialect Selection** screen (Figure 2.17), either choose the same COBOL dialect you chose earlier, or choose **Full function**. X/Open COBOL, incidentally, is UNIX-compatible COBOL.

```
COBOL Dialect Selection - This screen allows you to select the default
installed COBOL dialect.
    ( )   Full function (Includes ANSI'85, MF extensions, X/OPEN, and SAA)
    ( )   IBM(R) OS/VS COBOL
    ( )   IBM VS COBOL II R2 or R3-CMPR2
    (*)   IBM VS COBOL II R3 (NOCMPR2)
    ( )   X/Open (XPG3)
    ( )   SAA COBOL
    ( )   ANSI'74
    ( )   ANSI'85 (without nested program support or MF extensions)
```

Figure 2.17 Setup screen: COBOL Dialect Selection

The **Default Compilation Options** menu (Figure 2.18) lets you set up a file of compiler directives that will be the defaults under Workbench unless you override them at compile time. Mainframe programmers will most likely want to emulate the behavior of their own mainframe COBOL dialect, even in its less desirable features. The COBOL/2 Operating Guide gives details on the purpose and function of all of the compiler directives. Most of them won't apply to your particular situation.

```
            Default Compilation Options
    [X]   Bound checking on subscripts
    [X]   COMP fields are not truncated
    [X]   OS/VS COBOL and VS COBOL II PERFORM behavior
    [X]   OS/VS COMP data storage allocation scheme
    [X]   ANSI'85 Nested call support
```

Figure 2.18 Setup screen: Default Compilation Options

The first option provides checking for runaway indexes and subscripts; this takes some overhead but is desirable for testing. The second option works somewhat like the mainframe TRUNC or NOTRUNC option. In a COBOL COMP (hex) field, the number of digits in the COBOL PICTURE clause may be less than the number of digits that could physically be represented in that field in storage. This is because the amount of data storage for COMP fields is allocated in increments of two bytes at a time. This SETUP menu selection lets you choose whether or not to truncate the numeric value stored in a COMP field to the size of the field's PICTURE clause, when the PICTURE clause is smaller than what the storage location can hold.

The third option on this menu duplicates the somewhat erratic behavior of mainframe COBOL when nested PERFORMs share a common exit point. The fourth option simulates storage layout of mainframe COMP fields. The last option allows the use of ANSI '85 nested programs; select it if you have any VS COBOL II programs containing nested subprograms.

The next set of choices applies to those who plan to link-edit some modules. Unless you are doing PC programming and distributing standalone program modules, select the shared runtime library. Select DOS or OS/2 depending on where you plan to do most of your work (Figure 2.19):

```
                    Default Linking Libraries
    (*)   Shared run-time system, COBLIB, on OS/2
    ( )   Shared run-time system, COBLIB, on DOS
    ( )   Static linked run-time system, LCOBOL, on OS/2
    ( )   Static linked run-time system, LCOBOL, on DOS
```

Figure 2.19 Setup screen: Default Linking Libraries

As we will see later, the COBOL/2 compiler lets you generate several different types of object code. Figure 2.20 lets you set the default for the Workbench system. If you are planning to do your testing under the Workbench menu system, you might as well accept the default, .GNT object code. (You can also produce .OBJ object code for later link-editing.) Libraries are another Micro Focus feature that can be used by the mainframe programmer; they are a way of keeping track of copy members, routines, and so forth.

```
        Default Compilation Options
    [X]   Produce GNT format object code
    [X]   Allow copy files to be in libraries
```

Figure 2.20 Setup screen: Default Compilation Options

The **Customize System** menu will reappear with **Return to Main Menu** already highlighted (Figure 2.21). Press the enter key to continue.

```
                Customize System
              Select Components
              Configure Compiler
              Return to Main Menu
```

Figure 2.21 Setup screen: Customize System menu

When the main menu reappears, choose **Start the installation.** The **Installation Details** screen should appear (Figure 2.22).

```
Micro Focus COBOL/2 Workbench(tm) Version 2.5.18 - Installation
Installation Details
From : A:              Type : 3.5 inch diskette - high density
Use on : DOS and OS/2
Directories : Default multiple directories (K:\COBOL\...)

                      Installation
The Installation details above will be used to guide this installation
process. If these details are not correct, you may change them now.

              Continue with installation
              Change installation details
              Preview installation

Select using [arrow keys] and press Enter to perform selected function

F1=Help     Enter=Perform selected function    Escape=Main Menu    =Select
```

Figure 2.22 Setup screen: Installation Details

Be sure that the installation details are correct and change them if they are not! In particular, check your drive and directory path, and make sure that you are installing for the right operating system(s). Use **Change installation details** to fix any problems. **Preview installation** lets you find out how much disk space you will need to install the modules you have selected. When you are ready to go, select **Continue with installation.**

Verifying that the Micro Focus Workbench will start up under MS-DOS or OS/2. Once installation is complete, reboot your system to activate the SET, PATH, and LIBPATH commands. Before proceeding any further, make sure that the Workbench base product was installed correctly by attempting to bring it up on your machine.

Under MS-DOS, presumably you'll be using the Extended Memory Manager. Enter **XM WB** at the MS-DOS command prompt to start up Workbench. If you've installed everything correctly, the Workbench banner screen (opening menu) should appear.

Under OS/2, enter **WB** at the OS/2 full screen or windowed command prompt. Workbench will run in either mode, but it will run faster in full screen mode. **XM will NOT run under OS/2.**

XM requires at least 1.5 megabytes of memory on your machine. If you aren't sure how much is available, enter **XM +X** at the MS-DOS command prompt, followed by **M,0**. The amount of memory will appear in a message following the words **free size**. This works under plain vanilla MS-DOS, but might not work properly under Windows.

If you are still having problems with XM, then make sure you are not trying to run it alongside other memory management software or alongside terminate-and-stay-resident (TSR) programs such as Sidekick. Check your AUTOEXEC.BAT and CONFIG.SYS files to make sure that you are not loading an incompatible device driver at boot time. XM works with extended memory; it is incompatible with EMS (expanded memory) device drivers except for those specifically designed to coexist with extended memory managers.

Running XM on PC clone machines. Compatible workstations not made by IBM contain ROM BIOS chips different from those supplied by IBM. If you find that you cannot bring up the Workbench by keying **XM WB** at the command prompt, but that you can bring it up by keying **WB**, then you might need to adjust the settings for XM. The exact values might vary from one version to another. An appendix in *Getting Started with Workbench* lists switch settings for some clone machines, as well as switch settings needed for use with IRMA cards, token ring networks, and so forth. Some workstations may need different switch settings for XM depending on processor clock speed. A text file called XMCLONES.DOC, in the Micro Focus distribution diskettes, contains detailed information on runtime switches to use with XM on various non-IBM workstations.

Early Release diskettes. Once you've installed the Workbench, check through your package to see if you also have any Early Release diskettes. These are not automatically installed along with the rest of the Workbench product. Early Release diskettes, as the name implies, contain new versions of products that are not yet fully supported. You can experiment with them at your own discretion. Micro Focus product announcements will explain the purpose of each Early Release module. If you choose to install any of them, place the diskette in the drive and enter **SETUP** at the command line prompt just as you did for the Workbench installation itself.

After you select **Continue with installation,** SETUP will tell you how much disk space will be needed to install the modules you selected. It will ask you whether to go ahead. If you proceed with the installation, SETUP will list its activities on your screen and record them in a file called MFINS.LOG. You can look at that file later to see exactly what was installed. If you have changed your CONFIG.SYS or AUTOEXEC.BAT, reboot your system after installation is complete.

Update diskettes. Wait, we aren't finished yet! Check again through your package to see if you have any Update diskettes. These bring your Micro Focus Workbench up to a more current release. They are installed after you have finished installing everything else. The automated update process is controlled by another program called UPDATE. It checks the software you already have installed on your hard disk and replaces any obsolete modules with new ones. **UPDATE will not install new versions of any programs that are not already on your hard disk.** When using UPDATE, start with the Micro Focus Workbench update diskette, then load the Toolset update diskette, then the COBOL/2 update diskette. In each case, make your diskette drive the current drive and type **UPDATE** at the command prompt.

Finally, if you have any Micro Focus add-on products such as the CICS OS/2 Option, install those after you are finished applying the updates to the Workbench itself. Once you are finished, start up the Workbench again to verify that everything still works properly.

Running Workbench v2.5 under Windows. Figure 2.23 shows how the Workbench looks when it is running in windowed mode. To set up the Workbench under the Windows Program Manager, you'll need to use the WB.PIF file provided with the Workbench. Under the Program Manager, select the **File** pull-down menu, select **New,** then select **Program Item.** Enter the drive, directory path, and filename of the .PIF file in the **command line** box. Enter something like "Workbench" or "Micro Focus WB" in the description. Then, choose **Properties** on the **File** pull-down menu, and select an icon from PROGMAN.EXE or another file containing Windows icons. (See Figure 2.24.)

If you are concerned about getting Workbench v2.5 to run faster under Windows, or if you need the characters on the screen to be a little bigger and easier to read, you can use the Windows PIF Editor utility to change the Workbench PIF to run in full-screen rather than windowed mode. You'll still be able to bring up the Workbench by clicking on an icon, and you'll still be able to use **Ctrl+Escape** to switch to other Windows applications when the Workbench is running in full-screen mode. You can also use **Alt+Enter** to toggle back and forth between windowed and full-screen mode.

The PIF editor is in the "Accessories" group that is installed automatically along with Windows. Select the PIF Editor, then choose the **Open** option

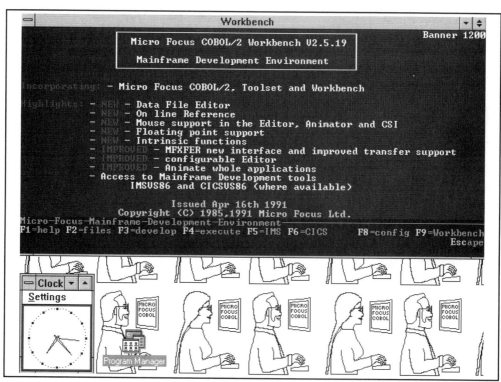

Figure 2.23 Appearance of Workbench v2.5 in a window

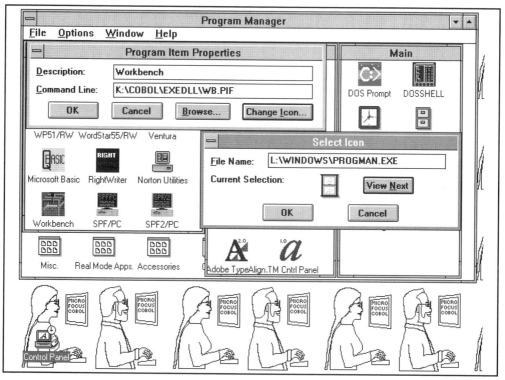

Figure 2.24 Installing Workbench v2.5 under Windows

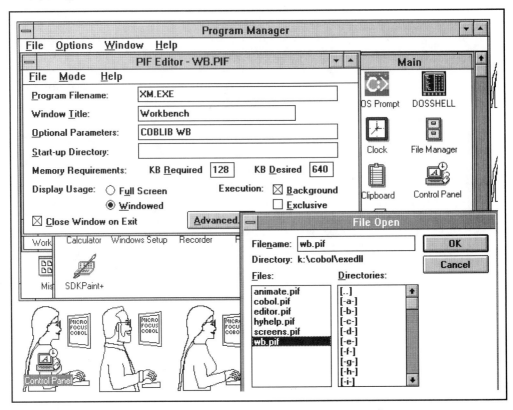

Figure 2.25 Using Microsoft Windows PIF Editor

on the **File** pull-down menu and specify the WB.PIF file. Once you bring up the current settings, you can switch the radio buttons from windowed to full screen mode and save your changes. (See Figure 2.25.)

2.3 Sample and Demo Programs Provided with the System

Once installation is complete, you'll find various sample programs in your \COBOL\DEMO subdirectory and in various subdirectories beneath DEMO. Some of these programs are intended to be used with the tutorials in the booklets supplied with the Micro Focus package. Others contain examples of different types of PC-based applications that can be done with the Workbench. The \COBOL\SOURCE subdirectory contains several copy library members that you may need, including one for the OS/2 Extended Services SQL communications area.

2.4 Exercises

1. The SETUP program lets you make choices with check boxes and radio buttons. What is the difference between these two devices? How do you use them?

2. What mainframe COBOL dialects are used in existing programs in your installation? What dialect is used for new program development?

3. Describe the purpose of the following files: AUTOEXEC.BAT and CONFIG.SYS under MS-DOS, AUTOEXEC.BAT and CONFIG.SYS under OS/2, WB.PIF under Microsoft Windows. Why do you need to modify configuration files to run the Workbench? Compare and contrast SET commands and other system configuration commands with mainframe JCL.

4. What is the difference between installation diskettes, Early Release diskettes, and Update diskettes? In what order should you install these diskettes? Which diskettes require you to run the SETUP utility and which require the UPDATE utility?

3

Becoming Familiar with the Workbench Menu System

3.1 Concept of Integrated Menu System

The Micro Focus Workbench is a big product. Its size and variety of features can make it look intimidating at first glance. In this chapter, you will learn some basic principles of how the menu system is organized, so that you can find the functions you need.

The Micro Focus Workbench **integrated menu system** provides seamless access to all Micro Focus Workbench functions, and to a variety of add-on products. Without leaving the menu system, you can develop applications, simulate the mainframe testing environment, and transfer files to and from the mainframe.

The **Micro Focus Menu Handler** program is the main driver for the Workbench. It displays menu screens, accepts user input, and runs programs and utilities. When you type **WB** or **XM WB** at the system prompt, the Menu Handler brings up the Micro Focus main menu and any other menus you select. Even if you run a Micro Focus utility separately from the command line by typing **WB [command],** the menu handler runs the desired program.

Micro Focus add-on products use the same menu system. Since the Micro Focus Workbench menu system is configurable, the SETUP utility for certain add-on products automatically changes the menu on your system. When you bring up the menu once again, it will contain new menu items for the functions in the add-on product.

Customizing menus for each site. Micro Focus provides everything you need to set up different menus for different users' needs. For instance, you can omit some features for security reasons or because you do not need them at your site. You can add your own programs, utilities, and submenus to the Workbench menu system to handle specialized situations. You can even call the Micro Focus Menu Handler program from your own PC COBOL applications. It lets you provide a menu facility to your users without having to design one yourself.

You can do practically everything without exiting to DOS. You can use operating system commands from within the Workbench. You don't have to shut down the Workbench (under vanilla MS-DOS) or bring up a separate DOS or OS/2 prompt window (under Windows or OS/2). The key combination **Shift+Ctrl+Break** will bring up the operating system command prompt from wherever you happen to be in the system. When you finish using the system prompt and wish to get back to the Workbench menu system, type **Exit** at the prompt. We will see later that the **Execute** submenu also offers an operating system command function, **F4=OS-command.** It lets you enter an operating system command on the command line at the bottom of the Workbench screen. You can run various small programs in this way, depending on how much memory they require. Use common sense here; never run system maintenance software such as CHKDSK or disk defragmentation utilities while the Workbench is running.

3.2 Menu Structure

All menus within a given Workbench system follow a common format. Text mode menus under Workbench up to version 2.5 use function key or hotkey menus at the bottom of each screen. These look somewhat like Lotus 1-2-3 or Microsoft Word menus. Graphics-mode menus in later versions of the Workbench follow the IBM SAA CUA standards for graphics-mode applications.

Under the covers... Even though Micro Focus uses a consistent format for its text-mode menus, some of the lower-level menus you see do not actually come from the configurable menu system itself. These menus come from individual program modules such as the editor or the checker, and are not configurable by the user.

```
                                                        Banner 1200
                    Micro Focus COBOL/2 Workbench V2.5.19


                       Mainframe Development Environment


Incorporating: - Micro Focus COBOL/2, Toolset and Workbench
Highlights: - NEW - Data File Editor
            - NEW - On line Reference
            - NEW - Mouse support in the Editor, Animator and CSI
            - NEW - Floating point support
            - NEW - Intrinsic functions
            - IMPROVED - MFXFER new interface and improved transfer support
            - IMPROVED - configurable Editor
            - IMPROVED - Animate whole applications
            - Access to Mainframe Development tools
                    IMSVS86 and CICSVS86 (where available)


                    Issued Apr 16th 1991
                Copyright (C) 1985,1991 Micro Focus Ltd.
Micro-Focus-Mainframe-Development-Environment──────────────────────────────
F1=help F2=files F3=develop F4=execute F5=IMS F6=CICS F8=config F9=Workbench
                                                              Escape
```

Figure 3.1 MDE main menu

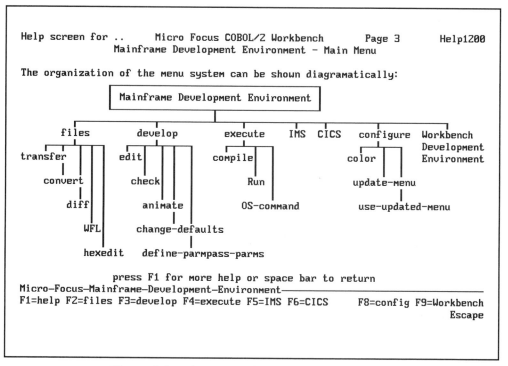

```
Help screen for ..    Micro Focus COBOL/2 Workbench      Page 3      Help1200
                  Mainframe Development Environment - Main Menu

The organization of the menu system can be shown diagramatically:

              ┌─────────────────────────────────────────┐
              │  Mainframe Development Environment       │
              └─────────────────────────────────────────┘

      files        develop        execute    IMS  CICS   configure  Workbench
                                                                    Development
   transfer        edit           compile               color      Environment

   convert         check           Run                 update-menu

      diff         animate        OS-command           use-updated-menu

       WFL         change-defaults

   hexedit     define-parmpass-parms

            press F1 for more help or space bar to return
Micro-Focus-Mainframe-Development-Environment──────────────────────────────
F1=help F2=files F3=develop F4=execute F5=IMS F6=CICS      F8=config F9=Workbench
                                                                        Escape
```

Figure 3.2 Help screen showing menu hierarchy

3.2.1 Parts of the Screen

By default, you will see a banner screen each time you start up Workbench. Figure 3.1 shows the Mainframe Development Environment banner screen that appears with version 2.5. It contains general information about the current release of the Workbench.

- Lines 1–20 of the screen form the **text area** for whatever program or data is being processed. If you are editing program code, for example, the source lines will appear in the text area. The text area on a banner screen, on the other hand, contains fixed data that conveys information about the Workbench system.

- Line 21 is the **information line.** It shows what system settings are in effect for the facility you are using. On editing screens, it will show your current position within the file, as well as various toggle-key settings. For instance, it will tell you whether you have **Caps Lock** or **Insert** on or off. On program compilation screens, the information line will show what set of directives is active. In the default Workbench color set for toggle-key indicators on the information line, yellow means "off" and white means "on."

- Lines 22–23 are the **function key menu lines.** They tell you what keys to use to select various facilities or subordinate menus. If you see the words **Alt** or **Ctrl** in the function key menu lines, additional menu functions will appear if you press and hold these keys.

- Line 24 is the **message line.** Error messages or normal completion messages will appear on that line.

3.2.2 Selecting Options

You can select an option by pressing the function key associated with it on the function key menu lines. On the Mainframe Development Environment main menu screen, every function key selection represents a subordinate menu except **F1=help.** F1 represents help on every Workbench menu.

Press the F1 key now and watch what happens. You will get a screen of help text with a message at the bottom, **press F1 for more help or space bar to return.** If you keep pressing F1, more help text screens will appear. One of these is a useful tree-structure diagram of the facilities available from the main menu (Figure 3.2). When no more help screens remain, pressing F1 will return you to the main menu.

3.2.3 How the Submenus Are Accessed

The Micro Focus menus are arranged in a hierarchy or tree structure, as shown on the help screen in Figure 3.2. You can use the function keys to go down one branch of the hierarchy or to go back up to the main menu. You cannot jump directly from one branch of the hierarchy to another without going back up to a menu screen. Here is a brief example:

- Start at the MDE main menu shown in Figure 3.1.
- Now press the F3 key. The menu lines shown in Figure 3.3 should appear at the bottom of your screen. This is the **F3=develop** submenu. It contains the functions that you will probably use most often: editing program source code, syntax checking, and animated debugging. You'll probably spend most of your time working with this menu and the submenus under it.
- Press the **F2=edit** key to get to the Micro Focus COBOL Editor. On a color monitor, the screen colors will change. You will get a screen resembling Figure 3.4.
- Now let's examine the **Edit** menu. Notice that the information line tells you what the edit function is doing. **Edit-new-file** shows that you are in the editor and that you have not yet loaded a file into the editor or saved one under a new name. Otherwise, the filename would appear on the information line in place of **new-file. Line-1** and **Col-8** show the cursor position. **Wrap-Ins-Caps-Num-Scroll** shows the status of settings that can be toggled on and off. For example, if **Ins** is highlighted, then insert mode is on. In insert mode, the editor will push existing characters to the right to make room for new ones. We will discuss the specific functions on this menu in Chapter 4, when we take a look at the Micro Focus Editor.

```
Program Development─────────────────────────────────────────────────
F1=help F2=edit F3=check F4=animate F5=change-default-directives        Escape
F6=define-parmpass-parms F7=data-file-editor
```

Figure 3.3 Develop submenu

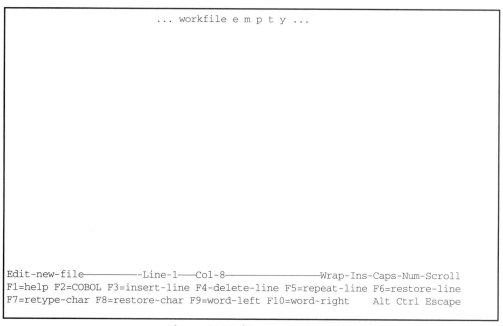

```
                      ... workfile e m p t y ...
```

```
Edit-new-file──────────Line-1──Col-8──────────Wrap-Ins-Caps-Num-Scroll
F1=help F2=COBOL F3=insert-line F4-delete-line F5=repeat-line F6=restore-line
F7=retype-char F8=restore-char F9=word-left F10=word-right   Alt Ctrl Escape
```

Figure 3.4 Editor main menu

3.2.4 Navigating with CTRL, ALT, and Function Keys

Notice that this menu contains the words **Alt Ctrl Escape.** Each of these three keys has specific effects on this menu. In particular, **Alt** and **Ctrl** bring up other menus that contain more functions used in the Editor. If you press and hold the **Alt** key, the menu shown in Figure 3.5 will appear:

```
Edit-new-file────────────────Line-1──Col-8───────────Wrap-Ins-Caps-Num-Scroll
F1=help F2=library F3=load-file F4=save-file F5=split-line F6=join-line F7=print
F8=calculate F9=untype-word-left F10=delete-word-right
```

*Figure 3.5 Editor **ALT** menu*

As soon as you let go of the **Alt** key, the regular Editor menu will come back. To use any of the functions on this menu, simply hold down the **Alt** key and press one of the function keys. Holding down the **Ctrl** key will bring up the menu shown in Figure 3.6 in much the same way. We will discuss the specifics of the editor in Chapter 4. Our purpose for the time being is only to show you how the Micro Focus menu system works. **If you see the words Ctrl or Alt on any Micro Focus menu, this means that you can view another submenu by holding down that key.**

```
Edit-new-file────────────────Line-1──Col-8───────────Wrap-Ins-Caps-Num-Scroll
F1=help F2=find F3=block F4=clear F5=margins F6=draw/forms F7=tags F8=word-wrap
F9=window F10=scroll  /  (move in window) Home/End (of text) PgUp/PgDn
```

*Figure 3.6 Editor **CTRL** menu*

3.2.5 Moving Back to Higher Menus with Escape Key

On any **Alt** and **Ctrl** menus, releasing the **Alt** or **Ctrl** key that you are holding will cause the "regular" menu to reappear. On all other Micro Focus menus other than the main menus, the **Escape** key will return you to the next higher level menu. On the Editor menu, pressing the **Escape** key once will get you back to the **Develop** menu. Pressing it again will get you back to the MDE main menu. The **Escape** key is a safety feature; you can use it to get out of menus without updating any data.

3.2.6 The Help System and On-line Reference

Help screens. On all Micro Focus menus, the **F1=help** key brings up a help screen telling you about the options on that menu. These screens are kept in a library and displayed by the Menu Handler. Up to now, this has been the usual way of providing help screens within the Workbench itself or for user-written applications.

Hypertext help. As of version 2.5, Micro Focus began replacing this form of help processing with a new On-line Information system that allows you to create **hypertext** help screens. Hypertext is a method of presenting data on a screen that is more flexible than plain scrollable text. Hypertext contains highlighted keywords or **hot spots** that the user can select with the mouse or cursor keys. Some hot spots let the user see more detailed subject matter related to the current topic. Others return the user to the previous screen or display an index or a table of contents. Each hot spot is associated with a piece of text that appears on screen when the user activates the hot spot. The user can navigate through the reference file to find related information by clicking on one hot spot after another. Text information from the file can be extracted and printed or copied into other documents.

Later, we will see that the new On-line Information system consists of a hypertext file compiler and a screen driver program that displays the hypertext files. You can make your own hypertext help files to run on the PC. Once you have defined all of the information that will go on the screens, including the hot spots and other cross-referencing information, you can compile the hypertext file. At runtime, you can invoke the screen driver program from within your application to show whatever screens the user requests.

The On-line Information system comes with a ready-made example containing a complete reference for the COBOL compiler directives and language syntax. COBOL syntax is shown with the "railroad track" form of diagrams used in Micro Focus and IBM language syntax manuals. The On-line Reference system will come up if you press **Alt+1** within the Editor, or type **HYHELP** at the operating system prompt.

3.2.7 The Operating System Prompt

We have already mentioned that you can use the key combination **Shift+Ctrl+Break** to bring up the operating system command prompt from anywhere in the Workbench menu system. When you are finished using the command prompt, type **Exit** to return to the Workbench menu system.

The **Execute** menu offers an alternative method to get to the MS-DOS or OS/2 command line prompt from within the Workbench. Let's use this method to view some system information:

- Press the F4 key (**F4=execute**) on the MDE main menu.
- Then press the F4 key again (**F4=OS-prompt**) on the **Execute** menu. You should see a system prompt command line at the bottom of the screen.
- Type the word **SET** at the prompt and press the enter key. You should see all of your MS-DOS or OS/2 environment settings displayed on the screen. The text area will scroll upward as needed.
- Type **DIR /P** at the prompt and press the enter key. This will show you a disk directory one screen page at a time.
- Press the F2 key (**F2=dir/w**) to see a short form directory listing.
- When you finish using the system prompt, press the **Escape** key once to return to the **Execute** menu.
- Then press **Escape** again to return to the MDE main menu. You'll still see the last display in your screen's text area until you invoke some other function that places data in that area.

3.3 Mainframe Development Environment (MDE) Main Menu

Let's look at the major functions available from the MDE main menu.

3.3.1 Help Screen Showing MDE Menu Structure

The **F1=help** key has the same function on all Micro Focus menus in that it always shows you a help screen. Different help information will appear depending on where you are in the system. On the MDE main menu, help screens show basic information about using function keys and cursor keys, together with a short description of the submenu associated with each function key. If you get lost navigating within the menu system, keep pressing the **Escape** key until you get back to the Mainframe Development Environment menu. Then, press the **F1=help** key repeatedly until you see the tree structure map showing the hierarchy of menus under the MDE main menu.

3.3.2 Files: Data Conversion Utilities

The **F2=Files** menu contains all the file-oriented utilities for mainframe upload and download, ASCII/EBCDIC conversion, file type conversion, building indexed files, source code comparison, hexadecimal editing, and the Data File Editor, a formatted editor that lets you edit data files field by field.

3.3.3 Develop: Editing, Checking, Animating (the Functions Most Often Used)

The **F3=Develop** menu contains the COBOL Editor that you will use for entering and updating source code. The COBOL Editor, in turn, provides access to other functions such as COBOL syntax on-line reference and Cobol Source Information (CSI). The Check function is actually the first pass of the COBOL/2 compiler. It checks your program's syntax and creates all of the executable and diagnostic files needed for testing it under the Animator. The Animator (with advanced features available under the Workbench) provides animated debugging showing program execution flow through your source code. You can change default compiler directives on this menu. You also can set up a file of parameters to pass to your program at runtime. Finally, this menu also provides access to the Data File Editor.

3.3.4 Execute: Compiling and Running Programs, Access to MS/DOS or OS/2 Prompt

The **F4=Execute** menu allows you to compile and run COBOL programs without the overhead associated with the animation process. You can use this to run parts of your application that you have already tested. This menu also provides access to the operating system prompt.

3.3.5 Add-On Products, if any (IMS, CICS)

The **F5=IMS** and **F6=CICS** keys bring up the IMS Option and CICS Option emulation systems, if they are present on your system. The IMS Option, formerly called IMSVS86, emulates the IMS database and data communications environment on the PC. The CICS Option, formerly called CICSVS86, emulates the CICS data communications environment on the PC. Both add-on products emulate software available in the IBM mainframe environment, for program development. **If you don't have these products installed, it's a good idea to reconfigure your Workbench menu system to eliminate these function key selections.**

Users of the CICS OS/2 add-on product will notice that CICS OS/2 does not appear as a function key on the MDE menu. CICS OS/2 was written by IBM and is sold in two ways. IBM sells CICS OS/2 on a mainframe tape for downloading to PC workstations for production use. Micro Focus resells CICS OS/2 on diskette as a Workbench add-on product for program development. The installation script for CICS OS/2 creates an entirely new "front end" menu to the Workbench, with features tailored specifically for CICS. On this front end menu, you would press the F9 key to get to the Workbench main menu. Details of these add-on products are in Chapters 12 and 13.

3.3.6 Configure: Customizing the Workbench Menus

On the **F8=Configure** menu, **F2=color** lets you set different color combinations for various situations within the Workbench. **F9=update-menu** lets you customize the Workbench menu system for your site. **F10=use-updated-menus** causes the updated menus that you created with the previous function to take effect.

3.3.7 Workbench: Developer's Environment (Alternative Main Menu)

Pressing **F9=Workbench** on the MDE main menu accesses the complete Workbench Development Environment alternative main menu system. Features used most often by developers of PC applications are on this menu. A few of those features are useful to mainframe developers under certain circumstances.

3.3.8 Toggling between the MDE and WDE Main Menus

Although you press the **F9** key to get from the MDE main menu to the WDE main menu, you do not press the **F9** key again to return to the MDE. Instead, press the **Escape** key on the WDE main menu. You will see a message at the bottom of the screen that says, **Exit from the Micro Focus COBOL/2 Workbench ? Y/N.** Despite what you might think, pressing **Y** will not shut down the Workbench; instead, it will simply get you back to the MDE.

3.3.9 Exiting from the System

If you press the **Escape** key on the MDE main menu, you will see this message at the bottom of the screen: **Exit from Micro Focus Mainframe Development Environment ? Y/N.** If you answer **Y,** the Workbench will shut down. You will return to your operating system prompt, to the Windows Desktop Manager, or to the OS/2 Program Manager, depending on how you started Workbench.

3.4 Exercises

1. Notice the tree structure diagram in Figure 3.2. Bring it up on your screen and describe the keystrokes needed to make this diagram appear.

2. Describe the two methods for accessing the operating system command line prompt from within the Workbench environment.

3. Explain the function of the escape key within the Workbench environment.

4

The Micro Focus COBOL Editor

4.1 Concept of ASCII Editor

When you first think of doing mainframe program development on the PC, this question always comes to mind: *How do you get the program source code onto the PC?* If you are writing new programs, you use a **text editor** to create source from scratch on the PC. If you are maintaining old programs stored on the mainframe, you use a download facility to copy source files from the mainframe to the PC. (We'll look at how to do this in Chapter 9.) Either way, once a complete program is on the PC, you continue to use a PC-based text editor to make changes and corrections.

The COBOL Editor is useful for COBOL programs, copy library members, command files, test data. To write COBOL applications efficiently on a PC workstation, you will need a convenient way to enter and edit ASCII text files. ASCII text is used for program source code, copy library members, AUTOEXEC.BAT, CONFIG.SYS, other .BAT or .CMD files, and possibly some input test data files. Even when you download an EBCDIC source code file from the mainframe, the conversion process creates an ASCII file on your PC. The reverse happens when you upload the finished program to the mainframe.

Not every PC file is an ASCII text file! A common example of an ASCII text file is the "READ.ME" or "README.TXT" or "README.DOC" instruction file often supplied with packaged software. Program source files for dBASE III or IV, FoxPro, or similar database programming environments are ASCII text files. So are MS-DOS .BAT files, program source files for C, Basic, Pascal, or Assembler, and even Adobe Postscript files. However, Lotus 1-2-3 spreadsheet files (.WK1), word processor document files, compiled programs, and graphics (picture) files other than .EPS files are *not* ASCII text files. You cannot view non-ASCII files with the Micro Focus COBOL Editor. For these, you use either the Workbench Hex Editor or the Workbench Data File Editor. For the sake of brevity, in this chapter we will often refer to the Micro Focus COBOL Editor simply as the "Editor," even though Micro Focus also provides editors for other types of files.

ASCII text files on a PC are stored differently from EBCDIC program source files on a mainframe. A **line sequential file** contains **variable length records**, with each record representing a line of ASCII text. An ASCII **carriage return/line feed (CRLF)**, hex value "0D0A", marks the end of each record. An ASCII text editor places this character combination in your file when you

press the enter key. It begins a new line on the screen whenever it finds a CRLF. This saves space by eliminating the need to pad each record with blanks to make all lines the same length. The Micro Focus Editor will handle up to 250 columns of data by scrolling horizontally. You can use it to edit any ASCII text file whose records are no longer than 250 bytes. Thus, the file should contain CRLF end-of-record delimiters no more than 250 bytes apart.

Unlike EBCDIC, ASCII was originally a seven-bit standard. Only the seven low-order bits of each data byte were meaningful in defining the character. The eighth bit was ignored. Seven bits gave room for 128 characters, including numerals, upper- and lowercase alphabetics, special characters (symbols), and nonprinting control characters. However, in the IBM PC environment, the eighth ASCII byte made room for 128 more ASCII values to define new special characters such as accented vowels, line drawing characters, and math symbols.

How do you know when you have reached end-of-file? In an ASCII text file, the end-of-file character is hex "1A." If no such character is present, then the file length in the directory indicates the file's actual length. On the other hand, if the file is not an ASCII text file, the hex "1A" character might mean something different. In that case, the I/O routine that reads the file must use the file length in the directory to know when it has reached end-of-file.

How is a text editor different from a word processor? Word processors are best suited for writing paragraphs of printed text intended to be read by humans: letters, memoranda, instructions, program documentation, and so forth. Text editors are most useful for creating text files intended primarily for use by machines. Word processors contain features for paragraph reformatting, headers and footers, chapter and page numbering, mail merge, and printer font handling. These features are useful for printed output but not for source code. Word processors lack specialized features for convenient editing of source code. For example, a word processor might have spell checking, but for COBOL programming you need COBOL syntax checking.

Can you use a word processor to edit program source code? It depends. Some word processors use high-order ASCII characters as control characters for handling hyphenation, line breaks, and other text formatting. The Micro Focus COBOL/2 compiler and other facilities that use COBOL source code will not accept program source files with those control codes. So, you can use a word processor to edit program source only if it will write plain vanilla ASCII files.

The COBOL Editor contains features to make it easy to enter COBOL source code. The Micro Focus COBOL Editor is designed around the idea of creating lines of COBOL source code rather than printed documents. While you can easily print your COBOL source listings, the Editor provides features that make it convenient to work without having to print listings as often. The Editor is fully integrated into the rest of the Micro Focus Workbench, so you can use other Workbench tools while editing is in progress. Margins and tabs within the Editor are set up by default for COBOL source files. However, you can change them for more convenient editing of other types of ASCII files.

The COBOL Editor works with your directory structure. The Editor interfaces with the Micro Focus directory facility that lets you specify what directories and filename extensions you want to scan. It provides a point-and-shoot list of text files from which to choose. You can look up existing copy library members, create new members, and import and export blocks of data from other files. You can edit two or more source code files at the same time by using Editor windows.

Checker, Animator, CSI, and On-line Information are available from the COBOL Editor menus. In the previous chapter, we mentioned that the Checker, Animator, and COBOL Source Information (CSI) facilities were available on the Program Development menu. These same facilities also can be reached from within the COBOL Editor by pressing **F2=COBOL** on the Editor main menu. This will bring up another menu with those selections on it (Figure 4.1), so that you can syntax check and then animate your program while editing is in progress. If syntax errors are present, the Checker will return you to the Editor with the cursor positioned at the first error. The CSI facility performs certain types of searching and scanning that otherwise would require printing out a listing and figuring out the program's structure by hand. You also can look up COBOL syntax through the On-line Information System by pressing **Alt-1** on the Editor main menu, as described in Section 4.15.6.

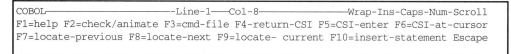

```
COBOL————————————————-Line-1——-Col-8————————————Wrap-Ins-Caps-Num-Scroll
F1=help F2=check/animate F3=cmd-file F4-return-CSI F5=CSI-enter F6=CSI-at-cursor
F7=locate-previous F8=locate-next F9=locate- current F10=insert-statement Escape
```

Figure 4.1 Editor COBOL support functions menu

4.2 Getting into the Editor

To get to the COBOL Editor from the Mainframe Development Environment (MDE) menu, press **F3=develop** and then press **F2=edit,** as we did in the previous chapter on menu navigation. To get to the Editor from the Workbench Development Environment (WBE) menu, press the **F2=edit** key. The Editor main menu is shown in Figure 4.2.

4.2.1 Items Appearing on the Editor Information Line

Throughout the Workbench environment, the **information line** tells you the status of your current activities. This may sound obvious, but the first word or phrase on the information line tells you what function you are in; in this case, **Edit.** Following that is the filename; if you have not yet loaded or saved a file so far in the editing session, the phrase **New-file** will appear in place of the filename. In this case, the comment **... workfile empty ...** at the top of the screen indicates that no data is present in the temporary work area. **Line-1** and **Col-8** shows your current cursor position within the file. Because the Editor assumes you may be creating a new file, the cursor will be in column 8 of the first line, where you would begin entering the first line of a COBOL program. The default COBOL margin settings make it unnecessary to use spaces or tabs on each line to get past the unused area.

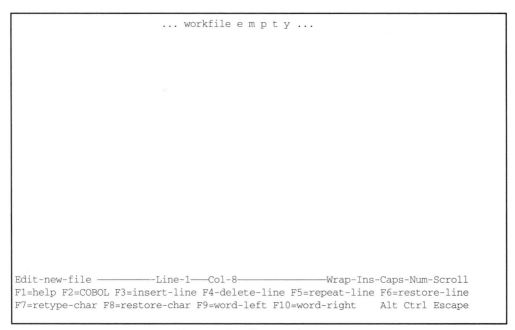

```
                      ... workfile e m p t y ...




















Edit-new-file ─────────Line-1──Col-8──────────Wrap-Ins-Caps-Num-Scroll
F1=help F2=COBOL F3=insert-line F4-delete-line F5=repeat-line F6=restore-line
F7=retype-char F8=restore-char F9=word-left F10=word-right   Alt Ctrl Escape
```

Figure 4.2 Editor main menu

Further to the right on the information line are the words **Wrap-Ins-Caps-Num-Scroll.** These show **toggle switch settings.** The **Ins, Caps, Num, and Scroll** indicators change color depending on whether or not insert mode, caps lock, num lock, and scroll lock are in effect. If you are using the default Workbench screen text colors, white means "on" and yellow means "off". The **Wrap** indicator appears if word wrap is on and disappears if word wrap is off.

The Editor main menu contains indicators for the **Alt** and **Ctrl** edit submenus. In general terms, the Editor main menu contains functions that deal with lines. The Editor **Ctrl** menu contains functions that deal with multiple lines. The Editor **Alt** menu contains functions that deal with files.

4.3 Loading Files to Be Edited

4.3.1 Choosing Files from the Directory

Suppose you want to edit an existing file rather than creating a new one. Pressing **Alt-F3** on the Editor main menu will bring up the load file menu (Figure 4.3):

```
COBOL───────────────────────────────Wrap-Ins-Caps-Num-Scroll
F1=help F2=directory F3=backup-file F7-files-in-window f8-all-files   Escape
File K:\COBOL\DEMO\                                                   Ctrl
```

Figure 4.3 Editor load file menu

When this menu comes up, the **file prompt** line will contain the current default drive and directory path, which in this case happens to be **K:\COBOL\DEMO**. If you know the name of the file you want to edit, you can enter the filename following the directory path. Pressing the enter key will load the file into the Editor.

You can choose a different drive and directory path by keying over what is in the filename prompt area. Here are some shortcuts: If you press the space bar within one of the file or directory names within the path, the directory system will clear out the trailing portion of that name. If you enter a letter followed by a colon, the system will clear out the current drive/path and replace it with that letter followed by a colon as the new disk drive designation.

Suppose you want to see a directory list so that you can choose a file from it. Press **F2=directory** to get a directory of the drive and path shown in the file prompt at the bottom of the screen. In this case, Figure 4.4 shows a screen containing the DEMO directory, which contains Micro Focus–supplied sample programs.

The Micro Focus directory facility. Every Workbench function that needs to load files or search for filenames on disk will need a directory facility. The Micro Focus directory facility that we have just seen is a subprogram that provides certain menu functions for listing directory contents and for loading and saving files. The directory function looks the same, regardless of which Workbench screen you use to invoke it.

```
List files :   K:\COBOL\DEMO\*.CBL,CPY,.
Date          Time      Size    Name

 3-Apr-91    5:17am     2473    CALLHYH.CBL
 8-Apr-91    5:23am    19981    CALLFDEM.CBL
 8-Apr-91    5:23am     3044    EXTFHWR.CBL
 8-Apr-91    5:23am     8567    BYTEIO.CBL
 8-Apr-91    5:23am     1186    BUILDMN.CBL
 8-Apr-91    5:23am     1073    BUILDSUB.CBL
 8-Apr-91    5:23am    23019    FSTEST.CBL
 8-Apr-91    5:23am    12834    WR1TEST.CBL
 8-Apr-91    5:23am    11231    MTHELLO.CBL
 8-Apr-91    5:23am    28497    RTSMOUSE.CBL
 8-Apr-91    5:25am    83967    SORTDEMO.CBL
 8-Apr-91    5:25am     9795    TICTAC.CBL
 8-Apr-91    5:25am     3320    ADMOUSE.CBL
 8-Apr-91    5:25am     8739    CALC.CBL
 8-Apr-91    5:25am     7172    CALENDAR.CBL
 8-Apr-91    5:25am    45918    CASE.CBL
 8-Apr-91    5:25am     2013    DECLARE.CBL
 8-Apr-91    5:25am     4811    DIOPHANT.CBL
Default—-K:\COBOL\DEMO\——————————————Asc-unsorted-Ins-Caps-Num-Scroll
F1=help    <-'=select-file F2=list-files          F3=list-dirs F4=delete-file
F5=sort-name F6=sort-time F7=unsort F8=list-asc/desc F9=drive    Ctrl Escape
total size= 33,454,080 available space= 14,553,088    listed files=   790,648
```

Figure 4.4 Directory display

Additional features on directory display menu. These function keys let you display the directory sorted in various different ways:

- **F5=sort-name** sorts the display by filename.
- **F6=sort-time** sorts by the age of each file.
- **F7=unsort** shows the actual order of your files in the directory.
- **F8=list-asc/desc** reverses the order of a sorted display.
- **F9=drive** lets you enter a letter to select a different disk drive for display.

Never delete files that Workbench is using!

When the directory display comes up, it shows only the actual files under the current directory, not the subdirectories. Pressing **F3=list-dirs** removes the files from the display and shows only a list of the subdirectories. You can use the enter key to select the highlighted subdirectory from the display to "drill down" further into the directory hierarchy, or you can select the parent directory to move back upward. If you want to switch back to the display of files, press **F2=list-files.**

F4=delete-file lets you delete the file whose name is highlighted in the list. **Warning: Never delete or rename any files that are currently loaded into the Editor. Never delete or rename a backup (extension .BAK) of a file you are editing, or any temporary Editor files (extension .$$?). Doing this will make the Editor crash.**

If you press the **Ctrl** key on the directory display, you'll see two more choices for directory sort order: **F5** for sort by file size and **F6** for sort by filename extension (Figure 4.5). On the **Ctrl** menu, **F8=browse-file** lets you scroll through a file (selected at current cursor position) with read-only access.

Choosing a file for editing from the directory display. The entire directory display is actually a **moving light bar menu.** If the file you want to edit is present, use cursor keys to scroll up and down in the directory list until you have highlighted the desired file, and press the enter key. This will take you back to the load file menu, but this time the selected filename will appear in the file prompt area. To load that file into the Editor work area, press the enter key again. For example, if you load the sample program DIOPH-ANT.CBL, your screen should look like Figure 4.6.

If you are entering filenames directly at the prompt, here is a shortcut. You can clear the old filename from the prompt area by pressing the space bar once. Pressing the space bar again will clear out the filename extension.

```
Default—K:\COBOL\DEMO\——————————Asc-unsorted-Ins-Caps-Num-Scroll
F1=help
F5=sort-size F6=sort-ext        F8=browse-file
```

*Figure 4.5 Directory display **Ctrl** key menu*

```
DIOPHANT.CBL
        $set ans85 noosvs mf

      PROGRAM-ID. DIOPHANT.
      *****************************************************************
      *
      *                  (C) Micro Focus Ltd. 1989
      *
      *                       DIOPHANT.CBL
      *
      * DIOPHANTINE - solve linear equation Ax + By = C
      *                 for integers x and y.
      *
      * Method:
      *          if A > B
      *              swap A and B
      *          fi
      *
      *          when A = 0
      *              set x = 0, y = C/B as solution, and fail if non-integer
Edit-DIOPHANT───────────────143-lines──Line-1──Col-8────-Wrap-Ins-Caps-Num-Scroll
F1=help F2=library F3=load-file F4=save-file F5=split-line F6=join-line F7=print
F8=calculate F9=untype-word-left F10=delete-word- right
```

Figure 4.6 File loaded into Editor work area

4.3.2 Default File Extensions

You might not see all the files that you thought would be in the directory listing. This is because the directory facility is set up to look for COBOL source files by default. It looks for certain filename extensions. If you specify a drive and path but no filename, the directory will show only those files having a filename extension of .CBL, .CPY, or spaces. If you want to see all files, type ***.*** after the directory path designation in the file prompt line, and press the enter key. You can substitute other MS-DOS wildcard characters to select various combinations of filenames and extensions. For example, ***.BAK** will show you your backup files, if you have named them with that extension. If no files with the requested extension are in the directory, the system will display the message, **File not found with defined extensions.**

4.3.3 Inserting Another File with Load Operation

Many programmers like to save time by cloning new programs from their collection of old programs and routines. They start with a skeleton or template program having the desired control logic, and then copy various subroutines into it while making minor changes. The Micro Focus Editor makes it easy to gather the needed files.

Suppose you have loaded your main program file into the Editor work area and you want to insert a subroutine file into it. To do this, use cursor arrow keys or other methods to position your cursor to the place where you want to insert the new file. Then, press **Alt-F3** to bring up the file load menu and select the desired subroutine. The Editor will load the entire subroutine into that position in your existing file. The Micro Focus Editor behaves differently in this regard from most editors; if you load a new file into a mainframe editor or most other PC editors, it will replace the old file.

4.3.4 Clearing the Editor Work Area before Loading the Next File

Suppose you want to load a new file in place of the existing file in the Editor work area. If you don't clear out the existing file first, the Editor will insert the new file somewhere within the old one, as we have already seen. If this is not what you want, then before you load the new file, clear the work area by pressing **Ctrl-F4.**

4.4 Creating a New File

To create an entirely new file, make sure the Editor work area is empty and then start entering data on the screen. When you save the file for the first time, type the drive, the path, and the new filename in the file prompt area at the bottom of the screen.

4.5 Saving a File to Disk

To save a new file to disk, or resave an existing file, hold down the **Alt** key and press **F4=save-file.** The Editor save file menu is shown in Figure 4.7. Be sure that the correct drive, path, and filename are in the file prompt area and press the enter key to save your file.

```
Save-file─────────────────────────────────────Wrap-Ins-Caps-Num-Scroll
F1=help F2=directory F3=backup-file   F7=files-in-window F8=all-files   Escape
File D:\cobol\programs\myprog.cbl                                        Ctrl
```

Figure 4.7 Editor save file menu

4.6 Changing Editor Settings

4.6.1 Insert

Pressing the **Insert** key toggles insert mode on and off. When insert mode is on, the **Ins** indicator will be highlighted on the information line. This is fairly straightforward: in insert mode, when you type in the text area, the Editor will push existing text to the right to make room for new text. In overtype mode, new text replaces existing text. **Be aware that insert/overtype mode also affects the behavior of function keys during certain copy and move operations.**

4.6.2 Caps Lock

Pressing the **Caps Lock** key toggles caps lock mode on and off. This causes all of the alphabetic keys to produce uppercase letters when pressed. When caps lock mode is on, the shift key will temporarily toggle into lowercase. If you are a mainframe COBOL programmer, you are probably accustomed to entering all of your COBOL source code in uppercase only. Mainframes for many years didn't support lowercase. However, uppercase is less readable. The Workbench and the COBOL/2 compiler let you use both upper- and lowercase letters for reserved words, data names, and procedure names. In other words, the compiler is not case sensitive regarding these items. Before you upload the source program back to the mainframe, you can use the Workbench DIFF (source file comparison) facility to convert all lowercase alpha characters to uppercase. DIFF will not convert lowercase characters within literals.

4.6.3 Num Lock

Pressing the **Num Lock** key toggles numeric lock mode on and off. Numeric lock lets you use the numeric key pad to enter numerals. Otherwise, with numeric lock off, the numeric key pad is "shifted" so that the cursor movement and scrolling keys will work. Whether it is convenient to use this setting depends on what kind of keyboard your machine has.

4.6.4 Scroll Lock

Pressing the **Scroll Lock** key toggles scroll lock mode on and off. When scroll lock mode is on, the cursor arrow keys will make the whole screen display in the text area scroll up and down, but the cursor will stay on the same screen line. When scroll lock mode is off, the cursor is free to move up or down on the screen. Scrolling does not take place until the cursor reaches the bottom or top of the screen.

4.6.5 Word Wrap

Pressing **Ctrl-F8** toggles word wrap mode on and off. When word wrap mode is on, the indicator **Wrap** will be visible on the information line. Suppose you are typing a word at the end of a line of text, and the text is becoming too long to fit within the margins. If word wrap mode is on, the Editor will move the entire word to the beginning of the next line. If word wrap mode is off, the Editor will split the word at the margin. (The Editor considers a word to be any character string delimited by spaces, or a string of two or more spaces.) Word wrap will be on by default unless you reconfigure the Editor to turn it off by default. We will describe Editor configuration later in Chapter 11.

4.6.6 Margins

The margins in the COBOL Editor work a little differently from margins in a word processor. The margin settings do not prevent you from entering text outside the boundaries. You can do this by moving to the desired location with cursor arrow keys and keying data. While all of the executable logic is between columns 8 and 72, you may also need to enter data outside those margins. The COBOL language uses columns 1–6 for sequence numbers, column 7 for asterisks to designate comment lines, column 72 for hyphens to designate continuation lines, and columns 73–80 for the optional identification field.

The purpose of the margins is to make the text cursor move in a way that is convenient for entering source code. When you reach the right margin, the cursor will return automatically to the left margin so that you can begin entering the next line. (See discussion of word wrap above). By default, the Editor assumes that filename extensions .CBL, .COB, .CPY, .BAK, or spaces indicate COBOL source program or copy library member files. This means that when you load a file with that extension into the Editor, the margins will automatically be set to columns 7 and 73. The cursor will come to rest at column 8 at the beginning of each line.

```
┌DIOPHANT.CBL────────────────────────────────────────────────────────────◆
│      █set ans85 noosvs mf                                              █
│                                                                        █
│      PROGRAM-ID. DIOPHANT.                                             █
│     *×××××××××××××××××××××××××××××××××××××××××××××××××××××××××××××××××█
│     *                                                                  █
│     *               (C) Micro Focus Ltd. 1989                         █
│     *                                                                  █
│     *                    DIOPHANT.CBL                                  █
│     *                                                                  █
│     * DIOPHANTINE - solve linear equation Ax + By = C                  █
│     *               for integers x and y.                             █
│     *                                                                  █
│     * Method:                                                          █
│     *        if A > B                                                  █
│     *            swap A and B                                          █
│     *        fi                                                        █
│     *                                                                  █
│     *        when A = 0                                                █
│     *            set x = 0, y = C/B as solution, and fail if non-integ█er
├Margins─────────────143─lines──────Line─1────────Col─8─────────Wrap─Ins─Caps─Num─Scroll
│F1=help F2=Cobol-margins F3=left-margin-to-cursor F4=right-margin-to-cursor
│F5/F6=left-out/in F7/F8=right-in/out F9=fullpage-left  F10=fullpage-right Escape
│             Left Margin = 7        Right Margin = 73
└────────────────────────────────────────────────────────────────────────
```

Figure 4.8 Editor margin menu

The column numbers used to set margins are the columns immediately *outside* the text area you want to enter. So if you want to enter most of your data in columns 8 through 72 for a COBOL program, set margins in columns 7 and 73. The tab key will move the cursor to the right four bytes at a time, so that you can get to column 12 by pressing the tab key once. If you load a file into the Editor with a filename extension different from those listed above, the left and right margins will default to columns zero and 81 respectively. This is useful for editing batch or command files. You can permanently configure the Editor to have other default margin settings for various filename extensions.

To change the margin settings from the default, hold the **Ctrl** key and press the **F5=margins** key to see the Margins menu (see Figure 4.8).

When you bring up the margins menu, the existing margins appear in the text area as highlighted vertical bars. Margin settings always exist; there is no switch to "shut off margins." To deactivate them, you set them outside the record boundaries. The maximum record length that the Editor will accept is 250 bytes. If you want the entire 250 bytes to be available within the margins, set the margins to the maximum settings, zero and 251. The Editor lets you set the left margin to zero even though the actual record begins at column 1, because the margin columns are *outside* of the text entry area. In fact, **F9=fullpage-left** sets the left margin to zero and **F10=fullpage-right** sets the right margin to 251. To reset the margins to the COBOL settings, 7 and 73, press **F2=COBOL-margins.**

The Editor provides several ways to make finer adjustments to the margins. You can move the cursor to the column you want to use for the left margin setting and press **F3=left-margin-to-cursor** to make that column the new left margin. Similarly, you can move the cursor to the column you want to use for the right margin and press **F4=right-margin-to-cursor** to make that column the new right margin. Alternatively, you can move the margin settings in and out one column at a time. **F5** moves the left margin out one column each time you press it. **F6** moves the left margin in one column. **F7** moves the right margin in one column. **F8** moves the right margin out one column. Unlike on a typewriter, you can move the margin settings through your current cursor position. The limitation is that you cannot move the margins any closer than one column apart.

4.7 Navigating through the File

4.7.1 Using the Cursor Keys

You can think of the screen display as a window into the file being edited. The cursor arrow keys, the **Home** and **End** keys, the **PgUp** and **PgDn** keys, and the function keys move your cursor position within the file. They also determine what portion of the file will be visible on the screen. The cursor arrow keys will move your cursor position on the screen until you reach one of the edges of the screen. When you get to that point, if more data remains to be displayed, the display contents will scroll in that direction.

Moving left and right on a line. The **F9=word-left** and **F10=word-right** keys move the cursor left and right one word at a time. Micro Focus considers a "word" to be a character string delimited by spaces, or a string of two or more spaces. The cursor position will wrap to the previous or next line once you have stepped through the words in the current line.

In overtype mode, the **Tab** and **Shift+Tab** keys move the cursor right or left four characters at a time. In insert mode, the **Tab** key indents the entire line of text. It shifts existing text from the cursor position rightward four positions at a time.

If you press the **Home** key once, the cursor will go to the left margin. Pressing it twice will move the cursor to column 1, even if column 1 is outside the left margin. This makes it convenient to enter data such as sequence numbers outside the margin. Pressing it a third time will move the cursor to the upper-left corner of your screen. Similarly, if you press the **End** key once, the cursor will move to the position just after the last character on the current line. Pressing it twice will move the cursor just outside the right margin so that you can enter data there. Pressing **End** a third time will move the cursor to column 250 of the current line. Pressing it a fourth time will move the cursor to column 250 of the last line displayed.

Paging through the file. The **PgUp** and **PgDn** keys move the screen display up and down by one page. How big is a page? A page is always one line less than the number of lines visible in your text window. If you are using a full screen text area of 19 lines, a page will be 18 lines. If you page down, the last line on your previous display will become the first line on the next page. This helps you to remember where you are in the file. In a larger file, you might need to move up and down more quickly than this. Commands for that purpose are available on the Editor **Ctrl** menu (Figure 4.9). **Ctrl+PgUp** and

Ctrl+PgDn will move the cursor up and down by 200 lines. **Ctrl+Home** and **Ctrl+End** will move the cursor to the beginning and end of the entire file.

```
Edit-new-file──────────Line─1──Col─8──────────────-Wrap-Ins-Caps-Num-Scroll
F1=help F2=find F3=block F4=clear F5=margins F6=draw/forms F7=tags F8=word-wrap
F9=window F10=scroll  /  (move in window) Home/End (of text) PgUp/PgDn
```

*Figure 4.9 Editor **Ctrl** key menu*

Scrolling vs. cursor movement. You can scroll the screen display without moving the cursor from its current position. Holding down the **Ctrl** key and pressing the left or right cursor arrow keys will scroll the screen display left or right along the current line *without moving the cursor*. Holding down the **Ctrl** key and pressing the up or down cursor arrow keys will scroll the screen display up or down without moving the cursor. If you are editing a very large file and you want to move much faster than that, press **Ctrl+F10** to bring up the Scroll menu. On that menu, you can use the up or down cursor keys to move much more rapidly. You can set the scrolling speed by pressing numeric keys 0 through 9: 0 represents the minimum speed and 9 the maximum.

4.7.2 Setting Cursor Position with the Mouse

Mouse support in the Editor became available with Workbench version 2.5. As of that release, the mouse cursor is available if you are running under MS-DOS or OS/2, but not under Windows. Workbench 2.5 runs under Windows as a text-mode application, so that Windows retains control over the mouse cursor for its own purposes.

So how do you use the mouse to set the cursor position? The text cursor appears as a blinking horizontal line, while the mouse cursor appears as a solid rectangle. Moving the mouse on your desk or mouse pad will move the mouse cursor on the screen. Clicking the left mouse key will set the text cursor to the current position of the mouse cursor.

4.8 Copying, Deleting, and Restoring Lines

4.8.1 The Internal Stack and How it Affects "Cut-and-Paste"

The Editor has an **internal stack** to hold lines being copied or moved. If you aren't already familiar with the concept of a stack, you can think of it as working in much the same way as a spring-loaded stack of trays in a cafeteria. You can add or remove an item only at the top of the stack. When you add a new item to the top of the stack, the item below it is pushed down (becomes unavailable). When you take an item from the top of the stack, the item just below it pops up (becomes available). If you retrieve one item after another from the top of the stack, the first item you get will be the item that was most recently added to the stack. In other words, you'll get the items back in the *reverse* of the order that you placed them on the stack.

The Editor's internal stack is used as a temporary buffer or clipboard within the Editor session. You can store any line of source code as an item on the stack. Whenever you delete (cut) a line from your file, it goes onto the stack. You can retrieve source lines from the stack in **last-in-first-out (LIFO)** order. You push new lines onto the top of the stack, and you also pop existing lines from the top of the stack. Thus, whenever you use a command to remove a line from the stack and restore (paste) it into your file, the line that comes off the stack will be the line that you most recently added to the stack. The same stack is common to all files being edited in your Editor session. This lets you use the stack to move lines from one Editor window to another.

4.8.2 Function Keys for Editing Lines

Inserting a line. You can insert a new blank line by pressing **F3=insert-line**. Move the cursor to anywhere on the line just below where you want to insert the new line and press **F3**. The cursor will move up to the new line. This process works by adding a carriage return to the file just before the beginning of the current line. A carriage return is all you need to define a line.

You also can insert a new line by pressing the enter key when you are in insert mode. Check the **Ins** indicator on the information line and press the **Insert** key to toggle that indicator on if needed. If you press the enter key with the cursor at the beginning of a line, you will insert a new line before the current line. If you press the enter key with the cursor at the end of a line, you will insert a new line after the current line. If you press the enter key with the cursor in the middle of a line, you will split that line into two lines at that point. In all cases, the cursor will move to the lower of the two lines. However, if you are in overtype mode, pressing the enter key will simply move you to the next line and will not insert a carriage return.

Deleting a line. To delete a line, move the cursor to that line and press **F4=delete**. This deletes the current line and moves it to the top of the stack. The lines below the deleted line on the screen display will move upward. Note that you cannot delete a line by pressing the **Delete** or **Backspace** key on your PC. You can delete printable characters or spaces with those keys, but not carriage returns.

Restoring a line. Restoring a line means removing one line of data from the top of the stack and pasting it into your file. To do this, move your cursor to the line just below where you want to restore the line, and press **F6=restore-line**. You can keep doing this until there are no more lines of data in your stack.

To move a series of lines from one part of your file to another, place your cursor on the first line that you want to move. Press **F4=delete-line** repeatedly until you have copied all of the lines to the stack. Then place your cursor on the line just below where you want to restore the lines. Press **F6=restore-line** repeatedly until you have inserted the lines into the file.

Repeating a line. Repeating a line means inserting a copy of the current line just above it. To do this, press **F5=repeat-line**. Repeating a line does not affect stack contents.

Copying lines with the stack. Let's say you want to copy a series of lines into your stack without deleting them from the current location. Position the cursor on the first line you want to copy. Alternate between pressing **F5=repeat-line** and **F4=delete-line** until each desired line has been repeated and deleted one time. Then, place your cursor on the line just below where you want to copy the new lines. Press **F6=restore-line** repeatedly until all lines have been copied.

Splitting a line. Commands for splitting and joining lines are on the Editor **Alt** menu (Figure 4.10). Holding the **Alt** key and pressing **F5=split-line** will split the current line at the cursor position. Splitting a line does not affect the stack. As we have seen, if you are in Insert mode you also can split a line by pressing the enter key with the cursor at the desired location.

Joining two lines. To join the current line with the line after it, hold the **Alt** key and press **F6=join-line**. Usually, the new text will be merged in just after the end of the existing text on the current line. No spaces will intervene between the old text and the new. However, if you position the cursor to a column after the end of the existing text on the current line, the new text will be merged in at the cursor position. One or more spaces will separate the existing text from the new text.

```
Edit-new-file———————————-Line-1——Col-8————————-Wrap-Ins-Caps-Num-Scroll
F1=help F2=library F3=load-file F4=save-file F5=split-line F6=join-line F7=print
F8=calculate F9=untype-word-left F10=delete-word-right
```

*Figure 4.10 Editor **Alt** key menu*

4.9 Deleting and Restoring Characters

In an earlier section, we discussed the use of insert mode versus overtype mode. Inserting text is simple: make sure you are in insert mode, move the cursor to the desired position, and begin typing. In overtype mode, you can replace existing text with other text or with spaces by typing over it. It's also important to know that whether you are in insert mode or overtype mode affects the way Editor commands delete and restore characters.

All characters that you overtype go into in a character buffer. This includes blank characters. The character buffer will let you save up to 250 characters (one maximum-length line.) You can use this buffer to move characters from one Editor window to another.

Deleting characters. The **Delete** key deletes the character at the current cursor location. It works the same regardless of whether insert mode is on. Text to the right of the cursor moves left one position. In insert mode, the **Backspace** key deletes the character immediately to the left of the cursor location. Here again, text to the right of the cursor moves left one position to close the gap. In overtype mode, the **Backspace** key acts differently. When you press the **Backspace** key, the character immediately to the left of the cursor position will be replaced with the character that was most recently overtyped.

Restoring characters. F8=restore-char restores the last character that you overtyped or that you deleted with the **Delete** key. The Editor inserts the restored character at the current cursor position. All other characters to the right of the cursor will move further to the right to make room. In other words, the **F8** key will insert the restored character regardless of whether insert mode is on.

   F7=retype-char retypes only those characters that you have deleted with the **Backspace** key. In overtype mode, **F7** replaces the character at the cursor position with the character from the buffer. In insert mode, **F7** inserts the character from the buffer at the current cursor position, moving the rest of the line to the right to make room.

4.10 Deleting Words

Deleting and restoring words. The two function keys for deleting words are also on the **Alt** menu shown earlier in Figure 4.10. No specific function keys are provided for restoring *words*; the function keys for restoring or retyping *characters* will retrieve the stored data. The Micro Focus Editor considers a word to be any character string delimited by spaces, or any string of two or more spaces. If the cursor is on a nonblank character, deleting a word left or right means deleting all characters up to the next blank. This means that if your cursor is in the middle of a word, you can delete the leading or trailing portion of the word by pressing a function key. If the cursor is on a blank character, deleting a word left or right means deleting all blanks until you reach the next nonblank character.

Deleting to the left. Holding down the **Alt** key and pressing **F9=untype-word-left** will delete words to the left of the cursor. This key works much like the **Backspace** key, except it deletes a word at a time. In insert mode, **Alt+F9** deletes the word to the left of the cursor. The text to the right moves left to close the space. In overtype mode, **Alt+F9** deletes the word to the left of the cursor, but the same number of characters is replaced by the most recently overtyped characters from the buffer. In either case, you can bring back the deleted word by pressing **F7=retype-char** until the complete word reappears.

Deleting to the right. Holding down the **Alt** key and pressing **F10-delete-word-right** will delete words to the right of the cursor. This works the same regardless of insert/overwrite mode. You can bring back the deleted word by pressing **F8=restore-char** until the complete word reappears. This key works much like the **Delete** key, except it deletes one word at a time.

4.11 Block Operations

The Micro Focus Editor lets you define a **block** of text lines and move, copy, or delete that block. You can edit the contents of that block or write it to another file. Blocks of text are kept in an internal block stack. The stack processing used with blocks works much like the stack processing used with lines, discussed in a previous section. You can get at the block menu by holding down the **Ctrl** key and pressing **F3=block**, as shown in Figure 4.11:

```
Block─────────────────143-lines──Line-1───Col-8────────────Wrap-Ins-Caps-Num-Scroll
F1=help F2=edit-block F3=insert-block F4=define-block    F6=restore-block Escape
```

Figure 4.11 Editor block menu

4.11.1 Defining a Block to be Manipulated

The first step in working with blocks is marking the beginning and end of the desired block of text within the file. Before doing anything else, move the cursor to the first line that you want to mark. Pressing the **F4=define-block** key brings up the block definition menu (Figure 4.12):

```
Block─────────────────143-lines──Line-1───Col-8────────────Wrap-Ins-Caps-Num-Scroll
F1=help F2=find F3=copy-to-block F4=remove-to-block Escape

cursor movement extends marked text
```

Figure 4.12 Editor block definition menu

Press the "down" cursor arrow key until you have highlighted every line that should be in the block. (You can press the "up" arrow key to backtrack if you find you have highlighted too many lines.) Once you have highlighted the desired block, you can press **F3=copy-to-block** if you want to copy the highlighted block into the stack. You can press **F4=remove-to-block** if you want to remove the highlighted block from the text and place it into the stack. In other words, use **F3** if you want to make a copy of the block without affecting its current position in the text. Use **F4** if you want to remove that block from its current position in the text for a move or delete operation. You can press the **Escape** key if you decide not to mark a block at that point in the file.

The **F2=find** key on this menu allows you to use a text string search to find a desired part of your file to mark a block. In other words, you can use it to find the first line that you want to define as your block. We will describe text search methods in a later section.

4.11.2 Copying or Moving a Block

The block that you have defined will now be at the top of the block stack. To get it back into the text, move your cursor to the line just above where you want to insert the block, and press **F3=insert**. Since this function does not remove the block from the stack, you can do this as many times as you want.

4.11.3 Deleting a Block

To delete a block of text from your file, simply use **F4=remove-to-block** on the block definition menu as described above, and leave it in your stack. The Editor clears the block stack when you exit from the Editor session.

4.11.4 Using the Block Stack

Pressing **F6=restore-block** will "pop" (remove) a block from the top of the stack and insert it just above the current line. You can do this only once for each block on the stack. If you have copied or moved a series of blocks onto your stack, you can use **F6** repeatedly to restore each block into your file.

Blocks will come off the stack in the order of newest to oldest. To use this feature effectively, you'll need to remember the order of blocks that you put onto your stack.

4.11.5 Editing a Block

To edit the block on the top of the stack, press **F2=edit-block** on the block menu. The Editor main menu will reappear. In place of the filename on the information line, you will see the word **Block**. From this Editor menu you can reach all the Editor functions, including the block menu. Since you are editing a temporary work area and not a file, you do not need to save the block to make the editing changes take effect. When you have finished making all your changes, press **Escape** to get back to the Editor main menu and your current file. From the Editor main menu, you can select the block menu again to insert or restore the edited block into your current file.

To edit a block that is not at the top of the stack, press **Ctrl+F3** and then **F2** to move down one level in the stack. Do this repeatedly until you have reached the desired block. You can use the **Escape** key to move back up in the stack.

Merging two blocks. Let's say that you have two blocks on the stack and you want to make them into a single block. From the block menu, edit the block on the top of the stack by pressing **F2=edit-block**. Within the first block, move the cursor to the line just above where you want to insert the second block. Then, bring up the block menu again by holding down the **Ctrl** key and pressing **F3=block**. Press **F6=restore-block** to remove the second block from the stack and insert it into the first block. The newly merged block will be at the top of your stack. Since you are still in the block editing function, you can either save the block as a new file as described below, or you can press **Escape** twice to get back to the original file you were editing.

4.11.6 Saving a Block as a New File

When you are in the block editing function, you can access the file save function by holding down the **Alt** key and pressing **F4=save-file.** Supply a drive, path, and filename in the file prompt area and press the enter key to save your file.

4.12 Find and Replace

A frequent task performed while editing source code is that of searching for and replacing text strings. You might want to do this if you are changing data names or cloning new programs from parts of old ones. The Micro Focus Editor provides a **find** menu for this purpose.

You can bring up the Editor find menu from the main menu by holding down the **Ctrl** key and pressing **F2=find**, as shown in Figure 4.13.

```
Find--------stp-143-lines--------Line-73--Col-8--------Wrap-Ins-Caps-Num-Scroll
F1=help F2=set F3=line F7/F8=REPLACE-back/fwd F9/F10=FIND-back/fwd    Ctrl Esc
Find FROG                                      Replace PRINCE
```

Figure 4.13 Editor find menu

The FIND function on this menu lets you search for a text string in your file. If the Editor finds the string, the cursor will move to the beginning of that string. Otherwise, the words **not found** will appear on the message line. Using the FIND function does not modify your file, regardless of whether there is anything in the Replace buffer. Searching proceeds sequentially, either backward or forward from the current position in the file. **F10** looks for the next occurrence of the string specified in the Find buffer. **F9** looks for the previous occurrence of that string. You can press these function keys repeatedly to get to the next instance of the string. In the example shown in Figure 4.13, pressing **F10** would locate the cursor at the next instance of the character string "FROG".

When the Editor finds the string, the following message will appear: **"F8=forward" to replace, "F10=forward" to find next**. This means that you have the option to replace this occurrence of the string or to move on to the next occurrence.

The REPLACE function works like the FIND function, with one exception: **The REPLACE function lets you substitute the contents of the Replace buffer for the original string once the Editor finds it. F8** looks for the next occurrence of the string specified in the Find buffer, while **F7** looks for the previous occurrence of that string. In the example shown in Figure 4.13, pressing **F8** would position the cursor to the next instance of the character string "FROG". Pressing **F8** again with the cursor on "FROG" will replace "FROG" with "PRINCE".

If your Replace buffer is empty, the replace function will simply delete the original string from your text. Trailing data in your text file will move left to close the gap.

Going to a specific line. Suppose you want to position your cursor at the hundredth line in your file. Pressing **F3=line** gives you the option to enter a line number. In this example, you would enter 100 and press the enter key. Note that this line number refers to the actual position of the record in your source file. It has nothing to do with COBOL sequence or identification numbers embedded in the records.

How margins affect searching. If your cursor is within the Editor's margins when you begin a search, the searching will take place only within the portion of the record within the margins. For example, suppose you are using the default COBOL margins of 7 and 73, and your cursor is on column 12 when you begin the search. The search process will look only at columns 8 through 72. For a COBOL program, this is probably the area you want to search.

On the other hand, if you begin a search with the cursor *outside* the margin, then the search process will confine itself to the portion of the file *between the record boundary and that margin.* If your cursor is in column 1 and you are using COBOL margins, then the search process will look only at columns 1 through 7. You might use this to look for a specific COBOL sequence number. If a margin column setting bisects (cuts through) a text string, then the search process will never locate that string. This is because only part of the string is inside the search area. You may need to change the margin column temporarily to get it out of the way of the text string. This normally would not happen in a COBOL program, except possibly in comment lines.

4.12.1 Entering Find and Replace Arguments

Pressing **F2=set** moves the cursor to the Find buffer at the bottom of the screen. This lets you key new text into the Find buffer. You can move the cursor to the Replace buffer either by pressing the **Tab** key or by pressing **F2** again. Pressing **F2** a third time moves the cursor back up to the text area. Thus, **F2** cycles the cursor from the text area to the Find buffer, to the Replace buffer, and back to the text area.

Important: When you key text strings into the Find and Replace buffers, be aware that spaces are significant. Do not use the space bar to clear data from these buffers unless you want spaces to become part of the search or replace strings. Ordinarily, you should clear the Find and Replace buffers with the delete key, the backspace key, or the clear key as shown below. **Under some circumstances, you *will* want spaces to be part of your search or replace strings.** You can search for a text string that consists of more than one word, such as "STOP RUN". You also can use spaces to isolate a character string when you want to find only those instances in which the string forms a separate word. This lets you ignore those instances in which the string occurs as part of another word. For instance, if you are looking for PAYROLL but not for PAYROLL-MASTER, you can add a trailing space after PAYROLL in your Find buffer to exclude the latter possibility.

From the Editor find menu, you can reveal some additional options by holding down the **Ctrl** key, as shown in Figure 4.14.

```
Find────────stp-143-lines────Line-73───Col-8──────Wrap-Ins-Caps-Num-Scroll
F1=help F3=cursor Find F4=clear F5=punc F6=case F9=repl-mode(step,all)
Find FROG                           Replace PRINCE
```

*Figure 4.14 Editor find **Ctrl** key options menu*

On this **Ctrl** menu, the **F4=clear** key will clear unwanted data from either the Find or Replace buffers without introducing unwanted space characters. Use **F2** to select the Find or Replace buffer you want to clear, and then press **Ctrl+F4** to clear it.

The **F3=cursor Find** option provides another way to put data into the Find buffer. Suppose your file contains many instances of a word you want to find or replace. Move your cursor to the first instance of that string in the text area, press **F2** to select the Find buffer, and then press **Ctrl+F3** to copy the word into the Find buffer. If you use **F2** to select the Replace buffer, you can then use **Ctrl+F3** to copy another word from your text area into the Replace buffer. **Ctrl+F3** copies one word of text into the buffer, which means that it will copy characters until it reaches the next space character.

4.12.2 Changing Default Settings for Find and Replace

Case sensitivity. By default, the Find process is case insensitive. If your Find buffer contains FROG, you will find frog, Frog, FROG, and so forth. If you only want to find FROG, then you need to turn on case sensitivity. Do this by pressing **Ctrl+F6**; the **case** indicator will appear on the information line. **Ctrl+F6** is a toggle switch that will turn case sensitivity on and off as needed.

Punctuation sensitivity. By default, the Find process treats three punctuation characters as spaces during searching: the comma, the period, and the semicolon. This helps you search for separate words even when they occur before a punctuation mark. If your Find buffer contains the word PAYROLL followed by a trailing space, the Editor will search for "PAYROLL ", "PAYROLL.", "PAYROLL," and "PAYROLL;". However, it will exclude other strings such as "PAYROLL-MASTER". If you want to turn this feature off so that the search process will distinguish commas, periods, and semicolons from spaces, press **Ctrl+F5** to turn on punctuation sensitivity. When you do this, the **punc** indicator will appear on the information line.

Stepwise versus global replacement. On the information line, the indicator **stp** ("step") shows that stepwise replacement is on by default. Thus, when you press **F7** or **F8** in step mode, you will replace no more than one text string occurrence at a time. To change this, press **Ctrl+F9** to change to global replacement mode. The indicator **all** will appear on the information line. In global mode, pressing **F8** lets you replace all string occurrences from the current cursor position forward to the end of the file. Pressing **F7** lets you replace all string occurrences from the current cursor position backward to the beginning of the file. Although a message will warn you that the next keystroke will replace all remaining occurrences, this can be a risky option if you make a mistake in entering data. It might be a good idea to save your text file before making any global replacement changes.

4.13 Multiple Editor Windows

Editor windows let you edit several files at a time. When you first bring up the Editor, the text area contains one **window**. You can load a file into the original window, and then open a second window to let you edit some other file at the same time. As mentioned above, the block, line, and character cut-and-paste commands can be used to move text between windows. You can open many of Editor windows, depending on system resources. Every window, including the original one, has a border; you can turn the border off later if desired. The window that is currently selected is called the **active window** and has a highlighted border. To see the window menu shown in Figure 4.15, press **Ctrl+F9**.

```
Window-Control─────────────────────────────Wrap-Ins-Caps-Num-Scroll
F1=help F2=border-on/off F3=size F4=move F5=open-window F6=show-windows
F7=previous-window F8=next-window F9=max/restore-window F10=close-window  Escape
```

Figure 4.15 Editor window control menu

4.13.1 Editor Window Commands

Creating a window. On the window control menu, pressing **F5=open-window** opens a new Editor window. The new window will become the active window. When first created, the new window will cover the lower half of the text area, letting you view more than one window at a time. The new window will be empty until you load or enter something into it.

Switching between windows. **F7=previous-window** and **F8=next-window** cycle backward or forward through the set of available windows, so that first one window and then another becomes the active window. You will see them in the order in which you created them. The display sequence wraps around from the most recent window back to the oldest window. **F6=show-windows** brings up a window navigation listbox, which lets you choose an existing window or open a new one.

Closing a window. **F10=close-window** closes (gets rid of) the active window. If you have made changes to a file in that window, the Editor will ask you, **Exit without saving? (Y/N)** to prompt you to save the file before closing the window.

Window configuration. If you need more room to work, **F9=max/restore-window** lets you toggle the active window from its current size to maximum (full screen) size and back to its original size. **F2=border-on/off** lets you toggle the border on and off for the active window. The border does use a little space on the screen, but it shows you where one window leaves off and another begins. If you want to move or size windows with the mouse, the borders must be on.

Resizing the active window with the keyboard. To change the size of the active window with keyboard commands, press **F3=size**. This will activate the window resizing function and deactivate all other window control functions. You change a window's size by moving its borders in and out. It is not possible to adjust all four borders at once. You can select two of the borders for resizing at any given time: one vertical border (either right or left) and one horizontal border (either top or bottom). The first cursor arrow key you press will select and highlight the corresponding border to be moved in or out. The right or left arrow selects the right or left border respectively. The up or down arrow selects the top or bottom border respectively. Once you've selected the two borders, all further use of the cursor arrow keys will move those selected borders in or out. When you have finished resizing the window to your satisfaction, press the **Escape** key to reactivate the other window control functions.

For instance, to make the window taller and narrower, press the up arrow key to select the top border and press the left arrow key to select the left border. Then, press the up arrow key to raise the top border and press the right arrow key to move the left border to the right. Press **Escape** when the window is the correct size and shape.

Moving the active window with the keyboard. To reposition the active window, press **F4=move**. This will activate the window move function and deactivate all other window control functions. Use the cursor arrow keys to move the active window around on the screen. Press **Escape** when you are satisfied with its position.

4.13.2 Mouse Support

As of Workbench version 2.5, mouse support is available if you are running the Workbench function key menu system under MS-DOS or OS/2, but not under Windows. You can use the mouse to select, move, resize, or maximize a window.

Selecting a window. Suppose you want to select a different window from the one that is now active. If any part of the desired window is visible on the screen, you can select it by clicking on it with the left mouse button. When that window becomes active, the text cursor will return to the position it had when that window was active before. Double-clicking (clicking twice rapidly) with the left mouse button will select the new window. It will also reposition the text cursor to wherever you are pointing with the mouse cursor, if it is a valid location.

Moving a window. To move a window, point the mouse cursor to the top border of the window, press the left mouse button, and drag the window by moving the mouse. Release the button when the window has reached the desired position. To move a window with the mouse, window borders must be on.

Sizing a window. To size a window, point the mouse cursor to the left, right, or bottom border (not the top), press the left mouse button, and drag the border in or out. Release the button when the border has moved the desired amount. To size a window with the mouse, window borders must be on.

Maximizing a window. To maximize a window means to make it grow to its maximum size. In the upper-right corner of the active window's border is a window size indicator. If the window is already taking up the whole text area, the indicator will be a diamond. If the window is smaller than that size, the indicator will be an up-arrow symbol. Clicking with the left mouse button on the indicator will toggle the window back and forth between the current size and maximum size.

Using the window listbox. To see the window listbox, click with the mouse on the Editor menu area. The window listbox will show what windows are available and what files are being edited within them. If the list is too long to fit in the listbox, a scroll bar will appear. Clicking above and below the slider indicator will page the listbox contents up and down.

Clicking once on any entry will highlight it; double-clicking will select that entry to be the active window. To open a new window with the listbox, double-click on the entry "Open New Window." **Escape** will terminate the listbox function.

4.14 Printing ASCII Files

4.14.1 The Print Function

Pressing **Alt+F7** on the Editor main menu causes the print menu to appear, as shown in Figure 4.16:

```
Edit-DIOPHANT————————143-lines—Line-1——Col-8———-Wrap-Ins-Caps-Num-Scroll
F1=help F2=cancel-print F3=pause-at-new-page F4=no-pause Escape
```

Figure 4.16 Editor print menu

To print your entire file without pausing at page breaks, make sure your printer is on and press **F4=no-pause**. The print routine does not send a page eject to your printer at end-of-file. On page printers, you may need to press the page eject button to get the last page to come out.

A page break will occur whenever a slash character ("/") is in the left margin column. The slash character is the COBOL program listing page break indicator. In a COBOL program, it is used in column 7, the left margin column. The Editor transforms the slash character into a printer control command; it does not actually appear on the printed listing.

F3=pause-at-new-page also will print your entire file, but it will pause each time it finds a slash character in the left margin column. To resume printing after the pause, press the space bar.

F2=cancel-print will cancel the print run and return you to the Editor main menu.

4.14.2 Printer Setup Considerations

Many printers look for printer control commands in the form of strings consisting of an escape character followed by other values. Printer control commands precede or are embedded within the text to be printed, to control such things as spacing, printer fonts, and so forth. You may want to use these in your documentation files to improve the appearance of printed output. How do you get an escape character into your edited text? When you press the **Escape** key from the Editor, you simply exit from your current function and go back to the next higher menu level. No escape character goes into your file.

To place an escape character into your text, hold down the **Alt** key and press the numeral **2** followed by **7**. **Alt+27** is another code for the ASCII escape character (ESC). A left arrow key will appear in your text file on the screen, but the Editor converts it into a printer control command when printing takes place. The escape sequence will neither appear nor take up a column of space in your printed output. This method is available as of Workbench version 2.5.

You can place printer codes that consist of values other than the escape character in your text in the same way. Hold down the **Alt** key and press the sequence of numerals for the ASCII value. These will differ depending on your printer. See your printer manual for available control commands.

4.15 Editor Tips and Tricks

4.15.1 Using Tags ("Bookmarks")

Suppose you are working with several different parts of a very long source file. To go back to important parts of the file quickly, you can set temporary tags. To reach the tag menu, press **Ctrl+F7** on the Editor main menu (Figure 4.17).

- **F2=set-file-tag** sets a tag at the current line.
- **F3=clear-tag** clears a tag from the current line.
- **F4=clear-all-tags** clears all tags from your file or block.
- **F7=prev-tag** and **F8=next-tag** move the cursor position to the previous and next tag position in the file.

```
Edit-DIOPHANT————143-lines————Line-1——Col-8———Wrap-Ins-Caps-Num-Scroll
F1=help F2=set-file-tag F3=clear-tag F4=clear-all-tags F7=prev-tag F8=next-tag
                                                                        Escape
```

Figure 4.17 Editor tags menu

4.15.2 Changing the Default Directory

You can reach directory functions by holding down the **Ctrl** key on the Editor load file menu (Figure 4.18). On that menu, **F2** shows which directory is the current default directory. **F3** returns the directory display function to using the default directory, in case you have changed the file prompt. **F4** lets you enter a new default directory for Workbench. **F5** and **F6** let you specify (or cancel) use of a Micro Focus library file. **F8=brs** allows browse access to a file in the directory display, meaning that you can page through it with read-only access. **F9=ren** and **F10=del** allow you to rename and delete files from the directory display.

```
Load-file———————————————————————————————Wrap-Ins-Caps-Num-Scroll
F1=help F2/F3/F4=show/use/set-def-dir F5/F6=call/cancl-lbr F8=brs F9=ren F10=del
File K:\COBOL\DEMO\
```

*Figure 4.18 Editor load file **Ctrl** key menu*

4.15.3 Line Drawing

You would not ordinarily need to use line drawing in programs intended to be loaded back up to the mainframe. However, you may want to draw lines and boxes in program documentation or help files. Also, if you plan to customize the Workbench menu system, you can use the Editor line drawing feature to make your own menu screens more attractive.

The line drawing feature is part of the forms menu. Other functions on the forms menu will not be discussed here because they are not relevant to the mainframe programmer. You can reach the forms menu by pressing **Ctrl+F6** from the Editor main menu (Figure 4.19).

```
Edit-SQUARES————————-19-lines————-Line-13——-Col-45——Wrap-Ins-Caps-Num-Scroll
F1=help F2=draw F3=text-to-forms F4=forms                              Escape
```

Figure 4.19 Editor forms menu

On the forms menu, press **F2=draw** to reach the line drawing menu shown in Figure 4.20. When you create lines and boxes, the Editor places high-order ASCII line drawing characters in your text file. **The line drawing menu operates in three modes: draw, move, and erase.** Pressing **F2** cycles among

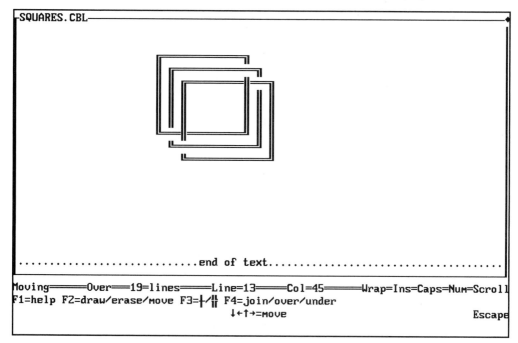

Figure 4.20 Line drawing function

these modes. An indicator on the information line shows which mode is active. In draw mode, moving the cursor will cause a line to be drawn where the cursor has been. In erase mode, moving the cursor will erase the position where the cursor has been. In move mode, moving the cursor will not change anything on the screen.

F3 toggles between single and double lines. The horizontal rule in the information line will be single or double depending on the current toggle setting of that function key.

F4=join/over/under cycles among the three ways of treating the situation in which lines meet. **Join** connects the two lines. **Over** causes the new line to appear to pass over the existing line. **Under** causes the new line to appear to pass under the existing line. The example shows the use of over and under modes in the interwoven boxes. An indicator on the information line shows which mode is active.

4.15.4 Using the Calculator

The Micro Focus Editor contains an arithmetical calculator function. Press **Alt+F8** on the Editor main menu to enter calculator mode. The plus, minus, asterisk, and slash keys perform addition, subtraction, multiplication, and division, respectively. Whenever you press one of these keys, the Editor will search your file for the next numeric character string. It will perform that arithmetic operation on the string, placing the result in a **Tally** field at the bottom of the screen. Pressing the equal sign key will insert the **Tally** value at the current cursor position in your text file, and reset the **Tally** to zero. The **Escape** key exits from the calculator function.

4.15.5 Editing Files Named in COPY Statements

Depending on which library utility is used on the mainframe, a COBOL program may refer to copy library members and subprograms by CALL, COPY, INCLUDE, ++INCLUDE, and -INC statements. Micro Focus supports all of these. When you are editing a program source file, you might need to view or change the contents of a copy library member. The Micro Focus Editor provides a convenient way to look up that member quickly.

Position the cursor on the line containing one of the above-mentioned statements. Hold down the **Alt** key on the Editor main menu and press **F2=library**. The Editor will begin searching for a filename matching whatever is in your copy statement. If the filename in your copy statement has no extension, the Editor will look for a filename having an extension of .CBL, .CPY, or spaces. If your copy statement contains a directory path, the Editor will search that directory. Otherwise, it will check to see whether that file is already present in an Editor window. If not, it will check the current directory and the COPCPY directory.

If a file with the correct name exists, the Editor will make it available in your current window. In effect, the second file is "stacked" above the original file in that same window. The Editor does not open another window to display the second file. You can edit and save it if desired. To get back to the main source file, press the **Escape** key. If no file exists with the correct name, the Editor will create a new one in the current directory.

4.15.6 Using On-line Information (Hypertext-Based Help)

You can reach the On-line Information function by pressing **Alt+1** from anywhere within the Editor. On-line Information is a **hypertext-based help facility** that lets you look up COBOL syntax, directives, error messages, called subroutines, and other information while you are editing a program. Hypertext is a method of presenting text on screen that lets you select more information about those topics that particularly interest you. You also can reach the On-line Information function by typing **HYHELP** at the operating system command line prompt. Figures 4.21 through 4.26 show examples of On-line Information screens used for looking up COBOL syntax.

Help information is stored in one or more help files. The actual location of help information is mostly transparent to the user. If you want to see what help files the system is using, you can bring up a menu by pressing **F** for Files on the On-line Reference menu. You can jump from one help file to another by selecting a topic that happens to be stored in another file. Several help files come with the Workbench, containing information that is also in the printed manuals. In the help files, the information is organized to make it easier to look up topics while you are working. The On-line Information system looks for its help files in the paths specified in the **SET COBHNF** environment variable.

Navigating through On-line Information. Obviously there is a treasure trove of information here. How do you get to the part you want? Since this is a hypertext system, you navigate through it by selecting and activating various **hot-spots** or **text buttons**. Buttons on the screen are separated from the rest of the text by triangular markers. In the default Workbench screen color set, the

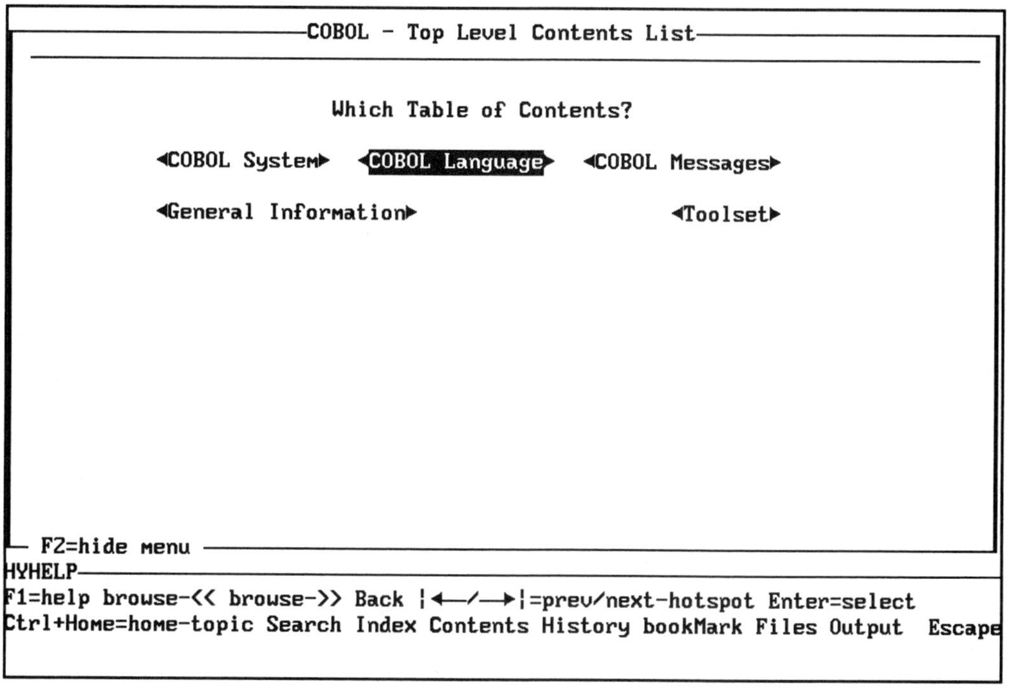

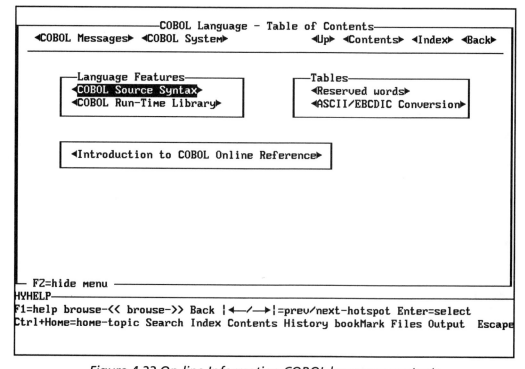

Figure 4.21 On-line Information top-level contents

Figure 4.22 On-line Information COBOL language contents

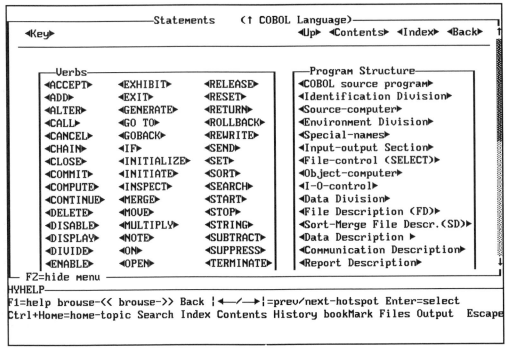

Figure 4.23 On-line Information COBOL language contents

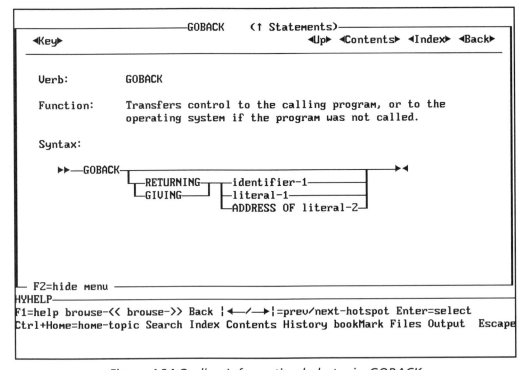

Figure 4.24 On-line Information help topic: GOBACK

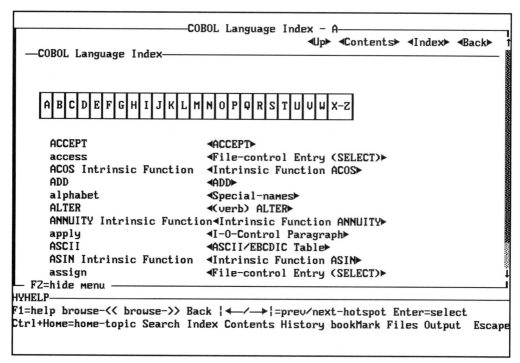

Figure 4.25 On-line Information COBOL language index

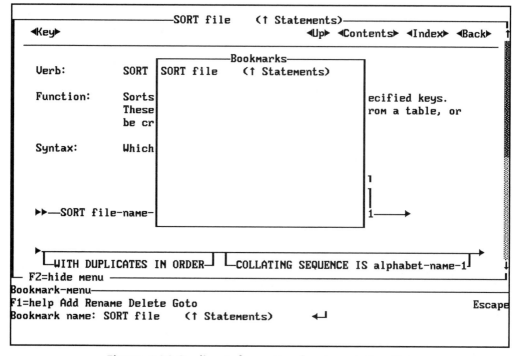

Figure 4.26 On-line Information bookmark function

triangular markers will be blue. Selecting a button is different from activating it. When you select a button, it becomes highlighted, but nothing else happens yet. You can see highlighted text buttons in Figures 4.21 and 4.22. Selecting a button means that it will become activated if you press the enter key. Activating a button will change the screen display contents to show the text indicated by that button.

If you are using a mouse, you can select a text button by moving the mouse cursor to that button and clicking on it once with the left mouse button. Otherwise, you can use the **Tab** or **Shift+Tab** key to highlight the next or previous text button on the screen. Pressing the **Tab** key repeatedly will cycle through each text button currently available on the screen. You can activate a text button by double-clicking on it with the left mouse button. You can also press the enter key to activate a text button that is already highlighted (selected).

Here is an example of screen navigation. The Top Level Contents List screen shown in Figure 4.21 is the main menu for the system. If you choose COBOL Language on that menu, the COBOL Language Table of Contents screen will appear, as shown in Figure 4.22. If you then select COBOL Source Syntax on that screen, the Statements screen shown in Figure 4.23 will appear. From there, choosing the GOBACK statement will display the syntax information shown in Figure 4.24.

Tables of contents and indexes. Some help screens are made up entirely of lists of text buttons arranged in a meaningful order. These screens can provide a table of contents or an index in the form of a text-button menu. For example, the COBOL keyword index works with a set of 26 alphabetical character text buttons, as shown in Figure 4.25. When you select a letter, the rest of the screen will show an index of COBOL keywords beginning with that letter. Hypertext systems often provide multiple pathways to the same piece of information. On this alphabetical index screen, if you select the letter G, and then select GOBACK, you will get the same display shown earlier in Figure 4.24.

Some help screens contain an **Index** text button that will bring up an index pop-up window containing a **moving light bar menu**. To use a light-bar menu, you select the desired topic with cursor keys or by clicking with the mouse, and activate the selected topic by pressing the enter key. You also can activate a topic directly by double-clicking with the mouse.

Rapid keyword lookup. Here is a shortcut for looking up a specific keyword quickly: Within the text file you are editing, move your cursor to a COBOL reserved word or some other meaningful keyword. When you press **Alt+1**, the help system will look up that word for you and display whatever information screen it finds. If it doesn't find anything relevant, it will display the top level help system menu. Within the help system itself, even if you double-click on some display text that is not a hot-spot or text button, the system will try to find a help topic with that name.

Scrolling a help topic. Some help screen topics contain too much text to fit on a single screen page. When you have selected a topic like this, a **scroll bar** will appear at the right side of the text window. If you are an experienced user of Microsoft Windows or OS/2, then you've used graphics mode scroll bars. In text mode, used in Workbench version 2.5, scroll bars do not look as detailed, but they still perform the function of showing where you are in the text and helping you to scroll more conveniently. Within the scroll bar, the **slider** indicates the part of the text that is visible in the window. The slider appears as the highlighted part of the scroll bar. The size of the slider relative to the rest of the scroll bar shows how much data remains to be displayed in the file. If you use the cursor arrow keys, the **PgUp** or **PgDn** keys, or the **Home** or **End** keys to move your current position in the text, the slider will move up or down within the scroll bar accordingly. **Clicking on the scroll bar above the slider moves the current position up one page in the text display. Clicking on the scroll bar below the slider moves the current position down one page.** Clicking on the slider itself, or attempting to drag it with the mouse, has no effect.

Not everything in the On-line Information system is done with text buttons. As with other Workbench screens, a function key menu at the bottom of the screen shows the available keyboard functions. The cursor arrow and paging keys work as they do in the Editor. The **Home** or **End** keys moves quickly to the beginning or end of the current topic. **Ctrl+Home** moves you all the way back to the home topic (top level) for the current help file. The "<" (less-than) key and the ">" (greater-than) key move you to the previous or the next topic in the current help file. This is known as the browse function. Pressing the **O** key to select the **O**utput function brings up a submenu that lets you copy the help text to an output file for printing or for merging into another document.

Backtracking. Pressing the **H** key to select the **H**istory function, or clicking with the mouse anywhere in the function key menu area at the bottom, will bring up the history pop-up window. The history window shows a light-bar menu of the 40 most recent topics displayed. You can reactivate one of those topics from that list if you want to see it again. Activating the **Back** text button will always redisplay the most recent prior topic.

Creating your own bookmarks. When using printed manuals, many people find themselves referring to certain topics again and again. This happens when you use some language features occasionally, but too seldom to memorize all of the particulars. In a printed manual, you can use pieces of paper or clips as bookmarks so that you can find your favorite topics quickly. How do you do that with an on-line help file?

Pressing the **M** key will bring up the book**M**ark menu, shown in Figure 4.26. This menu lets you define new bookmarks or use existing ones to find desired help topics. Suppose, for example, that you have trouble remembering the syntax for the COBOL internal sort. You can reach that information by activating text buttons for **COBOL language**, **COBOL source syntax**, and **SORT** on successive menu screens. Once the desired help text is visible on your screen, you can set up a bookmark to get to that topic again quickly. Press **M** to reach the bookmark facility. A bookmark pop-up window will appear, along with a different function key menu at the bottom. Press **A** to add a new bookmark that refers to the help topic now being displayed behind the pop-up window. When you do this, the text line at the bottom of the menu will contain the same title as the help topic itself. If you find that this title is, for your purposes, a suitable description of the desired help topic, simply press the enter key to add the new bookmark. Otherwise, retype the description as you prefer, for example, "Internal SORT syntax," and press the enter key to add the bookmark. The Workbench stores your bookmarks in an ASCII text file called ONL-BMK.TXT, so they will be available when you bring up the Workbench again.

To use an existing bookmark, press **M** again to view the pop-up window. You can activate the desired bookmark from the light bar menu in the pop-up window in two ways. You can double-click on it with the mouse, or select it with the cursor keys and then press the enter key.

For more information: Chapter 11 contains detailed information about the structure of help system files, so that you can set up your own if desired. The help system contains more than just COBOL syntax information; for instance, Chapter 11 shows you how to use On-line Information to look up error messages. Chapter 11 also contains a guide for finding answers to your questions in the Micro Focus printed manuals.

4.16 Starting Editor from the Command Prompt

Practically all Workbench facilities can be run separately from the operating system command prompt, without going through the menu. You can start the Editor directly from the command prompt by entering **EDITOR** for OS/2 or **XM EDITOR** for MS-DOS, assuming you are running Workbench under XM with MS-DOS.

4.17 Exercises

1. Bring up the Micro Focus Editor on your screen. Use appropriate function keys to view the subdirectory containing the demo programs supplied with the Workbench. (The drive- and pathname will vary depending on where it was installed on your system. By default, these will be in the DEMO subdirectory.) Then view a list of the subdirectories under that directory. Select one of these subdirectories and view a data file within that subdirectory.

2. Load one of the Micro Focus–supplied demo program source files into the Editor. Choose a fairly large file for this example. Then use the save function to make another copy of that file with a different name of your own choosing. Create the new file in one of your own subdirectories. (See the Appendix if you don't know how to create a new directory.)

3. Try out each of the cursor movement and paging functions to move up and down within the file you just created. Then use the clear function to remove this file from the Editor work area.

4. Examine various Micro Focus–supplied demo programs until you find a COBOL source file that contains at least one COBOL copy or include statement. Use the find function to search for these statements, examining several

source files as needed until you locate at least one such statement. Use the library function to bring one of these copy library member files into the Editor. Then use the escape key to go back to the original file.

5. Bring the source file you created in exercise 2 into the Editor. Open another window and bring a different text file into that window. Try out the functions that move and resize that text window. Use the mouse if you have one; otherwise, use keyboard commands. Using the block operations within the Editor, define a block of lines within the second file and copy them into the first file (the one that you created). Then close the second window; this will leave the first file occupying the entire text area. Add some new lines to that file. Then use the escape key to get out. When you see the "Exit without saving" message, save the file with your changes.

6. Bring up any COBOL source file on your screen. Move the cursor to any COBOL reserved word. Then bring up the On-line Information System. Does the help text explain that reserved word?

7. Clear the Editor screen. Enter the copy library member shown in Figure 4.27. Save it in the directory you are using for your own source programs, under the name CUSTMST.CPY. Enter the COBOL program shown in Figure 4.28 and save it in that same directory, under the name CUST.CBL. **We will use this program again in exercises in later chapters.**

```
* CUSTOMER MASTER RECORD.
 01   CUSTMST-REC.
      05   CUST-KEY.
           10   CUST-NO          PIC X(6).
      05   CUST-NAME             PIC X(25).
      05   CUST-PHONE            PIC X(10).
```

*Figure 4.27 Copy library member **CUSTMST.CPY***

```
 IDENTIFICATION DIVISION.
 PROGRAM-ID. CUST.
 AUTHOR. ALIDA M. JATICH.
*****************************************************************
* SAMPLE PROGRAM FOR LEARNING TO USE THE MICRO FOCUS WORKBENCH. *
* THIS PROGRAM ACCEPTS CONSOLE INPUT (CUSTOMER NUMBER, NAME,    *
* PHONE NUMBER) AND WRITES IT TO A FILE.                       *
*                                                              *
*                                                              *
*                                                              *
*                                                              *
*****************************************************************
 ENVIRONMENT DIVISION.
 INPUT-OUTPUT SECTION.
 FILE-CONTROL.
     SELECT CUSTMST
         ASSIGN TO "CUSTMST.DAT"
         ACCESS MODE IS SEQUENTIAL.
 DATA DIVISION.
 FILE SECTION.
 FD CUSTMST
     RECORD CONTAINS 41 CHARACTERS.
     COPY CUSTMST.
 WORKING-STORAGE SECTION.
 01   WS-COUNT             PIC 9(7) VALUE 0.
 PROCEDURE DIVISION.
 MAIN SECTION.
     OPEN OUTPUT CUSTMST.
     PERFORM UNTIL CUST-NO = "QUIT"
         DISPLAY "Enter customer number (6 digits) or QUIT"
         ACCEPT CUST-NO
         IF CUST-NO NOT = "QUIT"
             DISPLAY "Enter customer name (25 characters)"
             ACCEPT CUST-NAME
             DISPLAY "Enter phone number (10 digits)"
             ACCEPT CUST-PHONE
             WRITE CUSTMST-REC
             ADD 1 TO WS-COUNT
         END-IF
     END-PERFORM.
     DISPLAY "End of program CUST, "
         WS-COUNT " records added."
     CLOSE CUSTMST.
     STOP RUN.
```

*Figure 4.28 COBOL program **CUST.CBL***

5

The Micro Focus Syntax Checker

5.1 Basic Syntax Checker Concepts

5.1.1 What Is the Syntax Checker?

The first pass of the COBOL/2 Compiler. In many ways the COBOL/2 Compiler is the heart of the Micro Focus Workbench. For the mainframe applications developer, the Syntax Checker is, in turn, the most important part of the COBOL/2 Compiler. If you use the PC workstation only for coding and testing mainframe applications, and not for PC COBOL applications, you may find that the Micro Focus Checker alone is adequate for your purposes. You might not have occasion to use the code generation phase that makes up the rest of the COBOL/2 Compiler.

You may be wondering how this could make any sense. After all, running a mainframe or minicomputer COBOL compiler with "syntax checking only" usually means that the compiler flags syntax errors in the source code *without* producing an object code output file. In contrast to this, the Micro Focus Syntax Checker puts out an **intermediate code output file**. It's true that you cannot run an intermediate code file directly from the operating system command line prompt as a standalone program. However, within the Workbench environment, the intermediate code file is executable. You can test an intermediate code output file under the Animator facility of the Workbench. You can also run it under the Toolset Run-Time Environment (RTE).

PC versus mainframe development cycle. Let's look at typical methods for developing new programs. In a mainframe environment, you develop programs by editing the source code, then by compiling, link-editing, and running the program. You repeat this process as needed until the program finally works. Once it does, you move the source code to the mainframe production source library. Then you can compile and link-edit the program to the mainframe production executable library, or simply move existing load modules. On a PC workstation, you develop programs by editing the source code, then by syntax checking and animating the program until you are sure that it works. At that point, you upload the source code to a mainframe source library, then compile and link-edit it to a mainframe executable library, as

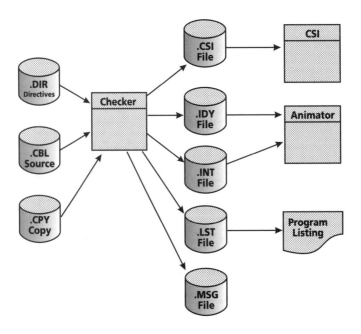

Figure 5.1 Syntax Checker

usual. Then you make up mainframe JCL, do a final system test, and put the system into production.

5.1.2 Files Used and Produced by the Checker

Checker input files. In this section, we will discuss the input and output files that the Checker uses (Figure 5.1). The Editor, the Checker, and the Compiler all rely on the Micro Focus directory search process. How do they find the files they need? If you run the Checker or the Compiler from the command prompt, it will look for a source input file having the extension .CBL unless you specify another extension. If you run the Checker from within the Editor, it will take its input from whatever source file is in the currently active Editor window. Suppose several Editor windows are open. If you start the Checker, it will take COBOL source input from the active Editor window, not from the others.

The Checker tries to expand COBOL COPY, INCLUDE, and similar statements in your source file by locating the actual data files. If your program contains the statement **COPY PAYMASTR**, then the Checker will look for PAYMASTR.CPY, PAYMASTR.COB, or PAYMASTR files. If your program contains the statement **COPY PAYMASTR.OLD**, then the Checker will look only for the PAYMASTR.OLD file. It searches for copy member files, first in the current directory, then in the directory paths specified in the SET COBCPY environment variable. (Recall that SET statements for environment variables are in either the MS-DOS AUTOEXEC.BAT file or the OS/2 CONFIG.SYS file.)

The Checker also reads directives from a directives file. If you run the Checker from the command line prompt, it uses **COBOL.DIR** by default. (You can specify other directives files also.) If you run the Checker from the Workbench Editor or Checker menus, the Workbench will substitute various directives files according to function key selections on the menu. We will discuss this in more detail later.

Checker output files:

- **.CSI** Files needed for Cobol Source Information (to be discussed later) have the extension .CSI.
- **.IDY** A cross-reference file needed for program animation will have the filename extension .IDY. This file correlates the .INT file with the animation process.
- **.INT** If you are checking a program that you intend to animate, the intermediate code file will have the filename extension .INT. Files of this type are executable under the Workbench.
- **.LST** Listings from the Syntax Checker can go to the screen, to the printer, or to a disk file, depending on the directives you provide. Program source listing files have the filename extension .LST.
- **.MSG** Files containing syntax error messages will have the filename extension .MSG.

It's important to have standardized places to put each file type. The Checker stores its output files where the runtime facilities of the Workbench can find them again. SET environment variable statements determine the search paths. For example, the Animator will look for .IDY files either in the same directory as the .INT file, or in the path specified in the SET COBIDY environment variable. By contrast, executable files with extensions .EXE, .DLL, or .GNT go into the directory path specified in the SET COBDIR environment variable.

5.1.3 Bringing Up the Checker from Workbench

The Checker menu. The Workbench MDE main menu provides two ways to get into the Syntax Checker facility: directly or through the Editor. Let's take another look at the program development menu (Figure 5.2). Pressing **F3=check** on the program development menu will take you directly to the Checker menu (Figure 5.3). We will discuss its menu options in the next section.

```
Program Development────────────────────────────────────────────────
F1=help F2=edit F3=check F4=animate F5=change-default-directives        Escape
F6=define-parmpass-parms F7=data-file-editor
```

Figure 5.2 Program Development menu

```
Check──Pause-Print───────────────VSC2(3)──────CSI───────────Ins-Caps-NumScroll
F1=help F2=dir F3=pse F4=list F5=anim F6=lang F7=x/ref F8=csi F9/F10=options Esc
File K:\COBOL\MFWBBOOK\CUST.CBL                                            Ctrl
```

Figure 5.3 Checker menu

Accessing the Checker from the Editor menu. You also can use most functions of the Micro Focus Checker facility from within the Micro Focus Editor. Load your source file into the Editor. On the Editor main menu (Figure 5.4), press **F2=COBOL** to see the Editor COBOL menu (Figure 5.5). Then press **F2=check/animate** to see the Editor's check/animate submenu (Figure 5.6). This menu allows you to use both the Checker and the Animator from within the Editor. We will discuss the Animator in the next chapter.

Saving your changes. If you have modified your COBOL source file, you'll need to save it before you begin checking so that you don't lose the changes you have made. If you press **F2=COBOL** and you have not saved your file, you'll see a message, **Unsaved files exist - exit without saving? Y/N.** If you answer Y, the Checker will work with the last saved copy of your program, and your changes will be lost.

```
Edit-CUST.CBL──────────Line-1──Col-8──────────────Wrap-Ins-Caps-Num-Scroll
F1=help F2=COBOL F3=insert-line F4-delete-line F5=repeat-line F6=restore- line
F7=retype-char F8=restore-char F9=word-left F10=word-right     Alt Ctrl Escape
```

Figure 5.4 Editor main menu

```
COBOL──────────────Line-1──Col-8──────────────Wrap-Ins-Caps-Num-Scroll
F1=help F2=check/animate F3=cmd-file F4=return-CSI F5=CSI-enter F6=CSI-at-cursor
F7=locate-previous F8=locate-next F9=locate- current F10=insert-statement  Escape
```

Figure 5.5 Editor COBOL menu

```
Checker-Check──Pause-List-Con──────────Strc+Anlz-VSC2(3)─XRef─────────CSI────
F1=help F2=check/anim F3=pause F4=list F5=strc/anlz F6=lang F7=ref F8=CSI    Esc
F9/F10=directives       check K:\COBOL\MFWBBOOK\CUST.CBL
```

Figure 5.6 Editor Check/Animate menu

Notice that the menu in Figure 5.6 is not the same as the Checker menu in Figure 5.3. How do you tell which menu you are seeing? Look at the word appearing in the leftmost portion of the information line. In version 2.5, if it is **Check**, you are seeing the standalone Checker menu. If it is **Checker**, you are seeing the Editor check/animate menu. Another clue: the standalone Checker menu has a few additional functions, which you can reach by holding down the **Ctrl** key.

5.2 Checker Directives

5.2.1 Types of Directives

As we have already seen, directives customize the Checker and Compiler according to your needs. Some directives control the Checker's user interface and its role as part of the testing and debugging facilities within the Workbench. Other directives control the use of COBOL language features and interfaces with other products. You will need to work with both types of directives.

The Micro Focus Workbench supports over a hundred directives. Don't worry, you don't have to memorize all of them to get your programs to work. **All Micro Focus directives have built-in default values.** If you do not specify a value for a directive, you are accepting its default value. Some directives have a default setting that represents "on" or "off," while other directives have other types of default values. Most directives deal with fairly specialized situations; you can ignore them unless you are doing something unusual.

Many of the Micro Focus manuals discuss the use of directives in various contexts. A complete reference guide to directives appears in Appendix B of the *COBOL/2 Operating Guide.* You can also look up directives in the On-line Information hypertext help system, discussed in Chapter 4.

Directives important for the mainframe programmer. The alphabetical listing of directives in the Operating Guide describes the parameter values you can use with each directive, including the default value. This listing also tells you what phase of compiler operation each directive will control. **Some directives take effect during the Syntax Checker phase, others during the object code generation phase, still others during both phases.** For testing mainframe programs within the Workbench, you will primarily work with directives that control the syntax checking phase.

A separate list in the *COBOL/2 Operating Guide* groups each directive by purpose:

- Compiler control
- Compiling for debugging
- Allowing language features
- SQL
- Choosing run-time behavior
- Object code size and optimization
- Format of your data files
- Reserved directives

The directives most useful to a mainframe programmer are in several of these groups. Certain other groups can be ruled out entirely. For example, "Reserved Directives" are marked "Do not use" in the manual: they make the Workbench compatible with older products or with add-on features.

Mainframe versus PC programming. A mainframe programmer can safely ignore those directives having to do with compiling programs to be run in the PC environment. Directives listed under "Object Code Size and Optimization" and "Format of Your Data Files" are primarily intended for PC applications development. For testing mainframe applications, you can ignore these directives by accepting their default settings.

Under the group "Allowing Language Features" is a subgroup, "Dialect." Directives in that subgroup let you make the COBOL/2 Compiler compatible with various mainframe, minicomputer, and PC COBOL language dialects. For example, the ANS85, OSVS, VSC2, and FLAG directives pertain to IBM mainframe compatibility. Another group, "Choosing Run-time Behavior," contains more directives that make the COBOL/2 Compiler compatible with mainframe COBOL dialects. For example, you can choose CHARSET (ASCII) or (EBCDIC). We will discuss these below.

Directives for using COBOL with add-on products. A few directives control the use of COBOL with add-on products such as CICS. Some of these directives are in the "Allowing Language Features" and "Reserved Directives" groups. See the printed documentation and "read-me" text files provided with the add-on products. When you install certain add-on products, the Micro Focus setup utility program will create special directives files for you to use with those products. You can ignore these directives unless you plan to use these add-on products with the program you are checking.

Checking/compiling for debugging. Most of the time, you will probably be testing your programs with the Workbench debugging tools. To do this, you must first check or compile your programs with certain directive settings. These directives, which we will discuss below, cause the Checker to produce output files needed during testing.

The group "Compiling for Debugging" also contains a subgroup called "Add-on Products." These directives tell the Checker to produce output that will let you test the program with various Workbench or Microsoft debugging tools. The *COBOL/2 Operating Guide* calls these Workbench facilities "add-on products" only because they are not part of the COBOL/2 Compiler itself. The Animator base product comes with the COBOL/2 Compiler, while the Advanced Animator is part of the Workbench utilities.

SQL. Micro Focus supports SQL-based database management systems (DBMS), including IBM's OS/2 Extended Services Database Manager. The DBMS itself is a separate product not supplied with the Workbench. However, the COBOL preprocessor and runtime support for using embedded SQL commands in COBOL programs is part of the COBOL/2 Compiler product. A separate group of directives controls the use of SQL support. A mainframe programmer can use SQL on the PC workstation to simulate mainframe DB2 databases.

What about using SQL with CICS? The CICS OS/2 option runs under OS/2 Extended Services. Therefore, the SQL-based OS/2 Extended Services Database Manager is available to users of CICS OS/2. (Other SQL-based databases, including XDB, also work with CICS OS/2 and the CICS Option product.) If you install the CICS OS/2 add-on product, the setup utility will create directives files that let you embed SQL commands in your CICS programs. You can safely ignore SQL directives when compiling or checking CICS, IMS, or plain vanilla COBOL programs that do not use SQL.

Compiler control directives. These directives control the following activities: syntax error flagging, contents of printed listing, screen display behavior, and the compiler's use of input and output files. Some of these directives are purely cosmetic. You can use them as personal preference dictates. A few compiler control directives are quite useful, such as the DIRECTIVES directive.

More information. Also see Appendix F, "Checker Directives Related to Mainframe Development," in the *Micro Focus Workbench Mainframe Programmer's Guide.* This appendix contains a list of directives that could be of use to the mainframe program developer. As you get more familiar with the Workbench, it's a good idea to review the available directives to see whether any of them apply to situations at your mainframe site.

5.2.2 Passing Directives to the Checker

Order of priority of directives. How does the Checker find the directive values it will need? The Checker will look for directive values from five specific sources, in order. **Directives that come in later will override directives from an earlier source.** Let's look at each source in turn:

- Default values built into the COBOL/2 Compiler
- The COBOL.DIR file
- The WBxxxx.DIR directives files
- Directives entered in the directives buffer on a Micro Focus Checker menu
- $SET statements within your program source files

Default values. As we mentioned, every directive has a default value. Since most directives are for specialized situations, their default values are frequently "NO" followed by the directive name. This means that the directive is "off" by default. Default values for each directive are listed in Appendix B of the *COBOL/2 Operating Guide.*

The COBOL.DIR file. COBOL.DIR is an ASCII text file containing directive settings. A COBOL.DIR file is built during the Workbench installation process, according to choices you make on the SETUP menus. Experienced users can change the COBOL.DIR file or create new ones to suit specialized needs. The Workbench will pick up the COBOL.DIR file from a subdirectory designated in the SET COBDIR= environment variable, if a COBOL.DIR file exists there.

What does a directives file look like? A directives file is an ASCII text file containing directives. If you wish, you can specify several directives on the same line, separated by spaces. The most convenient and tidy way is to specify one directive per text line. For example, Figure 5.7 shows the COBOL.DIR file created automatically during the installation process in Chapter 2.

```
NESTCALL
OMF(GNT)
COPYLBR
```

Figure 5.7 COBOL.DIR file

Let's take a look at the directives supplied in this example of COBOL.DIR. All three override system defaults.

- **NESTCALL** directive enables the ANSI '85 nested programs feature, so that nested programs will compile successfully. The default is NONESTCALL.
- **OMF"GNT"** tells the Compiler to produce generated (GNT) code to be run using the Micro Focus shared runtime system. The alternative is to produce

standard object code files (OBJ) that need to be link-edited for standalone use. For testing under the Workbench, GNT is what you want. The default is OMF"OBJ".

- **COPYLBR** tells the Checker that any qualified filename mentioned in a COPY statement refers to a Micro Focus library file, not to a directory path. These library files can be used to simulate mainframe partitioned datasets (PDSs) on the PC. The default is NOCOPYLBR. You can omit COPYLBR if you do not reference copy library members from a Micro Focus library file.

The COBOL.DIR file is a good place to put those directives that you want to take effect every time you sign on to the Workbench. For example, if you want the Checker to look for program source filenames with an extension other than .CBL, then you would place the OSEXT directive in the COBOL.DIR file. Suppose your existing COBOL source files or copy library members had an extension of .COB instead of CBL. To get at those without having to specify an extension, you would place the directive OSEXT "COB" in the COBOL.DIR file.

Some directives take one or more parameters after the directive name. In most cases, you have the option of surrounding your parameter with either parentheses or quotes. A few directives require you to delimit parameters by parentheses only. In other situations, the reverse is true. If your parameter value contains spaces, you must use quotes instead of parentheses.

The WBxxxx.DIR directives files. The WBxxxx.DIR files are separate directives files that come into play when you choose a language dialect on the Workbench Checker menu. The Workbench installation procedure sets up these files to let you make the Workbench compatible with mainframe language dialects. Their names follow the format **WBxxxx.DIR,** where the xxxx refers to a COBOL language dialect such as OSVS or VSC2. For example, the directives file for VS COBOL II(3) is named WBVSC23.DIR, shown in Figure 5.8. **Don't worry, you need not learn all of these directives to compile or syntax check VS COBOL II programs!** You just need to know how to choose the right set of directives for the language dialect you plan to use.

So how do you choose the directives file for the mainframe language dialect(s) you use? Pressing **F6=lang** on the Checker menu will cycle through the available language dialects. You can choose OSVS COBOL or any of the three levels of VS COBOL II. The current selection appears on the information line. A language setting of "blank" results in no language directives file. This represents Micro Focus COBOL (PC COBOL). You can use this setting for compiling some of the demo programs that come with the system. It does not simulate the IBM mainframe environment.

Directives in the directives buffer on the Checker or Editor Checker menu. You can enter directives on the Checker menu that affect that one checking session only. Pressing **F10** opens an area at the bottom of the Checker menu for entry of directives. After entering the directives (with a space between each), press the enter key. This in itself does not *activate* the directives. To use the directives you have entered, you must press **F9** to make the indicator **opts-on** appear on the information line.

```
ANS85
CANCELLBR
COPYLBR
CHARSET(EBCDIC)
DBCS
DEFAULTBYTE(00)
FLAG(VSC2)
FLAGAS(S)
FLAGCD
HOST-NUMCOMPARE
IBMCOMP
INFORETURN(0)
MAPNAME
NOMF
NOMFCOMMENT
NESTCALL
ODOSLIDE
NOOPTIONAL-FILE
NOOSVS
PERFORM-TYPE"OSVS"
NORESEQ
NOSEG
STICKY-LINKAGE
NOTRACE
VSC2(3)
WARNING(3)
ZEROLENGTHFALSE
NOZWB
```

Figure 5.8 WBVSC23.DIR file

The DIRECTIVES directive causes the Checker to read directives from a file. For example, if you enter DIRECTIVES (MYFILE.DIR) on the Checker menu or on the command line, the Checker will use directive values in the file MYFILE.DIR, overriding any others supplied earlier. If you see any mention of the USE directive in the manuals, be aware that the USE directive and the DIRECTIVES directive are the same except in name. If you specify a DIRECTIVES directive within another directives file, the Checker will switch over from the original directives file to the one you specified. It will not go back to process the rest of the directives in the original file. If you enter DIRECTIVES or USE as a directive on the Checker menu with the F9/F10 keys, the Checker will read directives from a file for that session only. You can set up separate directives files for different projects, depending on individual needs.

$SET statements within program source files. $SET statements in the program itself are the last directives that the Checker/Compiler finds. They can override directives at all previous levels. Most of the time, the $SET statement(s) will be at the beginning of your program. Enter the directives through the Editor, leaving a space between each directive. A few directives may be used in $SET statements elsewhere in your program (not at the beginning, although most cannot. (The list in Appendix B of the *COBOL/2 Operating Guide* indicates which directives can be used in $SET statements other than at the beginning of a program.) $SET commands embedded within the program might be useful for changing directives that affect the appearance of the printed output.

The syntax of a $SET command is the word $SET beginning in column 7, followed by directives. Allow a space between each directive. You can use additional $SET commands to hold more directives. Do not try to break or continue a directive from one $SET command to the next.

If you use $SET statements in programs intended for porting back to the mainframe, remember to comment out the $SET statements before you try to compile on the mainframe.

5.2.3 Directives for the Checker's User Interface

The two forms of the Checker menu shown in Figures 5.2 and 5.5 work in much the same way. Various toggle switch settings bring in the directives that people use most often. Indicators on the information line show which toggle switch settings are active. The **F3=pause** toggle switch tells the Checker whether or not to pause after each error. Most programmers turn it off to make the Checker collect all errors before pausing. The F3 key turns the ERRQ (pause on error) directive on and off.

F4=list-con tells the Checker where to send its output listing. Pressing that key repeatedly cycles through several choices. **List-con, print,** and **list-file** send output to the screen, to the printer, or to a disk file, respectively. **Nolist,** the default, suppresses listing output completely. If you are in a hurry, suppressing the output will make the checking go much faster. Most programmers set this option to **list-con** for screen (console) output. This F4 toggle switch works by setting the LIST(*filename*) directive. You can use only parentheses with the LIST directive, not quotes. The *filename* may be a disk file or a device such as CON or LST.

F7=ref tells the Checker whether to produce a cross-reference list. Pressing that key repeatedly cycles through the choices on the information line. **xref** provides a procedure division cross-reference, **ref** provides a data division cross-reference, **x+ref** provides both, and "blank" provides neither. In effect, this key turns the REF and XREF directives on and off.

What's going on "under the covers?" The Workbench menu system interprets the function key toggle settings as directives before it invokes the checking process. The Workbench passes the directives to the Checker much as though you had entered them following the program name on the MS-DOS or OS/2 command prompt. Feeling a bit confused about what directive settings are being used? Let the Workbench show you what it is doing. Placing the CONFIRM directive at the beginning of your COBOL.DIR file and your other directives files will make the Checker show the directives on your screen.

5.2.4 Directives for Debugging: Animation, CSI

If you plan to test with the Animator, the Analyzer, the Structure Animator, or COBOL Source Information (CSI), first you must check or compile the program with the required directives. The directives tell the Checker what files to produce to suit the needs of these testing tools. The Checker menu automatically provides the **ANIM** directive for you. Function keys let you set the **ANALYZE, STRUCT,** and **CSI** directives from the Checker menu as desired. Pressing **F5=strc/anlz** repeatedly will cycle through **Struct, Analyze,**

Strc+Anlz, and neither of the above. Pressing **F8=CSI** toggles the CSI directive on and off.

Don't confuse these with other similar directives in the list. **GANIM** lets you test with Xilerator, another debugging tool used mainly for mixed-language programs. **RNIM** is used at the command prompt; it causes the Animator to run instead of the Compiler. **XNIM** compiles your program for animation and then invokes the Animator.

The **COBIDY** directive lets you override the SET COBIDY= environment variable that tells where to find the Animator .IDY file. The default setting is NOCOBIDY, indicating that the .IDY file will be stored in the same directory as the .INT file.

Subscript and index bounds checking. The BOUND directive causes the Checker/Compiler to generate code to check for indexes and subscripts that are out of bounds. This feature is set on by default.

Programs containing COBOL READY TRACE verbs. We recommend that you avoid using COBOL READY TRACE, RESET TRACE, and EXHIBIT NAMED verbs in programs that you test with the Workbench. These verbs represent obsolete language features dropped under VS COBOL II. Even under ANSI '74 COBOL, TRACE verbs are useful only when no other testing facilities are available. Unless you are careful, these verbs rapidly dump out much more data than you would ever want to view, print, or store on disk. The Workbench interactive animation facilities are far better for tracking flow of control and changes to data values. The **NOTRACE** directive, the system default, causes embedded COBOL trace verbs to have no effect.

5.2.5 Directives for Compatibility with Mainframe COBOL

Let's take a quick look at several of the directives supplied automatically in the WBVSC23.DIR file shown in Figure 5.8.

- **CHARSET"EBCDIC"** sets the system character set to EBCDIC instead of the default ASCII. CHARSET"EBCDIC" causes literals and collating sequences (for comparisons and sorting) to use EBCDIC. Use of CHARSET"EBCDIC" also causes certain other directives to be set: SIGN"EBCDIC" for the sign conventions in numeric display conventions, and NATIVE"EBCDIC" for the default collating sequence.
- **ANS85, VSC2(3),** and **NOOSVS** tell the Checker which words are to be treated as COBOL reserved words. In addition, the ANS85 directive changes runtime behavior to conform to the ANS85 standard. The various **FLAG** directives control the types of syntax error messages that the Checker will produce.
- **DEFAULTBYTE"00"** causes your program to initialize all Data Division storage bytes to nulls if no VALUE clause exists. The system default is the ASCII space character, DEFAULTBYTE"32". Since we are using EBCDIC, this is undesirable.
- **FLAGCD** causes the Checker to flag all other directives that are incompatible with the selected language dialect. Thus, if you use VSC2(3) and you

specify some other directive that conflicts with VSC2(3), the Checker will flag it.

- **IBMCOMP** makes COMP fields occupy either two or four bytes so that they will line up the same way they would on a mainframe. You will need to use this directive if you plan to use the Micro Focus PARM Passer facility to simulate MVS JCL PARMs.

- **PERFORM-TYPE"OSVS"** affects the way that the program will return from nested PERFORMs. The system default, PERFORM-TYPE"MF", is straightforward and flexible in that it recognizes only the return point from the innermost PERFORM. However, PERFORM-TYPE"OSVS" provides a closer imitation of the behavior of mainframe COBOL. With PERFORM-TYPE"OSVS", the program will take whatever exit point it reaches first, whether innermost or not. PERFORM statements with the same exit point can be nested no more than two deep. The end of a section has the same exit point as the end of its last paragraph. Old programs with untidy nested PERFORM statements may run differently depending on the way this directive is set.

- **STICKY-LINKAGE** applies to called subprograms. Suppose you CALL a subprogram that has more than one entry point. STICKY-LINKAGE preserves the calling parameters in the called subprogram's linkage section. If you call the same subprogram again, even through a different entry point, the parameters from the previous CALL will still be available in the linkage section.

An unusual situation. In versions of Workbench prior to 3.0, complications arise when the first CALL to a subprogram is *not* to the name in the PROGRAM-ID, but to a different entry point. The PC has no facility for setting up an "alias" for an alternative entry point. Therefore, on the PC, the first CALL must be to the name in the PROGRAM-ID. You may need to place a "dummy" routine with GOBACK at the beginning of the subprogram's PROCEDURE DIVISION, and CALL it before doing anything else. For other options, see the section "Initial Call of an Alternate Entry Point" under "Compatibility Issues" in the *Micro Focus Mainframe Programmer's Guide*.

QUOTE vs. APOST. Because the COBOL language uses quotes as data value delimiters, COBOL provides a figurative constant, QUOTE, for placing a quotation mark in a data field. The **QUOTE** directive (the system default) equates the COBOL figurative constant QUOTE to the double quotation mark character. The **APOST** directive equates the COBOL figurative constant QUOTE to the single quotation mark character. QUOTE and APOST are opposites. Once you specify one of them, you cannot override it later with the opposite directive. **You will need to use the APOST directive only with COBOL programs that use the figurative constant QUOTE to place single quotes in data fields.**

Copy members in Librarian or Panvalet. Does your site uses Librarian or Panvalet to store program source and copy library members on the mainframe? If so, your mainframe programs will contain Librarian -INC or Panvalet

++INCLUDE statements instead of COBOL COPY statements. **Using the LI-BRARIAN or PANVALET directives will enable the Checker to expand -INC or ++INCLUDE statements.** Be sure that all needed copy members have been moved to the PC. Keep them either in the current directory in which your source program is stored, or in the directory specified in the SET COBCPY= environment variable.

Old programs and obsolete language features. Are you using the Workbench to maintain old mainframe COBOL programs? For programs that use the ANSI '68 form of COPY statements, the **OLDCOPY** directive will allow the Checker to expand COPY statements properly. For programs that use the COBOL ALTER verb, check the programs with the **ALTER** directive, at least until you get a chance to remove all dependency on this rather disreputable language feature.

Truncation of data in COMP (hex) items. The TRUNC, TRUNC"ANSI", and **NOTRUNC** directives control how much data will be stored in COMP fields. **You can usually allow this directive to default to TRUNC"ANSI" unless it is vital to duplicate the exact behavior of a mainframe program as it encounters overflow on COMP fields.** You can run into a slight discrepancy because the COBOL PICTURE length may be shorter than the physical data length (the maximum binary value that fits into that field). When a COBOL MOVE is taking place, TRUNC will truncate the value in decimal to the size of the COBOL PICTURE clause. NOTRUNC will truncate the value in binary to the size of the physical data length; that is, to the maximum capacity of the allocated storage item. TRUNC"ANSI" acts like TRUNC on nonarithmetic moves. For arithmetic operations that store data into the COMP field, you must use ON SIZE ERROR to trap an overflow condition; otherwise, the result will be undefined.

More information about mainframe compatibility. Some mainframe compiler control options have counterparts (more or less) among Micro Focus Checker directives. The "MDE Menu System" chapter in the *Micro Focus Mainframe Programmer's Guide* contains a chart showing how certain Micro Focus directives compare with OS/VS COBOL or VS COBOL II mainframe compiler options. Also see the section "Compiler Options versus Checker Directives" under "Compatibility Issues" in the *Mainframe Programmer's Guide.*

Micro Focus does not support the use of hard-coded CBL, *CBL, PRO-CESS, or *CONTROL statements at the beginning of COBOL program source files. If these are present in source files downloaded from the mainframe, you must comment them out before syntax checking on the PC. If these statements contain mainframe compiler options that you need to duplicate on the PC, you can supply Checker/Compiler directives in $SET statements, directives files, or on the menu screen.

5.2.6 Directives to Tailor Programs for Different Countries

If you write programs for use in countries other than the United States, you may need to set one or more of these directives:

- **CURRENCY-SIGN"*integer*"**, where *integer* is the decimal ASCII code of the currency sign character. The default is CURRENCY-SIGN"36", the dollar sign.

- **CURRENT-DATE"*format*"**, where *format* is DDMMYY or YYMMDD. This controls the order of the date in the CURRENT- DATE COBOL special register. The default is MMDDYY.

- **DBCS"*integer*"**, where *integer* specifies the level of support. This turns on two levels of support for double byte character set. DBCS(2) represents the full IBM SAA version. DBCS lets the computer represent languages such as Japanese, Chinese, and Korean that have more characters than can be expressed in a single ASCII or EBCDIC byte. Micro Focus recommends that you contact Technical Support for more information if you plan to use the Workbench with DBCS languages.

- **DBCSSOSI"*integer*" "*integer*"**, where the two parameters specify the ASCII codes of the shift-out and shift-in characters. This tells the Checker what characters indicate a shift between DBCS and single-character mode.

- **DBSPACE,** which tells the Checker to use the standard DBCS space rather than two ASCII spaces.

- **SAA** (Systems Application Architecture), which enables use of the DBCS"2" and DBSPACE directives listed above.

5.2.7 More about the Checker Menu

The Ctrl key menu. If you hold down the **Ctrl** key on the Checker menu, you will see a Micro Focus directory maintenance screen. It looks just like the one that comes up when you hold down the **Ctrl** key on the Editor file load menu. This menu, shown in Figure 5.9, lets you change default directories, browse, rename, or delete files, or use Micro Focus library files. It works the same as the Editor file load **Ctrl** key menu described in the previous chapter (see Section 4.15.2, "Changing the Default Directory"). This **Ctrl** key menu exists only on the Checker menu that is a submenu of the Develop menu, not on the Checker menu within the Editor facility. It would be redundant to place this submenu on the Editor Checker menu when the Editor itself already has that feature.

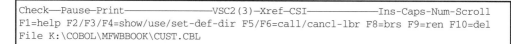

```
Check—Pause—Print————————————VSC2(3)—Xref—CSI——————————Ins-Caps-Num-Scroll
F1=help F2/F3/F4=show/use/set-def-dir F5/F6=call/cancl-lbr F8=brs F9=ren F10=del
File K:\COBOL\MFWBBOOK\CUST.CBL
```

*Figure 5.9 Checker **Ctrl** key menu*

Starting the syntax check process. Once you have all of the toggle switch settings and directives specified to your liking, press the enter key to begin the checking process.

5.3 Correcting Syntax Errors from the Checker

The Checker, like the Editor, the Compiler, and the Animator, is integrated into the Workbench menu system to make it more convenient for you to fix program errors. When the Syntax Checker finds errors in your program, it stores the error messages in a file named xxxxxxxx.MSG, where xxxxxxxx is the name of your program. This file acts as a pointer to errors in the source. When the Checker finishes, the system will return you to the Editor, load your program, and position the cursor to the first error. If more than one error is present, you can use **F8=locate-next, F7=locate-prev,** or **F9=locate-current** to reposition the cursor to other errors in the source file. If an error is in a copy library member, the system will load that copy member on top of the main source program in the same Editor window. Once you have finished fixing the errors in the copy library member, you can save the copy member and then press the escape key to get back to the main program. This automatic integration of the Checker with the Workbench Editor takes effect only when you use the Checker from the Workbench menu system, not by invoking the checker directly from the command line. However, certain other third-party editors are capable of interfacing with the Checker.

Figure 5.10 shows what the Checker screen looks like when it finds an error. Figure 5.11 shows the screen display after control has returned to the Checker. Notice the error message on the last line of the screen.

```
* Micro Focus COBOL/2 Version 2.5.27 L2.4 revision 002
* Copyright (C) 1985,1991 Micro Focus Ltd.     URN AXUPA/ZZ0/86353
* Accepted - CONFIRM
* Checking  K:\COBOL\MFWBBOOK\CUST.CBL

        DATA DIVISION.
        FILE SECTION.
        FD CUSTMSTR
            RECORD CONTAINS 41 CHARACTERS.
            COPY CUSTMST.
        * CUSTOMER MASTER RECORD.
        01  CUSTMST-REC.
            05  CUST-KEY.
                10  CUST-NO              PIC X(6).
            05  CUST-NAME                PIC X(25).
            05  CUST-PHONE               PIC X(10).
        WORKING-STORAGE SECTION.
        PROCEDURE DIVISION.
        MAIN SECTION.
            MOVE 0 TO COUNT.
*   13-S*******************                                        **
**     User-name required
CONTINUE CHECKING PROGRAM ?   Yes/No/Zoom

Checking CUST, Ctrl+Break to Stop
```

Figure 5.10 Checker screen display: pausing at error

```
CUST.CBL
        ■MOVE 0 TO COUNT.
         OPEN OUTPUT CUSTMST.
         PERFORM UNTIL CUST-NO = "QUIT"
             DISPLAY "Enter customer number (6 digits) or QUIT"
             ACCEPT CUST-NO
             IF CUST-NO NOT = "QUIT"
                 DISPLAY "Enter customer name (25 characters)"
                 ACCEPT CUST-NAME
                 DISPLAY "Enter phone number (10 digits)"
                 ACCEPT CUST-PHONE
                 WRITE CUSTMST-REC
             END-IF
         END-PERFORM.
         DISPLAY "End of program CUST.".
         CLOSE CUSTMST.
         STOP RUN.
.............................end of text.....................................



Edit CUST          42 lines     Line 27     Col 26      Wrap Ins Caps Num Scroll
F1=help F2=COBOL F3=insert-line F4-delete-line F5=repeat-line F6=restore-line
F7=retype-char F8=restore-char F9=word-left F10=word-right        Alt Ctrl Escape

*  13 User-name required
```

Figure 5.11 Editor screen after returning from Checker with an error

5.4 Running the Checker from the Command Line Prompt

You can run the Checker from the operating system command line prompt or from a command file (MS-DOS .BAT or OS/2 .CMD file). The command for this is **WB CHECK** followed by the program name and any directives you want to use, delimited by spaces. Using a command file for batch operation is convenient if you want to syntax check many programs when the computer is unattended. A command file of this type repeatedly invokes the Checker, supplying a different program name each time. You can start the job, go out to lunch, and look at the listings files on disk when you come back.

If you enter **WB CHECK** at the command line prompt, the Checker will use the same COBOL.DIR file that it would use under the Workbench. It also will use the system default WBxxxx.DIR file, unless you specify some other file in a DIRECTIVES directive on the command line or in a $SET command. The default will be WBOSVS.DIR unless you have reconfigured the Editor to use another default. (You can invoke the Compiler, rather than the Checker, by typing **COBOL progname** at the command line prompt. The Compiler will use directives from COBOL.DIR, but will not automatically pick up any of the WBxxxx.DIR directives files.)

5.5 Exercises

1. Using the Editor, print out the COBOL.DIR file and the other WBxxxx.DIR files on your system. These should be in the directory specified in the SET COBDIR= environment variable.

2. Using the Editor, load the program CUST.CBL that you entered as one of the exercises in the last chapter. Examine the program before checking it. Do you see any ANSI '85 (VS COBOL II) language features? What does that tell you about the language toggle setting to use? Make the program listing output go to your screen. Check the program CUST.CBL from the Editor Checker menu. If you made any keying errors while entering the program, the Checker will let you know. Fix any errors that it finds.

3. This time, suppress the Checker program listing output. What does the checking process look like to the user once the source program is free from errors?

4. Check the program CUST.CBL from the Checker menu instead of from the Editor Checker menu.

5. Bring up a MS-DOS or OS/2 command prompt and check CUST.CBL from the command prompt.

6. Experiment with checking some of the demo programs provided with the Micro Focus Workbench. What language toggle settings does each program need so that it will syntax check without errors?

6

The Micro Focus Animator

6.1 What Is the Animator?

6.1.1 Interactive Testing

Nobody is looking over your shoulder. Your boss doesn't know what you are thinking, so you might as well tell yourself the truth about your mainframe testing activities. **Do you *always* test your applications as well as you think you should?** Or do you and your colleagues sometimes feel compelled to cut corners? How often have you (or your end users) found bugs in programs that have just been put into production? Don't get us wrong; we are not accusing you of being careless about the quality of your work. After all, nobody wants

Installing poorly tested applications

to put faulty applications into production. Nobody wants to spend more and more time "fighting fires" in production systems. Why, then, do so many conscientious programmers skimp on testing? Let us answer that question with another question. **How many project budgets allow enough time and money for thorough testing?** How much is enough? That depends on what tools are on hand. We believe that no one can test complex programs thoroughly in any reasonable amount of time without the proper tools.

If you have never used an animated debugger, you may wonder what it means to "animate" a program. Animation sounds like something that is fun to use, and it is. No, you won't see Bugs Bunny or Bart Simpson on your VGA screen. Instead, you will see each line of program source code light up as the Animator executes it. You will see data element contents change. You can view the user's screen display as needed. You can change data contents or program execution sequence, or even add new statements, while your program is running. You can vary the execution speed to move rapidly through areas that do not concern you. You can slow down or stop where you want to take a closer look. You can capture and review execution statistics. You can even animate a block diagram of your program. With the Animator, program testing can be the best part of your job, rather than a chore you dread.

The benefits of thorough testing. Let's take a moment to think about two major purposes of testing: troubleshooting and quality assurance. Good testing

97

and debugging tools address both purposes by showing you how an application *actually* works as opposed to how you *think* it should work. Troubleshooting is the art of fixing known problems such as abnormal termination, poor performance, or unexpected results. Troubleshooting should address the underlying conditions instead of covering up the symptoms. Testing is vital to troubleshooting because it uncovers the roots of program and system problems. With that knowledge, you can solve problems without resorting to aimless trial and error. Once you have completed a "bug fix," thorough testing should verify that the fix solved the original problem without introducing new flaws.

As part of quality assurance, testing shows whether the program or system does what the end user wants it to do in a reasonably efficient way and without interfering with other work. It's important to realize that quality assurance, by itself, does not build quality into any system; only good analysis, design, and coding methods can do that. Instead, quality assurance either assures you that the expected level of quality is present, or indicates where quality falls short. When all new applications must meet standards of quality, there is less need to spend time "fire-fighting" production problems.

Reengineering old programs. In a typical mainframe shop, one of the least pleasant tasks is "archaeology": maintaining unstructured programs that seem to be left over from the days when dinosaurs roamed the earth. The original programmers have been gone for years, maybe decades. Someone else has to pay for their mistakes, probably you. Any documentation that still exists is outdated and misleading. You can't clean up this mess until you figure out what the programs do and how they fit together. Several Workbench testing tools, particularly the Advanced Animator and COBOL Source Information (CSI), offer diagnostic features that help you tackle old programs. This knowledge will let you restructure or rewrite programs that have become maintenance nightmares.

Interactive testing: PC versus mainframe. Interactive testing packages that run on the mainframe tend to be expensive and fairly complex to use. Some of them force the programmer to learn many cryptic commands. For batch COBOL programming, many installations cannot spare the mainframe CPU cycles needed for interactive (foreground) testing. This is why mainframe programmers still rely heavily on COBOL DISPLAY statements, printed trace output, and memory dumps for debugging batch programs. Mainframe CICS programmers generally can test their on-line programs interactively, but the available testing tools all have their drawbacks. For example, the CEDF transaction is part of CICS. CEDF is easy to use, but it traps only CICS commands and it can be slow on a heavily loaded system. Third-party CICS testing tools are more powerful but are harder to use and sometimes create security problems. It's too easy to damage system tables accidentally and lock yourself out of the system, or worse! Because of these problems, the memory dump with trace table is still a much-used mainframe CICS debugging tool.

Testing on the PC requires an interactive approach. When we got our first PC in 1983, one of our first complaints was, "We have an assembler, but no memory dump utility! How are we supposed to troubleshoot programs?" Even then, it would have taken time to print out 64K memory dumps on a dot matrix printer at 80 characters per second. Now, laser printers are faster and quieter, but our computer has eight megabytes of memory. It still does not make sense to print memory dumps on a PC. In any case, dumps and trace output are tools for tracking down problems after the fact. On a PC, with the whole system dedicated to your use, you might as well do your testing while the program is running, in "real time."

6.1.2 Basic Animator versus Advanced Animator

The Workbench Animator actually comes in two versions, basic and advanced. The basic Animator comes with the COBOL/2 Compiler product. A user who had only the COBOL/2 Compiler and not the complete Workbench would run the basic Animator from the command line prompt. The Advanced Animator comes with the Workbench product. It contains all of the basic Animator features plus some others: the Analyzer, the Structure Animator, and access to CSI (COBOL Source Information). This chapter will cover all Animator features, basic and advanced. The next chapter will cover CSI.

We described the Workbench setup procedures in an earlier chapter. One of the installation choices in the setup utility script lets you install either the full set of Advanced Animator features, or just the basic Animator. Here again, we assume that you have installed the full set of Advanced Animator features. If not, you can reinstall the Workbench to add any features you left out earlier.

6.2 Files Used by Animator

Checking your program with the right directives. As we mentioned in a previous chapter, you have to check your program with the proper directives for animation before you can "animate" it (test it with the animator). On the Workbench Checker menus, you can choose directives for animation by using function key toggle switches. These Checker directives will determine what Animator features will become available to you later when you test the program:

- **ANIM** enables the use of the Animator
- **Struct** enables structure animation
- **Analyze** enables the execution analyzer
- **Strc+Anlz** enables both structure animation and the execution analyzer
- **CSI** enables COBOL Source Information

If you try to animate a program without first checking it with the ANIM directive, the program will still run, but at "machine speed." It will not animate your program (run it in debugging mode). Sometimes this is what you want. If you are testing an application consisting of many program modules, you probably will not want to animate the parts that you have already tested. In that case, you would set the ANIM directive to check only those modules that still need testing.

Note: This information regarding directives applies only to animation within the Workbench function key menu system. As we will show in Chapter 15, you will not have to set these directives in order to animate a program within the newer GUI Workbench environment.

For each program module to be animated, the Animator needs certain input files:

- **.CBL** and **.CPY** files: this is the complete source program.
- **.INT** file: this is intermediate object code, created when you check with ANIM.
- **.IDY** file: Animator information file, created when you check with ANIM, and updated during animation. Execution counts from the Analyzer are kept in this file.

During animation, depending on what you choose to do, you may create output files:

- You can print structure diagrams on various types of PC workstation printers. The Animator will create a file formatted for printing with filename extension **.PRT** that you can route to your printer.
- Using the "Do At Breakpoint" function, you can enter new lines of source code. The Animator will interpret and execute them when it reaches the breakpoint. Lines of source code entered in this way are stored in an **.EDO** file so that you can merge them with your source code later if desired.
- You can also create a "query dump" file of data element values so that you can test your program again using those same values. A query dump file has filename extension **.ILS.**

An important tip: Suppose you have already checked or compiled a program without setting the ANIM directive, and you want to recheck it for animation. Delete all of the old non-Animator object files (filename extension .GNT or .OBJ) before you recheck. Otherwise, the Animator will find those old object files and run your program at machine speed instead of animating it.

Note: Be aware that the material in this section applies only to the function key based Workbench menu system that we have been discussing. Graphics-mode Workbench facilities may rely on other methods of specifying directives and other file naming conventions. Refer to Chapter 15 for more information.

6.3 Getting Ready to Animate

6.3.1 Bringing Up the Animator Menu

The Animator initial menu. Selecting **F4=animate** on the Develop menu will bring up the Animator initial menu. This menu, shown in Figure 6.1, lets you start the animation process. Directory functions, for selecting a program for animated debugging, are on the **Ctrl** key menu. The Animator directory menu is the same as the directory menu you use with the Editor, so we will not repeat it here. Alternatively, you can type the program filename directly at the bottom of the screen.

```
Animate-(Advanced)-with-Parmpass────────────────────Ins-Caps-Num-Scroll
F1=help F2=dir F3=switches F4=zoom F5=strc/anlz F6=Parmpass-off  F9/F10=opts Esc
File K:\COBOL\MFWBBOOK\CUST                                              Ctrl
```

Figure 6.1 Animator initial menu (before program is loaded)

Passing directives and parameters. Pressing **F10** opens an area at the bottom of the Animator initial menu for entry of Animator directives. After you finish entering directives, press the enter key. This in itself does not *activate* the directives. To use the directives, you must press **F9** to make the indicator **Options-on** appear on the information line. If you are writing mainframe programs, you probably won't need to change the Animator directives from their default settings.

　　F4=Parmpass-on turns on the Workbench Parmpass facility. Parmpass offers a way to simulate mainframe operating system parms. You set up a parameter file ahead of time with the Parmpass facility. This switch allows your program to receive the parm file. If Parmpass is on, the information line will say **Animate-(Advanced)-with-Parmpass.** Chapter 8 will show you how to set up the parameters under Parmpass.

　　F3=switches brings up a menu that lets you set COBOL runtime switches, if you are testing a program that requires them. We will look at the runtime switch menu in Chapter 8, where we discuss compiling and running programs.

Starting animation. Pressing the enter key begins animation. When the animation process is about to begin, you will see a message, **Preparing to animate [your program name].** The Animator main menu, shown in Figure 6.2, will then appear.

```
   33 MAIN SECTION.
   34     OPEN OUTPUT CUSTMST.
   35     PERFORM UNTIL CUST-NO = "QUIT"
   36         DISPLAY "Enter customer number (6 digits) or QUIT"
   37         ACCEPT CUST-NO
   38         IF CUST-NO NOT = "QUIT"
   39             DISPLAY "Enter customer name (25 characters)"
   40             ACCEPT CUST-NAME
   41             DISPLAY "Enter phone number (10 digits)"
   42             ACCEPT CUST-PHONE
   43             WRITE CUSTMST-REC
   44             ADD 1 TO WS-COUNT
   45         END-IF
   46     END-PERFORM.
   47     DISPLAY "End of program CUST, " WS-COUNT " records added.".
   48     CLOSE CUSTMST.
   49     STOP RUN.



Animate-CUST───────────────────────Level=01-Speed=5-Ins-Caps-Num-Scroll
F1=help F2=view F3=align F4=exchange F5=where F6=look-up F9/F10=word- </> Escape
Animate Step Wch Go Zoom nx-If Prfm Rst Brk Env Qury Find Locate Txt Do Alt Ctrl
```

Figure 6.2 Animator main menu (after program is loaded)

```
Checker-Chk+Anim——Pause-List-Con————————————-Strc+Anlz-VSC2(3)—XRef——-CSI
F1=help F2=check/anim F3=pause F4=list F5=strc/anlz F6=lang F7=ref F8=CSI    Esc
F9/F10=directives        check+anim K:\COBOL\MFWBBOOK\CUST.CBL
```

Figure 6.3 Editor Check/Animate menu

Let's look at another way to get into the animator function. Pressing **F2=COBOL** on the Editor main menu brings you to the Editor check menu (Figure 6.3). On this menu, pressing **F2=check/animate** repeatedly will toggle you through three selections on the information line: **Check, Chk+Anim,** and **Animate.** We already showed you how to use the Checker function from this menu. Selecting **Chk+Anim** will animate your program immediately after checking it, if there are no syntax errors. (If there are errors, you will go back to the Editor instead of the Animator.) Selecting **Animate** will animate the main program in your Editor work area, if you have already checked it with the **ANIM** directive. Note that this menu does not have all the features present on the standalone Animator menu. The standalone Animator initial menu lets you pass parms and switch settings to your program at runtime. We will discuss this in Chapter 8. **To avoid losing your most recent changes, remember to save your COBOL source file before checking and animating.**

You can animate your program in various different ways. The methods you choose depend on how much time you want to take and how much detail you want to see at each point in your program.

6.3.2 Navigating through the Source Program Display

When the animation process begins, your source code will appear on the screen. The first line of executable code (or the first section or paragraph name) will appear in highlighted type. Nothing will execute until you press a key to tell the Animator how to begin. Before execution begins, or whenever program execution has stopped, you can use the paging and cursor keys to examine various parts of your source code. These keys work as they do in the Micro Focus Editor. Moving the cursor or scrolling the screen lets you view the source code without executing anything. Changing cursor position does not in itself affect program execution sequence.

You will find that you can scroll upward into the Data Division and File Section. This shows the initial definition of your data elements, not their contents at runtime. The Animator does let you view and modify data element contents at runtime, but through a different method. This view of your data elements is for inquiry purposes only. It lets you refresh your memory about how your fields are defined and initialized in your File Section, Working Storage, or Linkage Section COBOL statements.

Structure versus code mode. If you have checked your program with the **Struct** directive set, you may see a program structure diagram superimposed on the program source code when you begin animating (Figure 6.4). The Animator works differently depending on whether the cursor is in the structure diagram or in the source code. We will discuss structure animation later. For now, you can move the cursor back into the source code by holding down the **Alt** key on the Animator main menu and toggling **F3=structure/code** to highlight the word **code.**

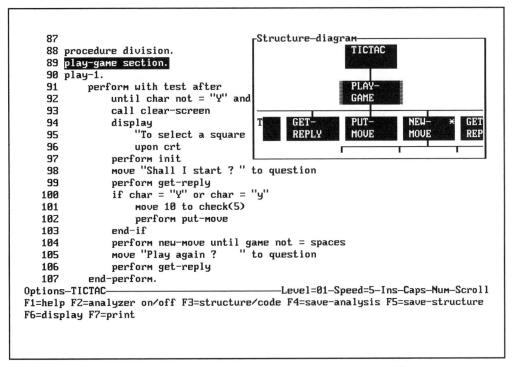

```
87
88 procedure division.
89 play-game section.
90 play-1.
91     perform with test after
92         until char not = "Y" and
93         call clear-screen
94         display
95             "To select a square
96             upon crt
97         perform init
98         move "Shall I start ? " to question
99         perform get-reply
100        if char = "Y" or char = "y"
101            move 10 to check(5)
102            perform put-move
103        end-if
104        perform new-move until game not = spaces
105        move "Play again ?      " to question
106        perform get-reply
107    end-perform.
Options-TICTAC────────────────────Level=01-Speed=5-Ins-Caps-Num-Scroll
F1=help F2=analyzer on/off F3=structure/code F4=save-analysis F5=save-structure
F6=display F7=print
```

Figure 6.4 Animator ALT options menu and structure diagram

Locating source lines. Pressing the **L** key for **Locate** will bring up a menu that allows you to locate various features in the source code (Figure 6.5).

```
Locate-declaration────────────────────Level=01 Speed=5 Ins Caps Num Scroll
F1=help F2=view F3=align F4=exchange F5=where F6=look-up  F9/F10=word-</> Escape
Cursor-name Enter-name Up-perform-level Down-perform-level
```

Figure 6.5 Animator Locate menu

The Locate menu is an inquiry-only menu, intended for looking at your program rather than executing it. Moving the cursor or repositioning the source code on the screen will not change program execution sequence. However, the Locate function can come in handy for finding places to set breakpoints in your program.

Suppose you already know what line number you want to see. In that case, press **F6=look-up**, enter the line number, and press the enter key. The Animator will reposition the source code on your screen so that the desired line number will be the third from the top of the screen display.

Suppose you want to locate a particular data or procedure name in your program. Pressing the letter **E** for **Enter-name** will open a box on the screen for you to enter the name you want to search. You can enter a data field name, a filename, or a paragraph or section name. Keying the name and pressing the enter key will reposition the program source display to the definition of that item in your program. For a filename, this will be the SELECT statement. For a data name, this will be the field definition in the data division. For a paragraph or section, this will be the label in the procedure division.

If the desired name is visible on your screen, you can position the cursor on that name and press the letter **C** for **Cursor-name**. Once again, this will reposition the source display to the definition of that item in your program.

Pressing the letter **U** for **Up-perform-level** will reposition the source code display to the routine that called the module that is now being executed. The cursor will be on the line just after the PERFORM statement in the calling module. Pressing **D** for **Down-perform-level** will reverse that effect.

More inquiry functions. Here are more inquiry functions available from the Locate menu as well as the Animator main menu:

- **F2=view** shows the screen that the terminal user would see while running your application. If you press this key before your program has displayed any data, you will see whatever else was there before you began animating. This might be a blank screen or a Micro Focus banner screen. How do you get back to the animation process? By default, the Animator will return to the source code animation display as soon as you press any key.
- **F3=align** repositions the program source code on the screen, so that the line containing the cursor will be the third line from the top of the display.
- **F4=exchange** switches to the other part of the display if you have defined a split screen.
- **F5=where** moves the cursor back to the next source line awaiting execution. The Animator will reposition the source code display to make that line visible on the screen, if need be. This is useful for returning quickly to the current line after you have been scrolling through other parts of the program.
- **F9** and **F10** move the cursor left and right one word at a time.

6.4 Executing under the Animator

User display versus program display. Most of the time when you are animating a program, the screen will show a display of your source code. Many application programs also need to use your keyboard and screen to do their own I/O. If you execute a source line that requires the user to enter some data, such as an ACCEPT statement, then the user screen display will appear. If that happens, perform the required action on that screen, as you would in a production environment. After the ACCEPT is complete, the Animator will redisplay the program source.

In the rest of this section, we will examine the various ways of animating a program.

6.4.1 Step (Manual Single Step through Program)

Let's take another look at the Animator main menu. On this menu are the functions that actually let you run the program. Suppose you want to step through the program at your own pace, to find out whether program execution flows the way you think it does. Pressing **S** for **Step** will execute the current source statement. You will see the highlighting on your screen move from the current line to the next line awaiting execution. The Animator will wait there for you to take the next step. You can keep pressing **S** repeatedly to track execution flow through your program.

6.4.2 Go (Automatic Step through Program with Adjustable Speed)

If you just want to watch the program run with source code animation, press **G** for **Go** on the Animator main menu. Here again, the program will pause for user input on COBOL ACCEPT statements. By pressing numeral keys 0 (zero) through 9, you can change the execution speed from 0 (paused) to 9 (fast), or anything in between; 5 is the default.

Animator information line. The information line will display the current execution speed setting for Go mode. Figure 6.5, for example, shows **Speed=5** on the information line. Another item on the information line is the **perform level,** shown here as **Level=01.** This is the nest level of the module you are executing. The count increments whenever it reaches a PERFORM statement for some other paragraph(s) or section(s), and decrements after the return from that PERFORM.

6.4.3 Zoom (Execute Until End of Program, or Next Breakpoint, Without Animation)

Pressing the letter **Z** for **Zoom** will take you out of animation mode for the time being. Your program will still be running under the Animator, but it will run at machine speed, without showing the source code animation. Suppose you have already found a program bug after processing only a few records, and you want to finish the program, but there are a hundred more records in the file. You can use Zoom mode to finish program execution quickly and gracefully once you've completed debugging.

Even in Zoom mode, program execution will stop at a **breakpoint.** Breakpoints are traps that stop program execution; we will discuss these later. You can set a breakpoint and then Zoom up to that breakpoint. Using Zoom mode saves time, so that you need not step through other routines to get to the part of the program that you want to see.

Getting out of Zoom mode. At any time, you can get out of Zoom mode and back to the Animator main menu by pressing **Ctrl+Break.**

6.4.4 Watch (Single Step Showing Data Fields)

The Watch function is an Advanced Animator feature. It works much like the Step function, except that it also shows you the data fields used by the COBOL statement before and after execution. Pressing the letter **W** for **Watch** will cause **watch monitors** to appear for each data field referenced in the current (highlighted) Procedure Division statement. These watch monitors are little boxes that contain the value of each field before execution. Pressing **W** again will execute the COBOL statement and update the field values in the watch monitors. The highlighting will move along to show the next COBOL statement awaiting execution. The Animator creates watch monitors for filenames as well as for field names. For example, when you open a file, the watch monitor will show you the return code and tell you whether the file opened successfully. Figures 6.6 and 6.7 show the contents of a watch monitor before and after opening a sequential output file. The last status code field is the same as the file status code that you see in mainframe COBOL programs.

```
 33 MAIN SECTION.
 34     OPEN OUTPUT CUSTMST.
 35     PERFORM UNTIL CUST-NO = "QUIT"
 36         DISPLAY "Enter customer number (6 digits) or QUIT"
 37         ACCEPT CUST-NO
 38         IF CUST-NO NOT = "QUIT"
 39             DISPLAY "Enter customer name (25 characters)"
 40             ACCEPT CUST-NAME
 41             DISPLAY "Enter phone number (10 digits)"
 42             ACCEPT CUST-PHONE
 43             WRITE CUSTMST-REC
 44             ADD 1 TO WS-COUNT
 45         END-IF
 46     END-PERFORM.
 47     DISPLAY "End of program CUST, " WS-COUNT " records added.".
 48     CLOSE CUSTMST.
 49     STOP RUN.  +CUSTMST———————————————————+
                   |Closed              Last status unset|
                   +—————————————————————————————————————+

Animate-CUST——————————————————————————Level=01-Speed=5-Ins-Caps-Num-Scroll
F1=help F2=view F3=align F4=exchange F5=where F6=look-up  F9/F10=word- </> Escape
Animate Step Wch Go Zoom nx-If Prfm Rst Brk Env Qury Find Locate Txt Do Alt Ctrl
```

Figure 6.6 Watch monitor before file open

```
 33 MAIN SECTION.
 34     OPEN OUTPUT CUSTMST.
 35     PERFORM UNTIL CUST-NO = "QUIT"
 36         DISPLAY "Enter customer number (6 digits) or QUIT"
 37         ACCEPT CUST-NO
 38         IF CUST-NO NOT = "QUIT"
 39             DISPLAY "Enter customer name (25 characters)"
 40             ACCEPT CUST-NAME
 41             DISPLAY "Enter phone number (10 digits)"
 42             ACCEPT CUST-PHONE
 43             WRITE CUSTMST-REC
 44             ADD 1 TO WS-COUNT
 45         END-IF
 46     END-PERFORM.
 47     DISPLAY "End of program CUST, " WS-COUNT " records added.".
 48     CLOSE CUSTMST.
 49     STOP RUN.  +CUSTMST———————————————————+
                   |Open  output        Last status 00   |
                   +—————————————————————————————————————+

Animate-CUST——————————————————————————Level=01-Speed=5-Ins-Caps-Num-Scroll
F1=help F2=view F3=align F4=exchange F5=where F6=look-up  F9/F10=word-/ Escape
Animate Step Wch Go Zoom nx-If Prfm Rst Brk Env Qury Find Locate Txt Do Alt Ctrl
```

Figure 6.7 Watch monitor after file open

Watch monitors are temporary. When you execute a new statement, watch monitors left over from the previous statement will disappear from the screen. Monitors for the data fields in the new statement will appear instead. The Animator will not create a watch monitor for a field that already has some other type of monitor.

6.4.5 Animate (Automatic Step Showing Data Fields)

The Animate function is an Advanced Animator feature. It steps through your program automatically much as Go mode does. The difference is that Animate mode also shows watch monitors for data fields on each line before and after execution. Pressing the letter **A** for **Animate** will begin this processing. Here again, you can use numeral keys 0 through 9 to regulate the speed of animation.

6.5 Querying Data Values

6.5.1 Displaying and Updating Data Fields

Now suppose you are especially interested in viewing and perhaps updating one or more data fields in your program. You want to keep monitor windows for those fields visible on the screen throughout the animation process. You do not want them to vanish as soon as the next statement executes. The Query function lets you set, update, and clear permanent monitor windows for desired fields. This mechanism lets you change the contents of data fields at runtime.

6.5.2 Creating and Deleting Monitor Windows

Pressing **Q** for **Qry** brings up the Query Data menu, shown in Figure 6.8.

```
Query-data─────────────────────────Level=01-Speed=5-Ins-Caps-Num-Scroll
F1=help F2=view F3=align F4=exchange F5=where F6=look-up F9/F10=word-</> Escape
Cursor-name Enter-name Repeat Monitor-off Dump-list Hide/Org-monitors Watch-off
```

Figure 6.8 Query Data menu

Figure 6.8 shows an information line followed by two menu lines. The second menu line on the Query Data menu shows commands for selecting data items for querying. Pressing the letter **E** for **Enter-name** will open a box on the screen for you to enter the name of the field or dataset you want to query. Keying the data name and pressing the enter key will cause a query window to appear on the screen, showing the contents of the desired field. Alternatively, if the name of the desired field is visible somewhere on your screen, you can position the cursor on the data name and press the letter **C** for **Cursor-name.**

Making a query monitor permanent. When you first create a query window, the menu will change to the Query [field name] submenu, shown in Figure 6.9. On that menu, you can use the **F4=monitor** command to make the query window permanent. Otherwise, the query window will disappear from your screen when you leave that submenu. How permanent are these monitors? As of Workbench v2.5, permanent query monitors remain on screen until you delete them. In fact, if you go back into the Animator in a later Workbench session and reanimate the same program, you will see query monitors for all the fields you originally requested. The data contents will be new. However, if you recheck or compile your program, the old monitors will disappear.

Removing unwanted monitors. You can crowd your screen with so many monitor windows that you can no longer see your source code. Nothing will stop you from creating more than one monitor for the same field. How do you get rid of unwanted monitors? Pressing **M** for **Monitor-off** deletes the last monitor created. Pressing **H** for **Hide-monitors** makes all the monitors disappear temporarily. They will reappear when the data field contents changes or when you use the **Org-Monitors** command discussed below. Finally, pressing **W** for **Watch-off** removes watch monitors from the screen.

Several more commands appear on this menu. The Query **Repeat** command reexecutes the most recent query and redisplays the Query [field name] submenu. Injudicious use of this command can cause duplicate queries into the same data field. The **Dump-list** command writes out a file containing Animator test data. You can create this test data with functions on the Query Alt menu, discussed below.

The Query Organize Monitors command. Pressing **O** for **Org-Monitors** on the Query menu will move any monitors on the screen back to their default positions. If you have any watch monitors on the screen, the Org-Monitors command will convert those temporary monitors to permanent status. They won't go away when the next COBOL statement executes. If you have both watch monitors and query monitors on the screen, the watch monitors will sometimes display on top of the query monitors.

If the Animator creates a *watch* monitor for a subscripted field, the subscript of the field being monitored will remain fixed after you convert the watch monitor to permanent status. For example, suppose the watch monitor originally showed the contents of TAB-ITEM (SUBX) when SUBX = 1. The monitor will continue to show the value of TAB-ITEM (1) even if SUBX changes. This is not always true of monitors you create with the Query menu. By default, query monitors will follow any changes made to the subscript value, so that if the subscript changes you will be looking at a different data item.

Once you have selected a data item to query, the Query [field name] menu will appear, as shown in Figure 6.9. Figure 6.10 shows the Query [field name] CTRL key menu. We will discuss the Query [field name] ALT key menu in a later section.

```
Query:    CUST-NO────────────────────Level=01-Speed=5-Ins-Caps-Num-Scroll
F1=help F2=clear F3=hex  F4=monitor                   ^ v=up/down data
F7=containing F8=contained F9=same level           Alt  Ctrl  Escape
```

Figure 6.9 Query [field name] menu

As we mentioned, the Query [field name] menu appears when you select a data name for querying. The field name visible in the menu title shows that all functions on this menu apply to this query field.

- If the data is too long to show completely in the monitor window, you can scroll up and down with the up and down cursor arrow keys.
- **F2=clear** clears field contents to zeroes or spaces so that you can enter some other test data.
- **F3=hex** toggles the query window into hex mode. The window expands to show both the hex values and the character translation side by side. Pressing **F3=text** again toggles the query window back into text-only mode. You can alter queried data by overkeying it in either mode.
- **F4=monitor** makes the current query window into a permanent monitor window that will remain on the screen after you exit from this menu.
- If the selected query field is a table item, you'll see the current subscript value alongside the field name in the menu title. In that case, **F5=up-table** and **F6=down-table** will display the previous and next table entries. The current subscript value in the menu title will change accordingly.
- **F7=containing** changes the query to display the group item that contains the data field that you originally selected.
- **F8=contained** changes the query to display the first detail item contained within the data field that you originally selected.
- **F9=same level** changes the query to display the next data item at the same level as the one that you originally selected.

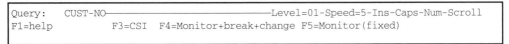
```
Query:    CUST-NO──────────────────────Level=01-Speed=5-Ins-Caps-Num-Scroll
F1=help          F3=CSI   F4=Monitor+break+change F5=Monitor(fixed)
```

Figure 6.10 Query [field name] **Ctrl** *key menu*

Several more functions appear on the Query [data field] CTRL key menu:

- **F3=CSI** lets you use the COBOL Source Information facility, discussed in a later chapter.
- **F4=Monitor+break+change** sets a breakpoint that takes effect whenever the contents of the selected field changes. We will discuss this type of breakpoint later.
- **F5=Monitor(fixed)** applies only if you are monitoring a subscripted data field; in other words, a table entry. The default behavior of the Workbench as of version 2.5 is to follow any changes in the subscript. If the subscript changes, the monitor will change so that it now shows a different table entry. Using **F5=Monitor(fixed)** causes the monitor to stay with the original value of the subscript from when the monitor window was created.

6.6 What Is a Breakpoint?

A breakpoint is a trap that you put into your program to cause execution to halt at a particular place, or when certain conditions become true, or both. The purpose of a breakpoint is to get you more quickly to the part of the program that you want to examine in detail. To use this feature effectively, you can set one or more breakpoints and then run the program at machine speed, using Zoom mode. When a breakpoint is reached, program execution stops and you see the Animator display. You can examine your data fields, make changes, reset execution sequence, step through certain routines, and so forth.

The Animator supports both local and global breakpoints. A local breakpoint is associated with a particular source line in your program, so that execution halts when program execution reaches that point. Local breakpoints can be unconditional, so that they always trigger when program execution reaches that point, or conditional, so that they trigger only when a certain condition is true. A global breakpoint is associated only with a data field, so that program execution halts whenever the value of that data field changes. It makes no difference what Procedure Division source line changed the field.

6.7 Using Breakpoints on a Source Line

Pressing **B** for **Brk** on the Animator main menu brings up the breakpoint menu, shown in Figure 6.11. This menu lets you set, clear, and examine breakpoints that apply to a particular Procedure Division source line. You can use the breakpoint menu before program execution begins or whenever program execution is halted. It does not matter what statement is currently being executed. You can move your cursor to any Procedure Division COBOL statement and set a breakpoint there. Within an ordinary Animator session, up to 100 breakpoints can be active at any time. (However, it is possible to configure the Workbench system to enforce a lower limit.)

```
Break-points-On-count=unset────────────Level=01-Speed=5──Ins-Caps-Num-Scroll
F1=help F2=view F3=align F4=exchange F5=where F6=look-up  F9/F10=word-</> Escape
Set Unset Cancel-all Examine If Do On-count Zoom
```

Figure 6.11 Breakpoint menu

6.7.1 Setting Unconditional Breakpoints

To set a breakpoint on a line, move the cursor to that line and press **B** for **Brk** to see the breakpoint menu. Then press **S** for **Set** to activate a breakpoint on that line. On a color monitor using the default colors of Workbench v2.5, the line with the breakpoint will display in highlighted blue text.

6.7.2 Setting Periodic Breakpoints

The Animator uses a counter to handle periodic breakpoints. Program execution halts each time the line containing the breakpoint has been executed a specified number of times. For example, you can make the program halt every tenth time the program reads an input record. To set a periodic breakpoint, press **O** for **On-count**. You'll see a small window labeled **Enter-On-count**. Enter a number for the desired breakpoint frequency, such as 10 for every tenth time, and press the enter key. Then press **S** for **Set** to set a breakpoint with that frequency.

6.7.3 Setting Conditional Breakpoints

To set a conditional breakpoint, move the cursor to the Procedure Division line where you want the program to stop. That line will become highlighted. Press **I** for **If** on the Query menu. You'll see a window labeled **Enter-condition:**.

```
33 MAIN SECTION.
34     OPEN OUTPUT CUSTMST.
35     PERFORM UNTIL CUST-NO = "QUIT"
36         DISPLAY "Enter customer number (6 digits) or QUIT"
37         ACCEPT CUST-NO
38         IF CUST-NO NOT = "QUIT"
39             DISPLAY "Enter customer name (25 characters)"
40             +Enter-condition:——————————————————————————+
41             |CUST-NO = "QUIT"                          |
42             |                                          |
43             +——————————————————————————————————————————+
44             ADD 1 TO WS-COUNT
45         END-IF
46     END-PERFORM.
47     DISPLAY "End of program CUST, " WS-COUNT " records added.".
48     CLOSE CUSTMST.
49     STOP RUN.




Break-points—On-count=unset——— ——————————Level=01-Speed=5-Ins-Caps-Num-Scroll
F1=help F2=clear                                                      Escape
```

Figure 6.12 Breakpoint If menu

Enter a comparison that refers to a data field name in your program. Use the same type of condition that you would use in a COBOL IF statement. Do not enter a complete COBOL IF statement. Enter only the comparison. Figure 6.12 shows how to enter a breakpoint condition. In this case, the breakpoint is being set on the PERFORM statement.

6.7.4 Viewing Breakpoint Settings

Pressing **E** for **Examine** positions your cursor at the next line in your program that contains a breakpoint. After the last breakpoint in your program, the cursor position will move back up to the first breakpoint. If the breakpoint is a periodic one, a message will show the contents of the execution counter for that breakpoint. If the breakpoint is a conditional one, a message will show the condition in effect.

6.7.5 Clearing Breakpoints

Pressing **U** for **Unset** clears the breakpoint at the current cursor position. Pressing **C** for **Cancel-all** clears all breakpoints from your program.

6.7.6 Animating with Breakpoints

Suppose you have set up one or more breakpoints. If you press **Z** for **Zoom** on the Animator *main* menu, the program will execute at machine speed (without animation) until it reaches a breakpoint. Then, the Animator display will return, with the words **Break-point encountered** visible on the last line of the screen. At that point, you can examine data items with the Query function, reset program execution sequence, resume step-by-step animation, or do whatever else is needed.

The **Zoom** function on the *breakpoint* menu works a bit differently. You can use it to zoom to the cursor location without setting a permanent breakpoint. Move the cursor to the location to which you want to zoom. Then, press **Z** for **Zoom** on the breakpoint menu. As long as you don't have any other breakpoints that come first, program execution will zoom up to the cursor location, then break.

6.8 Using Global Breakpoints Associated with Data Items

6.8.1 Usefulness of Global Breakpoints

As we mentioned earlier, a global breakpoint is associated with a data field, not with a Procedure Division statement. A global breakpoint halts the program whenever the value of a field changes or when a certain condition becomes true for that data item.

How does bad data get into a field? Global breakpoints are useful for troubleshooting program checks. Suppose you want to know how bad data is getting into a field. For example, nonnumeric characters in a numeric field have caused a data check. You don't know which source line is the offender. You can set a global breakpoint that stops program execution on any instruction that is putting bad data into your field.

6.8.2 Setting, Clearing, and Using Global Breakpoints

The Workbench offers two types of global breakpoints, available on two different Query submenus.

Break on any change to the field. Pressing **F4=Monitor+break+change** on the Query [data field] CTRL key menu sets a break point that takes effect whenever the value of that field changes. To set this type of breakpoint quickly, position the cursor on the name of the data item and press **Q**, then **C**, then **Ctrl+F4**. As of Workbench v2.5, you can set only one global breakpoint of this type at a time.

Break when a specific condition becomes true. Pressing **E** for **Env** on the Animator main menu brings up the Environment menu, shown in Figure 6.13. On that menu, press **U** to see the **Until** menu, shown in Figure 6.14. Then press **S** for **Set**. You'll see a window labeled **Enter-condition:**. Enter a comparison that refers to the data field name that you want to use to trigger the breakpoint. Use the same type of condition that you would use in a COBOL IF statement. Do not enter a complete COBOL IF statement. Enter only the comparison. For example, suppose you set the condition **CUST-NO = "QUIT"**. Program execution will halt as soon as you enter **QUIT** in the CUST-NO field. Here again, as of Workbench v2.5, you can set only one global breakpoint of this type at a time.

```
Environment——————————————————————————————-Level=01-Speed=5-Ins-Caps-Num-Scroll
F1=help F2=view F3=align F4=exchange F5=where F6=look-up  F9/F10=word-</> Escape
Program-break Threshold-level Until Backtrack Flash(step/zoom) Mon-slide(on/off)
```

Figure 6.13 Environment menu

```
Until————————————————————————————Level=01-Speed=5-Ins-Caps-Num-Scroll
F1=help F2=view F3=align F4=exchange F5=where F6=look-up  F9/F10=word- </> Escape
Set Unset Examine
```

Figure 6.14 Environment Until menu

The **Unset** and **Examine** functions on the Until menu also let you unset and examine the global breakpoint, much as the Breakpoint menu lets you do with local breakpoints. As of Workbench v2.5, only one of these global breakpoints can be set at one time.

6.8.3 Animator Environment Settings

The Environment menu lets you set other global characteristics of the Animator's operation. Before we go any further, let's look at several other settings on the Environment menu.

- **Flash(step/zoom)** affects the way the Animator displays or "flashes" the user screen. By that we mean the screen display that the program's user would see. The default setting, Flash(zoom), shows the user screen only when a program I/O statement affects it or when entering Zoom mode. The other setting, Flash(step), shows the user screen before executing each COBOL statement. Pressing **F** repeatedly toggles back and forth between the two settings. You might want to use Flash(step) if you are calling non-COBOL routines that do screen I/O.

- **Mon-slide(on/off)** lets you toggle "monitor slide" on and off. If monitor slide is on, new monitors will appear at the current source line. They will slide outward toward their final positions near the edge of the monitor. Monitor slide is a "gee-whiz" feature that makes the Animator display look a bit more exciting. If monitor slide is off, new monitors will first appear at the edge of the screen. They will not slide into that position. Pressing **M** repeatedly toggles this setting on and off.

- **Program-break** lets you set a control break to take place when a particular program begins to run. Program-break is useful only for applications made up of more than one program module. When you press **P** on the Environment menu, three functions appear on the second menu line: **This, Select,** and **Unset.** Pressing **T** for **This** sets a breakpoint the next time "this program" (the current program) begins to run. Pressing **S** for **Select** lets you enter the name of the program that should trigger the control break. Pressing **U** for **Unset** clears the program break.

- **Threshold-level** lets you choose to animate only the upper levels of program logic, so that the lower levels run in Zoom mode. You would use this if you are interested in logic flow among the main routines but you don't want to animate low-level PERFORMed or CALLed subroutines. Find some source code that represents the lowest PERFORM level that you still want to see in detail. Move your cursor to that source code. When you press **T** on the Environment menu, two functions appear on the second menu line: **Set** and **Unset.** Pressing **S** for **Set** sets the threshold level to the PERFORM level of that routine, so that everything below that level will execute in Zoom mode.

Pressing **U** for **Unset** clears the threshold level so that all program code will execute in animated mode.

6.9 Backtracking from a Breakpoint

6.9.1 Purpose of Backtracking

Suppose you want to halt program execution when a certain event takes place, and then see how the program got to that point. Backtracking is an Animator function that keeps a record of the program execution path through each COBOL statement. When the program halts at a breakpoint, you can examine this audit trail to see the path the program took to get to that breakpoint. Backtracking is especially useful for working with global breakpoints that could be triggered from many places in the program.

When you examine the backtracked execution path, you can use up and down cursor arrow keys to move backward or forward in the execution sequence. *Viewing backtracked data is purely an inquiry function. It does not update anything.* Viewing the saved execution path in forward or reverse order will neither execute any COBOL statements nor "back out" the results of previous COBOL statement execution.

6.9.2 How to Use Backtracking

```
Backtrack = set──────────────────────────────Level=01-Speed=5-Ins-Caps-Num-Scroll
F1=help F2=view F3=align F4=exchange F5=where F6=look-up  F9/F10=word- </> Escape
Set Unset Examine
```

Figure 6.15 Query Environment Backtrack menu

You can reach the Animator Backtracking function through the Query Environment menu. Here is how to set up and use the backtracking function:

- Bring up the Environment menu by pressing **E** for **Environment** on the Query main menu. Bring up the Backtrack menu by pressing **B** for **Backtracking** on the Query Environment menu. Figure 6.15 shows the Query Environment Backtrack menu.
- Turn on backtracking by pressing **S** for **Set** on the Backtracking menu.
- Set any local or global breakpoints you plan to use.
- Execute your program under the Animator in Zoom mode until it halts at a breakpoint. The Query main menu should be visible.
- Press **E** and then **B** to bring up the Backtrack menu again.
- Press **E** for **Examine** to see the saved execution path. Use the up and down arrow keys to move backward and forward.
- When you no longer want to use backtracking, press **U** for **Unset** on the Backtrack menu. This will tell the Animator to stop saving execution path data.

6.10 Adding New Source Lines While Animating

6.10.1 Concepts of Do and Break-Do Functions

Did you leave out a source line? Program bugs often resemble "sins of omission": some vital piece of logic is missing. The normal programming mindset makes it harder to find such bugs. **When looking at code, programmers are likely to see the program logic that they *intended* to write, not what actually made it into the source file.** Without the proper tools, it's hard to spot a line of code that should be there but is not. Stepping through the program with the Animator can show you what the program is really doing instead of what you think it should do.

Suppose you have found some missing COBOL Procedure Division code that should be in your program. You can test that code without having to go back into the Micro Focus Editor to fix and then recheck your program. The Animator **Do** and **Break-Do** functions let you enter source code for the Animator to interpret and execute while you are testing.

The Animator **Do** function lets you enter one line of COBOL code on the screen. You can enter up to 71 characters. The Animator will interpret and execute that line of code *as soon as you enter it.* To execute more lines of code, use the Do function repeatedly. You can use the Do function before execution begins or at any program breakpoint.

Important: The Do function will *not* insert lines into your COBOL source code file or change it in any other way. Also, the Animator will not keep track of the current position in the source code from each time you have used the Do function.

The Animator **Break-Do** function lets you enter a line of COBOL source code at a breakpoint. The Animator will interpret and execute the new source code *just before it executes the source statement containing the breakpoint.* A breakpoint set with the Break-Do function does not look like other Animator breakpoints. Program execution does not stop in Zoom or Go mode. In Step mode, a message will appear at the bottom of the screen to say that the new source statement has executed.

The .EDO File. Source lines that you enter while using the Break-Do function go into a text file. The main part of its filename is the same as your program name, and the extension is .EDO. Using the Micro Focus Editor or another ASCII file editor, you can move COBOL statements from the .EDO file to your source program by using block copy or move operations. Recheck your program before you animate it again.

6.10.2 Using the Do Function

Pressing **D** for **Do** on the Animator main menu brings up the Do menu, shown in Figure 6.16. Enter the first COBOL statement in the box labeled **Enter-COBOL-statement-to-be-executed.** When you press the enter key, the Animator will interpret and execute your statement. The Animator main menu will reappear. To enter more source lines, repeat this process.

```
33 MAIN SECTION.
34     +Enter-COBOL-statement-to-be-executed——————————+
35     |INITIALIZE CUSTMST-REC.                        |
36     |                                             |T"
37     +———————————————————————————————————————————————+
38         IF CUST-NO NOT = "QUIT"
39             DISPLAY "Enter customer name (25 characters)"
40             ACCEPT CUST-NAME
41             DISPLAY "Enter phone number (10 digits)"
42             ACCEPT CUST-PHONE
43             WRITE CUSTMST-REC
44             ADD 1 TO WS-COUNT
45         END-IF
46     END-PERFORM.
47     DISPLAY "End of program CUST, " WS-COUNT " records added.".
48     CLOSE CUSTMST.
49     STOP RUN.



Do————————————————————————————Level=01-Speed=5-Ins-Caps-Num-Scroll
F1=help F2=clear                                            Escape
```

Figure 6.16 Animator Do menu

6.10.3 Using the Break-Do Function

You set up the Break-Do function in much the same way as you set up the Do function. The only difference is that *you reach the Break-Do function from the Break-points menu,* instead of the Animator main menu. To use Break-Do, move your cursor to the Procedure Division line on which you want to set the breakpoint. Then press **B** for **Brk** on the Animator main menu to bring up the Break-points menu. Press **D** for **Do** on the Break-points menu. You will see a Break-Do menu that looks exactly like the Do menu in Figure 6.16. Nonetheless, Break-Do is not the same function as Do. Code entered with Break-Do does not execute as soon as you finish entering it. Instead, it is executed only when the Animator reaches the source line on which you set the breakpoint.

6.11 Next-If and Perform Functions

6.11.1 Zooming through Portions of Code

Even when you animate step by step, you may want to zoom through portions of code that are not of interest to you. The Next-If function lets you execute in zoom mode until you get to the top of an IF statement. The Perform function lets you zoom through performed routines.

6.11.2 Using the Next-If Function

Pressing **I** for **Nx-If** (Next-If) on the Animator main menu makes the Animator execute in zoom mode until it reaches the next COBOL IF statement. If you select this function while already in the midst of an IF statement, the Animator will go into zoom mode immediately. Suppose you are performing an IF statement repeatedly within a loop. Zoom mode will stop when you reexecute the IF statement you just left.

6.11.3 Using Perform Functions

The Perform function on the Animator main menu lets you zoom through performed routines. By that we mean separate paragraphs or sections, not ANSI '85 inline PERFORM statements. When you press **P** for **Prfm** on the Animator main menu, two functions appear on the second menu line: **Step** and **Exit.**

- If the current source line awaiting execution is a PERFORM or CALL statement, **Perform Step** will cause the Animator to zoom through that routine. From your point of view, it will look as though the current line was executed in one step. The Animator will pause on the next statement.
- If the current source line is within a routine being PERFORMed or CALLed from elsewhere, **Exit** (Exit Perform) will cause the Animator to zoom until it gets to the end of the PERFORM range. The Animator will pause on the statement after the PERFORM or CALL statement.

6.12 Reset Function to Skip Execution of Portions of Code

Suppose you want to skip execution of certain passages of code. You don't want to zoom through them quickly, you want to bypass them entirely. Instead of coding program stubs for modules that are not yet complete, you may want to skip execution of the CALL statement. Maybe you want to interrupt testing and "take it from the top": restart animation at the beginning of the current program. Maybe you just want to get out of the current routine being PER-FORMed. The Reset function lets you do all of these things.

Pressing **R** for **Rst** (Reset) on the Animator main menu brings up the Reset-execution menu, shown in Figure 6.17. Here are the functions on this menu:

- To reset program execution to another line in your program, move the cursor to that line. Pressing **C** for **Cursor-position** will make that line the new current line. Program execution will continue from that point.
- To skip the current line without executing it, press **N** for **Next.** The next line will become the new current line. Program execution will continue from that point.
- To get out of a PERFORMed routine or range of routines without executing anything, press **Q** for **Quit-perform.** The line following the PERFORM statement will become the new current line. Program execution will continue from that point.
- To go back up to the top of the program without executing anything else, press **S** for **Start.** The first executable line of your program will become the new current line. Program execution will continue from the beginning of your program. **Warning: The program will not reinitialize itself.** Files will still be open and data fields will not contain their initial values. Both situations can cause your program to fail. You may have to close files and restore initial values manually with the Do function. If this is too much trouble, you might be better off exiting from the Animator and then starting a new Animator session.

```
Reset-execution————————————————Level=01-Speed=5-Ins-Caps-Num-Scroll
F1=help F2=view F3=align F4=exchange F5=where F6=look-up  F9/F10=word-</> Escape
Cursor-position Next Start Quit-perform
```

Figure 6.17 Animator Reset menu

6.13 Split-Screen Function

Splitting the Micro Focus Animator display lets you look at file or field definitions while you are animating the procedure code. The split screen function is available on the Text menu.

Splitting the Animator screen. Pressing **T** for **Txt** (text) on the Animator main menu brings up the Text menu, shown in Figure 6.18.

```
Text————————————————————————Level=01-Speed=5-Ins-Caps-Num-Scroll
F1=help F2=view F3=align F4=exchange F5=where F6=look-up  F9/F10=word- </>Escape
Split Join Refresh Edit
```

Figure 6.18 Animator text menu

Pressing the letter **S** for **Split** will split the Animator screen display at the cursor location. The cursor must be at least four lines away from the top or bottom of the text area. This is because the minimum size for a split screen is four lines. Your program will be visible in both viewing windows, but you can scroll each window independently. Pressing **J** for **Join** rejoins the split screens. Pressing **R** for **Refresh** will redisplay your screen. This cleans up the Animator display if it somehow becomes corrupted.

Exit to the Editor. On the Text menu, pressing **E** for **Edit** takes you completely out of the Animator. It brings up the COBOL Editor screen, with your source program loaded into the work area.

6.14 Query Dump Files

As we discussed earlier, query monitors continue to exist from one Animator session to the next. They go away only when you recheck your program or when you delete the monitors. When you are working with query monitors, you can create a "query dump" file of data element values. This will let you test your program again using those same values. A query dump filename has the extension **.ILS.** Once you have built a query dump list, selecting **D** for **Dump-list** on the Query Data menu will write the list to the query dump file.

We have mentioned that the Mainframe Development Environment defaults to EBCDIC for the purposes of program literals and sequential datasets. If you look at the .ILS file with an ASCII editor, the stored data values will be unreadable. You'll need to use the Micro Focus Hex Editor or the Data File Editor to see character translations of the stored values. The same is true of sequential output files that have not specifically been defined as ASCII files.

Holding down the **Alt** key on the Query [field-name] menu will bring up the Query [field-name] ALT key menu (Figure 6.19). This menu lets you work with the list of items that make up a query dump file. All of the functions use the query monitor window as an area for you to enter the values to be saved or retrieved.

- **F2=update list** replaces the current value in the query dump list with whatever you have just typed in the query monitor window.
- **F3=add** adds the current value in the query monitor window to the end of the query dump list.
- **F4=delete** deletes the current value in the query monitor window from the query dump list.
- **F5/F6=up/down list** scrolls up and down in the query dump list. The different values present in the query dump list will cycle through the query monitor window. You can use this to select an item to be deleted, or to retrieve a value into the query monitor window for testing.
- **F7/F8=insert list left/right** adds the current value in the query monitor window to the list. F7 puts it before the current item, and F8 puts it after the current item.

```
Query:  CUST-NO────────────────────Level=01-Speed=5-Ins-Caps-Num-Scroll
F1=help F2=update list F3/F4=add/delete list F5/F6=up/down list
F7/F8=insert list left/right F9=locate F10=alter-window
```

Figure 6.19 Query [field name] **Alt** *key menu*

6.15 Adjusting Viewing Windows

You can set the position of a query monitor window. On the Query [field name] ALT key menu, pressing **F10=alter-window** brings up the alter window menu, shown in Figure 6.20. On this menu, you can use the up, down, right, and left cursor arrow keys to move the monitor window in each direction.

If you are monitoring a large data field, you may also want to change the size and shape of the window. To resize the window, use the **F5, F6, F7,** and **F8** keys to move the cursor to where you want the lower-right corner of the monitor window to be. Place the cursor position inside the current window to shrink the window, or outside the current window to expand it. Nothing will happen to the monitor window until you press **F9=redraw.** As the name implies, this redraws the monitor window with the new size and shape. **F4=monitor** works the same way as it does on the Query [field name] menu: it makes the query monitor permanent.

```
Alter window────────────────────Level=01-Speed=5-Ins-Caps-Num-Scroll
v > < ^ =move-window
F1=help F4=monitor F5/F6/F7/F8=window-size-left/right/up/down F9=redraw    Escape
```

Figure 6.20 Alter Window menu

6.16 Analyzer (Statement Execution Counts)

6.16.1 Analyzer Concepts

Testing coverage. Think for a moment about the last few programs you unit tested. One of the goals of unit testing is to exercise all parts of the program.

You choose a set of test data that you hope will cause execution of all source lines. After you finish running the test, how do you know that every source line was covered?

Performance bottlenecks. Does your mainframe installation have some programs that seem to take more than their share of execution cycles? These are usually big, complex programs. Optimizing compilers only go so far. Maybe it's time to reevaluate what the programs are doing. You will need to roll up your sleeves, dig into the program code, and find the bottlenecks within each program. How do you make sure that you have targeted the source lines in each program that are executed most frequently?

Automated execution counts. The Analyzer is a Workbench facility that keeps track of how many times each COBOL statement has been executed. You can see the totals during animation, but it makes more sense to execute in Zoom mode and check the totals after execution is complete. Numbers alongside each source line indicate how many times that line was executed. It's easy to find lines that have not been executed at all because they are marked with a hyphen. In this way, you can determine whether all parts of the program have been tested. The execution totals also will pinpoint the lines of code that are executed most often, so that you can target your effort to make those lines more efficient.

6.16.2 Setup and Execution

To use the Analyzer, you must first check or compile the program with the Analyze directive set. The Analyze directive is a toggle switch setting on the Checker menu. Then, on the Animator initial menu (shown earlier in Figure 6.1), toggle **F5=strc/anlz** until the **Analyze** directive appears on the information line. That will enable the Analyzer when animation begins. If you have checked the program with *both* the Struct and the Analyze directives, you can toggle **F5** until the **Strc+Anlz** appears on the information line. That will enable both the Analyzer and the Structure Animator when animation begins.

If you have enabled the Analyzer, then the word **Analyze** will appear instead of **Animate** on the first line of the Animator main menu. Before you begin animating, a hyphen will appear on the right side of the screen, opposite each source line. As you execute each source line, the hyphen changes to a numeral "1". The Analyzer increments the counter whenever the line is executed again. See Figure 6.21 for an example of an Analyzer display after program execution.

Varying Analyzer display format. You can use several options to change the appearance of the Analyzer screen display. Figure 6.4, earlier in this chapter, shows the Animator Options menu that becomes visible when you hold down the **Alt** key on the Animator main menu. Pressing **F6=display** on the Options menu brings up *another* Options menu, showing Analyzer settings. This menu is shown in Figure 6.22.

```
 32 PROCEDURE DIVISION.
 33 MAIN SECTION.
 34     OPEN OUTPUT CUSTMST.                                           1
 35     PERFORM UNTIL CUST-NO = "QUIT"                                 4
 36         DISPLAY "Enter customer number (6 digits) or QUIT"         3
 37         ACCEPT CUST-NO                                             3
 38         IF CUST-NO NOT = "QUIT"                                    3
 39             DISPLAY "Enter customer name (25 characters)"          2
 40             ACCEPT CUST-NAME                                       2
 41             DISPLAY "Enter phone number (10 digits)"               2
 42             ACCEPT CUST-PHONE                                      2
 43             WRITE CUSTMST-REC                                      2
 44             ADD 1 TO WS-COUNT                                      2
 45             PERFORM HELLO-ROUTINE                                  2
 46         END-IF                                                     2
 47     END-PERFORM.                                                   3
 48     DISPLAY "End of program CUST, " WS-COUNT " records added.".    1
 49     CLOSE CUSTMST.                                                 1
 50     STOP RUN.                                                      1
 51*
Analyze-CUST─────────────────────Scale=001-Level=01-Speed=5-Ins-Caps-Num-Scroll
F1=help F2=view F3=align F4=exchange F5=where F6=look-up  F9/F10=word-/ Escape
Animate Step Wch Go Zoom nx-If Prfm Rst Brk Env Qury Find Locate Txt Do Alt Ctrl
STOP RUN encountered with RETURN CODE = +00000: ESCAPE to terminate
```

Figure 6.21 Display with Analyzer execution totals

```
Options-CUST─────────────────────Scale=001-Level=01-Speed=5-Ins-Caps-Num-Scroll
F1=help                                                                  Escape
                         F7=figures/graph F8=color F9/F10=scale up/down
```

Figure 6.22 Options menu with Analyzer settings

Pressing **F7=figures/graph** on the Options menu (Figure 6.22) toggles the execution count display between numerals and a bar graph. In graph mode, a row of asterisks substitutes for the numerals. One asterisk represents one execution of that source line. Obviously, the rows of asterisks can grow too long. You can abbreviate the rows by adjusting the **scale factor.** Pressing **F10=scale down** raises the scale by a factor of two. For example, pressing **F10** once makes each asterisk in the graph stand for two executions of that source line instead of one. **F9=scale up** reverses the effect of **F10.** An indicator on the information line shows the scale factor currently in effect.

Pressing **F8=color** toggles "color mode" on and off. With color on, source lines will appear in different colors depending on how many times each one has been executed. Here again, the scale factor will affect the color assigned to each source line. If the scale setting is one, the color will change each time the line is executed. If the scale setting is four, the color will change only when a line has been executed four times.

6.16.3 Clearing Analyzer Counts

Analyzer execution counts stay with your program and keep increasing each time you animate. You can reset all counts to zero by rechecking the program or by clearing them manually. Pressing **Ctrl+F4** on the Animator main menu brings up the **Clear** function. On the screen, you will see a message: **Clear**

counts of all other active programs ? Y/N. This question applies to you if you are working with an application with subprogram calls. Answer **Y** if you want to clear counts for all programs in your application, **N** if only for the current program. If you are working with a standalone program, it doesn't matter whether you answer **Y** or **N**.

6.16.4 Printing Analyzer Totals

Pressing **F7=print** on the Animator Options menu shown in Figure 6.4 brings up a print menu that looks just like the one in the Micro Focus Editor. Selecting **F4=no-pause** on this menu will write the Analyzer totals to an output file. The main part of the filename will be the same as that of your program, and its extension will be .ANL. You can use an operating system command of the form **COPY progname.ANL LPT1** to send the file to a printer. You can substitute another printer address for LPT1 if your printer is connected to some other port. The Analyzer output looks much like the screen display: source lines on the left, execution counts on the right.

6.17 Structure Animation

6.17.1 Concepts

One common programming problem is that of "failing to see the forest for the trees." In a large program, a welter of detail can keep you from seeing how everything fits together. The Structure Animator keeps an animated structure diagram on screen while you are stepping through your code. The structure diagram contains a box for each of your program's sections or paragraphs, depending on how you set it up. The Structure Animator will highlight the box corresponding to the module being executed. In this way, you always know your position within the program. You can even print these structure diagrams on various types of PC printers. A printed copy of the structure diagram can become a useful part of each program's documentation. In effect, the Structure Animator provides "picture animation" as well as documentation for your application.

Structure Animator is most useful for large programs and for those that call other modules. If you use Structure Animator with a short, simple program, the diagram will be trivial. For example, the CUST program used as an exercise in the last two chapters would produce a structure diagram consisting only of a box containing the program name and one other box labeled MAIN. A structure diagram of a trivial program would not tell you anything you do not already know.

Structured walkthroughs play an important part in the quality assurance process. Code walkthroughs reveal how well the program source code follows the design specifications. Because the walkthrough process takes considerable time and effort, some installations avoid doing them. Using structure animation, printed structure diagrams, and COBOL Source Information can make structured walkthroughs proceed more quickly.

6.17.2 Using Structure Animation

Program setup. To use Structure Animation, you must first check or compile the program with the Struct directive set. The Struct directive is a toggle switch setting on the Checker menu. Then, on the Animator initial menu (Figure 6.1), toggle **F5=strc/anlz** until the **Struct** directive appears on the information line. That will enable Structure Animation when animation begins. If you have checked the program with *both* the Struct and the Analyze directives, you can toggle **F5** until the **Strc+Anlz** appears on the information line. That will enable both the Analyzer and the Structure Animator when animation begins.

Structure versus code mode. When you begin Structure Animation, you will see a program structure diagram superimposed in the upper-left corner when you begin animating. Certain Animator functions, such as the Step and Skip functions, work differently depending on whether the cursor is in the structure diagram or in the source code. The cursor location determines the Animator's operating mode. You can toggle the two modes by holding down the **Alt** key on the Animator main menu and toggling **F3=structure/code** to highlight either the word **structure** or the word **code.**

When you animate in code mode, the Structure Animator works the same as "normal" animation. The smallest unit of control is the program source line. Thus, the Step command executes one source line and positions the cursor at the next line. The major difference is the fact that a structure diagram will be visible on the screen along with the source code. The highlighted portion of the structure diagram shows what routine is executing. The structure diagram will scroll within the window as needed to show the box for that routine. In effect, the structure diagram display follows the animation process taking place in the source code.

When you animate in structure mode, the structure chart box (or node), rather than the program source line, becomes the unit of control. For example, the Step command executes the routine represented by the current structure chart box, and moves the highlighting to the next box. The source code will scroll on the screen as needed to show routines indicated in the structure diagram. In this case, the source code display follows the animation process taking place in the structure diagram window. In this chapter, we will be primarily concerned with animating in structure mode.

Navigating in structure mode. If your program is large, the complete structure diagram will not fit in the window. In structure animation mode, you can use the cursor arrow keys within the diagram window to scroll the diagram. Moving the cursor to any edge of the diagram window will cause the diagram to scroll in that direction.

Moving the cursor from one diagram box to another will scroll the source code on your screen. You will see the piece of source code corresponding to the box in the diagram that you select with the cursor. This operation is inquiry only and does *not* cause execution of any code. **F9/F10=node </>** will be visible on the Animator main menu when structure mode is active. This lets you use **F9** and **F10** to tab back and forth between diagram boxes, somewhat more quickly than with cursor arrow keys.

Printing a structure diagram. When structure animation mode is active, pressing **F7=print** on the Animator Options menu (Figure 6.4) brings up the Structure Analyzer print menu shown in Figure 6.23. Use the up or down cursor arrow keys to choose a printer configuration from the menu. Pressing the enter key on this menu will write the structure diagram to an output file. The main part of the filename will be the same as that of your program, and its extension will be .PRT. Send the file to a printer with an operating system command of the form **COPY progname.PRT LPT1**. Substitute another printer address for LPT1 if your printer is attached to some other port. Finally, selecting **F2=xref** before printing causes the Structure Animator to create a cross reference page for the structure diagram.

Why do you need to select a printer configuration? The Workbench supports a variety of hardware, and it needs to know what kind of output file to create. Different printers use different methods to represent page breaks, line drawing characters, and landscape-mode (sideways) output. For example, an ASCII printer with no graphics capability will substitute text characters to draw the boxes. An HP LaserJet printer uses control code sequences to switch between horizontal and vertical page orientation. Here are the choices on the printer configuration menu for Workbench v2.5:

- **IBM PC:** An IBM or Epson dot-matrix printer with graphics-mode capability, or any printer capable of emulating that mode.

- **6670 Laser:** An IBM 6670 laser printer.

- **ASCII:** Any printer that accepts ASCII files but does not recognize any special control characters.

- **ASCII (ANSI CC):** Any printer that accepts ASCII files and recognizes ANSI carriage control characters in column 1 of each record.

- **ASCII (ASCII CC):** Any printer that accepts ASCII files and recognizes ASCII carriage control characters.

- **HP Laserjet (Portrait):** An HP LaserJet or compatible laser printer. Choose portrait mode if you want the diagram to appear vertically on the page.

- **HP Laserjet (Landscape):** An HP LaserJet or compatible laser printer. Choose landscape mode if you want the diagram to appear horizontally ("sideways") on the page.

```
PRINTER NAME
_____

IBM PC
6670 Laser
ASCII
ASCII (ANSI CC)
ASCII (ASCII CC)
HP Laserjet (Portrait)
HP Laserjet (Landscape)

Options-TICTAC——————————————————Level=01-Speed=5-Ins-Caps-Num-Scroll
F1=help F2=xref                                              Escape
^ =up-name v =down-name                     <-'   =select-name
```

Figure 6.23 Structure Analyzer print menu

An ASCII printer pitfall. You will get disappointing results if you print a structure diagram on an ASCII printer using the default box spacing. The ASCII printer selections support printer devices that lack a graphics mode. For those configurations, the Workbench uses ASCII text characters to draw the diagram boxes. This results in coarse output. Some lines and connectors may be lost. To avoid confusion, you need to space the boxes further apart horizontally and vertically on your screen. In the next section, you will see how to adjust the diagram format.

Turning off Structure Animator. When you are in structure animation mode, you can turn off Structure Animator completely and return to "normal" animation mode. With the cursor in the Structure Animator diagram, press **Q** for **Qry**. You will see the usual main query menu. Then, press **C** for **Cursor-name.** You will see the menu shown in Figure 6.24. Pressing **F3=Structure-off** removes the structure diagram completely. To get back into structure animation mode, hold down the **Alt** key on the Animator main menu and toggle **F3=structure/code** to highlight the word **structure.**

```
Query structure────────────────────────────────Level=01-Speed=5-Ins-Caps-Num-Scroll
F1=help F2=alter-window F3=structure-off                                    Escape
```

Figure 6.24 Query Structure menu

6.17.3 Adjusting Diagram Format

Diagram window size and location. Pressing **F2=alter-window** on the Query Structure menu in Figure 6.24 will bring up the Alter Window menu. This menu looks and functions exactly the same as the menu shown in Section 6.15 (Figure 6.20) for altering query monitor windows, so we need not repeat the discussion here. You can use this menu to move or resize the window containing the structure diagram.

Level of detail. Several functions let you change structure diagram format. *These functions are available only when you are in structure animation mode.* Holding down the **Alt** key on the Animator main menu and pressing **F6=display** will bring up the Structure Alt-Options menu, shown in Figure 6.25. **Options selected on this menu affect the appearance both of the screen and of the printed structure diagram.**

Function keys **F2, F3, F4,** and **F5** let you choose the level of detail that the structure diagram will show. In each case, if the function key setting is selected, the item will appear highlighted on the first menu line. Once you have made your choices, press the enter key to redraw the structure diagram.

- **F2=paragraphs** causes the Structure Animator to show separate boxes for each paragraph. If this setting is not selected, the Structure Animator will show boxes only for sections.
- **F3=perform-thrus** causes the Structure Animator to show separate boxes for modules in a PERFORM THRU range.
- **F4=go-tos** causes the Structure Animator to show GO TOs.

- **F5=calls** causes the Structure Animator to show boxes for called subprograms. It makes no difference whether the CALL statements refer to modules written in COBOL or in other languages.

Reengineering old programs. Functions **F2** through **F5** on the Structure Alt-Options menu are handy for deciphering old programs that use GO TOs, PERFORMS, and PERFORM THRUs unwisely. For example, some old programs may PERFORM THRU a *mixture* of sections and paragraphs. Some may PERFORM THRU a *noncontiguous* sequence of routines, that is, where the first routine is actually later in the program than the second routine. Others may contain several PERFORM THRU ranges that *overlap*. Still others may GO TO, PERFORM, PERFORM THRU, and "fall into" the same routine *from several places in the code.* In some cases, program logic may even fall out of the physical end of the program without encountering a program exit statement. These are all dangerous programming practices. The Structure Animator can show how each paragraph, section, and subprogram is used, so that you can safely reengineer old programs.

Where should you begin? Animate the program, select all four of the function key options (**F2, F3, F4,** and **F5**), and then print a structure diagram containing this detailed information. The Structure Animator can provide a valuable "bird's eye view" of the entire application. COBOL Source Information (CSI), discussed in the next chapter, can provide a more detailed view of selected routines and data items.

```
Options-TICTAC────────────────────────Level=01-Speed=5-Ins-Caps-Num-Scroll
F1=help F2=paragraphs F3=perform-thrus F4=go-tos F5=calls            Escape
F9=box-dimensions                                      <-'  =select-options
```

*Figure 6.25 Structure **Alt** key Options menu*

Box size and spacing. Pressing **F9=box-dimensions** brings up a menu for adjusting diagram box size and spacing, shown in Figure 6.26. This is different from changing the diagram window size and position, which we discussed earlier. In this case, you are changing the boxes within the diagram to make the diagram more legible. If you are printing diagrams on an ASCII printer without graphics capabilities, you will need to space the diagram boxes further apart both horizontally and vertically. If you are working with a program that uses long data names, you may also want to make the boxes larger to allow more room for text. The trade-off is that larger boxes, or boxes spaced further apart, take up more room. Fewer of them will fit into a structure diagram window or on a printed page. You can vary box size and spacing only within limits set by the Workbench.

When this menu first appears, the menu line indicates that the cursor arrow keys affect **box size.** The left arrow key makes all boxes narrower. The right arrow key makes all boxes wider. The down arrow key makes all boxes taller. The up arrow key makes all boxes shorter.

Once you have chosen the box size you want, you can press **B=Box-separation** to work with box spacing, as shown in Figure 6.27. (Pressing **B** again returns to the box size function.) The menu line will indicate that the cursor arrow keys affect **box separation.** The left arrow key moves all boxes closer

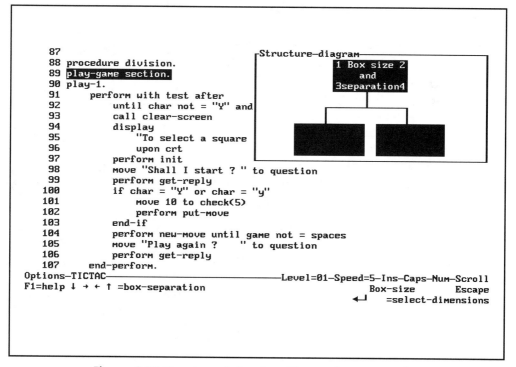

```
87
88 procedure division.
89 play-game section.
90 play-1.
91     perform with test after
92         until char not = "Y" and
93         call clear-screen
94         display
95             "To select a square
96             upon crt
97         perform init
98         move "Shall I start ? " to question
99         perform get-reply
100        if char = "Y" or char = "y"
101            move 10 to check(5)
102            perform put-move
103        end-if
104        perform new-move until game not = spaces
105        move "Play again ?    " to question
106        perform get-reply
107    end-perform.
```

```
Options-TICTAC─────────────────────────Level=01-Speed=5-Ins-Caps-Num-Scroll
F1=help ↓ → ← ↑ =box-size                                 Box-separation Escape
                                                          ↵    =select-dimensions
```

Figure 6.26 Structure Animator: Change box size

```
87
88 procedure division.
89 play-game section.
90 play-1.
91     perform with test after
92         until char not = "Y" and
93         call clear-screen
94         display
95             "To select a square
96             upon crt
97         perform init
98         move "Shall I start ? " to question
99         perform get-reply
100        if char = "Y" or char = "y"
101            move 10 to check(5)
102            perform put-move
103        end-if
104        perform new-move until game not = spaces
105        move "Play again ?    " to question
106        perform get-reply
107    end-perform.
```

```
Options-TICTAC─────────────────────────Level=01-Speed=5-Ins-Caps-Num-Scroll
F1=help ↓ → ← ↑ =box-separation                    Box-size        Escape
                                                   ↵    =select-dimensions
```

Figure 6.27 Structure Animator: Change box separation

together horizontally. The right arrow key moves all boxes further apart horizontally. The down arrow key moves all boxes further apart vertically. The up arrow key moves all boxes closer together vertically.

Compare the structure diagrams in Figures 6.26 and 6.27. Notice the expansion of both the box size and the box separation.

After adjusting both the box size and the box spacing, press the enter key twice to activate the changes and to get back to the Animator main menu.

6.17.4 What Structure Diagrams Reveal

Section and paragraph names. Each box in a structure diagram represents a routine. This can be a section or a paragraph, depending on the level of detail that you select. In this section, we will assume that you are viewing the diagram at the paragraph level. In that case, the Structure Animator will create a diagram box for each section and each paragraph. Suppose some program code is under a section label without a paragraph label. The Structure Animator will create a box for the section. Under that box will be another box labeled FILLER, representing the "assumed" paragraph name.

Symbols in boxes. Boxes in structure diagrams contain symbols that show how the program gets to that routine. The same routine can occur in several places within a structure diagram if it is used in different places within the program.

- No symbol at all means that the routine is being performed once.
- An asterisk shows that the routine is being performed repeatedly.
- A down arrow symbol shows that the routine is a subprogram referenced in a CALL statement. It makes no difference whether the subprogram was written in COBOL or another language.
- A "greater than" symbol (>) shows that the routine is part of a PERFORM THRU range.
- A degree symbol or small raised circle (°) shows that the routine is the target of a GO TO statement.

Format of printed diagram. The Structure Animator uses as many pages as it needs to show a printed diagram. If the entire diagram will not fit on one page, the print routine will place the remainder on other pages with appropriate references. The Structure Animator also creates separate printed diagram pages for items known as *common subtrees* and *widow subtrees*. Don't be intimidated by the word *subtree*. The structure diagram is a hierarchy, or tree structure, and a subordinate part of it can be called a subtree. A common subtree is simply a routine or group of routines that is used in more than one place in your program. The simplest example would be a section that is referenced in more than one PERFORM statement. A widow subtree is a routine or group of routines that is not referenced anywhere.

Figure 6.28, at the end of this chapter, shows a structure diagram created with the ASCII printer configuration. The program used in this example is TICTAC, one of the demo programs provided with the Workbench.

6.18 Animating from the Command Prompt

The following command will run a program under the Advanced Animator from the command prompt. Animator directives are optional and mostly pertain to testing PC applications (see *Workbench Reference*). Prefix the command with **XM** if you are running under MS-DOS.

```
[XM] WB ADVANIM program-name [animator-directives]
```

The following command will run a program under the basic Animator from the command prompt.

```
[XM] WB ANIMATE program-name [animator-directives]
```

The following command will run a program along with the Analyzer. The Analyzer will record statement execution statistics that you can examine later with the Animator.

```
[XM] WB ANALYZE program-name [analyzer-directives]
```

6.19 Exercises

Our purpose in these exercises is to give you some practice in getting into the Animator and using the basic functions. We will bring up the Animator first with a program that is simpler than anything you would need to debug in real life, so that you can concentrate on the mechanics of using the Animator. Later you can repeat some of these exercises with one of the more complex programs provided with the Workbench in the DEMO directory.

1. Refer once again to the CUST.CBL program from exercises in the last two chapters. Check that program using the Animator directive.

2. Bring up the animator with CUST.CBL. For now, use only the main Animator features (not the Analyzer or Structure Animator). Use the Watch function to execute several lines of code. How many times do you have to press a key to get one COBOL statement to execute? Then execute several lines of code with the Step function. What is the difference?

3. Now animate the program in Animate mode. What happens when you get to a user input screen? Show how to make the speed of animation faster or slower. Switch to Go mode. What is the difference?

4. How do you restart a program under the Animator once you've executed through it once? How does the Reset function differ from starting a new Animator session?

5. Set a breakpoint on any COBOL statement and animate in ZOOM mode until you get to that breakpoint. Then query a data field and change the contents of that field.

6.   Set a breakpoint with the Break-Do function (not the Do function.) After animating, look at the .EDO file associated with your program. Explain the contents of that file.

7.   Add the following section to CUST.CBL:

```
HELLO SECTION.
    DISPLAY "HELLO WORLD".
HELLO-EXIT. EXIT.
```

Place a PERFORM for that new section somewhere within the MAIN section. Now check the program using the directives for the Animator, the Analyzer, and the Structure Animator. Animate the program with *both* the Analyzer and the Structure Animator facilities. Can you see a box in the structure diagram for the new routine you just added? Is there also a box for the ANSI '85 inline PERFORM within the MAIN section? Move the cursor from one structure diagram box to the next. What happens to the source code display on the screen? Examine the Analyzer totals. Have all parts of the program been executed?

8.   Refer to the printed structure diagram of the TICTAC program shown in Figure 6.28. Explain the symbols used in the boxes that show how each routine is being accessed. What display options did we select in order to print the diagram in that form?

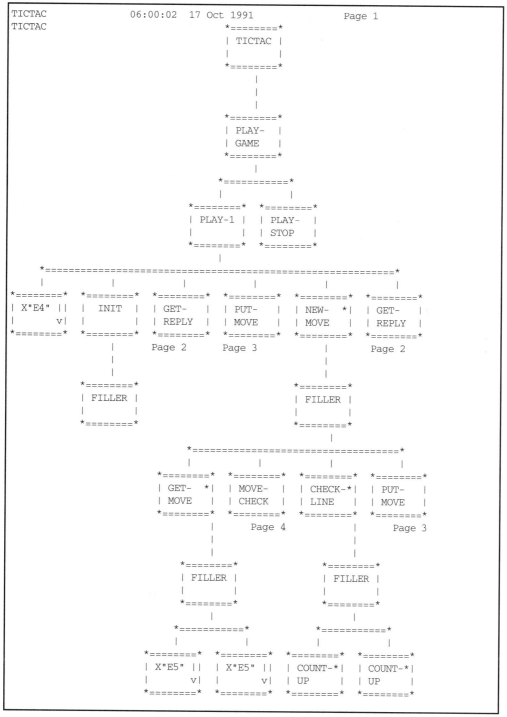

Figure 6.28a Printed structure diagram, page 1

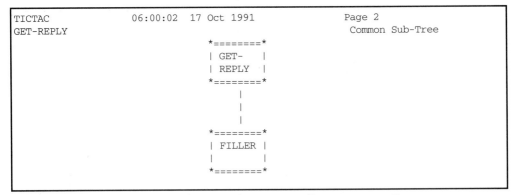

Figure 6.28b Printed structure diagram, page 2

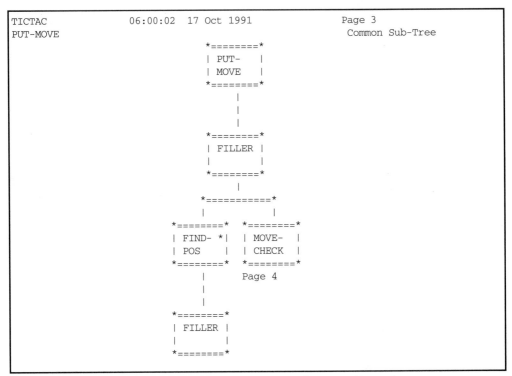

Figure 6.28c Printed structure diagram, page 3

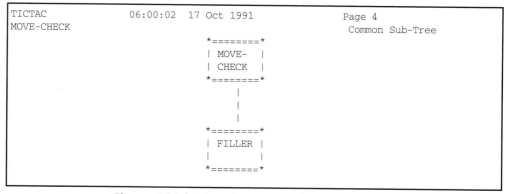

Figure 6.28d Printed structure diagram, page 4

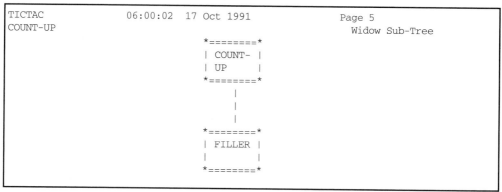

Figure 6.28e Printed structure diagram, page 5

COBOL Source Information (CSI)

7.1 Purpose of CSI

CSI saves time and reduces need for printed listings. We have a coffee mug on which an ecological message surrounds a drawing of a tree. *"Save me,"* reads the inscription. *"Think before you request that report."* With the present environmental concerns of forest preservation and waste disposal, many data processing sites are cutting down the amount of paper they use. From a programmer's point of view, program source listings take time to print and space to store. Any changes to a program make its printed source listing obsolete. Even so, some programmers print listings many times a day, while ignoring caustic remarks about how many trees die in vain each year. Other programmers pride themselves on never printing hard copy until testing for each program is complete, and sometimes not even then. *"Real* programmers don't need printed listings," they claim. We do not encourage anyone to choose work methods on the basis of ego or the desire to show off superior skills. On the other hand, nobody wants to squander valuable resources. The choice of methods and tools should be based on what gets the job done efficiently and effectively.

On the mainframe, working without printed listings has its own drawbacks. Typically, the programmer keeps the listing in the output spool queue and uses a utility to retrieve it on-line. Keeping extra spool files in the output queue will tie up system resources. It isn't always easy to find everything you want in a large spool file or print-image file. Spool display utilities are slow, especially with large files or a heavily loaded mainframe. In addition, a screen

shows fewer characters than a printed page. Most mainframe terminals show only 80 characters across, while spool files contain 132 characters preceded by a carriage control character. You can see only one screen of text at a time, unlike a printed listing that you can break apart and spread out over a desk. Even if your mainframe listing contains a cross-reference, no automatic lookup facility is available. To see all the source lines that update one data item, you have to page through the listing to find each reference yourself.

We don't claim that it is desirable or even possible to have a completely paperless DP installation. Yet the proper tools will reduce both the need for printed source listings and the time spent deciphering the contents of those listings. Stop for a moment to consider: Would you print fewer listings if you had an on-line utility that would give you all of the information you must now glean from a printed listing, *and give it to you more quickly?* What if this utility also could give you other useful information that might take you hours to put together by searching through the listing manually?

Extensive query function, not an update. COBOL Source Information (CSI), formerly called COBOL Source Intelligence, is a query function. It shows you the relationships between data items and routines in your programs. CSI is available both from within the Micro Focus COBOL Editor and from within the Advanced Animator. Although you access CSI through the Editor or the Animator, CSI neither updates source code nor executes any statements. It is purely a viewing facility.

You can select data or procedure names for CSI query directly from your Editor or Animator screen. You can scroll through the entire source file to choose items for querying. Once you have selected a data item or a procedure, CSI can give you detailed information about how it is used.

7.2 Preparation

7.2.1 Checking with the CSI Directive

Before you can use CSI with a program, you must syntax check it with the **CSI** directive. This directive tells the Checker to create a file with extension **.CSI,** containing information that CSI will use later. **F8=CSI** is a function key toggle switch available on both the Checker menu and the Editor check/animate menu. It turns the CSI directive on and off. Selecting the CSI directive causes an indicator to appear on the information line, as shown in Figure 7.1.

```
Check—Pause—Print————————————VSC2(3)——CSI——Ins-Caps-Num-Scroll
F1=help F2=dir F3=pse F4=list F5=anim F6=lang F7=x/ref F8=csi F9/F10=options Esc
File K:\COBOL\MFWBBOOK\CUST.CBL                                           Ctrl
```

Figure 7.1 Checker menu with CSI directive selected

You can use CSI with an unfinished program or with a program that still has syntax checker erors. As long as the Micro Focus Checker runs to the end of the program, even with errors, it will create a .CSI output file. CSI can provide a list of data items that still need to be defined, or paragraphs that have not yet been coded.

7.2.2 Running CSI

You can get into the CSI facility from the Editor COBOL support functions menu (Figure 7.2), reached by pressing **F2=COBOL** on the Editor main menu. Three function keys on this menu will get you into CSI:

- **F4=return-CSI** puts you into the CSI menus, displaying whatever query was active the last time you were in CSI. If you are entering CSI for the first time, no query will be active. In either case, you can request a new query once you are in CSI.

- **F5=CSI-enter** provides a box for you to enter a name to be passed to CSI. When CSI comes up, that name will be the object of the first query.
- **F6=CSI-at-cursor** picks up the name at the cursor position and passes that name to CSI. When CSI comes up, that name will be the object of the first query.

```
COBOL────────────────────────Line-1───Col-8─────────────Wrap-Ins-Caps-Num-Scroll
F1=help F2=check/animate F3=cmd-file F4=return-CSI F5=CSI-enter F6=CSI-at-cursor
F7=locate-previous F8=locate-next F9=locate-current F10=insert-statement Escape
```

Figure 7.2 Editor COBOL support functions menu

You also can get into CSI from the Advanced Animator. Holding down the **Ctrl** key on the Advanced Animator main menu brings up the Ctrl Options menu shown in Figure 7.3. From the Ctrl Options menu, **F3=CSI** puts you into the main CSI menu. **F5=CSI-enter** and **F6=CSI-cursor** on the Animator menu are the same as F5 and F6 on the Editor COBOL support functions menu shown above.

```
Options CUST                                  Level=01 Speed=5 Ins Caps Num Scroll
F1=help F2=find F3=CSI F4=clear F5=CSI-enter F6=CSI-cursor </> =page-left/right
F7=application-view                                         F9/F10=scroll
```

Figure 7.3 Animator Ctrl Options Menu

Still another way to bring up CSI is from the Advanced Animator. Query the desired field name. On the Query [field name] menu, hold down the **Ctrl** key to view the Ctrl menu shown in Figure 7.4. Press **F3=CSI** to perform a CSI query on the selected field.

```
Query:    CUST-NO───────────────────────Level=01-Speed=5-Ins-Caps-Num-Scroll
F1=help           F3=CSI   F4=Monitor+break+change F5=Monitor(fixed)
```

Figure 7.4 Animator Query [field name] CTRL key menu

7.3 Using the CSI Menus

Figure 7.5 shows the CSI main menu that appears when you first enter the CSI facility. This instance shows a query on the NEW-MOVE section within the TICTAC program. In this section, we will discuss functions available on this menu and on the submenus available from it.

7.3.1 Basic Query Functions

Procedure name query. Let's look at the CSI screen format shown in Figure 7.5. The source code display that occupies most of the text area looks similar to the source code display in the Animator. You can use cursor arrow or paging keys to move up or down through the display.

```
  125
  126 new-move section.                                              <--Defn
  127     perform get-move with test after until char9 not = 0       <--Exec
  128     perform move-check                                         <--Exec
  129     if game not = "stalemate"
  130         move low-values to check-array
  131         perform check-line varying i from 1 by 1               <--Exec
  132                       until i > 8 or game not = spaces
  133         if game not = "You win"          +Procedure————————————+
  134             perform put-move             |NEW-MOVE Section      |
  135         end-if                           |======================|
  136         if game = "I win" or game = "You wi|Executed from:-      |
  137             perform varying idx from a(j)|    PLAY-GAME PERFORM  |
  138                                       un|                        |
  139             move addr(idx) to locatio|Executes:-               |
  140             move entry-char(idx) to c|  PERFORM      GET-MOVE  |
  141             display char at location |  PERFORM      MOVE-CHECK|
  142         end-perform                  |  PERFORM      CHECK-LINE|
  143         end-if                       |  PERFORM      PUT-MOVE  |
  144     end-if.                          +————————————————————————+
CSI: NEW-MOVE————————————————————Executes-Exec-from————All———————————————
F1=help F2=posn-exit F4=compress F5=enter F6=csr F7/F8=prev/next F9/F10=</>  Esc
exec-From eXecutes Window Hide Locate/Return Tag Options Query Display
    6 line(s) highlighted
```

Figure 7.5 CSI main menu with procedure query

Unlike the Animator, the source code display also shows pointers in the margin that help you find the source lines that pertain to your query. In Figure 7.5, a "<—DEFN" pointer in the source code display shows the source line that defines the procedure name NEW-MOVE. "<—EXEC" pointers show lines within NEW-MOVE that execute other routines. Actually, there would be five pointers on this screen, but one of them is hidden behind the report box. Here are the source line pointers that CSI uses:

- **COPY**: beginning of copy library member.
- **DEFN**: procedure label (paragraph or section header) or definition of data item.
- **EFROM**: the procedure that you have queried is being executed from this line.
- **ENDCPY**: end of copy library member.
- **EXEC**: the procedure that you have queried executes another procedure.
- **MOD**: data item is modified.
- **QUAL**: data item is used as a qualifier for another data item.
- **TEST**: data item is tested in a comparison.
- **USE**: data item is used but not modified or tested.

At the bottom of the screen is a message, **6 line(s) highlighted.** CSI highlights all lines that pertain to the current query, whether or not they happen to be visible on the current screen. You can press **F7/F8=prev/next** to reach other pointers in the source code. In this case, the source line that performs NEW-MOVE is on a different screen page. Pressing **F7** would reposition the display to the source line that performs NEW-MOVE.

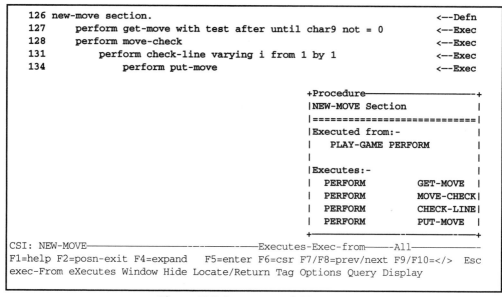

```
126 new-move section.                                              <--Defn
127     perform get-move with test after until char9 not = 0      <--Exec
128     perform move-check                                        <--Exec
131         perform check-line varying i from 1 by 1              <--Exec
134             perform put-move                                  <--Exec


                                          +Procedure------------------+
                                          |NEW-MOVE Section           |
                                          |===========================|
                                          |Executed from:-            |
                                          |   PLAY-GAME PERFORM       |
                                          |                           |
                                          |Executes:-                 |
                                          |   PERFORM      GET-MOVE   |
                                          |   PERFORM      MOVE-CHECK |
                                          |   PERFORM      CHECK-LINE |
                                          |   PERFORM      PUT-MOVE   |
                                          +---------------------------+
CSI: NEW-MOVE--------------------------Executes-Exec-from------All------------
F1=help F2=posn-exit F4=expand    F5=enter F6=csr F7/F8=prev/next F9/F10=</> Esc
exec-From eXecutes Window Hide Locate/Return Tag Options Query Display
```

Figure 7.6 Compressed CSI query

Pressing **F8** would simply move the cursor down through all the lines highlighted on the current screen.

The box at the lower-right corner of this display is called the **CSI report window.** The label at the top of this box, **Procedure,** shows that the query refers to a procedure name rather than a data name. The procedure being queried is **NEW-MOVE Section.** Below the double line, notice that this procedure is executed from a routine called **PLAY-GAME** with a **PERFORM.** NEW-MOVE Section, in turn, contains four other statements that execute other routines: **GET-MOVE, MOVE-CHECK, CHECK-LINE,** and **PUT-MOVE.**

Pressing **W** for **Window** switches the *focus* (the text cursor) between the source code display and the CSI report window. If the cursor is in the report window, it will show up as a light bar. You can move the light bar to some other name within that window, so that you can use the Locate function to get to that name quickly. By default, the cursor is in the source code display.

A large CSI report window on your screen can obscure part of the source code display. Pressing **H** for **Hide** repeatedly toggles the CSI report window off and on, so that you can see whatever source code is behind it. This function does not change window contents.

Compressing source display. Pressing **F4=compress/expand** on the CSI main menu toggles the source code display between expanded and compressed mode. Expanded (normal) mode shows everything. Compressed mode shows only those lines that have been highlighted for the current query. Figure 7.6 shows the same procedure query in compressed mode. Notice that there is now room to show all six flagged lines.

Level of detail. Two toggle switch settings on the CSI main menu govern how much procedure execution detail will be shown. Both settings are on by default. Pressing either key repeatedly will switch the function off and on.

```
 41      03 filler-8        pic x(64) value all spaces.
 42      03 tictac-00-1429 pic x(23) value "=======+=======+=======".
 43      03 filler-9        pic x(63) value all spaces.
 44      03 tictac-00-1535 pic x(17) value "1|      2|       3".
 45      03 filler-10       pic x(64) value all spaces.
 46      03 tictac-00-1636 pic x(09) value "|        |".
 47      03 filler-11       pic x(71) value all spaces.
 48      03 tictac-00-1736 pic x(09) value "|        |".
 49      03 filler-12       pic x(595) value all spaces.
 50 01 entry-array.
 51      03 entry-char      pic x              occurs 9 times.
 52 01 check-array.                                            <--Defn
 53      03 check           pic s99     comp  occurs 9 times.  <--Defn
 54 01 xcount              pic 9(2)     comp.
 55 01 ocount              pic 9(2)     +Data————————————————size-refs-+
 56 01 factor              pic s9(2)    |CHECK       Comp    sign    1    6m|
 57 01 char                pic x.       |Working-Storage Subscripted       |
 58 01 char9 redefines char pic 9.      |==================================|
 59 01 idx                 pic 9(2)     |Related definitions:-             |
 60 01 result              pic 9(2)     |CHECK-ARRAY Group             9   3m|
 61 01 cursor-pos.                      +—————————————————————————————————+
CSI: CHECK————————————————Executes-Exec-from-Related-All———————————
F1=help F2=posn-exit F4=compress F5=enter F6=csr F7/F8=prev/next F9/F10=</>  Esc
exec-From eXecutes Window Hide Locate/Return Tag Options Query Display
    9 line(s) highlighted
```

Figure 7.7 Querying a data name

- **F** for **exec-From** shows where the current procedure is executed from.
- **X** for **eXecutes** shows other procedures that are executed by the current procedure.

Data name query. Both data names and procedure names are selected for querying in the same way. The only difference is the type of response that CSI returns. Figure 7.7 shows the result of a query on the data name CHECK within the demo program TICTAC. For this query, the option switch for Related-data was on. Thus, it not only shows the query results for CHECK, it shows results for the group item, CHECK-ARRAY.

A data name query shows the item's data type and size, together with the number of times the program uses it. In this instance, the numeral **6** shows that CHECK appears on six source lines. The column at the right contains the **usage indicator.** A usage indicator of **m** shows that at least one of those source lines **modifies** CHECK. A usage indicator of **d** shows possible **dead code:** an item that is unreferenced within the procedure division. A usage indicator of **u** shows that the item is **used** (referenced) but not modified.

Navigating through a program. How do you move quickly to the parts of the program you want to see? Pressing **L** for **Locate** on the CSI main menu brings up the CSI Locate menu shown in Figure 7.8. On this menu are many shortcut commands for positioning the cursor within the source code. If the desired location does not exist within the source program, CSI will display the message, **Program position does not exist.**

- **P** for **Previous procedure** positions to the previous paragraph or section.
- **N** for **Next procedure** positions to the next paragraph or section.

- **T** for **file conTrol** positions to the first File Control statement for quick access to SELECT statements.
- **F** for **File section** positions to the first File Section statement for quick access to FD statements.
- **W** for **Working storage** positions to the first Working Storage statement.
- **L** for **Linkage section** positions to the first Linkage Section statement.
- **S** for **Start-procedure** positions to the Procedure Division header.
- **R** for **scReen section** positions to the first Screen Section statement. This is used for screen handling in PC-based and UNIX applications, not for IBM mainframe program development.
- **E** for **Enter** lets you enter a name to locate. This operation does not perform a query; it just locates the name.
- **C** for **Cursor** has no effect when the focus (the text cursor) is in the source display. When the text cursor is on a name in the report window, **C** locates that name in the source display. This operation does not perform a query; it just locates the name.

```
Locate─────────────────────────────Executes-Exec-from──────All──────────────────
F1=help F4=clear-return-stack Enter Cursor Previous/Next-procedure        Escape
file-conTrol File-section Working-storage Linkage scReen-section Start-procedure
```

Figure 7.8 CSI Locate menu

Finally, on the CSI main menu shown in Figure 7.5, pressing **R** for **Return** brings you back to the source line from which you previously used the Locate function. If you do not want to preserve this information, **F4=clear-return-stack** clears the stack of addresses from which previous LOCATE operations were performed.

Getting out of CSI. As with other Workbench facilities, the **Escape** key will move you back up to the previous menu each time you press it. Therefore, pressing **Escape** on the CSI main menu will take you back either to the Animator or to the Editor, depending on how you got into CSI. On the CSI main menu, pressing **F2=posn-exit** will return you to the Animator or the Editor *positioned at the current cursor position.* In the Animator, **F2=posn-exit** determines the position of the cursor within the Animator source code display. The cursor position does not affect program execution sequence once you get back into Animator.

7.3.2 Querying Additional Names

Once you are within the CSI facility, you can continue querying on more names. Pressing **F5=enter** brings up a prompt at the bottom of the screen to let you enter another name to query. You also can move the text cursor to a name on the screen and press **F6=csr** to pass that name to CSI for the next query.

Pressing **Q** for **Query** on the CSI main menu brings up the CSI query menu, shown in Figure 7.9. The basic query functions are still available here: you can press **C** for **Cursor** to query a name at the text cursor position, or **E** for **Enter** to enter a name directly. These work like **F5** and **F6** on the main CSI menu. The CSI query menu also offers several functions for changing data item queries:

- When the current query is a detail data item, pressing **R** for **paRent** does a query on its group item.
- When the current query is a group data item, pressing **H** for **cHild** does a query on the first detail item within that group.
- **S** for **Same-level** queries the next data item having the same COBOL level number.

```
Query----------------------------Executes-Exec-from------All--------------------
F1=help                                                              Escape
Cursor Enter Previous-queries paRent Same-level cHild
```

Figure 7.9 CSI Query menu

Returning to an old query. CSI preserves a list of previous queries. Pressing **P** for **Previous-queries** will bring up that list in a popup menu on the screen. You can use cursor arrow keys to move the light bar (highlighted line) within that menu to select an old query. Pressing the enter key reactivates the selected query.

7.3.3 Special CSI Query Keywords

As we mentioned earlier, using the function **F5=enter** brings up a prompt on the screen so that you can enter a name for querying. **F5=enter** also lets you supply other types of keywords and search criteria. This option greatly expands the power and flexibility of CSI.

Wildcards and qualified names. CSI allows you to query on **wildcard data names.** You can use wildcard characters to replace part of a data or procedure name: an asterisk (*) to replace a string of any length, or a question mark (?) to replace a single character.

To search on data names or procedure names only, enter the keyword DATA or PROC after the wildcard search string. In TICTAC, the wildcard search argument PLAY* DATA matches nothing, while the wildcard search argument PLAY* PROC matches the procedure labels PLAY-GAME, PLAY-1, and PLAY-STOP.

CSI also allows searches on **qualified data names,** such as EMPLOYEE-NO OF PAYMASTR.

COBOL verbs. Entering a COBOL verb at the screen prompt will cause CSI to search for all instances of that verb. For instance, if you query on PERFORM, "<—USE" flags will appear beside all PERFORM statements in the program. If you are maintaining old programs, you can use this feature to find verbs that you want to eliminate, such as GO TO and ALTER.

To limit the query to certain paragraphs or sections, follow the COBOL verb with a restrictive clause such as IN [routine-name-1] THRU [routine-name-2]. Make sure the second routine follows the first one in your program! For example, searching for SUBTRACT IN MAIN THRU MAIN-EXIT will find all lines containing the SUBTRACT verb in routines labeled MAIN through MAIN-EXIT.

In addition to COBOL verbs, CSI recognizes terms for certain other groups of COBOL statements, as follows:

- **ARITH** finds COBOL arithmetic statements.
- **DEPENDING** finds GO TO...DEPENDING ON statements.
- **END-SCOPE** finds ANSI '85 END- reserved words, such as END-IF and END-PERFORM.
- **EXIT-PROGRAM** finds EXIT PROGRAM statements, but not EXIT statements.
- **INLINE** finds ANSI '85 inline PERFORM statements.
- **I/O** finds COBOL file I/O statements.
- **PGMEXIT** finds GOBACK, STOP RUN, and EXIT PROGRAM statements.
- **PREPROCESSED** finds COBOL statements that an integrated preprocessor (such as CICS) has commented out and replaced.
- **STOP RUN** finds STOP RUN statements, but not STOP "literal" statements.
- **THRU** finds PERFORM THRU statements.
- **WHEN OTHER** finds WHEN OTHER keywords, but not WHEN keywords. WHEN OTHER is an ANSI '85 case structure keyword representing the default alternative.

Finding inactive code and "dead" data. Some old programs become more confusing over time because they become cluttered with unused code and data. This happens because maintenance programmers often make changes without understanding everything the program is doing. If a maintenance programmer is unsure about why a piece of code or data is there, he or she will probably leave it in the program, "just in case." With the aid of CSI, you can safely rid old programs of this burden.

Supplying the following search arguments at the **F5=enter** prompt can help you determine how code and data are actually being used:

- DEADDATA finds all dead data items. If neither the data item itself nor any of its **related data items** are used in any Procedure Division code, that item is "dead." Related data items are those dependent on the original item. These include data items defined over the same area of storage (e.g., REDEFINES and group items), the file definition for a data item occurring within a record, and the data item on which a condition name (88-level) depends. Note that DEADDATA may still find data names used in conditionally compiled code, which is not usually a concern for mainframe programming. It will also find data names used only in special clauses but not in the Procedure Division. For example, suppose a program contains a field called CUST-STAT used in the clause FILE STATUS IS CUST-STAT. If the program never checks this status code in the Procedure Division, CSI will consider CUST-STAT to be dead code. (Failure to check status codes is, of course, risky programming practice.) Once you have accounted for these few exceptions, it generally is safe to eliminate dead data items from your program.

- **UNEXEC** finds all paragraph and section names that are not referenced by name anywhere in the Procedure Division. *This does not automatically mean that the code is not being used, only that the procedure label is unreferenced.* In fact, the initial section and/or paragraph name in each program (the default entry point) is always "unreferenced," simply because no other routine executes it. In other cases, the routines may be part of a PERFORM THRU range. If a section is being PERFORMed, paragraphs within that section might not be referenced individually by name. Program execution can "fall into" a routine from the routine above it. When the code is still in use but the procedure label is meaningless, you might be able to eliminate the procedure label by merging the code into the routine that precedes it in the program.

- **UNREF** finds all data names that are not referenced by name in the Procedure Division. If a data item is unreferenced but is not dead data, then its storage allocation is still being used somewhere although the data name itself might not be. Using UNREF can help you to eliminate unneeded REDEFINES clauses from your data definitions.

- **UNDECL** finds all references to undeclared section or paragraph names. For example, if you have a PERFORM HELLO-WORLD statement but no paragraph or section named HELLO-WORLD, UNDECL will find the PERFORM statement. This is definitely an error! The Micro Focus Checker would have flagged the PERFORM statement also.

- **LABEL** finds all procedure names (paragraph or section) in the program.

- **ANALYZE** lets you view Source Code Analyzer execution statistics from within CSI.

The Source Code Analyzer. The ANALYZE search argument lets you restrict your CSI query to those Procedure Division source lines that have been executed a certain number of times. To do this, you must first check your program and test it with the Analyzer to accumulate runtime statistics. Then invoke CSI. Enter the **ANALYZE** search argument followed by an arithmetic expression and, optionally, by restrictive clauses such as a COBOL verb or a range of procedure labels. The first example finds unexecuted source lines:

```
ANALYZE < 1
```

The second example finds OPEN statements executed at least twice in the routines labeled MAIN through MAIN-EXIT:

```
ANALYZE > 1 OPEN IN MAIN THRU MAIN-EXIT
```

Measurements of program complexity. When you are about to embark on a program maintenance project, how do you estimate the amount of time it will take to change, compile, and test each program? Programs vary, not just in length, but in level of complexity. The more control structures in the program, such as IFs, PERFORMs, EVALUATEs, and nest levels, the longer it will take to understand what the program is doing. An unstructured program is difficult and risky to maintain. Overlapping PERFORM statements, GO TO, GO TO DEPENDING ON, or ALTER statements, and multiple program exit statements all indicate a lack of structure.

```
Statistics————————————————————————
Lines of Source        239
Lines of Code          151
Comment lines            9
Comments /100 lines      3
Statements             124
Sections                10
Paragraphs               2
Files                    0
Data-items              52
Condition                0
Screen Name              0
Report                   0
Level 78                 2
Call (by number)         2
Call (by name)           0
Call (data-item)         0

Verb Counts
WHEN                     4
MOVE                    40
ADD                      4
IF                      19
PERFORM                 13
CALL                     3
ACCEPT                   2
DISPLAY                  7
ELSE                     6
END-EVALUATE             1
END-IF                  17
END-PERFORM              3
EVALUATE                 1
PERFORM inline           3
STOP-RUN                 1
Program Exits            1
Arithmetic               4
ANSI'85 END-..          21

Maximum Nesting          4
Overlapping Performs     0
Program Volume        2178
```

Figure 7.10 CSI TIMES statistics for TICTAC program

CSI provides a quick way of evaluating the complexity of every program in your shop, even before you look at the source code.

Supplying the **TIMES** search argument at the **F5=enter** prompt will cause CSI to report statistics of program complexity, as shown in Figure 7.10.

What is program volume, and how do you use this figure? **Program volume is an assessment of program size and complexity.** To calculate program volume, CSI uses the formula **(A + B) LOG2(C + D)**, where A is the total number of COBOL statements, B is the number of references to identifier names, C is the number of unique verb types, and D is the total number of identifier names. To make use of program volume, begin by running CSI TIMES statistics for a variety of programs in your shop. The next step is to compare the program volume with the amount of time it actually takes to make a change to these programs. This process can give you an idea of how program volume can be used to estimate programming time requirements in your shop for future planned enhancements.

Here are some more uses for CSI TIMES statistics. Has your shop inherited bad programs from the years before structured programming came into vogue? CSI TIMES statistics can help you identify candidates for reengineering or replacement. CSI TIMES statistics also help you monitor program maintenance. Comparing CSI TIMES statistics taken before and after program maintenance shows whether the program has grown more complex (sometimes this is inevitable) and whether the programmer has cleaned up old unstructured code. If a maintenance programmer is "cutting corners" by introducing GO TOs, overlapping PERFORMs, or multiple program exits, CSI TIMES statistics will reveal that too.

Resources outside your program. To see all of the COPY statements used in your program, enter **COPY** at the **F5=enter** prompt. If your program has any nested copy library members, these will be indented.

To see all of the COBOL CALL statements in your program, make sure the **Exec-from** toggle is on (this is set on the main CSI menu). Enter **CALL** at the **F5=enter** prompt. Entering **CALL DATA** will show only calls to a data name (dynamic calls). Entering **CALL NAME** will show calls to a program name. Entering **CALL NUMBER** will find calls to Micro Focus–provided routines not used in mainframe programs.

7.3.4 Setting CSI Options: Types of Detail to Display

Switches that control how much query detail CSI will display are available on the **Options** menu. You can reach this menu, shown in Figure 7.11, by pressing **O** on the CSI main menu. Highlighted indicators on this menu show the current toggle switch selections. For instance, the function key selectors on the first menu line (**F2** through **F6**) will display in highlighted text when selected, and in normal intensity text when not selected. Indicators for **Data-selector** and **Related-data** will appear on the Options menu information line.

The function key selectors **F2** through **F8** all pertain to queries on procedure names (paragraphs, sections, or subprograms). The other two selectors, **D** and **R**, pertain to queries on data names.

- **F2=paragraphs** determines whether CSI will show paragraph names in "executes" and "executed from" queries on procedure names. This setting is on by default. If this setting is off, CSI will show only section names.
- **F3=performs** determines whether CSI will show procedures accessed by PERFORM statements. This setting is on by default.
- **F4=go-tos** determines whether CSI will show procedures accessed by GO TO statements. This setting is on by default.
- **F5=calls** determines whether CSI will show subprograms accessed by COBOL CALL statements. This statement is on by default.
- **F6=data-in-procedure** determines whether CSI will show a list of the data names referenced by the current procedure. The breakdown will show data names modified, used, and tested within that procedure. (The printed output in Figure 7.14 below shows an example of this type of query.)
- **D** for **Data-selector** determines what types of references to data items CSI will show. Press **D** repeatedly to cycle through the selections. Choices are

Uses (source lines that use the data item or modify it), **Mod** (source lines that modify the data item), **Defn** (source lines that define the data), or **All.** The value you select will appear on the information line. **All** is the default setting.

- **R** for **Related-data** determines whether CSI will show data items that are related to the item you are querying. Press **R** repeatedly to cycle through the selections. The value you select will appear on the information line. The default setting is "off" (blank), in which the query will ignore related data. **Child** will make the query include children of the selected data item (detail items defined within the group item). **Related** will make the query include all data related to the original item. This includes data items defined over the same area of memory, the file definition for a data item defined within a record, and the data field on which a condition name depends.

- **F7/F8=perform-level** lets you choose how many PERFORM nest levels you want to see. **F7** lowers the level and **F8** raises it. The current setting appears on the function key menu after the description **F7/F8=perform-level.** The default setting is 1, meaning that CSI will search for only one level of PERFORMs. Suppose routine A PERFORMs routine B, and routine B PERFORMs routine C. If the perform level is set to 1, a query on routine A would show only routine B. If the perform level is set to 2 or higher, a query on routine A would show routines B and C.

  Important: CSI does *not* immediately update the report window and highlighted lines to reflect any changes you have made to these settings. To refresh the query after making your selections, press the **enter** key to use the **Requery** function.

Tree structure of your program. You can use this feature to display or print a tree structure of your program. Set the perform level to the maximum of 255. Do a CSI query on the main routine in your program to get a hierarchy of all PERFORMed routines. If you want a report that shows how all data items in the program are being used, set the perform level to 255, set **F6=data-in-procedure,** and query on the main routine of your program.

```
Options————————————————Executes-Exec-from————All——————————————————————
F1=help F2=paragraphs F3=performs F4=go-tos F5=calls F6=data-in-procedure Escape
Data-selector Related-data F7/F8=perform-level:  1                   <-'=requery
```

Figure 7.11 CSI Options menu

7.3.5 Setting CSI Options: Display Format

Switches that control the appearance of CSI information are available on the **Display** menu. You can reach this menu, shown in Figure 7.12, by pressing **D** on the CSI main menu. Most menu functions control display appearance. We will discuss the printing and tags functions later on.

Moving the report window. First of all, notice the phrase on the first function key menu line: **Home/End/PgUp/PgDn=corner-report**. These four keys move the CSI report window quickly to the upper-left, lower-left, upper-right, and lower-right corners of the screen. The cursor arrow keys also move the CSI report window in each direction, but only one row or column at a time, not all at once.

Analyzer totals. If you checked your program with the ANALYZE directive, pressing **A** for **Analyzer** switches the display of Analyzer totals on and off.

Viewing PERFORM THRU ranges. Pressing **U** for **perform-thrUs** switches the display of PERFORM THRU indicators on and off. These indicators appear in columns 1 through 6, pointing out paragraphs that fall within a PERFORM THRU range. This function provides a good way to find paragraphs that the program can "fall into."

Comment lines in contrasting color. Pressing **C** for **Comment-color** lets you display comment lines in an alternate color. Pressing **C** repeatedly cycles through three choices: comment lines in the alternate color, all lines *except* comment lines in the alternate color, and all lines in the default color.

Sequence numbers. Pressing **N** for **seq-No's** switches the display of sequence numbers in columns 1 through 6 on and off.

7.3.6 Printing Results of a CSI Query

You can print the results of the most recent CSI query operation. Pressing **P** for **Print-to-file** on the CSI display menu will bring up the CSI print-to-file menu shown in Figure 7.13. On this menu, pressing **S** for **Source-only** prints only the highlighted (flagged) source lines. Pressing **R** for **Report-only** prints only the contents of the CSI report window. Pressing **B** for **Both-source-and-report** prints both the highlighted source lines and the report window contents. The example below, Figure 7.14, shows both.

CSI writes printable output to a file called **CSI.DAT.** You can print this file from the operating system command prompt with a command such as **COPY CSI.DAT LPT1.** Substitute another device address for LPT1 if your printer is attached to some other port. This output file is cumulative. Each time you tell CSI to write a query to this file, it appends the new information to the end. To clear old query information, delete the entire CSI.DAT file from the operating system command prompt. CSI will create a new output file the next time you request printed output.

```
Display───────────────────────Executes-Exec-from────All──────────────────
F1=help                    Home/End/PgUp/PgDn=corner-report ^v><=move-report  Escape
current-File Comment-color seq-No's Print-to-file Tags Analyzer perform-thrUs
```

Figure 7.12 CSI Display menu

```
Print-to-file─────────────────────Executes-Exec-from────All──────────────
F1=help                                                                  Escape
Source-only Report-only Both-source-and-report
```

Figure 7.13 CSI Print-to-file menu

```
Procedure
CHECK-LINE Section
============================
Executed from:-
    NEW-MOVE     PERFORM


Executes:-
    PERFORM          COUNT-UP
    PERFORM          COUNT-UP


Data-item   mods   uses tests
A                  -      3      -
B                  -      3      -
C                  -      -      3
CHECK              1      -      -
ENTRY-CHAR         -      -      2
FACTOR             7      1      -
GAME               2      -      -
I                  1      6      3
IDX                3      1      4
J                  3      2      1
OCOUNT             2      -      4
XCOUNT             2      -      7
```

Figure 7.14a CSI.DAT printed output (report window)

```
                                             130 lines unshown
131     '        perform check-line varying i from 1 by 1

                                              14 lines unshown
146 check-line section.
147     move zero to xcount,ocount,factor
148     perform count-up varying idx from a(i) by b(i)
                                               7 lines unshown
156              perform count-up varying idx from a(j) by b(j)
```

Figure 7.14b CSI.DAT printed output (source lines)

7.3.7 Tags (Bookmarks)

If you aren't using a printed listing, how do you mark important places in a big program? You can't use paper clips, Post-It™ notes, or fluorescent-marker highlighting on a scrolling screen display. The Tag function within CSI will do the job instead.

Pressing **T** for **Tag** on the CSI main menu will display the CSI Tags menu, shown in Figure 7.15. The Tag function lets you set tags anywhere in your program. Once you have set a tag, you can use that tag to reposition your source code display.

- To set a tag, move the cursor to the desired line and press **S** for **Set-tag.** A Tag indicator will appear in the left margin.
- To remove one tag, move the cursor to the line with that tag and press **U** for **Unset-tag.** The Tag indicator will vanish.
- To remove all tags from your source file, press **C** for **Clear-all-tags.** All Tag indicators will vanish.

```
        33 MAIN SECTION.
Tag—>       OPEN OUTPUT CUSTMST.
        35     PERFORM UNTIL CUST-NO = "QUIT"                          <—-Test
        36         DISPLAY "Enter customer number (6 digits) or QUIT"
        37         ACCEPT CUST-NO                                      <—-Mod
        38         IF CUST-NO NOT = "QUIT"                             <—-Test
        39             DISPLAY "Enter customer name (25 characters)"
        40             ACCEPT CUST-NAME
        41             DISPLAY "Enter phone number (10 digits)"
        42             ACCEPT CUST-PHONE
        43             WRITE CUSTMST-REC
        44             ADD 1 TO WS-COUNT
        45             PERFORM HELLO-ROUTINE
        46         END-IF
        47     END-PERFORM.
        48     DISPLAY "End of program CUST, " WS-COUNT " records added.".
        49     CLOSE CUSTMST.             +Data————————————————size-refs-+
        50     STOP RUN.                  |CUST-NO Alphanumeric    6    4m|
        51*                               |File Section                  |
        52 MAIN-EXIT. EXIT.               +——————————————————————————————+
Tag————————————————Executes-Exec-from———All—————————————————————————————
F1=help                                                           Escape
Set-tag Unset-tag Clear-all-tags Go-to-tag
```

Figure 7.15 CSI Tags menu

- To locate an existing tag, press **G** for **Go-to-tag**. This positions you to the next tag in the source file. Pressing **G** repeatedly cycles through every tag in the file.

7.4 Mouse Support in Text Mode

Micro Focus introduced mouse support with Workbench 2.5. As we mentioned earlier, mouse support is available under MS-DOS and OS/2, but not while running Workbench v2.5 in text mode under Microsoft Windows. Within CSI, you can use the mouse for several purposes.

Moving the text cursor. When mouse support is available, you will see both a mouse cursor and a text cursor. To position the text cursor, move the mouse cursor to the desired location and click the left mouse button. The text cursor will move to the position of the text cursor. By clicking in different areas, you can change the focus between the source code display and the CSI report window.

Querying another data or procedure name. Double-click the left mouse button on the desired name. This works the same as the **F6** query-cursor operation.

Moving the CSI report window. Position the mouse cursor to the top border of the CSI report window. Holding down the left mouse button, drag the window to the desired location and release the button.

Scrolling CSI report window contents. If the CSI report window contains more data than will fit in the boxed area, a scroll bar will be visible. Clicking on the up or down arrows will scroll up or down one line at a time.

Clicking above or below the slider will scroll up or down one page at a time. Clicking on the slider itself does nothing.

7.5 What About the Command Prompt?

As of Workbench v3.0, there is no method for running CSI independently from the operating system command prompt. Under the Workbench, CSI is available from within the COBOL Editor or from the Advanced Animator menus. Since you can run both the COBOL Editor and the Advanced Animator from the command prompt, you can access CSI from either of these utilities.

7.6 Exercises

1. Refer once again to the CUST.CBL program that was used and modified in Chapter 6. Check that program again, using the Animator, Analyze (or Strc+Anlz), and CSI directives.

2. Load CUST.CBL into the Micro Focus COBOL Editor. Bring up CSI from the Editor, using the **CSI Enter** facility. Query on the data name CUST-NO. How many source lines are flagged? What types of flags appear in the right margin? What does the report window show?

3. Return to the Develop menu and bring up the Advanced Animator. Execute CUST.CBL under the Animator, using the Analyzer to accumulate statistics. Now bring up CSI from within the Animator. Make the Analyzer totals visible from within CSI. Using the Analyzer totals, make CSI flag all lines that have been executed more than once.

4. Query on the procedure name MAIN. Turn on the **Data-in-procedure** toggle switch and refresh the query. What happened to the report window? How many data items are used in MAIN SECTION? Compress and expand the source listing portion of the display.

5. Let's practice navigating within the source code. Set several tags in the program. Use a menu command repeatedly to reposition the screen display to each of these tags. Now use a command on the Locate menu to position to the beginning of working storage. What commands did you use?

6. Move the report window around on the screen. What menu command moves the report window quickly to the upper-right corner? Use a menu command to hide the report window and then make it visible again.

7. Use a special query function to find all unexecuted procedure names. What is the result? Is it normal, or does it indicate that a problem exists? Is there any dead data?

8. What special query search argument will highlight the ANSI '85 inline PERFORM statement in this program?

9. Use a special query search argument to derive statistics on the program complexity of CUST.CBL (a fairly trivial program, we admit). Write the results

to an output file and print them. Compare these with the statistics shown for TICTAC.

10. Use a menu command to bring up a popup menu of your previous query operations. Choose one query from that list and reactivate it.

8

Compiling and Running Programs

8.1 Compiling/Linking/Running versus Checking/Animating

As a mainframe applications developer, you may wonder why we have a chapter on compiling, linking, and running programs on the PC. Why does Micro Focus provide this facility from the Mainframe Developer's Environment (MDE) menu? "After all," you might ask, "the Syntax Checker and Animator give me all the functions I need for testing, so why would I compile or link programs on the PC? I port everything back to the mainframe as soon as testing is done!" The answer depends on your situation. Perhaps you don't need these facilities, but perhaps you do. These scenarios show how PC programs fit into the "big iron" environment:

- As a COBOL programmer, you use the Workbench to develop customized tools and utilities for your own use on the PC. For example, you may want a program to delete and rebuild your test databases, or a small system to log mainframe downtime and problem reports at your computer installation. (We hope you don't need a *big* system to track problems!) Even though these in-house tools will be used only within your department, you still want them to run in "production mode" on the PC.

- You are using the PC to develop a mainframe application consisting of many programs. Some portions of that application are already complete. To test the new or changed portions of the application on the PC, you need to be able to run the entire suite of programs including the ones that need no further testing. Compiling, and perhaps linking, these other modules allows them to run faster and more efficiently.

- You are thinking about developing *cooperative processing* applications: those that run partly on the mainframe and partly on networked PC workstations. You plan to install CICS/OS2, APPC, or some other facility to make the programs cooperate over the network. At some point, you will need to compile and link certain programs on the PC as well as on the mainframe.

We mentioned earlier that the typical mainframe development cycle is edit, compile, link-edit, and go (execute). The typical Workbench testing cycle on the PC is edit, check, and animate. In either case, many iterations are needed before testing is complete. If the application is destined for mainframe use, you would move the completed source code to the mainframe production source library. From there, you would recompile it on the mainframe and link-edit it into the production executable library.

Even if your program consists of only one source file, it still uses subprograms to do I/O or make other calls to the operating system. In an assembler program, you would code these subprogram calls by using macros. In a higher-level language such as COBOL, the subprogram calls are transparent to you; the compiler puts them in where needed. This is true whether you run on the mainframe or the PC. Link-editing resolves memory addresses so that the modules can work together. There are several ways to link-edit. A link-editor can create one standalone executable file from the main program and all subprograms. Alternatively, it can link-edit the main program with code that will call some or all of the subprograms dynamically at runtime.

You may ask, "If every COBOL program calls runtime subprograms, how can the Micro Focus Animator let me test my programs without link-editing?" The Workbench calls all runtime subprograms on behalf of your program at runtime. Because the Workbench contains a **shared runtime system,** COBOL programs running under the Animator or under the Workbench Execute menu can access all required runtime support subprograms. You can make all of your COBOL programs share the same copy of the runtime system. Since the runtime service routines need not be duplicated within the COBOL programs themselves, the COBOL executable programs can be much smaller.

Important: If your application calls subprograms written in languages other than COBOL or mainframe assembler, you will need to link-edit. Why is mainframe assembler an exception? The MF/370 add-on product translates mainframe assembler programs to run on the PC. Recent versions of MF/370 support the RTS.

8.2 The Micro Focus Compiler

8.2.1 Files Used and Produced by the Code Generator

Input files. In an earlier chapter, we described the files used and produced by the Micro Focus Syntax Checker. You may recall that the syntax checker is the first pass of the compiler. The object code generation facility is the second pass. The code generator reads the **intermediate code file (.INT)** file from the checker. The code generator also can use the same **directives files** that the checker uses, such as COBOL.DIR.

Output files. Depending on the directive you specify, the generator can produce an object code file in one of two formats, **.GNT** or **.OBJ.**

- **Generated code file (.GNT):** According to Micro Focus, .GNT code executes faster than .INT code for CPU-bound operations. I/O-bound operations are substantially the same. Generated code program files are relocatable and must be run with the shared runtime system; .GNT files cannot be link-edited. (However, Micro Focus does offer a BUILD utility that combines .INT, .GNT, and .BIN files with the shared runtime system to create an .EXE file.)

- **Object code file (.OBJ):** The .OBJ file is the industry standard format for object code files on the PC. An .OBJ file is not executable; it must be link-edited to create an .EXE file. You can link an .OBJ file with programs written in languages other than COBOL. Only the required parts of the shared runtime system need to be linked into the .EXE file.
- **Printed output files.** If desired, you can also request a source listing file (extension **.LST**) or an object code listing in PC assembler language (extension **.GRP**).
- **Optional output files for debugging with Xilerator.** Depending on directives, the code generator will also produce .XLS and .PL output files for use with Micro Focus Xilerator.

If you want to animate: .GNT and .OBJ files cannot be animated. Only .INT files can be animated. If you want to animate, delete the .GNT and .OBJ files before you recheck the program with the ANIM directive. Otherwise, the Animator will find those old object files and run your program at machine speed instead of animating it. The presence of other executable files will make the Animator ignore the .INT file.

8.2.2 Compiler Directives

In Chapter 5, we introduced the concept of Syntax Checker and compiler directives. Most directives apply only to the syntax checking stage of the compilation process. The other directives apply to the code generation stage, or to both stages. We will not try to present every compiler directive here. Some directives support complex mixed-language programming on the PC, add-on products, or compatibility with older Micro Focus products. A complete reference guide to directives appears in Appendix B of the *COBOL/2 Operating Guide.* You can also look up directives in the On-line Information hypertext help system. You can supply directives in $SET commands in the program source file, in directives files, or as options on the Compile menu screen.

- **64KSECT** tells the code generator that your program has one or more sections that will generate more than 64K bytes of object code. To prevent overflow, the code generator will break up your program at paragraph boundaries rather than section boundaries. This directive is turned off by default.
- **ASMLIST** tells the code generator to produce a PC assembler language code listing. This listing shows both the assembler language statements and the PC object code. You can see what subroutines your program is calling from the runtime libraries. Used along with ASMLIST, **SOURCEASM** will include the COBOL source lines in the PC assembler language listing as well.
- **BOUND** tells the code generator to produce code for subscript and index range checking at runtime. This directive is on by default. It should be turned on during testing and debugging. For programs running in production mode on the PC, BOUND should be turned off for greater efficiency.
- **BOUNDOPT** internally truncates USAGE DISPLAY values that are being used as subscripts. The table addressing code will evaluate only the number

of digits needed to represent the actual number of table entries. The BOUNDOPT directive is on by default and should be left on, because it improves runtime performance.

- **CASE** keeps external symbols from being converted to uppercase. This lets you CALL subprograms in case-dependent languages such as C.
- **DEFFILE** makes the code generator produce a .DEF file. This is needed if you want to link-edit to create an OS/2 .DLL file.
- **DYNAM** works something like the mainframe DYNAM compiler option, in that it allows subprogram CANCEL statements to take effect. If NODYNAM is specified, called subprograms behave as though they are static; thus, CANCEL statements have no effect.
- **EANIM** sets up the .OBJ output file with information for runtime debugging utilities such as Microsoft CodeView.
- **GANIM** creates .XLS and .PL output files for use with Micro Focus Xilerator. Xilerator is used mostly for debugging mixed-language programs.
- **LIST** by itself tells the compiler to send the listing to the screen. **LIST**"*filename*" creates an output source listing file, with the specified filename. **LIST()** creates an output source listing file with the same name as your program, and with filename extension .LST.
- **LINKLIB**"*library1+...+libraryN*" lets you specify the names of the runtime support libraries that you will want the linker to use. The default is "COBLIB+COBAPI" which invokes the MS-DOS version of the shared runtime system. Other options are discussed below. Use a plus sign between each library name. If you omit a library filename extension, .LIB will be assumed. (At link-edit time, if you wish, you can still override these LINKLIB names by specifying the NOD option to the link-editor.)
- **LITLINK** tells the compiler to treat all subprogram names in COBOL CALL statements as external symbols. This allows subprogram linkage to be resolved at link-edit time rather than at runtime, to produce static subprogram calls. If LITLINK is off, which is the default, only subprogram names preceded by underscores are treated as external symbols.
- **NOTRICKLE** tells the compiler that you do not have any bad PERFORM ranges. These include overlapping PERFORM ranges, as well as routines that can be entered both by being PERFORMED and by having program execution sequence "falling into" it from the routine directly above. If your program abides by these restrictions, you can specify NOTRICKLE. This directive lets the code generator produce more efficient code. (See STATS directive, discussed below.)
- **OMF**"GNT" tells the compiler to produce generated (GNT) code for use with the Micro Focus shared runtime system. If you need to specify a name for your .GNT output file other than the default, supply the additional directive **GNT**"*filename*.GNT".
- **OMF**"OBJ" produces standard object code files (OBJ) to be link-edited for standalone use. If you need to specify a name for your .OBJ output file other than the default, supply the additional directive **OBJ**"*filename*.OBJ".
- **OPT**"0", **OPT**"1", **OPT**"2" represent compiler optimization levels. Ordinarily it is advisable to leave this at level 2.

- **OPTSIZE** and **OPTSPEED** let you choose whether to optimize the object code for small size (memory) or fast execution speed. These directives are mutually exclusive, with OPTSIZE the default.
- **STATS** produces a listing that shows overlapping PERFORM ranges or code that jumps out of a PERFORM range. If the STATS listing shows no bad PERFORM ranges, then it is safe to specify the NOTRICKLE directive the next time you compile.

8.3 The Execute Menu

8.3.1 Compiling from the Execute Menu

The Execute menu, shown in Figure 8.1, allows you to compile and run programs using the Micro Focus shared runtime system. It also provides access to the operating system command line prompt. To get to the Execute menu, press **F4=execute** on the Micro Focus Mainframe Developer's Environment main menu. Pressing **F2=compile** on the Execute menu brings up the Compile menu, shown in Figure 8.2.

```
Execute-COBOL-Application──────────────────────────────────────────────────
F1=help F2=compile F3=run F4=OS-command                          Escape
```

Figure 8.1 Execute menu

```
* Micro Focus COBOL/2 Code Generator        Version 2.5.27
* Copyright (C) 1985,1991 Micro Focus Ltd.       URN   AXUPA/ZZ0/86353
* Accepted - OMF(GNT)
* Accepted - OMF(gnt)
* Accepted - EDITOR(mf)
* Accepted - BOUND
* Data = 000001084 Code = 000001824 Dictionary = 000003286




Compile──────────────────────────────Nolist──Bound───────────Ins-Caps-Num-Scroll
F1=help F2=dir F3=asm F4=list F5=bound                   F9/F10=options Esc
File K:\COBOL\MFWBBOOK\CUST                                      <-' Ctrl
```

Figure 8.2 Compile menu with code generation messages

The Compile menu controls the object code generation facility, which is the second pass of the Micro Focus compiler. (The syntax checker is the first pass.) This menu facility does not compile your source code "from scratch." Instead, it takes the intermediate code output file (.INT) from the syntax checker and generates an object code file. By default, this menu facility produces a .GNT (generated object code) output file. By using the OMF"OBJ" directive you can make it produce an .OBJ file instead.

Directory of .INT files. **F2=dir** causes the screen to display a listing of all .INT (intermediate code files) in the current directory path. An .INT file is eligible for the code generation step, which is what the Compile menu provides. The directory menu at the bottom of the screen uses the same Micro Focus directory facility as the Editor and Animator file load function, so its operation should be familiar to you. The file directory forms a point-and-shoot light-bar menu for selecting an .INT file for compilation. Use the up and down cursor arrow keys until you have highlighted the program that you want to compile. When you press the enter key, the selected filename will appear at the **FILE:** prompt at the bottom of the menu. Pressing the enter key again will begin the compilation process.

Assembly code listing. **F3=asm** is a toggle switch for the ASMLIST directive. When this switch is on, **Asm** will appear on the information line. The code generator will produce an assembly language listing.

Where printed output will go. **F4=list** is a toggle switch for the printed output destination. Available settings are **List, Nolist,** and **List-File. Nolist** (or blank) produces no output listing. **List-File** passes the directive **LIST(*progname*.GRP)** to the code generator. **Print** passes the directive **LIST(lst)** to the code generator. If you did not request an assembly code listing, the printed output will contain only a short message showing the name and size of the generated code.

Index/subscript bounds checking. **F5=bound** is a toggle switch for the BOUND directive. This directive causes the checker/compiler to generate code to check for indexes and subscripts that are out of bounds. When you run your program, any subscript or index range violation will trigger an error message. When the BOUND toggle switch is on, the word **Bound** will appear on the information line.

Entering directives in the Compile menu buffer. You can enter directives on the Compile menu that affect that one compilation session only. Pressing **F10** opens an area at the bottom of the Compile menu for entry of directives. After entering the directives (with a space between each), press the enter key. This in itself does not *activate* the directives. To use the directives you have entered, you must press **F9** to make the indicator **opts-on** appear on the information line.

Beginning the compilation process. To begin compilation, enter the name of the .INT file at the filename prompt on the Compile menu, and press the enter key.

Stopping compilation. To terminate a compilation that is in progress, press the **Ctrl+Break** keys. However, if you use add-on products for SQL support such as the OS/2 ES Database Manager, stopping compilation could cause SQL database corruption. In that case, you would be better off to allow the compiler to finish on its own.

8.3.2 The Run Menu

Pressing **F3=run** on the Execute menu brings up the Run menu, shown in Figure 8.3.

```
Run-without-Parmpass───────────────────────────────Ins-Caps-Num-Scroll
F1=help F2=dir F3=switches F4=Parmpass-on           F9/F10=set-cmd-ln Esc
File K:\COBOL\MFWBBOOK\CUST                                   <-' Ctrl
```

Figure 8.3 Run menu

Directory of program files. **F2=dir** causes the screen to display a listing of all .GNT, .INT, .EXE, .BIN, and .LBR files in the current directory path. Here again, all of the usual Micro Focus directory display functions are available. The file directory forms a point-and-shoot light-bar menu for selecting a program file for execution. Use the up and down cursor arrow keys until you have highlighted the program that you want to run. When you press the enter key, the selected filename will appear at the **FILE:** prompt at the bottom of the menu. Pressing the enter key again will begin program execution.

Suppose you have more than one type of executable file for your program. If you enter the program name *with a filename extension* at the FILE: prompt at the bottom of the screen, the Workbench will run that file. Otherwise, if you enter just the program name with no extension, the Workbench will look for .GNT, .INT, .EXE, .BIN, and .LBR files in that order. If none of those are found, the Workbench will look for a filename without an extension. Incidentally, .BIN files are PC assembler language subprograms that observe certain conventions.

Passing parameters to your program. Many PC programs are designed to be run from the operating system command prompt. These programs require you to enter certain parameters or runtime switches after the program name on the command line. On the Run menu, you can enter command line parameters that the Workbench will pass to your program. Pressing **F10** opens an area at the bottom of the Run menu for entry of parameters. After you finish entering parameters, press the enter key. This in itself does not *activate* the parameters. To use the command line parameters you have entered, you must press **F9** to make the indicator **cmd-ln-on** appear on the information line.

At runtime, the COBOL program receives these command line parameters when it executes the following COBOL statement:

```
ACCEPT data-name FROM COMMAND-LINE.
```

That statement moves the entire series of command line parameters, delimited by spaces, into the field *data-name*.

The PARM Passer facility offers another way to simulate mainframe operating system job control language PARMs. You can set up a parameter file ahead of time with PARM Passer. Before running your program, use **F4=Parmpass-on** to turn on the Workbench PARM Passer facility. This switch allows your program to receive its entry from the PARM Passer file. If PARM Passer is on at runtime, the information line will say **Run-with-Parmpass** instead of **Run-without-Parmpass**. The next chapter will show you how to set up parm file entries under the PARM Passer.

Programmable runtime switches. **F3=switches** brings up a menu that lets you use function keys to set the value of COBOL runtime switches (Figure 8.4). Switches on this menu are logical-valued switches: off or on. If a switch is on, it will appear on the information line with a plus in front of it. Otherwise, it will appear with a minus. When you are finished changing switch settings, press the enter key to activate the new values.

- **Switches 0 (zero) through 8** are external switches for your program's use. A Micro Focus COBOL program can access switches 0 through 8 under the names **SWITCH-0** through **SWITCH-8**. External switches 0 through 7 also are available under the names **UPSI-0** through **UPSI-7.** The COBOL SPE-CIAL-NAMES paragraph lets you assign mnemonic names to these switches or to their "on" or "off" conditions. External switches may come in handy if you have inherited old IBM System/360-era DOS programs with UPSI switches.

- **Switch D** turns on ANSI COBOL debugging. This feature affects only those programs containing a WITH DEBUGGING MODE statement. If switch D is on, then all USE FOR DEBUGGING statements in your program will function.

- **Switch G** changes the size of buffers used for sequential file I/O. If switch G is off, buffers will be 4K bytes. Turning switch G on will reduce buffer size to 512 bytes. This can slow performance, but if you are really in a pinch for memory, it may give you a little breathing room.

```
Switches-(-0,-1,-2,-3,-4,-5,-6,-7,-8,-D,-G)----------------------------------
F1=help 0-8=Cobol-switches D=ANSI-Debug G=Run-Time-switch   <-'=set-switches Esc
```

Figure 8.4 Switches menu

Another way to enter runtime switches is through use of the COBSW environment variable. Here is the command for setting this variable:

```
SET COBSW=(switches)
```

where *switches* is a list of switch settings. Precede each logical-valued switch with a plus or minus to indicate whether it should be on or off. List the switch settings consecutively with no spaces in between. The COBOL compiler provides some other switches besides those specified on the Switches menu. Some are for compatibility with older Micro Focus products; others take advantage of certain PC hardware features. In general, these are not a major concern for mainframe programmers. If you are setting one of the few switches that take a numeric value (as opposed to off/on), precede it with a slash character ("/"). A discussion of some other programmable runtime switches is in the "Running" chapter in the *COBOL/2 Operating Guide*.

Starting program execution. To begin program execution, enter the name of the program file at the filename prompt on the Run menu, and press the enter key.

8.3.3 Operating System Command Prompt

The operating system command prompt is available both as an item on the Execute menu and as a hotkey combination. In either case, you can enter any operating system command, or the name of a program or command file to be run. In effect, the Micro Focus Workbench provides a **DOS shell.** This is somewhat similar to entering TSO commands while in mainframe ISPF/PDF. You can use all the features of TSO without having to leave ISPF/PDF.

Use common sense here. You can delete files, but be careful not to delete, rename, or move any files that any Workbench function is using! A DOS shell is no place to run disk reorganization utilities. Running CHKDSK from within Workbench may corrupt files. *Use disk maintenance utilities only when nothing else is running on your workstation.*

Do not try to use the MS-DOS or OS/2 **SET** command from the command prompt within the Workbench. The new environment variable settings will not become available to the Workbench session. You can, however, use the DOS shell prompt to change the current default directory for the Workbench session.

Shift+Ctrl+Break, the hotkey combination for the command line prompt, is available from any Workbench menu, not just from this one. It brings up an MS-DOS or OS/2 command line prompt at the bottom of the screen. Whatever text that was on the Workbench screen will scroll up out of the way to make room for command line input and output. Typing EXIT at the command line prompt and pressing the enter key will bring back whatever Workbench menu was active.

Pressing **F4=OS-command** on the Execute menu causes the OS-command menu to appear, shown in Figure 8.5. Here again, text from the Workbench screen will scroll out of the way to make room for command line input and output. The difference here is that the OS-command menu will reappear at the bottom of the screen as soon as the response to your command line input has finished. A shortcut key on this menu, **F2=dir/w,** displays the current directory in abbreviated form (filenames only). If you want a complete directory, type **DIR** on the command line and press the enter key.

```
OS-command──────────────────────────────────────────────Ins-Caps-Num-Scroll
F1=help F2=dir/w              Enter OS command below                    Esc
Command:
```

Figure 8.5 OS-command prompt menu

8.4 Compiling from the Command Line

You can run the Micro Focus COBOL/2 compiler directly from the operating system command line prompt. This method provides both the checker and code generator passes. Use the following syntax:

```
COBOL sourcefile,objectfile,sourcelist,objectlist,directives;
```

Use a comma to indicate the position of any parameter you omit. Omitting a parameter will cause the compiler to assume the default value. If you enter the word COBOL followed by no parameters at all, the compiler will prompt you to enter the parameters one by one.

- *sourcefile* is your program source file. If you specify no extension, the compiler assumes .CBL.
- *objectfile* is the name of the object output file. By default, the file will be named the same as your source file, but with extension .OBJ.
- *sourcelist* is the source code listing output file. By default, the file will be named the same as your source file, but with extension .LST. If you don't want a source listing, set this parameter to NUL. If you terminate the command line with a semicolon before you get to this parameter, no source listing will be produced.
- *objectlist* is the object code listing output file. By default, the file will be named the same as your source file, but with extension .GRP. If you don't want an object listing, set this parameter to NUL. If you terminate the command line with a semicolon before you get to this parameter, no object listing will be produced.
- *directives* are checker/compiler directives. Separate directives by spaces and do not break any directive at the end of a line.

8.5 Link-Editing and the Shared Runtime System

8.5.1 Using the Linker

The Workbench lets you link-edit your .OBJ files to create two types of .EXE (executable) files. One type is linked with the static-linked runtime system and the other type uses a shared runtime system. We will show how to link-edit both types of program files.

Throughout the Micro Focus manuals, you may see various references to *Microsoft utilities.* Micro Focus Incorporated is licensed to distribute certain Microsoft link-editing and debugging utilities along with the Workbench. If you have worked with the Microsoft C compiler or other Microsoft language products before, you might already be familiar with some of these utilities.

To run the linker from the command line prompt, use the following syntax:

```
LINK obj-file1+...obj-fileN,exe-file,map-file,linklib1+...+linklibN,
def-file,options;
```

All parameters are optional. If you simply enter LINK and nothing else, the linker will ask you for each filename. If you omit some other parameter, enter the comma delimiter so that the linker will know which parameter was omitted.

- *obj-file1* through *obj-fileN* represent your object file(s) that you plan to link-edit. You might need to link more than one object file if you have COBOL subprogram CALL statements.

- *exe-file* is the name of the executable output file. If you omit this parameter, the executable output file will have the name of the first .OBJ file, but with an extension of .EXE.
- *mapfile* is an output file with extension .MAP, showing linkage symbols and addresses.
- *linklib1* through *linklibN* are the link libraries containing runtime support routines. In the following sections we will discuss the link library names to use.
- *def-file* is an OS/2 module definition file. You would use this if you intend to create an OS/2 .DLL (dynamic linked library) instead of an .EXE file.
- *options* are optional linker directives, described in the chapter "Linking and Library Management" in the *COBOL/2 Operating Guide.*

8.5.2 Linking with LCOBOL: Static Linked Runtime System

Using the static-linked runtime system, you can make executable files that run without support from any other files. Each program must be linked with its own copy of the runtime support modules that it needs. As a result, the .EXE program files will be larger. To create a standalone .EXE file to run under MS-DOS, use link library names **LCOBOL+COBAPI.** To create a standalone .EXE file to run under OS/2, use link library names **LCOBOL+OS2.**

8.5.3 Linking with COBLIB: Shared Runtime System

When you link an .EXE file that is intended to use the shared runtime system, you don't actually link it with the runtime system itself. Instead, you link it with "stubs" that will call the required modules from the shared runtime system at runtime. The .EXE files will be smaller, but the runtime library must be present for the program to run. To create an .EXE file using the shared runtime system under MS-DOS, use link library names **COBLIB+COBAPI.** To create an .EXE file using the shared runtime system under OS/2, use link library names **COBLIB+OS2.**

The shared runtime libraries come with the COBOL/2 compiler. For MS-DOS, the runtime library is called **COBLIB.DLE.** For OS/2, the runtime library is called **COBLIB.DLL.** These files let you run your own .EXE programs on other PC workstations that do not have the Workbench. Check file creation dates to make sure that you are running with the most current versions of COBLIB.DLE or COBLIB.DLL. Delete all versions from your system except for the most recent. As a licensed Workbench user, you can package these COBOL/2 runtime system files along with your own .EXE programs without any additional charge.

8.5.4 Using RTE: Toolset Run-Time Environment

The Run-Time Environment (RTE) that comes with the Micro Focus Toolset is an enhanced version of the shared runtime system supplied with the COBOL/2 compiler. Since the Workbench includes the Toolset, all Workbench users have the Toolset RTE. The Toolset RTE lets you execute .INT or .GNT files without link-editing. It also accepts .EXE files linked for use with the COBOL/2 shared runtime system, shown in the previous section. (The RTE will *not* run .EXE files that use the *static-linked* runtime system; these have to run from the operating system prompt.) You can run large programs with the RTE. It contains a memory manager that cleans up unused memory and swaps storage out to disk. The RTE will run under XM, letting programs use memory in protected mode above the one-megabyte line under MS-DOS.

To run programs under the Toolset RTE, you do not necessarily need to have the Workbench available on the workstation. You will need to have **COBLIB.DLE** (for MS-DOS) or **COBLIB.DLL** (for OS/2). You also will need to have the RTE library **COBENV.DLE** or **COBENV.DLL,** and/or the RTE shell, which consists of **RUN.EXE** and **SHELL.LBR.** The Toolset RTE is part of the **Operating System Extension (OSX)** group of programs. This means that if you plan to distribute the Toolset RTE to other workstations along with your own applications, a license fee is involved.

8.5.5 Link-Editing from the WDE Menu

The WDE Compile menu. You can link-edit from the Workbench menu system, not just from the command line. This facility is available from the **Workbench Development Environment (WDE)** main menu, shown in Figure 8.6. To get to the WDE, press **F9=Workbench** on the Mainframe Development Environment (MDE) main menu. Then press **F5=compile** to get to the WDE compile and link menu, shown in Figure 8.7.

```
                  +—————————————————————————————+        Banner 0000
                  | Micro Focus COBOL/2 Workbench V2.5.19 |
                  |   Workbench Development Environment    |
                  +—————————————————————————————+


Incorporating: - Micro Focus COBOL/2, Toolset and Workbench

Highlights   - NEW - Data File Editor
             - NEW - On Line Reference
             - NEW - Mouse support in the Editor, Animator and CSI
             - NEW - Floating point support
             - NEW - Intrinsic functions
             - IMPROVED - MFXFER new interface and improved transfer support
             - IMPROVED - Configurable Editor
             - IMPROVED - Co-Writer user interface and access from Workbench
             - IMPROVED - Animate whole applications
             - Multi-dialect COBOL compiler with embedded SQL support for
               OS/2 EE and support for OS/2 PM programming
             - Mainframe size applications on DOS and OS/2

 Copyright (C) 1985,1991 Micro Focus Ltd.              Issued Apr 16th 1 991
Micro-Focus-COBOL/2-Workbench—————————————————————————————————
F1=help F2=edit F3=check F4=animate F5=compile F6=run F7=library F8=build F9=WFL
F10=directory                                           Alt Ctrl Escape
```

Figure 8.6 Workbench Development Environment (WDE) main menu

```
Compile-to-OBJ-+-Link—————————————Nolist—Bound—Litlink————Ins-Caps-Num-Scroll
F1=help F2=dir F3=asm F4=list F5=bound F6=GNT F7=litlink     F9/F10=options Esc
File K:\COBOL\MFWBBOOK\CUST                                           <-' Ctrl
```

Figure 8.7 WDE Compile (and link) menu

Returning to the MDE. Pressing **F9** on the WDE will *not* get you back to the MDE. Instead, press the **Escape** key on the WDE main menu. You will see a message at the bottom of the screen that says, **Exit from the Micro Focus COBOL/2 Workbench ? Y/N.** Pressing **Y** will not shut down the Workbench; it will simply bring you back to the MDE.

The WDE Compile menu is much like the MDE Compile menu shown above in Figure 8.2, except it has two more function key switch settings. These switch settings let you compile and link-edit in one session.

- **F6** cycles through three settings for the type of executable output you want to produce. The active setting is visible on the information line. **Compile-to-GNT** sets the OMF(GNT) directive. **Compile-to-OBJ** sets the OMF(OBJ) directive. **Compile-to-OBJ-+-Link** sets the OMF(OBJ) directive and also invokes the link-editor after compilation has finished. The link-editor will use the COBLIB+COBAPI link libraries for the COBOL/2 shared runtime system under MS-DOS.
- **F7=litlink** turns on the LITLINK compiler directive, discussed above.

The WDE Link menu. The link-editor is also available on the WDE Link menu. Holding down the **ALT** key on the WDE main menu brings up the WDE ALT key Options menu, shown in Figure 8.8. Pressing **F7=link** on this menu brings up the WDE Linker and Library Manager menu, shown in Figure 8.9. This menu gives you somewhat more flexibility in link-editing your compiled programs.

```
Micro-Focus-COBOL/2-Workbench——————————————————————————————————————————--
F1=help F2=screens F3=diff F4=hexedit F5=session F6=analyzer F7=link
F8=data-file-editor F9=file-finder F10=Co-Writer
```

*Figure 8.8 WDE **Alt** key Options menu*

On the WDE Linker and Library Manager menu, **F2=COBLIB/LCOBOL** lets you choose the type of executable file to produce. The **F2** key cycles through three settings that appear on the information line: **LCOBOL(EXE)**, **COBLIB(EXE)**, and **COBLIB(DLL)**.

- **LCOBOL(EXE)** creates an .EXE output file linked with the static-linked runtime system.
- **COBLIB(EXE)** creates an .EXE output file linked with the shared runtime system.
- **COBLIB(DLL)** creates an OS/2 .DLL (dynamic link library) output file, used for subroutines called by other programs.

Make sure that the current directory for your Workbench session contains the files that you want to link-edit. On the **Command Line:** at the bottom of this menu, enter the name of the .OBJ (object) file that you want to link-edit. Omit the .OBJ extension. If you have more than one .OBJ file, separate the filenames by plus signs ("+"). Once you have entered the names, press the enter key to activate the Microsoft link-editor.

```
                                                              BANN0014
                          The Link Menu
                          ──────────────

This menu allows you to easily create stand alone executable files from within
Workbench. You have two main options when Linking your programs :

LCOBOL   - Linking with LCOBOL places all of the Run Time support required into
           the .EXE file.

COBLIB   - COBLIB linking creates a much smaller .EXE file because the Run Time
           support is kept separately (in COBLIB.DLL/.DLE). This also means that
           on OS/2 only one copy of the Run Time support is loaded for ALL
           COBLIB linked applications running. Using COBLIB you also have the
           option of making your program into a .DLL which can be dynamically
           loaded by your main program.

   Please refer to your PC Programmer's Guide for more information on deciding
   how best to create your applications.

   Note that you should not specify any extension when typing the filenames
Linker-and-Library-Manager──-COBLIB(EXE)────────────────────-Ins-Caps-Num-Scroll
F1=help F2=COBLIB/LCOBOL F4=Link F5=Lib                                    Escape
Command Line:                                                              <-'
```

Figure 8.9 WDE Linker and Library Manager menu

On the WDE Link menu, the **F4=Link** key brings up the Microsoft link-editor, without passing any command line parameters to it. The link-editor will prompt you to enter each parameter one by one. In like manner, **F5=Lib** brings up the Microsoft Library Manager.

8.6 Running Programs from the Command Line

Running an .EXE program file. You can run .EXE programs from the operating system command line prompt simply by keying the program name (without the .EXE extension) and pressing the enter key. For example, to run the program **CUST.EXE**, type **CUST** at the command prompt and press the enter key. If the .EXE program was linked with the static-linked runtime system, it can run as a standalone module. If the .EXE program was linked with the shared runtime system, the runtime system library must be available at runtime. Here is the full command line syntax:

```
[path]progname [(switches)] [parms]
```

In this command, *path* is the drive and directory path of the program. You need this only if the program is not in the current directory. *progname* is the filename without the .EXE extension. *(switches)* are any programmable or runtime switches that the program uses. *parms* are any command line parameters required by the program.

Running .INT or .GNT program files. To run an .INT or a .GNT program file from the command prompt, you will need to run the Toolset Run-Time Environment with your own program as a subprogram under it. To do this, use the following format:

```
[XM] RUN [switches] progname
```

The RUN command initiates the runtime system. In this command, *progname* is the filename without the .INT or .GNT extension, and *switches* are any programmable or runtime switches that the program uses. You can also use this RUN command to run an .EXE program linked with the COBOL/2 shared runtime system, but not a static-linked .EXE program. Under MS-DOS, specify XM to use the runtime system under Micro Focus memory management.

If you enter RUN or XM RUN by itself, the RTE will act as a *runtime shell*. At the prompt, you can enter names of programs to be run or DOS commands.

Running programs with PARM Passer. If your .INT or .GNT program needs a PARM Passer file, you will need to run the program under the PARM Passer utility. Use the following command line format:

```
[XM] RUN PARMPASS progname
```

To animate a program that requires PARM Passer input from the command line, use the following format:

```
[XM] ANIMATE PARMPASS END progname
```

8.7 Performance Considerations on the PC Workstation

Micro Focus discusses some performance pointers in the chapter "Writing Programs" in the *COBOL/2 Operating Guide*. For large or frequently run programs on the PC, you may want to consider the following issues.

PERFORM and PERFORM THRU. The Micro Focus COBOL/2 compiler can optimize much more efficiently if you avoid using overlapping or unstructured PERFORM and PERFORM THRU ranges. Use the STATS directive to produce a listing of faulty PERFORM ranges. If the program is clean, then use the NOTRICKLE directive the next time you compile it. Also, remove ALTER statements from your program. Not only are they unstructured, they also prevent the COBOL/2 compiler from optimizing PERFORM statements in that program.

Memory alignment. Memory alignment can offer slight performance gains on 80x86-based workstations. Data items that are used most frequently should be aligned on even-byte boundaries. To force an item to align on an even-byte boundary, place it under a separate 01 level, or place it an even number of bytes from the beginning of an 01 level.

Conditions (comparisons). Conditions (in IF or PERFORM statements) are evaluated in the order that they appear, just as they are on a mainframe. If you put the condition first that is likeliest to evaluate to a false result, then in many cases the program will be able to skip the remaining conditions. Similarly, if you put the condition first that is easiest to evaluate, and the more difficult conditions later, then in many cases the program will be able to skip the more difficult tests. Comparisons that use EQUAL or NOT EQUAL evaluate faster than those using LESS THAN or GREATER THAN.

Tables. For table handling, turn off the BOUND directive (by using NOBOUND) after testing is complete. Use the BOUNDOPT directive to optimize subscript handling.

Internal sorts. The COBOL/2 compiler uses an internal sort algorithm that is fast, but may not work with large files. To use another algorithm at runtime intended for larger files, set runtime switch +B2.

Link-editing for CALLed programs. Programs using COBOL CALL statements will run faster if link-edited with the modules that they CALL. Within the called program, access to working storage fields is faster than access to linkage section fields. If you plan to use a parameter item frequently, move it from the linkage section to a working storage field before using it.

Libraries for floating-point support. If you use floating-point arithmetic with the shared runtime system, you will need to have the correct library module available at runtime. For MS-DOS, the module is **COBFP87.DLE.** For OS/2, the module is **COBFP87.DLL.** The shared runtime system will load floating-point support automatically if your program needs it.

If you link-edit with the static-linked runtime system, you will need to include the name of a floating-point library. For MS-DOS, use link libraries **LCOBOL+COBFP87D+COBAPI.** For OS/2, use **LCOBOL+COBFP87O+OS2** (the "**O**" is the letter **O,** not the numeral zero).

The floating-point support routines sense whether your PC workstation has an 80x87 math coprocessor. If present, it will use the coprocessor's instruction set. Otherwise, it will use floating-point emulation routines.

Large programs. The Intel 80x86 architecture addresses memory in 64K byte segments. If your program contains more than 64K of either executable code or data, you may have to make sure that code and data do not cross 64K boundaries. If you get a code generation error or runtime error for the code segment, you can use the 64KSECT directive, shown above. If data segment code is larger than 64K, recompile with the REF, CHIP"16", and FLAG(CHIP) directives. This gives you a listing showing exactly where data items cross 64K boundaries. Insert FILLER bytes or rearrange items as needed so that no data item crosses a 64K boundary.

8.8 Exercises

1. Bring up the Compile menu under the Workbench MDE. Compile the sample program CUST.INT to produce .GNT object code. Run CUST.GNT with the Workbench MDE Run menu. Run CUST.GNT again from the command line prompt under the Toolset RTE, using the RUN command.

2. Use the WDE menu to compile CUST.INT to produce .OBJ object code. Link-edit the program to produce an .EXE file that uses the COBOL/2 shared runtime system. Run CUST.EXE directly from the command line prompt.

3. From the command line prompt, link CUST.OBJ with the static-linked runtime system libraries. Run CUST.EXE directly from the command line prompt.

9

Mainframe Testing on the PC

9.1 EBCDIC versus ASCII Considerations

9.1.1 Bridging the Mainframe and PC Environments

The PC workstation has evolved with a much different design philosophy than the IBM mainframe. The mainframe serves the needs of a department or organization: large databases, scheduled batch jobs, and multiuser telecommunications networks. The PC workstation, though it may communicate with mainframes or other PCs, serves the needs of a single user with faster response and better user interface capabilities than a mainframe can provide. The PC is a much more recent machine; IBM mainframes inherit much of their instruction set, file handling methods, and job control language from the System/360. Since the architecture of the PC is unlike that of the mainframe, certain obstacles must be overcome to use the PC for developing mainframe programs.

Some issues affect program development more than others. The portability of ANSI COBOL largely insulates the programmer from the fact that the PC has its own architecture and instruction set. As long as the same COBOL source code produces the same test results, the source can be ported back to the mainframe and recompiled. Hardware representation can produce small differences in math precision, but in most situations, test results are the same. The main concerns arise from the fact that the PC is an interactive machine with a different file system, designed to use ASCII rather than EBCDIC to represent text data.

9.1.2 Which Files Need Translating?

Program source. To test a mainframe application on the PC, both program source and test data must be available. You can create new programs on the PC with an ASCII text editor. But what about maintenance? The vast majority of mainframe shops keep their program source libraries in EBCDIC on the mainframe. The COBOL/2 Compiler and Workbench accept COBOL source only in ASCII. Before using the PC to maintain an existing program, you must download the program and translate it to ASCII. Program source translation is straightforward. The Micro Focus conversion utilities even handle source program files that contain embedded non-ASCII bytes, such as control codes for screen processing.

Alternatively, if all program maintenance and development is done on the PC, it's practical to maintain the mainframe source and copy libraries in ASCII on a PC network server. This method lets you skip the initial download and ASCII translation steps. Whatever method you use, after testing is complete, you will need to upload EBCDIC source to the mainframe for the final compile and link-edit.

Test data. With test data, you also have the choice of downloading it from the mainframe or building it from scratch on the PC. The Workbench lets you work with both ASCII and EBCDIC formats for data files. The appropriate format to use depends on several factors.

There is no easy or practical way of dealing with a mixture of ASCII and EBCDIC data files and variables in the same COBOL program. You will need to settle upon one character set or the other, and convert data files as needed for consistency. The Mainframe Development Environment (MDE) defaults to the EBCDIC character set for data files and program literals. (As we have seen, you still use ASCII program source files.) If you plan to work primarily with ASCII data files, Micro Focus suggests that you consider using the WDE main menu instead of the MDE. How does the ASCII versus EBCDIC setting come into play? The mainframe language dialect toggle switches on the MDE Checker menu bring in directives files containing the CHARSET(EBCDIC) directive. Therefore, if you set the language toggle switch to OSVS, VSC2(1), VSC2(2), or VSC2(3), you will get CHARSET(EBCDIC). If you set the language toggle switch to blank, the CHARSET directive will default to ASCII.

Let's look at another EBCDIC/ASCII conversion issue. How do you convert a file when the same record definition contains both character (pic X) and numeric (COMP, COMP-3, etc.) data fields? The ASCII or EBCDIC character set applies only to text fields, not to packed, binary, or floating-point numeric. For example, suppose a COMP field in your file contains a numeric hexadecimal value not intended to be interpreted as a text character. If an ASCII/EBCDIC translation program mistakenly converts the COMP field to some other value, it will corrupt the hex value. Therefore, the conversion utility should perform ASCII/EBCDIC translation only on the character fields. The Workbench File Loader (WFL) utility lets you specify a set of translation masks to identify fields for conversion.

How character set affects test results. Using ASCII files will lead to some differences in test results when compared with EBCDIC. In the ASCII collating sequence, numeric characters zero through 9 precede uppercase alphabetics, which in turn precede lowercase alphabetics. In EBCDIC, lowercase alphabetics precede uppercase alphabetics, which in turn precede numeric characters. Not only that, but in EBCDIC, the alpha character ranges are interspersed with special characters. Spaces and other characters are represented with different hex values. With ASCII data, the expression **"1" > "A"** would evaluate as false. With EBCDIC data, that expression would be true.

How does this affect testing? Sequential files may sort differently. Comparisons in statements such as IF or PERFORM will sometimes have different results. Indexes and pointer files will be in the ASCII collating sequence. If your program retrieves records from an indexed file or database, they may arrive in a different order from what would be the case on the mainframe.

Should you translate test data files to ASCII? Most often, the answer is no. If you work with the MDE, you may have no need to translate data files to ASCII. Under most circumstances, it is easiest to keep all test files in EBCDIC. Nevertheless, you may find it necessary to translate test data files under certain circumstances:

- You plan to check and animate your program using CHARSET(ASCII), perhaps for compatibility with other modules.
- Your test files include floating-point fields. The PC stores numeric data in IEEE format, different from the System/370 format on the mainframe. Besides performing ASCII translation, the Workbench MDECONV utility intelligently converts floating-point data fields to the PC format.
- You plan to use the OS/2 ES Database Manager or any other add-on product that requires ASCII data. Note that you can get EBCDIC versions of the IMS Option and CICS Option. EBCDIC is preferable for most users. At the time this book was written, IBM does not offer an EBCDIC version of the Database Manager.

Limitations in EBCDIC mode. If you choose to keep all of your test files in EBCDIC, a few limitations apply. First of all, the Micro Focus COBOL Editor does not handle EBCDIC files. This is not a problem because you can use either the Workbench Hex Editor or the Data File Editor. Second, if your EBCDIC program CALLs a subprogram that expects parameters in ASCII, you are responsible for translating the parameters before issuing the CALL. Finally, when using CHARSET(EBCDIC), the COBOL/2 Compiler supports only the ANSI standard forms of the ACCEPT and DISPLAY statements. It will not support the Micro Focus extensions for screen handling in EBCDIC mode. This restriction does not affect mainframe program development, because mainframe compilers do not support that type of screen handling.

9.1.3 Source Programs with Embedded Hex Codes

Embedded hex codes can be a stumbling block for ASCII/EBCDIC conversion. They mostly occur in old mainframe programs that use attribute bytes or control codes for screen handling. VS COBOL II Release 3 allows the use of hex literals in the syntax **X"*nn*"**, where printable characters represent hex values. This is the preferred method, wherever practical. Older programs may have embedded hex values that are not printable. Someone may have used a hex editor to insert these unprintable hex values into the VALUE clauses of DISPLAY-type data. These **nontext characters** are the ones you may have to watch out for!

If you know that your source files don't contain this type of embedded hex, the normal File Transfer Utility can translate between ASCII and EBCDIC during the download or upload. Otherwise, you should transfer the files in binary format without conversion, and translate them on the PC with the MDECONV utility.

9.2 Mainframe versus PC File Types

Because the PC file system is different from that of the mainframe, all files and directories are stored differently. **Only sequential files can be downloaded from the mainframe to the PC. To download any other file type, you must convert it into a sequential file on the mainframe side.** The Transfer utility will send it as a binary data stream. As the file arrives on the PC, the operating system stores it as an EBCDIC record sequential file. You must rebuild it on the PC if you want to create some other file or database format.

PC file type internal layout. COBOL/2 programs do not have to deal with the minutiae of the internal representation of each PC file type. Just as on the mainframe, access method subprograms will present the right amount of data to your program. However, if you sometimes like to program right down to the "bare metal," you can view the files with the Workbench Hex Editor or Data File Editor. The "File Formats" chapter in the *COBOL/2 Operating Guide* describes the header records and control codes used with each file type.

9.2.1 Mainframe and PC Sequential Files

EBCDIC sequential files on the PC are always stored in **record sequential format.** Line sequential files are available only in ASCII. This is because line sequential files rely on the ASCII carriage return and line feed (CRLF) characters to mark the end of each record. Since EBCDIC naturally does not support the ASCII CRLF combination, the physical record length determines the end of data in each record. Record sequential files can contain fixed or variable-length records. If record length is fixed, programs that use the file must know the correct length. For variable-length records, control bytes indicate the length of each record.

ASCII sequential files typically use **line sequential** format. Line sequential records are variable-length, with each record representing a line of ASCII text. An ASCII CRLF, x"0D0A", marks the end of each record. A Ctrl+Z character, x"1A", marks the end-of-file, which may come before the physical end of space allocated to that file on disk. If there is no hex 1A character, the end-of-file will be the end of the physical space allocation in the directory.

Record sequential is the default format for sequential files in the Mainframe Development Environment. For PC programming, if you want to create an ASCII output file, specify ORGANIZATION IS LINE SEQUENTIAL or LINE ADVANCING in the SELECT clause. Alternatively, you can use the **SEQUENTIAL"LINE"** directive when checking or compiling; this affects all sequential files in the program.

What happens at runtime when a program checked with CHARSET(EBCDIC) uses an ASCII file? No, you don't have to translate all of the PIC X fields yourself. The I/O routine translates character data from ASCII to EBCDIC in a work area after reading each record, and translates from EBCDIC to ASCII before writing.

Simulating mainframe tape files. No, you don't have to buy a nine-track tape drive for your PC just to test mainframe programs that use sequential tape files. On the PC, you can ASSIGN the file to sequential disk. Use the diskette drive to simulate multireel tape files. Whenever it's time to mount another "reel," a console message will remind you to change diskettes. Obviously, mainframe sites use multivolume tape files for high-volume datasets. Since nobody wants to spend all day changing diskettes on the PC, we suggest using a subset of mainframe data for testing. Build no more test data than you need to exercise the multivolume processing.

For a description of the multireel "tape" header record, and for other details, see the chapter "File Handling on a Personal Computer" in the *COBOL/2 Operating Guide.*

Compatibility with the ASCII environment. The PC printer, keyboard, and screen, as well as the MS-DOS and OS/2 file systems, all use ASCII. Even when you check a program with CHARSET(EBCDIC), the program still must interface with these facilities in ASCII. Because PC printers are not equipped to take EBCDIC files, EBCDIC programs automatically create ASCII output files for the PC printer. **All files assigned to LPT1 or PRN become ASCII line sequential files, regardless of the checker directives that you use.** Because the PC keyboard and screen use ASCII, console I/O routines translate characters from COBOL ACCEPT statements to EBCDIC before presenting them to the program. Similarly, the console I/O routines translate COBOL DISPLAY characters to ASCII before putting them on the screen. Finally, because the PC file system relies on ASCII filenames, the program converts filenames to ASCII. These include program names in dynamic CALL statements and filenames in ASSIGN statements.

9.2.2 Mainframe and PC Indexed Sequential Files (VSAM)

VSAM files are a cornerstone of IBM mainframe installations. Neither the MS-DOS nor the OS/2 file systems provide indexed files. The Workbench makes up for this by providing its own indexed file system, V-ISAM, that simulates VSAM KSDS. It supports both fixed-length and variable-length records, in either ASCII or EBCDIC.

Within the COBOL program, I/O statements for indexed files work as they do on the mainframe. Outside the COBOL program, work methods differ. Because the IDCAMS utility does not exist in the PC environment, other utilities take its place. You can use the **Workbench File Loader (WFL)** to convert sequential files to the indexed format (and vice versa), and to rebuild existing indexed files. You can use MS-DOS or OS/2 commands to copy, rename, or delete indexed files.

The PC file system catalogues the indexed files the same way as it does other files. The index portion of the file will have an extension of **.IDX**. The data portion, by default, will have an extension of **.DAT**, unless you assign it another name. Indexed files are organized in B-tree format.

Limitations. V-ISAM simulates only VSAM key sequenced datasets (KSDS). It does not support entry sequenced datasets (ESDS) or relative record datasets (RRDS). For ESDS, use ordinary sequential files. For RRDS, use relative files (see below). The COBOL/2 compiler does not support syntax used for old ISAM and BDAM files. IBM announced the phasing out of these access methods some time ago.

VSAM under CICS OS/2. Users of CICS OS/2 take note: CICS OS/2 contains its own VSAM file access method, based on the proprietary *Btrieve* format. VSAM files created under CICS OS/2 have a filename extension of **.VSM.** The File Control command level application programming interface is identical to the mainframe implementation, so that you can migrate your CICS OS/2 programs to the mainframe after testing. Instead of using WFL, you define VSAM files under CICS Resource Definition Online using the IBM-supplied CEDA transaction. CICS OS/2 VSAM file support is part of CICS. It is not part of the OS/2 operating system (as is SQL), nor is it part of the Workbench or COBOL/2 compiler.

As of version 2.5, OS/2 COBOL programs could get at these local CICS VSAM files only through CICS commands. The Micro Focus V-ISAM support for batch programming differs from Btrieve. Workbench v3.0 introduced support for Btrieve files. In v3.0, DFED will edit Btrieve files. WFL will convert files between Btrieve and other formats. The runtime file handler routines will detect the presence of existing Btrieve files, so that existing mainframe COBOL VSAM syntax will work with either Btrieve or V-ISAM files.

9.2.3 Relative Files

No, a relative file isn't something you would get from a genealogist. It is a disk file composed of a fixed number of slots, each identified by a **relative record number.** The term "relative record number" in this context means "relative to the beginning of the file." The relative record number becomes the file access key. Each slot has room for one record. Unused slots in a relative file remain empty. If you define the file as having variable-length records, each slot must be the maximum length. The Micro Focus Workbench lets you work with relative files on the PC. The Workbench File Loader (WFL) will convert sequential files to relative format, and vice versa. Relative files can substitute for mainframe VSAM RRDS files or mainframe direct access files.

9.2.4 DL/I Databases

The Micro Focus IMS Option, formerly known as Stingray IMSVS86, allows you to simulate DL/I databases on the PC. Documentation supplied with the IMS Option shows how to transfer test data from mainframe DL/I databases to the PC.

9.2.5 SQL-Based Databases

To simulate mainframe DB2 or SQL/DS on the PC, you can use any of several SQL-based database managers. Micro Focus recommends **XDB-DB2 Workbench,** offered by XDB Systems, Inc., **SQL Precompiler Programmer's Toolkit,** offered by Gupta Technologies, Inc., and **OS/2 Extended Services Database Manager,** offered by IBM. Other options include the **Microsoft SQL Server** and **Oracle.** To transfer test data from mainframe SQL-based databases to the PC, see the documentation provided with these packages.

OS/2 Extended Services Database Manager versus DB2. If you plan to use the OS/2 Extended Services Database Manager to simulate mainframe DB2, be aware of some differences. Under the OS/2 ES Database Manager, the same EXEC SQL commands will work in much the same way as they do in mainframe DB2 or SQL/DS. However, the order of records retrieved from a SELECT with ORDER BY clause may differ because the database on the PC is in ASCII.

On both the PC and the mainframe, an SQL database is a collection of tables. One or more such collections may exist on a given workstation. Differences between mainframe and PC architecture can affect the way you set up databases.

In mainframe DB2, table space must be allocated on disk before any databases can be defined. Mainframes have large numbers of users and extensive needs for security, so it makes sense to define separate databases for separate groups of users. Each can have its own access security. **Under DB2, applications can use more than one database at a time, so that no real problems are created by splitting them up.**

Under OS/2, on the other hand, file allocation is dynamic. This is why you do not preallocate disk space with job control language before your program can write to an output file. There is no need to reserve a piece of unused disk space in case your program will need it later. Because OS/2 workstations have less disk space than mainframes, OS/2 attempts to conserve that space. OS/2 dynamic file allocation eliminates the need to use SQL commands to create table space on your OS/2 workstation before defining a database, as you must do under mainframe DB2. **The limitation is that an OS/2 program can attach itself to only one SQL database at a time.** This means that you will need to keep all tables together that will be needed by any one application. On an OS/2 workstation, with few users, local database security is less complex than it is on a mainframe. OS/2 programmers typically define only one database and keep all tables in it, for all applications being run on that workstation.

9.3 MS-DOS and OS/2 versus Mainframe JCL

9.3.1 What Mainframe JCL Actually Does

Another obstacle to mainframe program development on the PC is the fact that PC operating systems do not support mainframe job control language (JCL). On the mainframe, JCL is the primary means of allocating system resources to batch processes. (In this context, batch processes are sequences of programs that run with minimal user interaction.) Since the mainframe was originally designed for batch operation, mainframe JCL had to carry much of the burden of mainframe system operation. Interactive mainframe users can run batch jobs with JCL or with TSO CLISTs or REXX programs, in similar fashion.

On the other hand, the PC is primarily an interactive machine designed to serve the needs of a single user. PC operating systems provide comparatively little support for job streaming or unattended batch operation. Let's take a look at what mainframe JCL actually does, and how these same things might be done on the PC:

- A JCL stream can run a sequence of programs and system utilities without the operator or system user having to start each step separately. MS-DOS .BAT files and OS/2 .CMD files also do this.

- JCL passes job stream parameters to your programs and to system utilities. MS-DOS and OS/2 also pass command line parameters to your programs.

- You can embed a SYSIN file within a JCL stream. SYSIN files are sequential "card image" input files with 80-character records. They originated back in the era of punched cards. COBOL ACCEPT statements receive input data from SYSIN files, unless you specify ACCEPT FROM CONSOLE. Many mainframe system utilities take control statements from SYSIN files. However, SYSIN files as such are not available on the PC. Input data cannot be embedded in PC batch or command files. Input and output redirection can sometimes allow a system utility to read commands from a file instead of requesting responses from the user.

- JCL commands control memory allocation. Under MS-DOS, the application itself, or a memory manager running under MS-DOS, allocates whatever memory is available on the system. If a program needs more memory than is available on the system, some memory managers, such as XM, can swap memory pages to disk. OS/2 assigns real and virtual memory based on what each process needs. Here again, if processes need more memory than is available on the system, OS/2 will swap least-recently-used memory pages out to disk.

- JCL commands control how much execution time a job step (program) will get, and what priority it will have. This is much more important on a mainframe than on a PC because many batch jobs can run at the same time. MS-DOS was designed to run only one process at a time, so it makes no provision for allocating priorities among tasks. OS/2 assigns priorities depending on which process is active. Under OS/2, background processes run with leftover CPU cycles while you work with an interactive process in the foreground.

- JCL preallocates disk space for the files each job step will create. PC file systems allocate disk space dynamically, so there is no need to reserve disk space before a program uses it.

- A JCL stream can check return codes from completed programs. Based on those return codes, it can decide whether or not to run other job steps. The IF ERRORLEVEL syntax in MS-DOS .BAT or OS/2 .CMD files can substitute for this feature. When you use IF ERRORLEVEL, the COBOL program's return code can be one byte long under MS-DOS, and two bytes under OS/2.

- JCL lets you reassign filenames and devices, as well as other file characteristics, at runtime. On the PC, concerns such as blocking factor do not apply. However, you will likely need some flexibility in reassigning filenames at runtime. Micro Focus provides some features that let you do this. These will be discussed in the next section.

9.3.2 Methods for Allocating Disk Files to Programs

The SELECT/ASSIGN syntax is the COBOL method of mapping filenames within the program to actual files and device addresses. In this section, we will discuss options that give you flexibility in assigning files.

Standard mainframe SELECT/ASSIGN syntax. First, let's look at what happens on the PC when you use the same SELECT/ASSIGN syntax that a mainframe program uses, without any additional means of file allocation. The SELECT clause contains the logical filename by which the COBOL program will identify the file. The ASSIGN clause contains the external filename by which the operating system will identify the file. In mainframe programs, the external filename in the ASSIGN clause contains only an eight-character literal, the DDNAME, not the fully qualified dataset name. Mainframe JCL statements, in turn, equate the DDNAME to the fully qualified dataset name as it appears in the directory structure. You can keep the program's files wherever it is most convenient. What happens when you run the same program on the PC, which does not have the same type of JCL statements? The PC file system will simply look for that eight-character external filename in the current drive and directory. This method requires all of your program's disk files to be in the current drive and directory, giving you less flexibility than you would have on the mainframe.

Using SET commands to equate filenames. To equate the filename in the ASSIGN clause to an external filename, you need a mechanism that works somewhat like mainframe JCL. By using SET commands, you can establish environment variables that equate filenames in much the same way as mainframe JCL. Checking with the directive **ASSIGN(EXTERNAL)** tells runtime I/O support to look for environment variables for filenames. Alternatively, you can specify,

```
SELECT filename ASSIGN EXTERNAL environment-var-name
```

The corresponding SET command is in the format,

```
SET environment-var-name=drive:/path/filename.ext
```

One little wrinkle: if the *external-name* in the ASSIGN clause contains a hyphen, only the part after the last hyphen will be matched to the environment variable name.

Dynamic specification within the program. Checking with the directive **ASSIGN(DYNAMIC)** tells runtime I/O support to assign filenames "on the fly," using the contents of a program variable. Alternatively, you can specify SELECT *filename* ASSIGN DYNAMIC *COBOL-data-name*. Then, in the Procedure Division, you will move the desired filename to the *COBOL-data-name* in the ASSIGN statement. You can use a fully qualified data name with drive, path, filename, and extension.

MFEXTMAP.DAT File (External File Mapping). Micro Focus suggests using the External File Mapping facility as the easiest and cleanest way to allocate files to a program. Use the COBOL Editor to create an ASCII text file containing the file allocations. Use a separate record for each file allocation. Name the file **MFEXTMAP.DAT.** You can keep file allocations for all of your programs in the same MFEXTMAP.DAT file. Keep this file in the current directory or in the COBDIR path. Use the following format for each record:

```
assign-name drive:/path/filename.ext
```

Here is an example:

```
INFILE K:\COBOL\MFWBBOOK\AJINPUT.TXT
OUTFILE K:\COBOL\MFWBBOOK\AJOUTPUT.TXT
```

The Workbench will automatically look for an MFEXTMAP.DAT file at runtime. It will search the current directory and then the COBDIR path. If it finds MFEXTMAP.DAT, it will activate those file allocations automatically. If you don't want to keep MFEXTMAP.DAT in either of those two directories, use a SET MFEXTMAP *path* command to create an environment variable showing its location.

Ordinarily, the External File Mapper is available only when animating or running your program under the Workbench. (For PC-based applications, you can use the Toolset Build and Installf utilities to set up a free-standing application that will always look for file allocations from MFEXTMAP.DAT. The Build and Installf utilities are for PC program development and are outside the scope of this book.)

Device names. Where appropriate, you can assign files to device names other than disks. All of the MS-DOS or OS/2 system designations are available, such as COM1, LPT1, and so forth. CON (console) represents the keyboard and screen. You can ignore a file by assigning it to NUL.

9.3.3 Using the PC Printer and Other Devices

If you run a mainframe COBOL print program on the PC, will it produce the same print-image output file on disk? Definitely not. But will it produce the same output on paper? If the PC printer will print the same number of columns and lines on each page, the answer is yes. Mainframe printers accept EBCDIC files with either ANSI (DCB=RECFM=FBA) or IBM (DCB=RECFM=FBM) carriage control characters. PC printers accept only ASCII files and do not recognize any form of mainframe carriage control character. Nevertheless, the same WRITE AFTER ADVANCING syntax works in a PC program the way it does in a mainframe program. The COBOL/2 printer output support subprogram will insert the characters needed to advance lines and pages on the PC printer.

You can download mainframe print-image output files to your PC workstation. While they will not match the print-image output files that your PC COBOL programs create, there is a way to print them out on the PC printer. WFL lets you convert the carriage controls from mainframe to PC format.

Sending printer control codes. To get the most out of certain types of PC printers, you need to be able to embed specialized printer control sequences in your printer output file. Laser printers, inkjet printers, and other devices use control sequences to determine such characteristics as spacing, font, page size, and page orientation. For example, control sequences enable you to print a wide report horizontally on the page. Printer control sequences differ for each device. See your printer's technical documentation for more information.

How do you use these control sequences? If you do not need to change control codes within a report, you can build a printer setup file containing the desired control codes. Before running your program, you can use MS-DOS or

OS/2 commands to send the setup file to the printer. Afterward, if desired, you can send another setup file to reset the printer to its original format. Alternatively, you can build the control codes within your PC COBOL/2 program and send them to the printer. Mainframe programmers may need to isolate PC printer control logic in a called subprogram, because these control codes are not compatible with mainframe printers.

Printer control sequences obviously must contain bytes that are not printable ASCII characters. These nonprintable characters let the printer distinguish control sequences from output text. Some Hewlett-Packard products, for example, recognize control sequences that begin with the ASCII Escape character. The Escape character does not display on the screen or appear on a report. You cannot insert an Escape character into a file simply by pressing the Escape key, because Micro Focus products use the Escape key to exit from the current screen. So if you want to create a printer setup file, you must create it in hex format with the Hex Editor or Data File Editor.

Suppose you want to write a COBOL/2 program (or callable subprogram) that builds control sequences and sends them to the printer. In that case, you will need to specify the nonprintable characters in hexadecimal. VS COBOL II Release 3 lets you represent hex literals with the syntax **X"*nn*"**. In this syntax, *n* represents a hex digit in the range "1" through "9" or "A" through "F". These hex literals can be up to 120 bytes long and must contain an even number of hexadecimal digits.

Other devices. Micro Focus supplies a library of callable routines that allow a COBOL/2 program to interface more directly with the PC operating environment. They perform Boolean logic, file directory maintenance, filename parsing, upper-/lowercase conversion, and other functions including low-level I/O for the screen, keyboard, and mouse. Programs using these CALLs cannot be ported back to the mainframe. However, you may find these routines useful in your own utilities on the PC workstation. See the Appendices in the *COBOL/2 Operating Guide* for details.

9.3.4 Mainframe SYSIN and SYSOUT

MVS JCL lets you reassign COBOL ACCEPT statement input to SYSIN. You can reassign COBOL DISPLAY statement output to SYSOUT. This allows you to hard-code responses in your job stream, and to pass DISPLAYed output along to another job step. Since the Workbench is designed primarily for interactive testing, it does not support SYSIN or SYSOUT reassignment. ACCEPT and DISPLAY always refer to the keyboard and screen.

If you have a need to pass DISPLAYed output from one program to another, you can compile and link-edit the programs so that you can run them directly from the operating system prompt. From there, you can use MS-DOS or OS/2 I/O redirection to assign the data to a disk file. This batch file redirects the output of PROG1 to CONSOLE.TXT, and redirects that same file to be the input to PROG2:

```
REM RUN PROG1 AND PROG2
REM REDIRECTING SCREEN OUTPUT OF PROG1
REM TO ACT AS KEYBOARD INPUT TO PROG2
PROG1 > CONSOLE.TXT
PROG2 < CONSOLE.TXT
```

9.3.5 Using the PARM Passer Facility

In the previous chapter, we showed commands for running programs with the Micro Focus PARM Passer facility. The PARM Passer provides a substitute for MVS JCL PARMs. It lets you pass up to 100 characters of text data to each program. Data can include parameters or runtime directives.

Program setup. The receiving program can be either an intermediate code file (.INT) or a generated code file (.GNT). When you check the program, you must use the **IBMCOMP** directive so that the Linkage Section PARM byte count field will work properly. At runtime, the PARM character string will appear automatically in the Linkage Section of the receiving program.

At the beginning of the Linkage Section, create a work area of the following type:

```
01   PARMS.
     05   PARM-BYTE-COUNT    PIC S9(4) COMP.
     05   PARM-DATA          PIC X(100).
```

You can define PARM-DATA as a group item and define detail items under it, if desired. (Alternatively, you can define it as a COBOL array with OCCURS DEPENDING ON PARM-BYTE-COUNT.) As on a mainframe, the receiving program is responsible for breaking apart the input data and for making sure the correct number of bytes are present. PARM-BYTE-COUNT indicates how many bytes were actually passed in PARM-DATA. The byte count in that field does not include its own length. **Be careful never to access data past the end of the parameter byte count.**

In the Procedure Division header, use the name of the PARM area at the beginning of the Linkage Section:

```
PROCEDURE DIVISION USING PARMS.
```

Building the PARM Passer file. You can reach the PARM Passer menu by pressing **F6=define-parmpass-parms** on the Program Development menu, shown in Figure 9.1. (Reach the Program Development menu by pressing **F3=develop** on the MDE main menu.) The Program and Parameter Specification menu is shown in Figure 9.2. This is the menu that you will use to build a PARM Passer file.

The PARM Passer screen lets you create and update a file of parameter records. Each record contains parameters intended for a different program. The program name is in the first column. The second column lets you choose whether the parameters should be passed in ASCII or EBCDIC. The third column contains the actual parameter value. You may enter up to 100 characters of parameter data in a record. The screen will scroll horizontally as needed. You can move around within the parameter file with the usual cursor arrow and paging keys. The current line (record) within the file is highlighted.

When the PARM Passer screen first appears, it will contain any parameter entries that already exist on the system. The PARM Passer utility will look for an existing PARMPASS.DAT file, first in the current directory, and then in the COBDIR path. Data editing on the PARM Passer screen occurs in memory.

```
Program-Development─────────────────────────────────────────────────────────
F1=help F2=edit F3=check F4=animate F5=change-default-directives      Escape
F6=define-parmpass-parms F7=data-file-editor
```

Figure 9.1 Program Development menu

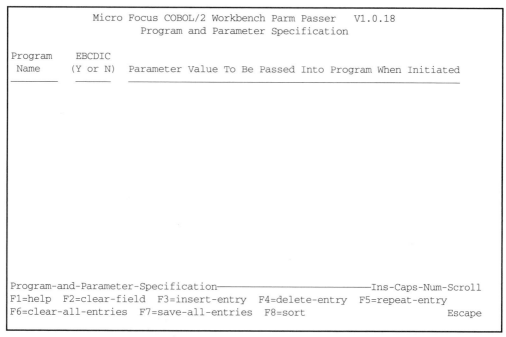

```
              Micro Focus COBOL/2 Workbench Parm Passer   V1.0.18
                      Program and Parameter Specification

Program    EBCDIC
 Name      (Y or N)  Parameter Value To Be Passed Into Program When Initiated
_____   _____  _____









Program-and-Parameter-Specification───────────────────────Ins-Caps-Num-Scroll
F1=help F2=clear-field F3=insert-entry  F4=delete-entry  F5=repeat-entry
F6=clear-all-entries  F7=save-all-entries  F8=sort                      Escape
```

Figure 9.2 PARM Passer screen

As with the COBOL Editor, you must save the file in order to apply the changes to the text file on disk.

The following functions appear on the PARM Passer menu:

- **F2=clear-field** clears the field at the cursor position.
- **F3=insert-entry** inserts a new blank record at the current line.
- **F4=delete-entry** deletes the record at the current line.
- **F5=repeat-entry** repeats the record at the current line.
- **F6=clear-all-entries** deletes all records.
- **F7=save-all-entries** saves the PARM Passer file to disk. If no PARM Passer file exists yet, this operation will create a new file in the current directory. Otherwise, this operation will update the existing file.
- **F8=sort** sorts the records in ascending order by program name (the first column). The sort process deletes any records having a blank program name.

Passing runtime directives. If you want to set any runtime directives within the 100-character PARM Passer record, put the directives *after* the parms that you actually want to pass to your program's Linkage Section. Precede the first runtime directive with a slash character ("/"). The slash, and any characters following it, are not passed along to your program.

Yes, you can use slash characters within parms that you pass to your program. The PARM Passer function looks for the *last* slash character to show where runtime directives begin. Thus, if your parameter data contains any slash characters, put an additional slash character after the end of the actual data. This will make the PARM Passer treat all previous slash characters as data to pass along to your program. The final slash character is not passed to your program. For example, suppose you want your program to receive the date **11/01/1991**. In the PARM Passer value field, add a third slash character so that it becomes **11/01/1991/**.

What about UPSI switches? Parameters are not the same as UPSI switches. If you maintain old mainframe programs that use UPSI switch settings, you will need to set the appropriate runtime switches. In the previous chapter, we discussed methods for setting these switches on the Animate and Run menus. You can also use the PARM Passer to set UPSI switches. Within the 100-character data field, you can enter UPSI switch values as a runtime directive in the following manner:

```
[parameters]/UPSI(nnnnnnnn)
```

Precede the first runtime directive, in this case **UPSI,** with a slash. Each UPSI switch value *n* is either a one or a zero. Enter no more than eight UPSI switch values.

9.4 Utilities on the Mainframe Side

To transfer programs and test data between the mainframe and the PC, you need certain utilities on both machines. This section will provide an overview of the utilities on the mainframe side.

9.4.1 IDCAMS REPRO

As we mentioned before, you can download only sequential files from the mainframe to the PC. The same is true in the reverse direction: you can upload only sequential files. To transfer any other file type, you must first convert it into a sequential file. IDCAMS is the primary system utility for managing mainframe VSAM files. To download the contents of a VSAM file, use the IDCAMS REPRO command to create a sequential file on the mainframe. If the VSAM file has an alternate index, use the alternate index path to build the sequential output file.

It's worth remembering that the IDCAMS REPRO command also can extract a subset of the mainframe production files for testing. This will save transfer time, as well as disk space and processing time on the PC.

9.4.2 VRECGEN (Micro Focus File Format Utility)

VRECGEN is a utility for the mainframe that comes with the Micro Focus Workbench. It converts mainframe files having variable-length records to a form that you can download to the PC. If you download variable-length records without using VRECGEN, record length information can be corrupted.

Installing VRECGEN. To use VRECGEN, you first have to install it on the mainframe. If it is not already installed, upload the source file VRECGEN.CBL using ASCII to EBCDIC conversion. Examine the source code on the mainframe; you may need to adjust the maximum record length or specify blocking information. Compile and link-edit VRECGEN on the mainframe. (Appendix A of the *Mainframe Programmer's Guide* describes compiler, linker, and runtime options to use on the mainframe side.)

Running VRECGEN. To run VRECGEN on the mainframe, you will need to set up JCL. Unless you have changed the program, the input file DD name will be **INPDD**; its DSN will refer to a variable-length file on the mainframe. The output file DD name will be **OUTDD.** You will need to supply appropriate space allocation, disposition, and DCB information. An example of JCL for VRECGEN appears in the "MDE Menu System" chapter of the *Mainframe Programmer's Guide.*

9.4.3 3270 Send-Receive or IRMA

To transfer files between the mainframe and the PC, your workstation must already be networked to the mainframe. The Micro Focus File Transfer Aid does not contain its own communications protocols. Instead, it provides an automated interface to the PC-to-mainframe protocols that already exist on your system. The File Transfer Aid supports 3270 Send-Receive (the default) and IRMA protocols.

9.5 Utilities on the PC Side

9.5.1 File Transfer Aid (Micro Focus Download Utility)

The Micro Focus File Transfer Aid is an interface to PC-to-mainframe communication protocols. It works with MVS/TSO and VM/CMS host systems. You can set up commands ahead of time to transfer many files at once. You can transfer files in either direction, with or without ASCII/EBCDIC translation. For program source files, you can choose whether or not to download copy library members that each program uses. You can even interface the File Transfer Aid to source control facilities such as Panvalet.

Bringing up the File Transfer Aid. Before you actually bring up the File Transfer function, you must use your connectivity software on the PC to log onto a mainframe session. Once this is done, you can bring up the File Transfer Aid either from the operating system command prompt or from within the Workbench menu system.

Within the Workbench menu system, you can bring up the File Transfer Aid from the File Utilities menu, shown in Figure 9.3. (Reach the File Utilities menu by pressing **F2=files** on the MDE main menu.)

```
File-Utilities───────────────────────────────────────────────
F1=help F2=transfer F3=convert F4=diff F5=WFL F6=hexedit F7=data-file-editor
                                                              Escape
```

Figure 9.3 File Utilities menu

You can bring up the File Transfer Aid from the command prompt with this command:

```
RUN MFXFER
```

File Transfer profiles. Pressing **F2=transfer** on the File Utilities menu brings up the File Transfer Profiles screen, shown in Figure 9.4. A profile is a list of files that the File Transfer Aid will transfer in one operation or "batch run." The profile list on this menu acts as a scrolling light-bar menu. You can use the cursor arrow keys to highlight the desired entry and press the enter key to select it for editing or execution. The list of profile names (not the profiles themselves) is in a file called MFAPPLS.DAT, either in the current directory or in the COBDIR path. If no MFAPPLS.DAT exists, an empty screen appears so that you can still create new profiles.

The options on Figure 9.4 let you update the list of profiles:

- **F3=add-profile** brings up another menu that allows you to create a new profile. You enter the profile name, the profile description, and the name of the file that will contain the profile details.
- **F4=delete-profile** deletes the currently highlighted profile.
- **F5=change-profile-name** lets you change the profile name, description, and details filename for the currently highlighted profile.

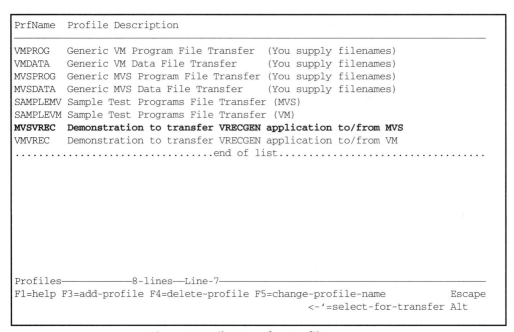

```
PrfName  Profile Description
─────────────────────────────────────────────────────────────────────
VMPROG    Generic VM Program File Transfer  (You supply filenames)
VMDATA    Generic VM Data File Transfer     (You supply filenames)
MVSPROG   Generic MVS Program File Transfer (You supply filenames)
MVSDATA   Generic MVS Data File Transfer    (You supply filenames)
SAMPLEMV  Sample Test Programs File Transfer (MVS)
SAMPLEVM  Sample Test Programs File Transfer (VM)
MVSVREC   Demonstration to transfer VRECGEN application to/from MVS
VMVREC    Demonstration to transfer VRECGEN application to/from VM
...............................end of list...................................




Profiles──────────8-lines──Line-7───────────────────────────────────
F1=help F3=add-profile F4=delete-profile F5=change-profile-name       Escape
                                          <-'=select-for-transfer Alt
```

Figure 9.4 File Transfer Profiles menu

```
Profiles──────────8-lines──Line-7───────────────────────────────────
F1=help F4=save-list
```

Figure 9.5 File Transfer Profiles ALT menu

```
PC Name  Ext  Host Name                              Member    Status
VRECGEN  CBL  COBOL.COBOL                            VRECGEN   Pending
..............................end of list..............................



















MVSVREC—all————————scan—upload-to-host————————————————————————————
F1=help F2=selection F3=copybook-scan F4=transfer-type F5=status-message  Escape
            F8=edit-list F9=edit-profile-defaults F10=start-transfer Alt
```

Figure 9.6 File Transfer screen

If you have made changes to the list of profile names, hold down the **Alt** key and press **F4=save-list** to save these changes to the MFAPPLS.DAT file. The Alt-options menu is shown in Figure 9.5. If you do not want to save the changes, press the Escape key to exit from the profile menu. In that case, answer **Y** to the question, **Exit without saving? Y/N.**

Using the File Transfer screen. If you use the enter key to select an item from the profiles menu, you will see the File Transfer screen shown in Figure 9.6. This screen shows the list of files that will be transferred when you execute that profile. The File Transfer screen is a scrolling light-bar menu. You can use the cursor arrow keys to highlight a file on the list for selection or editing.

For each file, this screen shows the PC filename and extension as well as the host dataset and member name. It also shows the **status** of the file transfer operation as it applies to that file. **Pending** means that the file is awaiting transfer. **Error** means that the previous file transfer attempt has failed. **Exists** means that the file already exists on the target system, so that there is no need to make another attempt to transfer it.

- **F2=selection** lets you choose which files on the list to transfer. Pressing **F2** repeatedly cycles through the choices of **all, current, pending, failed,** and **pending+failed.** "All," obviously, means all filenames in the profile. "Current" means the file on the currently highlighted line. The other options make it convenient to restart a file transfer operation that did not run to completion.

- **F3=copybook-scan** is for source program files. This option lets you choose whether to download all of the copy library members referenced in the source files.

- **F4=transfer-type** lets you choose the direction of file transfer. Choices include **download-from-host, upload-to-host, get-from-local-SCCS,** and **put-to-local-SCCS.** The first two choices let you download files from the mainframe or upload them to the mainframe. The latter two choices are intended for those who have a source code control system on the PC network or workstation.
- **F5=status-message** brings up a screen showing the status of the current file, shown in Figure 9.7.
- **F8=edit-list** brings up a menu, shown in Figure 9.8, that lets you update the list of files within the profile. Functions on this menu work in much the same way as on the Profile menu.
- **F9=edit-profile-defaults** brings up a menu, shown in Figure 9.9, that lets you control various details of the transfer process. We will discuss this menu below.
- **F10=start-transfer** activates the transfer process. The display shown in Figure 9.10 shows the progress of the transfer operation.

If you have made changes to the list of filenames or to profile defaults, and you want to save the changes, hold down the **Alt** key and press **F4=save-list-and-defaults.** This will update the details file for that profile. (The Alt-options menu is shown in Figure 9.11.)

If you do not want to save the changes, press the Escape key to exit from the file transfer screen. In that case, answer **Y** to the question, **Exit without saving? Y/N.**

```
+==============================================================================+
|                                                                              |
|        PC File Name: K:\COBOL\LBR\VRECGEN.CBL                                 |
|    Type of Transfer: Pending                                                 |
|      Host File Name: 'COBOL.COBOL(VRECGEN)'                                   |
|                                                                              |
|              Status: Pending                                                 |
|                                                                              |
|                                                                              |
|   Bytes Transferred:              0                                          |
|                                                                              |
+==============================================================================+




Transfer-Status──────────────────────────────────────────────────────────  --
F1=help                                                              Escape
```

Figure 9.7 File status inquiry display

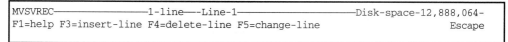

```
MVSVREC────────────────1-line──-Line-1──────────────────Disk-space-12,888,064-
F1=help F3=insert-line F4=delete-line F5=change-line                   Escape
```

Figure 9.8 File Transfer edit list screen

```
Defaults────────────────────────────────────────────────────────────────────
F1=help F2=PC-defaults F3=host-defaults F4=transfer-defaults           Escape
F6=pgms-to-ignore F7=copys-to-ignore
```

Figure 9.9 File Transfer defaults screen

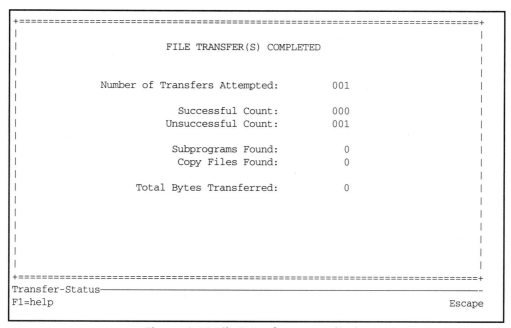

```
+==============================================================================+
|                                                                              |
|                         FILE TRANSFER(S) COMPLETED                           |
|                                                                              |
|                                                                              |
|           Number of Transfers Attempted:          001                        |
|                                                                              |
|                     Successful Count:             000                        |
|                   Unsuccessful Count:             001                        |
|                                                                              |
|                   Subprograms Found:                0                        |
|                    Copy Files Found:                0                        |
|                                                                              |
|            Total Bytes Transferred:                 0                        |
|                                                                              |
|                                                                              |
|                                                                              |
|                                                                              |
|                                                                              |
|                                                                              |
+==============================================================================+
Transfer-Status──────────────────────────────────────────────────────────-
F1=help                                                                Escape
```

Figure 9.10 File Transfer status display

```
MVSVREC──────────────────────────────────────────────────────────────────────
F1=help F4=save-list-and-defaults
```

Figure 9.11 File Transfer ALT screen

Changing profile default settings. Let's take another look at the File Transfer defaults screen, shown in Figure 9.9. Options on this screen let you decide exactly how the File Transfer operation should take place.

- **F2=PC-defaults** brings up the PC defaults screen, shown in Figure 9.12. On this screen, you can specify file extensions and drive/path designations on the PC side of the transfer process. When transferring source programs, you can specify whether the transfer process should also upload or download copy library members and CALLed subprograms referenced by the main program. If the copy member or called subprogram is already present on the target machine, then you can decide whether to overwrite it or not. The entries **Get from Local SCCS Command** and **Put to Local SCCS Command** are for users who have a source code control system on the PC workstation.

You can specify the name of a command file containing instructions for the SCCS.

- **F3=host-defaults** brings up the host defaults screen, shown in Figure 9.13. It lets you specify whether the host system is MVS or VM/CMS, as well as the file directory location on the host side. Here again, you can specify command files on the host side if you want to work directly with source code control systems such as Librarian or Panvalet. The *Workbench Reference* contains examples of how to set up these command files.

- **F4=transfer-defaults** brings up the transfer defaults screen, shown in Figure 9.14. This screen lets you specify whether you want EBCDIC/ASCII translation. If you do, specify **Y** for that option and for CRLF insertion. This will translate a fixed-length EBCDIC file to a line sequential ASCII file. **Use this translation facility only for source program files that do not contain embedded hex codes.** For source with embedded hex bytes, or for data files that contain a mix of character and other data types, specify **N** for EBCDIC/ASCII translation and **N** for CRLF insertion. Do the translation later on the PC workstation using MDECONV for source programs or WFL for data files. Finally, the transfer defaults screen contains the commands used for interfacing with the PC-to-host communications protocol. The default is 3270 Send-Receive. You can substitute other commands if you use IRMA.

- **F6=pgms-to-ignore** brings up a screen that lets you specify one or more CALLed program names that you want to exclude from the transfer operation.

- **F7=copys-to-ignore** brings up a screen that lets you specify one or more COPY member names that you want to exclude from the transfer operation.

```
+==============================================================================+
|                                                                              |
| File Extension for Source Programs: CBL                                       |
| File Extension for Copy Files      : CPY                                      |
|                                                                              |
| Drive:\Path for Source Programs    : $COBDIR                                  |
| Drive:\Path for Copy Files         : $COBDIR                                  |
|                                                                              |
| Scan for Called Subprograms?       : N   (Y or N)                            |
| Scan for COPY Files?               : N   (Y or N)                            |
| Scan for ++INCLUDE's?              : N   (Y or N)                            |
| Scan for -INC's?                   : N   (Y or N)                            |
|                                                                              |
| Overwrite existing subprograms?    : N   (Y or N)                            |
| Overwrite existing copy files?     : N   (Y or N)                            |
|                                                                              |
| Get From Local SCCS Command        :                                         |
| Put To Local SCCS Command          :                                         |
|                                                                              |
|                                                                              |
+==============================================================================+
PC-Defaults———————————————————————————————————————————————————————————————————
F1=help F2=clear-field                                          <-' Escape
```

Figure 9.12 PC defaults screen

```
+=============================================================================+
|Host system                       : MVS                                      |
|                                                                             |
|For MVS Systems:                                                             |
|                                                                             |
|Default PDS for Source Programs : COBOL.COBOL                                 |
|Default PDS for Copy Files      :                                            |
|                                                                             |
|For VM/CMS Systems:                                                          |
|                                                                             |
|File Type for Source Programs    : COBOL                                     |
|File Mode for Source Programs    : A1                                        |
|                                                                             |
|File Type for Copy Files         : MACLIB                                    |
|File Mode for Copy Files         : A1                                        |
|                                                                             |
|Host commands:                                                              |
|                                                                             |
|Get From Host SCCS Command       :                                          |
|Put To Host SCCS Command         :                                          |
+=============================================================================+
Host-Defaults─────────────────────────────────────────────────────────────────
F1=help F2=clear-field F3=host-system F4=MVS-dsnames            <-' Escape
```

Figure 9.13 Host defaults screen

```
+=============================================================================+
|                                                                             |
| EBCDIC/ASCII Translation?                     : Y  (Y or N)                  |
| Insert CRLF?                                  : Y  (Y or N)                  |
|                                                                             |
| Stop processing if error in any transfer? : N  (Y or N)                     |
| Display start transfer warning screen      : N  (Y or N)                    |
|                                                                             |
| Send/Receive message text prefix            : TRANS                         |
| Send/Receive successful transfer message  : TRANS03                         |
|                                                                             |
| Send command:                                                              |
| SEND %pcname %dsname %ascii %crlf                                           |
|                                                                             |
| Receive command:                                                           |
| RECEIVE %pcname %dsname %ascii %crlf                                        |
|                                                                             |
|                                                                             |
|                                                                             |
|                                                                             |
+=============================================================================+
Send/Receive-Defaults──────────────────────────────────────────────────────────
F1=help F2=clear-field                                           <-' Escape
```

Figure 9.14 Transfer defaults screen

9.5.2 MDECONV (EBCDIC/ASCII translation)

Purpose. The MDECONV utility provides a way to translate source program files that contain embedded nontext characters. MDECONV converts files in either direction between fixed-length sequential EBCDIC and line sequential ASCII. If you know that your source files are free of embedded nontext characters, it would be faster to translate them during the upload or download process with the File Transfer Aid utility. Otherwise, if you plan to use

MDECONV, transfer the files *without* EBCDIC/ASCII translation and *without* CRLF insertion.

MDECONV is not intended for data files whose records contain both character and numeric fields. To convert those, use the Workbench File Loader (WFL).

The MDECONV menu. To run MDECONV from the Workbench menu, press **F3=convert** on the File Utilities menu shown in Figure 9.3. The MF Source Converter menu will appear, as shown in Figure 9.15.

```
MF-Source-Converter————-Check-NTC's——LRECL=80————————-Ins-Caps-Num-Scroll
F1=help F2=dir F3=to ASCII/EBCDIC F4=NTC's F5=LRECL F9/F10=set-options  Escape
File K:\COBOL\MFWBBOOK\yourprog                                       <-' Ctrl
```

Figure 9.15 MDECONV menu

On the MDECONV menu, **F2=dir,** as well as the **Ctrl** key, provide the usual Micro Focus directory function to help you search for source files. **F3=to ASCII/EBCDIC** is a toggle switch that controls the direction of file conversion. The selected output format will appear in highlighted type. **F4=NTC's** is a toggle switch that controls whether or not MDECONV will check for nontext characters (NTC's). You will usually want to turn this on. **F5=LRECL** cycles through several choices for the logical record length of the EBCDIC file. Choices are 72, 80, and 132. It is important to choose the setting that matches the correct record length of the EBCDIC file. Finally, **F9/F10=set-options** lets you enter various directives for MDECONV. These control what MDECONV will do when it finds an error. Reference information for MDECONV directives appears in the chapter "Source Converter," in the *Workbench Reference.*

To begin the conversion process, enter the filename at the **File** prompt and press the enter key.

Running MDECONV from the command line. You can run MDECONV from the command line prompt by using the following syntax:

```
RUN MDECONV file1 [[TO] file2] [directives]
```

If you omit input or output filename extensions, MDECONV will assume .CBL for the ASCII file and .EBC for the EBCDIC file. If you omit the output filename (*file2*), MDECONV will use the input filename, substituting the appropriate extension. MDECONV will assume default values for any directives you omit. Specify the *direction* of translation (type of output file) by specifying **ASC** or **EBC.** If you specify neither, MDECONV will create an ASCII output file. MDECONV assumes a logical record length (LRECL) of 80 for the EBCDIC file. You can change this by specifying the directive **LRECL:*nn*** where *nn* is the record length.

If you have many files to convert and you don't want to keep entering commands at the PC, you can set up a command file as input to MDECONV. The command file must have a filename extension of .EBT. Run MDECONV using this command:

```
RUN MDECONV cmdfile.EBT
```

You can set up the commands in an .EBT file in various ways, as discussed in the "Source Converter" chapter in the *Workbench Reference.* An .EBT file is an ASCII text file. One way to set up the commands is to use a separate line for each file to be converted, in the following format:

```
infile.ext [directives] [TO outfile.ext]
```

If you omit the TO *outfile.ext,* MDECONV will create the output filename by using the input filename and substituting the appropriate extension. Unless you supply the EBCDIC directive, the conversion will be from EBCDIC to ASCII.

9.5.3 WFL (Workbench File Loader)

Purpose. The Workbench File Loader (WFL) is the primary tool for building test data files on the PC. It converts sequential files to other file organizations and vice versa. It performs intelligent field-by-field translation between ASCII and EBCDIC, and between mainframe and PC floating-point formats. It creates new indexed files by converting them from sequential organization, and it rebuilds existing indexed files for more efficient processing. It even lets you convert mainframe print files so that you can print them on the PC.

Invoking WFL. You can access WFL by pressing **F5=WFL** on the File Utilities menu. You can also run WFL from the command line with the command **RUN MFWFL.** Figure 9.16 shows the main WFL menu.

WFL conversion profiles. To make WFL convert a file, you need to tell it the input and output file characteristics. If the conversion is a onetime activity never to be repeated, you can simply enter the information on the WFL menu screen as you go. However, if you might need to convert the same file again later on, or if you have several similar files to convert, you can use a file conversion **profile.** WFL creates profiles with a filename extension of **.PRO**. A profile is a text file containing all required input and output file characteristics except for the filenames. On the WFL main menu, **F3=load-profile** lets you load an existing profile file into WFL for editing or reuse. This load function uses the Micro Focus directory menu facility. **F4=save-profile** lets you save changes to an existing profile file. It also lets you create a new profile file by specifying a new name at the filename prompt.

The WFL main menu screen does not work like an ordinary text editor. You cannot simply move the cursor to wherever you want on the screen to update a field. The WFL screen is divided into three parts: input file, output file, and conversion masks. You have to select a different submenu to work with each part of the screen.

- **F5=specify-input** lets you supply the input file characteristics (Figure 9.17).
- **F6=specify-output** lets you supply the output file characteristics (Figure 9.18).
- **F7=specify-mask-file** lets you load an existing file of record conversion masks.
- **F8=create/edit-mask** lets you update an existing conversion mask file or create a new one (Figure 9.19).

```
+==============================================================================+
| Name : K:\COBOL\MFWBBOOK\custmst.ebc                                          |
| Type : Record Sequential, Fixed Length        File is ASCII/EBCDIC           |
| Record Length Min :    41    Max    :    41    Floating Point Rep is IEEE/370 |
| Access Key Offset :     0    Length :     0                                   |
+==============================================================================+


+==============================================================================+
| Output File Details                                                          |
| Name : K:\COBOL\MFWBBOOK\custmst.dat                                         |
| Type : Indexed Sequential, Fixed Length        File is ASCII/EBCDIC          |
| Record Length Min :    41    Max    :    41    Floating Point Rep is IEEE/370 |
| Prime Key Offset  :     1    Length :     6    Alternate Keys? N             |
+==============================================================================+


+==============================================================================+
| Conversion Status   Convert EBCDIC to ASCII   No Floating point conversion  |
| using : No mask                                                              |
+==============================================================================+
Workbench-File-Loader─────────────────────────────────────────────────────────
F1=help F3=load-profile F4=save-profile F5=specify-input F6=specify-output
F7=specify-mask-file F8=create/edit-mask F9=rebuild-file F10=convert-file Escape
```

Figure 9.16 Workbench File Loader menu

```
+==============================================================================+
| Name : K:\COBOL\MFWBBOOK\custmst.ebc                                          |
| Type : Record Sequential, Fixed Length        File is ASCII/EBCDIC           |
| Record Length Min :    41    Max    :    41    Floating Point Rep is IEEE/370 |
| Access Key Offset :     0    Length :     0                                   |
+==============================================================================+


+==============================================================================+
| Output File Details                                                          |
| Name : K:\COBOL\MFWBBOOK\custmst.dat                                         |
| Type : Indexed Sequential, Fixed Length        File is ASCII/EBCDIC          |
| Record Length Min :    41    Max    :    41    Floating Point Rep is IEEE/370 |
| Prime Key Offset  :     1    Length :     6    Alternate Keys? N             |
+==============================================================================+


+==============================================================================+
| Conversion Status   Convert EBCDIC to ASCII   No Floating point conversion  |
| using : No mask                                                              |
+==============================================================================+
WFL-Specify-Input─────────────────────────────────────────────────────────────
F1=help F2=specify-file-name F3=specify-file-type       F4=toggle-ASCII/EBCDIC
F5=specify-access-key F6=toggle-IEEE/370                F10=specify-output-details Escape
```

Figure 9.17 WFL Specify Input menu

```
+==============================================================================+
| Input File Details                                                           |
| Name : K:\COBOL\MFWBBOOK\custmst.ebc                                          |
| Type : Record Sequential, Fixed Length        File is ASCII/EBCDIC           |
| Record Length Min :    41    Max    :    41    Floating Point Rep is IEEE/370 |
| Access Key Offset :     0  Length :     0                                     |
+==============================================================================+


+==============================================================================+
| Output File Details                                                          |
| Name : K:\COBOL\MFWBBOOK\custmst.dat                                          |
| Type : Indexed Sequential, Fixed Length       File is ASCII/EBCDIC           |
| Record Length Min :    41    Max    :    41    Floating Point Rep is IEEE/370 |
| Prime Key Offset  :     1  Length :     6    Alternate Keys? N               |
+==============================================================================+


+==============================================================================+
| Conversion Status   Convert EBCDIC to ASCII   No Floating point conversion   |
| using : No mask                                                              |
+==============================================================================+
WFL-Specify-Output────────────────────────────────────────────────────────────
F1=help F2=specify-file-name F3=specify-file-type       F4=toggle-ASCII/EBCDIC
F5=define-alternate-Keys F6=toggle-IEEE/370     F10=specify-input-details  Escape
```

Figure 9.18 WFL Specify Output menu

```
+==============================================================================+
|                                                                              |
| Description: Sample mask                                                     |
|                                                                              |
| Call:                                                                        |
|                                                                              |
|            No.  Description                    Type                          |
|            01   Sample #1                      New                           |
|                                                                              |
|                                                                              |
|                                                                              |
|                                                                              |
|                                                                              |
|                                                                              |
|                                                                              |
|                                                                              |
|                                                                              |
|                                                                              |
|                                                                              |
|                                                                              |
|                                                                              |
+==============================================================================+
New-Mask─────────────────────────────────────────────────Ins-Caps-Num-Scroll
F1=help F3=load F4=save F5=clear F6=repeat F7=relocate F8=delete  PgUp ^ v  Esc
F9=IDY/**manual** F10=external-call-off/on <-'=edit-selected-mask   PgDn Home End
```

Figure 9.19 WFL New Mask screen

The WFL Specify Input menu. On the WFL Specify Input menu, pressing **F2=specify-file-name** moves your cursor to the **Name :** prompt so that you can enter the input filename. You can enter a fully qualified name with drive and path if needed. Pressing **F3=specify-file-type** brings up a selection menu that lets you indicate the input file type. As of Workbench v2.5, WFL supports the following input file types:

- Line Sequential
- Record Sequential, Fixed Length
- Record Sequential, Variable Length
- Indexed Sequential, Fixed Length
- Indexed Sequential, Variable Length
- Relative, Fixed Length
- Relative, Variable Length
- VRECGEN
- Mainframe report format

We have already discussed most of these file types. **VRECGEN** refers to variable-length files downloaded from the mainframe after having been processed by VRECGEN. **Mainframe report format** refers to files that contain mainframe carriage control characters. WFL lets you translate mainframe report files into a form suitable for printing on the PC.

F4=toggle-ASCII/EBCDIC is a toggle switch that lets you indicate whether the input file is in ASCII or EBCDIC. The setting you select will be highlighted in the Input File Details portion of the screen.

If your input file is an indexed file on the PC, pressing **F5=specify-access-key** will let you specify the length and location of that key within the record. Within WFL, the first byte in the record is position 1.

If your file contains any floating-point fields, **F6=toggle-IEEE/370** lets you specify whether they are in PC (IEEE) or mainframe (370) format. During EBCDIC/ASCII translation, you will need to specify a conversion mask so that WFL will avoid corrupting floating-point fields. If your input file contains no floating-point fields, leave this toggle switch set to IEEE.

Finally, pressing **F10=specify-output-details** switches you into the submenu for specifying output file characteristics.

The WFL Specify Output menu. On the WFL Specify Output menu, most of the functions work similarly to the way they do on the input menu. **F10=specify-input-details** toggles you back into the submenu for specifying input details. WFL supports the following output file types:

- Line Sequential
- Record Sequential, Fixed Length
- Record Sequential, Variable Length
- Indexed Sequential, Fixed Length
- Indexed Sequential, Variable Length
- Relative, Fixed Length
- Relative, Variable Length
- PC Print format

PC print format lets you translate mainframe report files so that they can be printed on the PC. If you have selected mainframe report format for the input file, then select PC print format for the output.

If you specify an indexed sequential output file, data entry fields will open up so that you can supply the offset and length of the prime key. Within

WFL, the first byte of the record is position 1, not zero as you might assume. Pressing **F5=define-alternate-keys** brings up a popup menu that lets you specify alternate keys for the indexed file.

Data conversion masks. If your file contains some fields that you do not want to convert, you will need to specify conversion masks. If you already have created a mask file that applies to your situation, you can press **F7=specify-mask-file** to load it into WFL. A mask file will have a filename extension of .MSK. If you need to edit an old mask file or create a new one, press **F8=create/edit-mask** to bring up the mask menu shown in Figure 9.19.

A conversion mask file can contain several masks, each of which applies to a certain type of record in your file. Alternatively, if your file contains only one record type, your conversion mask file will contain only one mask. A scrollable list on this menu shows all of the masks in your current file. You can select a mask for editing by using the cursor keys to highlight the name of the mask and then pressing the enter key. Choosing the mask name *New* lets you create a new mask.

The functions **F5=clear, F6=repeat, F7=relocate,** and **F8=delete** let you rearrange the order of priority of masks on the screen. This is important because masks can contain selection criteria. At runtime, WFL uses those criteria to determine whether to use that mask to convert the record it is currently processing. The first mask whose selection criteria prove true becomes the mask that is used to convert that record.

To edit an existing mask file, press **F3=load** to load the desired .MSK file. To save a mask file, press **F4=save** and supply the filename.

The "WFL" chapter in the *Workbench Reference* shows several ways to create conversion mask files. On this menu, you have the choice of creating a mask manually or by copying a record description from an .IDY file from the checker.

Using masks from an .IDY file. To copy a record description from an .IDY file, use the cursor arrow keys to highlight the "New" line on this menu. Toggle F9=IDY/manual to the **IDY** setting and press the enter key. On the next menu, the FDs and 01 levels in that file will appear so that you can choose one.

Creating a new mask with manual input. Suppose you want to create a new mask manually. Use the cursor arrow keys to highlight the "New" line on this menu. Toggle F9=IDY/manual to the **manual** setting and press the enter key. The WFL Manual Editing screen appears in Figure 9.20.

On the manual editing menu, you can specify the lengths and offsets of each field to be translated or not translated. Be sure to specify the record length at the top of the screen. When you have entered all of the fields, press **F10=generate-mask.**

Multiple record types. If your file contains more than one record layout and you need to create more than one mask, you will need to establish the conditions for each mask. To do that, select **F7=rec-id/conditions,** which will allow you to enter the length and location of the record ID field.

If your record selection conditions are more complex than that, another menu will appear when you tab over to the **Conditions** field. This is the **Edit-Rec-Id-Conditions** popup menu shown in Figure 9.21. If you do not wish to use this popup, you can simply press the escape key to get back to the previous menu.

WFL also lets you write your own program or "user exit" to determine whether or not to use the current mask with each record. You can specify such a program by toggling **F10=external-call-off/on** and entering the program name on this menu.

Updating the mask. Once you have entered the record ID conditions, press **F10=generate-record-ID** to update the mask with that information. Be sure to save the mask file on the menu in Figure 9.19 after you have created all of the masks.

Running the file conversion. Pressing **F10=convert-file** on the WFL main menu screen begins the conversion process. A pop-up box on the screen will show you whether the conversion succeeded and how many records were converted, as shown in Figure 9.22. What do you do if WFL finds errors? If the error message shows a file status code, you can look it up in the "File Status" chapter of the *COBOL/2 Operating Guide.* WFL uses the extended file status codes for indexed files. More complete information about bad file status codes is in the *Error Messages Manual.* Other types of WFL error messages are described in the "WFL" chapter of the *Workbench Reference.* The likeliest source of WFL problems is "pilot error": supplying incorrect input, output, and mask information. Recheck your input parms against the actual files you plan to convert.

Using WFL to reorganize indexed files. Pressing **F9=rebuild-file** on the WFL main menu screen brings up the WFL Rebuild screen, shown in Figure 9.23. Most of the functions on this menu are the same as those on the file conversion menu. **F6=specify-rebuild-type** lets you decide whether to rebuild the index only, or both data and index. Which do you use? An index file can become corrupted if a program failure or system outage takes place while a file is open. If this happens, a flag in the file header will show that the index is corrupt. To recover from this condition, you need to rebuild the index portion.

On the other hand, an indexed file can become disorganized and inefficient as more and more updates take place. To reorganize the file to its optimal level of efficiency, you will need to rebuild both the index and the data portions of the file. When you rebuild both portions of the file, you will need to enter a name for the output file. Pressing **F8=output-file-name** allows you to enter the new name.

Micro Focus recommends that, once you have recovered a corrupt file by rebuilding the index, you also reorganize the complete file. This will restructure the file so that free space will become available for reuse.

Once you have entered all data required for rebuilding the file, pressing **F10=Rebuild** starts the rebuild process.

```
+===============================================================================+
| Mask:  1  Description: Sample #1                         Record-length:    20 |
|===============================================================================|
|                                    |Rec-id:01                                 |
|                                    |Offset:     1  Length: 2  Convert?:Y      |
|                                    |Conditions?             Created:manual    |
+===============================================================================+
  +=============================+ Offset Length              Convert?
  | This table shows the offsets|    1     2                    Y
  | and lengths which will be   |    3     4                    N
  | converted using this mask.  |    7    14                    Y
  | It should include any data  |    0     0
  | within the record which is  |
  | of display usage.           |
  +=============================+



Manual-Editing──────────────────────────────────────────────Ins-Caps-Num-Scroll
F1=help F4=delete                                            End ^ v <-' Esc
F7=rec-id/conditions F9=IDY     F10=generate-mask            Home  PgUp PgDn
```

Figure 9.20 WFL Manual Editing screen

```
+=================================================================================+
| Mask:  1  Description: Sample #1                           Record-length:    20 |
+=================================================================================+
|                                    |Rec-id:01                                   |
|                                    |                                            |
|                                    |Offset:     1  Length: 2  Convert?:Y        |
|                                    |Conditions?             Created:manual      |
+=================================================================================+
  +=============================+ Offset +=====================================+
  | This table shows the offsets|    1   | Condition  Value/Range-lo  Range-hi |
  | and lengths which will be   |    3   |              |=======     |======= |
  | converted using this mask.  |    7   |                                     |
  | It should include any data  |    0   |                                     |
  | within the record which is  |        |                                     |
  | of display usage.           |        |                                     |
  +=============================+        |                                     |
                                         |                                     |
                                         |                                     |
                                         +=====================================+



Edit-Rec-Id-Conditions──────────────────────────────────────Ins-Caps-Num-Scroll
F1=help F2=list F3=insert F4=delete F5=hex  F10=generate-rec-id  ^ v <-'  Escape
Enter the conditions, values & ranges above
```

Figure 9.21 WFL Edit Rec Id Conditions screen

```
+==============================================================================+
| Name : K:\COBOL\MFWBBOOK\custmst.ebc                                          |
| Type : Record Sequential, Fixed Length        File is ASCII/EBCDIC           |
| Record Length Min :    41    Max    :    41    Floating Point Rep is IEEE/370 |
| Access Key Offset :     0   Length :     0                                    |
+==============================================================================+
                  +===========================================+
+=================| File Conversion Completed Successfully  |==================+
| Output File Deta|                                           |                 |
| Name : K:\COBOL\|    Source records processed :    11       |                 |
| Type : Indexed S|                                           ||/EBCDIC         |
| Record Length Mi|    Minimum record size : 00041            ||t Rep is IEEE/370 |
| Prime Key Offset|                                           ||s? N            |
+=================|    Maximum record size : 00041            |==================+
                 |                                            |
+=================| Press any key to continue                 |==================+
| Conversion Statu+===========================================+oint conversion  |
| using : No mask                                                               |
+==============================================================================+
Workbench-File-Loader—————————————————————————————————————————————————————————————
F1=help F3=load-profile F4=save-profile F5=specify-input F6=specify-output
F7=specify-mask-file F8=create/edit-mask F9=rebuild-file F10=convert-file Escape
```

Figure 9.22 WFL menu showing conversion results

```
+==============================================================================+
| Input File Details                                                           |
+==============================================================================+
|                                                                              |
|                     Rebuild ISAM/VSAM Interface                              |
|                                                                              |
|==============================================================================|
|                                                                              |
| Input File Details                                                           |
| Name : K:\COBOL\MFWBBOOK\custmst.dat                                         |
| Type : Indexed Sequential, Fixed Length/Variable Length                     |
| Record Length Min :    41    Max    :    41    File is ASCII/EBCDIC          |
| Prime Key Offset  :     0   Length :     0                                   |
|                                                                              |
| Output File                                                                  |
| Name :                                                                       |
|                                                                              |
| Rebuild Type : Index Only/Data and Index                                     |
|                                                                              |
+==============================================================================+
WFL-Specify-Rebuild-Details————————————————————————————————————————————————————
F1=help F2=specify-file-name F3=specify-file-type        F4=toggle-ASCII/EBCDIC
F5=alternate-keys F6=specify-rebuild-type F8=output-file-name F10=Rebuild Escape
```

Figure 9.23 WFL Rebuild screen

```
=================================================================================
  000000    F0 F0 F0 F0 F0 F1 C3 96-87 89 A3 96 40 C3 96 99   000001Cogito Cor
  000010    97 96 99 81 A3 89 96 95-40 40 40 40 40 40 40 F3   poration        3
  000020    F1 F2 F7 F6 F7 F5 F6 F9-F1 F0 F0 F0 F0 F0 F2 C4   127675691000002D
  000030    81 89 A2 A8 7D A2 40 C6-89 A2 88 40 D4 81 99 92   aisy's Fish Mark
  000040    85 A3 40 40 40 40 40 40-F3 F1 F2 F7 F6 F7 F5 F6   et      31276756
  000050    F9 F1 F0 F0 F0 F0 F0 F3-E2 81 94 94 A8 7D A2 40   91000003Sammy's
  000060    C2 81 99 40 50 40 C7 99-89 93 93 40 40 40 40 40   Bar & Grill
  000070    40 F3 F1 F2 F7 F6 F7 F0-F0 F0 F0 F0 F0 F0 F0 F0    312767000000000
  000080    F4 D4 96 99 99 89 A2 40-40 40 40 40 40 40 40 40   4Morris
  000090    40 40 40 40 40 40 40 40-40 40 F3 F1 F2 F0 F0 F0            312000
  0000A0    F0 F0 F0 F0 F0 F0 F0 F0-F0 F5 D4 81 87 95 A4 94   0000000005Magnum
  0000B0    40 40 40 40 40 40 40 40-40 40 40 40 40 40 40 40
  0000C0    40 40 40 F3 F1 F2 F0 F0-F0 F0 F0 F0 F0 F0 F0 F0       3120000000000
  0000D0    F0 F0 F6 C6 99 85 83 92-93 85 A2 40 40 40 40 40   006Freckles
  0000E0    40 40 40 40 40 40 40 40-40 40 40 40 F3 F1 F2 F0               3120
  0000F0    F0 F0 F0 F0 F0 F0 F0 F0-F0 F0 F0 F7 D7 93 A4 A3   000000000007Plut
=================================================================================
  000100    96 40 40 40 40 40 40 40-40 40 40 40 40 40 40 40   o

Hexediting-CUSTMST.EBC—Len—0001C3-Adrs-000000————————————————————-
F1=help F2=hex/char F3=load-file F4=save-file F5=goto F6=display-all/ASC/EBC
F7=hex/dec-address F8=list-file F10=find                              Escape
```

Figure 9.24 HEXEDIT screen

New WFL capabilities in version 3.0. In Workbench version 3.0, WFL offers support for several more file conversion types. First of all, you can create mainframe format print files, so that you can route a file back to the mainframe for printing if you don't have a fast printer on your PC. You can also convert PC data files back to VRECGEN format so that you can send them back to the host, and, once there, import them into mainframe VSAM. This lets you continue using your PC test data files on the mainframe when you begin your system testing. Finally, you can convert Micro Focus V-ISAM files to and from Btrieve format. This makes it easier to share CICS OS/2 VSAM files with batch programs.

9.5.4 HEXEDIT (Hex Editor)

HEXEDIT is the original Micro Focus Workbench hexadecimal editor. The formatted Data File Editor, introduced with Workbench v2.5, takes the place of HEXEDIT for some purposes. Nevertheless, HEXEDIT remains a useful tool for examining data files when you don't know their structure ahead of time.

Invoking HEXEDIT. You can bring up the Hex Editor by pressing **F6=hexedit** on the File Utilities menu. Alternatively, you can enter the following command at the command line prompt:

```
RUN HEXEDIT filename
```

A sample HEXEDIT screen appears in Figure 9.24. If you invoked HEXEDIT from the command line and supplied the filename to edit, the screen will come up with the first page of file contents in the text area. Otherwise, you will need to load a file by using the menu. The HEXEDIT display format resembles a mainframe memory dump or file dump. The text area on the HEXEDIT screen contains three columns. The left column shows the data address expressed as an offset from the beginning of the file. The center column shows the contents of each byte in hexadecimal. The right column shows a character representation of the hex values, in your choice of ASCII or EBCDIC. In the character display, HEXEDIT substitutes dots for hex bytes that do not correspond to a displayable text character. The byte at the current text cursor position in the file will be highlighted in both the hex and character display.

Notice also that the first line in the text display area shows the last line from the previous display page, if any. The last line in the text display area shows the next line that will appear at the top of the next display page.

HEXEDIT function key usage. These functions appear on the HEXEDIT main menu:

- **F2=hex/char** lets you switch the text cursor between the hex and character display columns. By switching the cursor, you can edit file contents by overkeying data in either the hex or the character display columns. However, if you want to enter a hex value that does not represent a valid displayable character, you must enter it through the hex display.

- **F3=load-file** and **F4=save-file** let you load and save data files. These functions work in much the same way as they do in the COBOL Editor.

- **F5=goto** lets you move quickly to another part of the file. Pressing **F5** brings up a prompt for entering a data address. If you supply a new address (offset) and press the enter key, HEXEDIT will reposition your cursor to that byte. Supply the address in either hex or decimal, depending on your current selection of the hex/dec-address directive.

- **F6=display-all/ASC/EBC** selects the character set for the text display. **all** refers to the extended IBM PC ASCII character set. **ASC** refers to original standard ASCII. **EBC** refers to EBCDIC. If you are using HEXEDIT to examine unfamiliar disk files, and you want to know whether a file contains ASCII or EBCDIC text fields, toggle **F6** between ASCII and EBCDIC to see whether readable characters appear.

- **F7=hex/dec-address** switches the address representation between hexadecimal and decimal. HEXEDIT suppresses leading zeroes in the address column when displaying addresses in decimal.

- **F8=list-file** produces a file listing in printable format. Pressing **F8** brings up a prompt that lets you enter the output filename for the print file. Supply a filename and press the enter key. Then, HEXEDIT will prompt you for the beginning and ending of the range of addresses to print within the file. If you specify a zero address for the end of the address range, HEXEDIT will assume the end of the file.

- **F10=find** lets you search by file contents. Pressing **F10** brings up the HEXEDIT Find menu, shown in Figure 9.25.

HEXEDIT Find functions. You can bring up the HEXEDIT Find menu by pressing F10=find on the HEXEDIT main menu. Search arguments are entered as byte strings. In the **Find string** prompt area, you can enter up to sixteen bytes of data to use as a search argument. Pressing the enter key will begin a forward search for that string.

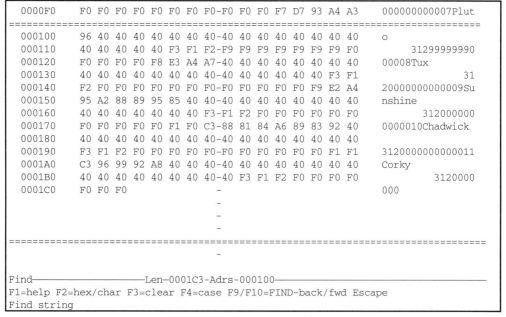

```
 0000F0      F0 F0 F0 F0 F0 F0 F0 F0-F0 F0 F0 F7 D7 93 A4 A3    000000000007Plut
============================================================================
 000100      96 40 40 40 40 40 40 40-40 40 40 40 40 40 40 40    o
 000110      40 40 40 40 40 F3 F1 F2-F9 F9 F9 F9 F9 F9 F9 F0          31299999990
 000120      F0 F0 F0 F0 F8 E3 A4 A7-40 40 40 40 40 40 40 40    00008Tux
 000130      40 40 40 40 40 40 40 40-40 40 40 40 40 F3 F1                     31
 000140      F2 F0 F0 F0 F0 F0 F0 F0-F0 F0 F0 F0 F9 E2 A4    20000000000009Su
 000150      95 A2 88 89 95 85 40 40-40 40 40 40 40 40 40    nshine
 000160      40 40 40 40 40 40 40 F3-F1 F2 F0 F0 F0 F0 F0 F0           312000000
 000170      F0 F0 F0 F0 F0 F1 F0 C3-88 81 84 A6 89 83 92 40    0000010Chadwick
 000180      40 40 40 40 40 40 40 40-40 40 40 40 40 40 40
 000190      F3 F1 F2 F0 F0 F0 F0 F0-F0 F0 F0 F0 F0 F0 F1 F1    3120000000000011
 0001A0      C3 96 99 92 A8 40 40 40-40 40 40 40 40 40 40 40    Corky
 0001B0      40 40 40 40 40 40 40 40-40 F3 F1 F2 F0 F0 F0 F0            3120000
 0001C0      F0 F0 F0                           -               000
                                               -
                                               -
                                               -
============================================================================
                                               -

Find────────────────────Len-0001C3-Adrs-000100────────────────────
F1=help F2=hex/char F3=clear F4=case F9/F10=FIND-back/fwd Escape
Find string
```

Figure 9.25 HEXEDIT Find menu

- **F2=hex/char** means approximately the same on the Find menu as it does on the initial HEXEDIT menu. It lets you decide whether to search on a hex or a character value.
- **F3=clear** clears the **Find string** prompt area.
- **F4=case** toggles case sensitivity on and off.
- **F9/F10=FIND-back/fwd** lets you choose whether to search backward or forward in the file. You must enter your search string before pressing these keys. The enter key initiates a forward search, as does **F10**.

9.5.5 Data File Editor (DFED)

The Data File Editor became part of the Workbench with version 2.5. You can use it in much the same way as the Hex Editor, to edit unformatted strings of data, or you can use it as an intelligent formatted file editor. If your data file is used in a program, the Data File Editor can use the program's record layout as a template. The Data File Editor will break out each field by name and type so that you can edit each one. You can read an indexed file in order by any of its indexes or search for a key value.

Invoking the Data File Editor. You can bring up the Data File Editor by pressing **F7=data-file-editor** on the File Utilities menu. You can also bring it up from the command line by entering either of these commands:

```
[XM] RUN DFED [filename] [-E] [-B]
[XM] WB DFED [filename] [/E] [/B]
```

In this command, the filename is optional. If you specify a filename, DFED will come up with the file already loaded into the work area. What about the runtime switches? The **-E** runtime switch specifies an EBCDIC character set.

You can switch between ASCII and EBCDIC in DFED also. The **-B** runtime switch causes DFED to make an automatic backup of the data file being edited. In this case, the backup filename will have an extension of .DBK. An index file backup will have a filename extension of .IBK.

Running DFED in 43-line or 50-line mode. If you have a monitor capable of displaying 43 or 50 lines in text mode, you can run DFED in that mode. DFED will look the same except for the fact that the characters will be smaller and the text area on the screen will show more lines. To set up the alternate mode under MS-DOS, you will need to include a **MODE CON: LINES=43** or **MODE CON: LINES=50** command in your AUTOEXEC.BAT file. You will also need to place a DEVICE command for ANSI.SYS in the CONFIG.SYS file. Under OS/2, ANSI.SYS is not used except in the DOS compatibility box. The OS/2 command to get into 50-line mode is different: **MODE CO80,50.** The MODE command applies to that one session only. Under either operating system, when you run your application, you would use runtime switch +C4 to get support of 43-line mode, or +C5 to get support of 50-line mode, or +C to default to the current setting. The switch can be placed either on the command line, in parentheses after the program name, or in the **SET COBSW=+C5** environment variable. In the case of DFED, you can use this command:

```
[XM] RUN +C DFED [filename] [-E] [-B]
```

Data File Editor (DFED) menus. Figure 9.26 shows the DFED main menu. If you have invoked DFED from the command line and you supplied a data filename, the screen will come up with the data file displayed in the text area. (Otherwise, you will need to use the DFED Alt key menu to load a file.) This example shows the CUSTMST.DAT file displayed in unformatted mode. Each record occupies one line with nothing to separate the data fields.

Record operations. The usual cursor and paging keys let you navigate in the data file. The following function keys are available on the main menu:

- **F7=previous-record** and **F8=next-record** will set the previous or next record to be the current record.
- A record number appears on the left of the unformatted DFED display, although you can turn off the record number with the **F5=hide-record-numbers** function.
- **F2=(un)format** is a switch that lets you toggle back and forth between unformatted and formatted mode. You can use formatted mode only if you have set up a record structure, as described below.
- **F3=insert-record** and **F4=delete-record** let you add a new record at the current position, or delete the current record. To update text data within the current record, overtype the data and press the enter key.

File operations. Figure 9.27 shows the DFED Alt key menu, but this time we have switched to a hex display.

- **F2=toggle-hex** lets you see the hexadecimal representation of the data. Hex mode lets you edit bytes that cannot be displayed in ASCII or EBCDIC.

- **F3=load-data-file** uses the Micro Focus directory facility to let you load a data file into DFED for editing.
- **F4=load-record-structure** lets you create record format templates from an .IDY file that you specify.

```
0000000001|000001Cogito Corporation        3127675691
0000000002|000002Daisy's Fish Market       3127675691
0000000003|000003Sammy's Bar & Grill       3127670000
0000000004|000004Morris                    3120000000
0000000005|000005Magnum                    3120000000
0000000006|000006Freckles                  3120000000
0000000007|000007Pluto                     3129999999
0000000008|000008Tux                       3120000000
0000000009|000009Sunshine                  3120000000
0000000010|000010Chadwick                  3120000000
0000000011|000011Corky                     3120000000
==========|==============================================================
          |
          |
          |
          |
          |
          |
          |
          |
          |
          |
CUSTMST--Key-Prime---Record-No-1---Record-Col-1--------------------------
F1=help F2=(un)format F3=insert-record F4=delete-record
F5=hide-record-numbers    F7=previous-record F8=next-record  <-' Alt Ctrl Escape
```

Figure 9.26 Data File Editor (DFED) main menu

```
0000000001|000001Cogito Corporation        3127675691
          |33333346666762467767676666222222233333333333
          |0000013F794F03F20F2149FE00000003127675691
          |
0000000002|000002Daisy's Fish Market       3127675691
          |33333346677272467624676672222223333333333
          |0000024193973069380D12B540000003127675691
          |
0000000003|000003Sammy's Bar | Grill       3127675690
          |33333356667272467222476662222223333333333
          |00000331DD9730212060729CC0000003127675690
          |
0000000004|000004Morris                    3120000000
          |33333346776722222222222222222223333333333
          |000004DF2293000000000000000000003120000000
          |
0000000005|000005Magnum                    3120000000
          |33333346666762222222222222222223333333333
          |000005D17E5D0000000000000000000003120000000
          |
          |
CUSTMST--Key-Prime---Record-No-1---Record-Col-1--------------------------
F1=help F2=toggle-hex F3=load-data-file F4=load-record-structure
F5=configuration-box F9/F10=select-prev-next-structure
```

Figure 9.27 DFED Alt key menu with hex display

```
0000000001|000001Cogito Corporation        3127675691
0000000002|000002Daisy's Fish Market        3127675691
0000000003|000003Sammy's Bar & Grill        3127670000
0000000004|000004Morris                     3120000000
0000000005|000005Magnum                     3120000000
0000000006|000006Freckles                   3120000000
0000000007|000007Pluto                      3129999999
0000000008|000008Tux                        3120000000
0000000009|000009Su+Configuration=========================+
0000000010|000010Ch| File:                             |
0000000011|000011Co|  Organization : Indexed 1 key      |
==========|========|  Type         : Fixed              |======================
          |        |  Length       : 612 bytes          |
          |        |  Character set: ASCII               |
          |        |  Record length : 41 bytes           |
          |        +====================================+
          |
          |
          |
          |
          |
Configuration-menu─────────────────────────────────────────────────
F1=help F2=toggle-character-set F3=save-defaults F10=commit-change
                                                             Escape
```

Figure 9.28 Data File Editor (DFED) configuration menu

- If you have already set up a file of record format templates, **F9** and **F10** on the Alt key menu let you select the previous or next structure in the file.

Configuration. Choosing **F5=configuration-box** on the DFED Alt-key menu brings up the menu shown in Figure 9.28. You will see a popup window showing the current file configuration.

- **F2=toggle-character-set** lets you switch between ASCII and EBCDIC display modes.
- Once you have chosen, press **F10=commit-change** to make the change effective.
- Finally, **F3=save-defaults** saves your editing configuration to the DFED.CFG file so that you can use the same settings next time you edit.

Editing files in formatted mode. When you press **F4=load-record-structure** on the DFED Alt key menu, you will see the menu shown in Figure 9.29. Pressing **F2=enter-structure-selector** on that menu lets you build file editing templates out of record definitions in .IDY files produced by the Micro Focus Checker. You can save these editing templates as a structure file. **F3=load-structure-file** lets you load an existing structure file created in a previous session. That function uses the Micro Focus directory facility to let you specify the structure filename you want to load.

```
Load-Structure-Defs─────────────────────────────────────────────────
F1=help F2=enter-structure-selector F3=load-structure-file
                                                             Escape
```

Figure 9.29 DFED Load Structure Definitions menu

```
                        Data Structure Selector


01   CUSTMST-REC                      (00001:00041)      Group
  02   CUST-KEY                       (00001:00006)      Group
    03   CUST-NO                      (00001:00006)      alphanumeric
  02   CUST-NAME                      (00007:00025)      alphanumeric
  02   CUST-PHONE                     (00032:00010)      alphanumeric









CUST————Depth 02—————————————————————————————————————————
F1=help F2=expand-item F3=select-IDY F4=save-list F5=picture F6=descend-level
                                                         <-'=select Esc
Select field to select this record structure.
```

Figure 9.30 DFED record structure selection screen

When you press **F2=enter-structure-selector** on the Load-Structure-Defs menu, you will see a Micro Focus directory function menu that asks you to supply the name of an **.IDY** file. The Checker produces an .IDY file when you compile your programs for animations. If any of your programs contain record layouts for the file you want to edit, you can use the .IDY file from one of those programs as a file editing template. When you supply the name of the .IDY file, the record structure selection menu shown in Figure 9.30 will appear.

When this screen first comes up, it will show a list of all of the COBOL 01 levels in your program, in the form of a scrolling light-bar menu. If your data file contains several record types with different layouts, then several different 01 levels in the program may be applicable. In any case, move the cursor to an 01 level that matches the records you want to edit. Press **F2=expand-item** to expand that field. The 01 level will expand to show the detail items under it, as in the example in Figure 9.30.

On this screen, **F3=select-IDY** lets you load a different .IDY file. **F4=save-list** lets you save the data structure that you have selected from the .IDY file. The newly saved structure filename will have an extension of .STR. **F5=picture** shows the location, length, and type of COBOL PICTURE clause associated with each data item on the screen. For example, Figure 9.30 shows that CUST-NAME begins in column 7 for a length of 25 and is defined as alphanumeric.

Suppose you want to extract a record structure from a subordinate group item that is below the 01 level. Selecting **F6=descend-level** will upgrade the data structures immediately below the currently selected item. These will become 01 levels in their own right so that you can select one of them to be an editing template.

This screen also lets you define an item as a record ID field. Pressing **F2=expand-item** on a detail item will invoke the Hex Editor function so that you can enter the record ID value that corresponds to this record layout.

When you go back to the DFED main menu, you will see your data file record formatted in accordance with the record structure you chose. Figure 9.31 shows an example of this type of display.

Editing functions on the DFED CTRL menu. Before we move on to the next topic, let's take a look at the functions on the DFED CTRL key menu shown in Figure 9.31. These functions have to do with the actual editing process.

- You can search for particular records in the file. If you are working with an indexed file, **F2=search-on-key** lets you specify a search argument (key contents). If the file contains a record with that key, DFED will display it on the screen.

- If your indexed file has alternate keys, **F3=change-key** lets you specify a different key sequence for the next search operation.

- You can also search for the occurrence of a text string, much as you would do in the COBOL Editor or the Hex Editor facilities. **F6=search-on-string** lets you specify the string you want DFED to find. **F7=repeat-string-search** repeats the search operation to find the next occurrence of that string in the data file.

- If you want to replace all of the contents of the current record, **F4=clear-record** will clear out existing field contents.

- F5=restore-record will restore them to previous values.

```
01 CUSTMST-REC
  02 CUST-KEY
    03 CUST-NO                [000002]
  02 CUST-NAME                [Daisy's Fish Market      ]
  02 CUST-PHONE               [3127675691]
============================= ===================================================




















CUSTMST──Key Prime──Record No 2──Field Col 1────────────────────────────
F1=help F2=search-on-key F3=change-key F4=clear-record F5=restore-record
F6=search-on-string F7=repeat-string-search F8/F9=scroll-field-name-left/right
```

Figure 9.31 DFED CTRL key menu with formatted display

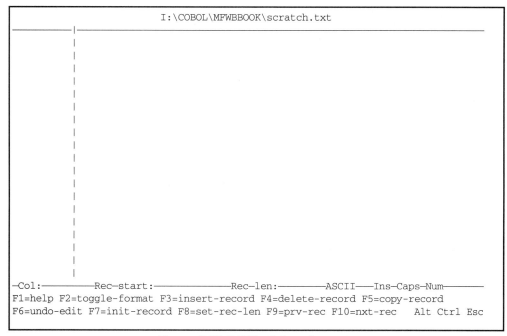

Figure 9.32 DFED v3.0 main menu

- Finally, if a name is too long to fit on the screen, **F8/F9=scroll-field-name-left/right** lets you see the rest of the name.

New DFED capabilities in version 3.0. Reorganized DFED menus appear in the function key Workbench v3.0 menu system. The primary aim was to make structure (field mask) selection easier to use. This version of DFED allows you to create new files of any supported Micro Focus file type. You can do full editing on all file types, including record sequential, line sequential, relative, V-ISAM, and Btrieve, with fixed or variable length records. Only V-ISAM and relative files were fully supported in v2.6. We will take a look at some of the new menu functions.

The DFED v3.0 main menu. Figure 9.32 shows the DFED main menu. This menu is primarily concerned with record-oriented operations.

- **F2=toggle-format** chooses whether to show the records as formatted (using a structure) or unformatted.
- **F3=insert-record** lets you insert a record just before the current record. If structures are available, you can pick a structure to use for building the new record.
- **F4=delete-record** deletes the current record. If you delete the last remaining record, the file will become empty, and the format will revert to unformatted mode.
- **F5=copy-record** copies the current record and inserts the copy following the current record.
- **F6=undo-edit** returns the current record to the contents it had before you moved the cursor to it.

- **F7=init-record** initializes the current record to spaces if it is unformatted, or to values dependent on the structure.
- **F8=set-rec-len** sets the record length to the cursor position in variable-length files.
- **F9=prv-rec** and **F10=nxt-rec** move to the previous and next records, respectively.

DFED v3.0 file operations. Figure 9.33 shows the DFED Alt key menu. This menu is primarily concerned with operations against the entire file.

- **F2=toggle-hex** lets you choose whether or not to see record contents in hexadecimal.
- **F3=load-file** brings up the menu in Figure 9.34 that lets you load an existing file for editing.
- **F4=save-file** saves the edited file to disk with the same name as before.
- **F5=create-file** brings up the menu in Figure 9.35 that lets you create a new file.
- **F6=save-as** lets you save an existing file under a new name.
- **F7=load-str-file** allows you to load a file containing record structures.
- **F8=structure-selector** lets you choose an appropriate record structure from within that file.
- **F9=record-group-edits** lets you edit more than one record at a time.
- **F10=file-info** shows information about the file currently being edited.

The DFED v3.0 Load file menu. Figure 9.34 shows the Load file menu, which lets you load existing data files. If you choose to load an existing fixed-length relative, fixed-length sequential, or line sequential file, DFED will prompt you for more information as needed. Let's look at the function keys on this menu:

- **F2=directory** lets you use the Micro Focus directory function to choose an existing data file for loading.
- **F3=toggle-backup** lets you decide whether to back up your old files automatically before saving changes. If this toggle is turned on, then DFED will rename .DAT files to .DBK, and .IDX files to .IBK.
- **F4=toggle-character-set** toggles the display translation between ASCII and EBCDIC.
- **F5=toggle-edt-mode** lets you choose between full edit mode and quick edit mode. Full edit will apply your edits only when the file is saved to disk. Quick edit applies edits immediately. The latter alternative is useful for files too large to be edited in any other way.

Using DFED v3.0 to create a new file. The **Create file menu,** shown in Figure 9.35, lets you specify the characteristics of the file that you want to create. Use the **Tab** and **Shift+Tab** keys to move back and forth among menu items. Reenter values as needed. Use the space bar to accept the current value of a menu item. Press the enter key when you are ready to create the file. This will return you to the DFED main menu so that you can create new records.

Performing searches with DFED v3.0. The DFED Ctrl key menu (Figure 9.36) lets you perform various search operations on a data file.

- **F2=search** lets you search on a file key, a character string, or a field value.
- **F3=repeat-search** lets you repeat the most recent search operation.
- **F4=compress/expand** changes the display format. Compress shows data items at the current COBOL level only; expand shows all data items.
- **F5=ascend-level** moves to the parent of the current field.
- **F6=descend-level** moves to the child of the current field.
- **F7=field/picture** toggles the left side of the display screen to show either the field name or the COBOL PICTURE.
- **F8=go-to-byte** moves the cursor to the Nth byte in the current record.
- **F9=go-to-Nth-record** moves to the Nth record in the file.
- **F10=toggle-character-set** toggles between ASCII and EBCDIC display translation.

```
—Col:————————Rec—start:——————————Rec—len:—————————ASCII——Ins—Caps—Num————————
F1=help F2=toggle-hex F3=load-file F4=save-file F5=create-file F6=save-as
F7=load-str-file F8=structure-selector F9=record-group-edits F10=file-info
```

*Figure 9.33 DFED v3.0 **Alt** key menu*

```
Load—file————————Backup——————————ASCII——————————Full—edit——Ins—Caps—Num—Scroll
F1=help F2=directory F3=toggle-backup F4=toggle-character-set F5=toggle-edt-mode
File I:\COBOL\SOURCE\                                                    <—' Ctrl
```

Figure 9.34 DFED v3.0 Load file menu

```
+————————————————————————————————————————————————————————————————————+
|                          Create new file.                           |
+————————————————————————————————————————————————————————————————————+
|   Filename: [I:\COBOL\MFWBBOOK\scratch.txt        ]                  |
|                        +—————————————————————+y  list:              |
|   Organization: [Line sequential]|Line sequential |osition:length    |
|                                  |Sequential       |————————————————+ |
|          Format: [Variable]      |Indexed          |             | | |
|                                  |Relative         |             | | |
|   Record length:                 +—————————————————+             | | |
|                                                    |             | | |
|                 Minimum: [    0]  Maximum: [    0] |             | | |
|                                                    |             | | |
|   Character set: [ASCII ]                          |             | | |
|                                                    |             | | |
|Data compression: [Off]                             |             | | |
|                                                    |             | | |
|     File format: [Micro Focus   ]                  |             | | |
|                                                    +—————————————+ | |
|       Edit type: [Full ]                                          | |
+————————————————————————————————————————————————————————————————————+
Create-file—————————————————————————————————————————————————————————————
F1=help F2=define-key F3=edit-key
|<—=previous-option —>|=next-option space=accept-item <—'=create-file Esc=cancel
```

Figure 9.35 DFED v3.0 Create file menu

```
—Col:————————Rec—start:————————Rec—len:————————ASCII——Ins—Caps—Num————
F1=help F2=search F3=repeat-search F4=compress/expand F5=ascend-lvl F6=descend-lvl
F7=field/picture F8=go-to-byte F9=go-to-Nth-record F10=toggle-character-set <— —>
```

*Figure 9.36 DFED v3.0 **Ctrl** key menu*

9.6 Processing Sequence for Downloading and Converting Each File Type

Suppose you have several mainframe files that you want to transfer to the PC. Here is a checklist of steps for downloading and converting mainframe files.

1. If the mainframe file is anything other than a sequential file, you will need to run a utility on the mainframe side to create a sequential file for downloading. If this step is needed, it will be the first step in the conversion process. For example, if the mainframe file is a dataset within a database, you would extract a sequential file with a database utility. If the mainframe file is VSAM, you would extract a sequential file with IDCAMS REPRO. If the file on the mainframe side is larger than what you would want to use for PC testing, adjust the IDCAMS parameters to extract only a subset of the original data.

2. At this point, you will have a mainframe sequential file. If this file contains variable-length records, run the VRECGEN utility on the mainframe to change the variable-length information to a format that can be downloaded safely.

3. Now it's time to do the actual download. Use the File Transfer Aid utility to download the data. If the file being downloaded contains only EBCDIC text (no embedded nontext characters, no packed or binary fields), and you wish to translate to ASCII, then set the File Transfer Aid parameters to do EBCDIC/ASCII translation. If the file is of any other type, then set the File Transfer Aid parameters to do a simple binary download.

4. At this stage you will have a sequential file on the PC. It will be either ASCII or EBCDIC depending on whether you translated it during the downloading process. If the file is an EBCDIC data file with fixed-length records, and you do not wish to translate it, then you're done. If the file contains program source code without embedded nontext characters, and you translated it to ASCII during the download, you're done. For other file types, continue with this checklist.

5. If the downloaded file consists of EBCDIC program source code containing embedded nontext characters, use MDECONV to convert the file to ASCII. If needed, use the Hex Editor or DFED to assign correct values to those characters on the PC side.

6. Alternatively, if the downloaded file consists of test data, and you want to use it in any format other than EBCDIC fixed-length sequential, use WFL to convert it to a PC file of the appropriate type. Also use WFL if some fields within the file require translation and others do not.

How does this work in practice? For example, if the mainframe file is a VSAM file with variable-length records, use IDCAMS REPRO to extract a sequential file. Use VRECGEN to convert the record length information. Use the File Transfer Aid to download the file in binary form. Finally, use WFL to create an indexed file on the PC workstation.

9.7 Exercises

1. Animate or run the CUST.CBL program example that we used in previous chapters. If you checked CUST.CBL with CHARSET(EBCDIC), which will be the default if you used one of the language dialect settings in the MDE, the CUSTMST.DAT file will be an EBCDIC sequential file. Rename the CUSTMST.DAT file as CUSTMST.EBC and use WFL to convert it to an indexed sequential file. Your result should be an ASCII data file named CUSTMST.DAT and an index file named CUSTMST.IDX.

2. Use the Hex Editor to examine the files created in the previous step.

3. Use the Data File Editor (DFED) to examine CUSTMST.DAT. Use the record description in CUST.CBL as a template for editing records. Use the key search feature in DFED to position the cursor to one of the records you have entered.

4. Choose an existing application at your mainframe site that might be a candidate for program maintenance on the PC. Do an inventory of the program source and data files that you would need to download to the PC. Classify the files by type (database, VSAM, sequential; source program or data file; fixed or variable-length records). For each type of file, identify the steps needed to make that file available on the PC.

Other Useful Utilities

10.1 Introduction

In this chapter we will discuss various Micro Focus functions and utilities that are useful for mainframe program development but that are not discussed in any of the other chapters.

Getting into the WDE menu. Some of these utilities that we will discuss in this chapter are available from the **Workbench Development Environment (WDE)** main menu, shown in Figure 10.1. Even though the WDE is intended primarily for PC application developers, it contains some tools that mainframers can use as well. To get to the WDE, press **F9=Workbench** on the Mainframe Development Environment (MDE) main menu. The submenus in the WDE work much the same as the submenus in the MDE that we have been using. Figures 10.2 and 10.3 show the WDE Alt-key and Ctrl-key menus that you can access from the WDE main menu.

Returning to the MDE. Pressing **F9** on the WDE will *not* get you back to the MDE. Instead, press the **Escape** key on the WDE main menu. You will see a message at the bottom of the screen that says **Exit from the Micro Focus COBOL/2 Workbench ? Y/N.** Pressing **Y** will not shut down the Workbench; it will simply bring you back to the MDE.

```
Micro-Focus-COBOL/2-Workbench────────────────────────────────────
F1=help F2=edit F3=check F4=animate F5=compile F6=run F7=library F8=build F9=WFL
F10=directory                                            Alt Ctrl Escape
```

Figure 10.1 WDE main menu

```
Micro-Focus-COBOL/2-Workbench────────────────────────────────────
F1=help F2=screens F3=diff F4=hexedit F5=session F6=analyzer F7=link
F8=data-file-editor F9=file-finder F10=Co-Writer
```

Figure 10.2 WDE Alt-key menu

```
Micro Focus COBOL/2 Workbench─────────────────────────────────────
F1=help F2=not used                F3=update-menu F4=use-updated- menu
F5=batch-files F6=concurrent-environment F7=OS-command F8=config F10=user-menu
```

Figure 10.3 WDE Ctrl-key menu

10.2 File Finder

10.2.1 What File Finder does

Have you ever misplaced a file on your PC workstation's disk drives? Have you forgotten exactly what you named it or which subdirectory you stored it in or even whether it is on your machine at all? This can happen to anyone, including ourselves. It's a consequence of working on large projects or on several projects at once. You can misplace files on a mainframe too, but in that case you can sometimes look at CLISTs or batch JCL to remind you of where your files might be. You can also ask for help. Mainframe sites often have staff whose duties include data library management. These include systems programmers, security managers, database administrators, data librarians, and source code control committees. On the PC, you are usually responsible for managing your own disk files. The File Finder is a tool that can help you keep track.

You might ask, "Why do I need a separate File Finder utility? Shouldn't I be able to locate all of my files with simple MS-DOS or OS/2 DIR commands?" Actually, you could, but it would take much more time and effort. The operating system DIR command is less powerful than File Finder. DIR lets you look at only one subdirectory at a time. For example, if you issue a DIR command on the root directory, you will see the files only in the root directory itself, not in any of the subdirectories. You will see only the names of the subdirectories that are immediately below the root directory, not their contents. If the file you want is somewhere further down in the hierarchy of subdirectories, you will have to issue a separate DIR command for each subdirectory in the hierarchy until you find what you are looking for. By contrast, unless you tell it to do otherwise, **File Finder will search not only the current directory but also the complete hierarchy of subdirectories below it.** It will also search for members within Micro Focus library files (.LBR).

Suppose you remember only part of the filename or extension you are looking for. The DIR command lets you use the wildcard characters "*" and "?". In this command, "*" substitutes for a string of any length and "?" substitutes for any single character. The DIR command allows you to use a wildcard character as a suffix, or as a replacement for the entire filename, extension, or both. For example, **DIR *.*** shows all files in the current directory regardless of filename or extension. However, DIR does not allow the use of a wildcard character as a prefix. In other words, you cannot get a list of all filenames ending with "FOO" by issuing the command **DIR *FOO.***. **File Finder, on the other hand, does allow you to use wildcard characters as either prefixes or suffixes.** (However, you cannot use wildcard characters as both prefix and suffix for the same filename, and you cannot embed wildcard characters inside a filename.)

```
                            File-Finder                        Banner 0015
Command line format is:
MFFINDER [directives ][drive:][path\][library-spec\]file-spec

- Search starts with specified path and includes subdirectories and libraries.
- If path is omitted current directory is assumed - use \ to get all.
- Library-spec (eg *.LBR\) forces search of just libraries.
- Library-spec and file-spec may include wildcards (* or ?).
- Wildcards allow "*abc" as well as "abc*" formats (but not "ab*cd" or "*bc*").
- Directives may be added before or after the filespec as follows:
  These take the form "/alphabetic-char", a single / may introduce several.
  /ADSHRE or perms thereof display only files with one of these attributes:
      A = updated since last BACKUP.  D = subdirectory.
      S = system file.                H = hidden file.
      R = read-only file.             E = program entry-point (in library).
  /B displays filenames without the associated details.
  /P pauses after a screenful and waits for a key to be pressed
  /X restricts search to the specified directory.
  /F restricts search to real files.
  /L restricts search to library members (equivalent to library-spec of *.LBR).

File-finder─────────────────────────────────────────────Ins-Caps-Num-Scroll
Please enter command line then press <-'                                  Esc
MFFINDER \CUSTMST.DAT                                                      <-'
```

Figure 10.4 File Finder menu

```
MFFINDER V1.1.013  Copyright (C) 1988,1989 Micro Focus Ltd
\custmst.dat
Searching \ for CUSTMST.DAT...
Filename                                  Attrib    Size   Date   Time
\COBOL\EXEDLL\CUSTMST.DAT......................A..........451.28Nov91.10:43a
\COBOL\MFWBBOOK\CUSTMST.DAT.....................A..........656..6Dec91..8:20a
Search completed ok
File-finder─────────────────────────────────────────────Ins-Caps-Num-Scroll
Please enter command line then press <-'                                  Esc
MFFINDER \CUSTMST.DAT                                                      <-'
```

Figure 10.5 File Finder screen output

10.2.2 Using File Finder

From the Workbench, you can bring up the File Finder screen by holding down the **Alt** key on the WDE main menu and pressing **F9=file-finder**. You will see the screen shown in Figure 10.4. You can also run File Finder directly from the command line by entering **MFFINDER** followed by the same command line parameters that you would use on the File Finder screen itself.

The screen text in Figure 10.4 shows the available directives and options, so we will not repeat all of them here. The directives let you restrict the search in various ways. Those directives having to do with attributes /A, /D, /S, /H, or /R, for example, restrict the search to those files having those particular MS-DOS or OS/2 file attributes. /Frestricts the search to actual standalone files, excluding members within Micro Focus library files.

Possibly the commonest use for File Finder is to do unrestricted searches. To use File Finder to search an entire drive for a filename, specify the root directory followed by the filename, as follows:

```
MFFINDER \yourfile.ext
```

Figure 10.5 shows the results of the search that we requested in Figure 10.4. It shows two files with filename CUSTMST.DAT in two different sub-directories.

10.3 Source Comparison (DIFF) Utility

10.3.1 What DIFF Does

The DIFF utility is described as "Source Comparison Utility." While its primary use is for comparing two program source code files, it has other uses as well. It will compare any two ASCII line sequential files, so that you can use it for comparing test output disk or print files. When used on a single input file, DIFF will reassign sequence numbers and it will convert ASCII text between lower- and uppercase.

Like all other systems, source control systems are fallible. Problems occur whenever two or more programmers work with the same source files or

The wrong time to bypass source control procedures

copy members at the same time. Emergency situations, tight deadlines, and poor communications make this situation more likely. Suppose you are in the process of enhancing a program as part of a major project, and you have a working copy of that program on your PC workstation. Someone else applies an emergency "bug fix" to the production version of that same program. Unless you merge that same bug fix into your working copy of that program, you will lose the bug fix when you put your new version into production. Whenever you suspect that two modified versions of a source program exist, DIFF can show you what lines need to be merged.

Let's look at what happens when two program source code files differ. It is not always a simple matter of matching records one-to-one and flagging any records that differ. The first file might contain extra records that do not exist in the second file, and vice versa. In that case, the source comparison utility must "catch up" and resynchronize the two files. DIFF offers a look-ahead function that can find more matching records following each group of unmatched records. By default, DIFF looks ahead up to a limit of 100 records when it tries to resynchronize files.

10.3.2 Using DIFF

You can reach the DIFF function by pressing **F2=files** on the MDE main menu, and then pressing **F4=diff** on the **File Utilities** menu. You will see the screen display in Figure 10.6. Alternatively, you can run DIFF directly from the command line by entering **RUN DIFF** followed by the same command line parameters that you would use on the DIFF screen itself.

The DIFF screen display (Figure 10.6) shows the command format and describes some of the directives that you can use. The "Source Comparison" chapter in the *Workbench Reference* describes various other directives that DIFF accepts.

```
                                   +———————+
                                   | DIFF |
                                   +———————+
Common Directives:

- LIST lists to console (default)          - LIST"file-id" lists to a file
- EXTEND opens list file "extend"          - LPRINT is same as LIST"PRN:"
- FORM"n" sets form-size (default=NOFORM)  - ERRLIST only lists discrepancies
- RESEQ puts sequence number in cols1-6.   - COBOL sets FROM 7 TO 72
- FROM n TO n gives range of cols to compare
- & requests a continuation line of directives
- COPYLIST expands copy statements for comparison
- MATCH"n" specifies number of consecutive matches needed to end mis-matches
- STEP or PAUSE give menu options allowing "stepping" etc.
- If LIST specifies a file-id, ECHO echoes discrepancies to console (default)
  and ECHOALL echoes full listing




DIFF——————————————————————————————————————————————————————Ins-Caps-Num-Scroll
Please enter "old-file-id new-file-id [directive ...]" then press <-'       Esc
DIFF CUST.CBL CUST.BAK LIST"DIFFOUT.TXT" ERRLIST
```

Figure 10.6 Source Comparison (DIFF) screen

Many DIFF directives are cosmetic, having to do with the appearance of output, so we will not repeat all of them here. We will show how to use the directives that are most important.

The example in Figure 10.6 shows a comparison of two versions of the same program source file. **LIST "DIFFOUT.TXT"** causes the print-image output of DIFF to go to a disk file named DIFFOUT.TXT. The **ERRLIST** directive lets you decide whether to show every record in both files, or just the mismatches. Since we have specified ERRLIST, DIFF will list only the discrepancies between the two files, as shown in Figure 10.7. If we had not specified ERRLIST, then all records in both files would show in the report. In that case, DIFF would have flagged some sequences of records as matching and others as mismatched.

If you want to watch the progress of DIFF as it compares the two files, you can use the STEP or PAUSE directives. When you run DIFF, a little menu line will appear on the screen, that looks like this:

```
Step Pause Zoom Echoall-on/off Beep-on/off Escape
```

You can single-step through the DIFF process by pressing the letter **S** on each line. Pressing **P** for Pause will cause DIFF to pause only when it finds a discrepancy. **Escape** interrupts DIFF processing.

COBOL and other source files. For a COBOL program source file, only the portion between columns 7 and 72 is significant to program logic. You may want to ignore discrepancies having to do with sequence numbers and record ID columns. Using the **COBOL** directive lets you confine the comparison to columns 7 through 72. The COBOL directive also excludes blank comment statements (those containing just asterisks and spaces) from the comparison.

For other types of source files, you can set a column range with the **FROM** *n* **TO** *n* directive.

The **COPYLIST** directive expands all copy members before doing the comparison. If you do not specify COPYLIST, only the COPY statements themselves will be compared, not the members they reference.

Comparing other file types. Suppose you want to compare two files that are not ASCII line sequential files. Since DIFF works only with ASCII line sequential files, how do you convert the files into that form without corrupting nontext fields? Load each file into the Hex Editor and use the Hex Editor's print function to write the hex/character display to a print file instead of the screen. Within Hex Editor, toggle the displayed character set to ASCII or EBCDIC depending on what you have in your file. Using the Hex Editor print function in that way will give you the equivalent of an IDCAMS file dump. Do this for both files that you want to compare. Since PC print-image files are ASCII line sequential, you can use DIFF to compare the two HEXEDIT print-image files. Used in that way, the DIFF report will show all mismatches in both hex and character format.

```
* Text File Comparison
*_____
* OLD=CUST.CBL
* NEW=CUST.BAK
*_____
* 000027/000027: extra NEW records :-
      * This is a comment line.
*_____
* 000029/000030: mis-matched records
* OLD :-
003000     PERFORM UNTIL CUST-NO = "QUIT"
* NEW :-
003000     PERFORM UNTIL CUST-NO = "QUIT" or "Quit" or "quit"
*_____
* 000039/000040: extra OLD records :-
                 PERFORM HELLO-ROUTINE
*_____
* 000048/000048: extra OLD records :-
      HELLO-ROUTINE.
           DISPLAY "HELLO WORLD".
      HELLO-EXIT. EXIT.
*_____
* end of comparison : CUST.CBL vs CUST.BAK
*      4 discrepancies involving     5 OLD,     2 NEW records
*=============================================================
```

Figure 10.7 Source Comparison (DIFF) output

Working with one file. You can also use DIFF to strip or renumber sequence numbers or to translate between lower- and uppercase ASCII. To tell DIFF that you are working with only one input file, substitute the slash character ("/") for the second filename input parameter. (Do not use a backslash character.) Following the slash character, enter one or more of the DIFF directives that pertain to single file processing. **UCASE** converts all lowercase alphabetic characters to uppercase. **LCASE** does the reverse. **RESEQ(*increment*)** renumbers the sequence numbers by the increment value. If you omit the increment value, DIFF increments by 1. If you use **RESEQ(0)**, DIFF will reset sequence numbers to zero. **ZEROSEQ** will put leading zeroes into the sequence number field.

The directive **LISTMARGINB** is used with **FROM *n* TO *n*** column limits. It causes DIFF to write only the specified columns to the output file. To strip sequence numbers and record ID field contents from COBOL source input, enter a DIFF command of the following type:

```
YOURPROG.CBL / FROM 7 TO 72 LIST"YOURPROG.NEW" LISTMARGINB
```

10.4 Concurrency

10.4.1 Concurrency Concepts

Concurrent processing simply means "performing two or more actions at the same time." As we discuss in Appendix A, one of the design limitations of MS-DOS was that it is intended to run only one program at a time. Over the years, software designers attempted to get around this limitation with various strategies. The OS/2 operating system eventually came to be offered as a replacement for MS-DOS for high-end workstations. But for those who are running under MS-DOS, other software must handle the administrative effort of running several things at once. Within the Micro Focus Workbench, the Concurrency function lets you keep several processes running at once, and switch between them. These can be Workbench utilities or your own programs.

Under OS/2, you don't need to use the Concurrency function just to run several processes at once. OS/2 lets you start up several Workbench sessions or other applications. However, there is a reason why you might still want to run Concurrency under OS/2. **The Concurrency function also lets you syntax-check your program while you are editing.** As you edit, the Concurrency function passes source lines to the Checker for checking while editing is still in progress.

Concurrency "under the covers." So how does it work? Concurrency sets up a separate virtual screen buffer in memory for each process. This lets a process update the "screen" even while it does not have access to the PC's actual screen. In any case, the user can switch between processes. The **active process** is the one that currently is visible on the screen. The keyboard and mouse are available only to the active process. However, under MS-DOS, Concurrency provides a **COBOL scheduler function** that provides CPU time to each process in turn. If other processes are not waiting for user input, they can continue running in the background even when they are not visible on the screen. The COBOL scheduler function is used only under MS-DOS, not under OS/2.

The Concurrency function uses the concept of **run unit.** A run unit consists of a main program and all of the subprograms that it calls. You can think of a run unit as an independently running process. The Concurrency scheduler itself and the Workbench menu system each represent a run unit. Any other process you begin, either a Workbench facility or any of your own applications, will create another run unit.

In this section, we will not attempt to cover all possible ways of using the Concurrency function. Further details about Concurrency are in the "Concurrency" chapter in the *Workbench Reference.*

10.4.2 Starting Concurrency

The Concurrency function is available on the WDE by pressing **F6=concurrent-environment** on the WDE Ctrl-key menu shown above in Figure 10.3. You will see the Concurrency menu shown in Figure 10.8. Alternatively, you can bring up the Concurrency menu from the operating system command line prompt with any of the following commands:

```
[XM]  WBCON
[XM]  RUN CONCLI
[XM]  WB CONCLI
```

In each case, specify XM only if you are running under MS-DOS. The first two command formats bring up Concurrency directly. The third format brings up Concurrency through the Workbench system, but shows you the Concurrency menu rather than the hierarchy of Workbench menus.

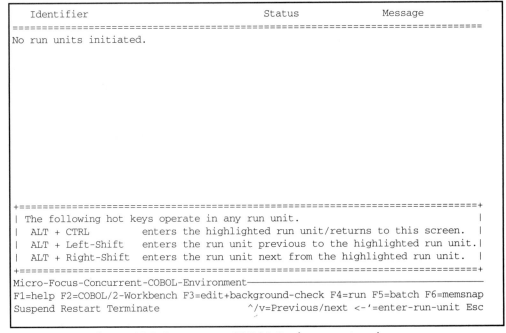

Figure 10.8 Concurrent COBOL Environment main menu

```
Run───────────────────────────────────────────────────Ins-Caps-Num-Scroll
F1=help F2=dir F3=switches              <-'=run-file         F9/F10=options Esc
File K:\COBOL\EXEDLL\                                             <-' Ctrl
```

Figure 10.9 Concurrency Run menu

```
                    +=====================+            Banner 0010
                    | Batch File Facility |
                    +=====================+

   - F3 will pass the program name below to the batch file CGR.CBT which
        will compile (check/generate) the program and then run it

   - F4 allows you to edit any file as specified in the prompt below
        This allows you to alter or create a batch file

   - F5 allows you to run the batch file specified in the prompt




Batch-file-handling───────────────────────────────────Ins-Caps-Num-Scroll
F1=help F2=dir F3=Check-Gen-Run F4=edit-file F5=run-batch              Esc
File K:\COBOL\EXEDLL\                                             <-' Ctrl
```

Figure 10.10 Concurrency Batch menu

10.4.3 Starting and Switching between Concurrent Processes

Under the Concurrency function, you start each new run unit with selections on the function key menu. When you start the first run unit, you can press the **Alt+Ctrl** keys at the same time to get back to the Concurrency menu. Each time you return to the Concurrency menu, you can start a new run unit, up to a maximum of ten. The **Alt+Left-Shift** and **Alt+Right-Shift** keys switch to the previous or next run unit, respectively.

What types of run unit can you start in the Concurrent COBOL Environment? **F2=COBOL/2-Workbench** brings up the entire Workbench menu system as a concurrent process. **F3=edit+background-check** brings up the COBOL Editor in such a way that you can syntax-check source lines without leaving the Editor. We will discuss this in a later section. **F4=run** lets you run your own COBOL or other program files. This menu, shown in Figure 10.9, works much like the Run menus provided in the regular Workbench environment. **F5=batch** lets you submit background program compilations or run other batch files as a concurrent process. The batch concurrency menu is shown in Figure 10.10.

Memory snapshot facility. Are you curious about how much memory each run unit is taking? Pressing **F6=memsnap** on the Concurrency main menu brings up the Run Unit Summary menu, shown in Figure 10.11. Like some other Workbench screens, the run units on this menu form a scrolling light-bar menu. You can highlight the run unit you want and select **M** for **More-details**

to see a detailed display of the memory resources used by that run unit. This display is shown in Figure 10.12. It contains a menu showing the individual program modules within that run unit. Here again, you can highlight a program and select **M** for **More-details** to see the memory resources used by that module (Figure 10.13).

```
 More-details  Next-page  Prev-page  Refresh  prinT  Exit  Help

MEMSNAP  V1.2.05              Run Unit Summary                    MEMS0001

Run Unit     Heap   Heap Size      Data      Code     Ovly    Dyn.     File
     ID      Size    (Disk)        Size      Size     Size    Size     Size

       2    15872         0       39088     71408        0   16176        0
       1        0         0         752      1024        0       0        0
       0     1536         0       24512     79648        0   10000        0
```

Figure 10.11 MEMSNAP Run Unit Summary

```
 More-detail  Next-run-unit  Prev-run-unit  Exit  Help

MEMSNAP              Summary for Run Unit No. :       0          MEMS0002

     Program Name         Prog    Data Size    Root Size    Ovly Size
                           ID

     CMENU.GNT           16240        8784        34864            0
     CONCLI.GNT          16128        6944         9920            0
     CLI.GNT             14960        8784        34864            0
```

Figure 10.12 MEMSNAP Run Unit Display

```
 Next-program  Prev-program  Exit  Help

MEMSNAP          Program Details for Run Unit No. :     0        MEMS0003

Program Name       : CMENU.GNT          Program ID          : 16240
Program Entry Point :
                                        File Usage :
Data Size          :     8784
Root Size          :    34864           No. of Files        :        0
Overlay Size       :        0           Size of File Buffers :       0

Heap Usage :
                                        Dynamic Memory Usage :
No. of Heaps       :        0
Size of Heaps      :        0           No. of Dynamic Areas :        5
Size of Heaps (disk):       0           Size of Dynamic Areas:      912
```

Figure 10.13 MEMSNAP Program Details

10.4.4 Background Syntax Checking While Editing

To invoke background checking from the COBOL Editor, press **F3=edit+back-ground-check** on the Concurrency main menu. You will see the same COBOL Editor main menu that you would ordinarily see. Load your source code file into the Editor. Press the **F2=check/anim** key repeatedly to cycle through the options until the **Background** indicator appears on the information line. The background checking process will begin when you press the **Enter** key. Once checking begins, a new menu line will appear on the Edit menu, as shown in Figure 10.14.

An indicator for the current status of the checking process appears in the lower-left corner of the screen. In this case, the indicator is **Wait**. Here are the possible indicator values:

- **Check:** Syntax checking is in progress. The number of the source line currently being checked will appear on the last line of the screen.
- **Complete:** The syntax checker has checked all lines in the source file.
- **Error:** The syntax checker has stopped at a line containing an error. The number of the faulty source line will appear on the last line of the screen. To see the error message, press **F4=view**. To position the cursor to the faulty line, press **F10=to-error**. You can restart checking with the Go function.
- **Paused:** You have paused the syntax checker with the Pause function **Shift+F3**. To restart it, press the same key combination again to invoke the Go function.
- **Wait:** The checker is waiting for you to enter more source lines or to move the cursor position further down in the source file. If you want to check the rest of the source file below the current cursor position, without having to move the cursor, press **F5=finish**. If you want to discontinue the checking process, press **F6=kill**. Finally, if you save the edited file and press the Escape key to get out of the Editor, the Editor will ask you whether you want to finish checking the file before exiting.

```
Edit-CUST————————50-lines————————Line-1—Col-8————————————Wrap-Ins-Caps-Num-Scroll
F1=help F2=COBOL F3=insert-line F4=delete-line F5=repeat-line F6=restore-line
F7=retype-char F8=restore-char F9=word-left F10=word-right      Alt Ctrl Escape
Wait                 Shift+F3=pause/go +F4=view +F5=finish +F6=kill +F10=to-error
```

Figure 10.14 Background Checking menu

Before you begin checking, you can change background checking options. To do this, hold down the **Ctrl** key. You will see the Background Checking Ctrl key menu shown in Figure 10.15.

```
Background—Line——Pause-Auto-Restart————————————————————————————
F1=help F2=limit F3=pause F4=auto-restart
```

Figure 10.15 Background Checking Ctrl key menu

The functions on this menu are toggle switch settings that let you select the exact way you want background checking to proceed. The selected settings will appear on the information line.

- **F2=limit** is a toggle switch that lets you decide how many lines to syntax-check at a time. **Line** is the default. If you set the limit to Line, the syntax checker will check all lines up to the current cursor line. To check more lines, move the cursor downward in the file. If you set the limit to **Screen,** the syntax checker will check all source lines in the file above the current screen image. Here again, to check more lines, page the display downward. If you set the limit to **End,** the syntax checker will check all lines in the file.
- **F3=pause** will pause the checking function.
- **F4=auto-restart** toggles the auto-restart function on and off. Suppose checking is in progress and you change a source line that has already been checked. If auto-restart is on, the checking process will restart at the line you just changed. Otherwise, checking will proceed to the end of the source file regardless of changes to any earlier lines.

Finding information in the manuals. Concurrency is a Workbench function; therefore, most of the information about Concurrency can be found in the "Concurrency" and "Memsnap" chapters in the *Workbench Reference.* However, since the Editor is a Toolset function, the details about background syntax checking are in the "Editor" chapter in the *Toolset Reference.*

10.5 Keystroke Macros (MFKEYMAC)

10.5.1 Keystroke Macro Concepts

What is a keystroke macro? A keystroke macro is a short keystroke combination that stands for a much longer keystroke sequence. A **keystroke macro translator** lets you define macros by equating the shorthand key combinations with the desired values. Any word, phrase, or command sequence that you type often could be a candidate for a keystroke macro definition. For example, one of the default Workbench keystroke macro values equates **Alt+H** with the string **HIGH-VALUES.** Instead of typing HIGH-VALUES directly, you can press Alt+H to insert that reserved word into your COBOL statement.

The benefit of using keystroke macros is that you can save time typing. The cost is a slight increase in performance overhead. This is because the keystroke macro translator must trap every keystroke as you type it. You must load the macro translator along with the Workbench at startup time. If the keystroke (or alt-key combination) matches a macro definition, the translator will pass the translated keystroke sequence to the Workbench. Otherwise, if the keystroke does not match a macro definition, the translator will pass it along unchanged to the Workbench.

The Keystroke Macro facility does not trap keystroke values in response to ACCEPT FROM CONSOLE or ACCEPT FROM DATE/TIME statements.

10.5.2 Starting Up Workbench with Keystroke Macros

To start up Workbench with the Keystroke Macro facility enabled, use either of the following command line parameters:

```
[XM] WB MFKEYMAC

[XM] RUN MFKEYMAC
```

If you are using the command line interface to bring up various Workbench facilities directly without viewing the Workbench menu system, you can still use the Keystroke Macro facility. Simply insert the keywords **MFKEYMAC CLI** after the WB, XM WB, or RUN in the command line interface. For example, instead of **WB EDIT**, you would enter **WB MFKEYMAC CLI EDIT**. Incidentally, the command line interface will not work for loading the Keystroke Macro facility with Concurrency. This is because the Keystroke Macro facility traps keystrokes only for the run unit with which it was loaded. Under Concurrency, the initial run unit is the Concurrency Scheduler (CONCLI) itself. In that case, the macro facility would not trap keystrokes for the other run units that do your actual work. If you need to use Keystroke Macro with Concurrency, you will need to modify the CONCLI.MNU or CONCLI.CFG files, or customize the Workbench menu system. Instructions for how to do this are in the "Keystroke Macro" chapter of the *Workbench Reference.*

10.5.3 Defining Keystroke Macros

Default keystroke macros. Certain keystroke macros are built into the Workbench configuration file, **MFWB.CFG.** These macros are automatically available when you start up Workbench with the Keystroke Macro facility. You can find them by loading MFWB.CFG into the COBOL Editor and searching for the tag **[MF-KEYMAC]**, as shown in Figure 10.16.

```
[MF-KEYMAC]
{Alt+A}   "AFTER "
{Alt+B}   "BEFORE "
{Alt+C}   "COMP-"
{Alt+D}   "DISPLAY "
{Alt+E}   "ELSE "
{Alt+F}   "FILLER "
{Alt+H}   "HIGH-VALUES"
{Alt+I}   "INSPECT "
{Alt+L}   "LOW-VALUES"
{Alt+M}   "MOVE "
{Alt+N}   "NEXT SENTENCE"
{Alt+O}   "OCCURS "
{Alt+P}   "PERFORM "
{Alt+R}   "REDEFINES "
{Alt+S}   "SPACES"
{Alt+T}   {Right}{Home}{End}*2{Btab}*9"TO "
{Alt+U}   "UNTIL "
{Alt+V}   "VALUE "
{Alt+W}   "WRITE "
{Alt+X}   {Right}{Home}{End}*2{Btab}*9"PIC X("
{Alt+Z}   "ZEROES"
{Alt+9}   {Right}{Home}{End}*2{Btab}*9"PIC 9("
```

Figure 10.16 Default macros in MFWB.CFG file

The macro key combination is followed by the macro definition. Most of the default macros are self-explanatory, in that they equate Alt-key combinations with COBOL reserved words. **Alt+T, Alt+X,** and **Alt+9** move the cursor to column 40 of the current row and enter the strings **TO, PIC X(,** and **PIC 9(** at that location. Values between quotation marks represent character strings to be entered. Values between curly brackets represent *key mnemonics* (labels of keys or key combinations) to be "pressed." When a key mnemonic is followed by an asterisk and a numeric value, that key combination is to be pressed the number of times indicated by the numeric value.

The Keystroke Macro facility does not toggle insert mode on or off. If insert mode is off, the keystroke macro value will overtype whatever data is present at the cursor position. **Caps Lock** and **Num Lock** do not affect keystroke macro output. You will get exactly what is in the macro definition.

Defining your own macros. You can define your own macros, using the same format shown above. Use the COBOL Editor to put them into the MFWB.CFG file after the **[MF-KEYMAC]** tag. Reloading the Workbench (beginning a new session) will activate the new macros.

Other key mnemonics exist besides those that happen to be used in the default macros. For example, key labels **{Left}**, **{Right}**, **{Up}**, and **{Down}** refer to the four cursor arrow keys. Therefore, **{Ctrl+Left}** would equate to "hold down the **Ctrl** key and press the left arrow key." You can also define key combinations in the form of hex literals, although this makes your configuration file less readable to human eyes. A full list of available keystroke mnemonics and hex values appears in the "Key Mnemonics" appendix to the *Workbench Reference.* Refer to this list when creating macros of your own.

If you choose to define keystroke macros, be careful about reusing a keystroke combination that already has another meaning. Defining it as a keystroke macro will keep you from using it for its original purpose.

Special functions. The Keystroke Macro facility provides two functions that you can place within a macro definition. Place the function label between two colon characters (":") to indicate that it is a function.

- **:olr:** invokes an interface to the On-line Information System. The interface program, HYH-INTF, looks for a word at the current cursor position and passes it to the On-line Information System. This system will look up that word in its topic index to display context-sensitive help, if available.
- **:reload:** causes the Workbench to reload the macros from the MFWB.CFG file. If you have previously defined a keystroke macro to reload the macro definitions, then you can use it to implement new macro definitions without having to restart the entire Workbench session.

10.6 Session Recorder for Regression Testing

10.6.1 What Is Regression Testing?

Has this happened to you? Have you ever found that an eagerly awaited program enhancement somehow made another part of the program *work differently*...and not in a way you would have chosen? Have you found that a desperately needed emergency bug fix introduced an even worse malfunction into one or more systems? It's true that structured programming techniques help to reduce the amount of interaction between modules. Even so, the risk remains that program changes will damage existing functionality. **Regression testing** is a way to manage that risk.

Regression testing. Let's look at what this means. To regress means to return to a previous state. Regression testing means that you reproduce previous testing conditions whenever you update a program. In particular, you will test the new version of a program with the same input data used for testing the previous version. Regression testing lets you make sure that the new version's output differs from the old version's output *only in desired ways.*

What is required? How much extra work does regression testing involve? That depends on the tools you use. A good regression testing methodology will help you maintain a library of test input for future program enhancements. For batch COBOL programs without keyboard and screen interaction, regression testing simply requires that you back up and restore input files, databases, and job control or command files. Operating system commands or backup utilities will do the job. What about test results? You can compare old and new batch COBOL program output with the Micro Focus DIFF function, as we described in an earlier section.

On the other hand, you may need to perform regression testing on programs that rely heavily on user interaction. These may be CICS programs, IMS/DC programs, or COBOL programs with ACCEPT and DISPLAY statements. This is less straightforward. You can't rely on the programmer or quality-assurance person to enter exactly the same sequence of keystrokes every time the program needs to be tested. Similarly, you can't rely on human memory to verify that screen output is identical from one testing session to the next. Regression testing of interactive programs requires a method for recording keystrokes and capturing screen displays. The Micro Focus Session Recorder serves this purpose.

Making initial testing easier. You may want to use the Session Recorder even while testing an interactive program for the first time. Programmers commonly begin testing by entering random sequences of menu selections and input data, just to make the new screens come up. Suppose you find a bug while testing in this way. Will you remember the exact keystroke sequence that revealed that malfunction? To fix a bug, you need to be able to reproduce it. Otherwise, you cannot even be sure which problem you are trying to solve! It's true that you could write down each keystroke on paper as you test. Besides being slow and error-prone, that method is as low-tech as using a trail of bread crumbs to find your way out of the woods. With Session Recorder, you can let the computer do the tiresome record-keeping for you!

10.6.2 Session Recorder Concepts

Parts of Session Recorder. The Micro Focus Session Recorder actually consists of three utilities. **Session Recorder** records keystroke input during initial testing. Later, it plays back that same keystroke input so that it tests the program again, the same way each time. The application behaves as though a terminal user is entering the keystrokes by hand. Session Recorder also captures screen image snapshot files from each testing session. The **MFREVIEW** utility lets you view and compare screen image snapshot files, so that you can see whether anything has changed from one testing session to the next. The **MFKTRANS** utility translates keystroke input files to compressed or uncompressed format. Session Recorder automatically calls MFKTRANS to translate keystroke files as needed. You can also use MFKTRANS to create readable documentation files that show exactly what testing was done.

Interaction with the Workbench session. You can run Session Recorder either from the Workbench menu system or directly from the operating system command line prompt. If you run Session Recorder from within the Workbench, you will record or play back your Workbench interactive session. This includes selections from Workbench menus as well as terminal I/O for programs that you animate or execute under the control of the Workbench. The recorded session will show the path you navigated through the Workbench menu system to select, load, and run your program. Running Session Recorder from the Workbench menu system adds more variables to the testing scenario. This has little effect on initial program testing but can sometimes complicate data gathering for future regression testing. Changes to the Workbench menu system or to your directories may cause your original keystroke sequence to fail to load the program you want to test. (You can modify or recombine keystroke files to get around this problem.) However, for testing CICS or IMS programs that must be run from the Workbench menu system, you will need to use this method.

On the other hand, if you execute a program under Session Recorder directly from the command line prompt, the recorded session will contain only keystrokes and screen displays pertaining to that program. For programs that can be run from the command prompt, this is the best way to build test data for regression testing. Once you have captured a keystroke file in this way, you can use it to animate or run the same program again from the command line prompt.

Interaction with the Animator. With regression testing under the Animator, you might want to use the same test data each time, but you might not always want to use the same Animator commands. The purpose of Animator is to give you many different options for examining your program while it is running. Because of this, Animator uses Session Recorder to supply program input, but it lets you control the Animator options from the keyboard. Session Recorder actually runs under Animator from the command line prompt. In effect, you are animating Session Recorder and then running your program under it.

Limitations. There are a few limitations that you must keep in mind. Session Recorder concerns itself only with user-terminal I/O. If your program also requires other test files or databases, you are responsible for backing up and restoring this data. Session Recorder will *not* verify that other test files are identical to those used in the first program test. For a valid regression test, all file input must be identical.

If you record a Workbench session, beware of situations that depend on directory structure or contents. While recording keystrokes, avoid using the "point-and-shoot" method for selecting a program or file from a directory list. Session Recorder records your selection as a series of cursor key movements followed by the enter key. The directory function will build a new display each time it runs. If the directory display contents change in any way, those cursor movements will guide the directory function to select a different file from what you intended. This defeats the purpose of regression testing. Similarly, Session Recorder will keep track of the current directory and command line contents from when the recording was made. However, you are responsible for making sure that those directories still exist at playback time!

Session Recorder works only with programs running under the control of the shared runtime system, in other words, .INT or .GNT programs. It will not work with those that use the static-linked runtime system (standalone .EXE modules). Recheck your programs with different directives if this situation applies.

You are responsible for knowing what parts of your application are intended to be different in the new version. Fields that show current date and time, or new fields added to the screen display, are obvious examples. You can tell the snapshot comparison function to ignore screen areas that you know will be different. Be aware of changes to input as well as output. If the new version requires some new keyboard input that the old version did not use, you must either supply the data by hand or modify a copy of the keystroke file to supply it automatically.

More information. The Workbench manuals contain over a hundred pages of information about using Session Recorder. Obviously, we do not attempt to cover every option here. This section will present an introduction so that you can get started. For more detailed information, see the "Session Recorder" and "Snapshot" chapters in the *Workbench Reference,* as well as the brief example in the "Session Recorder" chapter in the *Workbench Tutorials* manual. Some of this information is also in the **F1=help** displays attached to the Session Recorder menu and its submenus.

10.6.3 Recording a Testing Session

The keystroke file. Session Recorder records keystrokes into a file with filename extension **.KYS.** This file is in compressed format so that the Session Recorder will run more quickly. It is not designed for human readability. Session Recorder also calls the Keystroke Translator utility (MFKTRANS) to produce a translated version of the keystroke file with filename extension **.KTX,** as shown in Figure 10.17.

At playback time, the **:init:/:end-init:** section will start your program, while the **:play:/:end-play:** section will provide the keystroke values. If you modify the .KTX file, Session Recorder will call MFKTRANS to create a new .KYS file from it. By editing the .KTX file, you can change keystroke timings and sequences. You can even combine keystroke sequences from several .KTX files.

```
* Session recording TICTAC.KYS
*     translated to TICTAC.KTX
*_____
:init:
:ref: 51
:series: 01
:date: 920105
:time: 03222336
:lines: 25
:attributes: X"004E060E0B0F038F004E060E00000007"
:snap-control: 01
:comm-byte: 17
:end-control: 01
:cd: K:\COBOL\DEMO
:cmd: TICTAC
:ins: ON
:end-init:
*_____
:play:
:ins: ON
:delay: 732
"y"
:delay: 1896
"8"
:delay: 1269
"7"
:delay: 1796
"1"
:delay: 975
"n"
:delay: 1
:stop-run:
:end-play:
*_____
* End of Recording
*======================================
```

Figure 10.17 Session Recorder .KTX file

Delay statements. The :**delay:** statements contain numeric values that define how long Session Recorder should pause between keystrokes. This causes the playback to occur at approximately the same speed as the original recording. Why does Session Recorder include these delays? If your program or Workbench session contains a time-dependent process, and if you press a key to interrupt that process, the outcome may depend on the exact time you pressed that key. The delays make the processing reproducible from one run to the next.

Access through command prompt. The following command will start Session Recorder from the command prompt. It will run the program specified in *progname,* recording keystroke input. The **/S1** directive tells Session Recorder to take a screen image snapshot at every keystroke. The **/R** directive specifies that you want to record keystrokes (as opposed to playing them back), and specifies the filename to contain the keystrokes. The ***progname*** name at the end of the command is the program whose keystroke input you want to record. Other directives are displayed on the Workbench menu screens and listed in the manuals mentioned above.

```
WB SESSION /S1 /R(progname) progname
```

```
                   Micro Focus Session Recorder Utilities              Banner 0020
                   ─────────────────────────────────────

 Session Recorder
         - record and playback keyboard inputs to a COBOL session, either
           for a full Workbench session or for a specified program.
         - translates keyboard inputs to an easily editable text script.
         - "snapshots" screen changes; this may occur at every keystroke
           or just at specified points.
         - used with Animator it allows a program to be debugged with
           Animator input supplied from the keyboard and program input
           supplied from playback of a session recording.
 MFktrans - keystroke file translator
         - invoked automatically by Session Recorder.
         - optionally translates to a more compact documentation-only format.
 MFreview - snapshot file analyzer
         - Analyzes and displays snapshot files produced by Session Recorder.
         - Allows stepping and backstepping from one screen to the next.
         - Compares two snapshot files, for example one produced by playback
           of a test script and a control version, and reports the differences.

 Refer to Help screens and your Session Recorder documentation for more detail.
 Micro-Focus-Session-Recorder-Utilities─────────────────────────────────────
 F1=help F2=session F3=mfktrans F4=mfreview F5=session+animate Escape
```

Figure 10.18 Session Recorder main menu

```
                   Session Recorder Command Interface                  Banner 0024
                   ──────────────────────────────────

   This menu sets up directives for Session Recorder and then executes the main
 Session Recorder program when you press <-'. Note that File prompt specifies a
 recording filename; use F9/F10 to specify the program to run under Session.
   The following table shows the relationship between the text shown on the
 information line and the directives passed to Session Recorder.
   %F% = filename shown at the File prompt, %P%%N% = filename with no extension.
      +=================================================================+
      | F3=play/rec                        | F5=bstep    +Bkstep    /S5 |
      |       Playback        /P(%F%)      |                            |
      |       Record          /R(%F%)      | F6=fast     FF         /F  |
      |       Play+Rec        /P(%F%)/R    |                            |
      | F4=snap                            | F7=att      Attribs    /A  |
      |       Snap-all-Keys   /S1(%P%%N%)  |             Att-off    /A0 |
      |       :Snap:          /S3(%P%%N%)  |                            |
      |       :Snap-Key:      /S2(%P%%N%)  | F8=end      EOF-end    /E  |
      |       :Snap-Key:Spc   /S4(%P%%N%)  |             EOF-mnu    /E1 |
      |       No-Snapshots    /S0          |             EOF-kbd    /E3 |
      +=================================================================+
 Refer to Help screens and your Session Recorder documentation for more detail.
 Session-Play+Rec-Snap-all-Keys──────────────────────────────Ins-Caps-Num-Scroll
 F1=help F2=dir F3=play/rec F4=snap F5=bstep F6=fast F7=att F8=end F9/F10=cmd Esc
 File K:\COBOL\MFWBBOOK\CUST                                            <-' Ctrl
```

Figure 10.19 Session Recorder Command Interface

Access through Workbench menus. You can bring up the Session Recorder main menu by pressing **F5=session** on the WDE Alt-key menu shown in Figure 10.2. The Session Recorder main menu appears in Figure 10.18. Pressing **F2=session** on the Session Recorder main menu will bring up the Session Recorder Command Interface, shown in Figure 10.19.

On the Session Recorder Command Interface are various functions that control how Session Recorder will work. The screen display equates some functions with various command line directives. Other directives not on this menu are described in the "Session Recorder" chapter of the *Workbench Reference.*

- **F2=dir** brings up the Micro Focus directory function so that you can choose a program to run.
- **F3=play/rec** switches between three functions: **Record,** to record keystrokes; **Rec+Play,** to record keystrokes, play them back, and overwrite the previous file; and **Playback,** to play back a keystroke file. The first time around you will want to use **Record.** To play back the recording and capture screen images, change this setting to **Playback.**
- **F4=snap** sets a directive that tells Session Recorder when to take screen snapshots. A screen snapshot captures the appearance of the display screen. Session Recorder stores snapshots in a file with filename extension **.SNP.** Most of the time you will want to specify **Snap-all-Keys** because this takes a snapshot after every keystroke. This function also takes a snapshot whenever it finds a :snap: tag in the .KTX file. Alternatively, you can specify **:Snap:** to take a snapshot only when Session Recorder encounters a :snap: tag in the .KTX file. **:Snap-key:** will take a snapshot when the :snap: tag or the key combination Shift+F10 is encountered. **:Snap-Key:spc** will take a snapshot when the when the :snap: tag or the key combination Shift+F10 followed by the space bar is encountered. **No-Snapshots** inhibits snapshots altogether. You can change the snapshot key combination by inserting a :Snap-Key: tag into the header of the .KTX file.
- **F5=bstep** includes before images in the screen snapshot file. This lets the viewing program step backward in processing, if desired.
- **F6=fast** switches the fast-forward directive on and off. Fast-forward prevents delay statements from being recorded or played back.
- **F7=att** sets a directive telling Session Recorder whether or not to use the same display screen attributes at playback time. Unless you are running the same Session Recorder files on machines with different monitor types, this should not affect you.
- **F8=end** tells Session Recorder what to do at the end of your program or at the end of the keystroke file. **EOF-End** will end Session Recorder automatically if end-of-program does not coincide with the end of the keystroke file. **EOF-Mnu** will prompt you to continue or not. **EOF-Kbd,** the default, will switch over from Session Recorder input to keyboard input, giving control over the session back to you.
- **F9/F10=cmd** let you enter directives on the screen, much as you would do on the Syntax Checker screen. You can use this to enter directives that are not available as toggle switches on this menu.

Files created at playback time. If you requested screen snapshots to be taken during the Record process, Session Recorder will record the screen image output at the same time that it records the keystroke input. In that case, before playback begins, a screen snapshot file with filename extension .SNP will already exist. In effect, the Record process becomes the first test of your program.

When you play back the keystroke file, you are testing the program again with the same keystrokes you used before. Generally, you would do this after you have made some changes to your program. The second test will make a new screen snapshot file that you can compare with the old snapshot file. The playback process will rename your old .SNP file with a filename extension of .CTL, and will save the new snapshot file with extension .SNP. If a .CTL file already exists with the same name, Session Recorder will *not* rename the old .SNP file, but will discard it.

Playback from the command line. The following command will cause Session Recorder to play back the contents of *progname*.KTX. Before playing back the file, Session Recorder will call MFKTRANS to translate the .KTX file to .KYS format.

```
WB SESSION  /P(progname)
```

10.6.4 Comparing Screen Snapshot Files

Once you have created an old and a new screen snapshot file, you can compare the two sets of screen images with the MFREVIEW utility. Comparing the two snapshot files will show you whether your program changes have affected the program's screen output. Pressing **F4=mfreview** on the Session Recorder main menu brings up the MFREVIEW Command Interface shown in Figure 10.20.

```
  MFREVIEW Command Interface                    Banner 0026
  ─────────────────────────────
 This menu sets up directives for the MFREVIEW snapshot analyzer and then
executes the main MFREVIEW program when you press <-'.
 It also provides easy examination of the report file (MFREVIEW.LOG)
via F8=log.

 The following table shows the relationship between the text shown on the
information line and the directives passed to MFREVIEW.
 %F% = filename shown at the File prompt, %P%%N% = filename with no extension.

    +===================================================================+
    | F3=vu/comp                     | F5=heap                          |
    |    View            %F%         |               Heap         /X    |
    |    Comp-CTL        %P%%N%.CTL %F% | F6=go/zoom                     |
    |    Comp-SVD        %P%%N%.SVD %F% |            Go              /G    |
    | F4=att                         |               Zoom         /Z    |
    |    Text+Attribs+Cursor         | F7=dif                           |
    |    Text+Cursor     /A0         |               Diff         /D    |
    +===================================================================+

 Refer to Help screens and your Session Recorder documentation for more detail.
MFreview──Comp-CTL──Text+Attribs+Cursor──────────────Ins-Caps-Num-Scroll
F1=help F2=dir F3=vu/comp F4=att F5=heap F6=go/zoom F7=dif F8=log F9/F10=cmd Esc
File K:\COBOL\DEMO\TICTAC                                        <-' Ctrl
```

Figure 10.20 MFREVIEW Command Interface

F1=help, F2=dir, and **F9/F10=cmd** on the MFREVIEW Command Interface provide help, directory, and command line parameter support as they do in other Workbench facilities. Other functions on this menu let you choose runtime options for MFREVIEW. Once you have made the desired selections, press the Enter key to run the MFREVIEW program using those selections.

- **F3=vu/comp** gives you a choice of viewing one snapshot file or comparing two snapshot files. Three possible choices appear on the information line: **View** for viewing one file; **Comp-CTL** for comparing the current file with an old snapshot file with extension .CTL; and **Comp-SVD** for comparing the current file with an old snapshot file with extension .SVD. Unless you specify another filename extension at the **FILE:** prompt, MFREVIEW will assume a default filename extension of .SNP for the current snapshot file.
- **F4=att** lets you decide whether file comparisons will take into account differences in screen attributes. If you select **Text+cursor,** comparisons will ignore screen attributes and show only differences in the text. This function is useful if you are comparing snapshot files taken on machines having different video display support.
- **F5=heap** causes MFREVIEW to restructure your input files into heaps before displaying them. It will take longer to begin processing, but less time for each step after processing is under way. Backstepping (reverse) performance will be especially improved.
- **F6=go/zoom** determines the running mode of MFREVIEW. By default, MFREVIEW shows its initial menu display and then waits for you to tell it to step through each screen. In **Go** mode, MFREVIEW will keep displaying snapshots until it finds a mismatch, or you interrupt it, or it reaches end-of-file. In **Zoom** mode, MFREVIEW will not display snapshots. It simply compares the two files until it reaches end-of-file or it finds five consecutive mismatches.
- **F7=dif** tells MFREVIEW to place DIFF utility mismatch messages into the report file.
- **F8=log** brings up the ASCII Editor so that you can view the log file (MFREVIEW.LOG). Every time you run MFREVIEW, it appends information to this file. For each mismatched screen, this file indicates whether text, attributes, or cursor was responsible for the mismatch. It shows error counts for the run.

Controlling MFREVIEW processing. Suppose you have entered the selections to request comparison of two files, as shown in Figure 10.20. When you press the enter key, you will see the display in Figure 10.21. The message, **Screen 000001/000001 OK,** shows no mismatches in the first screen images in each file. An additional menu line on this display lets you step through the files and control the displays. With this menu, you simply press the key for the capitalized letter of each function.

- **New** displays the current screen image in the new snapshot file. Using the New function will make the new snapshot file into the current file for purposes of stepping through screen displays. To return from the screen display, press the space bar.

- **Old** displays the current screen image in the old snapshot file. This function applies only if MFREVIEW is performing a file comparison. Using the Old function will make the old snapshot file into the current file for purposes of stepping through screen displays. To return from the screen display, press the space bar.

- **Toggle** lets you switch back and forth between the old and new screen displays. The file most recently displayed will become the current file for purposes of stepping through screen displays.

- **Menu** lets you switch back and forth between the menu display and the current screen display.

- **Atts** lets you examine screen attributes as text characters.

- **Hide** lets you conceal those areas of the screen that you have specified as "variable." If you know that a certain part of the screen is supposed to be different from one version to the next, you can mask that area so that MFREVIEW comparison processing will ignore it.

- **Var** displays variable areas in reverse highlighting.

- **Ed-var** lets you use the cursor and tab keys to change the borders of defined variable areas.

- **Ins-var** lets you define new variable areas.

- **Step** tells MFREVIEW to compare the next matching pair of screen images.

- **Bstep** (backstep) steps backward to the previous pair of screen images.

- **Go** puts MFREVIEW into Go mode, as described above.

- **0-9** sets the speed for Go mode, with 9 being the fastest.

- **Zoom** puts MFREVIEW into Zoom mode, as described above.

- **sKip** tells MFREVIEW to skip to the next screen, but only in the current file. Use this if you know that the current file is intended to contain a screen image not present in the other file.

- **Esc** terminates processing after asking you to confirm with Y or N.

```
* MFREVIEW V2.2.041  Copyright (C) 1986,1991 Micro Focus Ltd
*  7-Jan-92  21:47
* MFREVIEW K:\COBOL\DEMO\TICTAC.CTL K:\COBOL\DEMO\TICTAC
* Comparing Old=K:\COBOL\DEMO\TICTAC.CTL vs New=K:\COBOL\DEMO\TICTAC.SNP
* Screen 000001/000001 OK
New Old Toggle Menu Atts Hide Var Ed-var Ins-var Step Bstep Go 0-9 Zoom sKip Esc
```

Figure 10.21 MFREVIEW submenu

MFREVIEW from the command prompt. As with other Workbench functions, you can run MFREVIEW directly from the command line prompt rather than by going through the Workbench menus. Once MFREVIEW comes up, the same submenu functions become available. You can compare two screen snapshot files with MFREVIEW with the following command:

```
WB MFREVIEW progname.CTL progname.SNP
```

Figure 10.22 shows the output with error count at completion.

```
[DOS] K:\COBOL\MFWBBOOK  0:30:09;
wb mfreview cust.ctl cust.snp
* MFREVIEW V2.2.041  Copyright (C) 1986,1991 Micro Focus Ltd
*  4-Jan-92  00:30
* MFREVIEW CUST.CTL CUST.SNP
* Comparing Old=CUST.CTL vs New=CUST.SNP
* MISMATCH found at screen 000001/000001 (Text,Attributes)
* Errors=000001
*==============================================================================

[DOS] K:\COBOL\MFWBBOOK  0:30:50;
```

Figure 10.22 MFREVIEW output from command prompt

10.6.5 Viewing Keystroke Files

Earlier in this chapter we showed a keystroke file in the translated (.KTX) format. These files can be used for documentation either in that form or after converting it further into report (.KPT) format. We also discussed the fact that Session Recorder automatically calls MFKTRANS to produce both compressed (.KYS) and translated (.KTX) versions of the keystroke file. You can change the testing procedure manually by using the COBOL Editor to change the contents of the .KTX file. The COBOL Editor lets you add, change, delete, or combine various parts of .KTX files. You do not have to bring up MFKTRANS to translate the file after you do this. MFKTRANS by default will automatically create a new .KYS file from the .KTX file before Session Recorder begins playback.

Pressing **F3=mfktrans** on the Session Recorder main menu brings up the MFKTRANS Command Interface, shown in Figure 10.23. Toggle switch functions on that menu let you set directives for the MFKTRANS process. Once you have made the required settings, pressing the enter key will begin the translation process.

- **F3=o/p-fmt** cycles through several options that define the type of output file. **KPT-format** produces a file with a .KPT extension. It looks somewhat like the .KTX file, but without the :delay: statements between keystrokes. An example of this appears in Figure 10.24. **KPT+NoXshift** omits statements that indicate extended shift status, such as :lalt: or :ralt:. **KPT+NoShift** omits all statements that include shift status and extended shift status, such as :alt:, :ctrl:, :lshift:, or :rshift:. Other designations, such as :ins:, :caps-lock:, :num-lock:, or :scroll-lock:, are retained. **KYS/KTX** translates between .KYS and .KTX files. This switch setting lets you translate in either direction. MFKTRANS determines the direction of translation from the filename extension of the input filename that you enter in the file prompt area. If that extension is omitted, MFKTRANS will assume that the imput file is .KYS and the output file is .KTX.

- **F4=cmpress** lets you choose options for text output compression. You can always use compression when producing a .KPT output file. When producing a .KTX output file, compression will work only if the .KYS file was recorded with the fast forward option. **Repeat** causes MFKTRANS to substitute {mnemonic}*n for n consecutive occurrences of {mnemonic}.

```
+----------------------------------------------------------------+
|                MFKTRANS Command Interface           Banner 0025 |
|                ------------------------                         |
| This menu sets up directives for the MFKTRANS keystroke translation utility |
| and then executes the MFKTRANS program when you press <-'.      |
|                                                                 |
| The following table shows the relationship between the text shown on the |
| information line and the directives passed to MFKTRANS.         |
|             +========================================+          |
|             | F3=o/p-format       KPT-format    /F   |          |
|             |                     KPT+NoXshift  /F/S |          |
|             |                     KPT+NoShift   /F/S0 |         |
|             |                     KYS/KTX            |          |
|             +========================================+          |
|             | F4=cmpress          Repeat+String /C   |          |
|             |                     Repeat        /C1  |          |
|             |                     String        /C2  |          |
|             +========================================+          |
|             | F5=us/uk            US            /U2  |          |
|             |                     UK            /U1  |          |
|             +========================================+          |
| Refer to Help screens and your Session Recorder documentation for more detail. |
| MFktrans—File->KPT+NoShift—Repeat+String-US——————————Ins-Caps-Num-Scroll |
| F1=help F2=dir F3=o/p-fmt F4=cmpress F5=us/uk F6/F7=ed-KTX/KPT F9/F10=cmd Escape |
| File K:\COBOL\DEMO\CUST                                    <-' Ctrl |
+----------------------------------------------------------------+
```

Figure 10.23 MFKTRANS Command Interface

```
* Session recording K:\COBOL\DEMO\TICTAC.KTX
*       translated to K:\COBOL\DEMO\TICTAC.KPT
*========================================
* Session recording TICTAC.KYS
*       translated to TICTAC.KTX
*_____
:init:
:ref: 51
:series: 01
:date: 920105
:time: 03222336
:lines: 25
:attributes: X"004E060E0B0F038F004E060E00000007"
:snap-control: 01
:comm-byte: 17
:end-control: 01
:cd: K:\COBOL\DEMO
:cmd: TICTAC
:ins: ON
:end-init:
*_____
:play:
:ins: ON
"y871n"
:stop-run:
:end-play:
*_____
* End of Recording
*========================================
```

Figure 10.24 MFKTRANS .KPT file output

String causes MFKTRANS to concatenate several consecutive ASCII text strings into one string.

- **F5=us/uk** enables display of the pound sign for those using the U.K. keyboard.

- **F6/F7=ed-KTX/KPT** lets you invoke the COBOL Editor to edit either the .KTX or the .KPT file, respectively.

MFKTRANS from the command prompt. You can run MFKTRANS from the command line prompt with the following command:

```
WB MFKTRANS [directives] input-file-ID [output-file-ID]
```

10.7 Exercises

1. Identify the logical drive containing the Micro Focus Workbench. Use the File Finder utility to list all files on that logical drive having filename extension .CBL.

2. Use DIFF to strip sequence numbers from CUST.CBL or from another COBOL source program file on your workstation.

3. Invoke the COBOL Editor under Concurrency with background syntax checking. Load CUST.CBL. Add some code to check for valid numeric input in the customer number and telephone number fields. Observe how the background syntax checking process processes each line of code.

4. Invoke Workbench with keystroke macros. Bring up the COBOL Editor. Experiment with the various Alt-key combinations that produce COBOL reserved words.

5. From the command line prompt, test CUST.CBL under Session Recorder. The first time you test, record the keystroke file and capture a screen snapshot file. The second time you test, play back the same keystroke file and capture a new screen snapshot file. Compare the two files with MFREVIEW. They should be the same.

11

Tools for the Workbench System Administrator

11.1 What the System Administrator Does

If your installation has many Workbench users, Micro Focus suggests that one person at your site be assigned the role of Micro Focus Workbench system administrator. With proper training, a PC coordinator or network administrator, a mainframe software support technician, or an experienced Workbench programmer can perform these duties. Note that if you are the first Workbench user at your site, these duties are likely to become yours, with or without a formal title.

You might ask, "Why do we need a software support person for PC workstations? I know how to use a PC. I thought the software department was for mainframes." It's true that any competent programmer can learn to set up and use all Workbench features; nonetheless, centralizing common tasks promotes consistency and eliminates wasteful duplication of effort. Some years ago, when entire mainframes were less powerful than PC workstations are now, mainframe shops typically had one or more software support staff members. They were available to install and upgrade products, set standards, diagnose and report problems, provide training, answer questions, and customize the system. All of these tasks still need to be done. Even though programmers using PC workstations can do much more for themselves than programmers formerly could on the mainframe, the need for software support never entirely goes away.

This chapter will introduce you to the tools that a Workbench system administrator can use for configuring the system. Even if you are not the administrator, this chapter is worth reading because it gives you a better idea of how the Workbench system works. It also contains a section describing how to use the Micro Focus reference manuals in an efficient, time-saving way.

11.1.1 Installing and Upgrading Workbench and Add-On Products

We have already seen that Workbench installation involves some informed decision making. Installation choices will be specific to each site. This is also true of add-on products. Therefore, if your site has licensed many copies of the Workbench and add-on products, then most likely all copies should be installed the same way. A Workbench system administrator can make sure this is done. When bug fixes or enhanced versions arrive, the Workbench administrator can make sure that everyone gets the same updates.

11.1.2 Training and Standards

An experienced Micro Focus system administrator can help introduce new users to the system by providing training and by answering questions. He or she can familiarize all users with site standards for filenames, checker directives, file transfer methods, network security, and source control procedures.

11.1.3 Contact Person for Micro Focus Product Support

The Micro Focus administrator should provide a central clearing house for questions and problem reports. Some problems result from programmer errors or from incomplete knowledge about how to use the system. Others require a bug fix or enhancement from Micro Focus or from the vendor of an add-on product. In either case, it sometimes happens that a Workbench user encounters a problem or question that someone else has already solved. No need for several Workbench users at the same site to call Micro Focus with the same problem. Allowing the site administrator to handle all communications with Micro Focus Product Support prevents delays and duplication of effort.

11.1.4 Customizing the Menu System

Many parts of the Micro Focus menu system are user configurable. The Micro Focus system administrator can supply all users with customized menu systems specific to the needs of their site.

11.2 Micro Focus Configuration Files

11.2.1 Overview of Configuration Files

Various configuration files govern the appearance and behavior of the Workbench. The setup procedure builds these files for you at installation time, in accordance with menu selections that you make. Once the Workbench is running, these configuration files establish defaults for checker and compiler directives, screen appearance, directory searches, behavior of the COBOL Editor, function key menu contents, help text contents, and other variables. Knowledgeable administrators can change the configuration files even more, to provide a customized Workbench menu system.

Checker and compiler directives files. We discussed directives files in the chapter on the Micro Focus checker. The setup procedure provides several files with extension .DIR, containing default directives appropriate for various COBOL dialects. Toggle switch settings on the Checker and Compiler menus select the desired COBOL dialect, and, therefore, the directives file. The ASCII Editor lets you make additional directives files or change existing ones to suit the needs of your installation.

Configuration (MFWB.CFG) file. The MFWB.CFG file is the global configuration file for the Workbench system. It contains information on such things as screen display colors, COBOL Editor settings, and printer support. This file is broken into sections by identifiers or **tags.** Each tag is a descriptive phrase enclosed in square brackets. All detail lines that follow that tag will pertain to the same subject matter, until a new tag is encountered. For example, the tag **[MFC-ATTRIBUTES]** indicates that the following detail lines pertain to screen display colors and highlighting. Detail lines contain a parameter followed by its value. For example, **SYS-ATT-16 : LIGHT GREY ON BLACK** indicates that text in certain parts of the Workbench display will show up as light grey on a black background. More details about the configuration file are in the "Configuration" chapter in the *Workbench Reference.*

Function key menu files. The configurable portions of the Micro Focus function key menu system are defined in ASCII text files that you can customize. The function key definitions, and the programs that run when function keys are selected, are kept in ASCII text files with filename extension **.MNU.** Some of the instructional text that accompanies the menu system is kept separately in **banner screen files.**

The Micro Focus menu handler program actually uses a compiled version of the menu file, with a filename extension of **.MNT.** If no .MNT file already exists, the Workbench will call a conversion program to create one from the .MNU version.

By default, the menu handler program will look for a menu file with the same name as itself. The Workbench main menu system is run by a program called CLI.GNT. That program looks for a menu file named CLI.MNT. More details about the function key menu system appear in the "Menu System" chapter in the *Workbench Reference.*

Concurrency configuration. The file **CONCLI.CFG** indicates what applications will automatically come up when Concurrency begins. You can change the default so that it automatically starts one of your own applications. The function key menu files used in the Concurrency function are **CON-CLI.MNU, CONCRUN.MNU,** and **CONCBAT.MNU.**

11.3 Customizing Menu Color Settings

You can change the screen display colors for the text mode Workbench menu screens. For most purposes, the default screen colors work well. These circumstances might justify changing text colors:

- **Running the Workbench on a workstation that has an unusual type of video display.** These include monochrome systems, certain laptop computers, or systems that drive translucent LCD displays for overhead projection. Setting different color combinations may improve contrast or visibility.
- **Setting up the Workbench for users with impaired color vision.** Some users have difficulty in distinguishing certain colors. Ask them whether switching to different colors or intensities would make it easier for them.
- **Catering to individual tastes.** The menus can be customized to match color scheme standards used on other screens at your site. If someone hates blinking error messages, you can turn that feature off.

```
Configure-Development-System─────────────────────────────────────────────
F1=help F2=color                    F9=update-menu F10=use-updated-menu Escape
```

Figure 11.1 Configure Development System menu

```
    +ATTRIBUTES──────────────────────────────────────────────────+
    |SYS-ATT-01 : BLACK ON BLACK               reserved           |
    |SYS-ATT-02 : YELLOW ON RED                reserved           |
    |SYS-ATT-03 : BROWN ON BLACK               MENU-TEXT          |
    |SYS-ATT-04 : YELLOW ON BLACK              KEY-TOPS           |
    |SYS-ATT-05 : LIGHT-CYAN ON BLACK          TELL-TALES         |
    |SYS-ATT-06 : WHITE ON BLACK               LOCK-ON            |
    |SYS-ATT-07 : CYAN ON BLACK                ANIMATED-TEXT      |
    |SYS-ATT-08 : WHITE ON BLACK BLINK         ERROR-MESSAGES     |
    |SYS-ATT-09 : BLACK ON BLACK               reserved           |
    |SYS-ATT-10 : YELLOW ON RED                MARGINS            |
    |SYS-ATT-11 : BROWN ON BLACK               NORMAL-TEXT        |
    |SYS-ATT-12 : YELLOW ON BLACK              CURRENT-LINE       |
    |SYS-ATT-13 : BLACK ON BLACK               reserved           |
    |SYS-ATT-14 : BLACK ON BLACK               reserved           |
    |SYS-ATT-15 : BLACK ON BLACK               reserved           |
    |SYS-ATT-16 : LIGHT-GREY ON BLACK          reserved           |
    +─────────────────────────────────────────────────────────────+

Color──────────────────────────────────────────────────────────
F1=help F2=set-colors F3=try-colors F4=save                    Escape
```

Figure 11.2 Color main menu

11.3.1 Configuring Colors

The Micro Focus Workbench offers an automated method of changing display colors. You can select colors on screen from a menu, without having to edit any configuration files directly. Pressing **F8=config** on the Mainframe Development Environment menu brings up the configuration menu shown in Figure 11.1.

On this menu, pressing **F2=color** brings up the Color menu shown in Figure 11.2. You will use the functions on that menu to select a new color scheme. Saving the color scheme updates the MFWB.CFG file.

Also on the configuration menu is **F9=update-menu.** This function brings up the CLI.MNU file under the COBOL Editor, so that you can make changes directly to the text file. In a later section, we will discuss methods for customizing the .MNU file. Once you have saved the changes, press **F10=use-new-menu** to compile the .MNU file to create a new .MNT file.

On the Color main menu shown in Figure 11.2, the text area shows the color combinations the Workbench is using for different types of display text. For example, normal text (most of the text that you would see in the COBOL Editor, for example) appears as brown type on a black background, by default.

Pressing **F2=set-colors** brings up the Set Colors menu shown in Figure 11.3. This menu lets you set the color combinations that the Workbench will use for each purpose. If you want to get back to the Workbench menu system with the new colors set temporarily, press **F3=try-colors.** The color settings will remain in effect only during that Workbench session. Previous settings will take effect if you exit and log on again. If you want to set the new color scheme permanently, press **F4=save** on this menu. This updates the [MFC-ATTRIBUTES] section in the MFWB.CFG file. The MFWB.CFG file is the source of the information that appears in the text area of Figure 11.2.

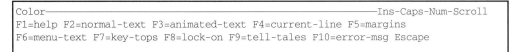

```
Color──────────────────────────────────────────Ins-Caps-Num-Scroll
F1=help F2=normal-text F3=animated-text F4=current-line F5=margins
F6=menu-text F7=key-tops F8=lock-on F9=tell-tales F10=error-msg Escape
```

Figure 11.3 Set Colors menu

On the Set Colors menu, select the function key for the type of text that you want to change.

- **F2=normal-text** includes most of the text appearing in the text area of Micro Focus screens. For instance, this category would cover nonhighlighted lines in the Editor or the Checker.
- **F3=animated-text** refers to program source code lines visible during animation.
- **F4=current-line** refers to the type of highlighting that distinguishes the current line of text.
- **F5=margins** refers to the highlighting used to denote the margin bars in the COBOL Editor. These are visible during the process of setting the margins. The same highlighting is also used to mark a block for copy and delete operations within the Editor.
- **F6=menu-text** refers to normal (nonhighlighted) text appearing in function key menus.
- **F7=key-tops** refers to the highlighted key identifiers appearing in function key menus. For example, function key names such as **F7** would fall into this category. It also refers to the settings used to indicate that toggle switch settings on the information line are "off."
- **F8=lock-on** refers to the settings used to indicate that toggle switch settings on the information line are "on."
- **F9=tell-tales** refers to other indicators that appear on the information line.
- **F10=error-msg** refers to error messages that appear on the last line of the screen.

If you select any of these options, the function key menu lines shown in Figure 11.4 will appear. These let you cycle among various options for background color, foreground (text) color, highlighting (normal or bright), and blinking. This screen shows you samples of the appropriate type of text so that you can experiment to find relationships among colors. Yellow, for example, is the high-intensity version of brown foreground text. Therefore, if you choose brown foreground text, and then switch to bright intensity, the text color will change to yellow.

When you are finished setting colors for whatever type of text you have chosen, press the Escape key to return to the Set Colors menu. From there, you can select another type of text to change, or you can choose Escape again to get back to the Color main menu.

```
      START-UP.
          Display space
          Call MOVE-CURSOR-ROUTINE using DUMMY, CURSOR-POSITION
          Call SCREEN-IO using WRITE-TEXT, FORM-PARAMS, READY-00
          Call SCREEN-IO using WRITE-TEXT, SCORE-PARAMS, SCORE-TEXT.
      LOOP.
          Move all "$" to SCREEN-ATTR-1
          Call SCREEN-IO using WRITE-ATTRIB, FORM-PARAMS, SCREEN-ATTR-1
          Perform DELAY-LOOP 30 times
      ************ Has a key been pressed?
          Call SCAN-KEYBOARD using SCAN-RESULT
          If SCAN-RESULT = 1
              go to CALL-INVADERS.
          Move all "" to SCREEN-ATTR-1
          Call SCREEN-IO using WRITE-ATTRIB, FORM-PARAMS, SCREEN-ATTR-1
          Perform DELAY-LOOP 30 times
      ************ Has a key been pressed?
          Call SCAN-KEYBOARD using SCAN-RESULT
          If SCAN-RESULT = 1
              go to CALL-INVADERS.
          Go to LOOP.
Color──Normal-text──────────Attribute-0000-0110-006-06h───────Ins-Caps-Num-Scroll
F1=help
F7=blink F8=background F9=intensity F10=foreground                     Escape
```

Figure 11.4 Color Normal Text menu

Tips for color selection.

- Use restraint in background color selection. When you install the Workbench, most background color settings default to black. You can change the background color for some or all types of text, but if you do, avoid using too many background colors. Otherwise, the Workbench screens can look like a patchwork.

- Avoid hard-to-read combinations of background and foreground color. For example, avoid dark blue on black, yellow on white, or red on turquoise. Text is more legible when the foreground and background differ in brightness as well as in hue. This is especially important for those users whose color vision is impaired.

- The blinking attribute should be used sparingly or not at all. Some users find blinking text to be too irritating even for error messages.

11.4 Customizing Editor Default Settings

11.4.1 Editor Configuration Information

When you begin a new Workbench session, the COBOL Editor uses a configuration derived from information in the MFWB.CFG file. (You may also find an EDITOR.CFG file. You can ignore that file; it is used only for running the COBOL Editor under the Toolset without the Workbench.) If you have installed the Workbench to use the Mainframe Development Environment, the MFWB.CFG file will contain an [EDIT-USER] section as shown in Figure 11.5. In the original version of that file installed by the setup procedure, the settings for margins and filename extensions are the same as the Editor's built-in defaults. In other words, if the Editor finds no configuration information, it will assume those defaults. More built-in defaults for the COBOL Editor are listed in Figure 11.6.

More detailed information about COBOL Editor configuration options is in the "COBOL Editor" chapter in the *Toolset Reference.*

```
[EDIT-USER]
lang osvs     use($cobdir\wbosvs.dir)
lang vsc2(1) use($cobdir\wbvsc21.dir)
lang vsc2(2) use($cobdir\wbvsc22.dir)
lang vsc2(3) use($cobdir\wbvsc23.dir)
margins {other} 0 81
margins cbl     7 73
margins cpy     cbl
margins {space} cbl
margins cob     cbl
margins bak     cbl
init-margins    cbl
extensions      cbl cpy {space}
```

Figure 11.5 COBOL Editor information in MFWB.CFG

```
CSI:ON
BACKUP:OFF
WORD-WRAP:ON
CHECK-MODE:CHECK
PAUSE:ON
LIST:CON
STRUCT:OFF
ANALYZE:OFF
REF:OFF
XREF:OFF
LIMIT:LINE
AUTORESTART:ON
```

Figure 11.6 Built-in COBOL Editor defaults

11.4.2 Word Wrap, Directives, and Other Toggles

Most of the built-in defaults govern toggle switch settings that appear on the COBOL Editor or Syntax Checker information line. To override any default settings, you can insert the override as a new line into the [EDIT-USER] section of MFWB.CFG. For example, to set word wrap off by default, insert **WORD-WRAP:OFF** into the [EDIT-USER] section of MFWB.CFG. If you want the Structure Animator and the Analyzer checker directives to be in effect by default, insert **STRUCT:ON** and **ANALYZE:ON** into the [EDIT-USER] section.

Each **lang** parameter line corresponds to a language toggle switch defined in the CLI.MNU file. It tells which directives (.DIR) file to use when that toggle switch is selected on the checker menu. In the parameter line **lang vsc2(3) use($cobdir\wbvsc23.dir),** the **$cobdir** will substitute the directory path from the COBDIR operating system environment variable. That particular setting applies to VS COBOL II Level 3. If you define additional language toggles, you can use these parameters to associate them with the desired .DIR files. You can define up to twenty toggle settings. The COBOL Editor automatically allows a blank selection for **F6=lang,** which corresponds to no language directives file. Since the language parameter for **osvs** appears first in the configuration file, OSVS will be the default setting when you first bring up the COBOL Editor. To change this, use the COBOL Editor to rearrange the order of the language parameter lines in MFWB.CFG.

11.4.3 Filename Extensions for Search

The **extensions** parameter line in the [EDIT-USER] section governs the default filename extensions that the Micro Focus directory facility will use when loading files into the COBOL Editor. If you do not specify a filename extension at the prompt, by default the directory facility will look first for a file with extension .CBL, then for extension .CPY, then for a file with an extension of spaces. If your site uses some other naming convention, such as .CCP for CICS OS/2 source files, you can place that extension before any of the others in the **extensions** parameter line. Filename extensions are not case sensitive. All are converted to uppercase.

11.4.4 Default Margin Settings

The default margin settings in the COBOL Editor are associated with the filename extension of the file being edited. When you load a source file with extension .CBL, the Editor sets its margins to columns 7 and 73. The **margins** parameter lines in the MFWB.CFG file equate filename extensions to margin settings. Filename extensions .CPY, space, .COB, and .BAK receive the same margin settings as do .CBL files. Because of the **margins {other} 0 81** setting, any other filename extension receives margin settings of columns 0 and 81. If you bring up the COBOL Editor without loading a file, the **init-margins cbl** parameter line sets margin columns to 7 and 73, as for .CBL files.

To change default margins for a specific filename extension, or to set default margins for a new filename extension, you can use the COBOL Editor to add or change the **margins** parameter lines in MFWB.CFG.

11.5 Creating New Banners and Text Screens

As we discussed previously, many of the instructional text displays in the Micro Focus function key menu system actually come from **banner screen files.** For example, many screens that come up from the function key menus when you press **F1=help** are actually banner screen files. So is the descriptive text appearing on the MDE and WDE main menus. These text files may be stored as individual screen-image files, under the naming convention **BANN*nnnn*.BAN**, where *nnnn* is a numeric value. Similarly, screens that you intend to use for customized **F1=help** displays are stored with the naming convention **HELP*nnnn*.HLP.** Alternatively, banner or help screen files may be stored as members within a Micro Focus library file (.LBR), with member names BANN*nnnn* or HELP*nnnn*. For those who are interested, the Library facility is described in the "Library" chapter of the *Toolset Reference.*

11.5.1 Using Forms Facility to Paint Text Screens

The Forms facility is primarily a screen painter used for developing COBOL applications to run on a PC workstation. You can also use Forms to make new banner text screens for the function key menu system. In this section, we will discuss only the features that you would use to create banner screens.

Invoking the Forms facility. You can bring up the Forms facility from the COBOL Editor main menu by holding down the **Ctrl** key and pressing **F6=draw/forms.** The opening menu of the Forms facility, shown in Figure 11.7, offers several functions:

- **F2=draw** gets you into the COBOL Editor line drawing function. We showed how to use line drawing in Chapter 4, so we will not repeat this information here. If you plan to use any box, border, or ruled lines in your banner screen, the Draw function is the easiest way to create them. Clear your Editor work area, draw the lines, and then use **F3=text-to-forms** to get this new data into the Forms facility. The line drawing function is also present on another menu within the Forms facility.

- **F3=text-to-forms** captures the data in the COBOL Editor work area, brings up the Forms main menu, and puts that data into the Forms editing work area.

- **F4=forms** gets you into the Forms facility, clearing the Forms editing work area.

```
Edit-new-file────────────────────Line-1──────Col-8────────Wrap-Ins-Caps-Num-Scroll
F1=help F2=draw F3=text-to-forms F4=forms                                   Escape
```

Figure 11.7 Forms opening menu

```
Forming-new-form-Text──Attribute-0000-0110-006──Cursor0101──Ins-Caps-Num-Scroll
F1=help F2=text/data F3/F4=insert/delete-line F5=repeat-line F6=restore-line
F7=retype-char F8=restore-char F9=repeat-ch F10=paint-attr     Alt Ctrl Escape
```

Figure 11.8 Forms main menu

Editing text on a banner screen. The Forms main menu (Figure 11.8) is used mainly for entering text on the screen. Most of the functions work much the same way as they do in the COBOL Editor, so we will not repeat all of that here. For creating banner screens, the **F3=text/data** toggle switch should be set to **text.** (The **data** setting is for defining data entry fields for PC COBOL applications programming.)

The information line shows numeric values for the current screen display attribute setting. This governs foreground and background color, intensity, and blinking. The word **attribute** on the information line shows what those attribute values actually look like in practice. Each new character you enter on the screen will have that attribute setting. If desired, you can use **F10=paint-attr** to change existing characters on the screen to the current attribute setting. Position the text cursor to the first character you want to change, and then press **F10** until you have repainted each character.

```
Forming-new-form-Text──Attribute-0000-0110-006──Cursor0101──Ins-Caps-Num-Scroll
F1=help F2=attr-on/off F3=load-form F4=save-form F5=generate-COBOL F6=clear-form
F7=blink F8=background F9=intensity F10=foreground
```

Figure 11.9 Forms Alt-key menu

Setting display attributes. Holding down the **Alt** key will reveal the Forms Alt-key menu, shown in Figure 11.9. This menu contains functions for loading and saving Forms files and for setting screen display attributes:

- **F2=attr-on/off** shows or hides the attribute indicators on the information line.
- **F3=load-form** and **F4=save-form** are the usual Micro Focus directory functions for loading and saving Forms files. By default, these functions will assume a filename extension of .FRM. When you are working with a banner or help screen, specify a filename extension of .BAN or .HLP in the file prompt.
- **F5=generate-COBOL** produces COBOL code from the screen layout, for use in PC-based applications.
- If you want to start over, **F6=clear-form** brings up a menu that lets you clear all text fields, clear all data entry fields, reset all screen attributes, or clear all data from the Forms editing work area.
- **F7=blink, F8=background, F9=intensity,** and **F10=foreground** let you change the current screen display attribute. Pressing these keys repeatedly will cycle through the available color and highlighting choices. The appearance of the word **Attribute** on the information line will show the effect of the currently selected values.

Inserting special characters. Holding down the **Ctrl** key will reveal the Forms Ctrl-key menu, shown in Figure 11.10. This menu contains functions for placing special characters on the screen. The last line of this menu lists all ASCII characters that will display on the screen. This line is a selection menu for choosing the ASCII character that you want; the currently selected character will be highlighted. It contains many ASCII characters that do not appear on your keyboard. Since there are too many ASCII characters to display at once, the last screen line will scroll horizontally.

- **F2=cursor^/->** is a toggle switch that determines whether the cursor will move one position to the right or one position downward each time you press **F5** to paint a character on the screen.
- **F3=char-left** and **F4=char-right** will select the character just to the left or right of the currently selected special character.
- **F5=select-char** will write the selected character at the text cursor position on the screen. Pressing **F5** repeatedly will produce a sequence of these characters along a row or column, depending on the direction of cursor movement that you have selected.
- **F6=draw** brings up the same line drawing menu that appears in the Forms opening menu and in the COBOL Editor itself.
- **F7=text->edit** brings up the COBOL Editor, loading the text from the Forms editing work area into the COBOL Editor. However, once you go into the Editor, you will no longer be working with a form or banner file!
- **F9=read-char** copies the character at the text cursor position into the character buffer. You can press **F9=repeat-ch** on the Forms main menu to reproduce that character elsewhere on screen if desired.

- **F10=read-attr** sets the current display attribute to the attribute of the character at the text cursor position.
- **End=menu-on/off** shows or hides the function key menu at the bottom of the screen, allowing you to see all 25 lines of the screen at the same time.

11.5.2 Installing New Banner Screens

What files to change. To make your new banner or help displays available within the function key menu system, you must complete the following steps. First, copy your new banner or help files into a directory named in your COBDIR environment variable. Second, update the .MNU file so that it invokes your new displays. Third, compile the .MNU file to produce a new .MNT file.

To update the .MNU file, press **F8=config** on the Mainframe Development Environment menu to bring up the configuration menu. Choose **F9=update-menu** on the configuration menu. The CLI.MNU file will come up under the COBOL Editor, letting you make changes directly to the text file. We will discuss those changes in the next section. Save the changes under the Editor, then press **F10=use-new-menu** to compile the .MNU file to create a new .MNT file. This will activate the changes you have made to the function key menu system.

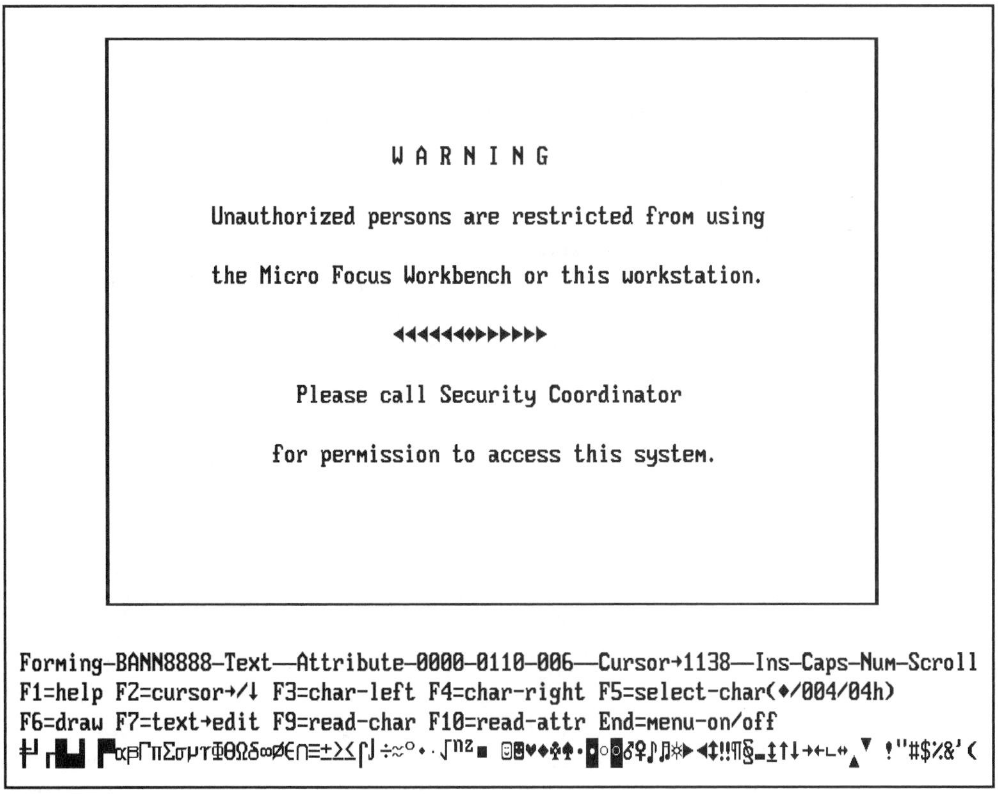

Figure 11.10 Forms Ctrl-key menu

```
MENU :menu: %
**************************************************************************
:new-menu: MAIN
**************************************************************************
:banner: 1200 :library: $COBDIR\WB2MDE
:title:
Micro Focus Mainframe Development Environment
:line1:
F1=help F2=files F3=develop F4=execute F5=IMS F6=CICS     F8=config F9=Workbench
hh      hh      hh         hh          hh      hh         hh        hh
:line2:
                                                                   Escape
                                                                   hhh

:library: $COBDIR\TOOLS.LBR
:library: $COBDIR\UTILS.LBR
:library: $COBDIR\WB2.LBR
*:opt-library: $COBDIR\MENU.LBR
:opt-library: $COBDIR\PARMPASS.LBR
*:opt-library: $CICS\CICSVS.LBR
*:opt-library: $IMSDIR\PCIMS.LBR
:efuncs:
F1 :help: 1200 :library: $COBDIR\WB2MDE
F2 :menu: FILES
F3 :menu: DEVELOP
F4 :menu: EXECUTE
F5 :call-menu: $IMSDIR\PCIMS.MNU
F6 :run: $CICS\CICSVS.LBR\CICSVS
F8 :menu: CONFIGURE
F9 :call-menu: WB2A.MNU
Esc :menu: :lastexitq:
:end-menu:
```

Figure 11.11 Excerpt from CLI.MNU (MDE main menu definition)

Banner and help statements in CLI.MNU. Figure 11.11 contains an excerpt from the CLI.MNU file. It shows only the portion pertaining to the MDE main menu display. The banner screen for any given menu will appear in the text area when that menu comes up. In this case, the default banner statement is **:banner: 1200 :library: $COBDIR\WB2MDE.** It refers to a member within the WB2MDE.LBR library file in the COBDIR path.

Suppose you have created a banner file and stored it as a separate file, under the name BANN8888.BAN. If you replace the existing banner statement with **:banner: 8888** and then recompile CLI.MNU, your banner file will appear on the MDE main menu in place of the Micro Focus display. For instance, your customized banner might contain your organization's name or logo, a security warning message such as that in Figure 11.10, and phone numbers for the Micro Focus system administrator or the help desk.

In similar fashion, the function key statement **F1 :help: 1200 :library: $COBDIR\WB2MDE** tells Workbench to load member HELP1200 from the WB2MDE.LBR library file in the COBDIR path. We do not recommend replacing a Micro Focus help file with your own displays. However, advanced users who add new menus to the Workbench menu system to run their own utilities would be well advised to add help displays to each new menu.

11.6 Customizing Function Key Settings

In the Workbench function key menu system, you can set up unused function keys to run your own programs or submenus. You can also turn off function keys for add-on products that you do not use. In this section, we will take a closer look at some of the statements that define menus. Further details are in the "Menu Handler" chapter in the *Workbench Reference.*

11.6.1 Function Key Menu Statements

The CLI.MNU file contains two sections. The first section is called the **command line section.** It determines how the Menu Handler will interpret command parameters when you run Micro Focus Workbench components directly from the command line. The second section is the **menu section.** It determines how the Micro Focus function key menus will work. This is the portion of CLI.MNU that concerns us here.

Figure 11.11 shows the statements that define the MDE main menu. Every menu definition within CLI.MNU begins with a **:new-menu:** statement and ends with an **:end-menu:** statement. As we have seen, the **:banner:** statement determines what, if anything, will display in the text area when this menu first comes up. The **:title:** statement provides the menu name that appears on the left side of the information line. In this case, the title is **Micro Focus Mainframe Development Environment.** If you define a new menu, give it a unique descriptive title so that users know where they are!

The **:line1:** and **:line2:** statements contain images of the first and second menu lines. Beneath each set of function keys is another line containing highlighting flags. Wherever the letter **h** appears below a character, that character will be highlighted with the attribute used for key tops. The highlighted characters should match the printing on the keyboard for those actual keys. If there is a third menu line, it is defined in a **:line3:** statement. However, this is best avoided if possible because line 25 is needed for error messages. The **:library:** and **:opt-library:** statements indicate Micro Focus library modules that the menu system can search.

Now for the function keys. The **:efuncs:** statement indicates that all function key designations are available, including the ones for Alt-key and Ctrl-key menus. The MDE main menu does not happen to use control and alternate menus, but some other menus do. You can use **:Alt-line1:, :Alt-line2:, :Ctrl-line1:,** and **:Ctrl-line2:** to define Alt-key and Ctrl-key menu contents. After you describe the menu lines, you need to specify the actions for each function key on them. Function key designations **F1** through **F10** represent the unshifted function key values. **F11** through **F20** represent the shifted function key values. **F21** through **F30** represent the Ctrl-key function key values. **F31** through **F40** represent the Alt-key function key values. For example, the combination **Alt+F3** becomes **F33** in the context of this menu system.

Let's look at some of the actions you can invoke with a function key. We have already discussed the **:help:** statement. To be consistent, **F1** should always be the help key. The **:menu:** statement designates a subordinate menu that appears when you press the function key. These menus are defined further down in the same .MNU file. The **:call-menu:** file is similar, but it refers to a separate .MNU file. The **:run:** statement actually runs an executable file. Finally, the **Esc** key should always let you out of the current menu. An application that won't let you out is no more trustworthy than a parachute that won't let you down. The **:lastexitq:** keyword allows the user to return to the previous menu, if any, or to get out of the system completely.

Here's an example of how you can use function key actions. The MDE main menu defines actions for eight function keys. This leaves F7 and F10 for user-defined actions, if desired. If you have only one or two programs that you need to put into the menu system, you can define function keys with the :run: statement. Otherwise, you can define a function key with :call-menu: to call a user menu file that you have prepared.

11.6.2 Customizing Default Checker/Compiler Directives

Previous chapters showed that the menus for the Syntax Checker and COBOL/2 Compiler use function key toggle switches to set certain directives on or off. Since these toggle switches are defined in the .MNU file, you can customize different default settings. Figure 11.12 shows another excerpt from the CLI.MNU file; in this case, the Check menu.

Before we get to the toggle switches, let's look at some other statements that make up this menu.

The **:name:** statement displays a file drive/path/name prompt to the user on the second menu line. Certain parameter variables make that name available to other menu statements. In this case, **%F%** refers to the fully qualified filename, and **%NE%** refers only to the eight-character filename and three-character extension.

The **:set-linein:** **SETDIRC** statement indicates that the SETDIRC menu, accessed when F10 is pressed, will pass a line of parameter data back to this menu system. The **%L%** parameter makes this data available when F9 is selected.

The **:runsys:** command works in much the same way as **:run:**, but it also lets you display a message. The accompanying **:message:** statement displays a message on the last menu line once the program begins running. In this case, pressing the enter key (here called **Ret**) runs the checker.

Now for the **:toggle:** statement itself. Each :toggle: statement is associated with a function key. The first line of the toggle statement lists all of the toggle values that cycle through the information line when you press that key. The **(u)** highlights that option on the information line. If you run the Workbench on a monochrome monitor, (u) represents underlined text. On a color monitor, the default is light blue.

The toggle switch setting that appears first in the list will be the default. In other words, this setting will be the one appearing on the information line when the menu first comes up. If a toggle switch value is a character string that contains spaces, surround it with quotation marks to show that it represents a single option. In the list of toggle switch settings, [], or square brackets, represents a *null* value. The null value is *not* equivalent to spaces; it represents a character string of zero length. The null value allows the user to turn an option off.

```
**************************************************************************
:new-menu: CHECK
**************************************************************************
:title:
Check
:line1:
F1=help F2=dir F3=pse F4=list F5=anim F6=lang F7=x/ref F8=csi F9/F10=options Esc
  hh      hh     hh     hh      hh      hh      hh       hh  hhh            hhh
:name: CBL
:library: $COBDIR\COBCLI.LBR
:library: $COBDIR\CHECK.LBR
:library: $COBDIR\ADVANIM.LBR
:set-linein: SETDIRC
:efuncs:
F1 :help: 1206 :library: $COBDIR\WB2MDE
F3 :toggle: (u)Pause [] :at: 9
       :return: "errq editor(mf)" editor(mf)
F4 :toggle: [] (u)List-Con (u)Print (u)List-File (u)Nolist  :at: 15
       :return: [] "list noform" list(lst) list() nolist
F5 :toggle: [] (u)Struct (u)Analyze "(u)Strc+Anlz" :at: 25
       :return: [] struct analyze "struct analyze"
F6 :toggle: (u)OSVS (u)VSC2(1) (u)VSC2(2) (u)VSC2(3) [] :at: 35
       :return: use($cobdir\wbosvs.dir)
                use($cobdir\wbvsc21.dir)
                use($cobdir\wbvsc22.dir)
                use($cobdir\wbvsc23.dir)
                []
F7 :toggle: [] (u)Xref (u)Ref (u)X+Ref :at: 43
       :return: [] xref ref "xref ref"
F8 :toggle: (u)CSI [] :at: 49
       :return: csi []
F9 :toggle: [] (u)Opts-on :at: 53
       :return: [] "confirm %L%"
F10 :menu: SETDIRC
Esc :menu: :lastexitq:
Ret :runsys: CHECK %F% anim ensuite(2)
:message: Checking %NE%, Ctrl+Break to Stop
:menu: :lastexitq:
:end-menu:
```

Figure 11.12 Excerpt from CLI.MNU (Check menu definition)

The **:at:** keyword indicates the column position on the information line at which the toggle setting will appear. Be sure to leave enough room to avoid overlapping. (Keep the **:title:** information separate from the toggle switches.)

The **:return:** keyword should contain as many returned values as you have toggle switch settings. They must be in the same order as the toggle switch values. A returned value can be null. If a returned value contains spaces, surround it with quotation marks to show that it represents a single option. On the Check menu, returned values are directives to be passed to the Checker.

Here is an example of the type of menu customization you might do. Suppose your site nearly always uses VS COBOL II level 3. For convenience, you want that to be the default language dialect for the **F6=lang** key. In that case, rearrange the order of the toggle settings in the **F6 :toggle:** statement so that **(u)VSC2(3)** is first. Rearrange the order of the returned values so that **use($cobdir\wbvsc23.dir)** is first. Then recompile the .MNU file.

11.7 Customizing On-line Information (HYHELP) Files

You can make up your own HYHELP files to use in addition to the ones that Micro Focus provides. For example, you can use HYHELP files to publish your organization's standards or to provide information about application programs.

Two Micro Focus facilities support hypertext help. **The On-line Information System Compiler (OLISC)** compiles hypertext help files into a form that will display as hypertext. The **HYHELP** program looks up and displays hypertext help information from these files. Complete information about creating hypertext files is in the "On-line Information" chapter in the *Workbench Reference.*

11.7.1 Where the System Finds HYHELP Files

The HYHELP program looks for help files with filename extension of **.HNF.** It searches the current directory path and the path designated in the **SET COBHNF** environment variable.

11.7.2 Creating New HYHELP Files

You can create a hypertext help source file as an ASCII text file with extension **.TXT.** From it, OLISC will compile an output file with extension **.HNF.** In this section, we will examine statements that make up a HYHELP source file. The sample HYHELP source file in Figure 11.13 shows many of these statements. Note that this example is somewhat abbreviated from what we would actually use to document an application. It is presented here to acquaint you with many of the HYHELP commands.

```
.title Help for Customer Master (CUST) application
.define @overview @1
.define @viewcust @2
.define @addcust @3
.define @chgcust @4
.define @delcust @5
.define @viewsale @6
.define @addsale @7
.comment The overview is the home topic
.context CUST
.context @overview
.topic Help for Customer Master (CUST) sample application
:ix1. overview
:ix1. Customer Master
:ix1. CUST
:ix1. CICS OS/2
:p. CUST is a CICS OS/2 application that updates customer
master and sales history records. It appears in the book
\bCICS Command Level Programming,\p Second Edition,
by Alida M. Jatich, John Wiley & Sons, Inc. 1991.

:p. On the main menu, choose the object that you want to work
with. Enter \b1\p for customer records or \b2\p for sales
history records. Then tab to the desired action on the action
bar and press the enter key. Before the next menu appears,
a popup menu will ask you to enter a starting customer number.
Supply this number and press the enter key
```

Figure 11.13 User-written HYHELP source file

```
:dl.
:dthd. Action
:ddhd.          Description
:dt. View
:dd.      \a<View customers>\v@viewcust\v or \a<view sales
history>\v@viewsale\v
:dt. Add
:dd.      \a<Add customers>\v@addcust\v or \a<add sales
history>\v@addsale\v
:dt. Change

:dd.      \a<Change customer records>\v@chgcust\v
:dt. Delete
:dd.      \a<Delete customer records>\v@delcust\v
:edl.
.context @viewcust
.topic View Customer Records
:ix1. view customer records
:ix1. browse customer records
:p. This screen lets you page through all of the
customer numbers and names in the file. You can restart
the browse at another position in the file by entering
a new customer number in the data entry field.

:dl.
:dthd. Function
:ddhd.          Description
:dt. PF3
:dd.     Exit to main menu.
:dt. PF7
:dd.     Page backward in the customer master.
:dt. PF8
:dd.     Page forward in the customer master.
:dt. PF10
:dd.     Move cursor to action bar.
:dt. PF12
:dd.     Cancel current action.
:edl.

.context @addcust
.topic Add Customer Records
:ix1. add customer records
:p. This screen lets you add a new customer record.
You cannot add a record if the customer number is already
on file.

.context @chgcust
.topic Change Customer Records
:ix1. change customer records
:p. This screen lets you change an existing customer
record. You cannot change current week sales, balance due,
or last bill date.

.context @delcust
.topic Delete Customer Records
:ix1. delete customer records
:p. This screen lets you delete an existing customer
record, provided that there is no current activity. You
will be asked to confirm the delete.

.context @viewsale
.topic View Sales History
```

Figure 11.13 User-written HYHELP source file (cont'd)

```
:ix1. view sales history
:ix1. browse sales history
:p. This screen lets you page through all of the
sales history for the customer that you selected on the
main menu.

.context @addsale
.topic Add Sales History
:ix1. add sales history
:p. This screen lets you add current week sales history.
Unit price and quantity must be numeric. Two decimal places
are assumed for the unit price.
```

Figure 11.13 User-written HYHELP source file (cont'd)

Control statements within a hypertext source file begin with a period or a colon to distinguish them from display text. Each hypertext file begins with a **.title** statement that describes that file. The title is for identification purposes and will not appear on help screens. You can place **.comment** statements anywhere in the file. OLISC will ignore any text on a comment line.

Defining hypertext topics. The HYHELP system is organized around topics. Each topic is associated with one or more **:context** statements. A context statement is a tag that allows you to look up a topic. If a context name begins with an "@" sign, it is a **local name,** available only from within that HYHELP file. Local names work more efficiently but you cannot look them up from outside the HYHELP file, as you can with external names.

Every context statement has a context number. You can use the **.define** statement to assign a context number to a context name, or OLISC will assign one automatically at compile time. The **.topic** statement assigns a title to the topic. This title will appear on the top border of the screen for that topic. If you tell OLISC to produce a table of contents, it will build it from the topic titles. Finally, the **:ix1.** statements specify index entries. You can assign as many index entries to a topic as you want. If you tell OLISC to produce an index, it will build the index from the :ix1. statements.

At display time, the forward and backward browse commands will navigate along a **browse chain,** if one exists. To specify a browse chain, use a series of **.browse** statements in the following format:

```
.browse #chain-number @topic-name @topic-name
```

A topic name of **@0** means that this topic is the first or last topic in the chain. Workbench v2.5 supports only one browse chain for each help file.

Defining display text. Now for the actual display text. The **:p.** keyword indicates the beginning of a paragraph. The paragraph continues until the next blank line. You do not have to concern yourself with the number of words on each line. At display time, HYHELP will flow (word wrap) all of the text between the :p. statement and the next blank line.

Suppose you want to create lines of text that will not flow. You can do this by specifying a block of fixed lines. Begin the block with a **:lines** statement, follow with each line of text, and end it with an **:elines** statement. If you want a block of fixed lines displayed in monospaced text, then begin and end it with **:cgraphics** and **:ecgraphics** statements. These tags refer to

character graphics. You can use this if you want to create lines and boxes that will always line up correctly. Finally, if a topic contains too much text to fit on one screen page, the screen image becomes scrollable at display time. If you want to create header lines that will not scroll with the rest of the text, put that text in a fixed-line block at the beginning of the topic. Use the **:freeze** *nn* statement to specify the number of lines that should be nonscrollable.

You can specify a list within a help topic. HYHELP supports various types of lists. The example in Figure 11.13 shows a **definition list.** A definition list begins with a **:dl.** statement and ends with an **:edl.** statement. Each entry in a definition list consists of a term, presented in a **:dt.** statement, and a definition, presented in a **:dd.** statement. Headers for the terms and definitions appear in **:dthd.** and **:ddhd.** statements.

Screen attributes let you highlight portions of text within a topic. OLISC offers four text attribute tags that each map to different colors on a color display screen. Bold is **\b,** italic is **\i,,** underline is **\u,,** and plain is **\p.**

Defining hot spots. A hot spot is a selectable part of the text display that allows you to reach a related topic. You can define a hot spot by embedding a topic name (actually a context name) within the text. The embedded topic name will be invisible on the help screen display. Surround the embedded topic name with **\v** flags. You can find examples of this on the first help screen within Figure 11.13.

Note that the embedded topic name is distinct from the hot spot itself. The embedded topic name identifies the topic that will come up when the user selects the hot spot. The hot spot is the selectable area within the text. This will be the word immediately before the first **\v** flag. As far as OLISC is concerned, a word is any text string delimited by spaces. If you want the hot spot to encompass more than one word, then use the **\a** (anchor) flag to delimit the beginning of the hot spot. The hot spot will cover everything between the **\a** flag and the first **\v** flag.

At display time, once the user tabs to a hot spot, that area will become highlighted. However, you will want to do something to distinguish those hot spots from the rest of the text even before the user tabs over to them. You can do that either by surrounding the hot spot by special characters, or by using a different color highlighting, or both. In this case, we used angle brackets (the less-than and greater-than signs) to distinguish hot spots. Whatever method you use, be consistent from screen to screen.

11.7.3 Compiling HYHELP Files

You can run OLISC, the hypertext help compiler, from the command line by using this syntax:

```
RUN OLISC filename [directives]
```

If you don't specify an extension for the input filename, OLISC will assume an extension of **.TXT.** The output file will have the same name as the input file, but with an extension of **.HNF.** You can provide several filenames or use wildcards if you want to compile several files together. Here are some OLISC directives you can specify:

- **/COBDIR** causes OLISC to place the output file in the COBDIR path instead of in the COBHNF path.
- **/CONTENTS** causes OLISC to create a table of contents topic. This topic will list every topic title in the source file. The HYHELP Contents function will allow access to this table of contents display.
- **/INDEX** causes OLISC to create an index topic. This topic will list every index item in the source file. The HYHELP Index function will allow access to this index display.
- **/LIST** causes OLISC to create a summary listing file. It will have the same name as the input file, but with an extension of **.LST**.

11.7.4 Testing HYHELP Files

To test your new hypertext file, enter the following command at the command line prompt:

```
HYHELP filename.HNF!topic
```

If you omit the exclamation point following the filename, the HYHELP system will default to showing you the Micro Focus Workbench help files rather than your own. If you specify a topic, HYHELP will position itself at the beginning of that topic within the help file. The topic must be an external context name; in other words, a context without an "@" sign preceding its name.

Figures 11.14, 11.15, and 11.16 show the results of compiling and testing the HYHELP file in Figure 11.13.

```
+-----------Help for Customer Master (CUST) sample application-----------+
| CUST is a CICS OS/2 application that updates customer master and sales |
| history records. It appears in the book CICS Command Level Programming,|
| Second Edition, by Alida M. Jatich, John Wiley & Sons, Inc. 1991.      |
|                                                                        |
| On the main menu, choose the object that you want to work with. Enter 1 for |
| customer records or 2 for sales history records. Then tab to the desired |
| action on the action bar and press the enter key. Before the next menu |
| appears, a popup menu will ask you to enter a starting customer number.|
| Supply this number and press the enter key.                            |
|                                                                        |
| Action     Description                                                 |
|                                                                        |
| View       <View customers> or <view sales history>                    |
|                                                                        |
| Add        <Add customers> or <add sales history>                      |
|                                                                        |
| Change     <Change customer records>                                   |
|                                                                        |
| Delete     <Delete customer records>                                   |
+------------------------------------------------------------------------+
HYHELP------------------------------------------------------------------------
F1=help browse-< browse-> Back |<—/—>|=prev/next-hotspot Enter=select
Ctrl+Home=home-topic Search Index Contents History bookMark Files Output  Escape
```

Figure 11.14 Appearance of home menu

```
+----------------------------View Customer Records----------------------------+
| This screen lets you page through all of the customer numbers and names in  |
| the file. You can restart the browse at another position in the file by     |
| entering a new customer number in the data entry field.                     |
|                                                                             |
| Function  Description                                                       |
|                                                                             |
| PF3       Exit to main menu.                                                |
|                                                                             |
| PF7       Page backward in the customer master.                             |
|                                                                             |
| PF8       Page forward in the customer master.                              |
|                                                                             |
| PF10      Move cursor to action bar.                                        |
|                                                                             |
| PF12      Cancel current action.                                            |
|                                                                             |
|                                                                             |
|                                                                             |
|                                                                             |
+-----------------------------------------------------------------------------+
HYHELP---------------------------------------------------------------------------
F1=help browse-< browse-> Back |<---/--->|=prev/next-hotspot Enter=select
Ctrl+Home=home-topic Search Index Contents History bookMark Files Output   Escape
```

Figure 11.15 Appearance of topic screen

```
+----------------------------View Customer Records----------------------------+
| This screen lets you page through all of the customer numbers and names in  |
| the file. You can restart the browse at another position in the file by     |
| entering a new custom+------------Contents------------+                     |
|                       |Help for Customer Master (CUST) |                     |
| Function  Description|View Customer Records           |                     |
|                       |Add Customer Records            |                     |
| PF3       Exit to mai|Change Customer Records          |                     |
|                       |Delete Customer Records         |                     |
| PF7       Page backwa|View Sales History              |                     |
|                       |Add Sales History               |                     |
| PF8       Page forwar|                                |                     |
|                       |                                |                     |
| PF10      Move cursor|                                |                     |
|                       |                                |                     |
| PF12      Cancel curr|                                |                     |
|                       +--------------------------------+                     |
|                                                                             |
|                                                                             |
|                                                                             |
+-----------------------------------------------------------------------------+
Contents-----------------------------------------------------------------------
F1=help                                                            Escape
```

Figure 11.16 Appearance of table of contents

11.8 How to Find Answers in the Micro Focus Manuals

No, it isn't *that* hard to find what you are looking for in the Micro Focus Workbench manuals. But you do get a large box of manuals with the Workbench. The sheer volume of reference information can seem intimidating until you understand how the manuals are laid out.

Micro Focus provides separate reference manuals for each part of the Workbench product; in other words, for the COBOL/2 Compiler, the Toolset, and the Workbench. Add-on products have their own manuals. Each of the three parts of the Workbench product has at least one *Reference* or *Operating Guide*, telling you how to use that product's features. For example, the COBOL/2 Compiler comes with several manuals. The *Language Reference* describes COBOL language syntax and indicates which COBOL dialects support each language feature. The *Operating Guide* describes how to set up and run the COBOL/2 Compiler, the Checker, the Animator, and other features that accompany this product. A *Pocket Guide* provides a pocket-sized quick reference to language syntax and to Checker/Compiler directives.

You need to know which book contains the Workbench function you are interested in. How do you do that? One way is to use the *Master Index*, which we will describe below. Another way is to look at the cover of each reference manual. The front cover contains a list of the major functions that make up that product. For example, if you want to read about the COBOL Editor, you will find "COBOL Editor" on the cover of the *Toolset Reference.*

```
+————————————Message 0326     (^ Syntax Messages)————————————+
|  <Key>                                  <Up> <Contents> <Index> <Back>  |
| ——————————————————————————————————————————————————————————————————— |
|                                                                        |
|   Message:      0326                                                   |
|                                                                        |
|   Text:         Literal cannot be receiving field                      |
|                                                                        |
|   Explanation:  You have specified a literal value as the receiving    |
|                 field in an operation involving an implicit or         |
|                 explicit move.  A receiving field must be a data item. |
|                                                                        |
|                                                                        |
|   Resolution:   Change the literal value to a reference to a data item |
|                 and resubmit your source code to your COBOL system.    |
|                                                                        |
|                                                                        |
|                                                                        |
|                                                                        |
|                                                                        |
+— F2=hide menu ———————————————————————————————————————————————————————+
HYHELP—————————————————————————————————————————————————————————————————
F1=help browse—< browse—> Back |<—/—>|=prev/next—hotspot Enter=select
Ctrl+Home=home—topic Search Index Contents History bookMark Files Output   Escape
```

Figure 11.17 Error message 0326 in HYHELP

11.8.1 Error Messages: Using the Error Manual

Nobody likes to think that he or she will get error messages, but it happens to all of us. The *Error Messages* reference manual contains sections for three types of errors: syntax checker errors, code generator errors, and runtime system errors. To use this manual, go to the section that corresponds to the source of the error message and look up the error number in that section.

Error messages in HYHELP. You can also look up error messages on-line with hypertext help. To do this, place the cursor at the beginning of the error number and bring up the HYHELP system by pressing **Alt+1.** You can also select **COBOL Messages** on the HYHELP main menu. This will get you to a submenu that lets you choose the class of error messages that you want to see, for example, syntax errors. Choose the error number from the next menu after that. Figure 11.17 shows an example of the results.

11.8.2 The Master Index Volume

The *Workbench Master Index* provides an alphabetical index to the entire set of Workbench manuals. While each volume concludes with its own index, that index contains page references to that manual alone. The *Master Index* lets you find all references to a particular topic. The *Error Messages* manual and the *Pocket Guide* are not included in the Master Index.

At the beginning of the *Master Index,* you will find a list of the codes used in the index. Each volume has its own code. For example, **WB GS** refers to the *Getting Started with Workbench* volume. These codes tells you which volume contains each index reference.

The index contains three columns. The first column contains the alphabetical index topic itself. The second column contains the code identifying the volume. The third column contains the chapter and page number. Each chapter is numbered separately. Tabs at the edge of each page help you find the beginning of each chapter. For instance, suppose you look up the topic **.MNU file.** In the index reference, the second column contains **WB Reference,** which means the *Workbench Reference* manual. The third column contains **22-5, 22-7.** Therefore, you will find information about the .MNU file on the fifth and seventh pages of Chapter 22 in the *Workbench Reference* manual.

11.9 Exercises

1. Using facilities on the Workbench configuration menu, describe the steps needed to change the error message attributes to nonblinking high-intensity white text on a red background. Test this answer on the Workbench.

2. Prepare a banner screen for your organization. Show the name and version of the Workbench inside a ruled box, followed by "Licensed to: *your organization*" and the telephone number of appropriate support personnel (this may be you).

3. Suppose your site is strictly an IMS DB/DC shop and does not use CICSVS86. Describe how to customize the MDE main menu to remove the function key option pertaining to CICS. Back up your menu file and test your answer.

4. Add a browse chain for the topics shown in the HYHELP file in Figure 11.13.

5. Use the Micro Focus HYHELP screens to look up syntax error code 0541. What does the message say?

Overview of Add-On Options

Simulating the complete mainframe environment. Thus far, we have shown how to use the Micro Focus Workbench to develop mainframe batch COBOL programs that use sequential, indexed, and relative files. You may be wondering, "What about CICS, IMS, IDMS, or SQL? What about COBOL programs that call mainframe assembler subroutines?" With the help of add-on options, you can use the Micro Focus Workbench to create and maintain these kinds of applications. **The availability of these add-on products makes the Workbench into a powerful, fully customizable mainframe application development environment.**

Other reasons to use add-on products are ease of learning, familiarity, and personal taste. Some applications developers have many years of mainframe experience using MVS JCL, CLISTs, and TSO/ISPF, or VM/CMS and XEDIT, but they have comparatively little PC experience. These users may prefer an interface to the Workbench that emulates the screens and commands they use on the mainframe. It takes them much less time to get up to speed with the Workbench if they have a front-end interface that uses the ISPF commands they already know. On the other hand, experienced PC "power users" are likely to prefer the standard Workbench menus, including the new graphical user interface (GUI) functions.

Purpose of this chapter. Many add-on products are available for use with the Workbench. This chapter will concentrate on those add-on products that have to do with mainframe compatibility. It will present an overview of the purpose and capabilities of each add-on product, and will tell you where to obtain more information. For some products, this chapter will show sample screen displays. In each instance, we assume that you have some familiarity with the mainframe counterpart of that add-on product. We will show you how to support that part of the mainframe environment on the PC workstation.

12.1 Mainframe Assembler Support

12.1.1 Micro Focus 370 Assembler with ANIMATOR/370

Overview. Since the PC workstation has a different instruction set from the IBM mainframe, native PC assembler language is not at all like its mainframe counterpart. **Micro Focus 370 Assembler (MF/370)** emulates mainframe assembler language on the PC so that you can work with assembler language

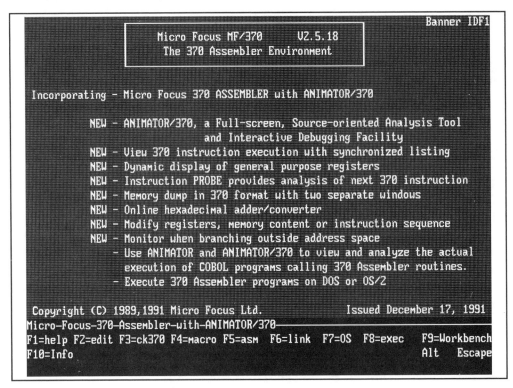

Figure 12.1 MF/370 Main Menu

main programs or CALLed subroutines. **ANIMATOR/370** is the animated debugging tool that works with the MF/370 product.

Attendees at the 1991 Micro Focus Users Conference in Orlando, Florida offered suggestions concerning the features an animated assembler product should have. These included displays of storage contents, register contents, and condition code settings. Users also requested that the debugger be able to step through a BAL program in much the same way the Animator steps through a COBOL program. ANIMATOR/370 came out just a few months later, incorporating these suggested features.

Product features. The MF/370 environment closely resembles the look and feel of the function key menus of the COBOL Workbench. Figure 12.1 shows the opening menu of the MF/370 product. Figure 12.2 shows the Alt-key options that go with the MF/370 main menu.

```
Micro Focus 370 Assembler with ANIMATOR/370
F1=info370      F3=ckalt        F5=linklib              F8=playback
```

Figure 12.2 MF/370 ALT-key menu

- **F1=info370** on the Alt-key menu provides a tutorial that introduces you to the system and explains the different types of input and output files used.
- **F2=edit** on the MF/370 main menu brings up a source code editor that works much the same way as the Workbench COBOL Editor.

```
K:\XMF370\TESTI370                          PAGE    1
MF/370 Assembler Compiler Options =LACED
  LOC          ADR1   ADR2 LINE LABEL    OP       OPERANDS
000000                       1 TESTI370 CSECT
000000                       2 ****************************************************************
000000                       3 * This program will execute the non-floating-point
000000                       4 * 370 instructions supported by MF/370.
000000                       5 * Standard 370 Assembler coding guidelines are
000000                       6 * used.
000000                       7 *     Position  1 - Optional Label
000000                       8 *     Position 10 - Mnemonic Opcode or Directive
000000                       9 *     Position 16 - Operands
000000                      10 *     Position 30 - Optional Comment
000000                      11 * The labels in this example are the mnemonic
000000                      12 * opcode preceded by an "I@". For example, a CLC
000000                      13 * instruction would have a label of I@CLC.
000000                      14 ****************************************************************
000000 05C0                 15          BALR     12,0        * PREPARE A BASE REGISTER
000002                      16          USING    *,12        * ESTABLISH BASE REGISTER
000002 5A40C376       0378  17 I@A      A        R4,HEX4     * ADD 4 TO REG-4
000006 4A40C374       0376  18 I@AH     AH       R4,HEX2+2   * ADD HEX-2 TO REG-3
00000A 5E40C372       0374  19 I@AL     AL       R4,HEX2     * ADD LOGICAL, REGISTER & STORAGE
00000E 1E34                 20 I@ALR    ALR      R3,R4       * ADD LOGICAL, REGISTER & REGISTER
000010 FA77C292C29A  0294 029C 21 I@AP  AP       D1,D2       * ADD DECIMAL
000016 1A34                 22 I@AR     AR       R3,R4       * ADD R4 TO R3, REGISTER & REGISTER
000018 45A0C01A       001C  23 I@BAL    BAL      R10,*+4     * LOAD R10 WITH LINK ADDR AND BRANCH
00001C 05A0                 24 I@BALR   BALR     R10,R0      * LOAD R10 WITH LINK ADDR
00001E 47F0C020       0022  25 I@BC     B        *+4         * BRANCH TO SELF PLUS FOUR
000022                      26 ****************************************************************
000022        00000022      27 I@BCR    EQU      *           +
000022 4180C02A       002C  28          LA       R8,BCREND   + LOAD BRANCH-TO ADDRESS INTO REG-8
000026 07F8                 29          BR       R8          + BRANCH TO ADDRESS SPECIFIED IN REG-8
000028 4700C026       0028  30          NOP      *           + THIS INSTRUCTION SHOULD NEVER EXECUTE
00002C        0000002C      31 BCREND   EQU      *           + LABEL FOR BCR-INSTRUCTION
00002C                      32 ****************************************************************
00002C        0000002C      33 I@BCT    EQU      *           +
00002C 41300003       0003  34          LA       R3,3        + LOAD 3 INTO REG-3 FOR DECREMENTING
000030        00000030      35 BCTLOOP  EQU      *           +
000030 4700C02E       0030  36          NOP      *           + NO-OPERATION TO SHOW BCT-LOOP
000034 4630C02E       0030  37          BCT      R3,BCTLOOP  +
000038                      38 ****************************************************************
000038        00000038      39 I@BCTR   EQU      *           +
000038 41300003       0003  40          LA       R3,3        + LOAD 3 INTO REG-3 FOR DECREMENTING
00003C 4140C03E       0040  41          LA       R4,BCTRLOOP + LOAD BRANCH-TO ADDRESS INTO REG4
000040        00000040      42 BCTRLOOP EQU      *           +
000040 4700C044       0046  43          NOP      BCTRNEXT    + NO-OPERATION TO SHOW BCTR-LOOP
000044 0634                 44          BCTR     R3,R4       + LOOP UNTIL REG-3 GOES TO ZERO
000046        00000046      45 BCTRNEXT EQU      *           +
000046 41300003       0003  46          LA       R3,3        + THE BCTR MAY BE USED TO DECREMENT REG
00004A 0630                 47          BCTR     R3,R0       + IF OP-2 IS 0 THEN DECR OP- 1,NO BRANCH
00004C                      48 ****************************************************************
00004C        0000004C      49 I@BXH    EQU      *           + BRANCH ON INDEX HIGH
00004C 41A0C06E       0070  50          LA       R10,BXHEND  + ESTABLISH BRANCH ADDRESS
000050 5840C062       0064  51          L        R4,BXHIDX   + ESTABLISH INDEX
```

Figure 12.3 Assembler output listing

- **F3=ck370** invokes three processing steps: the macro expansion, the assembly, and the linker. This process generates both intermediate code to run on the PC, and a printable assembly listing that looks like a mainframe assembler listing.

Part of an assembler listing is shown in Figure 12.3. Note that it contains the same machine instructions that you would get if you assembled that source code on a mainframe, showing machine addresses in base/displacement form. It also shows instruction offsets from the beginning of the program, just like a mainframe assembler.

Once you have checked your program successfully, you can animate it with ANIMATOR/370, available through the **F8=exec** option. The animator screen, shown in Figure 12.4, contains four panels:

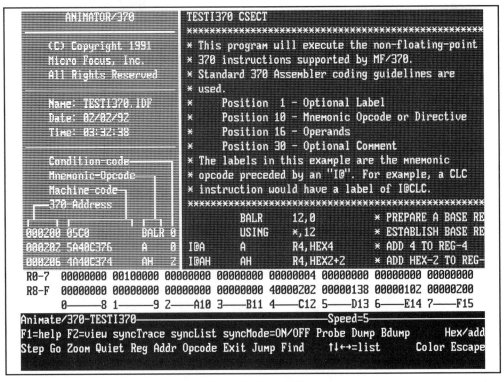

Figure 12.4 Animate/370 screen

- The **function key menu** offers many options, including stepping through the program one assembler statement at a time, setting breakpoints, and jumping to a different address.
- The **register panel** shows the contents of the sixteen general registers as the program is being executed. If you have a math coprocessor, you can also use floating-point instructions and display the floating-point registers.
- The **list panel** shows the MF/370 source code as it appears in your file, including the comment lines.
- The **trace panel** shows the 370 virtual machine address, the 370 instruction in machine code format, the mnemonic opcode, and the condition code setting. Line 18, the last line in the panel, is the line currently being executed.

Pressing **H** for **Hex/adder** on the animator menu opens up a hex converter/adder window.

Pressing **P** for **Probe** on the animator menu brings up the Probe function. This gives you a closeup view of the current instruction. The first panel, shown in Figure 12.5, explains how the instruction operates, displays the addresses of each operand, and shows how various results will affect the condition code setting. For instructions that reference main storage, pressing **P** a second time will bring up a memory dump panel for each storage operand, as shown in Figure 12.6. You can modify the contents of memory through these panels, much as you can in the COBOL/2 Animator.

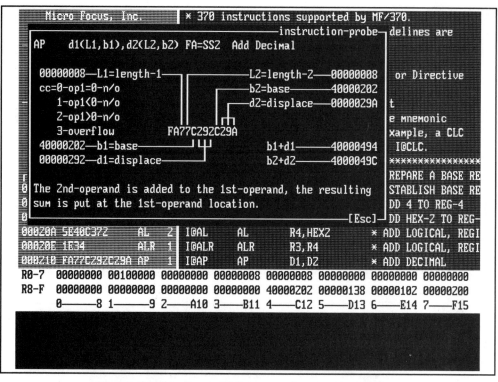

Figure 12.5 Animate/370 Instruction Probe screen 1

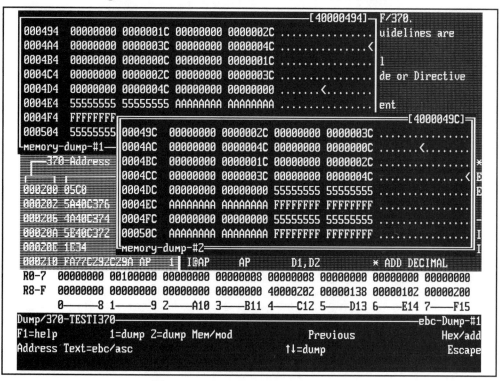

Figure 12.6 Animate/370 Instruction Probe screen 2

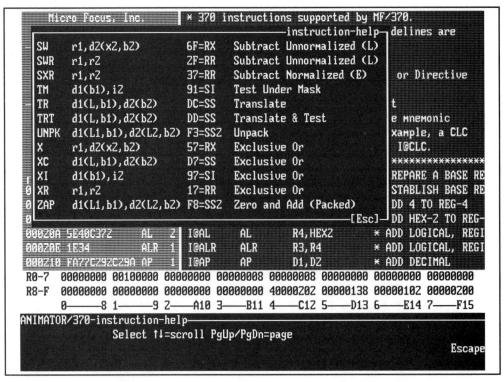

Figure 12.7 Animate/370 Instruction Help menu

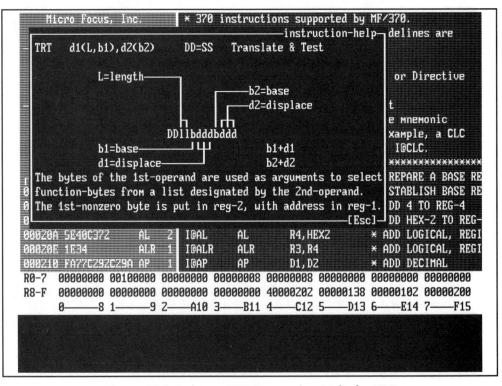

Figure 12.8 Animate/370 Instruction Help for TRT

If you don't have occasion to work with mainframe assembler very often, you may find that you have forgotten some of the subtleties of seldom-used instructions. Pressing **F10=Info** on the MF/370 main menu brings up the instruction help function. The first panel shows a summary for each instruction, including the hex opcode. This is shown in Figure 12.7. If you want a closer look at one instruction, pressing **S** for **Select** opens a dialog box that lets you specify the hex opcode of the instruction you want to see. Figure 12.8 shows a detailed explanation of the TRT instruction.

For more information.
Micro Focus, Inc.
2465 East Bayshore Rd., Suite 400
Palo Alto CA 94303
Voice: (415) 856–4161, Fax: (415) 856–6134

12.2 MVS JCL Support

12.2.1 Proximity Software ProxMvs

Overview. Proximity Software offers add-on options that let you run mainframe batch job streams on the PC workstation, under MS-DOS or OS/2. **ProxMvs** is an emulator for MVS JCL. Through an ISPF-like user interface, ProxMvs lets you create and test batch job streams using mainframe JCL on the PC. Figure 12.9 shows the ProxMvs Primary Selection Menu.

Included within ProxMvs are emulations of various mainframe facilities needed for batch job execution. As shown in Figure 12.10, ProxMvs uses **program aliases** to equate the names of ProxMvs utilities with the program names that you would use in mainframe JCL. Since MF/370 uses the Micro Focus Run-Time System, you can reconfigure function key usage through the Micro Focus menu system.

- The **Execution Manager** executes MVS jobstreams and PROCs, with support for PARMs, jobstream SYSIN records, and dataset allocations. It handles JOBLIB and STEPLIB statements for executable program libraries. If desired, the Execution Manager will scan jobstreams for correct MVS JCL syntax, similarly to mainframe TYPRUN=SCAN.

- The **Dataset Manager** supports dataset catalogs that let you define and manage mainframe file types on the PC. These file types include sequential, partitioned, KSDS VSAM, generation data groups, temporary datasets, and instream SYSIN records. You can list catalogs or edit, browse, copy, rename, delete, catalog, or uncatalog datasets. The browse (read-only) function is implemented within ProxMvs itself, while the edit function uses the Micro Focus COBOL Editor. When you get into the Editor, the margins by default will be set for COBOL, but we described how you can change that in previous chapters. Figure 12.11 shows the ProxMvs menu for using dataset functions interactively. Figure 12.12 shows the ProxMvs Dataset Information screen.

- The **SYSOUT Manager** emulates mainframe JES. It assigns reports to SYSOUT classes, so that each program can produce one or more report files.

It also manages the MVS system log dataset. Figure 12.13 shows a display of the ProxMvs output log, containing a JCL error.

- **PROXSORT** is the IBM DFSORT emulator. It lets you sort data files as you would on the mainframe, without having to code COBOL internal sort programs. It will let you test COBOL sort exit programs under the Micro Focus Animator. Figure 12.14 shows output from a job stream that contains a sort step followed by a program that prints out the sorted records.

- **PROXAMS** emulates VSAM Access Method Services (IDCAMS) command processing. This lets you embed IDCAMS steps in your job streams in the PC. Figure 12.15 shows the ProxMvs menu that lets you use IDCAMS functions interactively. Figure 12.16 shows simulated IDCAMS output from a ProxMvs job stream.

- **PROXIMS** emulates DFSRRC00, the mainframe IMS dispatcher program. It accepts the standard mainframe PARM for program type, program name, and PSB, and passes it to the Micro Focus IMS Option.

- **PROXDB2** emulates IKJEFT01, the mainframe DB2 dispatcher program. It uses the RUN PROGRAM command to connect to any SQL database engine supported by the Workbench.

- **PROXGENR** emulates IEBGENER, the mainframe dataset copy and conversion utility.

- **PROXBR14** emulates IEFBR14, the mainframe dummy program that is used to invoke the MVS JCL file management functions.

```
 ─────────────────── PROXMVS PRIMARY SELECTION MENU ───────────────────

OPTION ===> _____


        0  - PROXMVS PARAMETERS         C  - COMPILE
        1  - BROWSE DATASETS OR MEMBERS A  - ACCESS METHOD SERVICES
        2  - EDIT DATASETS OR MEMBERS   R  - RUN APPLICATION
        3  - DATASET UTILITIES          I  - IMS
        4  - EXECUTE JOBSTREAMS
        5  - SYSOUT UTILITIES
        6  - O/S COMMANDS

        ?  - PROGRAM INFORMATION
        X  - EXIT

SYSPARM: J:\CATALOG\SYSPARM.DAT
CATALOG: J:\CATALOG\CATALOG.DAT

 ──────────────────────────────────────────────────────────:000:─
```

Figure 12.9 ProxMvs Primary Selection Menu

```
┌─────────────────────────────────────────────────────────────────────────────┐
│ ─────────────────────── PROXMVS PROGRAM ALIASES ───────────────────           │
│                                                                               │
│     ALIAS NAME  PGM NAME      ALIAS NAME  PGM NAME                             │
│                                                                               │
│   1:  SORT____  PROXSORT   17:                       ASSIGN ALIAS NAMES        │
│   2:  IEFBR14   PROXBR14   18:                       TO PROGRAM FILES          │
│   3:  IEBGENER  PROXGENR   19:                                                 │
│   4:  IDCAMS    PROXAMS    20:                       FOR EXAMPLE:              │
│   5:  DFSRRC00  PROXIMS    21:                                                 │
│   6:  IKJEFT01  PROXDB2    22:                       ALIAS      PGM NAME        │
│   7:                       23:                       ─────────  ─────────      │
│   8:                       24:                       SORT     = PROXSORT        │
│   9:                       25:                       IEFBR14  = PROXBR14        │
│  10:                       26:                       IEBGENER = PROXGENR        │
│  11:                       27:                                                 │
│  12:                       28:                                                 │
│  13:                       29:                                                 │
│  14:                       30:                                                 │
│  15:                       31:                                                 │
│  16:                       32:                                                 │
│                                                                               │
│ ─────────────────────────────────────────────────────────────────:017:─      │
└─────────────────────────────────────────────────────────────────────────────┘
```

Figure 12.10 ProxMvs Program Aliases screen

```
┌─────────────────────────────────────────────────────────────────────────────┐
│ ──────────────────────── PROXMVS DATASET FUNCTIONS ────────────────────        │
│                                                                               │
│ OPTION ===> _____                                                          │
│                                                                               │
│   L  - LIST DATASET NAMES    X - COPY DATASET      C - CATALOG DATASET          │
│   I  - DATASET INFORMATION   D - DELETE DATASET    U - UNCATALOG DATASET        │
│   P  - PRINT DATASET NAMES   R - RENAME DATASET    J - SUBMIT JOB               │
│   B  - BROWSE DATASET        A - ALLOCATE DATASET  Z - SUBMIT JOB (SCAN)        │
│   E  - EDIT DATASET                                ? - SHOW FILE NAME           │
│                                                                               │
│ DATASET NAME ===>                                                             │
│    NEW NAME ===>                                                              │
│                                                                               │
│ ─────────────────────────────────────────────────────────────────:300:─      │
└─────────────────────────────────────────────────────────────────────────────┘
```

Figure 12.11 ProxMvs Dataset Functions menu

```
————————————————— PROXMVS DATASET INFORMATION —————————————————

DATASET NAME: TEST.SAMPLE.TEXT1
    FILE SPEC: J:\CATALOG\TEST\SAMPLE\TEXT1.DAT

        DSORG: SEQUENTIAL              CREATED DATE: 91/01/19
        RECFM: LSEQ                            TIME: 19:12:51
        LRECL:    80                            JOB: PROXMVS
        TRTCH: A                       USED DATE: 92/02/07
                                              TIME: 00:51:31
                                               JOB: PROXMVS

                                       SIZE:        528 BYTES

————————————————————————————————————————————————————————————:312A:—
                                                              READ
```

Figure 12.12 ProxMvs Dataset Information screen

```
       * * * * * * * * *   P R O X M V S   J O B   L O G   * * * * * * * * * *
       JOB: SAMPLE2   JOBN: 0003  DATE: 02/07/92  TIME: 00:59:54
       **** JOB FAILED - JCL ERROR
     1 //SAMPLE2  JOB 'PROXIMITY',CLASS=A,MSGCLASS=A
     2 ***————————————————————————————————————————————————————————
     3 ***     DEMONSTRATION JCL - SAMPLE2
     4 ***
     5 ***     THIS JOBSTREAM DEMONSTRATES THE FOLLOWING FEATURES:
     6 ***
     7 ***     - DETECTION OF A JCL ERROR
     8 ***     - SYSUDUMP IS IGNORED
     9 ***
    10 ***————————————————————————————————————————————————————————
    11 //STEP1     EXEC PGM=SAMPLE2
    12 //SYSUT1    DD DSN=TEST.SAMPLE.TEXT2DATA,DISP=(NEW,CATLG)
**** JCL ERROR MVS444F: INVALID DATASET NAME
    13 //SYSUT2    DD DSN=TEST.SAMPLE.TEXT2,DISP=(NEW,CATLG)
    14 //SYSUDUMP DD SYSOUT=*
    15 //

————————————————————————————————————————————————:100A:————————————
DATASET: SPOOL.SAMPLE2.00030000.000              COLS:     1 TO    80
COMMAND:                                 HELP: ? LINE:      1 TO    20
```

Figure 12.13 ProxMvs SYSOUT Manager screen showing JCL error

```
      * * * * * * * * * *    P R O X M V S   J O B   L O G   * * * * * * * * * * *
      JOB: SAMPLE10  JOBN: 0007  DATE: 02/07/92  TIME: 01:24:59
  1  //SAMPLE10 JOB 'PROXIMITY',CLASS=A,MSGCLASS=A
  2  ***──────────────────────────────────────────────────────────
  3  ***      DEMONSTRATION JCL - SAMPLE10
  4  ***
  5  ***      THIS JOBSTREAM DEMONSTRATES THE FOLLOWING FEATURES:
  6  ***
  7  ***      - EXECUTION OF A BATCH SORT (ALIAS=PROXSORT)
  8  ***         - SYSIN CONTROL STATEMENTS (RECFM=LSEQ,LRECL=80,EBCDIC)
  9  ***         - SORTIN FILE            (RECFM=LSEQ,LRECL=80,ASCII)
 10  ***         - SORTOUT FILE (TEMPORARY FILE PASSED TO SAMPLE8 DISPLAY
 11  ***           PROGRAM               (RECFM=F,LRECL=80,ASCII)
 12  ***      - DISPLAY UPON CONSOLE SCREEN MANAGEMENT
 13  ***
 14  ***──────────────────────────────────────────────────────────
 15  //SORTSTEP EXEC PGM=SORT
 16  //SORTIN   DD DSN=TEST.SAMPLE.TEXT10,DISP=OLD
 17  //SORTOUT  DD DSN=&&SORTED,DISP=(NEW,PASS),
 18  //            DCB=(RECFM=F,LRECL=80)
 19  //SYSOUT   DD SYSOUT=*
 20  //SYSIN    DD DSN=TEST.SORT.PARMS(SAMPLE10),DISP=SHR
 21  //SHOWIT   EXEC PGM=SAMPLE8,COND=(0,NE,SORTSTEP)
 22  //SYSIN    DD DSN=&&SORTED,DISP=(OLD,DELETE)
 23  //

**** EXECUTION SUMMARY ****
     01:25:00 SORTSTEP        - STEP STARTED
     TEST.SAMPLE.TEXT10                                    KEPT
     J:\CATALOG\TEST\SAMPLE\TEXT10.DAT
     &&SORTED                                              PASSED
     J:\CATALOG\TEMP\SORTED.007
     J:\CATALOG\SPOOL\00070100.003                         SYSOUT
     TEST.SORT.PARMS(SAMPLE10)                             KEPT
     J:\CATALOG\TEST\SORT\PARMS\SAMPLE10
     01:25:06 SORTSTEP        - STEP WAS EXECUTED   RC(0000)
     01:25:06 SHOWIT          - STEP STARTED
*MSG 00001 UNSORTED DATA RECORD 1
*MSG 00002 UNSORTED DATA RECORD 2
*MSG 00043 UNSORTED DATA RECORD 43
*MSG 00089 UNSORTED DATA RECORD 89
*MSG 00090 UNSORTED DATA RECORD 90
*MSG 00123 UNSORTED DATA RECORD 123
*MSG 00459 UNSORTED DATA RECORD 459
*MSG 03322 UNSORTED DATA RECORD 3322
*MSG 07654 UNSORTED DATA RECORD 7654
     &&SORTED                                              PASSED
     J:\CATALOG\TEMP\SORTED.007
     01:25:09 SHOWIT          - STEP WAS EXECUTED   RC(0000)
     01:25:09 SAMPLE10 (0007) - JOB ENDED
```

Figure 12.14 ProxMvs sort job output

```
────────────────────── PROXAMS ACCESS METHOD SERVICES ──────────────────

OPTION ===> _____

      1  - DEFINE CLUSTER    Define a new cluster
      2  - DEFINE AIX        Define an alternate index
      3  - DELETE            Delete an existing dataset
      4  - LISTCAT           List catalog entries
      5  - PRINT             Print a dataset
      6  - REPRO             Copy datasets
      7  - VERIFY            Verify VSAM file integrity

      X  - EXIT

────────────────────────────────────────────────────────────────:A00:─
```

Figure 12.15 ProxMvs Access Method Services menu

String testing. It's easy to see the practical benefits of using ProxMvs. For maintaining existing batch applications, you can download your mainframe JCL and translate it to ASCII with the Workbench file transfer utility, and use this JCL to test your programs on the PC. Using mainframe JCL makes it practical to set up string tests on the PC workstation. These string tests provide closer emulation of the way that batch portions of your system will work on the mainframe. In any mainframe installation, a large number of application programming errors are caused by faulty JCL. Using ProxMvs for new applications lets you debug your JCL on the PC before you port the application back to the mainframe.

For more information.
Proximity Software Inc.
408 Headquarters Drive, Suite 3C
Millersville, MD 21108
(410) 987–3400

```
PROXAMS Access Method Services Version 1.1
Copyright (c) 1991 Proximity Software, Inc.


                 DELETE TEST.SAMPLE.VSAM12
AMS115E(08) - ENTRYNAME [TEST.SAMPLE.VSAM12] IS NOT CATALOGED

                 SET    MAXCC=0
AMS140I(00) - MAX CONDITION CODE SET TO [000000000]

                 DEFINE CLUSTER                          -
                        (NAME(TEST.SAMPLE.VSAM12)        -
                        KEYS(20 0)                       -
                        RECSZ(100 100))
AMS113I(00) - ENTRYNAME [TEST.SAMPLE.VSAM12] DEFINED

                 DEFINE AIX                              -
                        (NAME(TEST.SAMPLE.VSAM12.INDEX)  -
                        RELATE(TEST.SAMPLE.VSAM12)       -
                        KEYS(10 20)                      -
                        NONUNIQUEKEY)
AMS127I(00) - ALTERNATE INDEX DEFINED
AMS128I(00) - [00000000] RECORDS INDEXED

                 REPRO  INFILE(FLATFILE)                 -
                        OUTDATASET(TEST.SAMPLE.VSAM12) REPLACE
AMS134I(00) - [00000003] RECORDS COPIED

                 PRINT  INDATASET(TEST.SAMPLE.VSAM12)
LISTING OF DATASET - TEST.SAMPLE.VSAM12
KEY OF RECORD - 3131313131313131313131313131313131313131
0000    31313131 31313131 31313131 31313131  31313131 41414141 41414141 41414141 *1111111111111111111AAAAAAAAAAA*
0020    41414141 41414141 41414141 41414141  41414141 41414141 41414141 41414141 *AAAAAAAAAAAAAAAAAAAAAAAAAAAAAAAA*
0040    41414141 41414141 41414141 41414141  41414141 41414141 41414141 41414141 *AAAAAAAAAAAAAAAAAAAAAAAAAAAAAAAA*
0060    41414141                                                                  *AAAA                            *

KEY OF RECORD - 3232323232323232323232323232323232323232
0000    32323232 32323232 32323232 32323232  32323232 42424242 42424242 42424242 *2222222222222222222BBBBBBBBBBB*
0020    42424242 42424242 42424242 42424242  42424242 42424242 42424242 42424242 *BBBBBBBBBBBBBBBBBBBBBBBBBBBBBBBB*
0040    42424242 42424242 42424242 42424242  42424242 42424242 42424242 42424242 *BBBBBBBBBBBBBBBBBBBBBBBBBBBBBBBB*
0060    42424242                                                                  *BBBB                            *

KEY OF RECORD - 3333333333333333333333333333333333333333
0000    33333333 33333333 33333333 33333333  33333333 43434343 43434343 43434343 *3333333333333333333CCCCCCCCCCC*
0020    43434343 43434343 43434343 43434343  43434343 43434343 43434343 43434343 *CCCCCCCCCCCCCCCCCCCCCCCCCCCCCCCC*
0040    43434343 43434343 43434343 43434343  43434343 43434343 43434343 43434343 *CCCCCCCCCCCCCCCCCCCCCCCCCCCCCCCC*
0060    43434343                                                                  *CCCC                            *

AMS135I(00) - [00000003] RECORDS PRINTED

                 LISTC  LEVEL(TEST.SAMPLE)
TEST.SAMPLE.GDG <GDG>
TEST.SAMPLE.GDG.G0001V00
TEST.SAMPLE.GDG.G0002V00
TEST.SAMPLE.TEXT1
TEST.SAMPLE.TEXT10
TEST.SAMPLE.TEXT12
TEST.SAMPLE.TEXT4
TEST.SAMPLE.TEXT5
TEST.SAMPLE.TEXT5A
TEST.SAMPLE.TEXT6
TEST.SAMPLE.TEXT6A
TEST.SAMPLE.VSAM12
AMS141I(00) - [00000012] DATASETS
```

Figure 12.16 ProxMvs IDCAMS output

12.3 CICS Support

Micro Focus offers two alternatives for CICS on the PC workstation. The appropriate choice for you will depend on how you intend to use CICS.

12.3.1 MCO2: Micro Focus CICS Option for OS/2 (CICS OS/2)

Overview. MCO2 is a PC implementation of CICS that can be used both for developing mainframe CICS applications and for running production CICS on a PC workstation. It facilitates micro-to-mainframe communications. MCO2 is provided as a Workbench add-on that runs under OS/2 Extended Edition using Presentation Manager, much as mainframe CICS would run under a mainframe operating system. The internal architecture of MCO2 bears no resemblance to any version of mainframe CICS, because the hardware platform and operating system is entirely different. However, the user interface and the application programming interface have been kept consistent with mainframe CICS as much as is practical.

MCO2 is more than a program development tool which allows a programmer to write and syntax-check command level programs to be run on a mainframe. In fact, it is a real version of CICS that can be used for both test and production purposes. Its capabilities are being enhanced with the passage of time. The prior version of CICS OS/2, version 1.10, was introduced early in 1988. It supported a level of functionality comparable with mainframe CICS 1.5. Version 1.20 supports a level of functionality comparable to CICS 3.x, with a few exceptions. In fact, MCO2 is so compatible with mainframe CICS that it does not even come with its own *Command Level Application Programmer's Reference Manual (APRM)*. You simply use the Command Level APRM for mainframe CICS/MVS or CICS/ESA. By using add-on products such as XDB, MCO2 lets you compile and run CICS COBOL programs that access various types of databases. VSAM support comes with the MCO2 product.

As of version 1.20, the most notable differences from mainframe CICS are the following:

- Basic mapping support is minimum-function, which means it handles neither BMS built-in paging nor unusual terminal devices such as bank teller machines. It will, however, handle the SEND TEXT command.
- It does not handle a two-phase commit under APPC. Usually, this would be needed only for complex recovery situations involving files updated on multiple machines.
- It does not support the JOURNAL command.
- It does not support macro-level calls. If you have old mainframe programs with macro-level calls, you can't download them to the workstation to maintain them. IBM has stopped supporting macro-level calls even in recent versions of mainframe CICS. IBM provides mainframe utilities to help you identify and convert macro-level CICS programs.
- It runs in ASCII rather than EBCDIC.
- It allows you to use certain COBOL statements in a CICS program that you would be restricted from using in a mainframe CICS COBOL program.

- It allows you to take advantage of the graphics capabilities of the OS/2 workstation. Using either COBOL or C, you can write a front-end graphical user interface program that uses OS/2 Presentation Manager calls in place of BMS commands. (This requires the Developer's Toolkit.) Alternatively, the CASE/PM product can be used to generate the PM interface. In either case, you can have a mouse-ready interface to your datasets that uses windows, buttons, scroll bars, and all of the other little goodies. But if you want to port the same CICS application back to the mainframe, you will have to provide an alternative front-end program using BMS commands. OS/2 programmers can also use the Dialog Manager from IBM or the Micro Focus Dialog System in conjunction with CICS. A new version of Dialog System II allows the application developer to paint PM graphical CUA-type applications that will also run under DOS in character graphics mode with no changes.

Figure 12.17 shows one of the Resource Definition Online (RDO) menus used for maintaining CICS system tables under MCO2. Figure 12.18 shows an example of a CICS application screen written with MCO2.

System requirements. MCO2 (CICS OS/2 1.20) needs OS/2 Extended Edition 1.1 or later, on an 80286 machine or better. CICS needs at least 1.3 megabytes of usable memory beyond that required by OS/2 EE; more for extra terminals. Plan on at least eight megabytes and preferably more, especially if you are using OS/2 EE Database Manager for SQL support. If you run OS/2 EE without enough memory, you'll get unpredictable, intermittent errors, possibly including trashed files or databases. While in theory you can install CICS in text mode under PC-DOS 3.3 or better, the PC-DOS environment doesn't provide CICS with enough memory to do anything of significance.

For more information. There is a detailed discussion of CICS in *CICS Command Level Programming, Second Edition,* by Alida Jatich, John Wiley & Sons, New York, 1991. This book addresses CICS programming and design, CUA compliance, CICS OS/2, SQL-based databases, and the OS/2 ES Database Manager. It shows you how to debug CICS programs using the Animator.

Licensing MCO2 for program development. As an add-on to the Workbench, MCO2 is available on diskette from Micro Focus, under a joint marketing agreement between IBM Corporation and Micro Focus, Inc. The MCO2 add-on is licensed for development purposes only. This is definitely the easiest way to go for the applications programmer. The Micro Focus SETUP script simplifies the install procedure to under 30 minutes and reduces the complexity of the install.

The MCO2 add-on lets you invoke CICS functions from the Workbench menu system. Also, the CICS translator (preprocessor) as well as the SQL preprocessor are integrated into the COBOL/2 compiler. This integration means that you will not have to debug the expanded code from the IBM CICS OS/2 translator. Instead, the Animator will debug your CICS COBOL program source (.CCP) file containing embedded EXEC CICS and SQL commands. The Animator will position on and execute the EXEC CICS...END-EXEC commands as if they were COBOL statements, simplifying the debugging task.

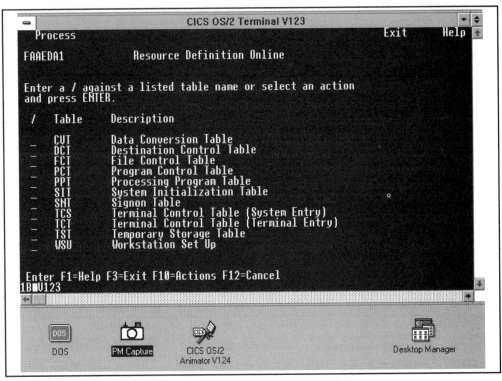

Figure 12.17 MCO2 Resource Definition Online menu

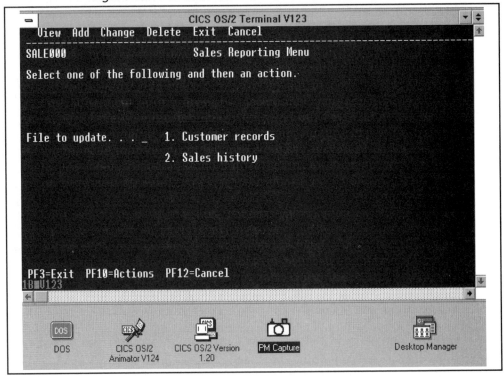

Figure 12.18 MCO2 CICS application program screen

For more information.
Micro Focus, Inc.
2465 East Bayshore Rd., Suite 400
Palo Alto CA 94303
Voice: (415) 856–4161, Fax: (415) 856–6134

Micro Focus Ltd.
26 West Street
Newbury, Berkshire, England RG13 1JT
Voice: 011–44–0635–32646, Fax: 011–44–0635–33966

CICS OS/2 for production use. You may also want to license copies of CICS OS/2 for production use instead of for program development. This allows the end user to run CICS OS/2 applications that were developed on some other workstation. If you want copies of CICS OS/2 to distribute to user PC workstations, without the Workbench, you will need to license the copies directly from IBM.

As of version 1.20, if you buy CICS OS/2 directly from IBM, it is not available on diskette for direct loading onto the microcomputer. (This may change in the future.) It has to be ordered in the form of a mainframe tape, loaded onto a mainframe under MVS or DOS/VSE, and downloaded to a microcomputer using the OS/2 ES Communications Manager or terminal emulator software, and appropriate software on the mainframe side. This process is described in the *CICS OS/2 System and Application Guide*. A separate license is required for each microcomputer workstation, but once you've purchased the license for a second workstation, you can copy the downloaded CICS from the first workstation to the second, and make diskette backups. According to IBM, you do NOT have to own or lease a mainframe to be allowed to purchase CICS OS/2 in that way. Once you have the tape and the license, you can take it to a service bureau to have it downloaded to your micro.

For more information.
IBM U.K. Laboratories Limited
Hursley Park
Winchester, Hampshire, England SO21 2JN
011–44–9628–44433

For location of IBM dealers, call (800) IBM–2468 in the United States, or (800) 465–1234 in Canada.

12.3.2 MCO: Micro Focus CICS Option (formerly ISI CICSVS86)

Overview. Micro Focus CICS Option (MCO) is intended purely as a mainframe applications development tool. While its capabilities are somewhat more limited than MCO2, it runs on both MS-DOS and OS/2 systems, and requires much less memory.

You can use add-on products such as XDB or the IMS Option along with MCO, so that you can develop CICS-DL/I or CICS-SQL COBOL programs.

For more information.
Micro Focus, Inc.
2465 East Bayshore Rd., Suite 400
Palo Alto CA 94303
Voice: (415) 856–4161, Fax: (415) 856–6134

Micro Focus Ltd.
26 West Street
Newbury, Berkshire, England RG13 1JT
Voice: 011–44–0635–32646, Fax: 011–44–0635–33966

12.4 SQL-based Database Management Systems

SQL-based database management systems bring the power and flexibility of relational databases to the mainframe and PC environments. If your mainframe shop uses DB2, SQL/DS, or another SQL-based DBMS, you will need to provide a compatible environment on your PC for program development. For your COBOL programs to access SQL-based databases, you'll need two utilities: an SQL command preprocessor for COBOL programs, and a runtime SQL engine. The SQL command preprocessor translates the EXEC SQL commands embedded in your COBOL source code. The runtime SQL engine provides database access services. Each of these add-on products will include these utilities. Some products include other utilities such as query languages, report generators, and connectivity tools.

12.4.1 XDB

Overview. XDB is the database management system that Micro Focus recommends for SQL-based databases. It is 100% compatible with IBM mainframe DB2. No reprogramming is needed when you port your XDB programs to the mainframe. XDB products run on MS-DOS, Microsoft Windows, OS/2, UNIX, and Novell Netware 386 systems. XDB supports both the EBCDIC and the ASCII collating sequences for text data. XDB supports COBOL programs that also use the Micro Focus CICS and IMS options. Micro Focus offers the **XDB Option for Micro Focus Workbench,** which includes the SQL database engine, the COBOL precompiler, and a subset of the XDB-Workbench utilities. These include Interactive SQL, DCLGEN, and Import/Export. Other XDB products that address the needs of the mainframe applications developer include the following:

- **XDB-Workbench for DB2** includes the COBOL precompiler, the SQL engine, a data dictionary, an interactive SQL query environment, a copy book generator (DCLGEN), and other migration and development utilities. Figure 12.19 shows an XDB COBOL program being animated under the Workbench. Note that the Animator display shows the actual SQL statements, not the preprocessor output. Figure 12.20 shows the results of a select statement performed in the interactive SQL (ISQL) environment. Figure 12.21 shows DCLGEN.

```
71* insert a data into specified table
72
73      EXEC SQL                                    ┌ZIP─┐
74        INSERT INTO EMPLOYEE                      │    │
75          (E_NO,LNAME,FNAME,STREET,CITY,ST,ZIP,   │    │
76           DEPT,PAYRATE,COM)                       └────┘
77        VALUES                                     ┌ST┐
78          (11,"McGruff","Jerry",                   │  │
79           "2345 Copeland Dr", "Byzan┌CITY──────  └──┘
80           "IL","60065","1050",45.5,.│
81      END-EXEC                                    │            │
82                                                  └────────────┘
83      MOVE SQLCODE TO DISP-CODE  ┌STREET──────────┐
84      DISPLAY 'insert ' DISP-COD │                │
85           ┌COM─┐                └────────────────┘
86*     No│00000594: 20 20 [   ]│s inserted  ┌FNAME─┐
87           └────────────────────┘            │      │
88      MO ┌PAYRATE─────────────────────────  └──────┘
89         │0000058C: 20 20 20 20 20 20 20 20 [            ]│
90*     Op └─────────────────────────────────────────────┘
91
Animate-TEST1──────────────────────Level=01-Speed=5-Ins-Caps-Num-Scroll
F1=help F2=view F3=align F4=exchange F5=where F6=look-up  F9/F10=word-</> Escape
Animate Step Wch Go Zoom nx-If Prfm Rst Brk Env Qury Find Locate Txt Do Alt Ctrl
```

Figure 12.19 Animating an XDB COBOL program

						Record 1 of 10	
e_no	lname	fname	street	city	st	zip	dept
1	Hurwood	Roger	1234 Stirrup La	Green Valley	MD	20441	2020
2	Kerin	Linda	802 Wilderness Dr	Wild Woods	VA	33256	2020
3	Gross	Mary	303 Stagecoach Rd	Green Valley	MD	20441	2020
4	Wilson	Arthur	211 Main Street	Yellow Fountain	VA	33210	2020
5	Chung	Yung	422 Maple St	Garden City	MD	20331	1050
6	Cox	John	555 Magnolia Dr	Garden City	MD	20331	2020
7	Crisp	Keith	Rt 2, Box 43	Yellow Fountain	VA	33210	1050
8	Hurwood	Susan	1234 Stirrup La	Green Valley	MD	20441	2020
9	Hopkins	James	345 Forest Dr	Yellow Fountain	VA	33210	1050
10	Haley	Olaf	334 Market St	Green Valley	MD	20441	1050

`== Bottom of Table ==`

```
F1             F2  print    F3            F4            F5            ?  help
F6             F7            F8            F9  goto      F10           Esc exit
```

Figure 12.20 XDB Interactive SQL screen: SELECT results

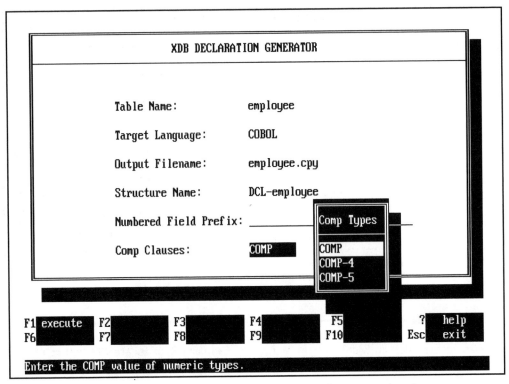

Figure 12.21 Using XDB DCLGEN to make a copy book

```
              XDB-SERVER  'XDBSERVE' USER ACTIVITY MENU
                                                        Page 1
USER           NODE         CURRENT              AUTO    LOGGED IN
NAME           ID           DATABASE   ILEVEL   COMMIT   SINCE
---------      -------      --------   ------   ------   ----------
SANDY          XDBCLIENT:5  TUTORIAL   CS       ON       12/13/1991  14:56:07
KAREN          XDBCLIENT:6  TUTORIAL   CS       OFF      12/13/1991  14:57:17
*DEBBIE        XDBCLIENT:7  TUTORIAL   CS       ON       12/13/1991  14:57:31
```

'*' in the first column denotes user is active
Press any key to return to XDB-SERVER Main Menu...

Figure 12.22 XDB-Server for OS/2 User Activity Menu

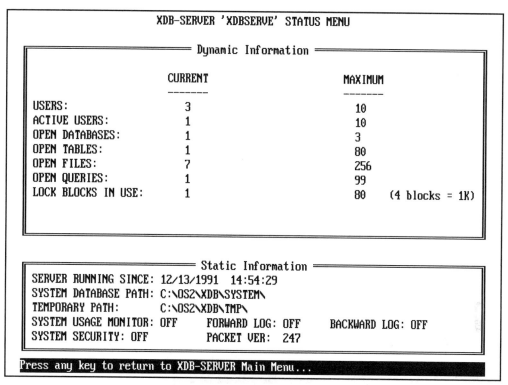

Figure 12.23 XDB Server for OS/2 Server Status Menu

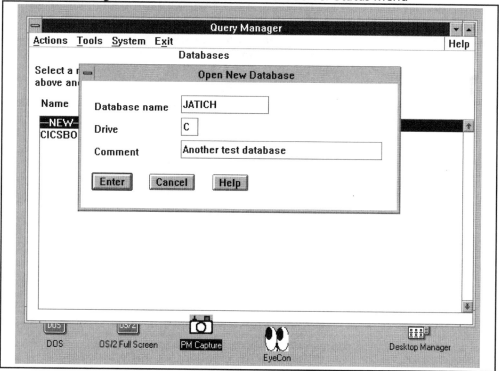

Figure 12.24 Creating a database with OS/2 ES Query Manager

- **XDB-Tools** is a prototyping toolkit that complements the XDB-Workbench. It contains a forms generator, a report generator, a menu generator, and various database utilities.
- **XDB-Server** expands the XDB-Workbench so that you can run it on a local area network. It includes password security, record locking, referential integrity, transaction processing, and backup/recovery facilities. Figures 12.22 and 12.23 show status menus for XDB-Server.
- **XDB-Link** lets you access mainframe DB2 databases from COBOL programs, C programs, or XDB interactive tools on the PC.
- **XDB-EXT** is a special version of the SQL engine that runs in MS-DOS above the 640K line in extended memory.

Other products include **XDB-C,** a C language preprocessor, **XDB-Windows Software Development Kit,** an SQL system that allows shared access under Windows, and **XDB-SQL PLUS,** an SQL engine packaged with 4GL utilities intended for PC applications development.

For more information.
XDB Systems, Inc.
14700 Sweitzer Lane
Laurel, MD 20707
(301) 317–6800

12.4.2 IBM OS/2 Extended Services Database Manager

Overview. This product was originally called the OS/2 Extended Edition Database Manager. It was part of the OS/2 Extended Edition. With OS/2 2.0, the DBMS, host communications, and networking services were unbundled from the base operating system and sold under the label **Extended Services.** The Database Manager runs only under the OS/2 operating system. It includes a preprocessor, a runtime database engine, and a Query Manager that resembles mainframe QMF. The Query Manager is convenient for testing because it lets you build test cases and view test results without having to write more programs. At this time, the OS/2 ES Database Manager supports text data only in the ASCII collating sequence. If you need EBCDIC compatibility, you can install the **Micro Focus Host Compatibility Option** add-on product. This product works as an interface between your application and the OS/2 ES Database Manager. Figure 12.24 shows a sample Query Manager screen.

The release of OS/2 2.0 saw a reconfiguring of the Database Manager. With OS/2 ES, you get a single-user version of the Database Manager that allows you to keep your database on the workstation. You also get OS/2 client support that lets your workstation access OS/2 ES databases on a server. To set up a shared OS/2 ES database on a PC server, you'll need the **Extended Services Database Server** package. If you want to use an existing DB2, SQL/DS, or AS/400 database system as a server, you'll need **Distributed Database Connection Services (DDCS).** DDCS lets an authorized workstation issue SQL commands on the mainframe or minicomputer. You can update as well as retrieve data. However, the workstation must be the requestor. The host (mainframe or minicomputer) cannot issue SQL commands against the PC workstation.

The OS/2 ES Database Manager provides a menu of OS/2 icons for the Recovery Tool, the Query Manager, the Command Line Interface (CLI) facility, the Directory Tool, the Configuration Tool, and the Database Messages on-line reference.

For more information.

IBM Corporation
11400 Burnet Road
Austin, TX 78758
(512) 823–0000

For location of IBM dealers, call (800) IBM–2468 in the United States, or (800) 465–1234 in Canada. For OS/2 help in the U.S., call the IBM Help Center at (800) PS2–2227 or (800)426–4238 (ASCII/TDD).

12.4.3 Microsoft SQL Server

Overview. Microsoft Corporation offers a set of products that provide SQL-based DBMS support for multiuser systems. The Microsoft SQL Server environment provides network security, fault tolerance, and transaction recovery processing. It enforces data integrity rules at the server.

- **Microsoft SQL Server** is an SQL-based database engine that runs on an OS/2 server. The server requires an 80286 or better processor, at least 8MB of memory, at least 20MB of free disk space, and network software that provides 100% compatibility with named pipes. Suitable network software includes Microsoft LAN Manager, Novell NetWare, Banyan VINES, and IBM LAN Server. Client workstations can run MS-DOS 3.3 or later, Microsoft Windows 3.0 or later, or OS/2 1.21 or later. Licensing is server-based. You can get a license to support up to ten simultaneous users on one server, or upgrade to a license that allows an unlimited number of users on one server.

- **Microsoft SQL Bridge** is a gateway that connects Microsoft SQL Server environments with SYBASE SQL Server environments. The SYBASE SQL Server is a compatible SQL environment that runs on UNIX, DEC VAX, and Apple Macintosh servers.

- **Microsoft Open Data Services** gateways provide access to other SQL-based databases, including IBM mainframe DB2, IBM minicomputer SQL/400, DEC RDB, Oracle, Ingres, and Teradata.

- **Microsoft SQL Server Programmer's Toolkit for COBOL** works with the Micro Focus COBOL Workbench or other compatible COBOL compilers. It lets you write applications programs that access SQL Server databases from an OS/2-based system. You'll need one Programmer's Toolkit license for each developer. There is no runtime royalty for applications developed using the Toolkit.

- **Other Programmer's Toolkits:** The Toolkit for Visual Basic works with the Microsoft Visual Basic Programming System under Windows 3.0 or later. The Toolkit for Basic works with Microsoft Basic Professional Development

System 7.0 or later, under MS/DOS or OS/2. The Toolkit for C Language works with Microsoft C 6.0 or later, or QuickC for Windows 1.0 or later, as well as other compatible compilers. The C Toolkit runs on MS-DOS, Windows, or OS/2 systems. It offers additional functionality not available with the other Toolkits, including two-phase commit processing.

- **Microsoft SQL Administrator for Windows** is a network administration tool that runs on Windows or OS/2 systems.

For more information.
Microsoft Corporation
One Microsoft Way
Redmond, WA 98052-6399
Voice: (206) 936–8361 or (800) 227–6444, Fax: (206) 93MSFAX

12.4.4 Oracle

Overview. Oracle Corporation supports a large variety of hardware and operating system environments. ORACLE SQL-based DBMS products are available for virtually all computers and operating systems, including MS-DOS, OS/2, UNIX, Apple Macintosh, Data General, DEC VAX, HP3000, IBM MVS and VM mainframes, and many other systems. Many types of network protocols are supported. Oracle offers precompilers for COBOL, FORTRAN, C, Ada, Pascal, and PL/I. If you require connectivity among a large variety of environments, this may be the way to go. Oracle Corporation offers other companion products, including the following:

- **SQL*QMX** is an emulator for mainframe IBM QMF that runs on other platforms, including the PC workstation.
- **SQL*CONNECT** products allow access to mainframe DB2 and SQL/DS, DEC RMS, and HP3000 TurboIMAGE databases.
- **SQL*NET** lets you use all standard network protocols to access databases distributed across multiple platforms.
- **SQL*TextRetrieval** lets you do text searches against data stored under Oracle DBMS.
- **CASE tools** are provided for analysis, design, data dictionary management, and forms generation.
- **Electronic mail,** spreadsheet, and business application software are also available.

For more information.
Oracle Corporation
500 Oracle Parkway
Redwood Shores, CA 94065
(415) 506–7000, (800) 633–0598, (800) 345–DBMS, ext. 57
International inquiries: 44–932–872–020

12.4.5 Gupta SQLBase

Overview. Gupta Technologies provides SQL-based DBMS support that can be used with the Micro Focus Workbench. This product handles text data in the ASCII collating sequence only. The Gupta SQL System consists of the following products:

- **SQLBase Server** is a multiuser SQL-based database engine designed to run on an MS-DOS, OS/2, UNIX, or Novell NetWare server. For an MS-DOS server, SQLBase Server requires an 80286 machine or better, at least 2MB RAM, and at least 10MB hard disk for the entry-level configuration. 4MB RAM is required for OS/2 or UNIX servers, and 8MB RAM on Novell NetWare servers. SQLBase Server comes with the **SQLPrecompiler for COBOL** and the **SQL/API for C** language support modules. SQLBase Server provides automatic recovery from failures, on-line backup, remote monitoring, and diagnostic tools.
- **SQLWindows** is a Windows-based application development system that provides graphical user interface 4GL support. It comes with a single-user database engine for development purposes.
- **SQLTalk** is an interactive data administration tool for SQLBase databases on a LAN. It runs in character or graphics mode.
- **Quest** is a graphical user interface 4GL that accesses data in SQLBase databases. It runs under Microsoft Windows 3.0.
- **SQLNetwork for Oracle** provides connectivity to Oracle databases.
- **SQLRouter** provides connectivity to Sybase/Microsoft SQL Server databases. This forms a bridge to VMS or UNIX systems.

For more information.
Gupta Technologies, Inc.
1040 Marsh Road
Menlo Park, CA 94025
Voice: (415) 321–9500, (800) 876–3267, Fax: (415) 321–5471

12.5 IMS Database and Data Communications Support

12.5.1 IMS Option (Micro Focus/Stingray Software)

Overview. The Micro Focus/Stingray IMS Option provides IMS database and data communications support for the PC. Micro Focus, Inc. is the owner of Stingray Software Company. The IMS Option, also known as IMSVS86, provides a complete PC emulation of the IMS environment, with utilities, program preprocessing, and runtime services. It supports batch DL/I, BMP, and MFS programs. You can use its IMS/DB (DL/I database) support to run CICS DL/I programs under MCO or MCO2, using the EXEC DLI or CALL CBLTDLI interfaces. You can use it with the Micro Focus MF/370 mainframe assembler emulator to support assembler language exits or assembler programs containing ASMTDLI calls. If you also have an XDB, Gupta, or IBM OS/2 database management system, you can access SQL-based databases from an IMS program. You may need to do this if you have both kinds of databases in your shop, or if you use IMS DC to access SQL databases on-line. The IMS Option will handle logical databases, secondary indexes, sparse index routines, and MFS field exits. It provides some support for fast path databases. A multi-user network version is available.

You can use the EXEC DLI in place of the CBLTDLI interface in batch COBOL DL/I programs or in CICS DL/I programs. Checker directives let you select the EXEC DLI preprocessor.

A separate add-on product, **MFSPAINT**, is a screen painter for MFS displays.

ASCII versus EBCDIC. The IMS Option is available in ASCII and EBCDIC versions. In either case, your program source code will be in ASCII. Only the database contents and sequence will be affected. You will probably want the EBCDIC version unless you need compatibility with some other product that is available only in ASCII, such as MCO2, Gupta SQLbase, or the OS/2 Database Manager. XDB can be used with either the ASCII or EBCDIC versions of the IMS Option.

Setup. Installing the IMS Option simply requires that you create a directory and run a setup program that unpacks the files into that directory from your distribution diskette. You'll need to add a new SET command to your AUTOEXEC.BAT under MS-DOS, or change your CONFIG.SYS under OS/2.

The IMS Option runs as part of the Micro Focus Workbench on MS-DOS and OS/2 systems, and under Microsoft Windows in text mode. Extended memory is required.

The IMS Option environment. Once you have installed the IMS Option, pressing **F5=IMS** on the MDE main menu will bring up the IMS Option main menu, as shown in Figure 12.25. On this menu, **F2=edit** brings up the Micro Focus ASCII Editor. **F3=check** checks your program. **F4=animate-IMS** allows you to animate an IMS program. You must use this selection instead of the ordinary animator menu selection in order to bring up the IMS control region (runtime services). **F5=MFSGEN** assembles your screens, as shown in Figure 12.26. **F6=RUN-IMS** brings up the IMS control region so that you can run an IMS application. Figure 12.27 shows one of the sample IMS applications running in the IMS control region. **F7=DBDGEN** invokes the database generation processor, as shown in Figure 12.28. **F8=ZEROLOAD** brings up a menu, shown in Figure 12.29, that lets you initialize an existing database before you load it. **F9=PSBGEN** invokes the program specification block processor, shown in Figure 12.30. **F10=IMSGEN** invokes the processor that lets you set parameters and define programs and devices to the IMS system. Figure 12.31 shows the appearance of the IMSGEN main menu, and Figure 12.32 shows the IMS system configuration menu. You can use this menu to display system resources and to delete unwanted or obsolete PSBs, DBDs, or MFS members.

Figure 12.33 shows the Alt-key option menu. **F2=run IMSPRINT** lets you print the results of an IMS trace. **F3=edit menus** and **F4=use new menus** let you change the PCIMS.MNU file. **F6=run MFSPAINT** runs a Stingray add-on product that lets you paint MFS screens. **F7=IMS SET's** will display current IMS variable settings. **F8=DBD Map** runs the DBDMAP utility to provide a hierarchical map of a single DBD.

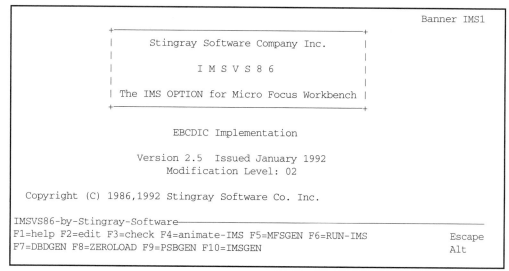

```
                                                              Banner IMS1
            +-------------------------------------------------+
            |         Stingray Software Company Inc.          |
            |                                                 |
            |                I M S V S 8 6                    |
            |                                                 |
            | The IMS OPTION for Micro Focus Workbench        |
            +-------------------------------------------------+

                        EBCDIC Implementation

                  Version 2.5   Issued January 1992
                      Modification Level: 02

      Copyright (C) 1986,1992 Stingray Software Co. Inc.

IMSVS86-by-Stingray-Software─────────────────────────────────────────
F1=help F2=edit F3=check F4=animate-IMS F5=MFSGEN F6=RUN-IMS      Escape
F7=DBDGEN F8=ZEROLOAD F9=PSBGEN F10=IMSGEN                        Alt
```

Figure 12.25 IMS Option main menu

```
MFSGEN─────────────Auto─────List─────────────────────Auto─────Ins-Caps-Num-Scroll
F1=help F2=dir F3=CopyExt F4=List F5=Model F6=/FOR F7=Stack F8=Echo       Escape
File K:\IMSDEMO\DEMO90.MFS                                              <-' Ctrl
```

Figure 12.26 IMS Option MFSGEN menu

```
MFDEMO
OTDEMO91   MICRO FOCUS LIMITED - TABLE FILE MAINTENANCE

SELECT ONE OF THE FOLLOWING FUNCTION CODES:

ADD      - TABLE FILE
CHANGE   - TABLE FILE
DELETE   - TABLE FILE
INQUIRE  - TABLE FILE

END      - TRANSACTION CODE

FUNCTION CODE C

TABLE-ID     TESTDEPT
PASSWORD

2-_
```

Figure 12.27 IMS Option sample application screen

```
DBDGEN starting
        DBD    NAME=DEMO03DD,ACCESS=(HIDAM,VSAM)
        DATASET DD1=DEMO03DD,DEVICE=3380,SIZE=4096
        SEGM   NAME=DEMOHDRS,PARENT=0,BYTES=144,PTR=TB
        FIELD  NAME=(SEQFIELD,SEQ,U),BYTES=40,START=1
        LCHILD NAME=(DEMOHDRI,DEMO03PD),PTR=INDX
        SEGM   NAME=DEMOELES,BYTES=224,PTR=(TB),                        X
               PARENT=((DEMOHDRS,DBLE))
        FIELD  NAME=(SEQFIELD,SEQ,U),BYTES=30,START=1
        DBDGEN
        FINISH
        END
DBDGEN for K:\IMSDEMO\DEMO03DD.DBD successful


DBDGEN————————Auto————List————NoMap———Normal————————————Ins-Caps-Num-Scroll
F1=help F2=dir F3=CopyExt F4=List F5=Map F6=Run-Type                   Escape
File K:\IMSDEMO\DEMO03DD.DBD                                           <-' Ctrl
```

Figure 12.28 IMS Option DBDGEN screen

```
ZEROLOAD———————————————————————————————————————————Ins-Caps-Num-Scroll
F1=help F2=directory                                                  Escape
Enter the Database name to Zeroload:            <-'
```

Figure 12.29 IMS Option Zeroload screen

```
PSBGEN starting
PSBGEN - Searching for PSBGEN macro
PSBGEN - Processing PSB
* DEMO001T WAS CREATED ON APRIL 30, 1985 AND CHANGED ON MMM DD YYYY
        PCB    TYPE=TP,MODIFY=YES,EXPRESS=YES
        PCB    TYPE=DB,DBDNAME=DEMO03DD,PROCOPT=AP,KEYLEN=80
        SENSEG NAME=DEMOHDRS,PARENT=0
        SENSEG NAME=DEMOELES,PARENT=DEMOHDRS
        PSBGEN LANG=COBOL,CMPAT=YES,PSBNAME=DEMO001T
        END
PSBGEN for K:\IMSDEMO\DEMO001T.PSB successful


PSBGEN————————NoVerify—List————Auto————————————————Ins-Caps-Num-Scroll
F1=help F2=dir F3=Verify F4=List F5=CopyExt                           Escape
File K:\IMSDEMO\DEMO001T                                              <-' Ctrl
```

Figure 12.30 IMS Option PSBGEN screen

DBUTIL, a supplied BMP transaction, lets you enter and run IMS database calls directly from the screen without having to write a program. Figure 12.34 shows the DBUTIL screen. The DBUTILF and DBUTILV utilities let you transfer data between mainframe IMS databases and the PC. You can also purchase a separate product, Compuware File-Aid/PC, that allows you to edit IMS Option databases as well as VSAM files on the PC.

For more information.
Stingray Software Co.
7612 Highway 60
Cedarburg WI 53012
(414) 375–9080

```
+-----------------------------------------------------------------------+
|                     I M S V S 8 6   IMSGEN Screen                     |
| Copyright 1986,1992 - Stingray Software Company Inc.                  |
+-----------------------------------------------------------------------+

                      1)  Define Transaction Codes
                      2)  Define Logical Terminals
                      3)  Configure IMSVS86 menu
                      C)  Define Database Catalog
                      4)  DBDGEN file maintenance
                      5)  PSBGEN file maintenance
                      5X) PSBGEN file maintenance - Expanded
                      6)  MFSGEN file maintenance
                      7)  Reorganize DBDGEN file
                      8)  Reorganize PSBGEN file
                      9)  Reorganize MFSGEN file




                  Enter selection number:        Start at name:
                  Press Enter key to invoke selection
                  Press F3/Esc key to exit IMSGEN
IMSLIB=Current Directory
Version 2.5.02
2-_
```

Figure 12.31 IMS Option IMSGEN screen

```
+-----------------------------------------------------------------------+
|                 I M S V S 8 6   General Configuration                 |
| Copyright 1986,1992 - Stingray Software Company Inc.                  |
+-----------------------------------------------------------------------+
 TRACING OPTIONS
 Call options
     PCB: N   SSA's: N   I/O Area: N   Call Stats: N          (Y,N)
 PCB type selection
     All PCB's: X   I/O PCB's only:    DB PCB's only:         (Select 1)
 Trace output options
     Trace output to screen: H   Pause after each CBLTDLI call: Y  (Y,H,N) (Y,N)
     Trace output to dataset name: BTS.LST

 OTHER OPTIONS
 Help messages for PCB status codes: Y                        (Y,N)
 Should screens beep when displayed: N                        (Y,N)
 Enable IMS/DB2 exits for vendor: N        (N=None X=XDB G=Gupta I=IBM OS/2 EE)
 OS/2 Extended Edition Database Manager database name:
 Emulate standard mainframe COBOL subroutine management: N
 Active IMSLIB variable for IMSGEN screen functions   : 1     (1,2,3)



 Press Enter to process changes, F3/Esc to cancel
 2-_
```

Figure 12.32 IMS Option General Configuration screen

```
IMSVS86-by-Stingray-Software——————————————————————————————————
F1=help F2=run IMSPRINT F3=edit menus F4=use new menus
F6=run MFSPAINT F7=IMS SET's F8=DBD Map
```

Figure 12.33 IMS Option Alt-key menu

```
                        I M S V S 8 6   Database Utility
    Copyright 1986,1992 - Stingray Software Company Inc.

  Dataset containing control cards:
   or,
  Enter interactive call parameters:

      Function  :
      PCB number:
      SSA #1    :
      SSA #2    :
      SSA #3    :
      SSA #4    :
      SSA #5    :
      PCB fdback:
      I/O area  :

  Enter options and press enter.  Press F3/End/Esc to exit
  2-_
```

Figure 12.34 IMS Option DBUTIL screen

12.6 Computer Associates DBMS Support

12.6.1 The CA-IDMS/PC and CA-DATACOM/PC Environments

CA-IDMS and CA-DATACOM are two separate families of database management systems offered by Computer Associates International, Inc. In particular, **IDMS/DB** and **DATACOM/DB** run on IBM MVS, VM, and DOS/VSE mainframes. **IDMS/VAX** and **DATACOM/VAX** run on DEC VAX VMS minicomputers. **IDMS/UNIX** and **DATACOM/UNIX** run on various UNIX workstations. **IDMS/PC** and **DATACOM/PC** run on MS-DOS and OS/2 workstations. Each of these products are compatible with their counterparts running on other machines, allowing applications to be ported.

CA-IDMS and CA-DATACOM each support their own navigational database application programming interfaces. In addition, both CA-IDMS and CA-DATACOM support SQL-based databases with the usual application programming interface of embedded SQL commands. In either environment, you can program in ANSI Standard SQL, Federal Information Processing Standard (FIPS) SQL, or CA Extended SQL.

12.6.2 CA-IDMS/PC

Overview. IDMS/PC consists of a database engine, multiple language support, an integrated data dictionary, an SQL reporting facility, and various utilities. A syntax conversion utility provides for uploading and downloading mainframe data dictionary entries. Other utilities provide for database definition, initialization, migration, reorganization, reporting, and repair. In addition, **CA-IDMS:SERVER** provides shared database and data dictionary support in a client/server environment. **CA-IDMS/DML ONLINE** provides a query-update facility resembling the mainframe version.

The application programming interface can consist of SQL statements or CODASYL DML statements. IDMS/PC supports COBOL, C, CA-IDMS/DML ONLINE, and CA-ADS/PC languages. COBOL programs may use batch, IDMS on-line, or CICS on-line processing.

IDMS/PC is integrated with Computer Associates fourth-generation languages and CASE tools such as **CA-DB:ARCHITECT, CA-IDMS/CONCEPTOR, CA-ADS/PC,** and **CA-ADS/GENERATOR for PC.**

CA-IDMS/PC RUNTIME and **CA-IDMS/PC RUNTIME SERVER** are database engines for those workstations and servers that are used only for production and not for development.

12.6.3 CA-DATACOM/PC

Overview. DATACOM/PC consists of three separate components. The **Data Base Component** supports both SQL and non-SQL (IDF) syntax. It is compatible with mainframe DATACOM/DB, although the User Requirements Table (URT) is optional on the PC. The **Data Dictionary Component** includes an Interactive Dictionary Facility, allowing you to model new entities from existing ones. The **Query Component** supports three levels of expertise. Expert mode lets you enter free-form SQL statements with the assistance of popup help menus. Intermediate mode provides a series of menus to lead you through the process of coding an SQL query, step by step. Novice mode lets you build simple point-and-shoot queries by choosing keywords and column names from menus.

DATACOM/PC supports the COBOL and C programming languages, as well as **CA-IDEAL/PC.** A transport utility allows you to port databases to and from the mainframe.

- **CA-DB:STAR/PC** supports distributed DATACOM/PC databases.
- **CA-DATACOM/PC RUNTIME** is a database engine for those workstations that are used only for production and not for development.
- **CA-CORTANA/PC** is a security manager that works with DATACOM/PC.

12.6.4 For more information.

To find out about IDMS/PC or DATACOM/PC, contact:
Computer Associates International, Inc.
711 Stewart Ave.
Garden City, NY 11530-4787
(800) 645–3003

12.7 VM/CMS Emulation

12.7.1 KEDIT: Emulator for VM/CMS XEDIT on the PC

Overview. KEDIT provides the functionality of XEDIT, IBM's VM/CMS editor, on the PC. It supports multiple files, multiple windows, block operations, character string find/change, DOS interface. It contains a built-in subset of

REXX, and will support full REXX with Quercus System's Personal REXX or the IBM OS/2 operating system. KEDIT supports macros written in the REXX language, but not mainframe CMS EXEC2 macros. You can assign REXX macros to function keys. KEDIT supports EGA 43-line or VGA 50- line mode.

For greater editing speed, KEDIT loads the entire file into memory. The DOS version edits files up to 350K in a typical 640K system. It also supports up to 8MB of EMS memory. Under OS/2, KEDIT supports up to 16MB of OS/2 virtual memory.

KEDIT handles only ASCII text files, not EBCDIC or binary. It accepts files with line lengths up to 4095 characters, delimited either with a carriage return or with a carriage return/line feed combination. Files can have fixed or variable-length records. If desired, you can configure XEDIT to ignore the ASCII end-of-file marker and to edit the entire data file up to the end of its physical allocation.

Setup. KEDIT is provided in separate versions for MS-DOS only and for OS/2. The OS/2 version also includes separate KEDIT executable files for the MS-DOS version. The OS/2 files are in the KEDITOS2 directory of the installation diskette. Installation is the essence of simplicity. Simply create a directory on the hard drive for the KEDIT program files. For example, create a KEDIT directory for MS-DOS. If you're running OS/2, KEDITOS2 might be an appropriate directory name. Load the KEDIT installation diskette into your **A:** drive, then copy all the files to the directory you've created for KEDIT.

It's possible to run KEDIT under Windows as a non-Windows application. You'll need to create or copy a .PIF file and assign an icon to the .PIF. See your Windows 3.x manual for more information about creating .PIFs.

As shown in Figure 12.35, you can set up a profile file to customize the appearance and function of KEDIT. You can change the position of screen elements, switch between cursor wrap and scrolling modes, set a new color scheme, or change default key assignments.

Appearance of KEDIT. Figure 12.36 shows an example of an editing session under KEDIT. A PC workstation has a more flexible user interface than a mainframe terminal. For example, a PC can process each keystroke as you press it, while a mainframe processes input a screen at a time. A PC also has Alt- and Ctrl-key combinations. KEDIT takes advantage of this additional flexibility.

You can enter program source code one line at a time by pressing the F2 key each time you want to insert a line. The F2 key inserts a new line below the cursor line and positions the cursor to the first column in that line. If the cursor is at the command prompt when you press F2, then the new line will appear under the current (highlighted) line. The WORDWRAP feature of KEDIT allows for continuous text entry in the same manner as a word processor. When the cursor reaches line 72, it automatically wraps to the next line.

Figure 12.37 shows a KEDIT directory display. KEDIT interfaces directly to the PC file system and does not attempt to simulate the mainframe VM file system.

```
k:\kedit\samples\profileb.kex      Line=21      Col=7      Size=51      Alt=0,0
* * * Top of File * * *
* PROFILEB.KEX - This is a sample profile
* It is an illustration of how a typical profile might be set up,
* and is not intended as a 'recommended' profile
* Version:  1.0 (May 1988)

* Don't display the time on the statusline
'set clock off'

* Adjust the colors of text within marked blocks, the current line when it
* is in a marked block and the normal text area
* Note - This is only meaningful for color displays
'set color block black on white'
'set color cblock bright blue on white'
'set color filearea white on blue'

* Position the current line at line 6 of the window
'set curline 6'

* Allow messages to overlay the window from lines 1 through 16
'set msgline on 1 16 overlay'

====>
KEDIT 4.0 Demo Files=4  Memory=865K                        11:25pm
```

Figure 12.35 Sample KEDIT profile file

```
k:\cobol\mfwbbook\lottery.cbl      Line=10      Col=1      Size=173      Alt=0,0
* * * Top of File * * *
        ************************************************************
        *                                                        *
        *                (C) Cogito Corporation 1991             *
        *                                                        *
        *                    LOTTERY.CBL                         *
        *                                                        *
        *    This program creates lottery wheels for Illinois    *
        *    Little Lotto                                        *
        *                                                        *
        ************************************************************
         identification division.
         program-id. Lottery.
         environment division.
         configuration section.
         source-computer. ibm-pc.
         object-computer. ibm-pc.
        *special-names.
        *console is crt.
         data division.
         working-storage section.
         01 seven- numbers.
====>
KEDIT 4.0 Demo Files=1  Memory=870K                        11:16pm
```

Figure 12.36 KEDIT editing session

```
k:\kedit\dir.dir              Line=21     Col=7      Size=34    Alt=0,0
* * * Top of File * * *
k: altered .kex      493    5-19-88    9:00    \kedit\samples
k: box     .kex     3904    5-19-88    9:00    \kedit\samples
k: boxfill .kex      868    5-19-88    9:00    \kedit\samples
k: caseword.kex     1317    5-16-89    9:00    \kedit\samples
k: colorfun.kex     1233    5-19-88    9:00    \kedit\samples
k: dirmac  .kml     2742    5-19-88    9:00    \kedit\samples
k: extrtest.kex      544    5-19-88    9:00    \kedit\samples
k: homend  .kml     1573    5-19-88    9:00    \kedit\samples
k: kexx    .hlp    24492    5-16-89    9:00    \kedit\samples
k: kexxhelp.kex     1683    5-19-88    9:00    \kedit\samples
k: kexxrexx.kex     2866    5-19-88    9:00    \kedit\samples
k: less    .kex      900    5-19-88    9:00    \kedit\samples
k: manyfile.kex     1713    5-19-88    9:00    \kedit\samples
k: misc    .kml     5292    5-19-88    9:00    \kedit\samples
k: more    .kex      744    5-19-88    9:00    \kedit\samples
k: profilea.kex     2656    5-19-88    9:00    \kedit\samples
k: profileb.kex     1692    5-19-88    9:00    \kedit\samples
k: profileb.kml     2453    5-19-88    9:00    \kedit\samples
k: ranger  .kex      878    5-19-88    9:00    \kedit\samples
k: reload  .kex      339    5-19-88    9:00    \kedit\samples
k: repeat  .kex     1064    5-19-88    9:00    \kedit\samples
===>
KEDIT 4.0 Demo Files=3  Memory=867K                  11:22pm
```

Figure 12.37 KEDIT directory display

For more information.
Mansfield Software Group, Inc.
P.O. Box 532
Storrs, CT 06268
Voice: (203) 429–8402, BBS: (203) 429–3784

12.8 Mainframe ISPF Emulation

12.8.1 CTC ISPF Editor (SPF/PC and SPF/2)

Overview. These products offer mainframelike text editing for those pro-grammers who are familiar with the mainframe ISPF/PDF environment. **SPF/2,** the more recent product, will work with any OS/2 system, as well as with MS-DOS systems on 80386-class or better workstations. **SPF/PC** has fewer capabilities but will work with MS-DOS systems running on any processor. **Details of how to install and use SPF/2 with the Workbench appear in Chapter 13.**

For more information.
Command Technology Corporation
1040 Marina Village Parkway
Alameda, CA 94501
Voice: (510) 521–5900, Fax: (510) 521–0369

12.8.2 Micro Focus/Stingray AD/MVS Menu System

Overview. Stingray Software **AD/MVS** is a front-end menu system that lets you access Workbench functions through an ISPF-like user interface. At the same time, it provides a front end to the Command Technology Corporation text file editor, **SPF/2.** The current version of this product requires you to have either SPFPC installed for DOS or SPF2 installed for OS/2. AD/MVS contains a special version of the ProxMvs mainframe JCL emulator. You can run external sorts and catalogue PC datasets in much the same way you would mainframe datasets. From the AD/MVS menu system, you can interface to the IMS Option, the CICS Option, and the MF/370 Assembler emulator. You can do foreground program checking; if an error is found, AD/MVS will position you to the error line in the SPF editor display. AD/MVS greatly reduces the learning time for mainframe programmers who are new to the Workbench. This product also offers support for some mainframe Dialog Manager functions so that you can write your own panels. Micro Focus, Inc. is the owner of Stingray Software.

A disclaimer. AD/MVS was still in beta test while this book was being written. **Screen images shown here may not contain all of the features in the finished product.** The production version may differ in certain details.

Installation and setup. Before attempting installation, it's a good idea to print, then read, all the README.* and *.DOC files from the installation diskette. You must create several ISPF directories on the hard drive where you intend to install the product. You may want to install this product on the same drive on which you've installed the Workbench. Once this process is completed, put the installation diskette into your "A" drive. Then get into the newly created ISPF directory and type **A:INSTALL**. All the necessary files will be automatically decompressed by PKUNZIP and copied to the appropriate directories on your hard drive.

There are two LOGONMVS files supplied with the installation diskette. If you're running under DOS, LOGONMVS.DOS is the file you'll copy to LOGONMVS.BAT. For OS/2 users, LOGONMVS.OS2 gets copied to LOGONMVS.CMD. Its a good idea to make copies of these files rather than simply renaming them since you'll need to make changes to the selected LOGONMVS file. These files contain various SET and other commands for AD/MVS. Once you've made the requisite changes to the LOGONMVS file to match your particular PC environment, you're ready to begin.

Primary menu options. Type LOGONMVS from the ISPF directory. You should see the **AD/MVS Primary Option Menu** shown in Figure 12.38. It should look similar to your mainframe ISPF/PDF Primary Option Menu.

Cataloging files. Just as the mainframe catalog supports 44 character dataset names and high level qualifiers, the AD/MVS catalog facility maintains this support on the PC. Selecting **Option 3** from the Primary Option Menu will bring up the **AD/MVS Utilities Menu** as shown in Figure 12.39. Selecting **Option 2**, CATALOG, from the Utilities Menu brings up the **AD/MVS SYSTEM CATALOG** menu shown in Figure 12.40.

```
───────────────────── AD/MVS PRIMARY OPTION MENU ─────────────────────
OPTION  ===>
                                                   USERID   - AD/MVS
   0   ISPF PARMS  - Specify terminal and user parameters   TIME     - 20:44
   1   BROWSE      - Display source data or output listings  TERMINAL - IBM
   2   EDIT        - Create or change source data            PF KEYS  - 12
   3   UTILITIES   - Perform utility functions
   4   FOREGROUND  - Invoke language processors in foreground
   5   BACKGROUND  - Invoke language processors in background (requires OS/2)
   6   COMMAND     - Execute DOS/OS2/TSO commands
   7   DIALOG TEST - Not Available
   8   IMS         - Invoke IMSVS86
   9   CICS        - Invoke CICSVS86 (Micro Focus CICS Option (MCO))
   A   ASM370      - Invoke MF370 Assembler
   C   CHANGES     - Not available
   E   EXTENSIONS  - User defined DOS/OS2 script processing
   T   TUTORIAL    - Not available
   U   USER        - Invoke user defined functions via Dialog Manager
   X   EXIT        - Terminate AD/MVS

Enter END command to terminate ISPF.
```

Figure 12.38 AD/MVS Primary Option Menu

```
───────────────────── AD/MVS UTILITIES MENU ─────────────────────
OPTION  ===> 2

   1   PDS SERVICES  -  Delete, Edit, Uncatalog, Zero, Copy PDS Members
   2   CATALOG       -  Catalog Management Services
   3   DEF           -  Data Editor Facility
   4   ETA           -  EBCIDIC  ASCII
   5   SORTMVS       -  Batch Sort
   6   FILE TOOL     -  Delete, Rename, Copy, Edit, Browse, Files in PC Syntax
   7   MFSPAINT      -  IMS/DC MFS Screen Generator
   8   SEARCH FILE   -  Search/Locate Files in PC Directories

Enter END command to terminate UTILITIES MENU.
```

Figure 12.39 AD/MVS Utilities Menu

```
───────────────────── AD/MVS SYSTEM CATALOG ─────────────────────
OPTION  ===> 1

   1   Catalog/uncatalog a dataset or partitioned dataset (PDS)
   2   Catalog/uncatalog a PDS member
   3   QUICKCAT - Update via PC subdirectory
   4   List catalog

Enter END command to terminate SYSTEM CATALOG.
```

Figure 12.40 AD/MVS System Catalog Menu

Selecting **Option 1** from the SYSTEM CATALOG panel brings up the **CATALOG** panel (Figure 12.41). This panel lets you connect your familiar mainframe dataset names to the actual dataset on the PC. To identify your file to the PC, use the same dataset information in the **Mainframe Designation** as you would use on the mainframe under ISPF/PDF.

```
                                          MVS86 CATALOG PDS DATASET CATALOGED
  COMMAND ===> C


   C  - CATALOG          U  - UNCATALOG


   DATASET TYPE:

    PDS X (DSORG=PO)  NON-PDS    (DSORG=PS)


   MAINFRAME DESIGNATION:
    PROJECT ===> BOOK
    LIBRARY ===> MICROF
    TYPE    ===> COBOL


    OTHER MAINFRAME DATASET ===>


   PC DESIGNATION:
    DRIVE          ===> K
    SUB-DIRECTORY ===> COBOL    ===> DEMO    ===>          ===>
    EXTENSION     ===> CBL


    OTHER PC DATASET ===>
```

Figure 12.41 AD/MVS Catalog panel

Then, fill in the **PC Designation** field with the correct disk drive, path, and file extension you want to reference. In the example in Figure 12.41, BOOK.MICROF.COBOL represents a mainframe PDS containing COBOL source code that we wanted to work with on our PC. We chose all the .CBL extensions from the Micro Focus COBOL\DEMO directory\subdirectory on our "K:" drive. We told ISPF to consider this file a PDS and to catalog it.

Unlike using the mainframe catalog facility, cataloging the PDS under AD/MVS does not automatically include all of the members in that PDS. Remember, these are not real PDS's, but PC emulations. Once the PDS has been cataloged, you're ready to catalog the members. While ISPF doesn't actually alter the PC file structure of directory\subdirectory\files, it treats this combination as part just as a mainframe would treat one of its PDS's. The F3 function key backs up one panel, just as the PF3 key does in mainframe ISPF/PDF. Use the F3 key to return to the AD/MVS SYSTEM CATALOG panel. There are two ways to catalog all the members into an existing PDS.

Option 2, from the System Catalog Menu in Figure 12.40, lets you catalog one member at a time. Using Option 2, it's possible to catalog members from different drive\directory\subdirectories under one PDS name. Ordinarily, you'd want to group PDS members the same way on the PC side as on the mainframe side; however, AD/MVS doesn't force you to do that.

A faster method is to use **Option 3, QUICKCAT**. Selecting the QUICKCAT option brings up the MVS BUILD CATALOG MEMBERS panel shown in Figure 12.42. The QUICKCAT catalogs the contents of an entire PC directory into the equivalent of a mainframe PDS. Pressing the ENTER key from this panel causes all files in K:\COBOL\DEMO with the .CBL extension to be cataloged under the BOOK.MICROF.COBOL mainframe designation. This two-step process applies only to PDS's. Sequential datasets can be cataloged in just the first step described above.

```
                                MVS86 BUILD CATALOG MEMBERS MEMBERS CATALOGED
COMMAND ===>


 MAINFRAME DESIGNATION:

   PROJECT ===> BOOK
   LIBRARY ===> MICROF
   TYPE    ===> COBOL

 PC DESIGNATION:

   DRIVE          ===> K
   SUB-DIRECTORY ===> COBOL    ===> DEMO     ===>            ===>
   EXTENSION      ===> CBL
```

Figure 12.42 AD/MVS Build Catalog Members panel

```
                                MVS86 LIST CATALOG
COMMAND ===>

PROJECT  LIBRARY  TYPE       MEMBER
BOOK     MICROF   COBOL
 PC NAME:  K:\COBOL\DEMO\*.CBL
BOOK     MICROF   COBOL      ADMOUSE
 PC NAME:  K:\COBOL\DEMO\ADMOUSE.CBL
BOOK     MICROF   COBOL      BUILDMN
 PC NAME:  K:\COBOL\DEMO\BUILDMN.CBL
BOOK     MICROF   COBOL      BUILDSUB
 PC NAME:  K:\COBOL\DEMO\BUILDSUB.CBL
BOOK     MICROF   COBOL      BYTEIO
 PC NAME:  K:\COBOL\DEMO\BYTEIO.CBL
BOOK     MICROF   COBOL      CALC
 PC NAME:  K:\COBOL\DEMO\CALC.CBL
BOOK     MICROF   COBOL      CALENDAR
 PC NAME:  K:\COBOL\DEMO\CALENDAR.CBL
BOOK     MICROF   COBOL      CALLFDEM
 PC NAME:  K:\COBOL\DEMO\CALLFDEM.CBL
BOOK     MICROF   COBOL      CALLHYH
 PC NAME:  K:\COBOL\DEMO\CALLHYH.CBL
BOOK     MICROF   COBOL      CASE
 PC NAME:  K:\COBOL\DEMO\CASE.CBL
```

Figure 12.43 AD/MVS List Catalog panel

To see all the files or members you've just cataloged, return to the AD/MVS System Catalog panel and select **Option 4**. Figure 12.43 shows the members cataloged under the PDS designation BOOK.MICROF.COBOL.

Compiling a program. Once you've cataloged a source program, either as a PDS member or sequential dataset, you're ready to compile it. We discussed the differences between checking and compiling in an earlier chapter. PC and mainframe terminology differ in this area. **Option 4** from the Primary Option Menu, the "foreground compile," actually calls the Micro Focus Checker. It produces .INT code suitable for animation. By using **Option 0** on the Primary Option Menu, you can set up AD/MVS to allow you to request the SPF editor whenever errors occur during program checking. Once any errors are corrected, and the program is rechecked without errors, **Option 3.1** from the Primary Option Menu allows you to begin animation.

Dialog Manager. Just as mainframe ISPF/PDF runs as a Dialog Manager application, AD/MVS runs under a PC version of Dialog Manager. The PC version may not possess all the features of its mainframe counterpart, but you can write your own panels, modify existing panels, and even write Dialog Manager applications on your PC. It's also possible to download Dialog Manager (DM) applications from the mainframe and run them on your PC, subject to the limitations of PC DM. One useful feature of DM on the PC is that you can customize your AD/MVS panels to resemble your mainframe ISPF panels.

For more information.
Stingray Software Co.
7612 Highway 60
Cedarburg WI 53012
(414) 375–9080

12.9 Source Code Management and Code Reusability

12.9.1 Reusable Code Manager

Overview. If you often clone or recycle new programs from parts of old programs, you may want to consider doing this work in a more efficient and systematic way. Reusable Code Manager (RCM), an add-on product from Micro Focus, addresses this issue. RCM is a utility for maintaining a library of existing, tested source code modules. Use RCM to identify, organize, and retrieve your site's inventory of tested modules and program logic structures. RCM helps you organize cooperative application development work without time-consuming regimentation. With RCM, you no longer have to rely on luck or on prior experience to know what reusable program modules are available at your installation.

RCM gives you more control than a 4GL or COBOL application generator. Rather than subjecting you to the rigidities of predefined logic, you can use RCM to generate exactly the program logic you want.

Once you find the reusable module that you want, you can tell RCM to create a new instance of it. The new instance will inherit all of the properties of the original, except for the changes that you tell RCM to make. You may be familiar with standard COBOL COPY statements that let you replace data names or prefixes in a limited way. RCM lets you perform more flexible types of replacement operations while creating the new instance of the source code or data definition module.

RCM is not limited to COBOL programs. Its usefulness extends to any ASCII text file. You can port the finished code back to the mainframe with Workbench conversion utilities, just as you would with any other applications you develop with the Workbench. Some examples of code that you can develop with RCM are JCL streams, IDCAMS statements, screens for CICS and IMS, SQL statements, and .BAT and .CMD files for PC applications. RCM's generic interface also lets you use it with commercial and home-grown CASE tools.

Like the Workbench, RCM is a PC-based product. There is no counterpart that runs on the mainframe. If you have been using the Workbench, you have already been keeping your copy library members and at least some source code on the PC. This leads to a question: what is the most efficient way of sharing your reusable code resources? If you have a PC network, store the shared library of reusable code on a PC network server where every programmer can reach it. Otherwise, you can keep the shared library on one workstation and distribute code on diskette as needed.

Licensing. Micro Focus Workbench licensing policies also apply to RCM. If you plan to install RCM on workstations, you purchase a separate license for each workstation, just as you do for the Workbench. If you plan to install RCM on a server along with a server-based Workbench, license agreements will follow Micro Focus policies for server-based products.

Terminology. Let's take a moment to discuss the terminology used within the RCM system.

- **Assets** are any reuseable code resources stored within the RCM system. These can be copy members, macros, models, and subroutines.
- **Copy members** in RCM contain the same data as copy members on the mainframe. RCM, however, associates descriptive information with each copy member, and makes it easy to look up the copy members you need for your project.
- A **macro** is a facility that takes one statement in your program and expands it into standard COBOL code as the program is checked or compiled. The RCM macro facility is only for COBOL programs. Mainframe BAL programmers will already be familiar with the concept of macros. RCM extends the benefit of macros to the COBOL environment, so that you can create your own COBOL verbs. For example, you could use macros to create standard error handlers that everyone in your shop can use. RCM supports nested macros.
- A **model** is mechanism for generating many programs that have substantially the same logic structure but use different inputs and outputs. Loops and if-then-else statements let you generate different source code based on input parameters. For example, you can use models to create file conversion routines and the JCL you need to run them. Since the turn of the century is rapidly approaching, many shops will need to convert the two character year fields in their files to four characters. Once you've set up new copy members, you'll need conversion programs for every sequential file, every indexed file, and every database. RCM lets you code each type of conversion program just once as a model, then generate all the other programs from it automatically.
- **Subroutines** in RCM refer to the CALL statements you use to invoke previously compiled external routines. When you put a CALL statement into your COBOL program, RCM prompts you for the correct parameter format.

- **List files** work with RCM models. They are parameter files that provide a greater degree of flexibility in the type of code you can build. For example, you can build a new paragraph of COBOL code for each record in a list file. Each instance of that paragraph will vary according to parameters in each list file record.

- **Project** is the highest level of grouping assets under RCM. Project names are user-defined. A project contains all of the macros, models, copy members, subroutines, and list files that RCM can access at any given time.

- **Class** is the next lower level of grouping reusable assets, below the project level. Available classes include COPY, LIST, MACRO, MODEL, and SUB-ROUTINE.

- **Type** is the lowest level of grouping assets. Type names are user-defined. For example, you can identify those macros that have to do with character string processing by assigning them a type of STRING.

- The **Locator/Selector Facility** is a library manager for your assets. You can retrieve, add, and update assets with this facility. You can supply parameters interactively to expand RCM assets into new source code. The Locator/Selector is also integrated with the Micro Focus COBOL Editor. For example, when you embed macro statements in a COBOL program, it will prompt you for the correct syntax.

- The **RCM Preprocessor** is invoked by the **PREPROCESS($RCMDIR\RCM)** Checker directive. It expands any macro statements and parameters to create standard COBOL source. You can check or compile the COBOL source on the PC, or port it back to the mainframe.

Setup. RCM uses the standard Micro Focus Setup utility. This product installs itself the same way the Workbench does. The setup script adds an option to the Micro Focus function key menu system. RCM also provides modules to run under the Workbench Organizer. See Chapters 14–16 for details about the Workbench Organizer.

To use RCM, you must have at least two megabytes of RAM memory under MS-DOS, and at least six megabytes under OS/2. RCM runs with MS-DOS 3.3 or higher, or OS/2 1.3 or higher. You'll need at least two megabytes of free space on your hard drive. You can use RCM with Micro Focus Workbench 2.4.15 or higher, but it's highly recommended that you upgrade to the current Workbench release.

Invoking RCM. You can reach RCM from the function key Workbench COBOL Editor menu, regardless of whether or not you are currently editing a program. Press **Ctrl+F6=draw/forms** on the Editor menu to bring up the forms drawing menu, as shown at the bottom of Figure 12.44. This function key menu will have one additional option: **F5=RCM.** The **RCM Locator/Selector Facility** will appear as a rectangular box superimposed over the Editor text area. The box will show some sample reusable assets that are supplied as part of RCM.

When RCM is visible on screen, its panel becomes the active window. RCM has its own function key menu line, showing what options are available while RCM is active. This function key menu line takes precedence over the

Editor menu line. Typically, you will use RCM to select something that you want to bring into the Editor. You can always select **F10=peek** from any RCM panel to see the underlying Editor screen without terminating RCM. Figure 12.44 shows the main RCM function key menu selections, while Figure 12.45 shows the Alt-key menu selections.

Selecting RCM assets. The RCM panel shows a sorted list of the assets in the categories that you have selected. Selecting **F2=type, Alt+F2=class,** or **Alt+F4=project** will invoke pulldown menus that let you change the subset of assets that RCM will display. For example, pressing **Alt+F2=class** will cause the Class pulldown menu to appear, as shown in Figure 12.45. These menus work in the usual manner, with a light-bar: use cursor arrow keys to highlight the desired line and press the enter key to select it. For example, if you select **COPY** on the Class menu, a display of copy members will replace the display of RCM macros, as shown in Figure 12.46. The Type menu additionally offers an entry for keyword search.

You can scroll up and down in the list of assets with the paging and cursor arrow keys. You can also move quickly to the desired letter of the alphabet by pressing that letter key. Pressing the same letter key more than once will step through the assets that begin with that letter. For example, to highlight the first entry beginning with T, press the T key once. To highlight the next entry, press the T key again or use the down arrow key.

Retrieving and using RCM assets. The entire RCM panel works as a scrolling light-bar selection menu for choosing the asset you want to retrieve. You highlight the desired asset and press the enter key. However, retrieving an asset can have different meanings depending on the class of that asset. Retrieving a COPY member lets you look at the member and insert a correctly formatted COPY statement into your program. Retrieving a subroutine or a macro is similar in that RCM prompts you to build the right CALL statement or macro statement. RCM inserts the resulting statement into your program, at the line above the cursor line. Retrieving a model is somewhat different, because it involves supplying parameters to expand the model into a separate output file. For example, this output file can be a COBOL program that you can check or compile.

Figure 12.47 shows a COBOL program supplied with RCM as part of a tutorial. If you place the cursor at the beginning of the line that says PERFORM DISPLAY-TITLES, and then invoke RCM to insert a line, the line will go just above that PERFORM statement.

Suppose you want to insert a macro call for SORT-TABLE. Figure 12.48 shows a **F3=details** display of that macro. You can page up and down in the display. To select the macro, press the Escape key to get back to the main RCM panel and then press the Enter key. This will bring up a parameter entry screen, as shown in Figure 12.49. The parameters you enter will appear in the completed macro statement for SORT-TABLE, as shown in Figure 12.50.

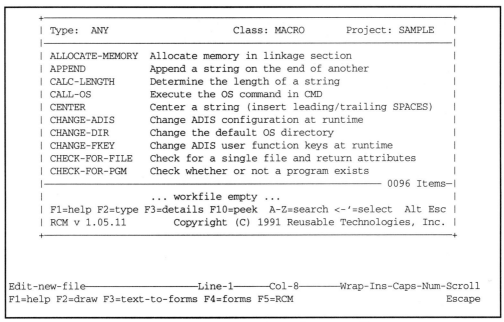

Figure 12.44 RCM Locator/Selector Facility

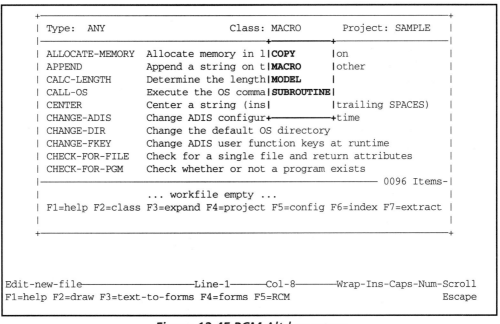

Figure 12.45 RCM Alt-key menu

```
+----------------------------------------------------------------+
|                                                                |
| Type:  ANY              Class: COPY         Project: SAMPLE    |
|----------------------------------------------------------------|
| A1PRT132 .CPY    Working Storage for PRINT132 macro           |
| A1PRT80  .CPY    Working Storage for PRINT80 macro            |
| A1PRT96  .CPY    Working Storage for PRINT96 macro            |
| A1WSDATE .CPY    Working Storage for DATE-AND-TIME macro      |
| FILEAREA .CPY    File control linkage area for demo programs  |
| MF_ADIS  .CPY    Copy automatically included with CHANGE-ADIS |
| MF_BYTST .CPY    Copy for byte-stream file processing macros  |
| MF_COLOR .CPY    Copy used by macros that address color attributes |
| MF_FKEY  .CPY    Copy automatically included with CHANGE-FKEY |
| MF_HEAP  .CPY    Copy for heap processing                     |
|------------------------------------------------------ 0018 Items-|
|                 ... workfile empty ...                        |
| F1=help F2=type F3=details F10=peek  A-Z=search -+=select  Alt Esc |
|                                                                |
+----------------------------------------------------------------+


Edit-new-file————————————————Line-1————Col-8————————Wrap-Ins-Caps-Num-Scroll
F1=help F2=draw F3=text-to-forms F4=forms F5=RCM                      Escape
```

Figure 12.46 RCM copy member display

```
      SPECIAL-NAMES. CONSOLE IS CRT CURSOR IS CUR-POS.
      WORKING-STORAGE SECTION.

      01  CUR-POS                    PIC 9(04) VALUE ZEROES.

      WS-TABLE TTL with 20 rows
      WS 07 TTL-NAME pic X(50)

      PROCEDURE DIVISION.

          CLEAR-SCREEN

          PERFORM LOAD-TITLES.

          PERFORM DISPLAY-TITLES
              VARYING TTL-NDX FROM 1 BY 1
              UNTIL   TTL-NDX  TTL-MAX.

          STOP RUN.

Edit-RCMTUTOR————————65-lines————Line-15————Col-8————————Wrap-Ins-Caps-Num-Scroll
F1=help F2=COBOL F3=insert-line F4=delete-line F5=repeat-line F6=restore-line
F7=retype-char F8=restore-char F9=word-left F10=word-right      Alt Ctrl Escape
```

Figure 12.47 Program supplied with RCM tutorial

```
     +--------------------------------------------------------------+
     | Type: TABLE              Class: MACRO      Project: SAMPLE  |
+------------------------------------------------------------------+
| SORT-TABLE               Details                   _SRT-TBL.MAC |
+------------------------------------------------------------------+
TITLE *Sort the rows of a standard table on a key.

TYPE  *TABLE

SYNTAX*SORT-TABLE %1 on %2 %3 [until %4]

DESC  *This macro sorts a standard WS-TABLE into ASC or DESC order
      *on a specified key.  The sort is performed in memory.  It will
      *be fastest if a STOP-VAL is specified.  When this STOP-VAL is
      *encountered in the table, the order of the rest of the table
      *will be ignored.  NOTE: A SORT-TABLE statement may take a long time
      *to Animate using Step — Perform-Step will be somewhat faster.
+-$RCMUSR\RCM-BASE.LBR------------------------------------ 0080 Lines-+
| F1=help F2=edit Home/End PgUp/PgDn ^ v              <-'=select Esc |
|                                                                    |
+--------------------------------------------------------------------+
Edit-RCMTUTOR--------65-lines--------Line-15--------Col-8--------Wrap-Ins-Caps-Num-Scroll
F1=help F2=draw F3=text-to-forms F4=forms F5=RCM                    Escape
```

Figure 12.48 RCM Details for SORT-TABLE macro

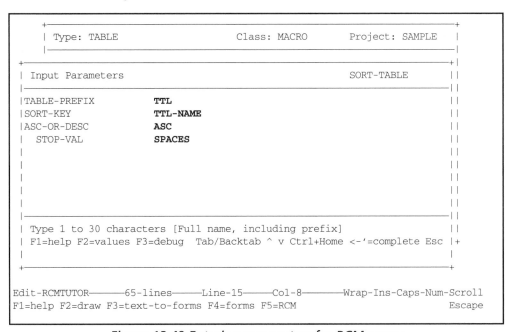

Figure 12.49 Entering parameters for RCM macro

```
        SPECIAL-NAMES. CONSOLE IS CRT CURSOR IS CUR-POS.

        WORKING-STORAGE SECTION.

        01  CUR-POS                    PIC 9(04) VALUE ZEROES.

        WS-TABLE TTL with 20 rows
        WS 07 TTL-NAME pic X(50)

        PROCEDURE DIVISION.

            CLEAR-SCREEN

            PERFORM LOAD-TITLES.

            SORT-TABLE TTL on TTL-NAME ASC until SPACES
            PERFORM DISPLAY-TITLES
                VARYING TTL-NDX FROM 1 BY 1
                UNTIL   TTL-NDX   TTL-MAX.

            STOP RUN.
Edit-RCMTUTOR———66-lines———Line-17———Col-12———Wrap-Ins-Caps-Num-Scroll
F1=help F2=COBOL F3=insert-line F4=delete-line F5=repeat-line F6=restore-line
F7=retype-char F8=restore-char F9=word-left F10=word-right     Alt Ctrl Escape
```

Figure 12.50 Sample program with RCM macro call

Creating new modules in your library. All of the RCM assets represent reusable source code or the parameter files used to generate source code. Even if you are dealing with subroutines, you use RCM to generate the subroutine CALL statements in your source code. The subroutine object code is kept in your link library or executable library, not under RCM.

Putting new assets into the RCM library involves a certain amount of effort. It is advisable to assign one person to coordinate that task. This person should identify the most up-to-date version of each source module. For copy library members, the task is simple. You need only put them into a subdirectory and then specify that directory name in the RCM.CFG file. To add a title and assign a type to each copy library member, you can bring up RCM from the Workbench Editor and go into Edit/Verify/Update mode to update each entry. You can reach this mode by scrolling to the desired member and pressing **F3=details** and then **F2=edit.**

To create other classes of assets, RCM needs appropriate header information. Select the desired class and then use the **Alt+F7=extract** function to create a new RCM library member from a template provided by the system. From there, you can go into Edit/Verify/Update mode to supply the particulars. You also can use the Micro Focus COBOL Editor or another ASCII editor to modify the file containing this asset.

To create a macro or a model, you start by identifying a routine or an entire program that lends itself to being generalized. If you intend to call the routine from within another program, you will want to create a macro. Otherwise, if you want to generalize your program to make other programs from it, you will want to create a model. The next step is to substitute RCM variables for each word in the source code asset that can take different values when the asset is reused. Finally, before making the new asset available to other programmers, use the Verify function to check its syntax, and test the code it generates in an actual program.

For more information. RCM is sold and supported by Micro Focus, Inc. Contact Micro Focus directly for technical support or to license copies of RCM for use at your site.

Micro Focus, Inc.
2465 East Bayshore Rd., Suite 400
Palo Alto CA 94303
Voice: (415) 856–4161, Fax (415) 856–6134

The SPF Editor

13.1 Why Use the SPF Editor?

You may ask, "Why use the SPF Editor when the Micro Focus Editor has so many features?" It's a matter of personal choice. Many MVS mainframe programmers already have years of experience working with the ISPF/PDF (Interactive Systems Productivity Facility/Program Development Facility) full screen editor. The browse and edit features of ISPF work equally well with source code and data files. So does the SPF editor for the PC. The PC SPF editor is always available. There's no downtime for mainframe system testing or mainframe system crashes. Once programmers have become proficient with the ISPF editor, they may be reluctant to change.

A good example of this came to light during the 1991 Micro Focus Users Conference in Orlando, Florida. The Micro Focus text editor was the topic of an evening special-interest group meeting. Most of the comments were directed toward making the Micro Focus editor more like the ISPF/PDF mainframe editor. The mainframe people in the group overwhelmingly preferred the SPF interface on the PC. This was noteworthy because the Micro Focus text editor, when used with the Workbench, offers some functionality that the SPF editors on the PC do not. For example, the Micro Focus Editor lets you expand copy library members while you are writing source code. The SPF editor does not. With version 2.5 of the Micro Focus Workbench, the Micro Focus Editor supports a mouse, while the SPF editor does not. For these reasons, PC programmers not accustomed to mainframe ISPF/PDF might prefer the Micro Focus COBOL Editor or the newer Micro Focus GUI Source Code Manager.

Meeting the need. Command Technology Corporation (CTC) provides two products for those MVS programmers who prefer an ISPF-like editor on their PC. SPF/PC is the editor for the MS-DOS or PC-DOS environment. It is intended for XT-class (Intel 8086 or 8088) or AT-class (80286) machines. (The Micro Focus Workbench, however, requires an 80286 machine or better to run.)

SPF/2 is the editor for 80386-class or better machines. It will run under MS-DOS, PC-DOS, or OS/2. Both editors, SPF/PC and SPF/2, contain most of the features you are familiar with on the mainframe. SPF/2 even supports REXX, IBM's command language that replaced CLISTs. Mainframe programmers already familiar with ISPF can begin using either SPF/PC or SPF/2 immediately.

SPF/PC is a subset of SPF/2. While SPF/PC will still be supported and sold as an entry-level product, all new features will be added to the SPF/2 product. Installation for both products is identical. Either product can be run as a non-Windows application under Windows 3.x. The remainder of this chapter will concern itself primarily with the features of SPF/2.

Purpose of this chapter. We will assume that you already know the ISPF/PDF commands from the mainframe, so we will not repeat the command syntax here. Instead, this chapter will show how to set up and configure the SPF/2 editor for the PC. It will show how to use those additional SPF/2 features on the PC that do not exist on the mainframe.

13.2 The SPF/PC and SPF/2 Menu Systems

13.2.1 Hierarchy of Functions

Many MVS shops have customized their ISPF menu system by adding features specific to that site. Your SPF/PC or SPF/2 menus may not look exactly the same as menus on your mainframe terminal. However, the user interface, particularly the directory and editing functions, work similarly. Figure 13.1 shows the SPF/PC Primary Option Menu, while Figure 13.2 shows the SPF/2 Primary Option Menu.

13.2.2 Using SPF/PC and SPF/2 with the PC File System

Both editors let you select files across drives, directories, and subdirectories. (See Appendix A for a discussion of the PC file system.) Like the mainframe editor, SPF remembers your last entry. In effect, these editors make the PC file system look like the mainframe file system as you would see it through the ISPF/PDF interface.

13.3 SPF/2 Setup

13.3.1 Installing SPF/2

Installation for SPF/2 is simple and straightforward. Place the installation diskette into your "A" drive and type "A:\install". Then press the ENTER key. During installation, you can accept the default directory and drivename, or change them to match you particular company standards. Accepting the installation defaults also allows SPF/2 to update your CONFIG.SYS file.

SPF/2 executes different programs at runtime, depending on whether you run it under OS/2 or under MS-DOS. Both programs are in the SPF2 directory created during installation. However, SPF2.EXE is the OS/2 version, while SPF386.EXE is the MS-DOS version.

13.3.2 Interfacing SPF/2 with the Workbench

As a COBOL programmer you'll want to know how to use the SPF/2 editor with the Workbench. This section will explore the possibilities.

```
SPF/PC1  331K ──────────── PRIMARY OPTION MENU ──────────── VER 02.10
OPTION ===>
                                                     USERID   - IBMPC
   0  SPF/PC PARMS - Specify terminal and user parameters    TIME     - 01:06
   1  BROWSE       - Display source data or output listings  TERMINAL - IBM
   2  EDIT         - Create or change source data            PF KEYS  - 48
   3  UTILITIES    - Perform SPF/PC utility functions
   4  FOREGROUND   - Invoke language processors in foreground
   5  SYSTEM INFO  - Display system information
   6  COMMAND      - Execute DOS commands
   C  CHANGES      - Display summary of changes for this release
   H  HELP         - Display information about SPF/PC
   U  USER         - Invoke user applications
   X  EXIT         - Terminate SPF/PC
Press [F3]  to terminate SPF/PC



        +────────────────────────────────────────────────────+
        |     (C)COPYRIGHT COMMAND TECHNOLOGY CORPORATION 1983-89     |
        |              ALL RIGHTS RESERVED                   |
        |          UNAUTHORIZED DUPLICATION PROHIBITED        |
        +────────────────────────────────────────────────────+
```

Figure 13.1 SPF/PC Primary Option Menu

```
─────────────────────── SPF/2 PRIMARY OPTION PANEL ───────────────
OPTION  ===>
                                                     USERID   - CTC
   0  SPF/2 PARMS - Specify terminal and user parameters    TIME    - 00:48
   1  BROWSE       - Display source data or output listings  PF KEYS - 48
   2  EDIT         - Create or change source data
   3  UTILITIES    - Perform utility functions
   4  FOREGROUND   - Invoke user applications in foreground
   6  COMMAND      - Execute system command
   C  CHANGES      - Changes from last version
   T  TUTORIAL     - Display information about SPF/2
   X  EXIT         - Terminate SPF/2

Enter END command to terminate SPF/2.

2.0.1 (C) COPYRIGHT COMMAND TECHNOLOGY CORP 1990, 1991
```

Figure 13.2 SPF/2 Primary Option Menu under MS-DOS

The "default" method. The simplest way, but the least effective, is simply to use SPF/2 as a standalone editor under MS-DOS. Place your source code in whatever PC subdirectory you use for source code, edit it through SPF/2, save it, terminate SPF/2, and get into the Workbench for checking and animating.

Separate Windows sessions. If you're using Microsoft Windows 3.0 or better, you can set up both SPF/2 and the Workbench to run as separate sessions under Windows. This lets you switch between them without having to terminate either application. Both SPF/2 and the Workbench function key menu system are text-mode, non-Windows applications. (In other words, they do not require Windows to run.) You can set up a .PIF file to run a non-Windows application in a Windows session. On the other hand, Windows applications use icons and .INI files instead of .PIF files. The new graphical user interface Workbench facilities can be run as Windows applications. The installation script will load all the files you need, including the icons and .INI files. Once you have both the SPF/2 editor and the Workbench installed under Windows, you can run both at once. After you have checked a program under the Workbench, you can use the split screen feature of SPF/2 to look at error messages in one panel and edit source code in the other.

Separate OS/2 sessions. Under OS/2, both SPF/2 and the Workbench run as OS/2 applications in separate sessions. You could use work methods similar to those that we just described for Windows. In this case, you could set up program icons for SPF/2 and for the Workbench within the OS/2 v1.3 Program Manager or the OS/2 v2.0 Desktop.

Since OS/2 supports the REXX command language, SPF/2 lets you use REXX macros when you run it under OS/2. A REXX macro, **MFCOMP,** entered on the SPF/2 command line, invokes the Micro Focus checker and checks the file you are currently editing. After checking is complete, error messages come back into the SPF/2 editor along with your source code. Each error message appears highlighted immediately above the line in error. You don't have to delete those messages. Just correct your syntax errors, save your source file, and issue the MFCOMP command again.

Adding SPF/2 to the Workbench menus. On diskette documentation accompanying SPF/2 describes a method of installing SPF/2 as a selection under the Micro Focus function key menu system. CTC provides a substitute function key menu (.MNU) file that contains a call to SPF/2 instead of the Micro Focus editor. At present, the version of the .MNU file supplied with SPF/2 2.0 supports only the WDE, not the MDE. Therefore, you might be better off creating your own .MNU file for the MDE environment and modifying it to invoke SPF/2 from an unused function key. For further details on customizing .MNU files, see Chapter 11.

If you're invoking SPF/2 from the Workbench under MS-DOS or Windows, you'll need to adjust memory usage. When you bring up the Workbench with the XM WB command, XM by default claims all the extended memory above the 1 megabyte line, leaving none for SPF/2. Thus, on an eight megabyte machine, XM will claim seven megabytes for the Workbench, which it doesn't need. You can limit the amount of memory available to XM by means of the /Z run-time switch. Changing your XM WB command to XM /Z4096 WB will limit the Workbench memory manager to four megabytes.

Under Windows, you may need to increase memory allocation in WB.PIF. Set the minimum allocation to 2MB and the maximum to 4MB. Improper memory allocation under Windows will result in paging errors (UAEs) or extremely slow response.

The AD/MVS menu system. Another possibility would be to use the AD/MVS menu system, described in Chapter 12. AD/MVS is is a separate product available from Micro Focus/Stingray Software. It runs both SPF/2 and Workbench functions from a mainframelike ISPF/PDF primary option menu.

```
———————————————————————— CHANGES IN VERSION 2.0 ————————————————
OPTION ===>

  This is of SPF/2 Version 2.0 from Command Technology Corporation.  Some
  of the changes since SPF/PC 2.1 or SPF/2 1.0 include:

     1.  Both DOS and OS/2 Compatible    16.  File Name Normalization
     2.  Maximum Record Length           17.  ISREDIT Short/Long Message
     3.  EBCDIC Editing                  18.  3.x Super Lists
     4.  Logical Printer Setup           19.  New File List Line Commands
     5.  Enhanced Foreground Panel       20.  Block Commands in Super Lists
     6.  DATA Primary Command            21.  INCLUDE / EXCLUDE in File Lists
     7.  DEFINE Primary Command          22.  Disable Data Shift
     8.  Compiler Error Parsing          23.  Text Highlighting
     9.  SEARCH File List Command        24.  Cursor Size Settings
    10.  SEARCH Abort                    25.  Screen Height Adjustment
    11.  MD, MDD, MDMD Line Commands     26.  XMACRO Exit Macro
    12.  Automatic Profile Migration     27.  Macro Access to PF Keys
    13.  Extended 3270 Emulation         28.  Count Save
    14.  Keyboard Typematic Adjustment   29.  Directory Maintenance
    15.  Row / Column Indicators



              (Press END key to return to main menu)
```

Figure 13.3 Screen showing changes in SPF/2 version 2.0

13.4 New Features of SPF/2 Version 2.0

13.4.1 Overview of New Features

Because the PC workstation is more powerful than a mainframe terminal, SPF/2 contains options that put these PC features to work for you. However, if you're not comfortable with these features, you can get by with using only the commands that exist on the mainframe. Figure 13.3 is a help screen that lists new SPF/2 features. You can obtain information about any feature by entering its number at the OPTION prompt.

13.4.2 Keyboard Mapping

One new SPF/2 option is **keyboard mapping.** There are three mapping options available. You can set up your keyboard to resemble an AT-style keyboard, a 101-key enhanced keyboard, or a 3270 keyboard. Simply pressing the ENTER key on an AT-style keyboard does not execute an entered command, it moves the cursor to the next line. So how can you get the enter key function? If you have selected an AT-style keyboard, you can do the following:

- Use the PLUS key from the numeric keypad, or
- Hold down the CTRL key while pressing the ENTER key to execute a command.

   There are more choices when using a 101-key enhanced keyboard:

- Use the right CTRL key, or
- Use the ENTER key on the numeric keypad, or

```
EDIT   K:\COBOL\MFWBBOOK\LOTTERY.CBL ───────────────── COLUMNS 001 072
COMMAND ===>                                            SCROLL ─── CSR
****** *************************** TOP OF DATA ***************************
000001         **************************************************************
000002         *                                                          *
000003         *                (C) Cogito Corporation 1991               *
000004         *                                                          *
000005         *                     LOTTERY.CBL                          *
000006         *                                                          *
000007         *     This program creates lottery wheels for Illinois     *
000008         *     Little Lotto                                         *
000009         *                                                          *
000010         **************************************************************
000011         identification division.
000012         program-id. Lottery.
000013         environment division.
000014         configuration section.
000015         source-computer. ibm-pc.
000016         object-computer. ibm-pc.
000017        *special-names.
000018        *console is crt.
000019         data division.
000020         working-storage section.
000021         01 seven-numbers.
```

Figure 13.4 SPF/2 screen showing text highlighting feature

- Hold down the left CTRL key while pressing the ENTER key to execute a command.

If you select a 3270-style keyboard, pressing the ENTER key executes the command that was entered. You can configure ENTER key behavior on SPF/2 options menu 0.1. *Note, however, that SPF/2 provides only the three keyboard mapping options mentioned above. You cannot arbitrarily reassign keys.*

The keyboard configuration also determines how many PF key combinations will be available to SPF/2. There are 48 PF keys available on the enhanced keyboard, but only 40 PF keys available on the AT-style keyboard.

Another new feature is the ability to edit in EBCDIC. Because PCs are ASCII machines, downloaded test data would normally have to be converted to ASCII. Since the Workbench can run COBOL programs that use EBCDIC data, SPF/2 now has the ability to edit your EBCDIC test data. Thus data files copied from the mainframe to the PC do not have to be converted to ASCII.

13.4.3 Text Highlighting

Text highlighting is a feature of SPF/2 not found on mainframe ISPF. This feature does not affect the text file itself, but only the way text is displayed on the screen. In a COBOL program, SPF/2 text highlighting looks for an asterisk in column 7 of your source text. Once SPF/2 identifies a comment line, it will highlight the remainder of the text to the end of that line. You can even set a highlight color. In 'C', 'C++', and 'PASCAL' program text, the comment character sequence starts the highlighting. You can even specify which column the highlight character appears in. This feature is very useful when scrolling through a program looking for comments. Figure 13.4 shows an editing screen with comment lines highlighted.

13.4.4 Super Lists

Option 18 on Figure 13.3 is **super lists.** This is a powerful utility not found on mainframe ISPF/PDF. This feature allows you to create a search list in almost any way you can image. The search list can span drives, search for text

strings, search directories or files or both, and do recursive searches. Not only that, using the super list feature, you can build the search list in any combination of the above items! Once the search list is created, you can save it for later use. When working with the search list, you can use some primary commands such as Include, Exclude, Search and Savelist, as well as the editor line and block commands. If your search extends across more than one drive, files found on different drives will display in contrasting colors.

Do you need tools to keep better track of your files?

Where possible, use your own knowledge to narrow your search criteria. Overly broad text searches can be most time-consuming and can return data other than what you had in mind.

Figure 13.5 shows the file and search utility selection menu. In this instance, we have chosen a complex search. This allows us to use multiple types of search criteria within the same search operation. Figure 13.6 shows the screen for entering complex search criteria. The example shown on this screen will search all directories on the **J:** and **K:** drives for files containing the character string **exedll.** Case sensitivity is turned off, so that the search will locate any upper-, lower-, or mixed-case representations of that character string. Figure 13.7 shows the search results.

```
———————————————————————— UTILITY SELECTION MENU ————————————————————————
OPTION  ===> C

   3   MOVE/COPY          -  Move or copy files
   4   FILE LIST          -  Display file names for selection

   A   DIRECTORY SEARCH - Build list of directories
   B   FILE SEARCH        -  Build list of files by name pattern
   C   TEXT SEARCH        -  Build list of files by text search
   D   COMPLEX SEARCH     -  Build list of files from multiple search criteria
   E   DRIVE SEARCH       -  Build list of files from drive list
   F   SAVED LISTS        -  Display list of saved lists.
```

Figure 13.5 SPF/2 search selection menu

```
——————————————————————— SUPER LIST: COMPLEX SEARCH ———————————————————————

COMMAND ===>


SYSTEM CUR DIR: K:\SPF2

FILE TYPES TO DISPLAY ===> B  (D = Directories, F = Files, B = Both)

SEARCH SUBDIRECTORIES ===> Y  (Y = yes, N = no)

PATH ===> J:\*.*
PATH ===> K:\*.*
PATH ===>
PATH ===>


TEXT ===> exedll                                    CASE SENSE => N
TEXT ===>                                            CASE SENSE => N
TEXT ===>                                            CASE SENSE => N
TEXT ===>                                            CASE SENSE => N
```

Figure 13.6 SPF/2 Super List complex search menu

```
——————————————————————— FILE SELECTION LIST ———————————————————————
COMMAND ===>                                      SCROLL ===> PAGE
J:\
  NAME                        SIZE      DATE      TIME

  K:\COBOL\SOURCE             <DIR>     6-22-91    9:45p
  K:\DATATOOL                 <DIR>     1-18-92    1:02a
  K:\ISPF                     <DIR>    12-12-91    8:39p
  K:\ISPMLIB                  <DIR>    12-12-91    8:40p
  K:\ISPPLIB                  <DIR>    12-12-91    8:39p
  K:\ISPPROF                  <DIR>    12-12-91    8:40p
  K:\MVS                      <DIR>    12-13-91   10:50p
  K:\SPF2                     <DIR>     9-19-91    8:46p
  K:\SPFPC                    <DIR>    11-02-91    4:52p
  K:\XMF370                   <DIR>     1-31-92   11:56p
  J:\COBOL\LBR\MFINS.ENV       6326     1-31-92    5:03p
  J:\COBOL\LOADWB.CMD           906     1-31-92    4:09p
  J:\COBOL\MFINS.LOG          34552     1-31-92    5:03p
  J:\COBOL\SET25.CMD            443     1-31-92    5:30p
  J:\COBOL\SET26.CMD            443     1-31-92    4:21p
  K:\COBOL\DOCS\WB-RN.DOC     30483     4-08-91    5:18a
  K:\COBOL\EXEDLL\SESSION.$$$   256     1-03-92   11:42p
  K:\COBOL\EXEDLL\TICTAC.KTX    781     1-03-92   12:18a
  K:\COBOL\EXEDLL\TICTAC.KYS    256     1-03-92   12:18a
```

Figure 13.7 SPF/2 Super List complex search results

13.5 Tailoring SPF/2

13.5.1 SPF/2 Options Menu

As in mainframe ISPF/PDF, option 0 (zero) on the main menu takes you to the menus for configuring the SPF environment. Figure 13.8 shows the SPF/2 Parameter Options menu.

- **1 TERMINAL** specifies terminal characteristics, such as enter key behavior.
- **2 PRINTER** specifies the printer type and page size.
- **3 PF KEYS** assigns commands to PF keys, as on the mainframe.
- **4 DISPLAY** selects screen display colors and highlighting.
- **5 OPTIONS** defines miscellaneous options. These include defaults for whether text searches should be case sensitive, and whether the cursor should wrap or scroll at screen boundaries.
- **6 PROF DEFAULTS** sets up a default template for creating new profiles.
- **7 PROFILES** creates editing profiles for different file types.

13.5.2 Profiles

By using profiles, you can configure the SPF/2 editor to work differently for different file types. Each profile applies to a filename extension. The NULL profile applies to those filenames lacking an extension. Figure 13.9 shows the profile for .CBL files.

The profile tells SPF/2 whether the file is ASCII or EBCDIC, how records are delimited, whether to highlight comment lines in the screen display, and whether to expand or compress tab characters when loading or saving the file. The input options refer to the process of loading the file into the editing work area. The output options refer to the process of saving the file.

```
———————————————————————— SPF/2 PARAMETER OPTIONS  ————————————————————————
OPTION  ===>

    1   TERMINAL       - Specify terminal characteristics
    2   PRINTER        - Specify printer characteristics
    3   PF KEYS        - Specify Program Function Key values
    4   DISPLAY        - Specify screen display characteristics
    5   OPTIONS        - Specify SPF/2 Environment Options
    6   PROF DEFAULTS  - Specify defaults for new profiles
    7   PROFILES       - Display, change, or delete profiles
```

Figure 13.8 SPF/2 Parameter Options menu

```
──────────────────────── PROFILE DEFINITION ────────────────────────

COMMAND ===>

PROFILE NAME            : CBL
MAXIMUM RECORD LENGTH   ===> 80   (1 - 4096)
CHARACTER SET           ===> A    (A- ASCII, E-EBCDIC)

INPUT RECORD FORMAT     ===> D    (D- Data delimited, L- Length delimited)
   LINE TERMINATOR      ===> CRLF (CR, LF, or CRLF)
   FILE TERMINATOR      ===> Y    (Y- Yes/stop at EOF char, N- No/entire size)
   TAB EXPAND AT        ===> 8    (0- Ignore tabs, 0 rep tabs with blanks)

OUTPUT RECORD FORMAT    ===> D    (D- Data delimited, L- Length delimited)
   LINE TERMINATOR      ===> CRLF (CR, LF, or CRLF)
   FILE TERMINATOR      ===> Y    (Y- Yes/set EOF char, N- No/set size only)
   TAB INSERT AT        ===> 0    (0- No tab insert, 0 rep blanks with tabs)
   PAD RIGHT W/BLANKS   ===> N    (Y- Yes/fill to max rec length, N- No/don't)

SAVE ON COUNT           ===> 0    (0- none, n- number of enters before save)
BACKUP ON SAVE          ===> N    (Y- Yes/copy old to *.BAK, N- No/overwrite)
CHANGE DATA SHIFT       ===> Y    (Y- Yes use ISPF Data Shift, N- No)
HIGHLIGHT CHARACTERS    ===> *    (1 or 2 characters to start highlighting)
HIGHLIGHT COLUMN        ===> 7    (Specific column number or 0 = any)
```

Figure 13.9 SPF/2 Profile Definition menu

The Graphical User Interface Workbench Organizer

14.1 Reducing the Intimidation Factor

With Workbench v3.0, Micro Focus introduced graphical user interface (GUI) Workbench support. The main menu for the GUI facilities is called the Organizer. You can customize the Organizer more easily than you can the Workbench function key menu.

The design of the Organizer is based on object-oriented principles. If you aren't familiar with object-oriented programming concepts, don't worry. **You don't need to know anything about object orientation to use the new Workbench menu environment. The Organizer is more powerful than the function key menu, but it is still a menu system for accessing data and programs.** It is more powerful because you can run both GUI and text-mode programs from it, and because you can customize it more easily and more extensively. The term "object-oriented," in this context, merely refers to the fact that the Workbench Organizer was written with the aid of object-oriented concepts and technology. We will show you how to use the new menu system to run any type of application, object-oriented or conventional: Workbench functions, add-on products, your own COBOL applications, or just about anything else.

You are not forced to go through the new menu system to run graphics-mode Workbench functions. You can run all GUI Workbench functions separately from the OS/2 command line or, in later releases, from Windows icons, much as you can run function-key Workbench utilities directly from the MS-DOS or OS/2 command line prompts.

On the other hand, if you do know something about object orientation, you will better appreciate the usefulness and flexibility of the Organizer environment introduced with version 3.0. For those who like to know what's happening "under the covers," the next section will introduce you to the purpose and basic concepts of object orientation.

A disclaimer: As this book went to press, not all GUI Workbench functions were completely implemented. Microsoft Windows support was not yet available. Production versions may differ in certain respects from what is shown in Chapters 14, 15, and 16. At press time, the Workbench Organizer was not yet in production (full release) status. Micro Focus often licenses new products in *early release* or *initial release* status to customers who want them. Micro Focus licenses early release products only for the purposes of testing and familiarization, not for production use. Early release participants are encouraged to provide feedback and suggestions. While the early release products have been through the beta test process, Micro Focus reserves the right to change them. In particular, Micro Focus does *not* guarantee that the production release will have the same features or work exactly the same way as the early release products.

An initial release product is a different matter. All of the features present in an initial release product will be carried over into the full release product. New features may be added later in the form of updates. Since initial release products might not be fully stabilized, Micro Focus suggests that they not be used for critical applications.

14.2 Workbench Organizer Concepts

14.2.1 What Object Orientation Means

Object orientation distinguished from GUI. Before we explain these concepts, let us clear up some confusion of terminology. **Object orientation is not the same as graphical user interface (GUI) processing.** Object orientation (OO) is a way of looking at the work that you do: the objects that you use, and the actions that you perform on those objects. A graphical user interface (GUI, pronounced "gooey"), is a way of displaying information to the user that takes advantage of modern pointing devices and bit-mapped screen displays. It's easy to get confused because OO applications generally have a graphical user interface. However, many GUI applications do not rely on object-oriented technology.

Limitations of conventional design. Conventional applications designers thought of data as being separate from the programs and processes that acted upon them. Files contained only the raw data, and programs contained all of the logic and intelligence needed for interpreting that data. Databases provided indexes and pointers that allowed programmers or interactive users to navigate from one record to another; however, the meaning of that data appeared only in the program logic or in the intelligence and skills of the interactive user.

This artificial separation between data and logic proved to be too limiting. Storing processing logic along with the data enforces consistency and prevents duplication of effort. One obvious example is a database management system that keeps tables of editing rules and data integrity constraints along with the data, so that you don't have to write separate programs or routines. You do not have to rely on every application program to call the correct set of routines; it's handled by the DBMS. The same program might even be able to work with another database that has the same structure, but somewhat different rules. Let us make it clear that this is not a full-blown implementation of object-oriented technology, only a step in that direction.

Objects and messages. In the object-oriented view, the data, and the intelligence having to do with the meaning and purpose of that data, are viewed as a unified whole: an **object.** This form of information-hiding is known as **encapsulation.** In engineering terms, the object is a "black box": external processes can interact with it if they know what input it uses and what types of output will result. External processes need only send messages to the object and receive responses from it. They do not have to know anything about what goes on inside the black box. Encapsulation provides more independence between modules, so that you can ignore the internal workings of the other modules with which your program will be interacting.

The versatility of objects. A given object can perform different tasks depending on the input, or message, you give it. Conversely, different objects can interpret the same message in different ways. For example, sending a PRINT message to a payroll check object will cause it to print a pay check. Sending a PRINT message to an on-line help system object will cause it to print a listing of help text. This variable behavior is called **polymorphism.** Each object contains **methods** that tell it how to handle the PRINT message or any other valid message it might get. In other words, objects are smart enough to recognize different types of input and handle them appropriately.

New objects from old. A good object-oriented development system will let you establish **classes** of objects and create new objects from existing ones. The new instance of the object will **inherit** all of the properties of its parent, unless you specify exceptions to this. Experienced programmers are all familiar with the process of cloning new applications from old ones. Object-oriented utilities can help you automate that process.

Recursion. An object-oriented language contains one other feature: it lets you write a **recursive** routine; that is, a routine that calls itself. A routine that calls itself must be reentrant. For each iteration of the routine, any passed parameters and work areas must be kept on a separate level of a stack. Thus it becomes possible to reenter the same program from the top before the previous iteration has completed.

The scope of the Organizer. The Organizer was written to implement OO concepts in its own conceptual scheme and user interface. The Organizer lets you run your own applications from its object-oriented menu system. However, it does not by itself provide a complete OO COBOL application development environment based on the use of an object-oriented programming language. For that, you will need an object-oriented COBOL language compiler. Micro Focus Corporation is participating in the development of standards for OO extensions to the COBOL language. In fact, the Organizer was written with the aid of internal prototype versions of OO COBOL tools.

The **Micro Focus Object Oriented COBOL Developer's Toolkit** became available in early release status in March 1992. It contains support for the proposed versions of the OO COBOL language extensions so that you can familiarize yourself with them for PC applications development. You will not be able to port source code containing OO COBOL language extensions back to the mainframe until mainframe OO COBOL compilers become available.

Contact Micro Focus Corporation regarding availability of the PC-based OO COBOL product.

Reusable Code Manager. RCM is a utility that uses object-oriented principles to speed the time-honored task of cloning new programs from combinations of existing routines and logic structures. It offers you a painless introduction to the use of object-oriented methods in COBOL applications development. You can use RCM to manage source code in the conventional ANSI standard COBOL language as well as source code that uses the proposed object-oriented language extensions. You can also use it to generate other types of source modules, such as mainframe JCL. Micro Focus Corporation offers RCM as an add-on product, with versions for both the function key and GUI Workbench. RCM will also be a part of the new OO COBOL product family. Chapter 12 provides more detailed information about RCM.

14.2.2 Advantages of Graphical User Interface

For readers unfamiliar with GUI applications, Appendix A explains the difference between text-mode and graphics-mode screen displays. It also describes the two major PC-based GUI environments: Microsoft Windows and IBM OS/2. Let's look at the benefits of the GUI Workbench facilities as compared with the text-mode Workbench function key menu system:

- A well-designed GUI-based application presents a more attractive and readable display than does a text-mode application. Pop-up menus, dialog boxes, push buttons, and scroll boxes are easier to see in the GUI environment than when simulated in text mode applications. A variety of screen fonts and type sizes are available. Graphical icons allow quick selection of functions.
- The GUI environment itself makes efficient use of the space on your display screen and of your own time and effort. By running applications in separate windows, you can keep several work activities on your screen at once, so that you can switch easily from one activity to another without having to terminate any of them. Whenever you no longer need to see a particular window, you can shrink it down to an icon or overlap other windows in front of it. You can expand a window to full screen size or use scroll boxes to see hidden data. A few mouse movements let you load and save files, start and end programs, choose menu options, pick items from lists, and move and resize windows.
- A GUI environment allows expert programmers to write PC-based applications that run in graphics mode. These include PC-based GUI front-end applications that access mainframe databases over a network.

Are there any drawbacks to using GUI-based utilities? Because the computer is doing more for you, GUI-based utilities require somewhat more memory, disk space, and execution time than do text-mode utilities.

14.2.3 SAA CUA Concepts

In this section, we will introduce you to another aspect of the design philosophy that governs the new graphical user interface of the Workbench. While you can still use the Workbench without being aware of these underpinnings, an understanding of the purpose of CUA standards will help you better appreciate what you see.

The SAA CUA standards. In the past, there was no preferred way to set up screen layouts and assign function key behavior for interactive applications. Some installations had their own written standards, others did not. In shops that lacked written standards, programmers often tried to follow the design conventions of various old applications that terminal users already knew. If the shop also had purchased applications from outside vendors, then each vendor's software would have its own design conventions. This made it harder for terminal users to switch from one application to another.

To alleviate this problem, IBM recommends that all of its customers follow a set of standards for user interface design. This set of standards is called **common user access (CUA).** CUA is a part of IBM's **Systems Application Architecture (SAA)** strategy. SAA endeavors to provide a consistent programming environment across IBM's various hardware platforms. Many screens that accompany IBM's own software, and software from other vendors, are being redesigned to comply with CUA standards. Because Micro Focus participates in the AD/CYCLE program, Micro Focus GUI Workbench screens follow CUA standards.

The CUA standards are updated and refined periodically. CUA '89 standards define two levels: basic and advanced. The basic interface standards apply to text-mode applications such as those using 3270-compatible mainframe terminals or text-mode MS-DOS programs. The basic standards are covered in an IBM manual called *SAA CUA Basic Interface Design Guide*. The standard tells how the cursor should behave and what the application should do when various keys are pressed. Applications that follow the basic standard will implement some of the simpler screen control structures by using ASCII text on a color or monochrome display. You can use the basic standard as a guide for designing your own text-mode CICS or IMS/DC screens for mainframe applications development.

The advanced CUA interface standards refer to GUI applications. These were introduced in an IBM manual called *SAA CUA Advanced Interface Design Guide*. In 1991, this standard was further refined in two manuals, *SAA CUA Guide to User Interface Design* and *SAA CUA Advanced Interface Design Reference*. You should become familiar with the advanced CUA standards if you plan to write GUI applications for the Windows or OS/2 PM environments.

The CUA object-oriented workplace environment. The CUA '91 standards also define the **workplace environment,** as seen in the OS/2 2.0 Desktop. The workplace environment attempts to portray an electronic version of an actual workplace, with various classes of objects represented by icons. Other applications can run within the workplace environment.

Version 3.0 of the Micro Focus Workbench Organizer is based primarily on the CUA '89 standard, with some features from the CUA '91 standard. This is because this version of the Organizer is intended to run under both OS/2 1.3 and OS/2 2.0. OS/2 1.3 does not fully support all CUA '91 features. In

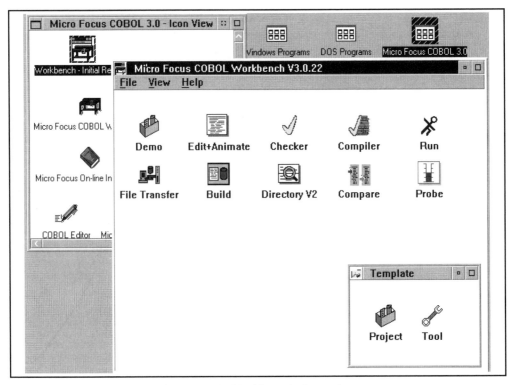

Figure 14.1 Workbench Organizer

addition, the Desktop in OS/2 2.0 contains some deviations from CUA standards. Where those deviations exist, the Workbench Organizer v3.0 is consistent with the OS/2 2.0 Desktop.

Objects and actions. Under CUA, the user works with menu options in **object-action** form. The objects appear in the central part of the menu (known as the **work area**) and the actions are listed in an **menu bar** on the top line of the menu. The user most often selects an existing object from a list by clicking on it with a mouse. Once this is done, the user selects an action by clicking on the appropriate action field on the menu bar, by clicking on a button, or by using a function key defined to invoke that same action.

Pull-down menus. Most applications support so many actions that it would be impractical for each to appear separately in the menu bar at the top of the panel. In that case, selecting a "main" action from the menu bar will cause a **pull-down menu** to appear immediately below the selected action. This pull-down menu is simply a boxed list showing "lower-level" actions. The user would then double-click on an item in the pull-down menu, or select a hotkey equivalent if it is provided.

Not all menus or menu options will be available at any given time, simply because they wouldn't make sense. For example, you can't animate a program that has never been checked. Selections that are not available are shown in gray to indicate that they are disabled.

In a CUA-compliant application, the first pull-down menu will be named after the class of object that the application uses. An application that deals primarily with files will have a **File** pull-down menu in the leftmost position on the menu bar. The exact contents of the File menu will vary depending on the nature of the application. Figure 14.1 shows the File pull-down menu in the Workbench Organizer, and Figure 15.3 in the following chapter shows the File pull-down menu in Animator V2.

The last selection on the first pull-down menu should always be **Exit**. Choosing Exit, of course, terminates the application.

Other CUA features. CUA supports other types of screen features. For example, each window or panel can have a variety of **controls,** such as scroll boxes, check boxes, radio buttons, push buttons, and window control buttons. **Dialog boxes,** sometimes called **secondary windows,** display a message or ask the user to enter data. Dialog boxes are superimposed over the main window. They handle temporary situations that don't belong on the permanent pull-down menus. **Help screens** are supported with similar logic. A help menu appears whenever the user presses the F1 key or selects the Help option on the menu bar. Tutorials, context-sensitive reference material, keyword indexes, and even help for using the help system are available from the Help pull-down menu. SAA CUA standards strongly recommend that programmers provide help screen support with their applications, whether in text or graphics mode.

14.2.4 Organizer Projects and Tools

The main menu of the Organizer handles two specific kinds of objects: **projects** and **tools.** Since the Organizer is intended for creating COBOL applications, a project is any COBOL source code module, a file, or a directory that forms "raw materials" for one or more of the tools. A tool is any executable module: Workbench utilities such as the Checker or the Data File Editor, your own executable applications, or third-party programs that you want to run from this menu. Each project and each tool has its own **icon,** not unlike those used in the Windows or OS/2 GUI desktop manager menu systems.

The strength of the Organizer menu system is the fact that it lets you associate other information with each object, such as default directives, command line parameters, and so forth. Furthermore, the system has intelligence built into it so that you can begin work by dragging a project icon with the *right* mouse button (instead of the usual *left* button) and dropping it onto a tool icon. This starts the tool working on that project. For example, if you drop a project icon for your source program onto the Checker icon, the Workbench will start checking your program with the directives you supplied.

14.3 Workbench Organizer Setup

14.3.1 Organizer System Requirements

The Organizer will run on systems with OS/2 1.3 or newer (including OS/2 2.0). You'll need one or two megabytes of memory beyond what the manufacturer recommends for running that version of OS/2 on your system. If your workstation has XGA high-resolution graphics support, the Organizer will take advantage of it.

The Organizer will also run as a Windows GUI application under Microsoft Windows 3.0 or newer.

14.3.2 Installing the Organizer

The Micro Focus SETUP script automatically installs the Organizer as a normal part of the installation procedure. It will ask you whether to create trigger programs and icons to make Workbench facilities available under OS/2. If you answer **Yes**, you will get a new group of icons for the function key menu Workbench and for several of the function key Workbench utilities, and you will also get an icon for the Organizer. A trigger program is simply a main routine associated with the OS/2 PM icon that starts the other routines needed to run the application.

14.3.3 Starting the Organizer

Micro Focus COBOL OS/2 icons. The Setup script will create separate OS/2 Desktop icons for the GUI Workbench Organizer, the GUI Workbench Tutorial, the function key menu Workbench, as well as the function key Animator, Compiler, Editor, Screens, and On-line Information System facilities. These icons will be in a *Micro Focus COBOL* program group or folder on the OS/2 Desktop. (Under OS/2 2.0, a *folder* is an object that contains other objects. When you open a folder by clicking on it, it becomes a window containing icons.) The *Micro Focus COBOL* folder appears in the background in Figure 14.1. The complete folder is visible in Figure A.5 in the Appendix.

Don't confuse the OS/2 icons within the *Micro Focus COBOL* folder with the icons that appear within the Organizer once it comes up. The Organizer is an object-oriented environment, not an OS/2 folder. Its icons represent objects that operate within that environment. Therefore, you cannot drag icons from the Organizer and deposit them onto the desktop.

Starting the Organizer from its icon. The most convenient way to bring up the Organizer is by clicking on the GUI Workbench icon provided during the installation procedure. When you do this, you will see a window labeled *Micro Focus COBOL Workbench,* followed by the current version number.

Using the command line interface. The following command will bring up the Organizer environment from the OS/2 command prompt:

```
WBPM
```

Appearance of Organizer. Figure 14.1 shows the appearance of the Workbench Organizer display. Certain utilities are supplied with it in the form of tool icons. A **menu bar** at the top allows you to reach pull-down menus by clicking the mouse on any of the actions, or by pressing a **hotkey**. Hotkeys are indicated by underlined letters within the actions or menu items. Figures 14.2 and 14.3 show the contents of the **File** and **View** pull-down menus.

Persistence. Whenever you use the object-oriented Workbench, it will create or update a file that indicates what projects and tools were present in your environment at the end of your session. When you come back into the Organizer session again, the objects you used in the last session will still be available through the icons you have defined. This phenomenon is known as **persistence.** Unless you specify otherwise, the Organizer will create or look for the Organizer environment files in the current directory. If you want to specify a different directory, you must use the following environment variable:

```
SET MFORG=d:\path;
```

where *path* is any valid directory path. If you use the MFORG environment variable, make sure that it points to a valid directory, even if the directory is empty.

14.4 Using Objects

14.4.1 Built-In Tools Supplied with Workbench

The default set of tools. Figure 14.1 shows the appearance of the Organizer, complete with the icons for the tool definitions provided with the Workbench. These tool definitions are loaded automatically the first time you activate the Workbench Organizer. If the Organizer does not find your desktop environment files from the last time you used the GUI Workbench, it will initialize the desktop environment by loading the default set of tool icons and creating new environment files.

Loading tool definitions. The **File** pull-down menu (Figure 14.2) lets you use an object definition file to load and store a set of tools and projects.

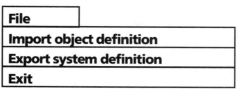

Figure 14.2 File pull-down menu

View
Arrange icons
Include

Figure 14.3 View pull-down menu

The **File** pull-down menu contains three options:

- **Import object definition** lets you load a set of tool and project definitions from a file.
- **Export system definition** is the inverse of the import operation. It lets you create a permanent file that saves all of your current tool and project definitions.
- **Exit** lets you terminate the Organizer environment.

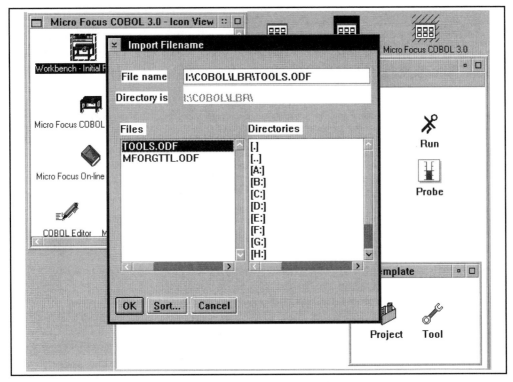

Figure 14.4 Importing tool definitions

If the tool icons are not visible on the Organizer desktop because they have been deleted, you can reload them from an object definition file. Select the **File** pull-down menu and select **Import object definition.** You will see a directory display labeled **Import Filename,** as shown in Figure 14.4. (More information about the GUI-based Directory V2 display is in Chapter 16.) The default set of Workbench tools will be **\COBOL\LBR\TOOLS.ODF.** Double-clicking on that filename will start a program that loads the icons. This method can be used to load icons for add-on products or for your own applications.

Rearranging icons. If you find that icons overlap, select the **View** pull-down menu from the menu bar. Then select **Arrange icons.** This will spread them out in an orderly manner. You can also move individual icons by dragging with either mouse button. **Include,** on the **View** pull-down menu, lets you show or hide the template window.

14.4.2 Using the Template to Define New Tools

The template window. The Workbench window contains a smaller window labeled **Template.** The Template window in turn contains prototype tool and project icons for creating new tools and projects. You can move the Template window around on the screen by dragging its top border with the *left* mouse button.

Defining a new tool. To define a new tool, use the *right* mouse button to drag the tool icon from the template window onto the main Organizer window.

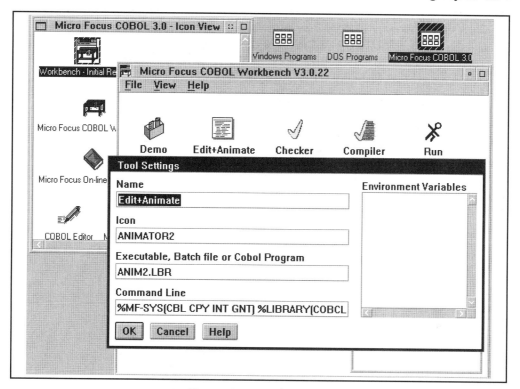

Figure 14.5 Tool settings

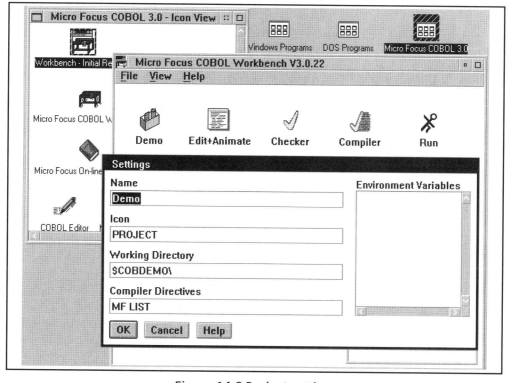

Figure 14.6 Project settings

As soon as you do that, you will see a **Tool Settings** menu. One example of a Tool Settings menu is shown in Figure 14.5. It lets you enter the information that Organizer will need in order to run your program. Here are the fields on the Tool Settings menu:

- **Name:** Supply the verbal description that should appear under the icon on the Organizer.
- **Icon:** Specify the icon that will identify this object on the Organizer. If you are creating a new tool, the default icon name will be **TOOL.** Icons provided with Micro Focus utilities will have other names.
- **Executable, Batch file, or Cobol Program:** Enter the filename of the batch file or executable module. You can enter a fully qualified filename with drive and path if needed.
- **Command Line:** Supply any other parameters that would follow the program name or batch filename on the command line.
- **Environment Variables:** You can use this scrollable box to enter SET commands for operating system environment variables that apply solely to this object. This makes it unnecessary to put them into CONFIG.SYS.

Once you have entered these fields, select **OK** to create the new tool. (If you change your mind, you can select **Cancel** and start over if desired.)

14.4.3 Using the Template to Create New Projects

Defining a new project. To define a new project, use the *right* mouse button to drag the project icon from the template window onto the main Organizer window. This will bring up the **Settings** menu, as shown in Figure 14.6. It lets you enter the information that Organizer will need in order to check or compile your program. Here are the fields on the Settings menu:

- **Name:** Supply the verbal description that should appear under the icon on the Organizer.
- **Icon:** Specify the icon that will identify this object on the Organizer. If you are creating a new project, the default icon name will be **PROJECT**.
- **Working Directory:** Enter the filename of the source program. You can enter a fully qualified filename with drive and path if needed.
- **Compiler Directives:** Supply any checker/compiler directives that you want to go into effect along with this source file.
- **Environment Variables:** You can use this scrollable box to enter SET commands for operating system environment variables to be used when processing this object. This makes it unnecessary to put them into CONFIG.SYS.

Once you have entered these fields, select **OK** to create the new project.

More about Organizer icons. If you use the Organizer's default icons for defining your own tools and projects, all of your tool icons will look like wrenches and all of your project icons will look like cartons. You might prefer something more distinctive, such as a fly swatter for debugging, a winged currency sign for a budget application, or perhaps a chainsaw for a program that purges old data from your database.

How do you go about creating new icons for the Workbench Organizer? On an OS/2 system, Micro Focus Workbench Organizer icons are provided in a file called **MFICONS.DLL.** A text file, **MFICONS.SF,** describes icons available to the system. Each icon within MFICONS.DLL is created with the OS/2 icon editor. IBM supplies the OS/2 icon editor as part of the OS/2 1.x Software Developer's Kit (SDK) and as part of the OS/2 2.0 base operating system. Micro Focus provides all of its icons in device-independent 32 x 32 pixel format. If desired, you can create other types of icons, such as device-dependent XGA format. Once you have created a new icon, you can use the Micro Focus **Panels 2** utility to add their names to MFICONS.SF. MFICONS.SF is a Panels 2 side file. The *Toolset Reference* describes how to use Panels 2 and side files.

You cannot use the Microsoft Windows icon editor to create icons for OS/2, or vice versa. The icon file format is different even when the resolution is the same.

Once you've added the new icon to MFICONS.DLL, use the **Icon:** field in the appropriate Settings menu to associate the icon with your tool or project. The Organizer uses a find file to associate icon settings with the contents of MFICONS.DLL.

14.4.4 Using Existing Tools and Projects

Figure 14.7 shows a **tool context menu.** It appears when you single-click either mouse button, or click both mouse buttons at once, on a tool icon in the Organizer environment.

Start Tool
Export Tool Definition
Delete
Settings

Figure 14.7 Tool context menu

You can select any option on a pull-down menu by double-clicking with the *left* mouse button.

- **Start Tool** begins executing the module.
- **Export Tool Definition** lets you write that tool definition to a file.
- **Delete** removes that tool definition from your Organizer window.
- **Settings** brings up the Tool Settings menu again, so that you can change fields on it.

Figure 14.8 shows a **project context menu.** It appears when you click the *left* mouse button on a project icon in the Organizer environment.

Export Project Definition
Delete
Settings

Figure 14.8 Project context menu

The project context menu works in much the same way as the tool context menu:

- **Export Project Definition** lets you write that project definition to a file.
- **Delete** removes that project definition from your Organizer window.
- **Settings** brings up the Settings menu again, so that you can change fields on it.

14.4.5 More about Starting Tools

Starting a tool from its icon. As we mentioned earlier, you can begin executing a tool by double-clicking on its icon with the *left* mouse button or by selecting **Start Tool** on the Tool context menu. What happens next will depend on exactly what tool you are starting. If the tool needs some raw materials to work on, such as an input filename or directory, you may see a dialog box that requests this information. Some tools have a default option. For example, if you start the Animator V2 tool icon and you don't specify an input filename, Animator V2 will assume that you want to create a new COBOL source file. In similar fashion, unless you tell it otherwise, Directory V2 will show you the contents of the current directory path.

Drag-and-drop. You can start some tools by using the "drag-and-drop" method. Drag the project icon with the *right* mouse button until you have superimposed it over the tool icon. Then drop it by releasing the mouse button. The Organizer will merge the project icon information with the tool icon information to build the correct command line options. It will create the desired operating system environment variables (SET commands) from those that you have supplied. It will set the drive and directory path to those specified in the Project Settings menu. It will prompt the user for any additional required information, such as a filename. Finally, the Organizer will start the executable module.

For example, suppose you keep COBOL source programs in the J:\COBOL\PROJECT1 directory. You can set up a Project icon associated with that path. The icon settings specify the directory path, command line options, directives, and SET commands needed to edit, check, and animate source programs within that project. Suppose you want to edit a program. The Animator V2 icon contains facilities for both editing and animation. If you drop the TICTAC.CBL project icon onto the Animator V2 tool icon, the Organizer will set your environment variables and will set the default directory to J:\COBOL\PROJECT1. The Organizer will pass your directives and command line options along to Animator V2. Because the Animator V2 Tool Settings contains the **%filename** parameter, the Organizer will prompt you to enter a filename. The default name in the **Enter Filename** dialog box will be the one you used the previous time, but you can select a different file if you wish. Animator V2 will begin running with your program loaded into its editing work area.

In summary, you can start a tool in two ways: by clicking on that tool with the mouse or by dragging a project icon and dropping it onto the tool icon. Dropping a tool icon onto any other icon, or dropping a project icon onto another project icon, will have no effect.

Projects and Tools for Checking and Compiling. Micro Focus recommends that you keep your Checker/Compiler directives with the source code icon and not with the Checker or Compiler icon. In other words, rather than creating several "flavors" of Checker icon settings for separate COBOL dialects and add-on products, you are better off using the same Checker tool icon for all COBOL source. You can govern Checker behavior by associating the right directive settings or .DIR file with each source code input file.

On the other hand, if you want to use several test environments separately from one another, you can SET environment variables in the Tool Settings menu. For example, you can use SET commands to tell the Checker to write its output to your local hard disk or to a network server. One tool icon could be labeled CHECK LOCAL and the other could be labeled CHECK SERVER. The only difference would be the environment variable settings.

14.5 Customizing the Environment

You can use runtime switches to affect the behavior of the Workbench Organizer and of the applications that run under it. For example, to keep error message windows from disappearing from the OS/2 PM desktop too rapidly to read them, set the runtime switch +K4 in OS/2 CONFIG.SYS with the following command:

```
SET COBSW=+K4
```

14.6 Exercises

1. Set up a project icon for CUST.CBL or one of your own COBOL source programs.

2. Install the Micro Focus tool icons and use the Checker icon to check CUST.CBL.

3. Now set up a tool icon for TICTAC.INT and click on that tool icon to execute TICTAC.INT under the Organizer. Notice the text-mode window that allows you to do ACCEPT and DISPLAY operations.

15

The GUI Animator V2

15.1 Animator V2 Concepts

15.1.1 Introduction

One of the strengths of the Micro Focus Workbench is the fact that it provides many options to suit individual needs and tastes. In Chapters 12 and 13, we showed how to use the Workbench and add-on products to provide a mainframe-like user interface for those Workbench users who prefer that environment. On the other hand, many experienced PC users are familiar with newer PC-based applications that run under Microsoft Windows or IBM OS/2. These users may prefer to access Workbench functions through a graphical user interface (GUI). Micro Focus developed Animator V2 to answer the requests of those users who prefer GUI-based applications.

A disclaimer: As this chapter went to press, not all Animator V2 functions were completely implemented. Subsequent production versions may differ in certain respects. The following known limitations are in effect: The initial release of Animator V2 will run only under OS/2. It will not contain the Source Code Analyzer and Structure Animator facilities. Missing functionality may be added later in the form of maintenance upgrades.

15.1.2 Overview of Animator V2

Despite its name, Animator V2 contains more than just the animation facility. Because Micro Focus Workbench users spend most of their time using the Editor, the Checker, and the Animator facilities, it makes sense to provide a seamless interface among them. In the function key Workbench menu system, to test a program you have just modified you have to switch to another submenu and load the .INT file. **Animator V2 lets you access the most frequently used Workbench functions from a single menu.**

Micro Focus designed Animator V2 to be compatible with the IBM SAA Common User Interface (CUA) standards described in Chapter 14. Even though the user interface is different, Animator V2 provides features similar to that of the corresponding parts of the function key menu Workbench. However, some features have received new names, because the new names provide a more logical arrangement, and because of the need for compatibility with IBM's Code/370 Debugger. Code/370 Debugger complements the Workbench in that it lets you use the PC workstation to debug programs running on the mainframe. Animator V2, and the rest of the Workbench, is intended for application development on the PC, while Code/370 Debugger assists final system testing of applications ported to the mainframe.

15.2 Animator V2 Setup

15.2.1 Installation

The Workbench Setup program installs Animator V2 automatically as part of the supplied GUI Workbench Organizer tools.

15.2.2 Starting Animator V2

Starting from the Workbench Organizer. You can start Animator V2 from the Workbench Organizer by double-clicking on the **Edit+Animate** tool icon. (An equivalent action would be using the *right* mouse button to bring up the tool context menu, then activating the **Start Tool** option.) When you start Animator V2 in this way, an **Enter Filename** dialog box will appear, as shown in Figure 15.1.

Enter Filename is a standard Micro Focus dialog box that contains entry fields for a filename and options. In the filename field, enter the name of a .CBL (COBOL source) file or an .INT (intermediate code) file from the Micro Focus Checker. Three buttons appear at the bottom of the **Enter Filename** dialog box: **OK, Cancel,** and **Find.** If you are unsure of the name or location of the desired file, click on the **Find** button. The Organizer will automatically run the File Open dialog from the Micro Focus Directory V2 facility. You'll see a point-and-shoot directory display that will let you search your disk drives for the desired filename. Chapter 16 contains detailed information about using Directory V2. If you select a filename and press the Enter key or click on the OK button, Animator V2 will start with that file loaded into its work area.

If you start Animator V2 without entering a filename in the filename field, it will assume that you want to create a new file. This is equivalent to the **Editing new file** situation in the function key Workbench. You can clear the existing contents of the filename field in the **Enter Filename** dialog box by positioning your cursor to the beginning of the field and pressing **Ctrl+End**. If you do this, the Animator V2 will start with nothing loaded into its work area. The window title bar will show **Edit:<New file>** until you save the new file with the **Save as...** function and assign a filename to it.

As described in Chapter 14, you can also start Animator V2 by dragging and dropping a project icon onto the Animator V2 tool icon. See Chapter 14 for complete information about setting up and using project and tool icons.

Starting from the OS/2 command prompt. The following command will bring up Animator V2 from the OS/2 command prompt:

```
ANIM2PM progname
```

where *progname* is the name of a previously compiled program or an editable text file.

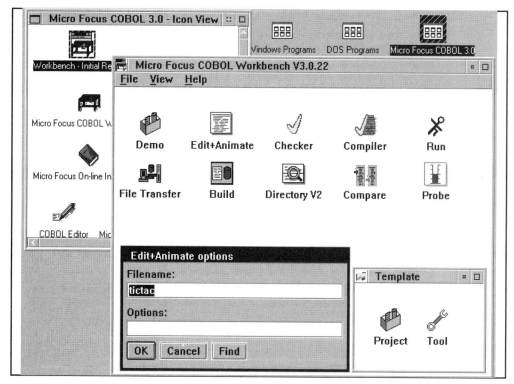

Figure 15.1 Enter Filename dialog box

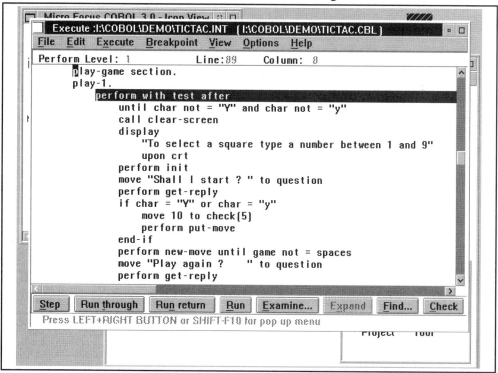

Figure 15.2 Animator V2 running TICTAC.INT

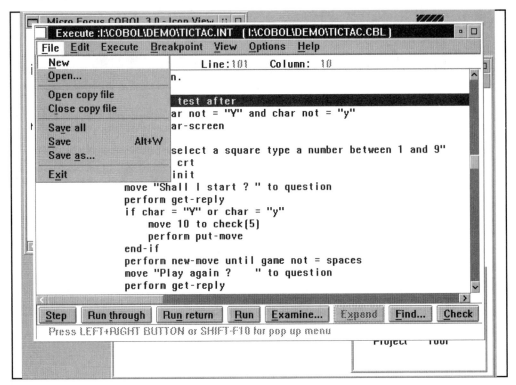

Figure 15.3 File pull-down menu

15.3 The Animator V2 Menu Structure

15.3.1 Appearance of Animator V2

The Animator V2 main window. Animator V2 displays a CUA-compliant GUI window that contains an action bar menu at the top, a text area for program source, and a row of push buttons at the bottom. We discussed CUA-compliant applications in Chapter 14. Figure 15.2 shows the Animator V2 main window, with a COBOL source program loaded into the text area. As in the Workbench Organizer, clicking on an action bar item causes a pull-down menu to appear. For example, the Animator V2 **File** pull-down menu is visible in Figure 15.3.

The push buttons perform some of the same actions that are already present on the pull-down menus shown in this chapter. Clicking on these buttons provides faster, more convenient access to commonly used features. For example, to step through instructions one at a time, you can select **Step** on the **Execute** pull-down menu, or click repeatedly on the **Step** button.

The information line. In Animator V2, the information line appears just below the action bar menu. It shows the current line and column number within your source file. During animation, it shows the current perform level.

The message line. The message line appears on the last row of the screen. The default message is **Press LEFT+RIGHT BUTTON or SHIFT+F10 to pop up menu.** The "LEFT+RIGHT BUTTON" mentioned here is the combination of the left and right *mouse* buttons. Pressing more than one mouse button at a time is called **chording.**

The COBOL text window. When required, Animator V2 also displays a second window called the **COBOL text window**. As the name implies, the contents of this window are in text mode. The COBOL text window somewhat resembles the OS/2 command prompt window in that it contains a black text area and it can be scrolled, moved, sized, and minimized to an icon. The COBOL text window serves two purposes. It displays runtime error and abnormal termination messages. Also, during animation, the COBOL text window allows your program to do character-mode I/O such as COBOL ACCEPT and DISPLAY statements. Animator V2 is intelligent enough to create the COBOL text window only when the window is needed.

For instance, if you animate TICTAC.INT, the game board will appear in the COBOL text window. You'll use the COBOL text window whenever TICTAC is waiting for data. Clicking the left mouse button anywhere on the COBOL text window will make it the active window and will position it in front of any overlapping windows, so that you can enter your data. You can also activate the COBOL text window by pressing **Ctrl+Esc** and selecting it from the list of active windows.

Editing versus animation mode. If you start Animator V2 with a COBOL source code (.CBL) file that has not been checked, Animator V2 will come up in editing mode. In editing mode, you can edit the program and check it, but you cannot animate it, because there is nothing to animate. The **Execute** and **Breakpoint** menu headers will appear in gray to indicate that they are disabled.

If you load Animator V2 with a program that has been checked, so that an intermediate code (.INT) file exists, Animator V2 will run in animation mode. In animation mode, you can edit, check, and animate your program; all menu headers will be visible. In either mode, the program source code will appear in the work area of the Animator V2 GUI window.

The Animator V2 window title bar. The title bar of the Animator V2 window tells you what action is in progress, what program is being edited or executed, and what source file is visible in the work area.

For example, start up Animator V2 and load K:\TEST\CUST.CBL into the work area. The title bar will show **Edit:CUST.CBL (K:\TEST\CUST.CBL).** The word **Edit:** tells you that Animator V2 is in editing mode, the first filename **CUST.CBL** tells you what program is being edited, and the second filename in parentheses tells you what source file is visible in the work area. If you move downward in the program and begin editing a copy file, say CUSTMST, the title bar will show **Edit:CUST.CBL (K:\TEST\CUSTMST.CBL).** If you check CUST.CBL, then after completion the title bar will show **Execute:CUST.INT (K:\TEST\CUST.CBL).**

Now, suppose you've made some changes to the TICTAC.CBL source file, but you haven't checked it again after making the changes. Suppose you have added some new source lines. The title bar will still show **Execute:CUST.INT (K:\TEST\CUST.CBL).** Your program is still executable, because an .INT file still exists, but the new source lines will not be reflected in the executable version yet. Just as in the function key Workbench, if you have not rechecked your program, you can get mismatched source and executable files. In that case, the Animator will display source lines that you can't actually execute. The date and time of the .CBL and .INT files will tell you whether you have changed the source code since the last time you checked your program.

Finally, if you select **New** on the **File** menu, you'll clear out the Animator V2 work area. The title bar will show **Edit:<New file>**.

Help functions. The **Help** pull-down menu, shown in Figure 15.4, provides access to hypertext help. It serves the same purpose as the On-line Information facility and the F1-key help screens provided with the function key menu system. Chapter 16 contains more details about how to use the hypertext help viewer. Because help information is updated with maintenance releases, the Help menu can give you more up-to-date information than the printed Micro Focus manuals.

- The **Help index** selection will show you a list of all help topics available. Clicking on a topic will cause that topic to appear in a separate scrollable window.
- The **General help** selection provides context-sensitive help pertaining to the current display.
- The **Using help** selection tells you how to navigate through the help system itself.
- The **Product information** selection on the **Help** menu will show you the complete version number of the Animator V2 software. *Important: If you need to call Micro Focus technical support, be prepared to give them this version number.*

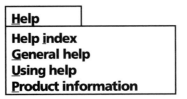

Figure 15.4 Help pull-down menu

15.4 File and Directory Facilities

15.4.1 Loading and Saving Files

The File menu. The File pull-down menu (Figure 15.3) lets you load and save program source and copy member files.

- **New** clears the text area and lets you create a new COBOL source file.
- **Open...** allows you to open an existing COBOL source file and load it into the text area. The three dots after the word Open on the menu tell you that another dialog box will appear if you select that option. In this case, it's the familiar File Open dialog used in other Micro Focus GUI functions. You can select a file from the directory display by clicking on it. See Chapter 16

for detailed information about the Micro Focus Directory function and the use of directory searches.

- **Open copy file** lets you open another source file that is associated with a COPY statement in your program. This lets you see the expansion of the COPY even before you check your program.

- **Close copy file** closes the copy file, writing the updated version back to disk.

- **Save all** lets you save not only your main program, but also all of the copy files associated with that program.

- **Save** will save your main program back to disk, under its current name.

- **Save as...** lets you save your main program to disk under a new name. The old version is unchanged.

- **Exit** terminates Animator V2.

15.5 Editing Facilities

15.5.1 Basic Editing Operations

The text cursor. In Animator V2, the shape of the cursor tells you whether you are in insert or overtype mode. If the text cursor is a vertical bar, you are in insert mode. If the text cursor is a rectangle surrounding the current character, you are in overtype mode. You can move the text cursor position by clicking with the *left* mouse button or by using the paging and cursor arrow keys. Using the window scroll bar will also change the cursor's position within the file. The cursor will remain in the same position relative to the window's borders, but since the file display has scrolled through the window, the cursor will be at a different position within the file.

Dragging the slider along the scroll bar will scroll the display through the text window. You can move the display a line at a time by clicking on the arrow buttons at either end of the slider. To move up or down a screen page at a time, you can click on the portion of the scroll bar above or below the slider.

The Edit menu. Figure 15.5 shows the Animator V2 Edit pull-down menu. This menu controls most of the basic editing operations.

- **Undo** will back out the effects of the last editing command that you executed. Undo is useful, for example, if you have just executed a Find and Replace operation with the wrong parameters. **Redo** reexecutes the command that you just undid with the Undo command.

- **Cut, Copy, Paste block,** and **Delete** all apply to block operations. You select a block of text by moving the mouse to the upper-left corner of the desired area and by dragging downward and to the right until you have covered all of the text to be selected. **Cut** deletes the selected text but saves it in the clipboard so that you can paste it somewhere else. **Copy** places a copy of the selected text in the clipboard, leaving the original in place. **Paste block** copies text from the clipboard to the current cursor location. **Delete** erases the selected text without copying it into the clipboard. For these block operations, the Edit Options menu gives you the choice of using either an internal clipboard or the OS/2 system clipboard. The latter option lets you share data with other OS/2 applications.

- The next group of operations all have to do with lines. They are *not* the same as the line operations in the function key Workbench. **Delete line** deletes the line at the current cursor position. You don't have to select the line by dragging the mouse through it. **Insert line** inserts a blank line above the line with the current cursor position. **Repeat line** inserts a copy of the current line *below* the current line, and moves the cursor down to that line. **Split line** splits the line at the current cursor position. All characters from the cursor position to the end of the line will move down to the next line, padded on the left with blanks. The cursor will remain on the current line. **Join line** reverses the effect of Split line. **Paste line** copies the clipboard contents as a block of lines into the current cursor location. If insert mode is on, existing lines will be moved down; otherwise, existing lines will be overwritten.

- **Edit command** lets you type the actual keywords for an edit command into a dialog box. The help button on this dialog box provides a list of available commands.

- **Find** brings up the dialog box for Find, Replace, and CSI functions. We will discuss this later in the section on CSI.

- **Select all** selects the entire file. The whole file becomes the equivalent of a block that you have marked with the mouse. **DeSelect all** deselects any block that you have marked.

Edit	
Undo	**Alt+Backspace**
Redo	**Alt+Shift+Backspace**
Cut	**Shift+Del**
Copy	**Ctrl+Ins**
Paste block	**Shift+Ins**
Paste lines	**Alt+Ins**
Delete	**Del**
Delete line	**Alt+D**
Insert line	**Alt+I**
Repeat line	**Alt+R**
Split line	**Alt+S**
Join line	**Alt+J**
Edit command...	**Alt+C**
Find...	
Select all	
DeSelect all	

Figure 15.5 Edit pull-down menu

15.5.2 Configuring Screen Appearance

The View menu. The View menu lets you configure the appearance and behavior of the Animator V2 editing function. During editing and animation, it also lets you move quickly to other parts of your source file.

Selecting some options on the View menu will cause a **cascaded menu** to appear, shown in Figures 15.6, 15.7, and 15.8. A cascaded menu appears to the right of the pull-down menu, so that you can make more selections. Whenever a pull-down menu option has a cascaded menu, you will see an arrow to the right of that menu option.

For example, in Figure 15.6 the **Include** option is shown with its cascaded menu. This menu lets you choose what features should be shown or hidden in the Animator V2 window. Clicking on an option turns it on or off. When an option is turned on, a tick mark will appear to the left of it. You can choose whether to show or hide the status line, the buttons at the bottom of the window, the information line, the COBOL sequence numbers, or the tag markers.

Tag markers represent a type of bookmark that you can assign to various source lines. Figure 15.7 shows the **Tag** option with its cascaded menu. You can **Set** or **Unset** a tag for the current line. The **Go to next** and **Go to previous** options position the current line to the next or previous tag in your file. **Clear all** removes all tags from the file.

Do you want to look at only those lines that have been specifically marked, or do you want to view the entire source file? The **Compress** cascaded menu, shown in Figure 15.8, lets you choose. **Breakpoints** will cause Animator V2 to show only those source lines that have breakpoints set on them. **Current finds** shows only those source lines that were marked in the most recent Find operation. **Tags** shows only those source lines to which you have assigned a tag. **Errors** shows error lines. Conversely, **Expand** restores the Animator V2 display to show all source lines.

The **Error** menu option offers two more choices, **Go to next** and **Go to previous.** They display to the next or previous error line in your file.

View menu options available during animation. Two options on the View menu are available only when you are working with a program that is being animated or is ready for animation. **Where** function moves the cursor to the line that will be executed next under the Animator. The **Align** function scrolls the display so that the line that will be executed next will be three lines from the top of the text area.

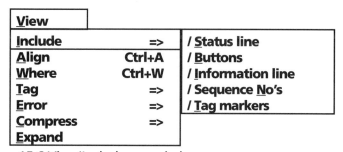

Figure 15.6 View/Include cascaded menus

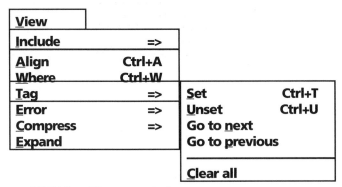

Figure 15.7 View/Tag cascaded menus

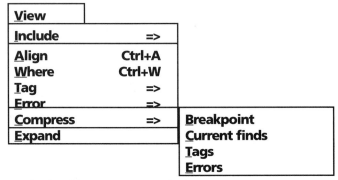

Figure 15.8 View/Compress cascaded menus

15.5.3 Configuring Editing Behavior

The Options pull-down menu. The Options menu in Figure 15.9 lets you configure the behavior of various parts of Animator V2, including the editor. **Short menus** and **Full menus** are mutually exclusive options. If you choose the former, certain options will be omitted from the menus to simplify operation for the new user. The **RCM Browse** option allows you to access the GUI Reusable Code Manager add-on product, if it is available on your system. The **Edit, Execute,** and **Find** options let you configure the editor, the animator, and the CSI functions of Animator V2.

Figure 15.9 Options pull-down menu

The Edit Options dialog box. Figure 15.10 shows the Edit Options dialog box. The options in that box all apply to one particular editing profile whose name appears on the **Base profile:** line. As we saw in Chapter 11, the editing

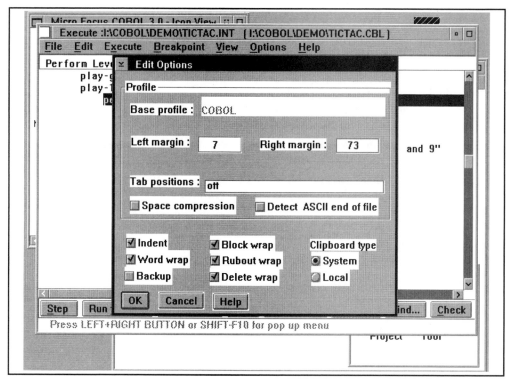

Figure 15.10 The Edit Options dialog box

profiles are defined in the Workbench configuration file. Each profile is associated with one or more filename extensions. When you load a filename with the specified extension into the editor, that editing profile will become active. You can assign a different profile to your file by entering the SET PROFILE editor command in the Edit Command dialog box. Because the Edit Options dialog box refers only to the profile currently active for your file, you cannot change the profile name within the Edit Options dialog box.

COBOL and SYSTEM are the default profile names supplied with the Workbench. If your filename extension does not match any other profile, the COBOL profile will become active. The SYSTEM profile has a different function. If you don't specify all of the available parameters for a new editing profile, the Workbench will default to using those settings defined in the SYSTEM profile.

- **Left margin** and **right margin** let you set the margins. These control the behavior for word wrap and find/replace operations.
- The **Tab positions** field lets you set the positions to which tab characters will align. In the disk file, the tabs are stored as embedded tab characters. Within the editor work area, and on the screen display, Animator V2 substitutes the correct number of spaces. Entering **Off** in this field will turn off tab character expansion.
- The **Space compression** check box lets you choose whether to compress out the space characters from your file when storing it on disk.

- The **Detect ASCII end of file** check box lets you choose whether to use the ASCII EOF character to signal the end of file, or to use the end of the physical space allocation.
- The **Indent** check box determines whether to indent the cursor automatically when moving to a new line.
- The **Word wrap** check box determines whether the cursor will move to a new line if the word you are typing overflows the right margin.
- Similarly, **Block wrap** determines whether or not inserted text blocks will wrap to another line or will overflow into the right margin if they don't fit.
- **Rubout wrap** determines whether the cursor will move back to the previous line if you press the backspace key in column 1.
- **Delete wrap** determines whether to wrap characters back from the next line if you use the delete key at the end of the current line.
- The **Backup** option determines whether to create a backup of the previous version of your file before you save the new version.
- The **Clipboard type** option allows two mutually exclusive selections, **System** and **Local.** The System option allows the OS/2 PM or Windows system clipboard to capture text from the Animator V2 window. The Local option restricts text data on the clipboard for use only within Animator V2.

15.6 Checking and Compilation Facilities

15.6.1 Checking a Program

Pressing the **Check** button at the bottom of the Animator V2 window will invoke the Checker, as will the **Check program** option on the Execute pull-down menu. An alternate method is to run the Checker as a separate session by clicking on the Workbench Organizer tool icon. Chapter 14 shows how to assign Checker directives to the Project icon for each group of source programs that you want to check.

Either of these commands will produce .INT output for animation:

```
COBOL progname ANIM,NUL;
WB CHECK progname
```

New directives with v3.0. Micro Focus has added some new directives to the Checker. The **DOSVS** directive causes the Checker to recognize mainframe DOS/VS COBOL reserved words. Similarly, the **COBOL370** directive causes the Checker to recognize mainframe COBOL/370 reserved words.

15.6.2 Compiling a Program

You can compile a program by using the Compiler tool icon in the Workbench Organizer, or by invoking it from the operating system command prompt. The Compiler is not built into Animator V2. From the command line, **COBOL progname** will compile .OBJ output. **COBOL progname OMF(GNT)** will compile .GNT output. If you have already checked your program, **WB progname GENERATE** will produce .GNT code from .INT code. **WB progname COMPOBJ** will produce .OBJ code from .INT code.

15.7 Animation Facilities

15.7.1 Animating a Program

The Execute menu. The Execute menu in Figure 15.11 lets you animate or run your program. Be aware that Micro Focus has changed the names of some Animator V2 features from those used in the function key menu. The initial release of Animator V2 provides no equivalent to the Watch or Animate functions in the original function key Animator.

- **Step** executes the next source line in your program's execution sequence. Animator V2 also provides a Step button at the bottom of the screen. Pressing this button repeatedly lets you single-step through the program.

- **Step All** is equivalent to the old Go function. It executes your program one line at a time and shows your position within the source code. A temporary dialog box allows you to change execution speed.

- **Run Through** is equivalent to the old Perform Step. If you are positioned on a PERFORM statement, it will run (zoom) until completion of that PERFORM.

- **Run Return** is equivalent to the old Perform Exit. If you are positioned within a PERFORMed routine, it will run (zoom) through the current PERFORM range and will stop at the statement immediately after the PERFORM statement.

- **Run to Cursor** sets a temporary breakpoint at the line containing the cursor, runs (zooms) to that breakpoint, and then removes that breakpoint.

- **Run** is equivalent to the old Zoom function. It will execute the program at machine speed, without animation, until you reach either a breakpoint or the end of the program.

- **Skip statement** bypasses execution of the next statement and positions the cursor to the statement after that one in the execution sequence.

- **Skip return** skips all remaining statements within the current PERFORM range. It will stop at the statement immediately after the PERFORM statement.

- **Skip to cursor** skips all statements between the current position and the cursor line. The cursor line will become the new current line.

- **Skip to Start** resets execution sequence to the beginning of the program. It will not reinitialize your data fields.

- **Examine** reveals the contents of the current data item and then gives you the choice of whether to add it to the monitor list. You can also select a data item for examination by double-clicking on it with the *left* mouse button. We will discuss this further in the section on monitoring data items.

- **Do statement** brings up a dialog box that lets you enter a COBOL statement to execute interpretively. Animator V2 will *not* automatically insert that statement into your program source code file.

- **Backtrack** lets you step backward and forward through the sequence of source lines that had been executed just before the most recent breakpoint. This is a viewing function only and does not execute any source lines, nor does it back out the effects of previous execution. Animator V2 will store this information only if the **Backtrack on** check box is selected in the Execute Options dialog box.

```
Execute
Step                Ctrl+S
Step all
Run through         Ctrl+P
Run return          Ctrl+N
Run to cursor
Run                 Ctrl+R
Skip statement
Skip return
Skip to cursor
Skip to Start
Examine...          Ctrl+X
Do statement...
Check program
Backtrack...
```

Figure 15.11 Execute pull-down menu

Configuring the Animator. To configure the behavior of Animator V2, select the **Execute Options** dialog from the **Options** pull-down menu. Three options appear in the Execute options dialog box in Figure 15.12.

- **Hide on run** hides the Animator V2 window when the Animator is executing at machine speed (run mode).
- **Backtrack on** records your execution path so that you can view it later with the Backtrack facility.
- **Threshold level** sets the nesting level of routines that will be run in step mode.

15.7.2 Monitoring Data Items

Now we've come to the most interesting part of using Animator V2: seeing what's happening to the data items while you animate your program. Either the **Examine** button at the bottom of the Animator V2 window, or the **Examine** option on the Execute pull-down menu, will let you do this.

Specifying the field name. When you select the Examine function, the first thing you'll see is a dialog box entitled **Examine.** This dialog box, shown in the lower-left portion of Figure 15.13, allows you to specify the data field or filename that you want to examine. You can type the name directly in the text area. Alternatively, if the text cursor is already on the data name that you want to monitor, you can press the **Cursor** button in the Examine dialog box. This will copy the data name into the dialog box. Once you have specified the data name, click on the **Ok** button in the dialog box.

The Examine Data Name window. Once you've selected the data name, you'll see another window with a title bar that reads *fieldname*:**Examine,**

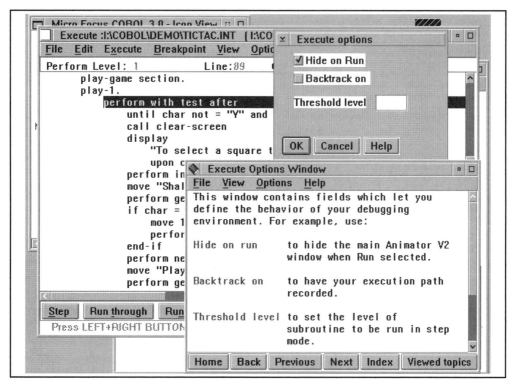

Figure 15.12 Execute options dialog box

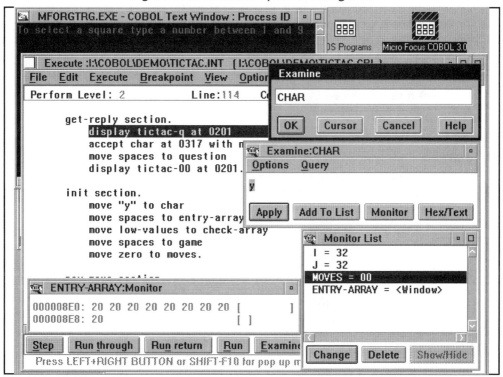

Figure 15.13 Using Examine and Monitor List dialog boxes

where *fieldname* is the field name that you have just specified in the Examine dialog box. A window labeled **CHAR:Examine** is visible at the right side of Figure 15.13. The text area in this window shows the current contents of the CHAR data field. Unless you add the item to the monitor list, the Examine window is temporary. It will disappear after the next source line is executed.

Updating and monitoring variables. The Examine window contains four buttons that provide functions for updating and monitoring data items.

- If you overtype the existing value, clicking on the **Apply** button will update the field with the new value that you have entered.
- Selecting **Add to list** will add the variable to the monitor list. The monitor list will appear as a separate scrollable window, labeled **Monitor List,** as shown in the lower-right corner of Figure 15.13. Each variable that you monitor will appear as an item in that same window. This is a good way to track any small data item that contains simple numeric or text data.
- Selecting **Monitor** will add the variable to the monitor list, and will also display that variable in a **monitor window.** A monitor window labeled **ENTRY-ARRAY:MONITOR** is visible at the bottom of Figure 15.13. The word **<Window>** will be substituted for the variable's value in the monitor list if the variable is being monitored in a window.
- Selecting **Hex/Text** toggles the Examine window display between hexadecimal and character mode. If you select the **Monitor** function while in hex mode, the monitor window will be created in hex mode, as shown in the **ENTRY-ARRAY:MONITOR** example in Figure 15.13. Hex mode will occupy more space on the screen, but it is useful for displaying group items containing binary, packed decimal, or other nontext fields.

Some of these functions are also available as selections on the **Options** pull-down menu in the Examine window, shown in Figure 15.14. Selecting **Clear** on this menu will clear the data item.

Once you have monitored a data item, its Examine window will disappear from the screen. You might need it again if you want to update the data item. To bring back the Examine window, click on the data item in the monitor list to highlight it, and then select the **Change** button in the monitor list window. In similar fashion, you can delete an unwanted monitor by highlighting the data item in the list and selecting the **Delete** button. The **Show/Hide** button temporarily hides the selected monitor.

Options	
C̲lear	**F2**
H̲ex/Text	
A̲dd to list	**F4**
M̲onitor	

Figure 15.14 Options pull-down menu in Examine window

Querying other data items. The **Query** pull-down menu in the Examine window (Figure 15.15) lets you select a different data item for querying.

- **Parent** looks for the group item containing the field you originally requested.
- If you are already examining a group item, **Child** looks for the first detail item within that group item.
- **Same level** will display the next data item at the same level as the one you are now querying.
- If you are examining a table item, **Next Occurrence** or **Previous Occurrence** will display the next or previous table item.

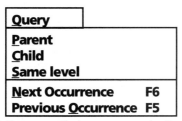

Query	
Parent	
Child	
Same level	
Next Occurrence	**F6**
Previous Occurrence	**F5**

Figure 15.15 Query pull-down menu in Examine window

15.7.3 Using Breakpoints

Breakpoint concepts. Breakpoints in Animator V2 work in much the same way as they do in the function key Workbench. The only real difference is the appearance of the menus and the display. A line containing a breakpoint will be flagged with the characters **BrkPt.** Breakpoints persist only until the end of the current Animator V2 session. In any execution mode, program execution will pause whenever a breakpoint is reached.

The Breakpoint menu. Figure 15.16 shows the Breakpoint pull-down menu. The selections on this menu let you create ordinary unconditional breakpoints on a COBOL statement.

- To set an unconditional statement breakpoint, move the cursor to the line that should have a breakpoint and select **Set**. You can also set an unconditional breakpoint for a source line by double-clicking in the left margin with the *left* mouse button.
- Conversely, **Unset** will clear a breakpoint at the line the cursor is on.
- **Clear all** will remove all breakpoints from your program.
- **Go to next** and **Go to previous** will scroll through your source file to locate the next or previous statement breakpoint.

Breakpoint	
Set	**Ctrl+B**
Unset	**Ctrl+U**
Set advanced...	
Go to next	
Go to previous	
Clear all	

Figure 15.16 Animator V2 Breakpoint pull-down menu

Advanced breakpoints. Other types of breakpoint are available from the Advanced Breakpoint dialog box, shown in Figure 15.17. You can bring up this dialog box by selecting **Set Advanced** on the Breakpoint menu.

The **Type** field lets you choose what type of breakpoint you want to set. The **Parameter** field lets you enter additional information required for certain types of breakpoints. The **Every** field contains a numeric value indicating how often the breakpoint should be activated. For instance, 01 pauses the program every time the breakpoint is reached, and 02 pauses every other time. For example, this feature would be useful if you want to pause the program every tenth time a certain statement is executed.

Here are the available breakpoint types:

- **Statement** is an unconditional statement breakpoint at the cursor line. This is the same type of breakpoint that you see on the Breakpoint pull-down menu.

- **Program** is a breakpoint associated with a program name. Enter the program name in the **Parameter** field. The breakpoint will be triggered whenever that module is entered or reentered. For example, entering the current program's name in the parameter field will trigger a breakpoint whenever you return to the current program from a subroutine call.

- **Data change** is a breakpoint that is triggered every time the contents of any data field changes.

- **Condition** is a conditional breakpoint associated with the COBOL statement at the cursor line. The breakpoint will be triggered only if the condition you enter in the **Parameter** field is true when that statement is reached.

- **Until** is a conditional breakpoint that can be triggered from anywhere in the program, if and when the condition you enter in the **Parameter** field becomes true.

15.8 COBOL Source Information Facilities

15.8.1 Performing Searches

In Animator V2, the Find/Replace and the COBOL Source Information (CSI) functions are consolidated into one menu. You can get to this menu by selecting **Find...** on the Edit pull-down menu, or by pressing the **Find...** button at the bottom of the Animator V2 window. Figure 15.18 shows the Find dialog box.

The Find dialog box contains a series of radio buttons. Choose one of them to indicate what type of item you want Animator V2 to find:

- **COBOL Item Information,** for a Find string representing a COBOL filename, data name, paragraph name, or section name. Do not confuse this with a simple text string search. This option performs an intelligent COBOL Source Information (CSI) search; using a dictionary built by the Micro Focus Checker. It provides full CSI cross-reference functions, returning the result in a CSI report window.

- **Text,** for a Find string representing a text string.

- **Labels,** for a Find string representing standard COBOL label such as WORKING STORAGE. To see what options are available, click on the down

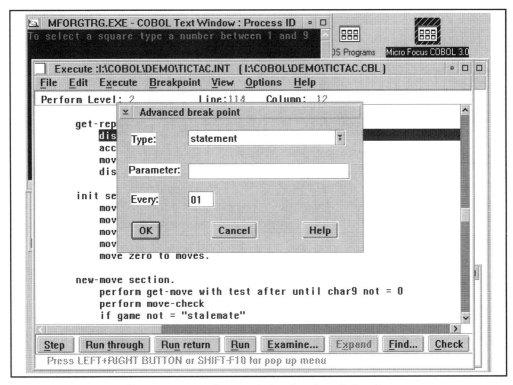

Figure 15.17 Advanced Breakpoint dialog box

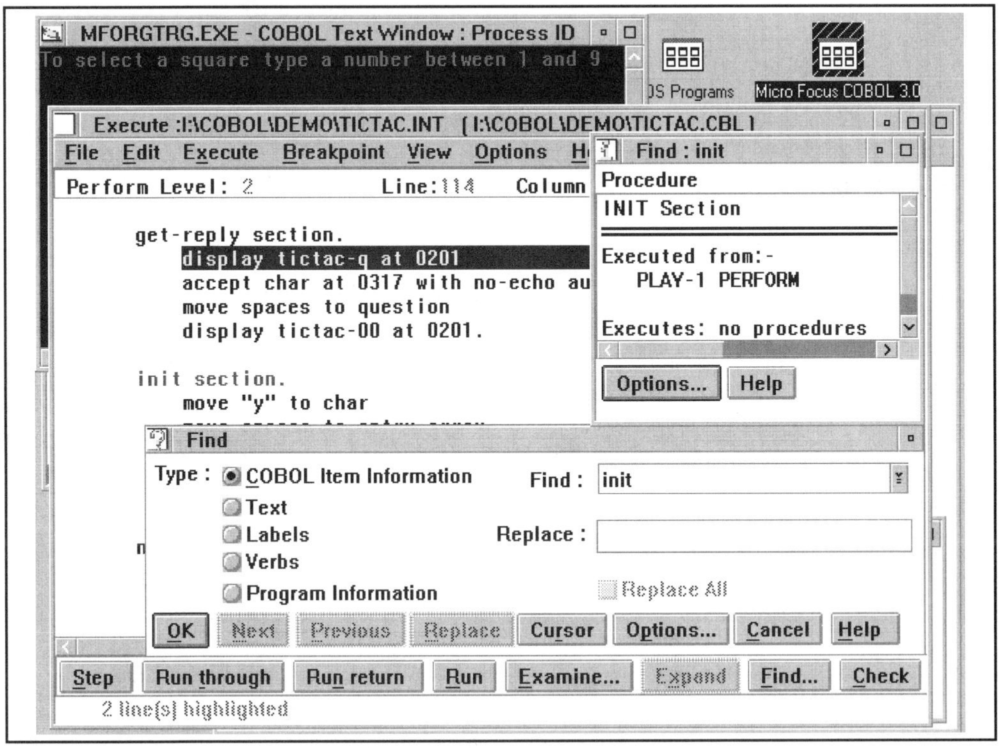

Figure 15.18 The Find function

arrow button immediately to the right of the Find string box. You can then select a search option by clicking on it.

- **Verbs,** for a Find string representing a COBOL verb.
- **Program Information,** if you want to view program statistics or flag unexecuted source lines or dead data. These resemble the specialized search options offered in the function key version of CSI. You may view available selections by clicking on the down arrow button next to the Find string box.

Entering the Find string. The Find string can be up to 30 characters long. If you want to search for more occurrences of a word or label that already is visible on your screen, move the cursor to the beginning of that text and click on the **Cursor** button at the bottom of the Find dialog box. This will copy that text into the Find string.

If you want to search for a string that includes trailing spaces, then follow those trailing spaces with a # character. If you want to search for a string only in the main program, not in any of the copy members, then terminate the string with the characters **#M.** The letter M, in this case, stands for "main file."

Performing the search. You can begin the search by clicking on the **OK** button in the Find dialog box. When the search is complete, another window will come up, entitled **Find: *string*,** where *string* represents the find string you have selected. This is the CSI report window. It provides information about the item you have found.

If the search item is a COBOL data item, source lines containing the string will be flagged with the indicators **Defn, Use, Mod, Qual,** or **Test,** depending on the way the item was used on that line. A copy library member will be bounded by **Copy** and **Endcpy.** If you are searching for a procedure, **Exec** and **Efrom** will indicate places where the searched procedure executes another procedure or is being executed from another line. If the search item is simply a text string, lines containing the string will be flagged with **Fnd.**

With all types of Find operations, you can use the **Compress** option on the Animator V2 View menu to display only the flagged lines. When you select **Compress,** you'll see a cascaded menu. Choosing **Current finds** on that menu will cause Animator V2 to show only the lines marked during the most recent Find operation. Choosing **Expand** returns the display to its original form to show all source lines.

This feature can be used to move around in the source file. Suppose you compress the display to show only the flagged lines, then move the cursor to one of those lines, then expand the display again. The Animator V2 display will move to the part of your text file that contains this particular flagged line.

Finding and replacing text strings. If you select the radio button for **Type: Text,** you can use the Replace option. Enter the replacement text string in the **Replace:** field. If you're feeling brave and you want to replace all instances of that text string in one operation, then select the **Replace All** check box. Otherwise, you can find each instance and decide whether or not to replace it. Clicking with the mouse on the **Next** or **Previous** buttons will move your display to the next or previous instance of the string to be replaced. If you want to replace the string in that line, click on the **Replace** button.

15.8.2 Setting Find Options

By using the **Find Options** selection on the Animator V2 **Options** pull-down menu, you can display a dialog box that lets you change the way the Find function will work. You can also get this display by clicking on the **Options** display at the bottom of the Find window. If you use this button, the Options display will show only those selections that pertain to the type of search that you are doing.

General options. The display in Figure 15.19 appears when you choose the **Find Options** selection. Because the **General options** radio button is selected by default, the **General Options** check boxes will appear. These allow you to choose whether or not to show the Find report box, and whether to adjust the size of the report box each time you do another Find operation.

COBOL Procedure finds. If you select the **COBOL Procedure finds** radio button, you'll see the set of options shown in Figure 15.20. Before you search for a COBOL procedure name, the check boxes let you decide how much information to show. They work in much the same way as the toggle switches in the function key CSI menu.

When you select the **Display PERFORMs, Display GO TOs,** or **Display CALLs,** check boxes will respectively display the names of routines accessed by PERFORM statements, GO TO statements, or CALL statements. Some check box selections work together with other options. For example, the **Display paragraphs** check box determines whether to display paragraph names or only section names when searching for **Display executed procedures** and **Display where procedure is called.** Similarly, the **Perform Level** setting lets you decide how many nest levels should be considered when searching for PERFORMing or PERFORMed routines. You can set the perform level up or down by clicking on the up or down arrow buttons.

COBOL data item finds. If you click on the **COBOL data item finds** radio button, you will see the set of options shown in Figure 15.21. These selections let you decide which source lines to highlight and which to ignore. Most of these are self-explanatory. **Display children of data item** will make the results include detail items within the group item you are FINDing. **Display related data** will make the results include all data related to the original item. Related data includes data items defined over the same area of memory, the file definition for a data item defined within a record, and the data field on which a condition name depends.

Text Finds. Finally, if you choose the **Text Finds** radio button, you will see the check boxes shown in Figure 15.22. You can choose whether to restrict your search to the area bounded by the margins, and whether the search should be case sensitive.

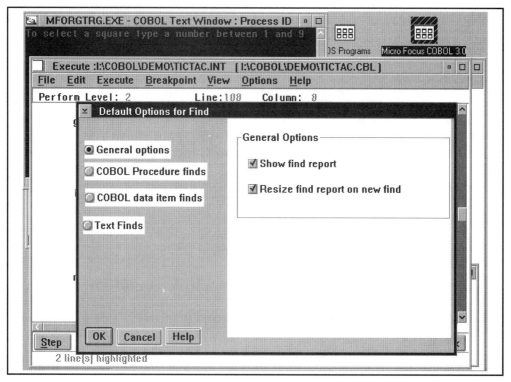

Figure 15.19 General find options

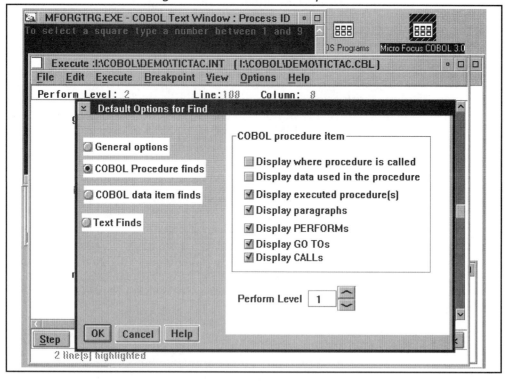

Figure 15.20 COBOL Procedure find options

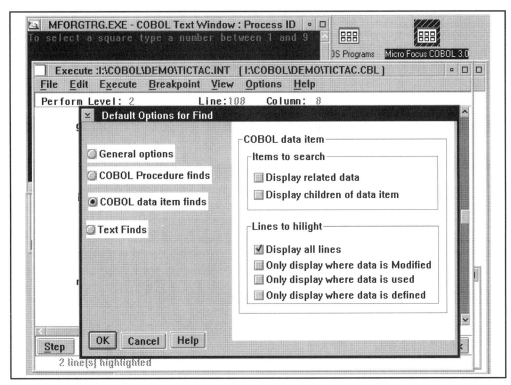

Figure 15.21 COBOL data item find options

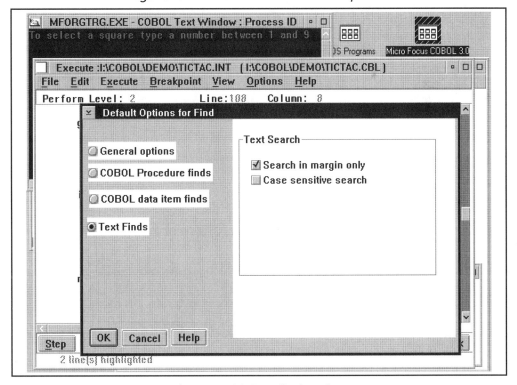

Figure 15.22 Text find options

15.9 Exercises

1.   Start Animator V2 from the GUI Workbench. Load CUST.CBL into Animator V2 so that you can edit it. Use the editor to add some field validation logic to this program. Experiment with using the mouse to perform block copy and move operations.

2.   Check the new version of CUST.CBL. (If you are using a version of Animator V2 that does not have the Checker implemented in it, then go back to the Workbench Organizer and bring up the Checker from its tool icon, check CUST.CBL, and load CUST.INT into Animator V2.)

3.   Animate CUST.INT. Use the Examine function to monitor the customer number field. Notice that the COBOL text window will contain the program's output. Whenever CUST.INT is awaiting user input, activate the COBOL text window and use the keyboard to enter data so that it appears in that window.

4.   Load TICTAC.INT into the Animator. (Recheck TICTAC.CBL if it has not already been checked.) Notice that, even though you are in animation (execution) mode, you can view and edit TICTAC.CBL. Use the **Save as...** option on the **File** pull-down menu to save a copy of TICTAC.CBL under another name. Use the **Find** button to perform searches on various data and procedure names within this program. Obtain program statistics for TICTAC.

16

Workbench GUI Utilities

16.1 Introduction

Micro Focus has implemented other utilities in graphics mode besides Animator V2. In this chapter, we will concentrate on the Workbench GUI utilities most relevant to the mainframe applications developer, particularly those that are fully supported with Workbench v3.0.

A disclaimer: As this chapter went to press, not all GUI Workbench facilities were completely implemented. Microsoft Windows support was not yet available. Some facilities, such as Session Recorder, were planned for early release status. Subsequent production versions may differ in certain respects. This chapter describes only those facilities that were scheduled for the initial GUI Workbench release. New facilities may be added later in the form of maintenance upgrades or GUI versions of add-on products.

Facilities that are supplied in early release status are for the purposes of familiarization and testing only. The early release license agreement does not permit use of those facilities for production use. This is because the functionality of Early Release products can change. *Early Release products are shipped on separate diskettes.*

16.2 Directory Facility (MFDIR V2)

16.2.1 Description

MFDIR V2 provides a graphical user interface to the MS-DOS or OS/2 file system. It combines the directory and File Finder (MFFINDER) facilities, allowing you to do the following:

- Display disk directories
- Move up and down in the directory hierarchy
- Display a directory tree structure diagram
- Select one or more files for copying or deleting
- Access files within Micro Focus library (.LBR) files
- Search for filenames within your directory structure
- Select a group of files for copying

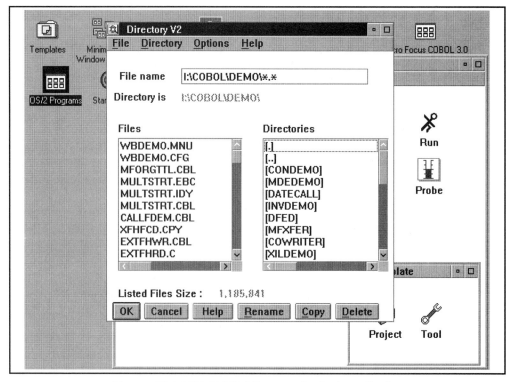

Figure 16.1 MFDIR V2 (directory) window display

The group copying function contains a useful new feature. If you select a group of files for backing up and run out of room on the first diskette, MFDIR V2 will automatically ask you to insert another.

Other Micro Focus GUI Workbench functions call the MFDIR V2 File Open dialog whenever the user selects a function that involves picking a filename from a directory list. The File Open dialog is a subset of the MFDIR V2 facility. In that regard, MFDIR V2 plays a role within the GUI Workbench similar to the role that the function key directory facility plays within the function key Workbench menu system. The function key directory facility handles the filename prompt and directory menu options that appear at the bottom of many text-mode Workbench screens. If you write PC-based GUI applications, your applications can call MFDIR V2 to prompt the user to specify a valid filename.

16.2.2 Invoking MFDIR V2

You can start MFDIR V2 by clicking on its tool icon in the Workbench Organizer. You also can invoke MFDIR V2 from the command line with the following command:

```
MFD2PM
```

Figure 16.1 shows the initial MFDIR V2 display. When it first appears, it will show the contents of the current directory. As MFDIR V2 reads the directory information from the disk, the size of the sliders on the vertical scroll bars will indicate how much of the information has been read into the display so far. The scroll bar slider has a specific meaning in the OS/2 PM and Microsoft Windows environments. The proportion of the length of the slider to the length of the entire scroll bar reflects the proportion of the amount of information visible in the window to the entire amount available by scrolling the display.

The name of the directory whose contents are being displayed is shown in the **Directory is** field. The **Files** scrollable box shows the filenames present in that directory. In the **Filename** field, you can enter *.* to display all files in the directory, or you can enter a partial or complete filename and extension to restrict what will be displayed. You can use wildcard characters in this field.

The **Directories** scrollable box shows all of the subdirectories beneath the current directory, followed by the drive letters for all of the logical disk drives available on your system. You can change to another drive or directory by clicking on one of these identifiers. If you want to move upward in the directory hierarchy to the parent of the current directory, click on the **[..]** directory name. That identifier always represents a pointer to the parent of the current directory.

16.2.3 Simple File Commands

You can configure the MFDIR V2 display and perform various operations by selecting various options from the pull-down menus. Figure 16.2 shows the contents of the MFDIR V2 **File** pull-down menu. Selecting **Exit** on this menu will terminate MFDIR V2.

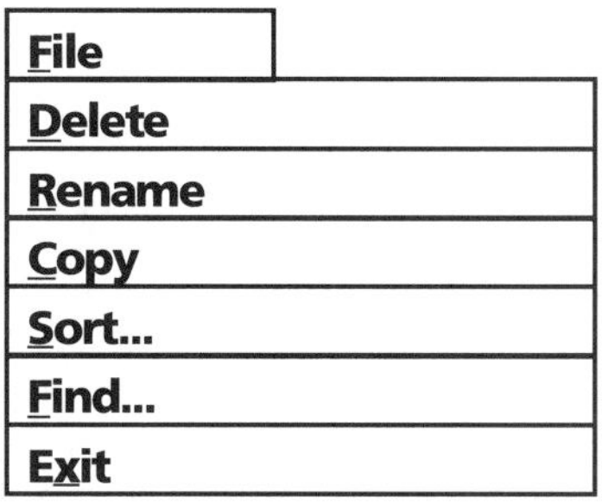

File
Delete
Rename
Copy
Sort...
Find...
Exit

Figure 16.2 MFDIR V2 (directory) File pull-down menu

The **Delete file, Rename file,** and **Copy file** options all work in conjunction with the **Files** scrollable list. Select an existing filename from the scrollable list by clicking on it. The selected filename will appear in highlighted text. Then choose the action from the **File** pull-down menu. If you choose **Delete file,** MFDIR V2 will ask you to confirm the delete before anything happens to the file. (You can turn off this safety feature if desired.) If you choose **Rename file** or **Copy file,** MFDIR V2 will ask you to enter the new filename in a field at the top of the window. You can precede the filename with any valid drive and directory path. You can also use wildcard characters such as *.* for the destination filename if you want to copy one or more files to a different drive or directory path using the same filenames as before.

Selecting multiple files. You can highlight more than one file at a time by holding the **Ctrl** key and clicking the *left* mouse button on each filename you want to select. Each file that you select will immediately appear in a separate window entitled **Extended Selection List.**

Sorting the filename display. The **Sort Files...** option on the File pull-down menu lets you choose the order in which MFDIR V2 will display its list of files. As shown in Figure 16.3, the **Sort Options** dialog box allows you to sort the display on filename, extension, date, or size. You can select ascending or descending order. If you select **Unsorted,** MFDIR V2 will display files in the order they actually appear in the disk directory.

16.2.4 Searching for Files

The **Find File** option on the **File** pull-down menu lets you search for filenames within your current directory and, optionally, within subdirectories below it. You can also search Micro Focus library (.LBR) files. Selecting the Find File menu option brings up a **FIND FILE** dialog box, as shown in Figure 16.4.

The **Search Spec** field lets you enter the directory path and filename you want to find. You can use wildcard characters as either prefixes or suffixes in the filename. If you want to begin your search at the root directory to search an entire drive precede the filename with a single backslash character ("\") to identify the root directory path. If you don't specify a path, Find File will begin its search with the current directory.

Once you have entered the search specification, you can go ahead with the search by clicking on the **Find** button in the **FIND FILE** dialog box. Any filenames that match the search criteria will appear in the **Extended Selection List** dialog box in Figure 16.4. This list allows you to gather a group of files to be deleted, renamed, or copied to another drive or directory.

Configuring Find File behavior. Pressing the **Options** button in the Find File dialog box will bring up the **Search Type** dialog box in Figure 16.5.

- If you select **Restrict search to specified directory,** Find File will look only at the directory path that you specified, and not at any subdirectories below that directory in the hierarchy. If you don't choose this option, Find File will search the entire directory tree below the directory you specified.
- The **Only search in libraries** radio button tells Find File to search only within Micro Focus library (.LBR) files. Conversely, **Do not search libraries** tells Find File to ignore the contents of Micro Focus library files. Obviously, these options are mutually exclusive. If you select neither option, Find File will search both the disk directory and the library files.
- The **File attributes** check boxes let you display only those files that have certain attributes in the disk directory.

16.2.5 Directory Commands

The **Directory** pull-down menu in Figure 16.6 lets you perform operations that involve directory names.

- If you select **Show default,** MFDIR V2 will show you a dialog box that contains the name of the current default directory.

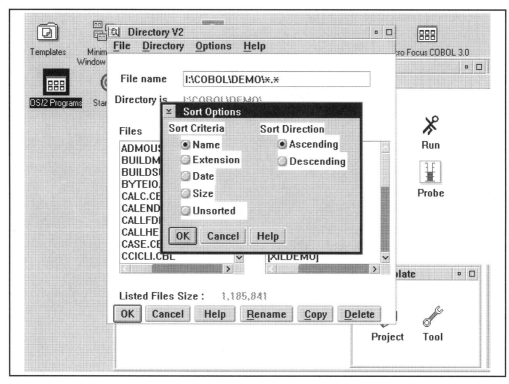

Figure 16.3 MFDIR V2 (directory) Sort Files dialog box

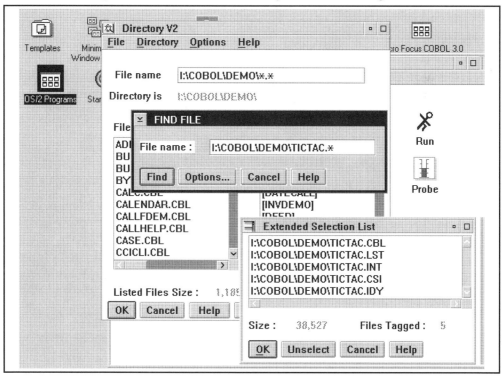

Figure 16.4 MFDIR V2 (directory) Find File dialog box

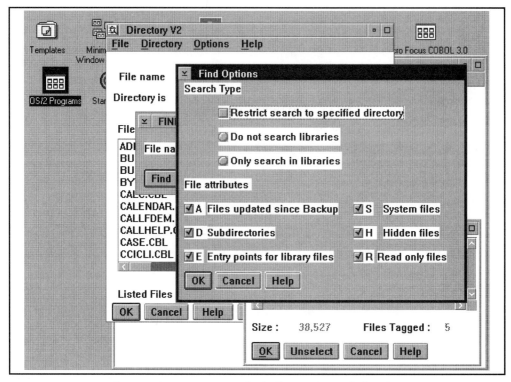

Figure 16.5 MFDIR V2 Find File Options dialog box

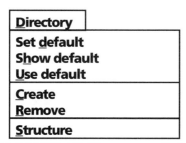

Figure 16.6 MFDIR V2 Directory pull-down menu

- To change to a new default directory, enter that path in the **Filename** field and select **Set default.** The pathname that you enter must actually exist.
- Depending on previous selections you have made, MFDIR V2 may be displaying a directory other than the default directory. The **Directory is** field will identify the directory being shown. If you want MFDIR V2 to display the default directory, select **Use default** from the Directory pull-down menu.
- **Create** will create a new subdirectory under the directory that is currently being shown. Enter the new directory name in the **Filename** field.
- **Remove** will delete the directory whose name is in the **Filename** field. The directory must not contain any files or subdirectories. By default, MFDIR V2 will prompt you to confirm the deletion.

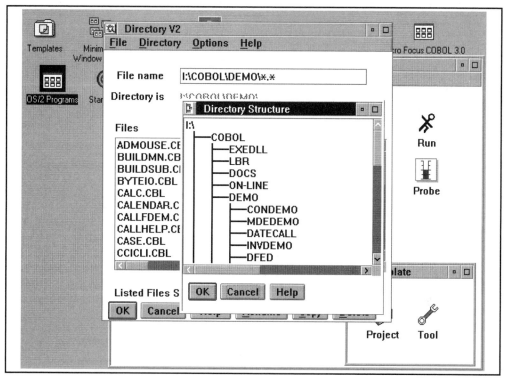

Figure 16.7 MFDIR V2 Directory Structure display

- **Directory structure** will display a scrollable directory tree structure diagram, as shown in Figure 16.7.

16.2.6 Configuration Options

The **Options** pull-down menu, shown in Figure 16.8, lets you configure the
operation of MFDIR V2.

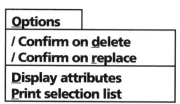

Figure 16.8 MFDIR V2 Options pull-down menu

- **Confirm on delete** and **Confirm on replace** let you turn off the safety feature
so that you will not have to confirm each delete or rewrite operation. A
check mark next to each option indicates whether it is turned on or off. This
can come in handy if you have an unusually large number of files to delete.
However, you would be well advised to check your filenames very carefully
before proceeding in this manner.

- **Display attributes** will show the file size and date along with each filename.
To see this information, you can scroll the file list box, or you can expand
the entire MFDIR V2 window to full-screen size.

- **Print selection list** will send a list of all files currently selected to the printer. This helps you to make sure that the right files have been selected for backup or deletion.

16.3 On-line Information System (GUI Hypertext Help)

16.3.1 Description

This product lets you view help files created to work with the On-line Information hypertext help system. You use it in much the same way you would use the text-mode hypertext help file viewer. The GUI version, however, comes up in a window, with improved visual appearance and more convenient mouse support.

All of the Micro Focus GUI Workbench tools, as well as the Workbench Organizer itself, provide **Help** pull-down menus on the action bar of each window. For example, Figure 15.4 in Chapter 15 showed the Help pull-down menu provided with Animator V2. Many GUI Workbench dialog boxes also provide **Help** push buttons where appropriate.

What's happening "under the covers?" Whenever the user requests a help function, the Micro Focus utility calls the On-line Information System, passing it a keyword that tells it what topic or index to display when it first appears. As in the function key menu system, you can also use the GUI On-line Information System from the command line prompt to display help databases you have created. Chapter 11 tells you how to create your own hypertext help source files and compile them through the On-line Information System Compiler (OLISC).

You can view the same help databases with both the GUI version and the function key version of the On-line Information System. The GUI version of the help system works much like the version provided with the function key Workbench, except for the fact that all screen features are in graphics mode.

16.3.2 Command line interface

You can invoke the On-line Information System from the command line with the following command:

```
RUNPM ON-LINE [file.HNF![topic]]
```

where *file* is the name of the hypertext help database, and *topic,* optionally, is a topic name within that database. If you omit the help database name, then the help system will default to showing you the Micro Focus COBOL help database, as shown in Figure 16.9. Available hypertext database (.HNF) files are present in the ON-LINE subdirectory supplied with the Workbench.

If you specify a topic name, the help system will look up that topic and show it to you, if it is present. Otherwise, the help system will start its display with the main table of contents. You must enter the exclamation point delimiter even if you don't specify a topic name.

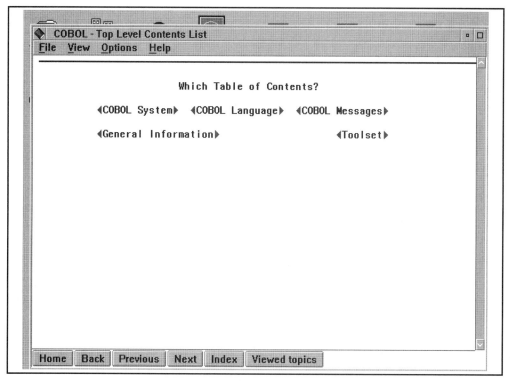

Figure 16.9 On-line Information (HYHELP) display

16.3.3 On-line Information menu options

The GUI version of the help system will display the help information in a graphics mode window with several mouse buttons at the bottom.

- **Home** will get you back to the home topic for the current help file.
- **Back** will return to the last display that you selected.
- **Previous** will show the topic that occurs just before the current topic in the help database.
- **Next** will show the topic that occurs just after the current topic in the help database.
- **Index** will display a help topic index in a separate scrollable window. You can double-click on any topic in that window so that its text will display in the main help window.
- **Viewed topics** will display a list of the previous topics that you have displayed in a separate scrollable window. You can double-click on any topic in that window so that its text will display in the main help window.

The File pull-down menu. The menu in Figure 16.10 lets you select the files that the hypertext system will be using.

- The **Open** selection on the File pull-down menu lets you open a different hypertext help file.
- **Copy to file** copies the text in the help topic display to a new ASCII text file.

- **Append to file** appends the text in the help topic display to an existing ASCII text file.
- **Print** sends the text in the help topic display to the printer.
- The **Exit** selection on the File pull-down menu terminates the help display. If you entered the help function from within some other application, you will return to that application.

File	
Open...	
Copy to file...	**Ctrl+F**
Append to file...	**Ctrl+A**
Print...	
Exit	**F3**

Figure 16.10 On-line Information File pull-down menu

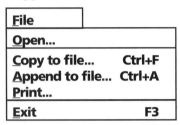

View		
Include	**=>**	**Buttons**
Next topic		
Previous topic		
Home topic	**Ctrl+Home**	
Most recent topic	**Esc**	
Viewed topics	**Ctrl+V**	
Index	**Ctrl+N**	
Contents	**Ctrl+C**	

Figure 16.11 On-line Information View/Include cascaded menus

The View pull-down menu. The menu in Figure 16.11 lets you choose the topics that will be displayed. Most of the options on the View menu are the same as those provided by the buttons at the bottom of the help display window. The **Most recent topic** selection is equivalent to the **Back** push button. Selecting **Include** reveals a cascaded menu that lets you choose whether or not you want the buttons to be visible. In addition, selecting **Contents** will display the table of contents within your current help file.

Options	
Search...	**Ctrl+S**
Repeat last search	**Ctrl+R**
Topic Search...	**Ctrl+T**
Bookmark...	

Figure 16.12 On-line Information Options pull-down menu

The Options pull-down menu. The menu in Figure 16.12 lets you perform customized searches of the help file contents.

- **Search** brings up a dialog box, shown in Figure 16.13, that allows you to search the current help file for a text string. Radio buttons allow you to set

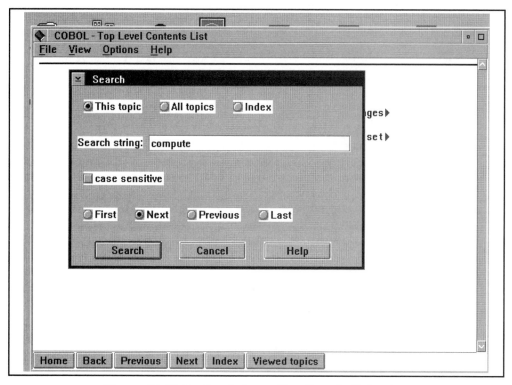

Figure 16.13 On-line Information Search dialog box

the scope of the text search: the current topic only, all topics in the file, or simply the index entries. A check box determines whether or not the search should be case sensitive. A second series of radio buttons lets you search backward or forward in the help file to find multiple instances of a text string.

- **Repeat last search** lets you redo the last search operation to find more instances of the same text string.

- **Topic search** brings up a small box that lets you enter a topic name. If that topic exists in the current help file, the help system will display it. Figure 16.14, for example, shows the first screen page of the COBOL SORT topic, obtained by entering the word SORT.

- **Bookmark** brings up a dialog box, shown in Figure 16.15, that lets you create your own bookmarks within the help system. If you often need to refer to the same help display, you can set a pointer to that display that will let you return to it quickly. The default name of the current display will appear in the text box at the top of the screen, although you can overtype it with something more to your liking. If you click on **Add,** the help system will use that name to create a pointer to your current screen. You can click on a bookmark name in the list to select it for **Rename** or **Delete** operations. To redisplay the screen that goes with a bookmark entry, you can highlight that entry and then click the **Goto** button, or you can simply double-click on the entry.

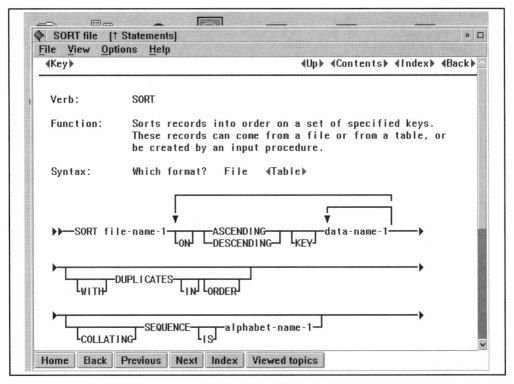

Figure 16.14 On-line Information COBOL SORT topic

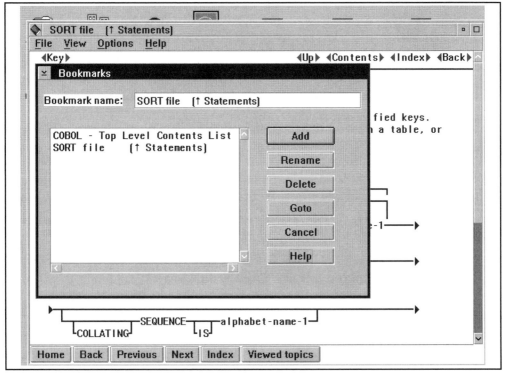

Figure 16.15 On-line Information Bookmark dialog box

16.4 Session Recorder

16.4.1 Description

The GUI Session Recorder lets you record keyboard and mouse input and screen output for any OS/2 applications that use the Presentation Manager GUI interface or the VIO interface. It lets you capture "old" and "new" snapshots of your application and compare the results.

16.4.2 Changes from the Text Mode Version

The GUI Session Recorder works differently from the text mode version in several ways. **The GUI version of the Session Recorder will work only with applications that use the OS/2 Presentation Manager or the OS/2 VIO interface.** This includes the rest of the Workbench GUI utilities, as well as text mode applications that run in an OS/2 window. You can easily use the GUI Session Recorder to record and play back an Animator V2 session, for example.

The GUI Session Recorder captures its information directly from OS/2 rather than from the Micro Focus RTS. **You can capture screen and keyboard I/O only from the application that is running under the Session Recorder.** It does not record anything outside the GUI application that you started up. Suppose you want to record a GUI animation session. You cannot start the GUI Session Recorder from within Animator V2. Instead, you start the Session Recorder first, then start the Animator V2 from within the Session Recorder, and then run your program under the Animator V2.

Instead of converting screen images to text files, the Session Recorder captures screen images as standard OS/2 PM bitmap files and stores them in compressed format. The PMView snapshot file viewer can view them on the screen or allow you to recapture them with the OS/2 PM clipboard.

Unlike the function key Session Recorder, version 3.0 of the GUI Session Recorder does *not* provide an editing facility to let you change the contents of the keystroke file.

Finally, PMView does *not* use the Micro Focus DIFF facility to compare screen snapshot files, because DIFF handles text files only.

16.4.3 Processing Flow

Suppose you want to use the GUI Session Recorder to find out how an application program change will affect the screen output. Here are the steps involved:

- Start the GUI Session Recorder from the icon or from the command line. You should see a screen display resembling Figure 16.16.
- Select the recording mode by clicking on the **Playback Test** check box until you have turned it off. You can tell that it is turned off because the **X** will disappear.
- In the **Test Filename** field, supply a filename for your keystroke recording file. This filename will also be used for the snapshot files. You don't need to enter the filename extension; Session Recorder will supply the appropriate extension for each file type.

- In the **Command line** field, enter whatever command line input is needed to start your application. If you want to record your program running under Animator V2, enter ANIM2PM *progname* on the command line. Then press the enter key.

- You should see a small control window with three push buttons, as shown at the bottom of Figure 16.17. To start your application running under the GUI Session Recorder in Record mode, click on the **Record** button. In this control window, the **Options** menu contains the same three selections that are on the push buttons. The **View** menu will let you see an error log file. When you want to end the GUI Session Recorder, select **Exit** from the **File** menu.

- Test your application by entering the keyboard or mouse input that it needs. The GUI Session Recorder will stop recording when the application terminates. If desired, you can stop recording by selecting the **Stop** button in the Session Recorder's control window. During this test, the GUI Session Recorder will create a keystroke file and an "old" screen snapshot file. See the On-line Information for the filename extensions used in your release of the GUI Workbench.

- Make your source code changes and recheck your application.

- Bring up the GUI Session Recorder and select the playback mode by clicking on the **Playback Test** check box. Supply the name of your test file and press the enter key. You'll see the GUI Session Recorder using your keystroke recording file to step through your application. Meanwhile, it will create a "new" screen snapshot file.

- Use the GUI Session Recorder's PMView facility to compare the screen images in the old and new screen snapshot files.

16.4.4 Invoking Session Recorder

You can start Session Recorder by clicking on the Session tool icon from the GUI Workbench Organizer. It will ask you for the name of a new or existing control file. Similarly, you can invoke the PMView facility by clicking on the PMView tool icon and entering the test filename in the dialog box. If you don't specify a filename extension, the snapshot viewer will assume you want to compare old and new snapshot files that have the default filename extensions.

- The **Playback test** check box on the GUI Session Recorder menu lets you switch into playback mode. If this button is not selected, you will be in recording mode, which preserves your keystroke input as well as the screen output. Playback mode will replay your existing keystroke file so that your application will generate new screen images. What filenames do you need in each mode? In recording mode, you must enter both the test filename and the command line information to start your application. In playback mode, just enter the test filename. Data in the keystroke file will restart your application for you at playback time, so that you don't need to specify the application command line information.

- The **Verbose Output** check box lets you switch into verbose mode. This option controls what happens when you are comparing the old and new screen snapshot files. If verbose mode is active, it will tell you whether each

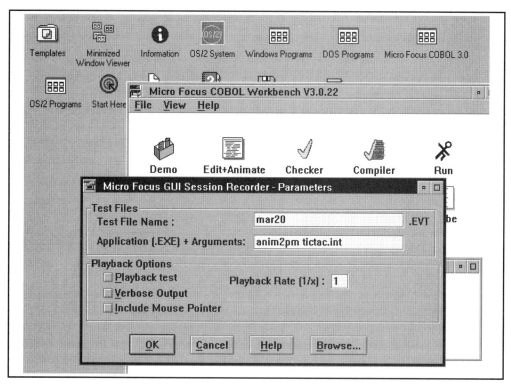

Figure 16.16 Session Recorder Parameters dialog box

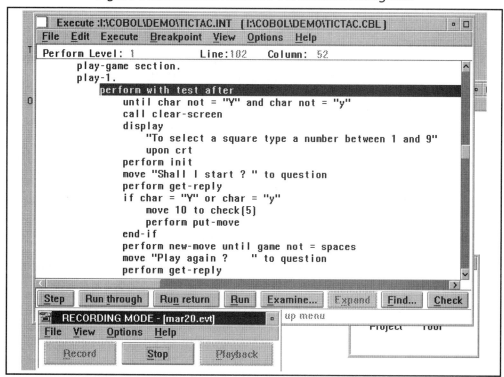

Figure 16.17 Session Recorder in recording mode

comparison resulted in a match or a mismatch. Without verbose mode, it will report only the mismatches.

- The **Playback Rate [1/x]** field lets you specify the playback speed as a ratio of the actual time spent during recording. The default is 1, which means that the application will play back at the same speed it was recorded. Playback rate values greater than 1 will work successfully only if your application is not time-dependent.

Using the command line. You can also invoke the Session Recorder from the command line with the following command:

```
SESS2PM flags test-file-name application-file-name application-arguments
```

In this command, *test-file-name* is the name of your keystroke capture file. *Application-file-name* and *application-arguments* are required only in recording mode, not in playback mode. They are used to start up the application that you want to record. *Flags* can be any of the following:

- **/p** switches the GUI Session Recorder into playback mode.
- **/v** switches the GUI Session Recorder into verbose mode.

16.5 GUI File Transfer Aid (MFXFER V2)

16.5.1 Description

MFXFER V2 is a utility for transmitting files to and from the mainframe. To use MFXFER V2, you must already have PC-to-mainframe communications hardware and software. MFXFER V2 gives you a higher-level user interface to that software. It lets you move a large number of files in one operation, convert between ASCII and EBCDIC, and copy programs along with the subroutines and copy library members that they need. Both the function key and GUI versions of MFXFER will work with IBM, IRMA, or any other PC-to-host protocol that has a similar command line interface.

MFXFER V2 provides a simplified graphical user interface that shows the progress of the file transfer operation. During transfer, you can see how many files have been transferred successfully, how many transfer attempts have failed, how many subprograms and copy libraries have been scanned, and how many bytes have been transferred.

MFXFER V2 supports user-installable transfer modules. It comes with two existing transfer modules. The first module, XFER, executes MS-DOS or OS/2 commands in a command line shell by means of DOSEXEC. The second module, WSP/2, interfaces to the WorkStation Platform/2 Library Services for use with IBM's host-based Software Configuration and Library Manager (SCLM).

Important: If you are transferring a source file containing embedded hex characters, do not use the ASCII conversion within IBM's 3270 Send/Receive protocol. If you do, you won't get the same file back when you convert it from EBCDIC to ASCII to EBCDIC again. The proper method is to transfer your file in binary format, without conversion, and then use MDECONV for the ASCII/EBCDIC translation. MFXFER V2 lets you invoke MDECONV automatically after completing the file transfer. Chapter 9 contains more details about choosing the right options for mainframe/PC file conversion.

16.5.2 Invoking MFXFER V2

You can invoke MFXFER V2 from the **File Transfer** tool icon in the Workbench Organizer. You can also invoke File Transfer from the command line with the following command:

```
MFXFERPM
```

16.5.3 Operation of MFXFER V2

File transfer profile names. When you bring up MFXFER V2, you'll see the File Transfer Utility main menu display shown in Figure 16.18. The text area contains a scrollable list of **file transfer profiles.** A profile lets you set up all of the parameters for transferring one or more files in unattended operation. Parameters include host and PC operating system, direction of file transfer, mainframe and PC file and directory names, conversion options, copy and subroutine library members, source control system commands, and so forth. You can use profiles supplied with the Workbench or create your own. (The **Edit** pull-down menu shown in Figure 16.19 lets you modify, copy, or delete existing profiles or create new ones.)

To choose a profile from the list, click on it with the mouse. The profile name will appear in highlighted type and it will also appear in the **Current**

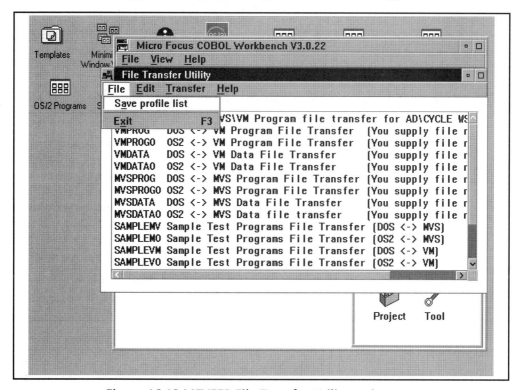

Figure 16.18 MFXFER File Transfer Utility main menu

profile selected text box. Double-clicking on a profile name will let you modify its filename, directory path, and description.

Figure 16.18 shows the **File** pull-down menu associated with the MFX-FER V2 main menu. On this menu, **Exit** terminates the application. **Save profile list** will save any changes you have made to the profile list on this screen.

The **Edit** option (Figure 16.19) on the MFXFER V2 main menu bar lets you copy, create, delete, or update profile names. These operations maintain the header information for each profile. You will specify details about individual files within each profile in the **Files to transfer** window.

Finally, the **Transfer** option (Figure 16.20) on the MFXFER V2 main menu bar lets you choose whether you want to transfer just one file or a preselected group of files. On the Transfer pull-down menu, **Single file transfer...** will bring up the single file transfer window shown in Figure 16.21. To set up a group of files for transfer, use the mouse to click on the name of the profile that defines this group. **Multi-file with profile** will fetch the selected profile and display it in the **Files to transfer** window in Figure 16.22.

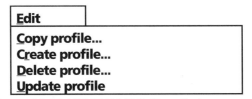

Figure 16.19 MFXFER V2 Edit pull-down menu

Figure 16.20 MFXFER V2 Transfer pull-down menu

Single file transfer. You can use the single file transfer window if you want to transfer only one file at a time. Enter the filename in the host and PC environments and select the radio buttons for host operating system type and transfer direction. If needed, use the check boxes to select ASCII conversion and carriage return/line feed insertion. Be sure that your PC is signed on to the host. Then click on the **Transfer** button to begin the transfer operation.

Multiple file transfer. To transfer a group of files, you'll need to select a profile from the MFXFER V2 main menu. The **Select profile** function will bring up the **Files to transfer** display shown in Figure 16.22. The profile that you have selected will be displayed in detail. It contains a list of the files that MFXFER V2 will transfer. You'll see the PC filename, the host filename, and the status (whether that file has already been transferred or not). Before starting a file transfer, you must edit the file list to make sure the right files are present.

The **Files to transfer** display also contains radio buttons that specify the direction of file transfer, and the status of the files that you want to transfer. Choosing **Current** will transfer the filename that you have highlighted on the

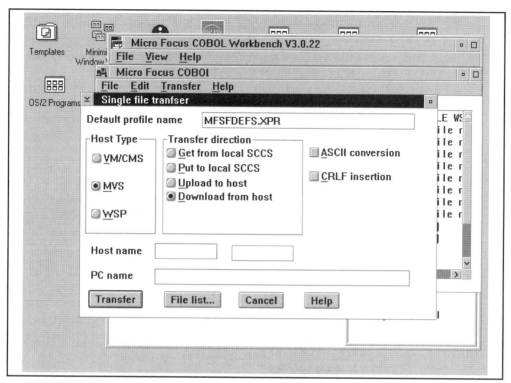

Figure 16.21 MFXFER V2 Single file transfer window

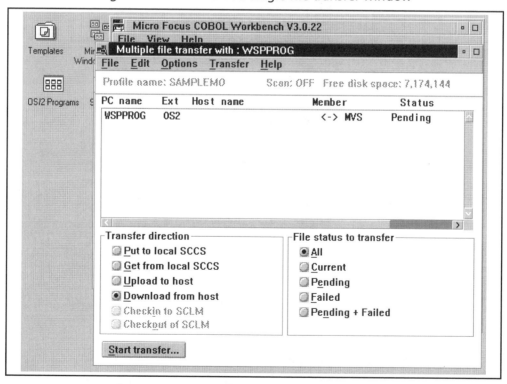

Figure 16.22 MFXFER V2 Files to transfer display

list. Choosing **All** will transfer all files on the list, even if some of them have already been transferred successfully. The other options let you resume a file transfer process following an interruption. Clicking on the **Start transfer...** button will begin the operation.

Each profile, or "file list," is stored in a separate file. The **File** menu in Figure 16.23 lets you update the file list file. **Save file list and defaults...** simply writes all of your changes back to disk. **File list location...** lets you select filenames from a PC directory list, so that you can add them to the file list. **Exit** gets you back to the main menu.

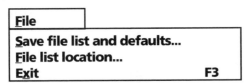

Figure 16.23 MFXFER V2 Files to transfer File pull-down menu

The **Edit** pull-down on the **Files to transfer** screen contains the same selections as the Edit pull-down on the main menu. It lets you change, copy, or delete existing filenames on the list, or add new filenames (Figure 16.24)

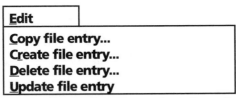

Figure 16.24 MFXFER V2 Files to transfer Edit pull-down menu

```
Options
PC defaults...
Host defaults...
Transfer defaults...
Conversion defaults...
Subprograms to ignore...
Copy files to ignore...
Display extended status...
Scan
Scan list...
Transfer mechanism...
```

Figure 16.25 MFXFER V2 Files to transfer Options pull-down menu

The **Options** pull-down menu in Figure 16.25 lets you specify groups of default settings much like those available on the function key MFXFER menus.

- **PC defaults** lets you specify the file directories and filename extensions on the PC side, as well as commands for a local source code control system if you use one.

- **Host defaults** lets you specify the mainframe operating system and the qualified filenames on the mainframe side, as well as commands for a mainframe source code control system if you use one.

- **Transfer defaults** lets you specify the SEND and RECEIVE command format. You can also use the check boxes to select ASCII conversion and carriage return/line feed insertion, if needed.

- **Conversion defaults** lets you specify whether to check for nontext characters, and whether to terminate processing if a nontext character or an error is found. You can also specify default filename extensions for ASCII and EBCDIC files, as well as the logical record length. You can use the check boxes to select ASCII conversion and carriage return/line feed insertion.

- If desired, MFXFER V2 will transfer copy members and subprograms along with your source file. If you want MFXFER V2 to omit certain modules that are already on your system, you can select **Subprograms to ignore** and **Copy files to ignore**. These selections provide scrollable list boxes into which you can enter the names that you want to ignore.

- **Display extended status** shows the fully qualified PC and host filenames and the status for the current file.

Scanning for related files to transfer. The **Scan** and **Scan list...** options let you choose whether or not to scan for copy member and subroutine filenames. The **Scan** selection in this menu is a toggle switch that sets the scanning function on or off. For example, if scanning is on and MFXFER V2 finds a COPY statement in your program, MFXFER V2 will transfer the copy member as well as the main program. The **Scan list...** function lets you add new types of statement to the list.

A default list of statement types to be scanned are already built into the MFWB.CFG file. You can add new permanent defaults by editing MFWB.CFG. MFXFER V2 will scan for up to 64 types of file statement.

- CALLed subprograms, where the subprogram is specified as a literal in a COBOL CALL statement.

- CHAINed subprograms, where the subprogram is specified as a literal in a COBOL CHAIN statement.

- COBOL COPY files.

- PANVALET ++INCLUDE files, where ++INCLUDE begins in column 8.

- Librarian -INC files, where -INC begins in column 1.

- Files named in EXEC SQL statements.

- Files named in EXEC CICS statements.

Starting the transfer. The **Transfer** push button starts the actual file transfer process. This function is also on the menu bar.

The SCLM interface. The interface to Software Configuration and Library Manager (SCLM) will be available only if you have IBM's WorkStation Platform/2 (WSP/2) installed on your PC. Otherwise, the "Check in" and "Check out" options in MFXFER V2 will be grayed out. SCLM is a host-based source code library manager. Both SCLM and WSP/2 are AD/CYCLE products.

WSP/2 interfaces to the host for transparent access to library modules on either the host or the PC workstation.

16.6 GUI Source Comparison Utility (DIFF V2)

16.6.1 Description

DIFF V2 (Source Comparison) lets you compare two source files to find the differences. It displays the old and new text files side by side, with differences highlighted. It performs the same function as the text mode version of DIFF, but the new version displays its data in CUA-compliant graphics mode windows.

16.6.2 Invoking DIFF V2

The DIFF V2 tool icon. If you click on the **Compare** tool icon in the Workbench Organizer, you'll see the **Micro Focus File Comparison Utility** dialog box shown in Figure 16.26. It lets you enter the names of the two files that you want to compare. The **List files...** button brings up the File Open dialog from the MFDIR V2 facility, so that you can select input files from the directory list.

The command line interface. You also can invoke DIFF V2 from the command line with the following command:

```
DIFFPM old-file-name new-file-name [directives]
```

DIFF V2 can use most of the same command line directives used with the function key version of DIFF. For example, you can set the number of lines to look ahead to reestablish matching. You can use a DIFF.DIR file to set default directives for DIFF V2. However, with the GUI version you cannot use those directives that control listing output, such as LPT, FORM, PAUSE, and so forth.

16.6.3 Operation of DIFF V2

DIFF V2 will compare the two files as they are being loaded. You'll see a small dialog box showing the progress of files being loaded as a percentage of the total length. A push button allows you to **Abort** the process before loading is complete.

Let Diff find the needle in the haystack.

Once DIFF V2 has started running, you'll see a display resembling Figure 16.27. The old and new source files will each be visible in separate scrollable windows. All lines that contain differences will be flagged and highlighted. The filenames will appear in the window title bars. You can move, resize, minimize, or maximize each window separately if desired. However, if you scroll the contents of one window, the position of the source file within the other window will remain synchronized with it, to make it easier to compare them line for line.

You will also see a small control window containing only a menu bar, shown in the upper-left corner of

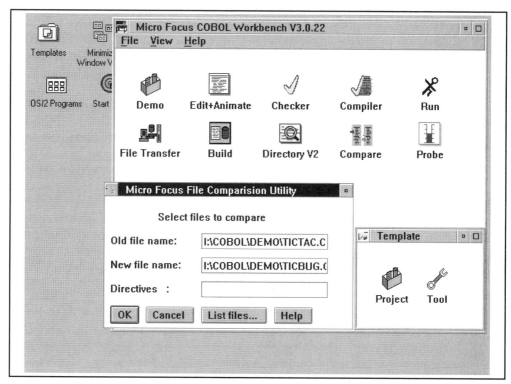

Figure 16.26 DIFF V2 dialog box for entering filenames

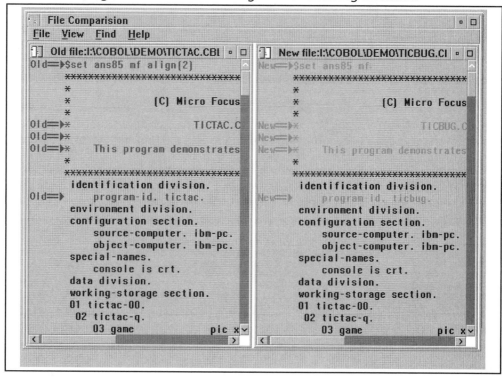

Figure 16.27 DIFF V2 comparison results, with File pull-down

Figure 16.27. The **File** pull-down menu is visible. It allows you to **Exit** from DIFF V2. It also contains a **New comparison** function that brings up the "Select files to compare" dialog box again. This dialog lets you enter a new pair of filenames to compare.

Configuring the DIFF V2 display. The **View** pull-down menu shown in Figure 16.28 lets you choose how DIFF V2 will display the two files.

- **Compress** will cause DIFF V2 to show only the flagged lines (the mismatched lines) in each source file.
- **Expand** will cause DIFF V2 to show all lines in each source file.
- **Mix** will merge the two windows into one file display, with **Old** and **New** lines placed together for comparison.
- **Split** will separate the file contents into two separate windows.

View	
Compress	Alt+O
Expand	Alt+E
Mix	Alt+M
Split	Alt+S
/ Show tags	Alt+H

Figure 16.28 DIFF V2 View menu

Positioning the DIFF V2 display. The **Find** pull-down menu in Figure 16.29 lets you search for source lines in the two files. Selecting the **Find** option on that menu will bring up a dialog that lets you enter a search string. If DIFF V2 finds the search string in the old or new file, it will highlight it and position the display to that line. **Next** and **Previous** will scroll the display forward or backward in the file to locate another instance of that string.

Find	
Next	Alt+N
Previous	Alt+P
Find...	Alt+I

Figure 16.29 DIFF V2 Find menu

16.7 Overview of Other New Workbench Functions

These utilities are not specific to the mainframe applications developer. We describe them here to make you aware of what is available, since you might find them to be useful for specialized needs.

16.7.1 Probe

Description. Probe is a utility that keeps track of memory usage and program module flow under OS/2. If you are running a large, complex application under OS/2, Probe will tell you how much memory is being allocated for each module and which programs and libraries are loaded or executing at each moment. Probe works somewhat like Structure Animator, but it concerns itself with programs within a system rather than modules within a program. Probe

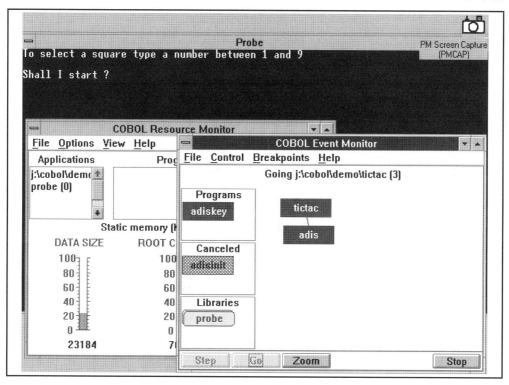

Figure 16.30 Probe display

will display a variety of sessions within an OS/2 system or across a network connected to an OS/2 server.

The Probe facility consists of two parts: the **Probe** module itself and the **Monitor.** Probe is written in COBOL and Monitor is written in SmallTalk, an object-oriented language. The Probe module gathers the information and the Monitor shows it to you.

In all cases, the Probe module must run on the same system as the application you want to view. The Monitor module must run on an OS/2 system. For example, if the application is running on an MS-DOS workstation connected to an OS/2 server, run the Probe module on the workstation and the Monitor on the OS/2 server. If the application is running on an OS/2 machine, both Probe and Monitor will run concurrently on that machine in separate OS/2 sessions.

Two types of monitors. Probe offers two types of monitors: the **resource monitor** and the **event monitor.** You can attach either or both types of monitor to an active Probe module. The resource module shows memory allocation, while the event monitor shows program module flow. In the event monitor window, each program and library module appears as an icon within a **container.** The container indicates whether the module is loaded, active, or cancelled. If you want a better view of how programs call one another, you can use the mouse to drag the program icons out of the container and onto the work area in the event monitor window. An example of Probe being run in this way is shown in Figure 16.30.

Behind the scenes. If you happen to be an OS/2 aficionado, here's how Probe and Monitor work. The Probe module is known as a **server application.** In other words, it is a "back end" application that specializes in handling that part of the work load that does not pertain to the user interface. In this case, Probe gathers data from the Workbench runtime system (RTS). The Monitor module is a **client application.** A client is a "front end" application that specializes in processing requests from the user. It communicates with its server application and passes that data back to the user. Probe and Monitor talk to each other through the Micro Focus COBOL Communications Interface (CCI). If you are connecting across MS-DOS and OS/2 machines, you'll need to specify Netbios as the connection method. Otherwise, you can use the default, which is CCI Named Pipes.

Starting Probe from the Workbench Organizer. You can start Probe from the Workbench by clicking on the Probe icon. Both the Probe and the Monitor modules will come up.

Starting Probe from the OS/2 command prompt. This is done in two steps:

- Start the Probe module by bringing up an OS/2 prompt window and entering **PROBE** at the command prompt. A text window will appear.
- Start the Monitor module by bringing up an OS/2 prompt window and entering **PRMON** at the command prompt. A graphics-mode window will appear.

Steps involved in using Probe. Once you've started Probe, you need to set up the monitor(s) and start your application from within a monitor. You'll need to decide whether you want to use the resource monitor or the event monitor or both. When you start the Monitor module, it always comes up as a resource monitor. If you want to use an event monitor, you have to start it from the resource monitor, as described below. Once you've started the event monitor, you can terminate the resource monitor if you no longer want it.

- If you plan to use the resource monitor, then go into the **File** pull-down menu of the resource monitor and select the option **Connect to Probe.**
- If you want to use *only* the resource monitor, and not the event monitor, then select **Start Application** on the **File** pull-down menu of the resource monitor. Enter the command needed to start that application. Probe will search the COBDIR path to find your application.
- If you plan to use the event monitor, you must select the **Monitor events** option from the resource monitor **File** menu. An event monitor window will appear. Connect the event monitor to the Probe and then start your application directly from the event monitor window. If you have not terminated the resource monitor window, you'll see your application being monitored in both the resource and event monitor windows.

Warning: Make sure that the Probe, the Monitor, and the Workbench itself are all from the same release of the Workbench. Otherwise, even if the executable filenames are the same across different releases, Probe and Monitor

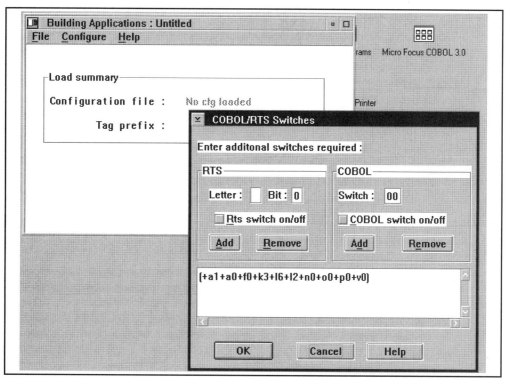

Figure 16.31 Build V2 display with COBOL/RTS switches

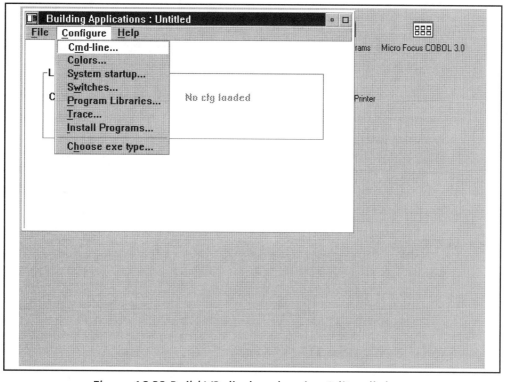

Figure 16.32 Build V2 display, showing Edit pull-down

might not be able to talk to each other or to the Workbench RTS. You can run into a problem with incompatible versions if you have more than one Workbench release on your system.

16.7.2 Build V2

Description. Build V2 is intended for packaging PC-based applications for distribution. It is the GUI version of the function key Build utility. It allows you to create executable files in .EXE format from .INT and .GNT files. By contrast, the linker creates .EXE files from .OBJ files. Because Build V2 is not for mainframe use, we will not discuss it in detail here. Complete information about using Build is in the *Toolset Reference,* one of the manuals provided with the Workbench.

Build V2 lets you set up a configuration (.CFG) file to specify parameters for your application. The .CFG file contains the name of the library files to load, the name of the main program, and the settings of runtime switches. Interactive screens let you specify this information, as shown in Figure 16.31. Incidentally, the main program doesn't have to be the first module in the .EXE file. Some of the flexibility of Build V2 is shown by the array of options on its Edit pull-down menu, shown in Figure 16.32. One useful feature of the .CFG file is that you can create applications that different users can colorize the way they want. One example of this is the MFWB.CFG file that specifies the colors that will appear in the Workbench function key menu system.

Build V2 lets you group modules together conveniently. If your application consists of several .INT or .GNT modules, you can put them together into one .EXE file. The disadvantage here is the large amount of memory that the .EXE file will require. You can avoid this problem by using a subroutine library. Build V2 lets you specify the name of the subroutine library that your application will use. What type of library? The .DLL files are not customarily used with Build V2. Instead, Micro Focus recommends that you use Build V2 to create an .EXE file from just the main program, and that you keep the remaining modules in a .LBR file.

Invoking Build. You can start Build V2 by clicking on the Build tool icon in the GUI Workbench Organizer. A dialog box will ask you to enter the name of a new or existing configuration file. You can also invoke Build V2 from the operating system command line with the following command:

```
BUILDPM
```

16.8 Other Enhancements with Workbench v3.0

Most of the enhancements provided with v3.0 have to do with GUI support, but some provide other forms of increased functionality. We have already discussed new Checker directives, as well as enhancements to the function key Workbench File Loader (WFL) and the Data File Editor (DFED).

16.8.1 Improved CICS Support

If you use either of the CICS options (MCO or MCO2) with Workbench v3.0, the Micro Focus Screens utility will create Basic Mapping Support (BMS) macros. Once you install MCO or MCO2, the Screens menu will contain an option for BMS. You can paint a screen and then convert it to BMS macros for use in your CICS programs. As of Workbench v3.0, the Screens facility is provided in text mode only.

16.8.2 Btrieve Support

The same COBOL syntax for indexed file I/O will work for Micro Focus V-ISAM files and for Btrieve files. If your program is creating a new indexed file, the new file will be created in V-ISAM format. (You can use WFL to convert it to Btrieve if desired.) If your program is using an existing file, the Micro Focus indexed file handler will recognize whether that file is in V-ISAM or Btrieve format and process it accordingly. Since MCO2 uses Btrieve files, this new feature makes it more convenient to share files between batch and on-line programs that you are testing on the PC.

16.8.3 The RUNPM Shell

The Workbench Organizer provides a **RUN** tool icon for running COBOL applications. It provides a runtime shell that lets you run both text-mode and GUI Workbench applications in a window. The executable program for this facility is RUNPM.EXE. The runtime shell for the function key Workbench, RUN.EXE, runs full-screen text-mode applications only.

A

Appendix A: PC Fundamentals for the Mainframe Programmer

If you have never used a PC before, or if you have not had enough PC exposure to be comfortable with using one, this introduction will help you to get started. Our purpose is to give you the information you need to run the Workbench under MS-DOS, Microsoft Windows, or OS/2.

A.1 Distinguish MS-DOS, Windows, and OS/2 Environments

The three operating environments most used on IBM-compatible PC workstations are MS-DOS (sometimes called PC-DOS when sold for IBM machines), Microsoft Windows, and OS/2. MS-DOS came into being when IBM first introduced the PC in 1981. It replaced CP/M, which had been the predominant operating system for earlier eight-bit microprocessors. Like CP/M, MS-DOS was, and is, quite limited in scope. MS-DOS is primarily a loader that allows one user to run one program at a time. It takes care of such chores as screen, keyboard, printer, diskette drive, and serial port I/O. It provides routines for language compilers to use. Program language compilers and interpreters make the correct operating system calls to MS-DOS on behalf of your program whenever I/O needs to be done. MS-DOS also provides a command interface to let you do housekeeping chores such as renaming files or copying files and diskettes. It formats blank disks by creating an empty directory and file allocation table, then adds, changes, and deletes directory entries whenever it creates, changes, or erases files.

The PC community soon began to outgrow MS-DOS. This operating system came from the days when the PC hardware had only a small fraction of the capabilities it has now. At first, a typical machine had one or two floppy drives, 64K of memory, and either a monochrome (text only) or a CGA (low-resolution graphics) monitor. The original version of MS-DOS addressed only 640K of memory. It did not support for disk subdirectories because the PC did not come with a hard drive. While Microsoft soon corrected the disk limitation, the memory limitation eventually became a serious problem as memory became cheaper and people wanted to run larger and larger programs.

PC users began to buy add-on products to extend the capability of MS-DOS. These included memory managers to address memory beyond 640K, graphics packages to make up for the lack of a built-in graphics protocol, and utilities that allow the PC to load two programs at once. These products were temporary stopgaps. For example, terminate-and-stay-resident (TSR) utilities such as Borland Sidekick became popular as a partial substitute for the multitasking that MS-DOS did not offer. A TSR utility reloads itself from a small "stub" in memory and reappears on the screen whenever the PC user presses a certain combination of keystrokes, or "hotkey." One can temporarily switch to an appointment scheduler or a screen capture utility while some other program is on the screen. However, TSRs were limited; they did not offer true multitasking under MS-DOS because the other application stopped running when the TSR was active. What is more, MS-DOS contained no mechanism to keep multiple TSRs from interfering with one another. They often did.

The question then became, "Where do we go from here?" Many people saw the need to get around the limitations of MS-DOS. From a practical standpoint, it took years to come up with alternatives that would give PC users the multitasking and graphics they wanted without requiring more memory or processing time than anyone can afford. Windows, for example, has been around since 1983. It reached a high level of popularity only when Windows 3.0 came out and 80386-class machines with several megabytes of memory became prevalent.

Over the years, Microsoft Windows and IBM OS/2 have emerged as the two primary alternatives to the unadorned MS-DOS environment. The Windows and OS/2 Presentation Manager screens look similar. Both work with a mouse. Both have windows, scroll bars (to scroll text or graphics displays within a window), and a point-and-shoot menu system complete with icons, action bars, pull-down menus, dialog boxes, and various types of push buttons. Both let you keep several tasks going at once. So what are the differences between the two environments?

The most obvious difference is this: Windows 3.x runs as an add-on to MS-DOS, while OS/2 is a full-blown operating system. To bring up Windows, you boot the computer under MS-DOS and then run the Windows program by using an MS-DOS command. When you shut down Windows, you're back to MS-DOS. To bring up OS/2, you must boot the system under OS/2. Shutting down OS/2 does not by itself get you back to MS-DOS; you have to reboot to do that. OS/2 2.0 introduced a **Shut down** function that performs some cleanup functions before rebooting or turning off power.

Both Windows and OS/2 let you select a DOS prompt **icon.** (An icon is a small symbol used as a push-button for starting a task or for bringing it up on the screen.) Clicking on the DOS prompt icon brings up a screen containing a simulation of the MS-DOS environment. This lets you run most MS-DOS applications and commands without having to shut down Windows or OS/2.

Another difference is that Microsoft Windows 3.x is intended for low-end and midrange use while OS/2 is intended for high-end use, especially for situations requiring networking or mainframe connectivity. OS/2 is a more robust operating environment than Windows. For example, it has safeguards to make sure one application does not use up more than its share of CPU cycles. OS/2 also works with IBM's Extended Services add-on products. These include an SQL-based database management system and a communications manager designed especially for networking your PC to other PCs or to larger

IBM systems. You can run CICS OS/2 with full capabilities under OS/2. OS/2 has much to recommend it as the Workbench environment for the mainframe programmer. Cost is the only real drawback: OS/2 is more expensive than MS-DOS or Windows, and it requires much more memory.

If you want to understand the difference between Windows and OS/2, here's where it can get *really* confusing. OS/2 2.0 actually contains special versions of Windows 3.0 (called WIN-OS2) and MS-DOS 5.0. IBM licenses the right to distribute this code from Microsoft. This code lets you run most MS-DOS and Windows applications directly from icons on the OS/2 Desktop. With OS/2 2.0, you don't have to reboot under MS-DOS just to run Windows. In fact, the OS/2 2.0 installation script lets you migrate your old Windows environment to WIN-OS2. However, you *cannot* run non-Windows MS-DOS applications under WIN-OS2; you must run non-Windows MS-DOS applications directly from a windowed or full-screen MS-DOS prompt.

Anything we say here about Windows versus OS/2 is likely to change. Microsoft and IBM are competing with one another in the Windows versus OS/2 arena, although they have cooperated in the past. No doubt that IBM and Microsoft will enhance these products in many ways as part of their marketing strategies.

A.2 Basic Concepts

A.2.1 MS-DOS and OS/2 Command Line Prompt

Let's start by describing some basic features common to all three environments. MS-DOS, Windows, and OS/2 all provide for a **command prompt** that allows you to enter operating system commands through the keyboard. At startup time and after each program or batch file finishes, the MS-DOS system will await your next command by displaying a command prompt on the screen. You can change the appearance of the command prompt. Many users set it up to show the current disk drive and directory. At the command prompt, you can type an MS-DOS command, the name of a program to be run, or the name of a batch file to be run. Figure A.1 shows a typical MS-DOS command prompt screen display, and Figure A.2 shows the DOS Shell user interface provided with MS-DOS 5.0.

Windows and OS/2 both provide point-and-shoot menu systems that let you select desired tasks without having to enter anything on the command line. To use the menu system, you first have to install each of your programs or batch files in the Windows Program Manager or OS/2 Desktop Manager menuing system so that you can select them later. Figures A.3, A.4, and A.5 show examples of Windows, OS/2 1.3, and OS/2 2.0 graphical screen displays.

In both Windows and OS/2, you can still get to a DOS command prompt by clicking on the DOS icon. To get back to the windowed task list when you are finished, press **Ctrl+Escape**. Under Windows and OS/2 2.0 (but not under OS/2 1.3) you can terminate the DOS prompt mode by typing **EXIT** at the DOS command prompt.

The DOS prompt under Windows will come up in full-screen mode, but you can switch it to windowed mode. Full-screen mode looks like normal MS-DOS; you won't see the windowing system while it is active.

```
[DOS] K:\COBOL  3:52:58;
dir

 Volume in drive K is COMPILERS
 Directory of K:\COBOL

.              <DIR>      06-22-91   9:42p
..             <DIR>      06-22-91   9:42p
DEMO           <DIR>      06-22-91   9:46p
DOCS           <DIR>      06-22-91   9:42p
EXEDLL         <DIR>      06-22-91   9:42p
INC            <DIR>      06-23-91  12:11a
LBR            <DIR>      06-22-91   9:42p
LIB            <DIR>      06-22-91   9:52p
ON-LINE        <DIR>      06-22-91   9:44p
SOURCE         <DIR>      06-22-91   9:45p
MFINS    LOG    2012 07-08-91   7:36p
      11 file(s)         2012 bytes
                  13959168 bytes free

[DOS] K:\COBOL  3:53:00;
```

Figure A.1 MS-DOS command prompt screen display

Under OS/2 1.3, you can run only one DOS session at a time. The DOS prompt will come up in full-screen mode. OS/2 2.0 provides icons for both a windowed and a full-screen DOS prompt. You can start as many DOS sessions as system resources permit.

Certain MS-DOS utilities access physical sectors on your hard disk drive, such as undelete and disk optimization programs. *Never* run MS-DOS programs of that type in a DOS session under OS/2; they can clobber your file system. Either boot under MS-DOS to run those programs, or use the OS/2 undelete command instead.

OS/2 allows you to enter commands at the **OS/2 command line prompt.** The OS/2 Desktop Manager lets you select either a full-screen OS/2 prompt or a windowed OS/2 prompt. The only difference is that the windowed prompt appears in a window and does not take up the whole screen. The OS/2 prompt works similarly to the MS-DOS command line prompt. In fact, most of the file and utility commands are the same. **Be aware that the OS/2 command line prompt is *not* the same as the MS-DOS command prompt, despite their similar appearance.** MS-DOS applications will *not* run from the OS/2 command line prompt, or vice versa, unless they have been written for use under both systems.

MS-DOS 4.0 and above provides a text-mode **DOS shell utility** that allows you to execute MS-DOS commands or view directories by selecting them with a mouse (Figure A.2). It also lets you set up a task-switching menu so that you can select programs you want to run. However, the DOS shell includes no multitasking or graphics support.

A.2.2 Directory Structure

Windows and OS/2 both support the same file system and directory structure that MS-DOS uses. OS/2 additionally supports an alternative directory struc-

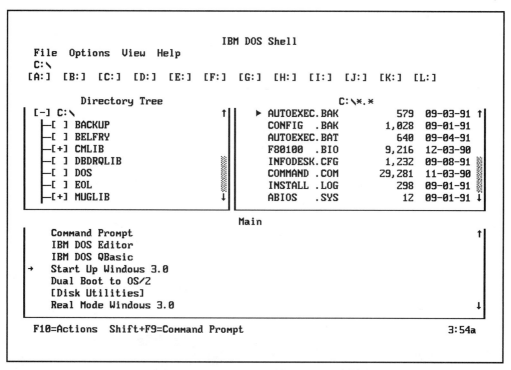

Figure A.2 MS-DOS 5.0 Shell display

ture called **High Performance File System, or HPFS,** which provides for longer filenames and additional directory information. Micro Focus supports HPFS directories as well as MS-DOS directories. Under OS/2, you can decide which file system you want to use when you initially format your hard disk drive. HPFS directories are OS/2 only and cannot be used for data shared with MS-DOS programs. In fact, if you format a drive under HPFS, MS-DOS will not be able to see that drive or any drivenames that follow it in alphabetical sequence.

Let's look at the MS-DOS file system. Whenever you format a diskette or hard disk under MS-DOS, you create an empty **root directory** and a **File Allocation Table (FAT).** The directory contains a list of filenames, sizes, and creation dates/times. The FAT contains a chained list of the sectors on disk that hold the data for each file. The FAT also keeps track of free space. When MS-DOS erases a file, it does not actually wipe out the data right away. It removes the directory entry and records the fact that the sectors used by that file are available for reuse. That is why undelete commands and utilities can sometimes recover deleted files. You should be aware that a file is not always stored in one contiguous piece. Whenever it needs to write data, the operating system uses the next piece of free space that it finds.

MS-DOS files are uniquely identified by the drivename, directory path, filename, and extension. The drivename will be a single letter from A to Z followed by a colon, with upper- and lower-case being equivalent. Drive names A: and B: are reserved for diskette drives. C: is your local hard disk drive. This leaves the other drivenames from D: to Z: available for more local

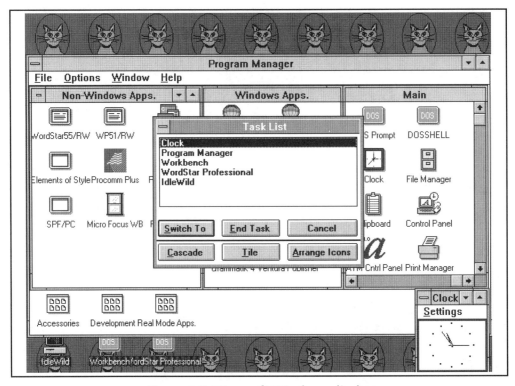

Figure A.3 Microsoft Windows display

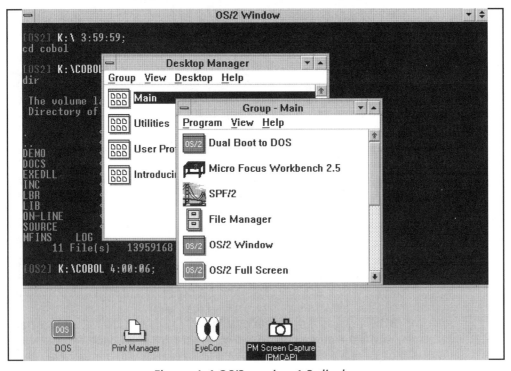

Figure A.4 OS/2 version 1.3 display

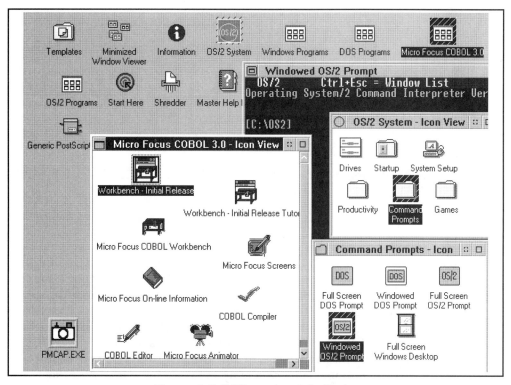

Figure A.5 OS/2 version 2.0 display

hard disk drives, network file servers, optical drives, and other devices. Depending on how you format your hard disk drive, you can have more than one **logical disk drive** on a single physical disk drive. This was originally necessary because older versions of MS-DOS could not address drives larger than 32 megabytes. Now this feature allows OS/2 users to define part of a large hard disk drive under the MS-DOS FAT file system and the rest of it under OS/2 HPFS.

The directory path shows whether the file is in the root directory or in a **subdirectory.** A large hard disk can easily have many thousands of programs and data files on it. You would become inundated with hopeless clutter if you kept all of your files in the root directory of a large hard disk drive. You need subdirectories to group related files so that you can find them and keep track of them. For example, when you install Micro Focus Workbench for the first time, the installation procedure creates subdirectories for the Workbench itself and for sample applications that come with it. Before you upgrade to a new release of Workbench, you can find and erase all files from the old release, because they will all be in subdirectories. You can view or print the contents of the root directory or subdirectories. MS-DOS commands allow you to switch the current default drive and directory so that you will be looking at the directory you want.

Suppose your current default directory is the root directory of the C: drive. If you create a subdirectory called SUB1, MS-DOS will place an entry for SUB1 in the root directory. Suppose you switch to SUB1 as your default directory and create another subdirectory under it called SUB2. MS-DOS will place an entry for SUB2 in the directory SUB1. MS-DOS subdirectories form a hierarchy or tree structure.

When you specify a directory path, you list the hierarchy of directories under which your file is stored. For example, if your file is stored in SUB2, the directory path would consist of SUB1 followed by SUB2. A **backslash character (\)** separates directory names. The fully qualified filename, also known as a **filespec,** would look like this:

```
C:\SUB1\SUB2\filename.ext
```

For a file stored in the root directory, the fully qualified filename would look like this:

```
C:\filename.ext
```

Here is how the defaults work: If you supply a directory path but omit the drivename, MS-DOS will look for your file on the current default drive in the directory path you specified. If you omit the directory path but supply a drivename, MS-DOS will look for your file in the current default directory of the drive you specified. If you omit both, MS-DOS will look for your file in the current default drive and directory path. MS-DOS keeps track of a default directory path for each drivename defined on your system.

MS-DOS filenames consist of up to eight user-assigned characters, followed by an optional extension of up to three characters. A dot separates the filename from the extension. In general, you can choose whatever you want for the eight-character name, except certain special characters and device names reserved for MS-DOS itself. MS-DOS allows only eight characters, so make your filenames descriptive. Some programmers make the mistake of wasting four characters on the word *file* as part of their filenames. Obviously, if it is on a disk drive, you already know it is a file of some kind; how could it be anything else?

The MS-DOS filename extension distinguishes various types of files, such as data files, source code, executable programs, subroutine libraries, and batch files. For example, standalone executable programs under MS-DOS have an extension of .COM or .EXE. MS-DOS batch files have an extension of .BAT. MS-DOS looks for these extensions when you enter the name of a program or batch file to be run. Other software, such as compilers, looks for specific filename extensions also. For example, the default extension for Micro Focus COBOL program source is .CBL. Use this when you enter a new COBOL source program. **MS-DOS subdirectory names are not given an extension.**

If you format a hard disk or a diskette as a **system disk,** you create a **boot sector** on that disk or diskette. That means you can start up the operating system from it. Booting a PC is much like IPLing a mainframe. Most computers have memory that loses its contents when power is off. The computer can do nothing unless a program is in memory. When you put the power back on, the hardware boot process reads a small loader routine into memory, which then loads the rest of the operating system so that the computer can go back to work. PC hardware is set up to look for the boot sector on the A: diskette drive if a diskette is loaded. If not, the hardware will look for the boot sector on the

C: hard drive. If your PC gets hung up because of software errors, you can always reboot by switching the power off and then back on. Usually, you can also reboot by pressing the Alt, Ctrl, and Del keys all at once. A bootable system diskette containing your system configuration files is a useful backup to keep on hand. You can start up your system from that diskette if you have problems with the system information on your hard drive. Lacking that, you can boot from your MS-DOS or OS/2 operating system installation diskettes.

You can set up your system to boot either MS-DOS or OS/2. Instructions for this are in Section A.4.

A.2.3 Batch Files (MS-DOS)

On a mainframe, programmers and operations staff use job control language (JCL) files to submit batch jobs for unattended operation. Although MS-DOS and OS/2 do not use IBM mainframe JCL syntax, both operating systems let you submit batch jobs on the PC. Under MS-DOS, batch files are given the extension .BAT. Batch files are ASCII text files containing one or more MS-DOS commands. When you run the batch file, each command will execute in sequence. You can create batch files with any word processor or text editor capable of producing ASCII text files. The Micro Focus Workbench editor is particularly convenient for maintaining your collection of batch files.

You may already be aware that the PC environment uses the ASCII character set, while the mainframe environment uses EBCDIC. MS-DOS, Windows, and OS/2 all operate in ASCII. This affects commands, filenames, system messages, and so forth. By default, any batch files, source code, and other text that you create on the PC will be in ASCII. Later, we will show that the Micro Focus Workbench provides routines for ASCII/EBCDIC conversion and various other tools for file transfer between the mainframe and the PC.

You can run a batch file by keying its filename (without the extension) at the MS-DOS prompt. In the Windows environment, you also can set up your Windows Program Manager to run a batch file when you click on its icon. Instructions for this are in the *Windows User's Guide* under "Program Manager." It makes sense to do this for any frequently used applications that run under Windows.

A.2.4 Command Files (OS/2)

Under OS/2, command files take the place of MS-DOS batch files. A command file contains one or more valid OS/2 commands. The filename extension for command files is .CMD. You can run a command file by keying its filename at the OS/2 command line prompt, or you can set up your OS/2 Desktop Manager to run a command file when you click on its menu item.

A.2.5 Environment Variables

MS-DOS and OS/2 both provide an area in memory called the **environment table.** Under MS-DOS, the environment table size is only 160 bytes unless you specify a larger number by using the **/E:nnnn** parameter with the SHELL command. OS/2 automatically allows you to use up to 64K for the environment table. Under both MS-DOS and OS/2, the environment table holds ASCII text variables that your application programs can examine by using an operating system call. Most of the variables in the environment are user-defined variables used in one application. For example, the Micro Focus COBOL compiler uses an environment variable to tell it what drive and directory contains the copy library. In some ways, this takes the place of mainframe JCL on your PC. Environment variables can be set at system startup time or later with batch or command files.

A.2.6 AUTOEXEC.BAT

MS/DOS looks for a file named AUTOEXEC.BAT at boot time. The commands that you put into this file will be run as the final step of the boot process. OS/2 also looks for the AUTOEXEC.BAT file the first time you begin using the MS-DOS command prompt. This AUTOEXEC.BAT defines the characteristics of the MS-DOS prompt handler running under OS/2. You can change this file to suit your needs. For example, MS-DOS does not have a built-in mouse driver, so many users put a command into AUTOEXEC.BAT to start up the mouse driver program. Most users include a **PROMPT PG** command in AUTOEXEC.BAT to make the MS-DOS prompt show the current default drive and directory path. If you want the computer to bring up a certain program automatically at startup time, such as Windows, you can supply the name of that application as the final command in AUTOEXEC.BAT. At startup time, the application will run just as though you had typed the program or batch filename at the MS-DOS command prompt.

If you change AUTOEXEC.BAT, you can put those changes into effect either by rebooting or by typing **AUTOEXEC** at the MS-DOS command prompt.

A.2.7 CONFIG.SYS

CONFIG.SYS is the name given to the system configuration file under both MS-DOS and OS/2. It takes effect at startup time, and specifies such items as the number of open files you will be using at one time, the number of buffers to assign, and device driver names. **If you change something in CONFIG.SYS, you must reboot to make the change take effect.**

Some commercial software installation routines take it upon themselves to change your AUTOEXEC.BAT or CONFIG.SYS files without asking you first. That is one reason it's wise to keep a backup copy of your AUTOEXEC.BAT and CONFIG.SYS files on a bootable system diskette. You will need to add some commands to those files to run the Workbench successfully, and you wouldn't want to lose them if something happened to these files. You can also use this bootable diskette to get back into your system if you have accidentally destroyed your AUTOEXEC.BAT or CONFIG.SYS files.

A.2.8 Text versus Graphic (Windowed) Environment

We mentioned before that the Windows and OS/2 environments are graphic environments. In other words, they use a **graphical user interface (GUI).** A GUI can display both text-mode and graphics-mode information on the terminal screen. To display graphics, the computer must have a graphical display device such as an EGA or VGA board and a compatible monitor.

Mainframe programmers are familiar with text-mode 3270-type terminals. Information sent to these terminals is in the form of **EBCDIC character data streams.** The green monochrome display and adapter board sold with some of the earliest IBM PCs was also an ASCII text-mode device. Text screen data is mapped into row and column locations, for example 24 x 80 on a mainframe terminal. A letter, numeral, special character, or space can occupy each of these screen locations. Since screen locations are fixed in size, only monospaced characters can be shown. The display does not allow for characters of varying width. **Text-mode terminals are incapable of displaying graphical information such as line art or bit mapped illustrations from a scanning device.** Some text-mode display controllers, including the old IBM monochrome display adapter (MDA), do allow for a line-drawing character set that permits lines and rectangular boxes to be drawn on the screen. This is not true graphics mode.

A graphical display device is one whose image is *dot-addressable*. Examples of this on the PC include Hercules, CGA, EGA, VGA, and XGA devices. The screen image is composed of dots; the software and display adapter can address each dot to determine what color it should be. This lets the device show pictorial information as well as text. Most, but not all, graphical display devices support color. The drawback to graphical displays is that it takes many more CPU cycles to generate a graphical image than it does to generate a screenful of text. Putting it simply, the computer runs slower when it paints a screen in graphics mode.

The graphical displays used on the PC can switch back and forth between text and graphics modes. The unadorned MS-DOS environment always stays in text mode unless you are running an application that switches temporarily into graphics mode. In Windows and OS/2, whenever you see a windowed display, the display adapter is in graphics mode. Some of the windows may contain nothing but text data. This is known as "text mode in a window" although the display adapter is in graphics mode. On the other hand, when you go to a full-screen DOS prompt, the display adapter switches to text mode. Screen displays from your own COBOL programs will be in text mode unless you call some outside program or routine to do graphics. COBOL programs that you write for mainframe use will be in text mode, since mainframes ordinarily don't have graphical terminal devices.

Micro Focus Workbench versions up to 2.5 run in text mode under MS-DOS. (Workbench v3.0 and above support graphics and text modes.) Under Windows or OS/2, you have the option of running the function key Workbench either in full-screen text mode, or in text mode in a window. The Workbench screen contents look much the same. The windowed display runs somewhat slower, but it has the advantage of letting you see other applications on your screen at the same time. However, Windows takes control of the PC system's mouse. This prevents the Micro Focus Workbench from making use of mouse support while running under Windows in version 2.5.

A.3 Commands Most Often Used

You need to know only a few operating system commands to make productive use of the Workbench. These simple commands are the same under MS-DOS and OS/2. You can use them either from the MS-DOS command prompt or from the OS/2 command prompt.

A.3.1 Viewing Directory Contents

Typing DIR at the command prompt will list the files in your current drive and directory. Alongside the filenames, you'll see the file sizes and the date and time of the most recent update. If the display scrolls off the screen too fast, you can use either of these variations:

```
DIR /P
DIR | MORE
```

Either of these will show the directory display one screen page at a time. You can "turn the page" by pressing the enter key. You can get an abbreviated directory display by typing the following:

```
DIR /W
```

If you want to list files in a different drive or directory, type the drive and pathname after the DIR:

```
DIR C:\COBOL
```

If you want to see only certain types of files, you can specify a partial filename and/or extension, using the asterisk as a wildcard character to match all trailing characters. This command will show all files in the current directory whose filenames begin with W and whose extensions are .CBL:

```
DIR W*.CBL
```

This command will route the directory listing to printer LPT1 instead of the screen:

```
DIR C:\COBOL LPT1
```

A.3.2 Making, Removing, and Changing Subdirectories

To make a new subdirectory under your current directory, type MKDIR (or MD) followed by the name of the new directory. You can use up to eight characters for the filename; there is no filename extension for a directory. To remove a directory, type RMDIR (or RD) followed by the directory name. The directory has to be empty of files before you can remove it with this command.

To change the default disk drivename, type the new drivename followed by a colon at the command prompt. For example, **C:** will make the C drive the current default drive. To switch to a different current directory, type CHDIR (or CD) followed by the path of the directory you want. For example, **CD ** will switch to the root directory of your current drive. If you specify only a subdirectory name instead of a complete path, the system will expect the desired subdirectory to be immediately under your current default directory. For example, if you are now in C:\SUB1, then **CD SUB2** will send you one level down in the hierarchy to C:\SUB1\SUB2. **CD ..** will always move you one level up within your current directory path, unless you are already in the root directory. In other words, it moves you up into the parent directory. For example, if you are now in C:\SUB1\SUB2, **CD ..** will move you back up to C:\SUB1.

When you get a box of unformatted blank diskettes, you will need to format them. The **FORMAT A:** command will format a diskette in the A: drive. To make a boot diskette, use the command **FORMAT A: /S**. Formatting a diskette creates a file allocation table and a root directory. You can create subdirectories on a diskette the same way you would on a hard drive. **Do not format your hard drive, or any diskette drive, when there are any files on it that you want to keep.**

A.3.3 Copying, Renaming, and Deleting Files

The COPY command will copy files from one drive or directory path to another. You can copy a file within the same directory as long as you provide a different filename or extension for the new file. To use the COPY command, type the word COPY followed by the old and new drive/path/filename designations. Omitting any designations will cause COPY to use the current default locations. This command will create a file named YOURPROG.CBL in the root directory of the A: diskette drive.

```
COPY C:\COBOL\YOURPROG.CBL A:\
```

Within your current default directory, this command will create backup copies of each of your COBOL source files with names beginning with W.

```
COPY W*.CBL W*.BAK
```

Printing with COPY. You can use device names in a COPY command. Suppose you have a file named DOCFILE.TXT. To copy this file to the printer, use this command:

```
COPY DOCFILE.TXT LPT1
```

You can substitute another device address for LPT1 if the desired printer is attached to some other port. COPYing a file to the printer works only when the input file is formatted properly for that printer. You won't have any problem sending an ASCII file to a dot matrix PC printer or to an HP-compatible laser or inkjet printer. If the records are short enough to fit on the page, the file will print correctly with no problems. The printer will use whatever font (type face) is the default. Suppose you want to print a plain ASCII file on a Postscript printer. You will need to use a word processor or a desktop publishing program to add some formatting information to the file before sending it to the printer.

To rename a file, use the RENAME command followed by the old and new filenames:

```
RENAME C:\SUB1\THISYEAR.TXT LASTYEAR.TXT
```

With the old filename, you can supply a drive and directory path if the file is not in the current default drive and directory. The RENAME command will not move a file from one directory to another, therefore you cannot supply a drive and directory path with the new filename.

To avoid running out of disk space, get into the habit of inspecting your hard disk contents regularly and deleting any files that are not being used. Seldom-used items can be copied to diskette, then deleted from the hard drive. To delete a file, use the ERASE or DEL command followed by the filename:

```
ERASE JUNK.TXT
```

If you want to get rid of everything in a directory, you can use wildcard characters:

```
ERASE C:\BADDIR\*.*
```

Before it purges the entire directory, the system will ask you, "Are you sure (Y/N)?" Double-check what you are doing before you answer this question!

A.3.4 Running Programs and Batch Files

To run an executable program, an MS-DOS batch file, or an OS/2 command file, type its filename (*without* the extension) on the command line and press the enter key. If the program needs user-input parameters on the command line, enter the parameters following the program name. For example, typing **WB** at the command prompt will start up the Micro Focus Workbench.

A.3.5 PATH Command

The PATH command places some information in the MS-DOS or OS/2 environment table that tells the operating system what directory paths to search for executable files. If you are using MS-DOS, use a PATH command in the AUTOEXEC.BAT file. If you are using OS/2, use a SET PATH in the CONFIG.SYS file. In either case, the PATH or SET PATH command is followed by a series of drive/directory paths, separated by semicolons. For example:

```
PATH C:\DOS;C:\UTIL;D:\WINDOWS;D:\COBOL;
```

Entering PATH without any parameters causes MS-DOS or OS/2 to display the current value of the PATH variable.

A.3.6 SET Command

You can SET other environment variables besides the PATH. The Workbench uses the SET command to determine where to look for files that it needs. For example, if you place this statement in your CONFIG.SYS file, then the Workbench will expect to find your COBOL copy library members in the C:\USERDSD\COPY subdirectory.

Entering SET without any parameters causes MS-DOS or OS/2 to display the current value of the SET variables.

```
SET COBCPY=C:\USERDSD\COPY
```

When entering a drive and directory path in an environment variable, **you must remember to put a colon after the drive designator.** Failure to do that will cause problems. Under MS-DOS, you can get messages saying "Out of environment space," even when you have plenty of space.

A.4 Installing Both MS-DOS and OS/2

A.4.1 Dual Boot Using MS-DOS or OS/2

What if you use MS-DOS (with or without Windows) part of the time, and OS/2 the rest of the time? MS-DOS and OS/2 have different boot routines. One of them has to be the default when you power on your computer. If OS/2 is the default, how do you boot under MS-DOS? That depends on the version of OS/2. OS/2 1.3 introduced an optional **dual boot** feature that lets you keep both boot routines on your hard disk drive. This makes it convenient to reboot under MS-DOS if you are under OS/2, and then return to OS/2 later if desired.

How does it work? **The BOOT command changes modes by swapping system files. Therefore, at power-up time, the computer will come up with the operating system that was active when you last powered down.**

When you are in MS-DOS mode, the MS-DOS boot routine will be in the boot sector. The MS-DOS AUTOEXEC.BAT and CONFIG.SYS will be in the root directory of your C: drive. The OS/2 AUTOEXEC.BAT, CONFIG.SYS, and boot file will be in the C:\OS2\SYSTEM directory under the names AUTOEXEC.OS2, CONFIG.OS2, and BOOT.OS2.

Switching to OS/2 mode will move the OS/2 boot routine to the boot sector. The OS/2 AUTOEXEC.BAT and CONFIG.SYS files will be in the root directory of your C: drive, and the MS-DOS versions will be in the C:\OS2\SYSTEM directory under the names AUTOEXEC.DOS, CONFIG.DOS, and BOOT.DOS. Here are some tips for using dual boot:

- Instructions for installing the dual boot option are in the v2.0 *Installation Guide* or v1.3 *Getting Started* manuals accompanying the OS/2 system. Follow instructions carefully; the installation routine will *not* set up dual boot unless it finds existing MS-DOS files in specific places. Before installing OS/2, put your MS-DOS files in the C:\DOS directory, except for AUTOEXEC.BAT and CONFIG.SYS, which belong in the root directory.

- If your system already contains the dual boot option from a previous version of the OS/2 operating system, you will need to preserve your MS-DOS boot capability when you upgrade to a new version of OS/2. To do this, **boot your system under MS-DOS just before you install the new version of OS/2.** This will store the MS-DOS boot routine safely in the boot sector of your primary hard drive where the OS/2 dual boot installation routine can find it. Otherwise, in the words of IBM technical support, the MS-DOS boot routine will be "toast." You'll have to reformat your primary hard disk partition, reinstall MS-DOS, and then reinstall OS/2 to get it back.

- When you install applications software, including the Workbench, you will often need to change the MS-DOS or the OS/2 versions of AUTOEXEC.BAT or CONFIG.SYS. Be aware of the effect of dual boot, so that you can apply changes to the correct versions of these files.

- With the Dual Boot option, MS-DOS and OS/2 share the same primary partition. If your existing primary partition (ordinarily your C: drive) is large enough to hold the files for both MS-DOS and OS/2, you won't have to reformat your hard drive. Section A.4.3 contains more information about defining and using hard disk partitions.

```
┌─────────────────────────────────────────────────────────────┐
│  ▭      ▭▭ ▭▭    ◇         ◯       ▭       ▭       ▭          │
│  ┌─────────────────────────────────────────────────────────┐ │
│  │ ⊟  Fixed Disk Utility                            ○ □     │ │
│ T│ Options  Help                                            │ │
│  │ ┌────────┐                                               │ │
│  │ │ ▬    1 │                                               │ │
│  │ └────────┘                                               │ │
│ ▌│─────────────────────────────────────────────────────────│ │
│  │ Partition Information                                    │ │
│  │                                                          │ │
│  │ Name          Status       Access    File System Type  MBytes │
│  │ ▓▓▓▓▓▓▓▓▓▓▓▓▓▓▓Startable▓▓▓▓:Primary▓▓▓BOOT MANAGER▓▓▓▓1▓▓▓│ │
│  │ MS-DOS        Bootable     :Primary   FAT                8 │ │
│  │ OS/2 2.0      Bootable    C :Primary   FAT               55 │ │
│  │               None       D :Logical   FAT               32 │ │
│  │               None       E :Logical   FAT               32 │ │
│  │               None       F :Logical   FAT               32 │ │
│  │               None       G :Logical   FAT               32 │ │
│  │               None       H :Logical   FAT               32 │ │
│  │               None       I :Logical   FAT               32 │ │
│  │               None       J :Logical   FAT               32 │ │
│  │               None       K :Logical   FAT               12 │ │
│  │                                                          │ │
│  │─────────────────────────────────────────────────────────│ │
│  │ PMCAP.EXE                                                │ │
│  └─────────────────────────────────────────────────────────┘ │
└─────────────────────────────────────────────────────────────┘
```

Figure A.6 FDISKPM after OS/2 Boot Manager installation

A.4.2 Booting from a Diskette

Another way to switch between MS-DOS and OS/2 is to keep the OS/2 boot on your C: drive and use a diskette in the A: drive when you want to boot MS-DOS. Using this method, the diskette contains the MS-DOS boot files and the MS-DOS AUTOEXEC.BAT and CONFIG.SYS files. All other MS-DOS files can stay in the C:\DOS directory, if you set a path to that directory in your MS-DOS AUTOEXEC.BAT.

The OS/2 AUTOEXEC.BAT and CONFIG.SYS are in the root directory of the C: drive, and the OS/2 boot sector will be on the C: drive. The rest of the OS/2 files can be in the usual OS/2 subdirectories. The PC will boot under MS-DOS if the boot diskette is present; otherwise, it will boot under OS/2 from the C: drive.

A.4.3 Boot Manager

With OS/2 2.0, IBM introduced a method for installing multiple operating systems, namely the Boot Manager. The Boot Manager allows you to boot from your choice of several versions of MS-DOS and OS/2 on the same machine, and even from a UNIX partition if desired. Every time you boot by turning on the power switch or by pressing Ctrl+Alt+Del, you'll see a menu asking you which operating system you want to start. Before installing Boot Manager, you may need to back up and reformat your hard drive to allocate the desired partitions. If you want to install only the current version of MS-DOS and the current version of OS/2, you can use either Boot Manager or the dual boot option that we described above. Having tried all methods, we prefer the OS/2 2.0 Boot Manager, even though it requires somewhat more effort to set up.

Hard disk drive partitions. The Boot Manager option requires that you use the **FDISK** utility to divide your hard disk into **partitions.** You will need to dedicate one **primary partition** solely to MS-DOS and one primary partition solely to OS/2. Both primary partitions will use the same drive identifier, generally **C:.** When you boot under MS-DOS, the system will see only the MS-DOS C: primary partition. Conversely, when you boot under OS/2, the system will see only the OS/2 C: primary partition. The MS-DOS C: partition is a good place to keep disk formatting utilities and other software that should be used only from the native-mode MS-DOS prompt. The OS/2 C: partition is a good place to keep the OS/2 swapper (virtual memory) file, along with utilities and games that come with the OS/2 system.

Any space remaining on your hard disk drive that is not needed for primary partitions will become the **extended partition.** Using FDISK, you can allocate one or more **logical drives** within the extended partition. This is where you store applications programs and data files, including the Micro Focus Workbench and your COBOL programs.

Boot Manager installation. Here are the steps for installing OS/2 Boot Manager with OS/2 2.0 and MS-DOS 5.0. It may seem complicated the first time you try it. If you are not an experienced OS/2 user, you might want to get some help from someone who has installed OS/2 before. This discussion is intended to be a supplement to the IBM manuals, not a substitute for them. Under no circumstances should you attempt to install Boot Manager without a careful reading of the *Installation Guide* for your current version of OS/2.

FDISK, the hard disk drive partitioning utility, is the primary tool for setting up your drive so that you can install each operating system. FDISK comes with OS/2. When you boot with the OS/2 2.0 installation diskette, it will ask you for diskette 1. Place that diskette in the drive and answer the questions on the screen. FDISK will begin running when you answer **Y** to "Change the drive." Once you've installed OS/2, you can also bring up a windowed version of FDISK by entering **FDISKPM** at the OS/2 windowed command prompt (Figure A.6).

Warning: Deleting or reformatting any primary partitions or logical drives on your hard disk drive will delete all data on those drives, including the boot sector. Either back up your data or move your data permanently to another drive if you plan to reformat any primary or logical partitions on your hard disk drive. However, deleting or reformatting one partition or logical drive will not affect data stored on other partitions or logical drives.

- Decide how to allocate disk space. Check the *OS/2 2.0 Installation Guide* for the latest information about space requirements for your release. OS/2 2.0 is quite demanding of disk space. A typical 32MB hard disk partition will not be enough to install the complete system.

- If necessary, use the FDISK **Delete Partition** option to free up enough space for the operating systems you want to install. We used FDISK to delete two *contiguous* 32K partitions in order to free up a 64MB block of free space. (You cannot install OS/2 in free space that is fragmented.) Whenever you delete any drive identifier or allocate new logical drives, FDISK automatically renames the other drives to avoid skipping letters of the alphabet. Whenever you finish using FDISK, remember to save and exit.

- Use the FDISK **Create Partition** option to create the Boot Manager partition and the other two primary partitions from that block of free space. We created 1MB for the Boot Manager itself, as well as an 8MB primary partition for MS-DOS 5.0, and a 55MB primary partition for OS/2 2.0.

- Use the FDISK **Add to Boot Manager** option to create entries on the boot menu to identify the MS-DOS 5.0 and OS/2 2.0 partitions.

- When installing the Boot Manager option, you'll need to install OS/2 2.0 first, and then install MS-DOS. This is the reverse of the installation process for dual boot. The partition you set as **Installable** will be the partition that will receive the new operating system when you boot from the installation diskette. Use the FDISK **Set Installable** option to set the OS/2 partition as installable, reboot from the OS/2 installation diskette, and follow instructions on the screen to complete OS/2 installation.

- Now set the MS-DOS partition as **Installable**, reboot from the MS-DOS installation diskette, and follow instructions on the screen.

- Use FDISK again. The MS-DOS and OS/2 partitions should be set as **Bootable.** Select the 1MB Boot Manager partition, set it as **Startable,** then save and exit. This should make your system reboot itself. If you have installed the Boot Manager option correctly, you should see a Boot Manager menu that lets you choose between MS-DOS and OS/2 by highlighting with arrow keys (Figure A.7).

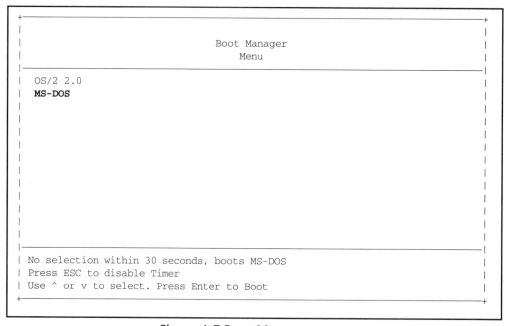

Figure A.7 Boot Manager menu

MS-DOS 5.0 upgrade. If you have purchased MS-DOS 5.0 as an *upgrade,* its installation program will look for an existing installed version of MS-DOS on your drive before it allows you to load the upgrade. The upgrade installation routine will *not* recognize the OS/2 Boot Manager environment, even when you have installed an older version of MS-DOS in the current installable partition. Before installing the MS-DOS 5.0 upgrade in a partition under the OS/2 Boot Manager, contact your IBM representative or call the IBM support 800-number on your OS/2 carton. Explain the situation and ask for the MS-DOS 5.0 upgrade enhanced installation utility. When you receive it, use the Boot Manager to boot the partition containing the older version of MS-DOS, and then run the enhanced installation program from the diskette. Don't boot with the MS-DOS upgrade diskette or the enhanced installation diskette.

A.5 More About the OS/2 2.0 Desktop

A.5.1 Objects on the OS/2 2.0 Desktop

The OS/2 2.0 Desktop is more flexible than the menu system in previous versions of OS/2. You can define icons for many different types of objects, not just for programs and command prompts. Among other things, icons can represent data files, disk drives, printer queues, folders, and the shredder. The **shredder** is exactly what it sounds like: a deletion tool. You can delete an object by dragging it to the shredder and dropping it. A **folder** is a window that contains other icons. A folder is *not* the same as a disk directory, although you can use a folder to display the programs and files within a disk directory. You can nest folders within other folders. Figure A.5, shown earlier in this chapter, contains several folders.

Double-clicking on an icon will open the object associated with the icon. What this means will depend on the type of object. Opening a program or command file icon will start running it. Opening a disk drive will display its directory structure. Opening a printer queue will show you what jobs are waiting to print. Opening a folder will show you what icons are in it. Opening a data file will display its contents in an OS/2 System Editor session.

You can move icons by dragging them with the *right* mouse button. You can create new objects by copying from existing ones or by dragging **template** icons out of the template folder and onto the Desktop. Each type of template icon has its own menu format for configuration settings.

The system menu button is in the upper-left corner of every window. Clicking on that button displays the pull-down menu for that window. If you choose to minimize the window to an icon, the icon will have hatch-marked shading behind it to indicate that a task is still active. You can click on the icon again to make the windowed or full-screen session visible once again. With OS/2 2.0, you have a choice of whether the minimized icon will be visible on the desktop or only in the folder from which you started the task. The Settings menu for each object lets you choose what type of session to run it in and what to do with the minimized icon.

A.5.2 The Settings Menu

OS/2 2.0 provides an interactive method for configuring the appearance and behavior of any object on the Desktop, namely, the Settings menu. The Settings menu differs for each type of OS/2 2.0 object, but some elements are common to all types. For example, the **General** section selects what icon is used.

If you click on any OS/2 icon with the *right* mouse button, you'll see a popup menu. The options on that menu will vary depending on the type of object, but you'll always see an **Open** option. Clicking on the arrow next to the **Open** option will bring up a cascaded menu. Click on the **Settings** option. A new window will appear, containing the Settings menu. The Settings menu resembles a notebook with divider tabs; clicking on a tab will turn to a different page of menu options. Each page has a help function for information about the menu options. When you are finished making selections, click on the button in the upper-left corner of the window frame, and select the **Close** option from the window popup menu. This will save your selections.

A.5.3 Shutting Down OS/2 2.0

OS/2 2.0 keeps track of your desktop configuration, so that you can restart where you left off the last time you used OS/2. You need to tell OS/2 that you are about to reboot or shut down, so that OS/2 can write some information back to disk. If you move the mouse to anywhere on the Desktop that does not contain an icon or a window, and then click the *right* mouse button, you'll see a popup menu for the Desktop itself. Click on the **Shut down** option. A message will tell you when it is time to power off or reboot. Don't flip the "big red switch" until disk I/O has stopped!

A.6 Where to Find More Information

A.6.1 The COBOL Language

Training new COBOL programmers. If you plan to use the Workbench to train new COBOL programmers, we recommend *Simplified Structured COBOL with Microsoft/Micro Focus COBOL,* by Daniel D. McCracken and Donald Golden, ©1990 John Wiley & Sons, New York. This book uses the Micro Focus COBOL/2 compiler for its examples. Both of us have successfully used McCracken's books in the past to teach COBOL programming.

Evolution of ANSI COBOL. If you are converting from mainframe OS/VS COBOL to VS COBOL II, we recommend *VS COBOL II for COBOL Programmers,* by Robert J. Sandler, ©1990 John Wiley & Sons, New York. This book shows the differences between the older and newer COBOL dialects and shows you how to migrate.

How do you get the most out of the latest ANSI Standard COBOL features? Need some good coding examples? Micro Focus offers a book by Jerome Garfunkel on "cutting-edge" ANSI COBOL features. Contact Micro Focus for title and availability.

A.6.2 The PC Operating Environment

MS-DOS commands and utilities. You don't need to know PC operating system internals to run the Micro Focus Workbench. You only need to know how to use the actual commands. Those given here are just a start. Many books, pocket references, and training aids tell you about other commands and options. Here are several books for MS-DOS:

- *Learning and Running MS-DOS®,* by Microsoft Corporation and Van Wolverton, Microsoft Press, One Microsoft Way, Redmond, WA 98052–6399. The book comes with tutorial diskettes. The current edition covers MS-DOS versions 2 through 5. The book, *Running MS-DOS,* is available separately.
- *Concise Guide to MS-DOS® 5,* by JoAnne Woodcock. This book is available from Microsoft Press.
- *DOS 5.0, The Basics,* by Ken W. Christopher, Jr., Barry A. Feigenbaum, and Shon O. Saliga, ©1991 John Wiley & Sons, New York.
- *DOS 5.0 Command Reference,* by Ken W. Christopher, Jr., Barry A. Feigenbaum, and Shon O. Saliga, ©1991 John Wiley & Sons, New York. This is a pocket-sized command reference.
- *PC Magazine DOS 5® Techniques and Utilities,* by Jeff Prosise, ©1991 Ziff-Davis Press. This large paperback comes with two diskettes.
- *MS-DOS® 5 Quick Reference,* Timothy S. Stanley, ©1991 Que Corporation. This is a pocket-sized command reference.
- *Using DOS,* developed by Que Corp., text by David W. Solomon, ©1989 Que Corporation.
- *Using MS-DOS 5,* Que Development Group, ©1991 Que Corporation.

Microsoft Windows.

- *Learning and Running Windows™3.1,* by Microsoft Corporation and Craig Stinson, Microsoft Press, One Microsoft Way, Redmond, WA 98052–6399. The book comes with tutorial diskettes. The current edition covers MS-DOS versions 2 through 5. The book, *Running Windows™3.1,* is also available separately.
- *Windows™ 3.1 Companion,* by The Cobb Group: Lori L. Lorenz and R. Michael O'Mara with Russell Borland. This book is available from Microsoft Press.
- *Concise Guide to Microsoft® Windows™3.1,* by Kris Jamsa. This book is available from Microsoft Press.

OS/2 books.

- *Using OS/2 2.0,* available from Que Corporation.
- Van Nostrand Reinhold also plans to offer a series of books on OS/2.

OS/2 on-line help. IBM now provides the command reference for OS/2 in the form of an on-line hypertext help system, the **OS/2 Command Reference.** Under OS/2 1.3, the **OS/2 Command Reference** appears automatically as a selection in your OS/2 Desktop Manager when you install the software.

Under OS/2 2.0, you'll get three icons on your desktop labeled **Start Here, Information,** and **Master Help Index. Start Here** provides a mini-tutorial that all new users should go through. **Master Help Index** provides a keyword index to all of the help information. Clicking on the **Information** icon opens up a folder, which is an OS/2 window containing other icons. In this case, you'll see icons for the **OS/2 Command Reference, REXX Information, Tutorial, Glossary,** and the **README** file. The README file contains information about OS/2 compatibility issues. You should examine it to see if any topic concerns you.

More information. If you are curious about the internal workings of OS/2, a good starting point is *Inside OS/2*, by Gordon Letwin, Chief Architect, Systems Software, at Microsoft. Another is *OS/2 Notebook,* edited by Dick Conklin of IBM. Complete information for programmers is available in the *OS/2 2.0 Technical Library,* available from IBM. For Microsoft Windows, see the *Microsoft® Windows 3.1™ Programmer's Reference Library.* These books are available from Microsoft Press.

B

Appendix B: Micro Focus Support Information

B.1 User Groups

The following section lists contact names and addresses for Micro Focus user groups. For the most current updates to this information, or if there is no user group in your area, call the Micro Focus User Group Coordinator at (415) 856-4161.

Southeast Area MUG (Atlanta)
Contact Roger Cravens, (404) 920–0563

Australia MUG (Victoria)
Contact Granville Parker, +61–3–882–7522

Mid-Atlantic MUG (Baltimore)
This group serves users in Delaware, Maryland, Virginia, and Washington DC.
Contact:
MAMUG
6400 Baltimore National Pike
Suite 170A–362
Baltimore, MD, 21226
John Finkbeiner, (410) 673–7151

Carolinas MUG (Charlotte)
Contact Liza McCullough, (215) 688–8200

Midwest Area MUG (Chicago)
Contact:
Midwest Area Micro Focus Users Group, Inc.
    3567–B Brand Avenue, Suite 260, Gurnee, IL 60031
Jim Daly, Baxter Healthcare Corp., 1400 Waukegan Rd., MPG–79,
    McGraw Park, IL 60085–6784, voice (708) 578–2631, fax (708) 473–3630
Art Gould, Micro Focus, 4239 Lee Street, Skokie IL 60076

Ohio MUG (Columbus)
Contact Mark Conway, (614) 431–2345

North Texas MUG (Dallas)
Contact Jim Gardner, (214) 580–6500

Rocky Mountain MUG (Denver)
Contact Jan Cunningham, (303) 665–0731

Michigan MUG (Detroit)
Contact Blair McDonald, (313) 356–1410

Finnish MUG (Helsinki)
Contact Antti Höyden, +358–0–436–1611

Houston MUG
Contact Harry Woodstrom, (713) 578-2059

Italian MUG (Rome)
Contact Giorgio Callegari, +39–6–5042646

Greater Los Angeles MUG
GLAMUG, PO Box 527, Canoga Park, CA 91305
Contact Lynn Mark, (213) 354–3435

Memphis MUG
Contact Ron Hughes, (901) 743–4440

Montreal MUG
Contact Catherine Bechamp, (514) 733–1377

New England MUG (Boston)
New England MUG
P. O. Box 804
Boston, Massachusetts 02103
Contact Martha Slocum, (617) 743–5029

Greater New York MUG
This group serves New York City, Long Island, and northern New Jersey.
Contact Nancy Draga, (215) 688–8200 or Bill Healey, (212) 623–6992

Philadelphia/Valley MUG
Contact Amy Abrams, (215) 964–1070

Arizona MUG (Phoenix)
Arizona Micro Focus User Group
P.O. Box 51326
Phoenix, AZ 85076
Contact Bob Katz, (602) 995–7240

Bay Area MUG (San Francisco)
Contact JoAnn Moisan, (510) 833–6723

Pacific Northwest MUG (Seattle)
This group serves Washington, Oregon, and western Canada.
Contact Lois Wyse, (206) 477–1034

Spanish MUG (Barcelona)
Contact Marc Perez, +34–3–410–0405

Toronto Area MUG
Contact Catherine Bechamp, (514) 733–1377

United Kingdom
Two groups exist, one for PC application developers and one for mainframers.
Contact Charles Gray in the UK, 011–44–0635–32646

B.2 The Micro Focus Bulletin Board System (BBS)

Micro Focus runs several bulletin board systems so that users can share public
domain software and demo programs, download new documentation, and
converse with one another. Each Micro Focus BBS allows users to submit
queries and problem reports to Micro Focus Product Support, and to transfer
files to and from Product Support to solve problems more quickly.

The message areas on the Micro Focus bulletin boards are divided into
special interest groups (subject areas) such as OS/2, SQL, networks, add-on
products, and Unix. You can also leave more general questions and requests
for assistance, as well as suggestions for Micro Focus.

The line protocol for all Micro Focus BBSs is as follows: **8 data bits, no
parity, 1 stop bit, and speeds of up to 9600 baud.**

Palo Alto, CA USA
(415) 855–9147, (415) 855–9132

Wayne, PA USA
(215) 687–0295

United Kingdom
011–44–0635–32622

Germany
089 42094 230

B.3 Micro Focus Offices

USA—West Coast (US Main Office)
Micro Focus
2465 East Bayshore Road
Suite 400
Palo Alto, CA 94303
Telephone voice: (415) 856–4161 fax: (415) 856–6134

USA—East Coast
Micro Focus (Philadelphia),
Suite 340
Eight Valley Forge Executive Mall
Wayne, PA 19087
Telephone (215) 688–8200

USA—Chicago Area (Training Facility)
1300 Iroquois
Suite 150
Naperville, IL

UK
Micro Focus Ltd.
26 West Street
Newbury, Berkshire, RG13 1JT
Telephone voice: 011–44–0635–32646 fax: 011–44–0635–33966

Japan
Micro Focus Japan (KK)
Mitsui Nishi Azabu Bldg. 4F
Nishi Azabu 4–17–30, Minato-Ku, Tokyo 106
Telephone (3) 486–7791

Germany
Micro Focus GmbH
AM Moosfeld 11
D-8000 München 82
Telephone (89) 42094–0

France
Micro Focus Sarl
Les Algorithmes
Batiment Epicure
St. Aubin, 91194 Gif-Sur-Yvette Cedex
Telephone (1) 6941–8962

Index

370 Assembler support
see MF/370
3270 Send-Receive, 183, 188
43- or 50-line display mode, 202

A

AD/CYCLE program (IBM), 325, 381
AD/MVS menu system, 297–301, 314
American National Standards Institute
(ANSI), v-viii, 7–9, 27, 85, 124, 145, 160,
169, 171, 178, 202, 292, 324, 410
1968 COBOL, 21, 91
1974 COBOL, 2, 7, 21, 89
1985 COBOL, 2, 8, 21, 27, 85, 95, 117, 130,
143, 151
1989 Addendum, 8, 21
See also COBOL language
Animator, 97-133
Advanced Animator, 11, 26, 84, 98–99,
105, 107, 129, 136–137, 151
backtracking from breakpoint, 75, 114
Break-Do function, 115–116, 130
breakpoint, conditional, 110
breakpoint, periodic, 110
breakpoint, unconditional, 110
Do function, 116
global breakpoints, 112–113
Go mode, 105, 107, 115, 129, 235
making a monitor permanent, 107, 119
Next-If function, 116
organizing monitor windows, 108
query dump files, 100, 118–119
removing unwanted monitors, 108
Reset function, 101, 106, 117–118, 121
Source Code Analyzer, 88, 99–100, 119–
124, 129–130, 144, 148, 151, 245, 337
Step mode, 115

Structure Animator, 88, 99, 120, 122–126,
128–130, 245, 337, 384
viewing user display, 104
watch monitors, 105, 107–108
Zoom mode, 105, 109, 113–114, 116, 120
See also COBOL Source Information (CSI)
Animator V2 (GUI edit/check/animate/
CSI), 337–361
animation functions, 349–350
edit configuration, 346–347
editing operations, 343
editing versus animation mode, 341
Find/CSI configuration, 357
invoking from command prompt, 338, 374
See also Checker, COBOL/2 Compiler
ANSI
See American National Standards Institute
ASCII versus EBCDIC considerations
ASCII/EBCDIC translation, 41, 169–171,
183, 190–194, 376, 399
CHARSET directive, 84, 87, 89, 170–173,
211
embedded hex in programs, 171, 188, 376
IMS Option, 288
MCO2, 276
SQL support, 280, 284, 287
See also File types, MDECONV, WFL
Associating files with COBOL programs
ASSIGN(DYNAMIC) directive, 177
External File Mapping, 177–178
using SET commands, 177
AUTOEXEC.BAT
See Operating system variables

B

Banner screens, 246, 248, 250
installing new banner screens, 249
using Forms facility to design, 246–247

Basic Mapping Support (CICS), 84, 276–277, 280, 284–287, 292, 322, 388–389
breakpoint
　See Animator, Animator V2
Build utility, 178
Build V2 (GUI), 388

C

Calculator function
　See COBOL Editor
Caps Lock toggle, 37, 52, 226
Checker, syntax, 79–96, 154
　$SET directives statement, 85, 87–88, 91, 94, 155
　access from function key Checker menu, 81, 88
　access from function key Editor menu, 82
　access from GUI Animator V2, 348
　Checker versus Compiler directives, 83
　COBOL.DIR file, 80, 85–86, 88, 94, 154
　language toggle, 81–82, 86, 102, 136, 245, 253
　running from command line, 94, 348
　WBxxxx.DIR files, 26, 85–86, 94
CICS OS/2
　See Micro Focus CICS Option for OS/2 (MCO2)
CICSVS86
　See Micro Focus CICS Option (MCO)
COBOL dialects, mainframe
　COBOL/370, 2, 8, 12, 21, 348
　DOS/VS COBOL, 12, 279, 292, 348
　OS/VS COBOL, 2, 7, 12, 21, 26–27, 91, 279, 292, 348, 410
COBOL Editor
　access to hypertext help, 47
　calculator function, 69
　configuring, 244
　editing copy members, 70
　internal stack, 56
　invoking, 47, 76
　line drawing, 68
　loading files, 48
　margins, 47, 53–55, 246
　mouse support, 66, 150
　word wrap, 48, 53, 245, 256, 347
　See also COBOL Source Information (CSI)
COBOL language, v-viii
　intrinsic functions, 8, 14, 21
　Object Oriented COBOL Task Group (OOCTG), 9
　object-oriented (OO) COBOL, 323–324
　See also ANSI, CODASYL

COBOL Source Information (CSI), 135-152
　inactive code and dead data, 143–144
　printing the results, 148–149
　procedure name query, 137
　purpose of, 136
　setting options, 146–147
　source line pointers, 138
　TIMES program statistics, 145–146
　using bookmarks, 149
　wildcard data names, 142
COBOL.DIR file
　See Checker, syntax
COBOL/2 Compiler, 7-11, 153-159
　access from GUI Workbench Organizer, 348
　directives, 85–87, 155–158, 165, 252, 332, 348
　internal sort, 20, 75, 168, 270, 371-372
　See also Link-editing
COBSW, 160
CODASYL, vi-viii, 293
Code/370, 337–338
Common User Access (CUA)
　1989 IBM standards, 325
　1991 IBM standards, 325
　cascaded menu, 345–346, 356, 370, 410
　context menus, 333–334, 338
　dialog boxes, 327
　menu bar, 326
　workplace environment, 325
Compiler, COBOL/2
　See COBOL/2 Compiler
Concurrency, 219-224
　background syntax checking, 223
　CONCLI menu files, 220, 222, 225, 241
　memory snapshot facility, 221–222
　run unit, 220–222, 225
　starting the environment, 220
CONFIG.SYS
　See Operating system variables
Configuration files
　CONCLI.CFG (Concurrency), 225, 241
　EDITOR.CFG (Toolset), 244
　WB.CFG, 225–226, 240, 242–246, 381, 388
Copy library
　.CPY files, 51, 53, 70, 77–78, 80, 100, 246
　COBOL COPY statement, 70, 78, 80, 85–87, 91, 138, 146, 188, 217–218, 301, 303–304, 343, 381, 404
　COBOL Editor, access from, 70
　correcting errors in copy member, 93
　Librarian, 70, 90–91, 381
　Panvalet, 70, 91, 381
CSI
　See COBOL Source Information (CSI)

D

Data File Editor (DFED)
  configuration, 203–204
  editing in formatted mode, 204
  from function key menu, 38, 81, 181, 201
  function key v3.0 changes, 207–210
  running from command line, 201
DATACOM (Computer Associates), 292–293
Debugging
  See Animator, Animator V2
Develop menu, 92, 100, 151
Dialog System (Micro Focus), 14, 277
DIFF
  See Source Comparison
Directives
  See Checker, Compiler
Directories on the PC
  default directory, 68, 161, 312, 334, 364, 366, 397–398, 402–403
  DIR command, 214
  See also MFDIR V2
Disk space allocation, 15, 17, 20, 24, 29–30, 175–176, 182, 285, 324, 404, 407
DL/I support
  See IMS Option

E

Early Release status, 22, 29–30, 33, 361
Editor, COBOL
  See COBOL Editor
Error messages, 37, 81, 92-94, 260–261, 297, 345
Executing compiled programs
  Execute menu, function key, 36, 41, 157, 250
  Run menu, function key, 157, 159
  RUNPM Shell (GUI Workbench RUN icon), 368, 389
Execution counts
  See Animator (Analyzer)
Exiting from Workbench
  See Function key menu
Extended Memory Manager (XM), 11, 13, 20, 24, 29, 35, 76, 129, 164, 167, 176, 201–202, 220, 225, 265, 270–272, 314–315, 318
External File Mapping
  See Associating files with COBOL programs

F

File Finder, 214–215, 238, 361
File Transfer Aid (MFXFER), 36, 183–184, 376–381
  GUI version, 376–381
File types
  Btrieve, 12, 174, 199, 207, 389
  line sequential, 45, 172–173, 188–189, 194, 207–208, 216, 218
  mainframe tape, 42, 172-173, 279
  MS-DOS filenames, 395-399
  printed output from COBOL programs, 178
  program source code, 45–47
  record sequential, 172, 192–194, 207
  relative, 173–174, 207, 263
  SYSIN and SYSOUT, 176, 179, 269–270, 272–273
  V-ISAM, 173–174, 199, 207, 389
  VSAM, 7, 173–174, 182, 199, 210–211, 269–270, 274–276, 290
Function key menu
  accessing command prompt from, 36, 40, 157, 161
  CLI.MNU file, 225, 241–242, 245, 249–253
  Configure menu, 242, 248, 250–262
  customizing default directives, 245
  ESCAPE key returns to higher menus, 40
  exiting from the system, 43
  help screens, accessing through F1, 40
  hypertext help, accessing through Alt+1, 47
  menu handler, 35, 40, 241, 251
  screen organization, 37
  See also Banner screens, Mainframe Development Environment (MDE), Workbench Development Environment (WDE)

G

Generated code executable file (.GNT)
  compiled from .MNU file, 241
  conflict with Animator, 100
  default path for, 81
  Organizer compile icon, 348
  running, 159-161, 163, 166-167
  versus .OBJ format, 28, 85-86, 154-158, 164-165
GUI File Transfer Aid (MFXFER V2), 376–381
GUI Hypertext Help, 368–371
GUI Source Comparison (DIFF V2), 382–384

GUI Workbench Organizer, 303, 321–335
compiling, 348
executing compiled programs
(RUNPM Shell), 368, 389
project icons, 330, 332
running GUI utilities, 361-389
templates, 326, 330-332
tool icons, 328–330, 332, 335, 338
See also Animator V2

H

Help screens
See Banner screens, Hypertext help
HEXEDIT (Hex Editor), 199–201, 218
Hypertext help (HYHELP), 83,155, 254-259
access from COBOL editor, 40, 47
bookmarks in GUI version, 371
bookmarks in text-mode version, 75-76
building custom help files, 254–256
compiled help (.HNF) output file, 18–19,
70, 254, 257–258, 368
from GUI menus, 328, 342, 368-372, 374
GUI version from command line, 368
hot spots, 40, 257
keystroke macros, using with, 226
On-line Information System Compiler
(OLISC), 254, 256–258, 368
rapid keyword lookup, 74
testing your custom help files, 258
text version from command line, 258
See also Banner screens

I

IDMS (Computer Associates), 12, 263, 292-
293
Ignoring a file, 178
IMS Option, 42, 171, 174, 270, 279, 287–
292, 297
IMSVS86
See IMS Option
Information line
in function key menu, 37
in Animator V2, 340
Insert versus overtype mode, 38, 48, 52,
55, 57–59, 226, 343–344
Installing Workbench updates
See UPDATE utility program
Intermediate code output file (.INT)
from AD/MVS foreground compile, 300
input to code generator, 154-155, 158-159
output from Checker, 79, 81, 100

under Animator V2, 337-338, 341-342, 348
under RTE, 79, 163, 166-167
Internal sort
See COBOL/2 Compiler
IRMA, 29, 183, 188, 376
ISPF Dialog Manager, 277, 297–298, 301
See also AD/MVS, SPF/2, SPF/PC

K

KEDIT, 293-296
Keystroke macros (MFKEYMAC), 224–225
default macros, 225
defining new macros, 226
purpose of, 224

L

Link-editing, 23, 27–28, 79, 86, 153–156,
162–166, 168, 170, 179, 183
See also Build V2

M

Mainframe Development Environment
(MDE)
installing, 25
contents , 36-37, 41-43
MDECONV (EBCDIC/ASCII translation),
171, 188–191, 210, 376
See also ASCII versus EBCDIC
considerations
Memory management
See Extended Memory Manager (XM)
RAM, 2, 15, 26, 51, 78, 90, 93, 143, 244,
270–271, 287, 299–300, 303, 319
Message (.MSG) output file, 81, 93
MF/370 (370 Assembler support),154,
263–266, 269, 287, 297
MFDIR (text mode directory), 49-51
MFDIR V2 (GUI Directory), 361–367, 382
file search options, 364
general options, 367
MFKEYMAC
See Keystroke macros
Micro Focus CICS Option (MCO), 42, 279-
280
Micro Focus CICS Option for OS/2
(MCO2), 42, 84, 276–279
See also Btrieve
Micro Focus, Inc., history of, 1-3

Micro Focus library (.LBR) files, 159, 164, 214-215, 246, 250, 253, 361, 364, 388
MS-DOS operating system
.BAT files, 399-400
bibliography, 410-411
commands, 401-404
concepts, 391-394
FAT file system, 17, 395, 397–399
MVS JCL support
external sort, 270–271, 273, 297–298
JCL versus batch files, 175-179, 399-400
using RCM to generate JCL, 302, 324
See also AD/MVS menu system, PARM Passer, ProxMvs

N

Novell Netware support, 14, 280, 285, 287
See also Btrieve
Num Lock toggle, 53, 226

O

Object code (.OBJ) output files, 28, 100, 154–156, 158, 162–163, 165, 168, 348, 388
Object orientation, 9, 321–325
classes, 325
encapsulation, 323
polymorphism, 323
recursion, 323
See also COBOL language, Reusable Code Manager
OMF directive, 85–87, 156–158, 165, 348
On-line Information
See Hypertext help
Operating system prompt
access to, 393-394
from function key menus, 36, 40, 157, 161
Operating system variables
AUTOEXEC.BAT, 17–20, 29–30, 33, 45, 80, 202, 288, 400, 404–406
CONFIG.SYS, 17–20, 29–30, 33, 45, 80, 202, 288, 312, 332, 335, 400, 404–406
Environment, 399-400
LIBPATH command, 17–19, 29
PATH command, 17–20, 29, 318, 404
SET command, 404
Optimization, 83, 120, 156-157, 167-168
OS/2
bibliography, 411-412
Boot Manager, 406–409
dual boot option, 19, 405–406, 408
folders, 409

HPFS file system, 17, 395, 397
icon format, 333
Presentation Manager, 14, 276–277, 373, 392
Program Manager, 20, 30, 43, 314, 393, 399
version 1.3, 303, 325, 327, 393–394, 405, 411
version 2.0, 284, 325–328, 333, 392–394
See also SQL (Database Manager)

P

PARM Passer (Parmpass) utility, 90, 159–160, 167, 180–182, 250
PC assembler (.GRP) output file, 155, 158, 162
PC clone machines, installing on, 29
PC-DOS
See MS-DOS
printer control, 67, 178–179
Probe utility, 266, 384–386
ProxMvs, 269–275, 297

R

Reusable Code Manager (RCM), 11, 301–309, 324, 346
Locator/Selector facility, 303, 305
macros, 302, 304, 307–308
models, 302
Runtime system, 11, 13, 85, 154–157, 162–168, 229, 261, 386
Toolset Run-Time Environment (RTE), 79, 163–164, 166–168, 273
See also Shared Run-time System, Static Linked Run-time System

S

SAA CUA
See Common User Access (CUA)
Scroll Lock toggle, 53
Session Recorder
comparing snapshot files (MFREVIEW), 228, 233–236, 238
from command line, 230, 233
keystroke files, 229–230, 232–233, 236-238
regression testing, 226–229, 231, 233, 235
screen snapshot files, 232–236
translating keystroke files (MFKTRANS), 228–229, 233, 236–238
Session Recorder (GUI), 373–376

SETUP utility program, 13, 15–18, 20–22, 24, 27, 30, 32–33, 35, 85, 277, 328
Shared Runtime System (COBLIB), 28, 156, 162–166
Sort, external
    See MVS JCL support
Sort, internal
    See COBOL/2 Compiler
Source Comparison (DIFF), 52–53, 216–219, 227, 234, 238, 373
    GUI version, 382-384
SPF emulation
    See AD/MVS menu system, SPF/2, SPF/PC
SPF/2, 296–297, 311–320
    keyboard mapping, 315
    Super Lists, 315, 317
SPF/PC, 296, 311–313, 315
SQL support, 84
    DCLGEN utility, 280
    Gupta SQLBase, 7, 174, 287–288
    Host Compatibility Option, 284
    Microsoft SQL Server, 174, 285, 287
    Oracle, 174, 285–287
    OS/2 Extended Services Database Manager, 7, 14–15, 84, 159, 171, 174, 277, 284–285, 288
    XDB, 7, 84, 174, 270–271, 276, 279–280, 282, 284, 287–288
Standalone executable (.EXE) output files, 16, 18–19, 30, 81, 154–155, 159, 162–168, 229, 312, 388–389, 398
Static Linked Runtime System (LCOBOL), 28, 163, 165–166, 168
System installation
    See SETUP utility program

T

Tags, use of, 39, 56, 67–68, 147–151, 241, 256–257, 345, 384
Toolset, 7, 11, 13, 333, 388
    See also COBOL Editor, Runtime system, SETUP utility, XM

U

UNIX, 2, 14, 26, 141, 280, 285–287, 292, 406, 415

UPDATE utility program, 30, 33
UPSI switches, 160, 182

V

VRECGEN (mainframe File Format Utility), 25, 182–183, 185–186, 194, 199, 210–211
VSAM
    Access Method Services (IDCAMS), 173, 182, 210–211, 218, 270–271, 275, 301
    See also File types (V-ISAM, Btrieve)

W

WB.DIR files
    See Checker, syntax
Wildcards in file names, 214–216, 402
Windows, Microsoft, 11, 13–14, 16, 31, 321, 328, 337, 361
    bibliography, 411-412
    Desktop Manager, 43, 393–394, 399
    icon format, 333
    mouse conflict, 150
    running add-on products, 280, 285, 287-288, 313
    PIF Editor, 20, 30–33, 294, 314
    scroll bar, 75, 363
    under MS-DOS and OS/2, 391-393
Word Wrap toggle, 53, 245
Workbench Development Environment (WDE)
    installing, 25
    contents, 164-166, 213-214
Workbench File Loader (WFL), 12, 170, 173–174, 178, 188, 190–199, 210–211
    enhancements in v3.0, 388-389
    mask file (.MSK), 195
    reorganizing V-ISAM files, 196
Workbench version 2.5, 12, 20, 30, 107, 110, 112–113, 124, 150, 193, 199, 256
Workbench version 3.0, 12, 151, 174, 207–210, 321, 326, 348, 361, 388–389, 401

X

XEDIT emulation
    See KEDIT
XILERATOR, 24

Let's Hear from You!

This book is intended to serve your needs as a COBOL applications developer and Micro Focus user. We would appreciate it if you would let us know whether we are "on target" and what we can do to meet your needs better in the future. **Please send your replies to Alida Jatich and Phil Nowak, 3835 West 56th Place, Chicago IL 60629.**

1. Did you find any errors in this book? If so, please include page number and description.

2. In your opinion, does this book cover all of the subject matter that a mainframe COBOL applications developer needs to begin using the Workbench effectively? If not, what is missing?

3. Are the writing style and the level of detail appropriate for your needs?

4. Did this book influence your decision to purchase the Workbench or any of its add-on products?

5. If you or your organization has already purchased the Workbench, did this book help you begin using the Workbench for developing COBOL applications?

6. What other topics would you like to see in future editions of this book, or in additional books intended for the applications developer?